4th Edition

Flea Market

Price Guide

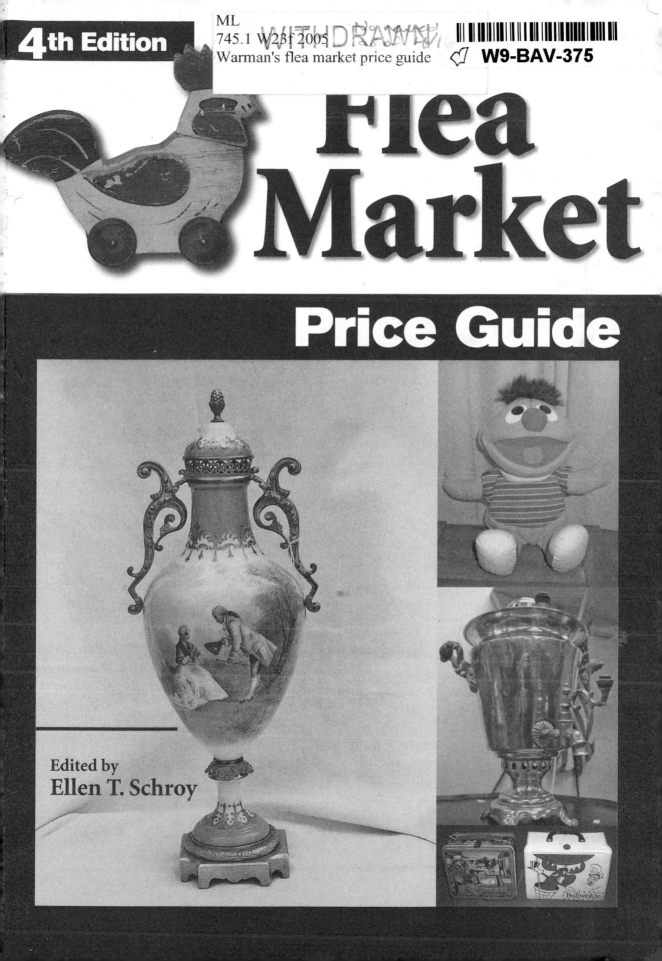

Edited by
Ellen T. Schroy

©2005 KP Books
Published by

kp books
An Imprint of F+W Publications

700 East State Street • Iola, WI 54990-0001
715-445-2214 • 888-457-2873

Our toll-free number to place an order or obtain
a free catalog is (800) 258-0929.

Photos featured on the front cover are, clockwise from top
left: wooden rooster pull toy, 6" h, 7" l, **$35**; Fitzgerald Magic
Maid electric mixer, green, **$115**; 25-year badge, International
Order of Odd Fellows, 1899 patent date, 1-1/2" d, **$15**; and
"Clifton Suspension Bridge" souvenir china teapot, 5" h, **$60**.
Photos on the back cover are: a lady's head vase, **$75**; and a
tin #12 Marx windup race car, metal wheels, 16" l, **$225**.

Library of Congress Catalog Number: 2004115472

ISBN: 0-89689-159-3

Designed by Jamie Griffin
Edited by Kristine Manty

Printed in the United States of America

Contents

Acknowledgments

Like building blocks from my childhood, this project has been filled with moments that when combined build up an even greater creation, making it unique to the moment. Do you remember the sounds that stacking blocks on top of one another made? Clink, clink.

CLINK. I owe a debt of gratitude to collectors and dealers for the enthusiastic response to the first editions of *Warman's Flea Market Price Guide*. Your thoughts, letters, and e-mails helped improve and refine the format for future editions.

CLINK. I say thank you to my editor, Kris Manty. Though we've worked from afar, your time, patience, and vision are always appreciated.

CLINK. I am so grateful to everyone who helped us obtain photographs for this book. My humble requests to take photos at dealers' booths are never refused, and usually met with offers to help, and to turn an object so it's very best side shows. Thanks!

CLINK. Thanks to those who know why they are special: the friends and family who encourage me to keep putting these price guides together. Many of these folks helped me build bigger and bigger castles when I was a child. Together today we still reminiscence about a back porch filled with villages built out of wooden blocks, with streets winding through them for our trucks and cars, with Barbies and Ginny dolls holding court in our finest castles.

Ellen Tischbein Schroy, January 17, 2005

Introduction

Ready for an adventure, ready to take a stroll among some of the treasures that make America a very special place? Great, join me as we head out for one of the best experiences we can share—going to a flea market! Whether we head for a large well-organized event that goes on for days, or a smaller market that springs up in the side yard of the local fire company, we're in for an adventure. Heading out with an open mind, a free spirit and willingness to enjoy the sunny skies, will only enhance our day of fun. With the help of this edition of *Warman's Flea Market Price Guide,* perhaps you will be a better-informed flea market browser, knowing where to look for great deals, and how to find those things that will make you smile every time you gaze on them. Get your favorite hat, your most comfortable sneakers, and let's head out. It's a family thing.

One benefit of today's flea market is the emphasis placed on the family. While some dealers at higher-end markets twitch nervously at the sight of strollers and young children, most flea markets are promoted as events for everyone, young and old. Look around the next time you're at an outdoor flea market. Notice the number of parents pulling children in wagons; and, pay close attention to the smiles on those kids' faces.

Where else are kids encouraged to dig through a box of fast-food toys or spend a portion of their allowance on a 10-cent baseball card? And when they're wearing down, an ice-cold drink or a soft pretzel is often all that's needed to give them a boost.

No segment of the antiques and collectibles industry does a better job catering to the interests of children than flea markets. These microcosms of the antiques trade offer youngsters appealing items at reasonable prices. For many adults, their love of collecting germinated in childhood and blossomed into adulthood. The legion of flea markets across the United States assures a bright future for the antiques and collectibles trade by creating tomorrow's collectors today.

And the fun isn't just for kids. If you haven't been to a flea market in a while, you're in for a treat. What are you waiting for?

Let the fun begin

The thrill of the hunt continues to drive the antiques and collectibles market. People delight in the search for treasured items. Nowhere is that hope more alive than at a flea market. Whether you're looking for that Partridge Family paper doll set you remember from your childhood or a plate to add to your collection of Depression glass, flea markets offer the realistic hope that the search will be successful. Better yet, chances are good the item can be purchased for a reasonable price.

Don't assume this book is another run-of-the-mill price

Many flea market dealers try to set up very interesting looking booths. This one featured a set of sturdy shelves holding antiques, while still more primitives and collectibles were laying within each reach on the top of their table. Covering their table with a cheerful blue and white checked tablecloth helped draw the shoppers eyes to their wares.

guide. It's much more than that! *Warman's Flea Market Price Guide* contains valuable information about attending flea markets, as this edition has been honed specifically toward your needs as a flea market shopper or seller. Believing that flea markets are fun, family oriented events, the tone of this edition has been kept somewhat lighthearted. A sufficient amount of information about each topic has been provided to give you a basic idea of its history or use. However, the listings are the backbone of the work, since that's what flea market enthusiasts really want.

In compiling the listings for *Warman's Flea Market Price Guide*, we put our fingers on the pulse of the marketplace, carefully checking to see what's being sold at flea markets. There's not much sense in listing prices for potholders if no one is collecting them. Instead, we've focused on what's hot, like NASCAR collectibles, which has its own heading in this edition. Other new categories include American Art Pottery, flue covers, and union-related collectibles.

Photographs are a key component of this work. *Warman's Flea Market Price Guide* contains more photographs, and this book illustrates more categories, than does any other flea market price guide. From the beginning of this project, photography has been a priority. While detailed listings are vital, clear photographs are invaluable for identifying an item. However, part of finding what you are looking for at a flea market can be fun—searching through objects and scanning tables to find that perfect piece. This edition has more "on location" photographs, showing what it really is like to browse at a flea market.

In preparation for this book we asked you, flea market buyers and sellers, to tell us what you think. That input allowed us to fine-tune the end product to fit your needs. This isn't just another general-line price guide with the upper-end merchandise stripped away and the words "Flea Market" added to the title. From start to finish, we've focused on creating the best flea market book possible. Included is inside information about what's happening on the flea market

scene, what's being offered for sale, and the value of that merchandise.

Our goal was to accurately reflect a typical flea market. We were literally thinking on our feet as we prepared this book. We walked hundreds of miles during a multitude of flea markets, talked to countless dealers, and listened to innumerable shoppers while observing the collectibles landscape. While hours are spent compiling the information and writing the photo captions, even more hours have been spent walking the aisles at flea markets, large and small, watching who's selling what, who's buying, and listening to what YOU think is important.

You'll find an intriguing mix of merchandise represented here, from things that are readily available to scarce objects that, much to the delight of collectors, do occasionally surface at flea markets. Values in this price guide begin at 25 cents for trading cards and range upward from there, highlighting the diversity of items that can be found even within specific categories.

Methodology 101

How do you combine roughly 1,300 photographs, nearly 600 categories, and thousands of listings into one cohesive unit? We started with "A." It's a pretty basic concept, but one that works just fine. Categories are listed alphabetically, from Abingdon Pottery to Zeppelins. Within each section, you may find the following:

Category: In an effort to make this book as enjoyable to read as it was to write, we intentionally omitted dry discourses on a category's history. If you wanted to do research, you'd be at a library, not at a flea market. Levity aside, that doesn't mean we shied away from useful information. Instead, we utilize a mix of key facts and fun tips. If you're not

smiling as you read this book, we haven't done our jobs. For anyone wanting additional insight into a topic, we encourage you to seek more information through the periodicals, reference books, and collectors' clubs that support the collecting hobby we all so passionately enjoy.

Reproduction alert: Reproductions remain a problem throughout the antiques and collectibles trade. When we are aware of reproductions within a specific category, we use this alert to call your attention to their existence.

Listings: Looking for the heart of this book? You just found it. The individual listings are short but sweet, giving detailed descriptions that aid in identification. You'll find the listings presented alphabetically, each with a current value.

What's a flea market?

Attempting to define a flea market is like trying to describe all restaurants with a single statement. Sure, McDonald's and the White House kitchen both serve food, but there's a world of difference between the two.

Flea markets suffer from the same identity problem. They come in innumerable varieties, from multi-thousand-dealer events at Brimfield, Massachusetts, to the local volunteer fire department's annual flea market and chili supper, featuring only a handful of merchants. The first may attract full-time dealers, while the latter may appeal to neighbors who have just cleaned out their garages. Yet, good sales and exciting buys can be made at both events.

One of the fun aspects of browsing at a flea market is finding ways in which old things can take on new useful lives. This dealer has taken small bottles, vases, etc. and turned them into decorative items by creatively adding wire and beads.

Typically, flea markets are stereotyped as having low- to middle-market merchandise displayed in a haphazard manner. Imagine a herd of nude Barbies sprawled on the bare ground under a wobbly folding table holding a scattered array of chipped glassware and musty *TV Guides*.

However, that's not always the case. In today's market, a shopper is just as likely to find a selection of 19th-century mechanical banks grouped in a professional setting, complete with risers and lights.

Additionally, a number of events considered flea markets are actually seasonal antiques shows, such as the Sandwich Antiques Market in Sandwich, Illinois. Ask someone in the Midwest to name his favorite flea market, and Sandwich is likely to be it. The Sandwich Antiques Market remains dedicated to providing both affordable and quality antiques and collectibles, while filtering out those dealers who carry bottom-of-the-line material. Is Sandwich a flea market? No, but it exhibits many of the qualities that attract flea market dealers and shoppers—a well-established event with indoor and outdoor spaces, good facilities, and the promise of finding a bargain.

The reputation of a particular market often dictates the quality of the merchandise presented. Better-known flea markets typically attract upper-end dealers who are just as comfortable at sophisticated antique shows, while lower-end markets tend to adopt a more laid-back approach. Booths may have a cluttered look, and there may be more merchants selling items from outside the antiques and collectibles field, including everything from ferrets to football jerseys.

Flea markets also run the gamut from daily markets held in strip malls to monthly shows at 4-H fairgrounds. Outdoor summer markets tend to be a favorite with shoppers. During good weather, the flea market becomes a haven for families wanting to do something together. Children who normally whine at the suggestion of going to an antiques mall or auction will often put on a happy face when told the destination is a flea market.

Long live flea markets!

Flea markets are alive and well. That's good news in an industry that is undergoing none-too-subtle changes, due in large part to the Internet. In a day when many antiques malls are losing dealers who have decided they can more easily do business selling online, flea markets still appear to be strong. What's their secret? Actually, it's the Internet!

An increasing number of people have discovered fun and profit through selling antiques and collectibles on the World Wide Web. Although they might have started by cleaning out the attic, they're soon looking for additional sources of inventory. Flea markets have proven to be the perfect place to find inexpensive items for resale.

Nor have seasoned collectors abandoned flea markets. Shoppers still root through showcases and

This old cabinet takes on a new life as a potting table with a shabby chic coat of white paint. It sold quickly at Renninger's Extravaganza in Kutztown.

This frame shows a neat way of displaying a group of post cards. Each one is original for a different holiday, but has a bell theme, tying the whole piece together in a decorative way, **$65.**

burrow under tables for prizes waiting to be found, sometimes at a fraction of their value. The thrill of the hunt continues to lure collectors and dealers to their favorite flea markets.

Those flea markets that serve as tag-team partners with more traditional antique shows are also doing well. Consider the Springfield Antiques Show & Flea Market, held monthly in Springfield, Ohio. While shoppers find a variety of upper-end antiques there, from American art pottery to country furniture, the show also attracts a number of dealers selling more affordable wares. Looking for Beanie Babies?

They're there. Need vintage hardware for a kitchen cabinet? No doubt, someone has it. Interested in Little Golden Books? Bring a large bag to carry them home.

Many promoters who combine traditional antiques shows with flea markets are careful to limit the number of dealers selling new items, such as T-shirts and shrubbery.

Because they are offered a range of items across a broad spectrum of prices, shoppers have the hope of finding exactly what they're looking for. Not even the Internet can dampen that enthusiasm.

The flea-market zone

If Rod Serling were still with us, he might sum things up this way: "There is a fifth dimension beyond that which is known to man. It is a dimension as vast as collectibles and as timeless as antiques. It is the middle ground between wanting and owning, between seeing and sacking, and it lies between the pit of man's coveting and the balance of his checkbook. This is the dimension of collecting. It is an area which we call The Flea Market Zone."

Is there a signpost up ahead? Collectors hope so, and they get excited when it reads "Flea Market" in large, bold letters. However, there are more efficient ways to find flea markets than by relying on chance. For starters, several guides have been published that cover American flea markets. These books are valuable for the detailed information they provide, listing flea markets, locations, dates, times, admission rates, dealer rates, and contact information. Check your favorite bookseller for titles and availability.

Trade publications are another excellent source of information. National and regional publications contain a fair number of advertisements for flea markets. In addition, don't overlook the free tabloids available at many flea markets, antiques shows and antiques malls. Ads for smaller flea markets and festival-related events can often be found in these publications.

Keeping in touch with others is a basic human need and when

If you were searching for fireplace accessories, this dealer may just have the thing you're looking for. Dealers that carry a lot of inventory make the task of outfitting a fireplace easier to offering good choices in different styles and metals.

you combine it with the allure of learning more about one's favorite objects, it's even better. Collectors' clubs offer many folks a marvelous way to learn more about their specific loves. If this is an aspect of collecting that appeals to you, you're bound to find kindred spirits at a flea market. Browse over that table of club announcements, show cards, and trade publications found at every flea market, and perhaps something will spark your interest. Stuff a few show cards into your pockets and then resolve to visit a couple of new shows and flea markets, to keep feeding that collecting spirit.

Of course, nothing beats a good recommendation from other collectors and dealers. Ask around, especially when at a flea market you like. Talk to the dealers to find out which markets they prefer and which venues offer similar types of merchandise.

Do plan on checking with a local newspaper, chamber of commerce, or neighborhood know-it-all to double check that super-duper tremendous flea market you heard about to make sure it really will be held on the date you think. Some flea markets are better on certain days of the week. Don't be afraid to ask the locals when they go to shop for antiques and collectibles, not vegetables.

The Columbus, NJ, flea market is a great example—plan to go there on a Thursday, not Saturday or Sunday, if you're looking for really great antiques and collectibles. If you happen to drive down popular Route 206, the signs for Columbus will tell you they are open on Saturday and Sunday— sure enough, but the really in-the-know dealers and collectors probably scooped up the best stuff on Thursday.

Don't go quite yet

You've done your homework. You've found a great-sounding flea market. You managed to finagle a Saturday off from work. The rest of the family is dressed and ready to go. Have you forgotten anything?

How about a phone call?

Sure, the flea market guide states that Billy-Bob's Flea-Spectacular is open every Saturday and Sunday. However, circumstances do arise that cause flea markets to change their hours, move to a different location, or even go out of business.

There's nothing more frustrating than driving 100 miles in the wee morning light, enduring two hours of your kids drubbing each other in the back seat, and drinking three cups of lukewarm coffee, only to find a "CLOSED" sign hanging crookedly on the chain-link fence surrounding what used to be Billy-Bob's. Such experiences can generally be avoided by confirming the details of the market ahead of time.

When contacting the promoter, double-check the date, hours of operation, and admission fees. If you aren't familiar with the area, ask for directions. And remember, if the drive involves much distance, find out if you will be changing time zones; otherwise, a road trip from Illinois to Michigan could find you arriving 45 minutes after the gate opened instead of 15 minutes early, as you had planned. Time zones have crushed more than one collector's hopes of getting into a market with the opening surge of shoppers.

Dealers at open-air flea markets must be prepared for sudden changes in the weather. Here dealer Gail Grimley has enclosed part of her space with large plastic sheets, protecting her merchandise and herself from impending showers at Renninger's Extravaganza in Kutztown.

While you're at it, don't forget to check the weather forecast. It might be sunny when you leave your home in San Jose, but Pasadena could be in the midst of a thunderstorm. Rain and outdoor flea markets are natural enemies. A quick check of The Weather Channel would have shown you that a low-pressure system had stalled directly above the Rose Bowl Flea Market and Swap Meet. Sure, the event might be held "rain or shine," but that doesn't mean you feel like slogging through puddles on your day off.

Using your best networking skills, ask favorite dealers if the hours posted in the trade paper ads are really reliable, or do

dealers have a habit of sneaking out early from certain flea markets. Many will tell that a few black clouds will send dealers in an unprotected field scrambling quickly if the crowds aren't buying. You really can't fault the dealers for protecting their investment, but when the sun is shining and the sign says "open 'til 5" and you get there at 10 and the most action you are seeing is the back of dealers as they pack up, that's not quite fair to the shoppers.

If getting up at the crack of dawn to encounter this, check out some other flea markets or better yet, patronize those who are willing to stay until the designated closing times.

Getting comfortable

Boy Scouts are pretty intelligent kids. They've got that neat hand sign, and they're good at expecting the unexpected. We should all be so smart.

Veteran flea market shoppers also know to be prepared. To begin with, they dress for success. Nothing will kill a day at a flea market faster than being uncomfortable, whether you're too cold, too hot, or suffering from achy feet. Dressing appropriately for the season and accounting for changes in the weather are essential components of an enjoyable hunt for flea market treasures. Two rules are key: dress in layers, and take a change of clothes.

Many flea market shoppers are early birds, wanting to jump into the action as soon as possible. When arriving at a Wisconsin flea market in the chill of the morning, a wool sweater and a cup of steaming coffee will keep you warm. But once the coffee cup is empty, Mr. Sun peeks from behind the clouds, and the temperature climbs, it's likely your wardrobe will become a hindrance. Suddenly you're concentrating on the hot, itchy sweater instead of the under-priced Art Deco candlesticks you just walked past.

At the very least, expect the temperature to fluctuate during the day. Layers of light clothing will prepare you for any variations in the weather. It's better to wear a light jacket that can be removed and carried in your cloth bag or backpack, serving as packing material if needed, than to be stuck in a heavy hooded sweatshirt all day because it's the only thing you tossed on that morning. And don't even think about breaking in a new pair of shoes at a flea market. You're just asking for trouble (read: blisters) if you think your new Nikes are going to travel miles of hot pavement and acres of uneven terrain at an outdoor market without revolting against your toes or heels. Comfortable, well-worn walking shoes are your best bet.

Don't forget something to cover your noggin, also. On cold days, nothing keeps you warm like a stocking cap. In hot weather, a wide-brimmed hat will protect your head, face, and neck, lessening the possibility of sunburn and headaches. At the very least, a baseball-style cap affords shade for your face, and it can easily be stuffed in a back pocket when no longer needed.

In addition to those items you're wearing, pack a second set of clothes to keep in your vehicle. Give yourself the option of warmer or cooler clothes, depending on the weather. You may start the day wearing long pants, but by noon the shorts in your car might feel more comfortable. A quick trip to change will be time well spent.

Don't forget to pack an extra pair of shoes and socks as well. More than one rainy day at the flea market has been salvaged when the cloudburst stopped and the shopper changed out of soaked sneakers and into a dry pair of shoes and socks. Better yet, pack a pair of boots. You'll be glad you did when the other shoppers are slogging through a rain-soaked field with mud oozing between their toes.

Fine art often makes it way to flea markets. Here a booth at Renninger's Extravaganza in Kutztown displayed a good selection of oil paintings, watercolors, and interesting framed mirrors, all ready to take home and hang.

The right stuff

The right clothes are important, but wise flea market shoppers know that it takes more than a comfortable pair of khakis to ensure a good day shopping. Here are some other items you'll find useful:

Cash: Money talks and speaks a universal language that everyone understands. Do more than just take along enough to get you through the day, keeping in mind that you'll probably eat and put gas in the car before returning home. Make sure you have a sufficient number of small bills, as well as some change in your pocket. Ones and fives come in handy when buying low-priced items, especially if a dealer has a handful of twenties or doesn't want to break your $100 bill for a postcard tagged $1.50. The quarters jingling in your pocket will speed the transaction at the concessions stand when all you want is a glass of iced tea before heading down the next aisle.

Other funds: Although not all dealers accept checks, many do. Before leaving home, make sure you have a sufficient number of checks with you. Credit cards are honored by some dealers, primarily at the larger events; however, don't expect to use your VISA at many of the smaller flea markets. An ATM/debit card offers the best of both worlds. When you unexpectedly find a Pairpoint cornucopia just as you are running low on cash, the dealer will likely hold it for you while you dart off to the nearest automated teller machine. Many large flea markets

These assorted clock faces represented a real decorator's accent bargain as they were priced at **$2** each.

now have ATMs available on the property.

Meals and snacks: Flea market food ranges from fantastic to repulsive, and to make matters worse, what some markets charge for a hot dog and a cold drink could finance a small Third World nation. Depending on the market, a better solution might be to pack your lunch and keep it in a cooler in the car. A quick trip to the parking lot will take less time than waiting in line for a greasy cheeseburger.

Pack high-energy food that's easily digested and, if desired, can be eaten while you walk. As a snack, fruit is always a good option, as are many sports-related energy bars. Don't forget to take along some drinks. A thermos of coffee, tea, or even soup is great for chilly mornings, while a cooler of iced soft drinks or juice will be worth its weight in gold by the end of the day. And don't forget the

water. Not only will it quench you thirst, but it can also be used to clean and cool your face, neck, and hands on hot, sunny days.

After a long day of shopping, you may be too tired (or too poor) to stop at a restaurant. A cold drink and that box of crackers you stashed in your vehicle might be just what it takes to see you through the miles home. A small bag of hard candies might also give you the sugar rush needed to get home. That's a better option than trying to starve off light-headedness by scrounging for gummy bears stuck to the carpet in the back seat.

The car kit: If you've spent much time at flea markets, you know how important it is to pack some things in the car "just in case." Among the items to consider are sunblock, lip balm, a travel-size medical kit, pain reliever, antacid, a small package of facial tissues, a container of anti-bacterial wipes or hand cleaner, bug spray, and even a hairbrush for those windy days at outdoor markets.

A box of your most frequently used reference books can serve as your traveling library. And don't forget to toss in some empty boxes, newspapers, wrapping supplies, and tape to pack your purchases safely for the trip home. A clipboard or several sturdy pieces of cardboard will protect items that are easily bent.

Some shoppers also include a black light, Bakelite and gold test kits, plastic bags for holding small items, maps, a flashlight, a tow chain, gloves, hand warmers, an umbrella, and a small bag of tools with screwdrivers of various types and sizes.

Tools of the trade: Although your goal is to travel as lightly as possible, you will still want to carry a number of items with you. Begin with a cloth bag, fanny pack, or backpack for storing needed tools of the trade as well as your

Flea markets are great places to find display cases appropriate for use in antique shops. This oak cabinet featured a glass top and sides and a sliding rear door with a mirror. It was priced at **$250.**

flea market finds. Some shoppers prefer to use collapsible carts.

A pen and a pocketsize notebook are useful for jotting down information on a dealer's location or for noting a specific item you want to quickly research using the reference books in your vehicle. A small tape measure can be used to determine whether the yellowware bowl you're

considering is the size needed for your nesting set, or whether the Victorian marble-top table will fit next to your sofa. A collapsible jeweler's loupe will prove invaluable in reading small marks or enhancing details in vintage photographs. Some shoppers prefer a magnifying glass with a battery-powered light.

A magnet can be used to determine if a painted frog doorstop is cast iron or brass, and a set of batteries will come in handy for testing toys or other battery-operated collectibles.

Handing out a want list or cards printed with your name, telephone number and what you collect can help secure items after the event. Most business supply stores and copy centers can create inexpensive versions. You might also want to carry an inventory to refer to so you don't purchase duplicate items.

Durable paper towels can be tucked in your pocket, serving a multitude of functions. They

Companies such as McCoy, Roseville, Weller, etc. commonly made two-piece jardinières, a top for holding a plant and a base to elevate the pretty plant. This green and brown glazed example shows that buyers need to carefully examine both parts as marriages between similar colored pieces often occur at flea markets. If you liked the colors and didn't mind a slightly mismatched set, this set of unmarked pieces priced at **$65** was a good deal.

can be used to wrap your newly acquired Davenport Cigars match safe so it doesn't get scratched, wipe a runny nose, clean up blood from a cut finger, or serve as a backup when the Port-A-John is out of toilet paper.

Communication: Cellular phones and walkie-talkies have become standard equipment for many flea market shoppers. The cell phone allows you to inform your spouse when you're running a little late, to ask a friend if he's interested in the Creature From the Black Lagoon model kit you just found, or to call to have someone check a reference book you forgot to pack.

Walkie-talkies and other two-way radios allow teams of shoppers to stay in contact with each other, checking to see if a Pepsi tray is a good buy or whether a team member still needs a specific Camp Snoopy drinking glass. However, remember to be polite to your fellow shoppers, don't carry on your conversations with such vigor that you walk into tables, or share all your "business" by loudly yelling into your phone.

On your mark...

When it comes to flea markets, most veteran collectors attack the event with forethought. There's method to their madness. Here are some of the approaches used.

Run and gun: In the run and gun, the shopper hurries down the aisles, glancing in each booth for certain items, but not stopping unless he sees something he wants to buy. Sometimes he resorts to shouting, "Got any...?" as he's scurrying past. After going through the entire show, he'll begin a second loop, this time checking each booth more carefully.

Slow and steady: In this approach, the shopper figures he has a better chance of finding something if he methodically looks at all of the merchandise in each booth. This method allows him to scrutinize the items in each booth, but by the time he gets to the last aisle, several hours may have passed. He feels what he might miss in those latter booths (because it's already sold by the time he gets there) will be offset by the treasures he discovers on.

FDS (Favored Dealer Status): Knowing certain dealers carry the type of merchandise he's looking for, the collector will immediately head to those booths. This is generally a good approach, and the dealers are easy to find since most flea markets allow them to reserve the same booth space for each show.

Walking advertisement: In this method, the customer wears a shirt or sign noting what he collects. Who could miss a neon-orange shirt with large black letters that read, "Old Cameras Wanted." Dealers with cameras for sale will eagerly flag down the shopper. No doubt, the resulting sale will be a Kodak moment.

A little diplomacy

It's well understood that most flea market dealers are willing to lower their prices. Surely you've had this experience: You're shopping a flea market when, out of curiosity, you pick up an item. Immediately, you are hit with a rapid-fire, "Icandobe'eronthat!" Translated, it means, "I can do better on that." It doesn't matter if you're holding a $125 Blue Ridge teapot, a $10 PEZ dispenser, or the gum wrapper your daughter just dropped on the ground: the phrase speaks volumes about the fact that flea markets are places where prices can be negotiated.

Some dealers will automatically volunteer to provide a discount, while others may have signs announcing, "Ask for a better price" or "No reasonable offer refused." Yet, often it's up to you to make the first move. Here are some rules for the game of dickering.

Rule No. 1: Politeness is everything. This is a good rule to follow in all your dealings at a flea market, from negotiating with a seller to ordering a hot dog at the concessions stand. Put a smile on your face and enjoy the day. When seeking a better price from a dealer, a cheery countenance can work wonders. Talk to him with the same tone and manner you would use when asking a friend for a favor.

You can never go wrong when treating people with kindness and respect.

Some dealers feel it's just as easy to put odd things together on one table and then add a sign reading "This table 25¢ each or five for $1." Items range from collectibles to useful household items, mugs, stemware, holiday decorations, a little something for everyone.

keep you from owning something you want, especially if it's already affordable. If you find a Hummel lamp worth $475 that's only priced at $200, it's okay to ask if the dealer will negotiate the price. However, don't be offended if he tells you the price is firm. Pay the $200 and be happy with your bargain. Remember, collecting should be fun. Don't let the absence of a discount ruin your day.

Rule No. 4: Know how to bargain. There are a number of methods that work for buyers. The one we prefer is a straightforward, non-threatening approach. Politely call the item to the dealer's attention and ask, "Is this your best price?" The dealer then has the option of quoting a lower figure or telling you the price is firm. If a discount is offered, we recommend you either accept it or thank the dealer and walk away.

Some people delight in dickering back and forth until a price is agreed upon. If that's your style, and the dealer doesn't mind, the best of luck to you both. But keep in mind that some dealers will be insulted if you respond to their offer by undercutting it with a counteroffer.

Rule No. 5: Bargain seriously. Don't ask for a discount unless you are truly interested in buying the item. Otherwise, you're wasting both your time and that of the dealer. We've all seen it happen. Someone picks up a Hubley airplane tagged $165 and asks the dealer, "Can you do any better on the price?" The dealer says he really wants to move merchandise, so he'll take $85 for it. The customer then mumbles something unintelligible, sets

Common courtesy will also put you in good stead when seeking additional information about an item that's for sale. You might want to know who previously owned a particular cedar chest or whether an oil painting has had touch-up work. Do as your mother told you, and mind your manners. A non-threatening approach will help put the dealer at ease and could put you both on the path to a sale.

Rule No. 2: Play with a poker face. Conceal your enthusiasm until after you've purchased the item. If you spot a Chef

egg timer you recall from your grandmother's kitchen, don't squeal, "OH MY GOSH!" and immediately rush into the booth to gleefully snatch the piece off the table. To a dealer, that's tantamount to announcing, "I hereby waive all my rights to bargain on the price of this item." The dealer knows you want the egg timer, and he sees a sale coming at full price. Instead, wait until you get the little Chef character back to the car before jumping for joy.

Rule No. 3: Be willing to pay a fair price. Don't let your pride

down the plane and walks out of the booth. Obviously, the individual never intended to buy the toy.

Rule No. 6: Be kind and courteous. Being polite and interested in what the vendors are selling will get you much further than being openly critical of their merchandise. Remember some of the folks you will find selling things will be professionals, those who make a large part of their income from buying and selling items at this level. However, there are others who are part timers, perhaps retired or between "real world" jobs that are there to supplement their income. Another group of vendors fall in to the "let's clean out the attic" school and they are more than likely selling off their own possessions. If they begin to tell you that it was their wedding present from Great Aunt Tilly, you know you've got folks who really are bringing fresh merchandise to the marketplace.

Also be kind to fellow shoppers. Keep an eye on your kids, don't let them wander too far ahead of you or play in the aisles. Some of us lose the ability to reconnoiter among little ones. And be kind to those using canes and wheel chairs. Cutting in front of them to grab that special bargain may come back to haunt you or at least your conscience. You'll find almost every one at the flea market is there for the same reason you are—a great outing with the added benefit of *perhaps* finding something to add to a treasured collection. Approaching the adventure with a positive attitude may reward your soul as much as your shelves.

And that's final!

Flea markets are a great place to find vintage architectural elements. This set of porch railings was priced at **$30** per section; other matching elements were also available. Be sure to bring a tape measure and your measurements if shopping for this type of antique.

They're just three little words, but they can have a big impact on your life. We're all familiar with the phrase "All sales final." The general rule at most flea markets is that the deal is finalized when money changes hands. If you experience buyer's remorse or find an identical item for less just two booths later, don't expect the seller to refund your purchase price or give you a rebate.

Even if the item is later determined to be a reproduction, your avenues of recourse may be limited. While reputable dealers will refund the purchase price if an honest mistake has been made, others will point out that you should not have bought the piece if you weren't sure of its authenticity.

The best thing you can do is to carefully examine all merchandise before you buy.

This Ironstone pitcher with a black Oriental transfer decorated with green and orange highlights, if perfect, would be valued at **$95-$115,** but it has a "make-do" repair, lowering its value to **$35-$65.**

Would you check on that?

You've found a McCoy cookie jar, the sticker price seems fair, and the dealer appears willing to negotiate. But before you strike a deal, there are some other steps you'll want to take.

Examine the item: Carefully check over prospective purchases. If the price seems low, the piece may be damaged. Examine glassware and pottery for chips and cracks. Check toys to see if all the parts are original and to determine whether the item has been repainted. Look for stains and holes in textiles and make sure you're dealing with an authentic item, not a reproduction.

Ask about it: Even if you are convinced the item is perfect, ask the dealer if he's aware of any damage. You might have missed a hairline crack or a carefully concealed repair. An honest dealer will tell you what he knows and most dealers are honest.

That Latin phrase

This is the part of the book in which we get to use the Latin phrase every antiquer knows, *caveat emptor*—let the buyer beware. Although flea markets are enjoyable and hold the promise of turning up a prized collectible at a reasonable price, there are also some pitfalls that seem more troublesome than in any other segment of the market.

We want to stress that most flea market dealers are honest, reputable sellers who enjoy what they're doing and wouldn't think of jeopardizing their business by cheating a customer. However, it's important to discuss the proverbial "one bad apple" that can spoil the rest of the fruit in the barrel.

Reproductions: Reproductions, fakes, and fantasy items are often found at flea markets. One must understand that sales of reproductions are not dependent on the items being represented as old merchandise. Quite the contrary. At some flea markets, reproductions are stacked ten-deep on the table and are offered at wholesale prices. That repro tin windup penguin may be bought as new here, passed off as authentic there. They may be no farther than three aisles away, so *caveat emptor.*

Knowledge is your best defense. If the price seems too good to be true, even at a flea market, then maybe it is. When examining an item, use all your senses. Look at it. Are the details crisp, or does a cast-iron bottle opener have the worn molding of many recasts? Examine the hardware. Are the screws in a mechanical bank the right type for when the piece was made? Study the lithography. Is the printing of a die-cut sporting goods sign a little fuzzy, indicating a later printing method? Feel the piece. Does the wear on the base correspond to the age of the planter? Some old merchandise even has a slightly different texture than the reproductions. Using your nose can also provide some clues about the item. Does a small curly maple candle box have the smell of a 150-year-old piece, or is the scent that of freshly cut wood or new varnish?

Tall tales: Unscrupulous dealers always have a story to tell about their merchandise. Listen carefully, and *caveat emptor*. You might be told that a crystal goblet traveled across the Atlantic Ocean with a family of Pilgrims aboard the Mayflower. But, if that goblet is pressed glass, you can rest assured it's not as old as the dealer suggests.

Some mistakes are made honestly, but they're mistakes nonetheless. How about the Lucy doll with a 1963 copyright date? The price tag read: "Lucy, 1963, all original, $45." But, Lucy's dress was fastened with Velcro tabs. Does anyone see a problem here? The Velcro shows the clothes to be of a more contemporary design.

Copyright dates are tricky things, and worth a brief mention. They indicate when a particular copyright was issued, not necessarily the date of manufacture for the object on which the copyright appears.

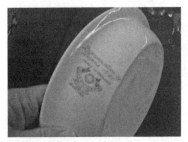
Mark on side of reproduction Staffordshire vegetable bowl.

Reproduction wares also show up at flea markets. This vegetable bowl is clearly marked on the side "Reproduction of Rogers 1780 Made in England," banner mark "John Steventon & Sons Ltd. Burslem." If this green transfer decorated bowl matched your set of dinnerware, it was a good bargain at **$5.**

G.I. Joes are a good example. Fuzzy-haired Joes first appeared in 1970, but the copyright date on each figure says 1964, so do your homework.

Look for clues that indicate an item's true age. For instance, a Royal Staffordshire platter marked "Dishwasher Safe" is definitely from the second half of the 20th century, not from the 19th century, no matter how old the transferware pattern looks. Knowledgeable collectors are always on the lookout for price tags with incorrect information. Among the common mistakes are pressed glass said to be cut glass, molded pottery marked as hand-thrown, machine-molded glassware claimed to be mouth-blown, plastic tagged as Bakelite or celluloid…Need we go on?

Knowledge is your friend. The best purchases you will ever make are good reference books. Some of your most productive time will be spent with dealers and collectors who allow a hands-on examination of authentic antiques and collectibles. Armed with knowledge, you can shop any market safely.

Absolutely positive

Don't let "The Bad and the Ugly" scare you away from flea markets. The nasties are far outweighed by "The Good" that can be found at these events. Topping the list of those positives is the family atmosphere at flea markets. Here's the perfect way to spend a day with loved ones. Because flea markets offer something for everyone, even children enjoy tagging along. The hunt for inexpensive collectibles will keep them interested for hours.

Although children seem to have a natural interest in the merchandise at flea markets, they don't always have the stamina to spend an entire day walking aisles and darting into booths. One popular solution is to take a wagon. Your youngsters will enjoy the ride, especially at outdoor markets. Toss in a coloring book or handheld video game, and you've made great strides toward boredom-proofing the day. Add a small cooler with juice and snacks, and you'll be a hero in their eyes.

Strollers can also be used, and they're particularly good

Watch for repaired items while browsing at flea markets. This decorated ironstone pitcher had a neat "make-do" repair, along with an old hand written explanation of who did it—"Grandmother Jane Hunter, hole plugged in her day"—explaining the hard blob. This pitcher must have been something special to that family for generations.

for infants. But whether you're pushing little Susie in a stroller or pulling Johnny Jr. in a wagon, don't be surprised if you get the evil eye from at least a few shoppers. Some adults think children should be banned from all markets. Don't let such cavalier attitudes ruin your day. Remember, you're spending time with your family, and there are few things in the world more important than that. Behaving courteously when maneuvering through the show and using common sense when parking your children to examine an item will certainly be appreciated though.

Due to the inexpensive nature of some of the merchandise, flea markets are good places for children to learn the value of money. Permitting them to spend their allowance on a collection of their own teaches them to make decisions regarding how that money is used.

The other side

What's more fun than shopping at a flea market? How about selling at one? Most flea markets are a mix of full-time dealers running a business and one-time sellers looking for a way to get rid of the stuff that has piled up in the garage. As such, these markets are perfect for anyone looking to make a little cash from the extra things around the house.

Here are some tips to help you succeed if you're new to the role of flea market dealer.

Finding fleas: The first thing you need to do is decide which flea market you want to try. Check flea market directories and trade publications to see which events are held in your area. Before making a commitment to take a booth, attend several flea markets. Ask the dealers what they like about the event and what they would change. Question them about what's selling well and what price ranges attract buyers. Decide whether your merchandise will fit in at a particular market. Inquire about other flea markets the dealers use, as well as the ones they like to shop. Don't forget to find out how and where the flea market is advertised. The greater the number of people who hear about the market, the more customers you will likely have.

Next, study the environment. Are there plenty of shoppers? Are the facilities well kept? Are there affordable concessions and clean restrooms? All of these are important considerations for keeping shoppers happy. As a dealer, you'll quickly learn that an

These flea market finds are actually clever re-uses of old parts, front: a baluster makes a handle for this caddy; put flowers or tools in it, the decision is up to the next user. In the back is a small side table made with a few slats of picket fencing, each painted green and white and priced at **$35**.

unhappy customer is less likely to make a purchase.

Calculating costs: It's important to know how much you'll have to spend to get started in the flea market business, whether you're interested in selling only once or want to set up every weekend. Talk to the promoter about rates and the availability of booth space. Do the dealers also rent tables for displaying their goodies, or will you need to bring some from home? Of course, don't overlook the incidental expenses, such as gas for travel, meals while away from home, and the cost of a motel if you're traveling any distance. All those things can quickly cut into your profit.

Factoring time: If you are retired, you might have unlimited time to devote to your new.hobby. But if you're still holding down a

9-to-5 job, can you get away from your desk in time to get on the road and set up at your favorite flea market? Before committing to a particular market, ask the promoter about the event's set-up policy. Because dealers often arrange their booths before the show begins, you may need to spend Friday traveling to your destination and setting up, in preparation for the crowd that will spill through the gates early Saturday morning.

One other factor to consider is how early you plan to arrive at your booth during the show. When we asked flea market dealers for tips, they repeatedly told us, "Arrive early." After only one flea market experience, you'll appreciate the need to be ready before the show opens, in order to maximize sales to early shoppers as well as other dealers.

Some dealers also mentioned that it's important to be willing to stay late at a show. Leaving too soon might get you home in time to catch that made-for-TV movie you wanted to see, but it can also mean you miss out on sales to last-minute bargain hunters.

Deciding what to take: In addition to your merchandise, you'll need the following.

Tables—Unless tables are provided by the promoter, you'll need something to display your items on. Card tables and larger folding tables are ideal.

Chair—Don't forget something to sit on during lulls in the action.

Cash box and change—A small locking cash box and adequate change, both bills and coins, will be essential.

Spending money—In addition to the money for your cash box, you'll want to take along some extra funds for any purchases you might make or to buy lunch.

Wrapping material—Newspapers, tissue, and bubble wrap will protect your customers' purchases on the trip home.

Who doesn't need a little extra shelf? This clever one was created with picket fencing and shelves, painted green and white; it was waiting for a new home for **$60.**

Tape—This can be used to secure the wrapping material around an item or for posting signs in your booth.

Bags and boxes—You will need paper or plastic bags to hold sold merchandise if the customer doesn't have their own carry-all. Cardboard boxes are good for packaging larger pieces or multiple items.

Receipt books—You'll want to record your sales, and your customer will appreciate a copy of the transaction.

Price tags—Pack some extra price tags for any items you purchase for resale while traveling to the flea market or while at the event. You might also discover you've forgotten to mark some

merchandise, and extra tags will come in handy.

Business cards—Don't be bashful about handing out business cards to anyone who is interested in your merchandise. It may result in a sale long after you've packed up and gone home. When a shopper has time to reconsider your *Wizard of Oz* book he walked away from at the flea market, knowing how to contact you could put that one in the sold column.

Price guides—Pack a few of your favorite price guides, including one general-line guide that covers the market as a whole. (Of course, we strongly recommend this book!) They'll come in handy for determining whether an Annie lunchbox is a good buy or for showing a customer an example just like the one for sale.

Showcase—Consider keeping any valuable small items in a showcase, which will discourage theft.

Sheets or tarps—You might also want to take some light, unfitted bed sheets to cover you merchandise when you're out of your booth, keeping ne'er-do-wells from being tempted by your miniature Blue Willow tea set. For outdoor shows, a light covering will also prevent dew from forming on your merchandise, while a water-resistant tarp will be more appropriate when the skies threaten rain.

Creating the display: There is no right or wrong way to display merchandise at a flea market. Some dealers achieve satisfactory

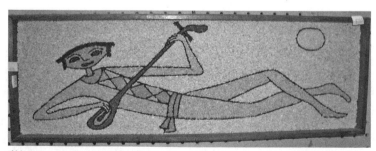

I'd be giving my age away if I admitted to creating wall art such as this when I was a kid, but I bet some of you did, too! The scary part is that examples of this are starting to show up at flea markets and antique shows. This orange and turquoise mandolin player had a price tag of **$45.**

results by simply placing their wares on a blanket on the ground. Others adopt a more professional approach, using tables with table covers, risers and lights. We believe the latter provides better exposure for your merchandise, and increased visibility can translate to increased sales.

One of the best things you can do to encourage sales is to price all of your merchandise. Some shoppers hesitate to ask for the price of an item that's untagged. Others may not ask out of principal, believing the dealer will quote a figure that's artificially inflated if the shopper is dressed nicely and appears to be financially fit. Don't run the risk of losing a sale because your merchandise isn't marked.

Many flea market promoters encourage local farmers to sell produce, helping the economy and providing yet another reason for folks to come shop at the flea market.

Providing customer service:

The manner in which you treat your customers is the single most important factor in ensuring your success as a flea market dealer. Never underestimate the importance of greeting every individual who enters your booth. A genuine smile and polite conversation might be all it takes to win over a shopper who's debating whether to buy your hula girl nodder. Customers treated with courtesy will remember you, and a friend you make today might well be a customer you keep for life.

Another voice heard from: We all figure we're beating out fellow collectors and dealers when we're buying at flea markets, but there is another character in the crowd that often will out-spend even a dedicated collector—and that's a decorator!

Professional decorators, and budding amateurs, too, frequent flea markets in search of accent pieces, and more and more are planning whole decors around their flea market find. We've got HGTV and some of the most popular television shows, like *Trading Spaces,* to thank for this. It's great fun to watch them, trying to match color swatches, or whipping out their tape measure to see if that architectural fragment is big enough, or if that kitsch lamp is the right size.

Add to that folks like me who sometimes take their flea market finds and transform them (or try to) into something more usable, giving a second lease on life to an outdated chandelier, or

Don't forget that you will need to get your flea market purchases home with you, fitting everything in can be as much a challenge as finding the treasure. This metal patio set was a real bargain at **$45.**

turning a planter into a place to stash kitchen clutter. Snapping up vintage linens to reuse as curtains turned out to be a rather inexpensive fix for my office. By adding small brass clip-on rings, I can simply take them off and fold up the linens to be used in another way.

At Christmas, I took an artificial wreath from last year and put it in the center of the dining room table. After putting three white pillar candles in the center, I tucked real holly, boxwood, and ivy in to fill in the spaces and elongate the arrangement a little. Then I tucked in some vintage cardboard putz houses, pinecones, and other bits and pieces of Christmas memorabilia that I found during a flea market trip. By placing another little house on each place setting and tucking in a name card in each, I had an interesting table setting for very little expense. My friends and family have grown accustomed to my eclectic table settings, mixing and matching early American pattern glass with Depression glass to favorite pieces of family china. I've got a hunch some of my guests even look forward to seeing what new flea market finds are going to be there, and who's going to get the "new goblet." No need for cutesy "wine glass charms" at our house; every wine glass is different and with flea market finds, there are always spare goblets to use for serving.

Here's wishing that you find bargains and exciting items awaiting you at the next flea market you visit.

Best Flea Markets

Ask any collector what their favorite flea market is and you'll probably get a smile with the answer. That's been my experience when posing that question through this and the preceding editions of *Warman's Flea Market Price Guide*. Most folks will answer with a name of a flea market that's pretty close geographically to them. They often continue to tell me that the market is within easy driving distance, that they know some of the dealers there and have developed relationships with them. Others tell me they like markets they find on their vacations, or that traveling several hours to get to a once a year or special flea market is really part of their overall antiquing pleasure.

Getting down to a nitty-gritty list of our readers collective favorite flea markets was a bit of a challenge because one really needs to define a flea market. Is it a spot where sellers and collectors come together to exchange goods for cash? That sounds simple enough, but it also describes antique shows, antique shops, antique malls, yard sales, and swap meets. The edges of where a flea market stops and where an outdoor show begin often are now blurring together and that's probably as it should be. Both offer collectors great places to scout for their treasures. Some folks will tell you they avoid flea markets that include vendors selling T-shirts, socks, and fresh produce. Others will tell you those are the best markets ever. Much depends on whether you're thinking about a salad as well as finding that vintage collectible that makes your heart sing.

The diversity of America's flea markets certainly speaks to the itch that we all experience when we're getting ready to take off to find something special. If you live in the warmer parts of our great country, you might be able to head off to a flea market every day of the week. I can do that too, but here in Pennsylvania, it's a pretty seasonal thing. The flea markets I most often find myself at range from markets held once a week, to once a month, to twice a year. Each is known for different things. On Monday I might be at Perkiomenville, "Perky" as the locals have dubbed it, where I can find all kinds of collectibles, antiques, fresh flowers, veggies, and even an auction or two going on. Sometimes the dealers who work the weekend circuit will try their hand there before heading back to their home states. Thursday might find me heading for Columbus, NJ, where flea market dealer Bob Zimmerman tells me he finds his best art pottery pieces. Weekends are reserved for finding treasures at either Golden Nugget in Lambertville, NJ, or perhaps taking in a theme market that might be hiding under the cooling shade of the tall trees at Shupp's Grove, or seeing who's set up at Renninger's or Black Angus in Adamstown, which is a short ride from Shupp's.

Several times a year I'm glad to hop in my car and travel a little further to get to a couple of the seasonal flea markets, the type that are organized and promoted for the same time every year, often three or so times a season. Renninger's Extravaganza is a good example of that kind of flea market. Dealers from all around the country congregate there for three days in April, June, and September. By visiting a seasonal flea market like this one, I get to see what dealers who travel the summer flea market circuit have. Author Walter Dworkin drives down for this event every time he can, looking for examples of Holt Howard or those 1950s ceramic collectibles he loves. He also likes the monthly flea market at Stormville, NY, where he looks for these same types of items, plus he often tells me about some great buys on Gloriosa daisies he's found there for his garden.

Warman's adviser Jerry Rosen, in New England, likes Todd's Farm Flea Market in Rowley, MA. He says it's small enough to be comfortable, usually about 100 dealers outside with more inside. Like many other folks, he tells me he likes that market because it's well run, the merchandise stays fresh, and it's close by for him. Many folks who I spoke with echoed Jerry's thoughts about patronizing a flea market that's well operated, friendly, where the dealers are honest, and is the kind of place you like to take your family. Many flea markets feature both indoor and outdoor dealers, something to consider when planning your trip. Look for flea markets operated by promoters who advertise their markets, and provide well-maintained parking lots and other facilities. Generally you'll find dealers here that are happy and ready to make good deals.

To give *Warman's Flea Market Price Guide* readers a little bit broader prospective, how about considering the list of the World's Best Flea Markets, as complied by the Travel Channel. This branch of the Discovery Channel did a thorough job of investigating flea markets and those who go to them in 2002, when their list was compiled by Constance Van Flendem. You can check out the list by going to www.travel.discovery.com. Her article for the Travel Channel describes the Top 10 Flea Markets in the world.

Interestingly enough, eight of the best fleas markets are in the United States. That either means we're really good at putting on flea markets, or that we have a lot more stuff to sell than the rest of the world.

The Travel Channel favorites were:

1. Brimfield Outdoor Antiques Show, Brimfield, MA. Held for a week each in May, June, and September.
2. Rose Bowl Flea Market, Pasadena, CA. Held the second Sunday of each month.
3. The Maxwell Street Market, Chicago, IL. Held on Sundays.
4. 127 Corridor, Jamestown, TN. Once a year, mid-August.
5. The All Night Flea Market, Wheaton, IL. Once a year, third Sunday of August.
6. Daytona Flea Market, Daytona, FL. Friday through Sunday, year round.
7. San Jose Flea Market, San Jose, CA. Wednesday through Sunday, year round.
8. Austin County Flea Market, Austin, TX. Weekends.
9. New Caladonia Market, London, England. Friday mornings.
10. Marche Aux Puces De Clignancourt, Paris, France. Daily.

Seasonal flea markets

Warman's Flea Market readers probably would agree with the Travel Channel's choice #1 as being the best flea market. This mecca for flea market lovers can be found in a succession of as many as 20 different weeklong markets that pop up in the fields, parking lots, etc. that put Brimfield, MA, on the map. You'll find it west of Sturbridge on Route 20. As many as 4,000-5,000 dealers descend on the area, with different markets opening from Tuesday through Sunday in May, July, and September. Check out its Web site at www.brimfield.com for dates and details such as parking and entrance fees. Devotees of Brimfield will tell you to come early, as many of the markets open at daybreak.

This dealer at Renninger's Extravaganza in Kutztown could park her van right at her space. Her informal style of setting up furniture, small decorative items, etc. is one that encourages collectors to browse.

If you like the idea of a seasonal market like Brimfield, perhaps Renninger's in Kutztown, PA, would also be enjoyable for you. It's a little smaller, but if the weather is good, it will attract dealers from far and wide, sometimes the same dealers who set up at Brimfield will set up at Kutztown and continue on to other summer flea market events. Unlike Brimfield, it has an indoor section that is open every weekend, offering even more dealers. Plus it has a fine farmer's market too, so it can be a great place to grab some better quality food if you're tired of flea market hot dogs.

Another great seasonal market touts itself as "America's Largest Antique & Collectible Sale"—if you feel this qualifies as a flea market, you will want to be at the Portland Multnomah County Expo Center, Portland, OR, in March, July, and October for these gatherings. It is a combination of indoor and outdoor vendors.

Every Memorial Day and Labor Day, the ball fields at the Amos Herr park in Landisville, PA, turn into a flea market. The event is sponsored by the Hempfield Women's Club and raises money for its scholarship funds.

Check out the promoter's Web site, www.palmerwirfs.com, for details about dates, prices, parking details, etc.

Annual event flea markets

It seems many flea-market devotees have a favorite annual event. You know, the kind that rises magically out of a ball field or behind the local firehouse. I happen to think the ladies of the East Hempfield Women's Club have it just about perfect when it comes to their annual flea market in Landisville, PA. Every Memorial Day weekend and Labor Day weekend, they transform the park at the Aaron Herr Homestead into a bustling event. Set-up is early that morning, and by noon the ladies have usually sold out the next event's spots. From the Boy Scouts who are there early on to direct the vendors to their spots to the caterer who comes to provide a lunch, everyone knows their job and does it well.

I find the dealers who set-up there are a good mix of professionals and those folks who like to set-up and help the charity while culling their own

Bargains for a quarter were a big hit with those who browsed through the boxes at the annual Women's Club Flea Market in Landisville, PA.

collections a little. One family I spoke with last September uses the Labor Day event to raise cash for their children's back-to-school shopping. The children had made jewelry, cleaned out their toy boxes, etc. and all was neatly displayed along with the candles and tie-dyed T-shirts that their Mother made. The dealer next to them had good quality primitive items, providing me with an interesting eclectic mix of items to choose from. It's one of those markets where I usually figure on taking along my wheeled bag as I find so many well-priced things and the walk back to the car can be long! The folks in the Landisville area often have their annual yard sales the same day, giving those who really want to spend the day browsing for treasures even more places to look.

Good Neighbors Show radio host Kathy Keene of WHBY, Appleton, WI, and *Antique Trader Weekly* editor Pat Duchene both told me they like the Cedarburg Maxwell Street Days which is a flea market run by firemen in Cedarburg, WI, three times a year. Held in May, July, and September, it certainly seems like this picturesque Wisconsin town is a great place to visit and explore. It also sounds like it's an event very much like the one I encounter at Landisville. These types of flea markets, run by community organized groups, really are a benefit to the whole community. Try to find one or more of these events and I'm sure you'll come away with a smile, too.

The Travel Channel's #5, The All Night Flea Market, Wheaton, IL, is one of the most unusual annual flea market events—it happens only at night! Dealers set up and await the shoppers who descend on this market like fireflies heading toward a lantern. Fabulous buys are made, usually right on the spot since shoppers tend to feel a real time pressure as the whole market folds up and disappears as the sun comes up.

Monthly flea markets

A few flea markets fall in to the once-a-month category. The Travel Channel's #2, Rose Bowl Flea Market, is one. On the second Sunday of every month, the Pasadena football stadium fills up with dealers carting in all kinds of things, from collectibles to useable second-hand items. It has an admission's fee, which lets early shoppers in very early, but for a premium price. California shoppers who miss the second Sunday market can flip their Daytimers to the third Sunday and plan to hit the Americana Enterprises, Inc., Long Beach Outdoor Antique & Collectible Market at Veterans Stadium in Long Beach. Monthly flea markets are great, but it can be a chore to remember what week they appear. If you are searching for a good monthly flea market in the Midwest, consider Kane County, Kane County

This Landisville flea market dealer offered a wide variety of things under their tent. They had created some tie-dyed shirts and hand-made candles. Their children had strung bead bracelets, hoping to generate a little spending money for back to school supplies. Dealers like this add some color and variety to America's flea markets.

Fairgrounds, St. Charles, IL, www. kanecountyfleamarket.com. The Cedars Flea Market, Cedars, PA, is a once-a-month Saturday market. It tends to attract more upscale vendors and shoppers who are out for a great day of antiquing. Finding rock-bottom prices at markets like these tend to be a little harder than finding a great bargain at a weekly or annual event flea market. If you are a flea market devotee that enjoys a leisurely stroll and less pressure to buy, this might be just what you are looking for.

The Ann Arbor Antiques Market is on the third Sunday of the month with some full weekends scheduled, too. Check out www.annarborantiquesmarket.com to get a full schedule.

Weekly flea markets

The Travel Channel's Nos. 3, 6, 7, 8, 9, and 10 all fall into the *Weekly Market* type category, and that's not surprising. Flea markets held the same time every week are probably the most popular with those who can't get enough of the flea market scene. Many of these markets are combined with indoor vendors who also offer interesting merchandise. It's not unusual to find some of the indoor vendors out browsing the outdoor exhibitors to add to their own stock, to see who's there selling and buying, etc. At all kinds of flea markets, you'll probably find the exhibitors knowing each other and freely exchanging opinions and supporting each other in various ways. Remember that outdoor exhibitors are probably just there for the day or perhaps the weekend in the same spot. They are most likely to make good bargains as they are setting up and closing up. The business from dealer to dealer during set-up is often a large portion of their daily revenue.

Weekly flea markets also attract more vendors selling household goods, second hand wares, tube socks, and produce. If you prefer to do one-stop shopping, these are probably the best markets for you. Tuck that shopping list into one pocket and the list of collectibles you're searching for into another. By frequenting a particular flea market for several weeks, you'll get a good feel for when the dealers

Beaded bracelets made with beads and buttons, colorful bargains at **$2.50** each. Their dealer mom told me it was an ongoing project for them, finding buttons and beads at yard sales and then stringing them to sell at this annual Labor Day flea market.

are starting to pack up, who may bring the freshest merchandise and where particular dealers like to set up. Don't be surprised to find that some Sunday markets have peaks which coincide with the times local churches end.

One weekly flea market popular with *Warman's Flea Market* readers that didn't make the Travel Channel's list is First Monday Trade Days, Canton, Texas. This popular market attracts upward of 3,000 dealers into a three-acre area. Like the name implies, some good old-fashioned trading goes on here, plus dealers are more than glad to trade their things in their inventory for cash. Check

This vendor at the Labor Day Landisville flea market offered flowers and bulbs.

out www.firstmondaycanton.com for details about dates, set-up, and parking. Admission is free, but plan to drive a good-sized vehicle so you can take home all your goodies.

Wonderful flea markets exist all across this great land. Each has its own special flavor and special attributes that beckon shoppers to each. Perhaps it's the easy walking layout, the great spirit of the vendors, the music drifting down the aisles, the best food, or just the lure of finding that next terrific example for a collection. Go, enjoy, and take your family and friends.

Flea Markets Around the Country

Here's a list of some of the great flea markets located all around America and some terrific Canadian markets, too. Be sure to call ahead and check for directions, when they are open and other details that will make your flea market excursion great.

The West Palm Beach Antiques Show, West Palm Beach, FL, is a good example of how Mother Nature can interrupt antiquers' best intentions. During the 2004 hurricane season, this great show was shut down *twice* when the fairgrounds location turned into a Red Cross evacuation center. Many flea markets co-exist at fairgrounds and other civic structures, so schedules get jiggled around a little. Plus, many of the open-air flea markets sit on prime real estate, so one just never knows.

This list is a partial listing at best. Many flea markets don't advertise far beyond the local level, making it really difficult to find them for a publication like this.

Many flea markets, their addresses, dates, etc. can now be found on-line. Try one of these Web sites before heading out, or use your favorite search engine for more information; http://collectors.org/FM/ www.fleamarketguide.com

Alabama

Attalla: Mountain Top Flea Market, 11301 US Hwy 278W, www.lesdeal.com

Bessemer: Bessemer Flea Market, 1013 8th Ave. North

Birmingham: Birmingham Fairground Flea Market, Alabama State Fairgrounds, Exit 120

Centeister: North Alabama Flea Market, Hwy 72

Clanton: KayeCee's Flea Market, 224 Town Rd

Collinsville: Collinsville Trade Day, Hwy 11, www.collinsvilletradeday.com

Cullman: Cullman Flea Market, 415 Lincoln Ave. SW

Dothan: Sadie's Flea Market, Route 231S near Route 109

Douglas: Douglas Flea Market, 614 Hambrick Rd

Eufaula: Gopher Hill Flea Market, Hwy 431 S

Florence: Trash & Treasures, Cloverdale Rd

Guntersville: All American Trade Day Flea Market, 11190 Hwy 431

Harpersville: Dixie Land Flea & Farmers Market, State Hwy 25

Huntsville: Huntsville Gigantic Flea Market, Memorial Parkway & University Drive

Jasper: Kelly's Flea Market, Hwy 78

Killen: Uncle Charlie's Flea Market, Hwy 72W

Madison: Limestone Flea Market, Hwy 72 at Burgreen Rd

Mobile: Flea Market Mobile, 401 Schillingers Rd

Montgomery: Blue Ridge Treasure Hunt; Eastbrook Flea Market, 425 Coliseum Blvd; Montgomery's Gigantic Indoor Flea Market, 2270 E South Blvd

Muscle Shoals: Fairgrounds Gigantic Flea Market, Fairgrounds, Hwy 43S

Scottsboro: First Monday Flea Market, Courthouse Square

Selma: Selma Flea Market, Hwy 80 Bypass at River Rd

Smiths: Lees County Flea Market, Route 431 and 280W

Sulpher Springs: JJ's Iron Dog, 789 Hwy 59N

Theodore: South Alabama Flea Market, 6280 Theodore Dawes Rd

Wetumpka: Hilltop Flea Market, Hwy 231N; Santuck Flea Market, 662 Dexter Rd; White Rail Flea Market, 10869 Central Plank Rd

Alaska

Anchorage: Downtown Wednesday Market, Fourth Ave. from C to F streets; Downtown Saturday Market, 3rd and E streets

Fairbanks: Fairbanks Flea Market, Tanana Valley Fairgrounds

Palmer: Alaska State Fair Flea Market, Glenn Hwy

Seward: American Legion Flea Market, American Legion Building, 402 5th Ave.

Soldotna: Soldotna Flea Market, 538 Arena Drive

Arizona

Apache Junction: American Park N. Swap, 2651 W. Apache Trail, www.americanparknswap.com

Blytheville: Blytheville Flea Market, 70 Terry Walters

Casa Grande: Shoppers Barn Swap Meet, 13480 West Hwy 84; Flagstaff Flea Market, 2530 N. 4th St.

Glendale: Glendale 9 Swap Meet, 5650 N. 55th Ave., www.centurytheater.com

Goodyear: Goodyear Market Place Swap Meet, 17605 W. McDowell Rd, www.fleaamerica.com

Mesa: JJ's Old West Flea Market, 9705 E. Apache Trail; Mesa Market Place Swap Meet, 10550 E. Baseline, www.fleaamerica.com/mesa.html

Phoenix: Phoenix Antique Market, Phoenix Fairgrounds, www.jackblack.com; Park N Swap, 3801 E. Washington St., www.americanparknswap.com; Paradise Valley Swap Meet, 2414 E. Union Hills Drive

Prescott Valley: Peddlers Pass, 6201 E. Hwy 69

Quartzsite: The Main Event, Business 1-10, Mile Post 17, www.quartzsite.com

Surprise: Surprise Swap Meet, 12910 Sante Fe Drive

Tucson: America Park N Swap, 2601 S. 3rd Ave., www.americanparknswap.com; Pima County Monthly Antique Fairs, Lew Sorenson Community Center; Tanque Verde Swap Meet, 4100 S. Palo Verde Rd, www.flash.net-tvsm

Yuma: Yuma Park N Swap, 4000 S. 4th Ave., www.yumafleamarket.com

Arkansas

Conway: The Rhino and the Lady, Hwy 66N, www.Rhino-Lady.com

Harrison: Trade Days in the Ozarks in Harrison, fairgrounds

Hot Springs: Central Station Marketplace & Flea Market, 3310 Central Ave.

Knoxville: Hwy 64 Flea Market, 23375 Highway 64W

Little Rock: Carrie's Collectibles, 8718 Geyer Springs Rd; Memphis Flea Market, Little Rock Expo Center, www.americanparknswap.com

Magnolia: Checkers Flea Market, 219 W. Main St.

Pine Bluff: Pinecrest Flea Market, 407 N. Blake St.

Redfield: County Fair Flea Market, S Hwy 365

California

Alameda: Alameda Antique Flea Market, 1150 Ballena Blvd, former Naval Air Station

Anderson: Jolly Giant Flea Market, 6719 Eastside Rd

Aromas: The Big Red Barn, 1000 Hwy 101

Azusa: Azusa Swap Meet, 673 E. Foothill Blvd

Bakersfield: Bakersfield Fairground Swap Meet, Kern County Fairgrounds

Bloomington: Bel-Air Swap Meet, 17565 Valley Blvd

Boonville: Boonville Veterans Annual Flea Market, Veterans Building

Ceres: Ceres Flea Market, 1651 E. Whitmore Ave.

Concord: Solano Drive-in and Swap Meet, Solano Drive-in Theater, www.centurytheater.com

Costa Mesa: Orange County Market Place, 88 Fair Drive, www.ocmarketplace.com

Cupertino: De Anza College Flea Market, 21250 Stevens Creek Blvd

Dominguez Hills: California State Univ Antique Flea Market, 1000 E. Victoria St. at Avalon

Earlimart: Earlimart Community Swap Meet, 159 S. Valente

Escondido: Escondido Swap Meet, 635 West Mission Ave.

Folsom: Annual Peddlers Faire & Antique Market, Sutter St.

Fresno: Big Fresno Flea Market, Fresno Fairgrounds; Cherry Lane Auction, Inc., 4640 Cherry Ave.

Fullerton: Troubleshooters Antiques & Collect Round-Up, Cal State University, www.rgcshows.com

Garden Grove: Main Street Flea, 12000 block Main St.

Glendale: Glendale City Community College Swap Meet, Mountain Ave. near Verdugo Rd

Goleta: Santa Barbara Swap Meet, 907 S. Kellogg

Hayward: Chabot College Flea Market, 25555 Hesparian Blvd, www.chabot.cc.ca.us

Long Beach: Americana Productions, Monthly Antiques,Collectibles & Home Furnishings Flea Market Long Beach Veterans Stadium, 3rd Sunday, www.longbeachantiquemarket.com

Hollywood: Eclectibles on Melrose, 7171 Melrose Ave.; Melrose Trading Post Antiques & Collectibles Market, Fairfax High School

Huntington Beach: Golden West College Swap Meet, Golden West St. & Edinger Ave.

Indio: Maclin's Indio Open Air Market, 46-350 Arabia St., www.maclinmarkets.com

King City: King City Rotary Flea Market, Salinas Valley Fairgrounds

Lancaster: Lancaster Chamber of Commerce Semi-Annual Flea Market, 155 E. Ave. I, www.richardmaries.com

Napa: Napa Flea Market, 303 S. Kelly Rd

Oceanside: Oceanside Swap Meet, 3480 Mission Ave.

Orange: YMCA Flea Market & Y's Buys, 146 N. Grand St.

Pasadena: Rose Bowl Flea Market and Swap Meet Pasadena Rose Bowl, Rosemont Ave & Aroyo Blvd

Petaluma: Petaluma Outdoor Antiques Faire Sonoma-Marin Fairgrounds, 4th & KY St.

San Bernardino: Pro-Swap-Meet, 632 S Mt. Vernon Ave

San Diego: Kobey's Swap Meet San Diego Sports Arena, 3500 Sports Arena Blvd

San Francisco: Cow Palace Cow Palace, Hwy 101

San Jose: Capitol Flea Market, 3630 Hillcap Ave.

San Mateo: San Mateo Flea Market—there are several different flea markets held in this town

Santa Cruz: Skyview Flea Market, 2260 Soquel Drive

Santa Monica: Santa Monica Outdoor Antiques Market, parking lot, Airport Rd & Bundy Ave.

Spring Valley: Spring Valley Flea Swap Meet, 6377 Quarry Rd

Stockton: San Joaquin Delta College Flea Market, San Joaquin Delta College

Colorado

Boulder: Boulder Market, Boulder High School, 14th and Arapahoe, www.bouldermarket.com

Colorado Springs: The Flea Market, 5225 E. Platte Hwy

Denver: Mile High Flea Market, 1-76 at 88th Ave; The Ballpark Market, 22nd and Larimer St., www.ballparkmarket.com; The Collectors Fair, National Western Complex

Englewood: Arapahoe Flea Market, 3400 S. Platte Dr.

Granby: Top O'The Rockies Flea Market & Auto Swap, 11034 Hwy 34

Pueblo: Sunset Flea Market, 2641 N. I-25

Redstone: Redstone Flea Market, 0373 Redstone Blvd

Connecticut

New Britain: New Britain Shopping Festival Flea Market, 723 Farmington Ave.

Plainville: Flea Market at the Crossing, 105 E. Main St.

Salisbury: Antiques in a Cow Pasture Barn Star Productions

Woodbury: Woodbury Antiques & Flea Market, Route 6

Delaware

Dover: Spence's Auction & Flea Market, 550 S. New St.

Laurel: Bargin Bill, Route 13 at Route 9 E., www.barginbill.com

Newark: Optimist Club Memorial Flea Market, Kirk Middle School

New Castle: Farmer's Market, 110 N. DuPont Hwy

Florida

Auburn: International Market World Inc., 1052 Hwy 92 W.

Bradenton: Eddie's Flea Market, 5715 15th St. E.

Daytona: Daytona Flea Market, I-95 and US 92

Deland: Deland Flea Market Volusia County Farmer's Market, E. New York Ave.

Fort Lauderdale: A-1 Flea Market, 1621 N. St. Rd 7; Oakland Park Blvd Flea Market, 3161 West Oakland Park Blvd

Jacksonville: Ramona Flea Market, 7059 Ramona Blvd

Kissimmee: Hwy 192 Flea Market, W. Irlo Bronson Hwy; Osceola Flea & Farmers Market, 2801 E. Irlo Bronsn Hwy

Lake Worth: Shoppers Depot, 3911 Jog Rd

Lecanto: Cowboy Junction

Melbourne: Super Flea & Farmers Market, 4835 West Eau Gallie Blvd

Mt. Dora: Renningers Florida Twin Markets, 20641 US Hwy 441

Okeechobee: The Market Place Flea Market, 3600 Hwy 441 South

Orlando: Colonial Flea Market, 11500 E. Colonial Drive

Pinellas Park: Wagon Wheel Flea, 7801 Park Blvd

Port Richey: USA Fleamarket, 11721 US Hwy 19

Sarasota: Flea Market & Collectibles Show, Sarasota Fairgrounds

St. Augustine: St. John County Beach Flea Market, I-95 and State Rd 207, exit 94

Stuart: B & A Flea Market, South US Hwy 1, across from Martin Sq Mall

Webster: Sumter County Farmer's Market, Inc., Hwy 471; Webster Westside Flea Market, 516 NW 3rd St., Hwy 478 at NW 3rd St.

West Palm Beach: 45th Street Flea, 45th St.; Beach Drive-In Theatre Swap, 1301 Old Dixie Hwy; Dr. Flea's Farmer's Market, 1200 Congress Ave.; West Palm Beach Antiques Show, www. dmgantiqueshows.com

Georgia

Atlanta: Lakewood Antiques Market, 2000 Lakewood Way; Pride of Dixie N. Atlanta Trade Center, 1700 Jeurgens Court; Scott Antique Market, A & C Show Atlanta Expo Center, 3650 Jonesboro Rd

Augusta: Augusta Barnyard Fleamarket, 1625 Doug Barnard Parkway, www.augustabarnyard. com

Blairsville: Blairsville Super Flea Market, 466 Orbit Drive

Carrollton: West Georgia Flea Market, 3947 Hwy 27N

Decatur: 285 Flea Market, 4525 Glenwood Rd, SE

Douglasville: Premier Flea Market, 1516 Muncipal Parkway

Macon: Smiley's Flea Market, Georgia Hwy 247

Mcdonough: Peachtree Peddlers Flea Market, 155 Mill Rd

Sanderville: WACO Flea Market, Hwy 15 South

Savannah: Keller's Flea Market, 5901 Ogeechee Rd

Summerville: Summerville Flea Market

Hawaii

Aiea: Kam Super Swap Meet, 98-850 Moanalua Rd

Honolulu: Aloha Stadium Flea Market, Aloha Stadium

Pearl City: Kam Drive-In, Kaonohi and Moanalua Rd

Wahiawa: Mango Marketplace, 620 California Ave

Idaho

Boise: Spectra's Flea Market, West Idaho Fairgrounds

Filer: Twin Fall County Fairgrounds Flea Market, Twin Fall County Fairgrounds

Ketchum-Sun Valley: Warm Springs Village Peddler's Fair Antique Show

Sagle: Sagle Flea Market, 130 Algoma Spur Rd

Illinois

Alsip: Tri-State Swap-O-Rama, 4350 W. 129th St.

Belleville: Belleville Flea Market, Belle-Clair Exposition Center, Fairgrounds; West Main Fea Market, 2615 W. Main St.

Bloomington: Third Sunday Market McClean County Fairgrounds, Interstate Center

Chicago: Ashland Avenue Swap-O-Rama, 4100 S. Ashland Ave.; Buyers Flea Market, 4545 W. Division St.; New Maxwell Street Market, Canal & Roosevelt St., www.openair. org/maxwell/newmaxwell.html; The Bull Ring, 10600 S. Torrence Ave.

Dixon: Sauk Valle Community College Flea Market, Route 2

Du Quoin: Giant Flea Market, State Fairgrounds

Freeport: Yellowcreek Flea Market, Stephenson County Fairgrounds

Grafton: Water Street Flea Market, Water Street

Gray Lake: Lake County Ant & Collect Show & Sale, Lake County Fairgrounds; Zuako Antiques & Collectibles Mart

McLean: Old Route 66 Country Market, Route 66

Melrose Park: Melrose Park Swap-O-Rama, 4600 W. Lake St.; Wolff's Flea Market, 2031 N. Mannheim, www.wolffsfleamarket.com

Morris: Grundy County Antiques & Flea Market, Grundy County Fairgrounds

Ottawa: Ottawa Riverfest Craft & Flea Market, Washington Square

Pecatonia: The Pec Thing, Winnebago County Fairgrounds, www.winnebagocountyfair.com

Pontiac: Pontiac Thueseman's Shows

Princeton: Princeton Flea Market, fairgrounds

Rantoul: Gordyville Flea Market

Rockford: Greater Rockford Antique & Flea Market, 3913 Sandy Hollow Rd

Rock Island: Rock Island Summerfest Antique Market, 18th St. between 2nd and 3rd Ave., www. antiquespectacular.com

Rosemont: Wolff's Flea Market, Rosemont Horizon, near intersection of I-90 and I-294

Sandwich: Sandwich Antique Market, Fairgrounds, State Rt. 34, www.antiquesmarket.com

Springfield: Giant Flea Market, State Fairgrounds

St. Charles: Kane County Flea Market, Kane County Fairgrounds, St. Charles St., www2.pair.com/ kaneflea

Sycamore: Antique, Craft & Flea Market, Sycamore High School

Tinley Park: I-80 Flea Market, 19100 Oak Park Ave.

Towanda: Towanda Antique Flea Market, NW of Bloomington at I-55, exit 171

Wheaton: All-Night Flea Market, 2015 Manchester Rd

Woodstock: Summer Collectors Fairs & Markets, McHenry County Fairgrounds, www. zurkantiquetours.com

Indiana

Cedarlake: Big Bear Flea Market, I-70; Uncle John's Flea Market

Evansville: Cain's Flea Market, 322 W Columbia St.; Collectors Carnival, Vanderburgh County 4-H Fairgrounds

Fort Wayne: Memorial Coliseum Flea Market, Memorial Coliseum

Indianapolis: Indianapolis Flea Market, Indiana State Fairgrounds

Shipshewana: Shipshewana Auction & Flea Market, State Route 5

Veedersburg: Steam Corner Flea Market, 2164 S US Hwy 41

Iowa

Davenport: Davenport Flea Market, Mississippi Valley

Fairgrounds; West Kimberly Market, 4004 West Kimberly Rd

Des Moines to Coon: Hwy 141 Garage Sale

Dubuque: Dubuque Flea Market, Dubuque County Fairgrounds

Fort Dodge: Hillbilly Sale & Flea Market, Webster County Fairgrounds

Hazelton: Open Air Flea Market, Hazelton Commercial Club, City Park

Lake Okoboji at Milford: Treasure Village Flea Market & Antiques Show, Treasure Village, 2033 Hwy 86

Perry: Perry Park N Swap, 1030 26th St.

Spirit Lake: Country Time Farm, 1060 N Hwy 86, www.angelfire. com/ia/countrytimefarm; Annual Antique Show & Flea Market at Vick's Corner, Wa-Hoo Flea Market, Hwy 9 and 86

Walnut: Whole town

What Cheer: Collectors Paradise Flea Market, Keokuk County Fairgrounds

Kansas

Hutchinson: Mid-America Flea Market, Kansas State Fairgrounds, www.midamericamarkets.com

Kansas City: Bouvelard Drive-In Swap & Shop, 1051 Merriam Lane

Kechi: Kechi Antique Swap Meet & Flea Market, downtown, 61st North & Oliver, www.kechiksoc.com

Opolis: Opolis Flea Market, US 171 and 57

Sparks: Sparks Flea Market, K-7 Hwy and Mission Rd, www. members.tripod.com/~sparks_flea_ market/index.html

White Cloud: White Cloud Flea Market, 103 Main St.

Witchita: Mid-America Flea Market, Kansas Coliseum; Mid-Town Flea Market, 430 E Harry; Village Flea Market, 2301 South Meridian

Kentucky

Ashville: Hillbilly Flea Market, Russell Rd, Rt 23

Bowling Green: Flea Land of Bowling Green, 1100 Three Springs Rd

Corbin: Cumberland Gap Parkway Flea Market, I-75 exit 29 & Cumberland Gap Parkway

Edmonton: Bargain Train, 1101 West Stockton St., www.kysavagegrocery.com

Elizabethtown: Bowling Lanes Flea Market, 4547 North Drive

Flemingsburg: Annual Old Fashioned Court Day, Main St., center of town

Georgetown: Country World Flea Market, US Route 460, off I-75, exit 125

Greenville: Luke's Town and Country Flea Market, Hwy 62 W.

Leitchfield: Bratcher's Flea Market, Hwy 62, 1 mile east of Leitchfield

Lexington: Lexington Center Antique & Flea Market, www.stewartpromotions.com

London: Flea Land Flea Market, Barberville Rd

Louisville: Derby Park Flea Market, 2900 S. 7th St. Rd, www.fleamarkets.com/derbypark/index.html; Kentucky Flea Market, Kentucky Fairgrounds & Expo Center, www.stewartypromotions.com

Madisonville: Madisonville Flea Market & Antiques, 4195 Anton Rd

Maysville: Maysville Old Fashioned Court Days, Market St.

Mount Sterling: Mount Sterling October Court Days, Main St., www.mountsterling-ky.com

Paducah: Traders Mall Flea Market, 6900 Benton Rd, www.tradersmall.org

Richwood: Richwood Flea Market, 10915 US 25, www.richwoodfleamarket.com

Simpsonville: Shelby County Flea Market, 820 Buck Creek Rd, www.shelbycountyfleamarket.com

Williamstown: Grant County Flea Market, 1418 N. Main St., www.grantcountyfleamarket.com

Kentucky, Tennessee, Alabama, plus

Longest Yard Sale US 127-South, www.450milefleamarket.org

Louisiana

Algiers: Algiers Flea Market, Anson St.

Denham Springs: Louisiana's Finest Antiques and Flea Market, 2360 S. Range Ave., Spring Park Plaza

Deridder: Pine Hill Trade Days, Beau. Par. Fairgrounds

Hammond: Hammond Flea Market, 14175 Hwy 190 W.

Jefferson: Jefferson Hwy Flea Market, Jefferson Hwy

Kenner: Original Jefferson Flea, 2134 Airline Drive

Lafayette: Lafayette Jockey Lot, I-49 North

Lake Charles: Family Flea Market, Widgeon St.; Front Porch Antique & Flea Market, Ryan St.; Kershaw's Cajun Festival City, 3401 East Prien Lake Rd

Leesville: Glenda's Place Pickering Flea Market, Building #6, 14004 Lake Charles Hwy

Marion: Little Bit of Everything, 320 Main St.

Minden: Deals, Deals, Inc., Main St

New Orleans: The Venue Outdoor Flea Market, 6611 Chef Menteur Hwy

Shreveport: Merchants Market, Pines Rd; Riverfront Trade Days, 3232 E. 70th St

Maine

Lincoln: Lincoln Flea Market, I-95 Access Rd

Searsport: Hobby Horse Flea Market

Maryland

Baltimore: Best Yard Sale; Patapsco Flea Market, 1400 West Patapsco Ave., Mountain Rd

Massachusetts

Brimfield: Brimfield's Heart-O-The-Mart A & C Show, several different flea markets held at the same time in this town

Chelmsford: Chelmsford Elks Flea Market, 300 Littleton Rd

Everett: Everett Flea Market, Ashland St.

Grafton: Grafton Flea Market, Inc., Rt 140 Upton-Grafton Town Line

Hadley: Olde Haldey Flea Market, Route 47

Holyoke: Pioneer Valley Fleamarket, 2200 Northampton St.

Hopedale: Hopedale Flea Market, 1 Spaceway Lane

Lancaster: Lancaster Flea Market, 1340 Lineburg Rd

Leominster: Four Seasons Flea Market, 38 Spruce St.

Lunenburg: Montuori's Flea Market, Massachusetts Ave.

Palmer: Tri-Town Flea Market, Route 20

Randolph: The Randolph Flea Market, Randolph High School Football Field

Reading: ABC Flea Market, 1 General Way

Rowley: Todd's Farm Antiques & Flea Market, Route 1A, Main St.

Seacoast: Seacoast Flea Market, 4 Ocean Front North

Taunton: Taunton Flea Market, 93 Williams

Worcester: Kelley Square Flea Market, 149 Washington St.

Michigan

Ann Arbor: Ann Arbor Antiques Market

Blissfield: Blissfield Markets, E. Jefferson

Centreville: Centreville Flea Market, St. Joseph County Fairgrounds

Lapeer: Lapeer Flea Market

Pontiac: Dixieland Telegraph & Dixie

Port Huron: Fort Gratiot Flea Marketm 4189 Keewahdin Rd

Utica: Red Barn Flea Marketm 47326 Dequindre

Minnesota

Albany: Pioneer Days Flea Market

Annandale: Wright County Swap Meet, 13594 100th St. NW

Belle Plaine: Emma Krumbee's Antiques in the Orchard, US Hwy 169, www.emmakrumbees.com

Cambridge: Cambridge Antique Fair, Isanti County Fairgrounds, 1 mile east of Hwy 65 on Hwy 95, www.cambridgeantiquefair.com

Detroit Lakes: Shady Hollow Flea Market, Hwy 59

Elko: Traders Market, I-35 at County Rd 2

Hinckley: Hinckley Flea Market, Hwy 48 & I-35

Lake City: Eighty-five-mile Garage Sale, Minnesota Hwy 61 & Wisconsin Hwy 35 around Lake Pepin, www.lakecity.org

Mankato: National Guard Armory, 2nd & Plum St.

Medina: Medina Entertainment Center Flea Market, 500 Hwy 55

Monticello: Orchard Fun Market, Orchard Rd, Route 75

Oronoco: Downtown Oronoco Gold Rush, Inc., whole town

Wabash: Wabash Indoor/Outdoor Flea Market, Hwy 61 & Industrial Court

Mississippi

Armory: Bigbee Waterway Trade Days, 3 miles north of Armory on Hwy 371

DeSoto: DeSoto Flea Market, 342 County Rd 690

Corinth: Corinth Flea Market, Hwy 72E

Jackson: Fairgrounds Antique Flea Market, State Fairgrounds

Philadelphia: Williamsville Flea Market, 1031 Rd 606

Ripley: First Monday Flea Market, Ripley Trade Days, 10590 Hwy 15S, www.firstmonday.com

Tupelo: Tupelo's Gigantic Flea Market, Tupelo Furniture Market Building, 1979 N Coley Rd

Vicksburg: Battlefield Trade Days, 3240 Brabston Rd, I-20 exit 15

Missouri

Asbury: Stateline Trade Center, Hwy 171

Aurora: Houn' Dawg 25, W. Locust St.

Branson: Confeit's Flea Market & Craft Village, Hwy 165

Cassville: Ole Home Place Flea Market, Business Hwy 37 at Hwy 112, www.oldhomeplaceantiques.com

Colony: Colony #1 Flea Market, Route V off Route K

Farmington: Fairgrounds Flea Market, St. Francois County Fairgrounds, Hwy 67

Imperial: Barnhart Flea Market, 6850 Hwy 61 & 67

Joplin: Joplin Flea Market, Old City Market, 1200 block of Virginia Ave.

Kansas City: Jeff Williams Flea Market, Kemper Arena Compex, Governor's Building; KCI Convention Center Flea Market, KCI Convention Center

Lake Ozark: Fiesta Flea Market, Hwy 54; Osage Beach Flea Market; Village Flea MarketPevely: Pevely Flea Market, I-55 S off Hwy 270

Neosho: Marco's

Rosati: Twin Gables Antique Mall & Flea Market, between Rolla & St. James

Rutledge: Rutledge Flea Market

St. Louis: Frison Flea Market, 7025 St. Charles Rock Rd

Sikeston: Tradewinds Flea Market, 875 W. Malone

Springfield: I-44 Swap Meet, 2908 N Neergard; Old P.O. Flea Market, 304 W. Commercial St.

Wentzville: Wentzville Flea Market

Montana

Columbia Falls: Glacier Flea Market, 5580 Hwy 2 West

Corvallis: Montana Marketplace, 1708 Simpson Rd

Great Falls: Great Falls Farmer's Market, civic center; The Market Swap Meet, 1807 W. 3rd St. NW

Lincoln: Lincoln Flea Market, Pit Stop Drive-In

Missoula: My Fair Lady's Market, 1001 S. Ave. W., Reserve St. exit

Nebraska

Brownville: Fall Flea Market, Main Street; Spring Flea Market, Main Street

Dwight: Dwight Czech Festival Flea Market, Hwy 66

Omaha: 60th Street Flea Market

Valentine: Valentine Masonic Lodge, 120 S. Green St.

New Hampshire

Amherst: Amherst Outdoor Market, 157 Hollis Rd

Derry: Grand View Flea Market, Rt. 28 and Bypass 28 South

Hollis: Hollis Country Store Flea Market, Silver Lake Rd; Silver Lake Flea Market & Antique Fair, 447 Silver Lake Rd

Lebanon: Colonial Plaza Antiques & Flea Market, Route 12A at I-89, exit 20

Meredith: Burlwood Antique Center, 194 Daniel Webster Hwy

New Jersey

Auburn: Auburn Antique & Flea Market, 773 Southbridge St.

Berlin: Berlin Farmer's Market, 41 Clementon Rd

Cherry Hill: Garden State Park Flea Market, Garden State Race Track, Rt. 295

Collingwood Park: Collingwood Auction & Flea Market, St. Hwy 33

Columbus: Columbus Farmer's Market, Rt. 206

Dover: Dover Flea Market, Rt. 80, exit 35A

East Rutherford: Meadowlands Marketplace, Giants Stadium, parking lot 17, Rt. 3 West, www.meadowlandsfleamarket.com

Edison: New Dover United Methodist Church Flea Market, 687 New Dover Rd

Englishtown: Englishtown Auction & Flea Market, 90 Wilson Ave., NJ Turnpike exit 9, www.englishtownauction.com

Flemington: Flemington Fair Flea Market, Flemington Fairgrounds, Hwy 31

Howell: Basics Flea Market, 2301 Hwy 9N

Jefferson: Jefferson Township Fire Company #2 Flea Market, Rt. 15S

Lakewood: Route 70 Flea Market, between Garden State Parkway and Rt. 9

Lambertville: Golden Nugget Antique Flea Market, Rt. 29

Manahawkin: Manahawkin Flea Market, 657 E. Bay Ave.

Mount Laurel: William Spencer's Antique Show & Sale, 118 Creek Rd

Neshanic Station: Neshanic Flea Market, 160 Elm St.

New Egypt: New Egypt Auction & Farmers Market, Route 537 between Routes 528 and 539

North Cape May: Victoria Commons Flea Market, Victoria Commons, Bayshore & Townbank Rds

Palmyra: Tacony-Palmyra Swap N Shop Market, Route 73

Vineland: U-Sell Flea Market, 2896 S. Delsea Drive

Stanhope: Waterloo Antiques Fair, Waterloo Village

Warren: Washington Valley Fire Company Flea Market, 140 Washinton Valley Rd

Woodstown: Cowtown Bawl, Route 40

New Mexico

Albuquerque: Fairgrounds Flea Market, State Fairgrounds; North Valley Indoor Flea Market, 1026 Candelaria NW; Star Flea Market, 543 Coors Blvd SW

Carlsbad: Rose Peddle Flea Market Standpipe Rd

Deming: Traders Village of New Mexico, 4725 Keeler Rd

Farmington: Farmington Flea Market, Hwy 550, between Farmington and Aztec

Gallup: Gallup Flea Market, Old Route 666, I-40, Exit 26 at Sheetrock

Las Cruces: Big Daddy's Market Place, Inc., 7320 N. Main St.

Moriaty: Moriaty Flea Market, Rt. 66

Taos: Taos Rendezvous, Paseo del Pueblo Sur, Hwy 522

Nevada

Hendersen: Silver State Marketplace at Sam Boyd Stadium, Russell Rd and Broadbent

Las Vegas: Fantastic Indoor Swap Meet, 1717 S. Decatur Blvd at West Oakley Blvd

North Las Vegas: Broadacres Open-Air Swap Meet, 2960 Las Vegas Blvd

Sparks: El Rancho Flea Market, 555 El Rancho Drive, www.centurytheaters.com

New York

Avon: East Avon Flea Market, 1520 W. Henrietta Rd

Bouckville: Bouckville Antique Pavilion, Rt. 20

Cheektowaga: Super Flea & Farmer's Market, 2500 Walden Ave.

Clarence: Antique World & Marketplace, 10995 Main St.

Conklin: Jimay's Flea Market, 1766 Conklin Rd

Fishkill: Dutchess Mall Flea Market, Route 9, www.dutchessfleamarket.com

Greenwich: Washington County Fairgrounds Antique Fair & Flea Market, Rt. 213

Madison: Country Walk Antiques Flea Market, Route 20 between Madison & Bouckville

Monticello: Village of Monticello Street Fair, on Broadway, Route 42, between Liberty & Bank streets

New York City: GreenFlea, Columbus Ave. at 77th St.; Soho Antiques Fair, Broadway & Grand St., Soho; The Annex Antiques Fair & Flea Market Ave. of the Americas, between 24th and 27th St., Manhattan; The Garage Flea Market, 112 W. 25th St., Manhattan; The Showplace, 40 W. 25th St.; 23rd & Broadway Flea Market, Manhattan

Port Chester: Empire State Flea Market Mall, Caldor Shopping Center, 515 Boston Post Rd

Queens: Aqueduct Flea Market, 108th St.

Rhinebeck: Rhinebeck Antiques Fair, Dutchess County Fairgrounds, Rt. 9

Staten Island: Antiques, Arts & Crafts Market, Staten Island Historical Society, 441 Clarke Ave.

Stormville: Stormville Airport Antique Show & Flea Market, Airport, Rt. 216

North Carolina

Charlotte: Metrolina Expo, 7100 Statesville Rd

Concord: Treasures & Collectibles, 789 Cabarrus Ave.

Fayetteville: Great American Flea Market, 4909 E. Raeford Rd

Goldsboro: Paradise Super Flea Market, 1015 N. Williams St.

Greensboro: Super Flea Market, Greensboro Coliseum Complex

Hampton: Vintage Village, I-77 and US Hwy

Monroe: Sweet Union Flea Market, 4420 Hwy 74 West

Selma: The Marketplace on I-95, 1501 Industrial Park Dr

Valdese: New 40 Flea Market, 5550 Paradise Ave.

Wilmington: The Starway, 2346 Carolina Beach Rd

Winston-Salem: Flea Country USA, 4267 N. Patterson Ave.

North Dakota

Dickerson: West River Regional Flea Market, Hospitality Inn

Fargo: The Indoor Flea Market, 2340 S. University Dr

Hettinger: Hettinger Area Chamber of Commerce Flea & Farmers Market, Armory St.

Minot: Magic City Flea Market, State Fairgrounds

Trenton: TISA Day Flea Market, Trenton Lake

West Fargo: All American Indoor Flea Market, 110 Sheyene St.

Ohio

Allensville: Cross Creek Flea Market

Callipolis: Gallia County Flea Market, Gallia County Fairgrounds

Cincinnati: Peddlers Flea Market, 4343 Kellogg Ave.

Hartville: Byler's Flea Market, 900 Edison St. NW; Hartville Flea Market, 788 Edison St. NW

Middlefield: Middlefield Flea Market

N. Ridgeville: Jamies Flea Market

Piketown: 23 South Flea Market, US 23

Rogers: Rogers Comm Auction & Open-Air Market SR 154, 10 miles N. of East Liverpool, OH

Springfield: Springfield Antique Show & Sale, Clark County Fairgrounds

Oklahoma

Anadarko: Anadarko Flea Market, Georgia St., http:fleamarketers.tripod.com

Cartwright: Lake Texoma Trade Days, corner 4th and Denison

Elk City: Western Oklahoma Historical Society Flea Market, Old Hwy 66

Oklahoma City: AMC Flea Market, 1001 N. Pennsylvania St.; Buchanan's Antique & Collectors Market, Oklahoma City Fairgrounds, I-40 at May Ave.; Mary's Ole Time Swap Meet, 7905 23rd St. at Midwest Blvd; Old Paris Flea Market, 1111 S. Eastern Rd

Tulsa: Great American Flea Market & Antique Mall, 9206-9244 East Admiral Place, www.gamarkets.com; Tulsa Flea Market, State Fairgrounds, 21st St. & Yale; Weekend Market & Bazaar, Catoosa, one block south of I-44 and 193rd St.

Yukon: Route 66 Traders Market, 3201 N. Richland Rd, www:route66tradeersmarket.com

Oregon

Albany: Willamette Collectors Market, Linn County Fairgrounds

Astoria: The Pacific Flea Market, Clastop Fairgrounds

Bend: Bend Public Market, Bend Armory, 875 SW Simpson Ave.

Eugene: Picc-a-dilly Flea Market, Lane County Fairgrounds, 796 W. 13th St.

Medford: The Original Medford Giant Flea Market, Medford National Guard Armory, 1701 S. Pacific Hwy

Ontario: Ontario Flea Mart, 1414 SE 5th Ave.

Portland: America's Largest Antique & Collectibles Sale, Multnomah County Expo Center, www.palmerwirfs.com; Fantastic Flea Market, 19340 SE Stark; #1 Flea Market, 17420 SE Division St., D Street Corral Dance Hall; Sandy Blvd Flea Market, 12021 NE 122nd St.

Salem: Salem Collectors Market, Oregon State Fairgrounds, 2770 17th St.

Sumpter: Sumpter Flea Market, 365 SE Ash St.

Pennsylvania

Adamstown: Renninger's #1 Rt. 272; Shupp's Grove; Stoudt's Black Angus Antique Mall, Rt 272

Barto: Jake's, 1380 Rt. 100

Butler: Clearview Flea Market, Rt. 8 North

Hazen: Warsaw Twp Volunteer Fire Co. Flea Market, Rt. 28

Kutztown: Renninger's #2 Antique Market, 740 Nobel St.

Lahaska: Rice's Market, 6326 Green Hill Rd

Landisville: Hempfield Woman's Club Flea Market, Amos Herr Park, East Hempfield Township

Latrobe: Hi Way Drive-In Flea Market, Rt. 30

Ligonier: Ligonier Fleatique, Rt. 30 and Rt. 259

Matamoras: Matamoras Drive-In

New Hope: New Hope Country Market, Rt. 202

Perkiomenville: Perkiomenville Flea Market, Rt. 29

Pittsburgh: Antiques Fair at the Meadowlands, I-79S, Exit 41; Castle Shannon Flea Market, Fire Hall; Eastland Mall, east of Pittsburgh

Quakertown: Quakertown Farmer's Market, 201 Station Rd

Saylorsburg: Blue Ridge Flea Market

Washington: The Meadows, Racetrack Rd

Rhode Island

Charlestown: General Stanton Inn, 4115A Old Post Rd

East Greenwich: Rocky Hill Flea Market, 1408 Division Rd

Providence: Cedar Street Flea Market, Cedar St.; Valley Street Place, 500 Valley St.

South Carolina

Anderson: Anderson Jockey Lot & Farmer's Market, Hwy 29 between Greenville and Anderson

Beaufort: Laurel Bay Flea Market, 922 La Chere St.

Charleston: Lowcountry Flea Market & Collectibles Show, Gaillard Aud, 77 Calhoun St.

Pickens: Pickens County Flea Market, 1427 Walhalla Hwy

South Dakota

Baltic: Treasures on I-29, I-29 at exit 94

Madison: Memory Lane Flea Market, Madison bypass curve

Sioux Falls: Benson Flea Market, W. H. Lyons Fairgrounds

Tennessee

Bristol: Greenway Flea Market, 511 Melrose St.

Chapel Hill: Dixieland, 4482 Nashville Hwy

Chattanooga: East Ridge Flea Market, 6725 Ringgold Rd; Monster Flea Market, 5615 Lee Hwy

Columbia: Blue Knight's Flea Market, 6201 Cayce Lane

Crump: Hilltop Flea Market, Hwy 64

Crossville: Dixon's Flea Market, Hwy 70 North

Greeneville: Fairgrounds Flea Market, 123 Fairgrounds Circle

Johnson City: US Flea Market Mall, Bristol Hwy

Knoxville: Knoxville Expo Center, Clinton Hwy at Merchants Rd

Lebanon: Old Boot Factory Flea Market, 125 East Forrest Ave.

Louisville: Green Acres, 908 Hillside Dr.

Memphis: Memphis Flea Market, Memphis Fairgrounds

Nashville: Expo Flea Market, 1-24 Expo Center (Smyra)

Old Hickory: Phoenix Flea Market, 1409 Robinson Rd

Paris: Old Shirt Factory Mall and Flea Market, 205 E. Washington St.

Sevierville: Flea Traders Paradise, 1907 Winfield Dunn Parkway; Great Smokies Flea Market, I-40, exit 407

Smyrna: Tennessee Expo Flea Market, 1412 Hazelwood Drive

Sweetwater: Fleas Unlimited, Exit 60, I-75

Telford: Jonesborough Flea Market, 2726 Hwy 11-E

Trenton: Gibson County Fairgrounds, First Monday Flea Market, Manufacturers Row

Tyler: Tyler Market Center, Hwy 69N

Texas

Canton: First Monday Trade Days, two blocks north of downtown square

Corpus Christi: Merchants' Square, 11330 W. Leopard St.

Dallas: Buckarama Fair Park

El Paso: Fox Plaza Mercado, 5559 Alameda Ave.

Ft. Worth: Henderson Flea Market, 1000 N. Henderson St.; Will Rogers Complex

Grand Prairie: Traders Village Ltd., RV Park, Rodeo Arena

Houston: The Market Place, 10910 Old Katy Rd

Roundtop: Marburger Farm

Waxahachie: Ellis County Trade Days, Hwy 287

Weatherford: First Monday

Utah

Kamas: People's Market, Kamas Rodeo Grounds

Salt Lake City: Redwood Swap Meet, 3600 South Redwood Rd

West Valley City: Salt Lake's Indoor Swapmeet, 1500 W. 3500 South

Virginia

Chantilly: DC Big Flea, Chantilly Convention Center

Front Royal: Double Tollgate Flea Market, 490 N. Commerce Ave.

Hillsville: VFW Labor Day Gun Show & Flea Market, VFW Complex, US Rt. 58-221 W.

Lynchburg: Market Antiques Fair, Old City Armory

Virginia Beach: Virginia Beach Antique & Collectible Expo, Virginia Beach Pavilion Convention Center

Vermont

Chelsea: Chelsea Flea Market, North and South Common of Chelsea

Fairlee: Whistle Stop Flea Market, US Rt. 5

Waterbury: Waterbury Flea Market, Rt. 2

West Topsham: East Corinth Flea Market, 450 Vt Rt. 25

Washington

Everett: Puget Park Swap Meet, 13020 Meridian Ave. South

Seattle: Midway Swap Meet

Tacoma: America's Largest Antique & Collectibles Sale, Tacoma Dome; Triphammer, 5202 Proctor St.

Toutle: Labor Day Weekend Swap Meet, 5050 Spirit Lake Hwy

Wenatchee: Wenatchee Valley Swap Meet, 1869 South Wenatchee Ave.

Washington, DC

Washington: Eastern Market, 7th St. & North Carolina, SE; Georgetown Flea Market, Wisconsin Ave. & S. St. NW

West Virginia

Charleston: Greenbrier Flea Market, Coonskin Park

Fayetteville: Bridge Day, New River Gorge Bridge

Harpers Ferry: Harpers Ferry Flea Market, Dual Hwy 340

Martinsburg: Berkeley Plaza Flea Market, 103 Berkeley Plaza

Milton: Milton Flea Market, US Route 60

Reedsville: Indian Rocks Flea Market, Rt. 1

Wisconsin

Caldonia: 7-Mile Fair, 2720 West 7 Mile Rd

Cedarburg: Maxwell Days, historic area

Dells: Wo Zha Wa Antique Market, downtown Wisconsin Dells

Elkhorn: Walworth Flea Market, Walworth City Fairgrounds

Milwaukee: Rummage O'Rama, State Fair Park Grounds

Mukwonago: Maxwell Street Days Flea Market, Field Park

Shawano: Shawano County Fairgrounds, Flea Market Hwy 29

Wyoming

Casper: Casper Flea Market, Central Wyoming Fairgrounds

Cheyenne: Cheyenne Flea Market, Lincolnway, right side

Jackson Hole: Mangy Moose Antique Show & Sale Teton Village

Laramie: Barts, 2401 Soldier Springs Rd; Golden Flea Gallery, 725 Skyline Rd

Canada

Alberta

Calgary: Crossroads Market, 2222 16th Ave.; Hillhirst-Sunnyside, 1320 5th Ave., NW; Swap-O-Rama, Stampede Park; Victoria Community Association Flea Market, 1302 6th St. SE

Edmonton: A-1 Flea Market, 11815 124th St.; Good Earth Flea Market, 9658 Jasper Ave.; Jasper Gales Flea Market, 15020 Stony Pin Rd; Lake Beaumarias Mall, 27-1533 Castle Downs Rd; Superflea Market, 12011 111th Ave.; Swap-O-Rama, Exhibition Grounds; Yellowhead Flea Market, 12112 67th St.; 68th Street Flea Market, 12115 68th St.; 99th Street Flea Market, 9908 65th Ave.

Spruce Grove: Spruce Grove Public Storage and Public Flea Market, 24 Alberta Ave.

British Columbia

Abbots Ford: Fraser Valley Swap Meet, Exhibition Park

Cloverdale: Cloverdale Flea Market, fairgrounds

Fernwood: Fernwood Community Center Flea Market, 1240 Gladstone Ave.

Kelowna: Elks Hall Flea Market, Springfield Rd

New Westminster: Downtown New Westminster Flea Market, Downtown New West Parkade; Front Street Flea Market, 525 and 527 Front Street

Manitoba: TransCanada-Routledge, 7 miles east of Virden; Winnipeg Flea Market Co-Op Inc., 100 Mandalay Drive

Port Edward: Mora Trade Centre, 704 Mora

Richmond: Delta Drive In Theater Shop N Swap, 340 No. 5 Rd

Surrey: HiWay 10 Flea Market, 17790 56th Ave. Hwy 10

Vancouver: Bennett's Antique Mall, #1 Alexander Street; Croatian Cultural Centre Flea Market 21st Century Promotions; Swap-O-Rama, PNE Grounds

Victoria: Victoria Flea Market, 3400 Tillican Rd

Nova Scotia

Amherst: Amherst Flea Market, 1 Crescent Ave.

Greenwood: Greenwood Flea Market, Greenwood Mall

Pictou: Pictou County Weekend Market

Tiverton: Tiverton Lions Flea Market, Hwy #121

Windsor: Windsor Country Fair, Exit 5A Hwy 101

Ontario

Aberfoyle: The Aberfoyle Antique Market, Brock Rd 46

Alton: Alton Antique Affair & Crafts, Millrun Inn

Angus: Angus Lions Flea Market, Lions Hall, 162 Mill St.

Aylmer: Aylmer Farmers Market, Aylmer Sales Arena

Barrie: The 400 Market, Hwy 400, Exit 85, Innisfil Beach

Bowmanville: Wellington Street Flea Market, 182 Wellington St.

Brampton: Bramalea Flea Market, 50 Kennedy Rd S. at Clarence St.; Snelgrove Flea Market, Hwy 10

Brantford: CrossRds Flea & Farmers Market, 1116 Colborne St.

Brighton: Brighton Flea Market, 25 Richardson St.

Brockville: Traders Post Flea Market, 14 Courthouse Ave.

Campbellford: Meyersburg Flea Market & Antiques, Hwy 30

Cambridge: Cambridge Antique & Flea Markets, 150 Holiday Inn Drive; Cambridge Farmers Market, corner of Ainslie & Dickson Street; Cambridge Flea Market, 261 Hespeler Rd

Chatham: Chatham Farmers Market, Chatham Sales Arena

Courtice: Courtice Flea Market, 1696 Bloor St.

Delaware: Hilltop Antique & Flea Market, Longwoods Rd

Durham: Super 6 Flea Market, 625 Garafraxa St. South

Elmvale: Elmvale Sales Barn & Flea Market

Essex: Essex County Flea Market, NE on County Rd 23

Grand Bend: The Pinery Antique & Flea Market, Hwy 21

Guelph: Guelph Farmers Market, Gordon Street & Waterloo Avenue; Guelph's Royal Flea Market, 340 Woodlawn Rd

Hamilton: Barton Street Flea Market, Barton Street & Rosslyn Avenue; Circle M Flea Market, Hwy 5; Millgrove Flea Market, Hwy 6

Jordan: Jordan Valley Flea Market, Regional Rd 91

Kingston: Kingston Market, behind City Hall off King St.

Lawrence: North York Flea Market, 2780 Dufferin St.

Lindsay: Lindsay Flea Market, Hwy 7 & Victoria City Rd #4

London: Gilbratar Weekend Market, corner of Dundas and 3rd St.; London Farmer's Market, London Sales Arena, Dundas Street East

Morrisburg: McHaffie's Flea Market, Hwy 31

Mississauga: Dixie Mall, 1250 S Service Rd

Niagara Falls: Niagara Falls Flea Market, 4735 Drummund Rd

Ontario: Newmarket Flea Market, Newmarket Plaza

Oshawa: Oshawa Bazaar & Flea Market, 727 Wilson Rd S.

Ottawa: Colonnade Flea Market, 155 Colonnade Rd; Ottawa By Ward Market, 55 By Ward, Market Square

Peterborough: The Barn, Fowlers Corner, Hwy 78

Richmond Hill: Richmond Hill Flea Market, 11300 Yonge St.

St. Andrews: Bonnville Flea Market, Hwy 139

St. Jacobs: St. Jacobs Farmers Market, Hwy 86

Stouffville: Stouffville Country Market, Hwy 47

Toronto: Dr. Flea's Hwy 27 & Albion Flea Market, Inc., 8

Westmore Dr., www.dr-fleas.com; Harbourfront Antique Market, 221 Queens Quay West; Hwy 27 & Albion Flea Market; Mega City Market, 30 Vice Regent Blvd; St. Clair West Fea Market, 404 Old Weston Rd

Trenton: Carrying Place Flea Market, Hwy 33

Waterloo: Stockyard Farmers Market & Flea Market, King & Weber streets

Windsor: Windsor Public Market, 195 McDougal St.

Quebec

Bromont: Hwy 10 Flea Market, Hwy 10; Marche aux Puces de Bromont, Motorway 10 at Bromont

Montreal: Finnigan's Market; Hudson Que; Lachute Flea Market; Lesage Flea Market; Marche aux Puces st-Michel, corner of St. Michel and Cremazie

St. Eustache: St. Eustache Flea Market, Hwy 640 West

Abbreviations

The following are standard abbreviations used throughout this book.

3D: three-dimensional
adv: advertising
approx: approximately
attrib: attributed
C: century
cond: condition
cov: cover, covered
d: deep
dec: decorated
dia: diameter
dj: dust jacket
doz: dozen
ed: edition, editor
emb: embossed
ext: exterior
ftd: footed
gal: gallon

ground: background
h: high
horiz: horizontal
hp: hand painted
illus: illustrated, illustration, illustrator
imp: impressed
int: interior
irid: iridescent
k: karat
kt: karat
l: long
lb: pound
litho: lithograph
MBP: mint in bubble pack

mfg: manufactured, manufacturing
MIB: mint in box
MIP: mint in package
mkd: marked
MOC: mint on card
n.d.: no date
No.: number
NOS: new old stock
NRFB: never removed from box
op: operated
opal: opalescent
orig: original
oz: ounce
pat.: patent
pc: piece

pcs: pieces
pg: page
pgs: pages
pr: pair
pt: pint
qt: quart
rect: rectangular
Soc: Society
sgd: signed
sq: square
unp: unpaged
vol: volume
w: width
yg: yellow gold
#: number, numbered

For exciting collecting trends and newly expanded areas look for these symbols:

Hot Topic   New Warman's Listing

Abingdon Pottery

The Abingdon Sanitary Manufacturing Company of Abingdon, Ill., was founded in 1908. Although originally created to make plumbing fixtures, an art pottery line was introduced around 1933. In 1945, the company's name was changed to Abingdon Potteries, Inc., with production of the art pottery line continuing until 1950, when fire destroyed the art pottery kiln. The company then focused its attention on plumbing fixtures, eventually becoming Briggs Manufacturing Company.

For additional listings, see *Warman's Americana & Collectibles*.

Abingdon Pottery, vase, blue, urn shape, handles, marked, **$30.**

Ashtray, #456 .... 35.00

Bookends, pr, goose, #98 .... 42.00

Bowl, Shell, #533, sea-green, c1940-48, 11-1/4" l, 8" w 35.00

Candlesticks, pr, 2 lite, rose glaze
.... 35.00

Centerpiece bowl
#5-11, semi-gloss white, blue oval ink stamp, incised 5-11, 14-1/2" l, 4" h 48.00
#377, yellow, handle continues into bowl, 3-3/4" h, 14" w 55.00

Compote, #568, white, 5" h, base 2" sq 25.00

Cookie jar, cov
Daisy............................... 45.00
Little Bo Peep 330.00
Pineapple, 10-1/2" h 95.00
Windmill, #678................... 250.00

Figure
Goose, #571, blue 45.00
Peacock, pink....................... 40.00

Flower pot, #151, white, hp floral dec, 5" h 25.00

Planter
#462, bow shape, pink, 7-1/2" l
.... 20.00
#484, fan with bow in center, ivory
.... 20.00
#616D, Mexican and cactus
.... 70.00

Salt and pepper shakers, pr, Little Bo Peep.................................. 48.00

String holder, mouse 90.00

Tray, green, 10-3/4" x 8" 22.50

Vase
#103, Chinese Red, incised and ink stamp mark, 10" h 150.00

Abingdon #435 wall pocket, **$35.**

#181, ivory, two handles 50.00
#482, double cornucopia, white
.... 35.00
#491, flared, pink matte, 5" h 65.00
#512, pink glaze, 7" h 20.00
#513, fan, salmon glaze, 9" h 30.00
#520, Baden, light blue ground, white int., floral dec, gold trim, two handles, 8-3/4" h 30.00
#538, pink, incised and ink stamp mark, 8-3/4" h 20.00
#560, Pink Cameo, Star Flower pattern, sgd "Special B, 4-16-42," 6-1/4" h........................... 125.00

Wall pocket, #377, flower, gray sticker, incised 377 .... 40.00

Action Figures

Action figures are posable models with flexible joints. Generally made of plastic, the figures portray real or fictional characters, and their clothing, personal equipment, vehicles and other accessories are collected as well. The earliest action figures were the hard-plastic Hartland figures that depicted popular Western television heroes of the 1950s. During the late 1950s, Louis Marx also produced action figures for a number of its playsets, but it was G.I. Joe, introduced in 1964, that triggered the modern action figure craze. Mego established the link between action figures and the movies when the company issued series based on "Planet of the Apes" and "Star Trek: The Motion Picture." Kenner jumped on the bandwagon with the production of "Star Wars" figures in 1977.

Action figure, Kiss, Spawn, Starchild, NRFB, **$8.50.**

Amy Allen, A-Team, Galoob, 6" h, MIP 30.00

Arachnid, Alien 20.00

Arzon, Visionaires, Hasbro, 1987, MOC 35.00

Baltar, Battlestar Galactica....... 35.00

Batman, Super Powers, Kenner, Canada, 1985, MOC 65.00

Betty Mustin, Mask, Kenner, MOC 20.00

Black Bolt, Fantastic Four, 1995, MIP 10.00

Action figure, Spawn, with skull launcher, NRFB, **$5.**

Boba Fett, Star Wars, two circles, MIP 25.00

Boss Hogg, Dukes of Hazzard, 3-3/4" h, MOC 15.00

Bug-Eye Ghost, Ghostbusters, Kenner, 1986-91, MIP 15.00

B-Wing Pilot, Kenner, sealed in bag 15.00

Charo, Clash of the Titans, Mattel, 3-3/4" h, MOC 35.00

Cryotec, Visionaires, Hasbro, 1987, MOC 35.00

Cyclotron, Super Powers, Kenner, Canada, 1985, MOC 75.00

Darkstorm, Visionaires, Hasbro, 1987, MOC........................... 35.00

Deadproof, #1, X-Men 25.00

Dorian, Mask, Kenner, MOC ... 20.00

Dr Zarkow, Flash Gordon, Mego, 1976, loose............................. 55.00

Flash Gordon, Defenders of the Earth, Galoob, 1985, MOC.... 35.00

Garax, Defenders of the Earth, Galoob, 1985, MOC.............. 35.00

General Ursus, Planet of the Apes, Kenner 25.00

General Vondar, Star Com, Coleco, 1986, MOC........................... 20.00

German Mechanic, Raiders of the Lost Ark, Kenner, MOC......... 60.00

Golden Pharoh, Super Powers, Kenner, Canada, 1985, MOC 125.00

Hannibal, A-Team, Galoob, MOC 20.00

Heads Up, Mask, Kenner, MOC 20.00

Hercules, swash buckling, loose 3.00

House Ghost, Extreme Ghostbusters, 1997, MIP 4.00

Human Torch, Fantastic Four... 7.50

Jon, Chips, 3-3/4" h, loose......... 10.00

Joker, Legends of Batman 15.00

Kato, Captain Action, MIP 20.00

Kimo, Chuck Norris, 6", MIP ... 12.00

Lexor, Visionaires, Hasbro, 1987, MOC 40.00

Long Ranger, GI-Joe, 1989, loose, 3-3/4" h 14.00

Luke, X-Wing, 3", loose 12.00

Mandrake, Defenders of the Earth, loose... 8.00

Action figure, Masters of the Universe, left: Tung Lashor; Beast Man, NRFB, each **$7.50.**

McDonaldland, Ronald McDonald, footed red hair, MOC 18.00

Ming the Merciless, Defenders of the Earth, Galoob, 1985, MOC 35.00

Mothra, Godzilla, boxed 10.00

Mystique, Marvel, loose, 10" h 15.00

Pandora, Bolt, MOC................. 15.00

Penguin, Super Powers, Kenner, Canada, 1985, MOC 65.00

Pfc John Jefferson, Star Com, Coleco, 1986, MOC................ 15.00

Phantom, Defenders of the Earth, Galoob, 1985, MOC.............. 35.00

Picard, Star Trek, loose 10.00

Power Drod, loose, 3" h 8.00

Quick Draw, Mask, Kenner, MOC 20.00

R2-D2, pop-up lightsaber, C-8 .... 135.00

Rogue, Marvel, loose, 10" h...... 12.00

Sabretooth #1, X-Men............. 10.00

Spiderman, super posable, 10" h 10.00

Spy, MAD Magazine, 6" h 12.00

Tornado, Mask, Kenner, MOC. 20.00

Tremor, Spawn, loose............... 12.00

Vampire, Spawn, loose............. 17.50

Werewolf, Spawn, loose........... 20.00

Wild Wolf, Mask, Kenner, MOC 18.00

Willie Mays, Starting Lineup .. 20.00

Witterquick, Visionaires, Hasbro, 1987, MOC............................ 35.00

Adams

For collectors, the name Adams denotes quality English pottery. Since the company's inception in 1770, Adams potteries have been located in seven locations. Various marks have been used over the years, ranging from a simple "Adams" to more complex variations of the name. Some pieces were not marked.

ABC plate, 7-1/4" d, horse head in center, alphabet letters around rim, chip on back 75.00

Creamer, scene of three people in front of English buildings, dark blue transfer, wishbone handle, imp "Adams" 165.00

Cup and saucer, handleless, Adam's Rose pattern, imp "Adams" . 225.00

Dish, Cries of London-Ten Bunches A Penny Primrose, rect............. 50.00

Mush mug, The Farmers Arms 90.00

Pitcher, 7-1/2" h, haying scenes, green transfer, imp mark, c1840 .... 385.00

Plate
   Abbey pattern, mulberry 25.00
   Adam's Rose pattern, early... 95.00

Italian Scenery pattern, gray transfer, red and green accents, relief molded border, 10" d 30.00

Shakespeare Series, Sir John Falstaff, black transfer, blue and green accents, orange border 35.00

The Sea pattern, red transfer, 8-1/2" d............................. 80.00

Platter, Calyx Ware, Carolynn pattern, 14" l.......................... 75.00

Teapot, Titan Ware, bulbous, dark red, purple, and blue flowers and green leaves in band, green lined rims and handle, green and tan knob, cream ground, 7" h...... 40.00

Vegetable bowl, Mazara pattern, 8-3/4" d................................. 24.00

Adams China, Adam's Rose pattern, late, 7" d plate, **$45.**

Advertising

Advertisers of the 19th and early 20th centuries understood the necessity of catching the attention of potential customers. Colorful graphics were an important feature of mass-produced advertising items beginning in the late 1800s. Not only did bright, creative packaging attract attention, it also helped customers identify and locate particular brands during an era in which many people could not read. Those same colorful designs serve as head-turners for today's collectors, just as they did for buyers of a bygone era.

For additional listings, see *Warman's Antiques & Collectibles*, *Warman's Americana & Collectibles* and *Warman's Advertising*, as well as specific categories in this edition.

Badge, Northwest's Market, St. Paul, 4" d cello suspended from 2-1/4" w diecut thin brass hanger bar inserted by cello strip with handshake gesture, double cornucopia and cartons, packages, orig cardboard back insert mkd "Western Badge & Novelty Co., St. Paul, Minn," 1910-20............. 30.00

Banner, Holsum Bread, illus by Howard Brown, 58" w 125.00

Billhook, Ceresota Flour.......... 50.00

Blotter
   Cotton Overshirts, 3" x 6" ivory white and black celluloid cover, bound at each corner by metal mount to two removable cardboard ink blotter sheets,

Oppenheim, Oberndorf & Co., late 1890s......................... 28.00

Rochester Gas & Electric Utility Co Mighty Midget, 3-1/2" x 6-1/4", 1940s 10.00

Booklet, Bromo-Seltzer, A Reel Story of Real Relief, New York World's Fair, 1939, photo endorsement by tennis champion Don Budge and golf champion Gene Sarazen. 25.00

Box opener, Wrigley's, 1940s .. 70.00

Bowl, Bird's Eye, General Foods 27.50

Champagne horn, Dry Monopole, Heidseick & Co., 3" x 3-1/2" x 13" h formed cardboard, 3-D cover for champagne bottle, glossy black,

Advertising, shoe horn, Shinola Shoe Polish, Chas S. Shank Co. Litho, Chicago, **$30.**

gold neck and molded cap, paper stickers, 1930s 5.00

Charm, Pet Evaporated Milk, figural can, red and white label wrapped around celluloid, small hanging loop, c1920............................ 12.00

Coat hanger, San Francisco Cleaning & Drying Works, wood 10.00

Coffee cup, White Castle 35.00

Coffee measure, "Coffee Satisfaction is assured by A & P Coffee Service," aluminum, 3-3/4" l 8.00

Cookie jar, Entenmann's, 11" h, heavy ceramic, 9" d baker hat lid, "Fine Baked Goods, Quality Since 1898" on lid, mkd "Exclusively for Entenmann's 1st Collectors Series/ JCK 1992, Made in Brazil" 20.00

Counter display sign, Look Better in a Mademoiselle Fifth Ave Sweater, cardboard, self frame 40.00

Desk calendar, Blue Ribbon Canned Foods, 3-1/4" x 4-1/4" ivory celluloid over tin, full-color pineapple, blue lettering "A Sure Foundation For A Good Table," 1916 paper calendar 24.00

Diecut, Compliments of C. A. Steely, Fancy Groceries, scene of little girl holding teddy bear, puppy, and kitten, multicolored............... 85.00

Doll

Jewel Skippy, 6" h, white soft vinyl, blue paint on nautical hat, collar and trousers, black facial features and chest buttons, molded hair curls, "Jewel Skippy" on rear of jacket, 1970s..................... 24.00

Regent Baby Products, 7-1/2" h hollow soft rubber, moveable head, painted blue eyes, squeaks,

Advertising trade card, Andes Stoves & Ranges, little dark haired girl in blue dress, framed, **$35.**

Advertising, fan, Pur-Ox Syrups, cardboard, back with advertising for M. F. Stintsman, Confectionary, Light Lunch, New Hope, PA, **$30.**

mkd "1973 © Regent Baby Products Corp, Made in Korea" 24.00

Emery board, Wead's Bread.... 20.00

Figure, Davison Chemical, 5-1/4" h, hollowed and glazed ceramic, glossy white face, hands, and jacket, black accented eyeglasses, small gauge in one pocket, hair, trousers, and shoes, dark green safety helmet hat, inscription in green across back shoulders, 1960s.................... 38.00

Flipper pin, Sunset Coffee, International Coffee Co., canister shape..................................... 12.00

Folder, Marcelle Face Powder, samples 18.00

Jar, Horlick's Malted Milk, orig lids, set of four............................ 125.00

Key ring, Bell Atlantic, Your Equipment Connection, combination key ring and bottle opener..................................... 7.50

Lapel stud, Garland Stoves and Ranges, white text, blue center, 7/8" d 15.00

Liquor jug, Fleischmann's, dark blue pottery 90.00

Memo book, Libby's Food Products, Libby, McNeill & Libby, celluloid cover, full-color view of Chicago factory, 14 pgs, printed by Whitehead & Hoag Co., 2-1/2" x 4-1/2" 55.00

Mending kit, Real Silk Hosiery. 5.00

Pail, Picwick Peanut Butter, faded and dented, 12-oz, 3-1/2" h, 3-1/4" d 25.00

Paperweight

Anderson Concrete Corp, 3" glass done, 1-1/2" x 3" x 3" black hard plastic base inscribed with name in orange, painted view of city, Progressive Products, Union, NJ, 1950s 24.00

Archies Lobster House, 3" d glass globe, 1-1/4" x 3" x 3" dark brown hard plastic base with inscribed sponsor name and "Roanoke, VA," white fishing boat, two red miniature lobsters 45.00

Maryland Casualty Co., 2-1/2" d, 1/2" h, black, white and gold text, red, black, and gold Maryland state seal in center, c1910 20.00

Vulcan Rail & Construction Co., 2-3/4" h, dark brass luster, image of early blacksmith on top of rocks, holding hammer, standing next to anvil, company name on base, 1930s 60.00

Pie pan, Enjoy Py-O-Ice Box Pies, raised letters in bottom 5.00

Puzzle, McKesson's Products, 11" x 14" manila envelope with art and text in black and white, red accents, 10-5/8" x 13-7/8" thin cardboard puzzle with images of 1833 and 1933 chemists in laboratory, three orig sheets to enter contest, 1933 .... 35.00

Ruler, Clark Bars, wood 8.00

Salesman's brochure, Superior Matches, matchbook covers, "Glamour Girls Series" 45.00

Salt and pepper shakers, pr, Sunshine Bakers, 2-1/2" h, white china, wearing chef hats........ 18.00

Sign

Butternut Bread, Gee! But It's Dandy Brandy, cardboard diecut, 7" x10", repairs 20.00

Carstairs Harmony Blended Whiskey, 16-1/2" x 21", wooden frame, high gloss slick cardboard art titled "There's always

Advertising, ink blotter, Bird Roll Roofing, O. E. Sherman, No. Scarboro, Me., unused, 6-1/4" x 3-1/2", **$2.50.**

Harmony here" with three customers enjoying highballs and singing....................... 25.00

Cat's Paw, emb black cat, scrolled ends, dirty 65.00

Occident Flour, tin over cardboard, 13-3/4" w, 9" h 75.00

Rainbow is Good Bread, 2-1/2" x 18", emb tin...................... 15.00

Snow Drift Fancy Patent Flour, Imperial Enamel Co., NY, heavy porcelain, two-sided, 1940s, 15" x 18"................................. 30.00

Spinner top, Hurd Shoes, black and white celluloid, wooden red spinner dowel, 1930s 20.00

Squeaker toy, Wrigley's Spearmint Chewing Gum, 1-1/2" x 2" x 7" soft vinyl, gum package, 1950s 35.00

Stickpin, Grand Andes Range, diecut thin celluloid red, white, and blue US flag, brass stickpin, 1905 patent date 10.00

Tape measure
Hawk Work Clothes, full-color brown half holding red, white, and blue sign from beak, yellow background, blue rim, blue lettering on reverse "Miller Co.," 1920s 35.00

Sears, Roebuck & Co., white lettering, black ground, lightning bolt-style lettering for "WLS" (World's Largest Store,) red, white, blue, and green stylized floral design on back........ 15.00

Tin
Hostess Holiday Fruitcake, 3-1/2" x 6" x 3" h, hinged lid, gold, red, and blue accent litho brocade

pattern, oval with young hostess portrait on lid, mkd "Metal Packaging Corp of NY," 1930s 12.00

Lorillard Tobacco, 8" x 9-1/2" x 7" litho tin, swivel carrying handle, early 1900s 30.00

Maryland Graham Wafers, green, gold, white, and black, round 25.00

Tip tray
Clysmic Water, woman, deer and giant bottle of product 45.00

Prudential Has the Strength of Gibraltar, rock in center, sailboat in foreground, green border, oval, 2-1/2" x 3-1/2" 15.00

Toy, Fort Bedford Peanut Butter, P-Nut Butter Game, 5" x 6-1/2", full color, cardboard, adv on back, © 1909 .... 25.00

Trade card
Armour Luncheon Beef, eight 3-1/4" x 4-1/2" cards bound by cord through two punched margin holes, numbered in sequence, full-color art on black background of monkey and parrot, text on back, early 1900s 18.00

Burdock Blood Bitters, 3" x 4-1/2", little girl holding doll next to box, black and white text on back 4.00

Dunham's Coconut, 2-3/4" x 4-3/4", browntone, red accent showing cut-away of coconut revealing six monkeys, c1880.................. 7.50

8th Wonder or Engle Clock, 3" x 5-1/4", Capt J Reid and wife standing next to giant

mechanical clock built by jeweler and watchmaker in Hazelton, PA, c1890 .... 5.00

Honest Abe Work Shirts-Overalls, 2-1/2" x 4-1/2", black and white, Lincoln type holding axe above text "Guarantee for Product" sgd by Abe N. Cohen, diecut hole for hanging, c1910................... 4.00

Swayne's Ointment, 2-3/4" x 4-1/4", Stanley in Africa, series, 1, Stanley asleep in hammock, monkeys pulling out cans of Swayne's Ointment from bag, red, white, and blue, black printed description on back, c1870 .... 4.00

Wall pocket, Compliments of H. B. Schanley, emb multicolored stuff paper, doves and water trough, text on fold-out pocket................. 35.00

Whetstone, Lavacide, For Fumigation, celluloid, Innis, Speiden & Co., N.Y., ... 35.00

Whistle
Atwater Kent Radios 15.00

Butter-Krust Bread, red and white celluloid, tin backing panel, 1930s 20.00

Old Reliable Coffee, tin litho 15.00

Visit Penny's Toyland, celluloid, 1920s 20.00

Wristwatch, Toppie the Elephant, Tip Top Bread, Ingraham, 7/8" chrome case, gray leather strap, pink polka dotted elephant wearing cape with "Toppie," 1951 .... 110.00

Yardstick, Smith's Furniture Store 10.00

Advertising Characters

Just as advertisers used colorful labels to attract attention, the use of characters became quite important. When consumers didn't know what brand to buy, they often decided to trust the character or personality promoting a product. Today many of these characters generate strong collector interest. From Mr. Peanut to the Campbell Kids, there is a plethora of items available to collectors.

For additional listings, see *Warman's Antiques & Collectibles*, *Warman's Americana & Collectibles* and *Warman's Advertising*, as well as specific categories in this edition.

Reproduction Alert.

Alka-Seltzer, Speedy
Figure, plastic, 1960s, 5-1/2" h 24.00

Sign, 20-1/2" x 28", stiff paper, multicolored Speedy, "Pron-Tito" on hat, Spanish slogans.... 65.00

Buster Brown
Pinback button, Buster Brown Shoes, sepia letters, brown rim 24.00

Shoe store mannequin, 32" h, jointed at shoulders, text on back

"Buster Brown Dress With Size 2 Garments Old King Cole Inc.," 1960s 50.00

Advertising character, Dairy Queen mascot, stuffed, brown and white plush ice cream sandwich body, stitched facial features, green and purple feet, original tag with 1999 copyright, **$2.**

Charlie the Tuna
Alarm clock, wind-up, brass, Lux Time Co. 65.00
Bracelet, 1-1/4" disk, c1970 .. 15.00
Doll, vinyl, 7-1/2" h 30.00
Drinking glass, 3-3/4" h, 3" d, clear, single image of Charlie in white, no inscription, heavily fluted base, c1970 .... 12.50
Necklace, 1-1/4" pendant with high relief image of Charlie on anchor 4.50
Watch, 1-1/8" gold-tone case, blue leather double strap, 1971, mint with offer insert 55.00

Dutch Boy Paint
Hand puppet, vinyl head, fabric body, orig cellophane bag, 1960s 45.00
Marker, diecut thin cardboard, wooden base, Dutch Boy on front, black and white paint can on back, inscribed "Paint with Dutch Boy White Lead," c1930 .... 20.00

Elsie the Cow, Borden's
Borden Cheese gift box, 9-1/2" x 12" x 3-1/2", vinyl over cardboard, solid dark olive green, gold emb Elsie head in center, holiday green int., 1950s 14.00
Drinking glass, Spirit of '76, red, white and blue patriotic dec, colonial garb, Elsie playing drum, Elmer playing fife, Beauregard playing small drum, 5-1/2" h, pr 28.00
Fun book, 7" x 10-1/4", 20 pgs, 1950s 18.00
Poster, Borden's Egg Nog, 20" x 14" 30.00

Energizer Bunny, wristwatch, black plastic case, black leather strap, pink bunny drumming on face, 1992 .... 20.00

Entenmann's, bank, 8-1/2" h, ceramic, piggy baker wearing hat and kerchief, black eyes and shoes,

glossy white body, orig box, early 1990s 30.00

Exxon Tiger
Bank, tiger, figural, plastic ... 35.00
Mug, 3-1/2" h, white glass, full color tiger portrait, 1970s .. 8.00

Florida Orange Bird, Tropicana, nodder 150.00

Green Giant
Doll, Little Sprout, 6-1/4" soft vinyl doll, movable head, orig mailing bag 25.00
T-shirt, 9" x 12" mailing envelope, folded white shirt, green at crew collar and short sleeves, "I feel like a Giant today," 3" button "Vote for The Green Giant or Your Leaves Will Fall Off," 1980s 15.00

Hawaiian Punch Punchy
Figure, hard plastic, orange . 12.00
Wristwatch, Swiss digital, rect gold-tone case, wide red leather strap with snaps, 1970s 110.00

Hostess Munchies, doll, 6" x 9" x 14" h, stuffed plush fabric, label "Best-Made Toys Ltd, Toronto," 1980s 10.00

Johnny, Philip Morris
Box, 3-1/2" x 5-1/4" x 10-1/2", plastic, hinged, 1950s 35.00
Pinback button, 1930s 35.00
Sign, emb tin, worn, 12" x 14" 95.00

Keebler Elf
Doll, Ernie, plus, talking 25.00
Mug, 3" h, hard plastic 20.00
Watch, silver-tone case, black leather strap, watch hands formed by Ernie's arms, 1980s, MIB 25.00

Kool Cigarettes
Pinback button, Willie between donkey and elephant, 1930s 25.00
Salt and pepper shakers, figural Willie and Millie, black and white plastic, yellow and red accents, c1950, 3-1/2" h ... 35.00

Little Hans, Nestle
Doll, 13" h, stuffed printed fabric, tiny Nestle copyright on foot, c1970 .... 28.00
Wristwatch, silver-tone case, Little Hans in center of face, eyes move from side to side, 1971 ..... 50.00

Michelin Man
Figure, 3-1/4" h hollow soft rubber ivory figure of Mr. Bib suspended on thin elastic stretch cord, 1950s 18.00

Key ring, 1-1/4" h white plastic figure, 2-3/4" long metal key ring, 1960s 15.00

Micro Mike, RCA, pinback, 3" d, ivory white cello, crisp red image, title of anthropomorphic figure of RCA radio tube torso, 1940s-50s 18.00

Mr. Bubble
Hat, blue and white striped canvas, 2" d stitched fabric patch . 15.00
Wash mitt, 6" x 6-1/2" printed blue image on peach-colored sponge, c1970, unused 7.00

Nestles Quik Bunny
Mug, plastic, two handles, 4" h 12.00
Pitcher, hard plastic, 9" h 22.00
Tin, teal blue, litho Victorian scene, rect 2.00

Nipper, RCA
Print, 7" x 9-3/4", full color, Nipper listening to record, reverse with text about award received at St. Louis Expo in 1904 .... 20.00
Record brush, 3-1/2" d celluloid, dark blue soft pile fabric brush, red and gold design, black rim, Nipper listening to Victrola, RCA circle logo, Philadelphia Badge Co. for Radio Corp of America, Camden, NJ, late 1930s-early 1940s 20.00

Pillsbury Doughboy, Pillsbury Co.
Cookie jar, 10-1/2" h, glossy white, blue accents, c1970 .... 30.00
Doll, vinyl, smiling, blue accent eyes, button on cap, copyright 1971 Pillsbury Co., Minneapolis, 7-1/4" h 18.00

Chiquita Banana stuffed toy, 14-1/2" h, **$20.**

Salt and pepper shakers, 4" h
Poppin Fresh, 3-1/4" h Poppie,
names on bases, copyright 1974
.... 28.00

Reddy Kilowatt
Ashtray, clear glass, red and white
reverse-painted image on
bottom, c1950, 4" d 38.00
Bib, 8" x 10" textured white fabric,
tied strings, verse "I Am Your
Pal, Bo-Peep, Boy Blue, Ready
to Help with Whatever You Do,"
unused 18.00
Comic book, 7-1/2" x 10", 16
pgs, full color, ©1946, based
on movie cartoon "Reddy
Made Magic" by Walter Lantz
Productions 20.00
Figure, 4-3/4" h litho cardboard,
flesh-tone face, black and white
bulb nose, red body, blue gloves
and boots, name and ©1940,
replaced cardboard base .. 60.00

Hard hat, 8-1/2" x 12", 6" h crown,
yellow hard plastic, 2" h Reddy
decal, black lettering "Reddy
Kilowatt Your Electric Servant,"
adjustable, 1960s 20.00
Magic slate, 4" x 6-3/4", wooden
stylus, red, and black cover,
white lettering "Reddy's Plus
12 Electric Aids," imprinted for
Washington Water Power Co.,
c1937, wear 20.00
Memo wallet, 4" x 6-3/4" black vinyl
folder organizer, inner slash
pockets, red Reddy image, slogan
"Make Every Day A Happier Day
Sell Electric All The Way," circle
logo for The Electrical Assoc of
Philadelphia, 1950s 15.00

Sandler of Boston, display figure,
13" w, 13" h, painted hollow latex,
Colonial man in smock with
hammer and ruler, Sculptural
Promotions New York City, late
1940s-50s 25.00

Tony the Tiger
Pencil sharpener, soft vinyl, orange
head, threaded black plastic
base, c1960 .... 80.00
Watch, Kellogg's Frosted Flakes,
Swiss wind-up, silver-tone case,
black vinyl strap with snaps, face
with Tony, 1976, MIB 215.00

Willie the Penquin, Kools, glass,
2-1/2" d, 5-1/2" h, frosted, 1950
.... 45.00

Willy Wiredhand
Ashtray, 5-1/4" sq translucent dark
glass, colorful image in center,
Lorain-Medina Rural Electric
Cooperative, 1960s 25.00
Button, 4" d, Pushin For Missouri,
yellow and black cello, gray
mule, pink and red image of
Missouri, 1960s 18.00
Hat, diecut 4" x 12" cardboard, late
1940s-50s 15.00

Airline Collectibles (Commercial)

Come fly with me! The friendly skies continue beckoning collectors today. As airlines merge, change names,
or even go out of business, interest in related memorabilia will increase.

For additional listings, see *Warman's Americana & Collectibles*.

Award plaque, 6-1/2" x 8-1/2" wood
shield, United Air Lines' 100,000
Mile Club, small red, white, and
blue logo, engraved inscription with
pilot's name, 1955 .... 30.00

Baggage sticker, 4" x 5-3/4" oval, The
Mercury Flight, American Airlines,

Airline collectibles, plaque, 100,000
Miles United Airlines, 1955, wood and
brass, 6-1/2" x 8-1/2", **$30.**

foil, late 1930s, unused
.... 15.00

Coin purse, CAAC, "Fly CAAC,"
beaded butterfly design, MIP
.... 20.00

Cup and saucer, Delta Airlines, for
VIP International flights, Mayer
China 25.00

Dinner plate, Delta Airlines, for VIP
International flights, Mayer China
.... 20.00

Cigar cutter, pocket, Pan Am, 1901
.... 70.00

Fan, 9" x 14", Cathay Pacific Airways,
full-color sketch montage of Mid-
East and Oriental tourists, 1960s
.... 9.50

Game card, 2-1/4" x 3-1/4", buff-
tone still paper, printed in red and
green, Soco side with math puzzles,
transatlantic side with pencil puzzle
game, C. Carey Cloud, Chicago
1946 copyright 8.00

Junior jet club kit, British Airways,
orig flight book, orig mailing
envelope, wings pin 10.00

Log book, transport pilot's, 3-1/2" x
6", hardcover, 104 pgs, ©1930
.... 15.00

Magazine
Popular Aviation, July, 1937 ... 6.50

Airline
collectibles,
Old Taylor
whiskey bottle,
glass, "Bottled
Especially for
Delta," 4-7/8" h,
$4.50.

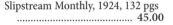

Slipstream Monthly, 1924, 132 pgs
.... 45.00

Paperweight, 1-1/4" x 4" triangular brown wood base, 10-1/2" h red, white and blue fabric 48 star flag with gold cords, symbol for PCA (PA-Central Airlines), opposite side with Pledge of Allegiance, 1950s
.... 20.00

Patch, Ozark Airline, 3" d......... 10.00

Pin, Winged Aces, 4" x 5" red, white, and blue card "Dedicated to the Aces of the Air," 2" w "Solid Bronze/Etched and Enameled" thin metal wings pin, 1930s.................... 14.00

Place setting, china, plate, bowl, cup and saucer, United Airlines... 42.00

Playing cards, Martin Aircraft, black styrene holder with two decks of cards, 1950s.......................... 24.00

Postcard, unused
Air Canada, preparing for takeoff, oversized 6.00
Alitalia, Caravelle III S.E. 210, radio print on back...................... 8.00
KLM, Douglas DC-6B, airline issued, slight crease............ 7.00
Pan American, Super 6 Clipper, color 8.00
TWA Jetstream, French text. 10.00

Promotional brochure, show schedule of Las Vegas acts, Frontier Airlines, Elvis, Ella Fitzgerald, Don Ho, Patti Page, and other celebrities, 1970..................... 15.00

Puzzle, Douglas DC-7, 8" x 10" frame tray, thick cardboard, Grosset & Dunlap publisher, © 1955 .... 8.00

Stewardess wings, United Airlines, silver accent wings, red, white and blue center logo, orig black and white card, c1960, unused, 2" w
.... 20.00

Toy plane, litho tin, friction
Corvair Inter-Continental Jet, 14" l, MIB 145.00
Pan Am Boeing 747, 7" l, MIB
.... 225.00
Royal Dutch Airlines, KLM Corvair jet, 14" l 95.00

Toy wristwatch, jet pilot, D-Luxe Toys, Japan, 1950s, 3" x 7" card with 1-1/4" d face.......................... 12.00

Akro Agate

Akro Agate began producing marbles in 1911. The company moved from Ohio to Clarksburg, W.Va., in 1914. By the 1930s, competition in the marble industry was fierce, and the company chose to diversify its product line. Floral dinnerware and children's play dishes were among its most successful products.

Reproduction Alert.

Children's play dishes

Beverage set
Concentric Rib, eight pcs, yellow plates, green cups, green water pitcher, white saucers, orig Play-Time box 135.00
Stacked Disk, green, pitcher and six tumblers, orig Play-Time box with slight wear............. 175.00

Cereal bowl
Concentric Ring, blue, large. 27.50
Interior Panel, transparent topaz, large, c1936-36................. 30.00
Stacked Disk and Interior Panel, blue, transparent, large.... 35.00

Creamer
Interior Panel, jade trans optic, small, c1935-36 .... 75.00
Octagonal, sky blue, open handle, large.............................. 25.00
Stacked Disk, green or pink, small
.... 10.00
Stacked Disk & Interior Panel, cobalt blue, small, 3-3/8" w, 1-1/2" h............................ 40.00

Cup and saucer
Chiquita, jade green, J. Pressman
.... 6.50
Interior Panel, jade trans optic
.... 32.00

Octagonal, green and white, large
.... 22.00
Stippled Band, transparent green, small................................ 30.00

Pitcher, small
Interior Panel, blue transparent
.... 35.00
Stacked Disk, blue opaque ... 15.00
Stippled band, green transparent
.... 18.00

Plate
Chiquita, green, J. Pressman, 3-3/4" d.............................. 8.00
Concentric Ring, dark blue, small
.... 6.50
Interior Panel, jade trans optic, large................................ 18.00
Octagonal, blue, or green and white, 4-1/4" d.................... 8.25
Stacked Disk, green or blue, small
.... 10.00
Stippled Band, topaz, large .. 10.00

Sugar, cov, small
Chiquita, transparent cobalt blue
.... 8.00
Stacked Disk, green............. 10.00

Teapot, cov
Chiquita, J. Pressman, jade green, 2-3/4" h............................ 28.00

Concentric Ring, pastel blue, white lid, crow and "A" mark, 3" h, c1930-40........................... 40.00
Interior Panel, cobalt blue teapot, cream lid, 3-1/2" h, 4-1/4" w
.... 90.00
Stippled Band, green, small . 35.00

Tea set
Concentric Ring, green plates, green cups, white saucers, blue creamer and sugar, blue teapot

Akro agate glass, assorted pieces of child's play set, Octagonal, green, **$145.**

with white lid, 16 pcs, orig box
.... **200.00**
Interior Panel, topaz transparent,
service for four, cups, saucers,
plates, creamer and sugar, teapot
with lid **215.00**
Swirl, jadite and lemonade, small
size, 12 pcs, each mkd with
flying A logo, orig box "Play-
Time Glass Dishes, No. 2340
Green & Yellow Tea Set," photo of
two children having a tea party
on lid, 1930s, box insert replaced
.... **275.00**

Tumbler
Interior Panel, green transparent,
2" h **12.00**
Stacked Disk, pink or white, 2" h
.... **16.00**
Stacked Disk and Interior Panel,
transparent topaz **18.00**

Household items

Apothecary jar, cov, 3-3/4" d,
6-1/2" h, black, very little gold paint
left........................... **45.00**
Ashtray
2-7/8" sq, blue and red marble **8.50**
4-1/2" w, hexagon, blue and white
.... **35.00**
Basket, two handles, orange and
white **35.00**
Cigarette set, 2-3/4" h cigarette jar,
four 2-7/8" sq ashtrays, red and
white marble.................. **160.00**
Cornucopia, 2" d base, 3" h, #765,
white **12.00**
Flower pot
2-1/4" h, Ribbed, green and white
.... **10.00**
2-1/2" h, Stacked Disk, green and
white.......................... **12.00**

4" h, Stacked Disk, blue and white
.... **25.00**
Mexicalli jar, covered, orange and
white **40.00**
Planter
Graduated Dart, oval, scalloped,
dark blue **30.00**
Narcissus, green and white or
orange and white, mkd "Made in
USA 57," flying wings mark
.... **15.00**
Powder jar, cov
Colonial Lady, yellow **65.00**
Scottie, pink milk glass, Scottie
finial, other Scotties along
bottom, 6-1/8" h **190.00**
Vase
3-3/4" h, green, marble **15.00**
4-1/4" h, lily, marble.......... **18.00**

Aladdin Lamps

Many collectors use the term Aladdin to refer to items produced by the Mantle Lamp Company of America. Founded in Chicago in 1908, the company was known for its lamps. Vintage Aladdin lamps are made of metal and glass, and Alacite is the name given to their popular creamy, translucent glass. Collectors insist that lamps possess all the correct parts, including original shades, which can be difficult to find.

The Aladdin Knights of the Mystic Light, (3935 Kelley Rd, Kevil, KY 42053) is a dedicated collectors' club for those who appreciate Aladdin Lamps of all types.

Aladdin lamps, tall Lincoln Drape oil lamp, Alacite, **$275.**

Electric

Alacite table lamp, ivory, embossed
leaf design, cut-through scalloped
base, wreath-shaped Alacite finial,
22-1/4" h **90.00**

G-217 table lamp, ivory Alacite, gold
metal base, vase design with leaf
spray in high relief, c1940..... **75.00**

M-123, lady figural, metal, orig fleur-
de-lis finial..................... **400.00**

Kerosene

**B-26 Simplicity "Decalmania"
lamp**, pink Alacite, c1948-53
.... **325.00**

Model 8, 401 shade **265.00**

Moonstone Quilt, green, B burner,
wick, Chimney, c1937 .... **335.00**

Washington Drape, amber, plain
stem, B burner, wick, chimney,
shade, c1940 .... **195.00**

Aladdin lamps, salesman's sample, original case with Aladdin lamp, two shades, mantles, chimney, and advertisements, **$250.**

Albums

Albums consist of a grouping of pages that are bound together and used for a similar purpose. Albums can range in size from small examples used for autographs to larger, more ornate types for storing photographs. They offer a unique glimpse into the life of their owner. An autograph album might show one's friends and their sentiments of a bygone era. Photograph albums filled with images of unidentified people are often found at flea markets. Usually the value of these individual "instant relatives" is minimal, but if the photographs happen to include a famous person, an interesting pose, or an unusual setting, the value of the album is enhanced.

Autograph
Leather cover, used, wear to cover 65.00
Velvet cover, "Autograph" emb on front, faded red, filled with autographs, some including caricatures 75.00

Daguerreotype, gutta percha, scrolling motif, dark brown .. 50.00

Photograph
Celluloid cover, floral motif . 85.00
Leather cover, brass closure, family photos, worn 80.00
Velvet cover, maroon, "Our Friends" in nickel plate metal, c1890-1900, filled with old photos, 11" x 9" 140.00
Wood, "Our Honeymoon" in relief, Silver Springs, Fla., hp flamingo motif, unused, 9" x 6" 36.00

Space exploration, P80-1 Satellite, 8-1/2" x 11" folder with 12 thin cardboard cut-out sheets, assembly instructions for 1/20 scale NASA spacecraft............................... 12.00

Stamps, Wildlife Poster Stamp Album, 8" x 11" stiff paper, 24 mounted full color 1" x 2" stamps, 1940 .... 5.00

Tintype, leather cover, holds 24 tintypes, 1-1/2" x 1-1/4" 225.00

Tobacco cards, 7-1/2" x 5", John Players & Son Imperial Tobacco, International Air Liners, 19 pgs, 50 cards 75.00

World's Fair, New York World's Fair Snapshots, 5" x 6-3/4", cardboard covers over 14 sheets of black stiff paper, red, white, and blue cover design and title, 1939 .... 20.00

Album, photo, gold embossed rose on cover, raised decoration, **$90.**

Album, open to show two photos, **$90.**

Album, red, black, and gold cover, Victorian palm plant, woman's profile in upper corner, **$35.**

Album, opened, front page inscribed with giver's name and Christmas 1887, filled with pasted diecuts, **$35.**

Aliens, Space-Related

From little green creatures to Martians, collectors are fascinated by science fiction and aliens. As you can see from this sampling, space-related items encompass a wide variety of collectibles, from scary and spooky to just plain fun. Any alien collection is sure to be out of this world!

Action figure
Clan Leader Predator, loose ... 5.00
Hicks, Kenner, MIP 20.00

Big Little Book, *The Invaders Alien Missile Threat*, by Paul S. Newman, Whitman #12, 1967 .... 8.00

Cap, from movie Alien, 1992, black, neon green writing, adjustable strap, officially licensed by Universal Industries, Inc. 10.00

Christmas ornament
Bird of Prey, Star Trek, Hallmark, 1994, MIB 30.00
Kringles Bumper Cars, Santa, reindeer and space alien, Hallmark, 1991, MIB 50.00

Comic book
Alien Nation, DC Comics, 1988, #1 .... 2.50
Alien Resurrection, movie related 2.00

Aliens, Dark Horse, movie sequel, #1 .... 12.00
Gargoyle, Marvel Comics, 1985 .... 3.00
Xenotech 2.50

Game, Alien, Kenner, 1979 ...... 80.00

Hood ornament, 5-1/2" h, space alien, plastic and pot metal, lights up 10.00

Keychain, Toy Story, Pizza Planet vending machine, antennae light, orig Basic Fun blister pack 4.75

Model, from movie Alien, Aurora, MIB 125.00

Magazine, Famous Monsters of Filmland #143, Close Encounters, Alien, and Star Wars 8.00

Puppet, Alf, red shirt and cap, Alien Productions, 1988, played with 10.00

Aliens, space-related, comic book, *Close Encounters of the Third Kind*, Marvel, No. 3, **$15.**

Almanacs

While few of us today rely on almanacs for forecasting the weather, it wasn't too long ago that many folks did. They got much more than weather information from these charming little booklets; beauty tips, household hints, and exercise regimens were also included.

Agricultural Almanac, 1932, John Baer's Sons, Inc., Lancaster, Pa. 15.00

Bell Telephone System, 1941, 32 pages 12.00

Dr. Jayne's Medical Aliment and Guide to Health, 1870 .... 35.00

Dr. Miles Almanac, 1934, red, white and blue cover, 32 pgs, cover loose, worn 7.50

Goodrich Almanac for Farm and Home, 1937 .... 10.00

Healthway Products Almanac, 1940, Illinois Herb Co. 12.00

Maine Farmer's Almanac, 1916, wear and stains 15.00

MacDonald's Farmer's Almanac, 1922, Binghamton, N.Y. 5.00

Rawleigh's Almanac & Catalog, 1936 .... 10.00

The Herbalist Almanac, 1942, Meyer trademark, cover shows Indians bringing in herbs to dry 9.00

The Ladies Birthday Almanac, 1937, Medlock's Drug Store, Roscoe, Texas 12.00

Uncle Sam's Almanac, 1941, compiled by Frederic J. Haskin, 64 pgs 24.50

Almanacs, 1774, John Anderson's Almanac and Ephemeris...Calculated For Newport, Rhode Island...London, printed in Newport, by Solomon Southwick, 7" h, 4-3/4" w, **$195.**

Aluminum, Hand-Wrought

The aluminum giftware market began in the 1920s, providing consumers with an interesting new medium to replace fancy silver and silver-plate items. In order to remain competitive, many silver manufacturers added aluminum articles to their product lines during the Depression. Many well-known metalsmiths contributed their skills to the production of hammered aluminum. With the advent of mass-production and the accompanying wider distribution of aluminum giftware, there was less demand for individually produced items. Only a few producers continue turning out quality work using the age-old and time-tested methods of metal crafting.

For additional listings, see *Warman's Americana & Collectibles*.

Aluminum, hand wrought, handbag, swing handles, pressed floral pattern, **$95.**

Basket, Chrysanthemum pattern, pierced, elaborate handle, mkd "Forman 4 Family".............. 30.00

Bowl
Chrysanthemum pattern, Continental Silverlook, 11-3/4" d
.... 20.00
Pine Cone pattern, Wendell August Forge, 8" d 45.00

Bread tray, Chrysanthemum pattern, Continental Silverlook, 13-1/4" l
.... 25.00

Butter dish, round, dome cov, double-loop finish, glass insert, mkd "Handwrought Buenilum"
.... 35.00

Candleholder, Buenilum, beaded edge base, aluminum stem with wood ball, 6" h..................... 12.00

Candy dish, curled handle, center china dish with Japanese floral dec, hand wrought aluminum edge with floral design, mkd "Farber and Shlevin"................................. 40.00

Casserole carrier, holds Fire-King casserole, moving the handle lifts the metal lid 35.00

Coaster, Bamboo pattern, Everlast Forged Aluminum, set of eight, matching holder 25.00

Compote, ftd, fluted edges, emb fruit motif, 6" h, 6-1/2" d.............. 10.00

Creamer and sugar, Chrysanthemum pattern, Continental Silverlook, matching tray... 35.00

Lazy Susan, Everlast, Art Deco leaping stag in relief, mkd on bottom 30.00

Nut bowl, footed, floral dec, 4" h, 9" l
.... 20.00

Pitcher, Regal, red, black handle
.... 15.00

Salad set, tulip dec, matching serving utensils, Buenilum Hand Wrought
.... 24.00

Aluminum, hand wrought, tray, china plate center, **$30.**

Silent butler, Chrysanthemum pattern, Continental Silverlook
.... 45.00

Tidbit tray, three tiers, Dogwood pattern, mkd "Wilson Specialties Co., Inc., Brooklyn, N.Y.," 10" h, 13" d..................................... 30.00

Tray
Barley pattern, Wendell August Forge, #606, 14" x 9" 35.00
Flying geese handles, mkd "Shup Laird Hand Wrought Argental Number 713".................... 55.00
Rose design, scalloped and pierced open-work edge, 12-1/2" x 7"
.... 14.50

Water pitcher, handle knotted and riveted to pitcher, mkd with globe logo and "World, Hand Forged," wear, 8-1/2" h......................... 35.00

American Art Potteries, Inc.

This American company was in existence from 1947 until 1961. Most of its wares included a figural element. Production catered to the florist and gift shop market and used clays and talented craftsmen from the Morton, IL, area. Many of its glazes were sprayed on, allowing for shading and subtle differences. Some of their wares were marked with paper labels.

American Art Pottery, vase, parrot on stump, **$25.**

Figure, 7-1/2" h, trumpeting elephant, gray spray glaze 20.00

Planter
  ABC blocks, bear atop B, pink and blue, hand dec 15.00
  Quail, natural colors 18.00
  Swan, pink and orchard spray glaze 15.00

TV lamp, 8" x 12", planter base, tufted titmouse on limb, natural colors, pr 35.00

Vase
  2" h, bluebird on limp, blue, brown, and green spray glaze 12.00
  6" h, six-sided, matt green, white gloss spatter 10.00
  7" x 10", conch shell, yellow and green spray glaze 15.00

American Art Pottery, planter, fish shape, original foil label, **$35.**

Wall pocket, 6" x 5-1/2", apple on three inverted leaves, natural colors 18.00

American Bisque

The American Bisque Company was founded in Williamstown, W.Va., in 1919. Although the pottery originally produced china-head dolls, it quickly expanded its inventory to include serving dishes, cookie jars, ashtrays, and other decorative ceramic pieces. B.E. Allen, founder of the Sterling China Company, invested heavily in American Bisque and eventually purchased its remaining stock. In 1982, the plant was sold and operated briefly under the name American China Company. The business closed in 1983.

Trademarks used by American Bisque included Sequoia Ware and Berkeley, the former used on items sold in gift shops, and the latter found on products sold through chain stores. Its cookie jars are marked with "ABC" inside blocks.

For additional listings, see *Warman's Americana & Collectibles* and *Warman's American Pottery & Porcelain*.

Bank, 6" h, elephant 95.00

Cookie jar
  Bear with Cookie, mkd "USA" 90.00
  Beehive, mkd "USA," 11-3/4" h 175.00
  Candy Cane Babies 200.00
  Cat, 5" w, 8-7/8" h 300.00
  Churn Boy 225.00

American Bisque, spotted pig pitcher, 7-3/4" h, **$77.50.**

  Cookie Sack 95.00
  Dutch Boy, sailboat 175.00
  Jack-in-the-Box 195.00
  School Bus 250.00
  Yogi Bear 300.00
  Wooden Soldier 100.00

Creamer, pig, red bow, 5" h 30.00

Food mold, fish, white, red trim, incised "ABC," ring for hanging, 10" l 20.00

Pitcher, chick, gold trim 48.00

Planter
  Baby carriage with lamp, pink and blue flowers 12.50
  Bear sitting on stump 20.00
  Lamb 15.00
  Tiger 28.00

Sugar bowl, pig, red bow, 3" h 30.00

Teapot, Red Rose, gold trim, 6-1/2" h 55.00

Vase
  6" h, white heart, blue bow .. 28.00
  7-1/4" h, green, fern frond handles 20.00

American Bisque, cookie jar, Eeyore, blue and gray body, pink flower as lid, **$200.**

Animal Dishes, Covered

These clever covered dishes were first popular during the Victorian era, when they were used to hold foods and sweets on elaborate sideboards. China manufacturers produced some examples, but most were made of glass, representing many of the major glass companies. They can be found in colored and white milk glass, clear glass, and many colors of translucent glass.

Animal covered dish, hen on nest, amber glass, painted details, modern reproduction, 7-1/2" l, **$10.**

Camel, white milk glass, Westmoreland 165.00

Cat, on hamper, green milk glass, V mark 115.00

Chick, on sleigh, white ... milk glass 115.00

Cow, white milk glass, Kemple 160.00

Dolphin, white milk glass...... 145.00

Duck, swimming, white milk glass, Vallerystahll......................... 145.00

Fish, flat, white milk glass, Atterbury 120.00

Hen, on nest
Marbleized, head turned to left, white and deep blue, Atterbury 185.00
Mirage (pale orchid), Boyd, 5-1/2" l, 4-1/4" w, 5-3/4" h 20.00
Transparent blue, Kemple Glass, mkd "K" 35.00

Kitten, ribbed base, Westmoreland, white 85.00

Lion, white milk glass, criss-cross base 135.00

Lovebirds, pink irid, Mosser, "M" in shield mark........................... 25.00

Owl, green slag, Imperial Glass, mkd "IG" 60.00

Rabbit, light blue, National Milk Glass Society mark 145.00

Animal covered dish, hen on nest, opaque blue top, white base, 5-1/2" l, 4-1/2" h, **$70.**

Robin, on nest, white milk glass, air bubbles, Vallerystahl 95.00

Swan, closed neck, white milk glass, Westmoreland 120.00

Turkey, white head, dark amethyst body 170.00

Annalee Mobilitee Dolls

Barbara Annalee Davis started making felt dolls and puppets in her home as a hobby in the 1930s. Initially her dolls were sold at craft outlets in New Hampshire and Boston. In 1941, she married Charles Thorndike and they settled in the Meredith, NH, area as poultry farmers. By the 1950s, the Thorndikes started making dolls and puppets full time, developing a unique wire infrastructure, allowing the dolls to have some flexibility and to be posed. As business prospered, some at-home workers are hired to supplement those who work directly with the Thorndikes. Designs centered around mice and Christmas related characters. In 1964, the first factory was built and 10 years later, the Thorndikes were honored as the New Hampshire Small Business of the Year. Annalee Mobilitee dolls were delivered to the White House as a Spirit of '76 tableau in 1989, and again in 1991 as part of a Desert Storm tribute. After its founder passes away in 2002, the business remains active and developing new characters, such as Snowboard Pete, honoring the US Olympics.

Christmas ornament, white felt angel, wings, gold foil halo, 1984, 2-3/4" w, 7-1/4" 18.00

Doll
Baby duck, 3" h..................... 12.00
Candyman Snowman, 2004 ... 8.00
Sir Christmas Frog, green body, red top hat and tails, white collar, 1969, 10" l......................... 15.00

Snowman, broom, black boots and hat, red scarf, green gloves and ear muffs, 1991, 20" h...... 28.00

Mice
Christmas, holding muff, 1966, 13" h 32.00
Christmas mouse in Santa's mitten, 1967, 9" l............................. 9.00
Sledding, 1997, orig tags...... 15.50

Mrs Santa, 1993, 8" h.............. 12.00

Santa
Holding book with his list, burlap bag of toys, candy cane, orig dated tags, 10" w, 17" h 35.00
Painting train, 1990............. 20.00
Sitting on White Moon, red cloth suit, white fur trim, three yellow felt stars, 18" h, 1981........ 24.00

Annalee Mobilitee, Mrs. Claus and Santa in long underwear, large size characters, each **$20.**

Annalee Mobilitee, Little Drummer Boy, **$12.**

Annalee Mobilitee, Patriotic Mouse, red and white striped vest, blue tricorn hat, blue coat, **$20.**

Anthropomorphic Collectibles

Even before the creation of "Veggie Tales," tomatoes and cucumbers had a life of their own. Merchants discovered years ago they could attract a customer's attention by giving human characteristics to inanimate objects. Flea markets are a great place to find anthropomorphic collectibles. Don't hesitate if you see something you like, since this area of collecting is heating up.

Anthropomorphic collectibles, ceramic figurine, man with onion head, made in Japan, 3-1/2" h, **$35.**

Condiment jar, banana boy, green bowtie and brown hat, slotted lid to insert spoon, worn, 5-1/2" h . 55.00

Condiment set
Tomato heads, mkd "Made in Japan," 3-1/2" w, 4" h........ 45.00
Train, red ink stamp Japan mark, 9" l, 2-3/4" h, slight wear.. 35.00

Figure, 4-1/2" h, Penny Pineapple, human head, green leaf necklace, 1942 Peedee ©, Carlton Ware 40.00

Head vase, apple, illegible incised mark and 97608, orig chenille bee insert..................................... 30.00

Rolling pin set, toothpick holder and salt and pepper shakers sit in rolling pin, four-pc set 24.00

Salt and pepper shakers, pr
Apples, full-figure, green-and-black dresses, applied black bead eyes, one with two holes, one with three, cork stoppers, 2-1/2" h 24.00
Cucumbers, green suits, one with four holes, one with three, missing stoppers 4-1/4" h 45.00
Mushrooms, Napco 36.00

Statuette, 7-1/2" h, 3" x 5" rounded base, Penny Pineapple, human head, hand tugging hair box, orig sticker, 1942 Peedee © 35.00

Anthropomorphic collectibles, chalkware fruit plaques, grapes, berries, cherries and banana, set of four, **$50.**

Teapot, pr salt and pepper shakers, one boy and one girl shaker in teapot form, orig corks.......... 60.00

Transfer patterns, The Vitamin Ball, 24 characters include 10 couples, 12-pc orchestra, conductor and singer, Joseph Walker Co., orig packet with split along top.... 32.00

Appliances

Appliances of all types fascinate collectors, with the most common question being, "Does it work?" Please exercise caution when attempting to see if an item functions. Damaged cords and frayed wiring can lead to unpleasant results. When considering a purchase, remember that original instructions, parts, and boxes add greatly to the value of vintage appliances.

For additional listings, see *Warman's Americana & Collectibles*.

Appliances, ice box, Gibson, white enamel body, original hardware, **$450.**

Advertisement, General Electric's New Line, shows can opener, toaster, coffee maker, iron, black and white, 9-1/2" x 12" 12.00

Blender, Chronmaster Mixall, chrome and black motor, single shaft on hinged black base, orig silver-striped glass,1930s 40.00

Buyer's Guide, Food is Fun, Gas Appliance Manuf Assoc, 1963 .... 10.00

Catalog, Trible's Appliance Parts Master Catalog, illus, 1959.... 25.00

Chafing dish, American Beauty, American Electrical Heater Co., three-part, nickel on cooper, black painted wood handles and knob, c1910...................................... 50.00

Drink mixer, Weining Made Rite Co., lightweight metal, cream and green motor, single shaft, 1930s 25.00

Egg cooker, Hankscraft Co., yellow china base, instructions on metal plate on bottom, 1930s 35.00

Flour sifter, Miracle Flour Sifter, electric, cream body, blue wood handle, 1934 .... 35.00

Grill, Sunbeam, model FP, 12" x 12" x 4"... 45.00

Hair dryer
Polar Club, AC Gilbert, orig box 15.00
Queen, Handy-Hannah Products Corp., Whitman, MA 15.00

Hot plate, El Stovo, Pacific Electric Heating Co., solid iron surface, clay-filled int., pierced legs, pad feet, c1910............................... 25.00

Juicer, Vita-Juicer, 1930s, Kold King Distributing Corp., cream-painted cast metal................................. 35.00

Milk shake mixer, A.C. Gilbert Co., restored................................ 125.00

Mixer, Montgomery Ward, electric beater with glass jar, green handle on beater................................. 65.00

Appliances, coffee pot, chromed, original cord, bulbous body, wooden handle, glass percolator top, **$45.**

Appliances, Kitchen Aid mixer, Model K-4-B, Hobart, 1939, **$75.**

Popcorn popper, Rapaport, 5-1/2" sq black base, metal legs, round aluminum upper part, red knob, chrome handle, 1920s 25.00

Record, Get More from your Kenmore, 33-1/3 rpm............ 10.00

Salt and pepper shakers, pr, Tappan Kitchen Ranges, heavy glass with glossy yellow or pale blue finish, baker figure on one panel, black plastic threaded cap, 1940s ... 20.00

Toaster, two slices, chrome body General Mills, wheat decor on side, black Bakelite base, early 1940s 35.00
Kenmore, black Bakelite handles, mechanical clock mechanism, early 1940s 30.00

Waffle iron
Coleman Waffle Iron, high Art Deco style, chrome, small black and white porcelain top impala insert, black Bakelite handles, early 1930s 85.00
Universal, electric, porcelain top, replaced cord.................... 65.00

Art Deco

The term Art Deco is derived from the French name for the Paris Exhibition of 1927, L'Exposition International des Arts Décorative et Industriels Mondernes. The style became quite popular, with its sleek, angular forms and simple lines reflected in everything from artwork to skyscrapers of the period.

For additional listings, see *Warman's Antiques & Collectibles*.

Bookends, pr, bronze clad, Egyptian scribes, greenish-black, lighter green highlights, c1920 .... 350.00

Brush, pearlized pink, matching comb, Fuller, 1925 .... 65.00

Chair, side, chromed metal rod frame, triangular back over triangular upholstered seat, 32" h, pr 100.00

Clock, 16" l, mantle, circular geometric form, green variegated onyx, Whithal electric movement, c1925, some repair, minor loss 100.00

Demitasse cup and saucer, cream ground, multicolor floral dec, stamped on base, Honiton Pottery, Devon, England.................... 90.00

Figure, Man Struggling with a Winch, seminude male figure winding a rope around a large turnbucke, green marble base, Marcel Bouraine (French, c1918-1935), bronze, 25-1/4" l, 27" l base,......... 1,750.00

Art Deco, silver-plated creamer and sugar, 4-1/4" h, pair, **$25.**

Fruit bowl, 12-1/2" d, Christofle silver plate, from the cruise ship L'Atlantique, c1930, flattened handles and stepped rim..... 350.00

Jewelry, 16" l necklace, 7" bracelet, rock crystal, sterling silver .. 470.00

Lamp, boudoir, Danse De Lumiere, 11" h, molded glass figure of woman with outstretched arms, bearing stylized feather drapery, oval platform base with internal light fixture, molded title and patent mark, c1930, mold imperfections 400.00

Lamp, table, 19" h, 11" d concentric ribbed pink satin shade with stylized rosebud center, shade emb "Vleighe France 1137," nickel-plated brass base with emb geometric designs, minor flakes on shade.................................... 520.00

Magazine rack, bronze, upright circular sides with openwork design of greyhound in stride, scrolling leaf border, c1930, 4-1/2" w, 11-7/8" l, 12" h..................... 375.00

Nutcracker, 9-1/2" l, 4-3/4" h, figural elephant, cast iron, orig orange/red paint, black and white details, twine tail....................................... 275.00

Salad servers, fork and spoon, Swedish, c1930-35, 11-3/4" l. 50.00

Vase, 12-1/4" h, 5-1/2" d, Wiener Werkstatte, bulbous, flaring neck, painted white and black geometric pattern, brown ground, stamped "WWW/Made in Austria/HB" 125.00

Wall sconce, 7" h, 3" d, nickeled brass plate and curved arm, frosted glass shade with raised geometric design, rim chips to shade, minor dents to sconce 90.00

Art Deco, perfume bottle, emerald green, woman with arms outstretched embossed on base, original stopper, **$125.**

Art Nouveau

Sensuous female forms with flowing lines are the signature motif of this style. The Art Nouveau period started during the 1890s and continued for the next 40 years, popular in both Europe and America. Leading designers of the time introduced the style's sweeping lines into their works. Florals, insects and other forms from nature were popular motifs.

For additional listings, see *Warman's Antiques & Collectibles*.

Belt buckle, polychrome enamel, silver mount 265.00

Bookends, pr, nude winged dancing nymph, flowing scarf, copper colored cast iron, stamped "Designe Pat. 1154" 285.00

Box, domed cov, paneled box of rust brown shaded to colorless cased glass, acid-etched dec with textured surface, gilt highlights, bottom mkd

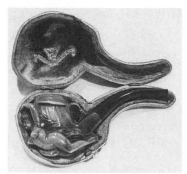

Art Nouveau, pipe, Meerschaum, nude, original case, 5-1/2" l, **$265.**

"H 57," Continental, early 20th C, 4" h.. 350.00

Brush, silver-plate
Nude woman on back, 7-1/4" l
.... 50.00
Scrolls, initials, dated 1916, 7-1/4" l
.... 50.00
Woman's face, 5" l................. 75.00

Bud vase, 8-3/4" h, glass, deep crimson, cut back to citron. 100.00

Candlestick, 11-3/8" h, patinated metal, figural, nymph standing on butterfly, holding flower form candle sconce, flower-form base, early 20th C 115.00

Case, sterling silver, Tiffany & Co., rect, engraved on both sides, monogram "AJC," suspended from silver chain, brown leather interior with two pockets, orig silver retractable pencil, sgd 215.00

Desk set, onyx, two inkwells, blotter, note pad, card holder and pen

holder, inlaid lapis lazuli band, imp hallmarks, London, c1921, six-pc set... 300.00

Dinner gong, mahogany, five graduated bronze bells, exotic wood floral marquetry on sides, bells restrung, 12" w, 10-1/2" d, 10" h 450.00

Figure, Fame, gilt-spelter, on marble base, figure after E. Villianis, French, 17" h 275.00

Inkstand, brass, two-tiered letter holder, hinged lid on inkwell, etched floral decor, base imp "D.R.G.M. 237670 Ges Gesch," 3-7/8" h 120.00

Lamp, polychromed, three lights with frosted shades issuing from foliate standard, classical maidens and child below on sq base, hoof feet, 40" h.................................... 300.00

Mirror, cast bronze, Rococo, kidney shape, 19-1/2" h................... 250.00

Notebook, hammered sterling silver, Tiffany & Co., flying bird and branch dec, entwined starfish on reverse, contains celluloid cards with days of week, sgd, additional hallmark for Shiebler 360.00

Picture frame, silver, English hallmarks, 4-3/4" h x 6-1/2" .. 90.00

Tumbler, 4" h crystal tumbler, acid stamped "WMF," hallmarked silver handled holders, set of four 175.00

Umbrella stand, cast iron, emb floral dec, old green repaint, 28-1/2" h, ... 150.00

Art Nouveau, matchsafe, woman with flowing hair and flowers, sterling silver, American, 1-5/8" x 2-1/2", **$150.**

Urn, 17-1/2" h, conical pottery body, large white and red spring garden flowers, painted blue shiny glazed body, artist sgd, Continental, triple griffin bronze holder base... 475.00

Vase
6" h, 6-1/2" d, silver plate, stylized relief waterlily dec, English, c1900-15......................... 175.00
7-1/8" h, glass, quarter form, ruffled rim, ribbed stem, bulbed base, green glass cased to opaque pink int., slight irid sheen, rough pontil, attributed to Union Glass Co., Somerville, MA....... 115.00

Arts & Crafts

Decorative arts in America took on an entirely new look during the Arts and Crafts movement. This period, from 1895 to 1920, was greatly influenced by leading proponents Elbert Hubbard and his Roycrofters, the brothers Stickley, Frank Lloyd Wright, Charles and Henry Greene, George Niedecken, and Lucia and Arthur Mathews. Individualistic design and a re-emphasis on handcraftsmanship were important features of their work. Most Arts & Crafts furniture was made of oak. The market for good-quality furniture and accessories remains extremely strong.

For additional listings, see *Warman's Antiques & Collectibles*.

Book stand, 45-3/4" h, oak, four open shelves with cutout sides and through tenons 500.00

Box, cov, 4-1/2" l, 2-3/4" d, 2" h, hammered copper, cloisonné enamel with pink flower and

cabochon on lid, scrolling sterling feet, natural patina 365.00

Bowl, 5" d, 1-3/4" h, hammered silver, stamped "Sterling, Hand Beaten at the Kalo Shops, Park Ridge, Illinois," 4 troy oz 395.00

Cabinet, 19" w, 15" d, 67" h, mirrored, single door painted with monk pouring wine, pewter strap hinges, paper "Shop-Of-The-Crafters" label on back, skinned finish................................ 1,300.00

Arts & Crafts, tankard, copper and brass, pewter lined, barley design, English, 14" h, **$295.**

Candlesticks, pr, 11-3/4" h, 3-3/4" d, cast copper, imp "1797" with double cross, no patina, unmarked 195.00

Chamberstick, 6-1/4" h, hammered copper, cup-shaped bobeche, riveted angular handle, flaring base, stamped "OMS" for Onondaga Metal Shops, old cleaning and verdigris to patina 175.00

China cabinet, 45-1/2" w, 17-1/4" d, 61-3/4" h, Rome Furniture Co, GA, two doors, orig glass in doors and in sides, three shelves, paneled back, paper label 1,200.00

Cigarette box, 2-1/4" x 5" x 4", hammered copper, riveted trim, emb circular medallions, cedar lining, natural patina, unmarked, attributed to England 260.00

Coat rack, 24" d, 67" h, brass, four-sided post, flaring base, four double hooks, old patina 200.00

Desk set, sterling on bronze, overlaid with pine bough motif, dark patina, pen tray, perpetual calendar/letter holder, blotter roller, inkwell, orig dark patina, stamp mark "Heintz," foil label 275.00

Inkwell, 5-1/4" sq, 3-1/2" h, faceted copper, curled, riveted feet, enameled green, red, and black, spade pattern, orig patina, unmarked Arts & Crafts Shop, couple of nicks to dec 250.00

Magazine stand, mahogany, four shelves over arched toe board, orig finish, 38" h, 18" w 350.00

Nut set, hammered copper, 8-1/2" d master bowl, six 3" d serving bowls, Benedict, some wear to patina, unmarked 290.00

Rocking chair, Gustav Stickley arm rocker, #311-1/2, mahogany, V-back, five vertical slats, orig worn leather cushion, 34" h 920.00

Sewing table, 18" l, 18" w closed, 29" h, drop leaf, two drawers with wooden pulls, tapering legs, orig finish, two splits to top 350.00

Smoking set, hammered copper, 12" d tray, match holder, cigarette

Arts & Crafts, candy dish, pewter, leaf and daisies decoration, marked "Kayserzinn #4065," **$120.**

holder, humidor with scrolled brass feet, stamped "Benedict Studios" marks, some cleaning to reddish patina, price for set 550.00

Trunk, 30-1/2" l, 16-1/2" d, 17-1/2" h, copper and iron, strapwork and pyramidal tack mounts, black paint, hinged slant lid revealing rect box 200.00

Umbrella stand, Gustav Stickley, #54, four tapered posts, orig copper drip pan, recent finish, unsigned, 34" h, 12" sq 575.00

Vase
8" h, 3-1/2" d, sterling on bronze, corset shape, flowering branch, dark orig patina, stamp mark "Heintz" 450.00
10" h, 3" d, sterling on bronze, cylindrical, overlaid with bird on branch, pewter finish, stamp mark "Heintz," small base dent 300.00

Vice cabinet, 20" w, 12-1/2" d, 32" h, backsplash, single drawer, carved door with green slag glass panel, new medium brown finish, replaced drawer bottom and glass 800.00

Ashtrays

Now that smoking is unfashionable in certain circles, ashtray collectors are finding more choices to pick from at their favorite flea markets. To narrow the field, many collectors specialize in a particular type of ashtray, whether advertising, souvenir, or figural.

Brass, Capitol Metals Co., embossed 10.00

Cast aluminum, Real Hoot Gas Ranges, 3" h, 4-3/4" l, figural duck, text on side, 1930s 25.00

Cast iron
Bum, holding no parking signs, cast iron, Wilton, 3-1/2" w at front, 4" w at back, 3-1/2" h 75.00

Donkey, 4-1/2" w, 4-1/2" h . 130.00

Ceramic
Coronation of Queen Elizabeth II, 1953, gold trim, 3-1/2" sq 15.00
Structural Waterproofing, 6-1/4" d, ceramic, center image of skyscraper office structure under umbrella, white, black

lettering, orange bowl, mkd "Made in Germany," 1960s 45.00
Tournament of Roses 9.00

Chalkware
Collie, ashtray with three cigarette holders, 3-1/2" d, dog 8-3/4" h, 7-1/2" w 22.00
Lion, few paint chips, 10-1/2" h, 9" w 30.00

Ashtray, Pennsbury Pottery, Kiwanis International, Wrightstown Bucks County, Penna, Indian Walk, symbol in center, **$7.50.**

China, New York World's Fair, 1964-65, 5-1/4" x 7-1/2", soft dark gray, vivid shades of blue flanked by yellow and brown sketch art of skyscrapers, gold hand lettering 10.00

Glass
  Amber, glass, molded eagle in center, 9-1/4" 8.00
  Akro agate, burgundy and amber swirls, lip to hold book of matches 125.00
  Esso, clear glass, blue and red dealer inscription, c1950, 4-1/4" x 4-1/4" x 1" h................... 35.00

  New York World's Fair, 4" x 4" x 1/2" h, dark finish, nigh scene, deep blue sky with gold and white fireworks over gold lettering............................ 15.00
  White Horse Whiskey 10.00
Metal
  Century of Progress, 3" sq copper metal, Art Deco, image of Chrysler Building in center 20.00
  Grand Canyon, silvertone, emb with attractions, 5-1/2" 12.00

Ashtray, advertising, stamped thin metal, Stegmaier's Gold Medal Beer, Since 1857, **$2.50.**

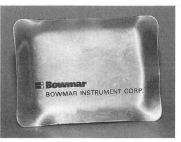

Ashtray, aluminum, advertising Bowmar Instrument Corp., 3-5/8" x 4-7/8", **$2.**

Plaster, Chicken Charlie, 8" h painted plaster figure, 4" x 4-1/2" base, raised inscription on base, two cigarette rests, Beaver Falls, PA, area, 1960s 40.00

Wood, N Brezner & Co., brown composition wood, contoured to 5-1/2" x 7" base, rising 5" at back, elfin-like shoe cobbler seated on storage check, titled "Mr. Cobbleright," slogan "Buy Right With Cobbleright-By Brezner Leahters," three cigarette rests, clear glass inset tray, green felt skid pad, 1940s...................................... 40.00

Aunt Jemima

The Pearl Milling Company first used the image of Aunt Jemima in 1889. The firm's owner, Charles G. Underwood, had been searching for a symbol his company could use for a new self-rising pancake mix. Reportedly, a team of blackface comedians performing a cakewalk to a song called "Aunt Jemima" served as his inspiration.

Aunt Jemima and Uncle Moses, salt and pepper shakers, plastic, **$35.**

Bank, cast iron, hands on her hips, blue and white polka dot bandanna, red dress, white apron, 5-1/2" h 175.00

Bell, ceramic, Japan, 1940s, 3-1/2" h 75.00

Button, "Aunt Jemima Breakfast Club," tin litho, color image of smiling Jemima, red ground, black text "Eat a Better Breakfast," c1960, 4" d... 35.00

Cookbook, *Aunt Jemima's Album of Secret Recipes*, 1935, 30 pgs, soft cover 35.00

Cookie jar, hard plastic, F&F Mold & Die Works, Dayton, Ohio 450.00

Creamer and sugar, plastic, Aunt Jemima and Uncle Moses, F&F Mold & Die Works, Dayton, Ohio 20.00

Doll, stuffed vinyl, 1940s, 12" h 165.00

Hat, Aunt Jemima's Breakfast Club, paper, fold-out style.............. 20.00

Aunt Jemima and Uncle Moses, creamer and sugar, F&F Mold & Die Works, pair, **$20.**

Magazine tear sheet, Aunt Jemima Pancakes, 1949, 13" x 5" **15.00**

Pancake mold, round with four animal shapes, aluminum, 1950s, 8-1/2" d **125.00**

Place mat, paper, Aunt Jemima's Kitchen, full-color, unused.... **20.00**

Pot holder, "There's Love in every Bite—Aunt Jemima," 6" sq **24.00**

Sheet Music, Aunt Jemima's Picnic Day, 1914 .... **25.00**

String holder, chalkware, 1940s-1950s, orig paint.................. **395.00**

Syrup pitcher, Made in U.S.A., 5-1/2" h **65.00**

Thimble, porcelain, Aunt Jemima and Uncle Mose, c1980, 1-1/8" h **12.50**

Automobilia

People have always had love affairs with their cars, and automobilia represents one of the biggest collecting areas in today's market. Flea markets are excellent sources for all types of materials relating to automobiles—parts, accessories, advertising, etc. Specialized flea markets held in conjunction with car shows offer the best opportunities for finding automobilia, but general flea markets can also hold some choice items for collectors.

For additional listings, see *Warman's Antiques & Collectibles*.

Automobilia, Ford key holder, blue leather, **$7.50**.

Ashtray, Chrysler, 1933............ **45.00**

Badge, attendant's hat, Sinclair Grease, celluloid, 3" d.......... **350.00**

Badge, driver's hat, Trailways Bus Lines, enamel **225.00**

Bank, shaggy dog, "Ford" on collar, marked "Florence Ceramics" **65.00**

Blotter, Sunoco advertising, Disney's Goofy character, near mint ... **60.00**

Book, Automobile Blue Book, Standard Road Guide to America, 5-1/2" x 9-1/4", 1,300 pgs, 1922 .... **30.00**

Box, Mobil oil "Gargoyle" logo, designed to hold lubrication charts **45.00**

Buckle clip, 1-1/2" x 1-1/2", silvered and lightly emb thin brass, turnbuckle clip on reverse, early 1900s vintage touring car profile, 1950s..................................... **12.00**

Calendar card, 2-1/4" x 3-3/4", Red Seal Dry Battery, motorist in

goggles holding battery, July 1916 calendar on back **7.50**

Can, motor oil, D-A Speed Sport, racing oil, yellow tin with black and white checkered flags, near mint full quart................................. **50.00**

Clock
Atlas Tires and Batteries, wall clock, 1950s **175.00**
Pontiac Service, glass front, dark blue painted rim **300.00**

Dealer brochure, Ford, 1954, shows all models, staple hole, unfolded 21" x 24".. **30.00**

Display cabinet
Auto Lite Spark Plug, 13" w, 18 1/2" h, painted metal cabinet, glass front....................... **125.00**
Gates fan belts, hangers inside for various sizes, painted tin front, 15" l, 30" w, 24" h **75.00**

Figure, 6" h, Champ Man, flexible vinyl, Champion Auto Stores/Home-Owned Auto Parts Stores, ©1991 .... **15.00**

Key fob, Esso Tiger logo, 1960s, engraved serial number for lost key return..................................... **10.00**

Lapel pin, Ford logo, cloisonné, 1-1/2" l **4.00**

Manual, 8-1/2" x 11", Graham Cars Instruction Manual and Parts Price List, 1940, orig mailer **20.00**

Pinback button, 3" d, red, white, and blue, blue hat circled by red ring, Valvoline Wins, 1960s **20.00**

Poster, 17" x 22", How Many of These Cars Can You Name, Goodyear Tires, 1962 .... **20.00**

Service mailer, 5-1/2" x 8-1/2", blue and white postal folder, Chevrolet's Mr. Super Service and Mr. Fitz-Rite characters, Baltimore dealer, late 1940s... **5.00**

Showroom catalog
7-3/4" x 10-7/8" folds to 15-1/2", Buick, 1952, 8 color pgs, wear **20.00**
10-3/4" x 12-3/4", Chrysler '61, 16 color pgs........................... **20.00**

Ticket, 2-1/2" x 7", Tournament of Thrills, pale blue card stock, red lettering, 1958........................ **10.00**

Watch fob, Good Roads, celluloid logo affixed to metal fob **75.00**

Automobilia, AAA bumper insignia, White Rose Motor Club, York County, painted black and white, **$35**.

Autry, Gene

One of the famous singing cowboys most Baby Boomers remember, Gene Autry spawned a wide range of items for collectors to enjoy. Since he delighted us on the movie screen, radio, and television, an interesting variety of collectibles can be found at today's flea markets. A visit to the Gene Autry Western Heritage Museum in Los Angeles is a must for all dedicated Gene Autry collectors.

Gene Autry, Better Little Book, *Gene Autry and the Bandits of Silver Tip*, 1949, worn, **$15.**

Arcade card, black and white, 1940s, 3-1/2" x 5-1/2"
Gene Autry and Champion .. 12.00
Head and shoulders pose 10.00
Playing guitar 10.00

Book
Gene Autry and the Big Valley Grab, 1952, 250 pgs, hardcover 15.00
Gene Autry and the Golden Stallion, Cole Fannin, 1954, 282 pages, hardcover 17.50
Gene Autry and the Thief River Outlaws, Whitman, 1944, 249 pgs, hardcover, dj 35.00

Cap pistol, silvered metal, simulated pearl handle, c1950, 8" l........ 35.00

Coloring book, Gene Autry Cowboy Adventures to Color, Merrill Publishing, ©1941, unused ... 20.00

Comic book, Gene Autry, Dell, #115 .... 22.00

Cookie jar, McMee Productions, signature across back, copyright 1955 Autry Museum of Western Heritage, 15" h 225.00

Guitar, Emenee, orig box......... 75.00

Handout, Sunbeam Bread, color photo of Gene and Champ, 1950s, 8" x 10"...................................... 5.00

Home movie, Shoot Straight, Carmel-Hollywood, 16 mm, orig box 35.00

Little Golden Book, Gene Autry and Champion, 1956 .... 25.00

Magazine ad, BF Goodrich tires, June, 1950............................... 8.00

Map, Gene Autry Adventure Story Trail Map, Sunbeam Bread premium................................. 50.00

Lobby card, Western Jamboree, Republic Picture, 14" x 11".... 35.00

Pennant, large 55.00

Record, Merry Christmas with Gene Autry, 45 rpm, 1950, orig box, four-record set............................... 40.00

Sheet music, Mister and Mississippi, 1951 .... 22.50

Gene Autry, comic book, *Gene Autry's Champion*, Dell, May, **$50.**

Songbook, Gene Autry's Sensational Collection of Famous Orig Cowboy Songs and Mountain Ballads, Cole, Chicago, 1932 .... 40.00

Watch 110.00

Writing pad, full-color cover, 9" x 5-1/2" 32.00

Autumn Leaf

A premium for the Jewel Tea Company, this dinnerware pattern was produced from 1933 until 1978. Autumn Leaf became so popular with American housewives that other companies began making accessories to complement the pattern.

Bean pot, two handles 295.00

Berry bowl, 5-1/2" d 6.00

Bread and butter plate, 6" d .. 12.00

Bud vase, 5-3/4" h 295.00

Cake plate, gold trim, 9-1/2" d 30.00

Canister, metal, plastic lid 25.00

Coasters, set of eight................ 48.00

Creamer and sugar, cov, ruffled 35.00

Cream soup bowl 20.00

Cup and saucer 17.50

Dinner plate, 9" d 25.00

Drippings jar............................ 40.00

Autumn Leaf, Aladdin teapot,
10-1/2" l, **$75.**

Fruit bowl, 5-1/2" d 12.00
Jug, ball form, 7" h 70.00
Pie plate, 9-1/2" d 18.00
Pitcher, gold trim worn, 7" h ... 40.00
Range set 42.00

Autumn Leaf, 46-piece set, including creamer and sugar, teapot, serving pieces,
mixing bowls, warming tray, **$350.**

Salad plate 12.00
Teapot, Aladdin, infuser 120.00
Tidbit server, three tiers 60.00

Tumbler, 5-1/2" h 35.00
Vegetable bowl 40.00

Aviation Collectibles

Flying machines continue to fascinate us, and aviation collectibles are soaring at flea markets around the
country. Collectors can find material related to hot air balloons, dirigibles and zeppelins, early flight, and
modern planes. From paper items to toys, the sky's the limit in this category.

For additional listings, see *Warman's Americana & Collectibles.* Also see Airlines, Lindbergh, and
other related categories in this edition.

Autograph
  Bishop, W. A., Lt. Col., 6-1/4" x
    9-5/8" paper sheet with sepia
    tone photo, 1920s **120.00**

Cessna, Clyde V., 2-3/4" x 4-1/4"
  clipped signature attached to
  white paper, 1930s 12.00
Cochran, Jacqueline, 7-1/8" x 9-1/4"
  cream colored stationery from
  Cochran-Odlium Ranch, Indio,
  CA, typed note, Aug. 24, 1967
  .... 60.00

Lee, Hamilton, clipped signature
  on triangular pc of white paper,
  1930s **15.00**
Merrill, Dick, 2-1/8" x 2-5/8"
  clipped signature attached to
  white paper, 1920s **10.00**

Aviation collectibles, needle
book, Trans-Atlantic Aeroplane,
Czechoslovakia, litho paper, original
needles, **$8.**

Aviation collectibles, playbill, Going Up,
musical comedy, Golden Theatre, New
York, **$20.**

Aviation collectibles, The American
Clipper postcard, unused, **$3.**

Robbins, Reg, 2-1/8" x 2-5/8" clipped signature attached to white paper, 1920s 10.00

Big little book
Air Races, Saalfield #1183, 1940 .... 35.00
Barney Baxter In The Air With The Eagle Squadron, Whitman #1458, 1938 .... 30.00
Jimmie Allen In The Air Mail Robbery, Whitman #1143, 1939 .... 30.00
Pat Nelson-Ace Of Test Pilots, Whitman #1445, 1937 ...... 30.00
The Great Air Mystery, Whitman #1184, Universal movie film version, 1936 .... 40.00

Booklet, Facts About the Sohio-Giro- And Other Aircraft, © 1931 .. 20.00

Business card, 1-3/4" x 3", Major H. J. L. Hinkler, Director of British Hospitals Air Pagents, c1930 .... 45.00

Cigarette lighter, desk type, chrome plated, lighter compartment in wing, c1937............................ 95.00

Comic book, *Jim Ray's Aviation Sketchbook*, #2, 1946, ink stain on front, wear, yellowing, 64 pgs 18.00

Gum cards, Aviation Pioneers, includes Hugo Junkers, Otto Lilienthal and Orville Wright, biographies in German, set of three 15.00

Magazine
Famous Flights of History, gravure, 48 pgs, 1929 .... 40.00
The Mentor, The Conquest of the Air, six supplement gravure plates, April 1, 1914 .... 40.00

Movie poster, Spirit of St Louis, starring James Stewart, Patricia Smith, Murry Hamilton, folded 90.00

Pennant, 29" l, National Air Races, red, white, pink, and blue accents, 1950s...................................... 35.00

Pinback button, 1-1/4" d button, red, white, and blue ribbon with figural plane on bottom, National Air Races Curtiss-Reynolds Airport, Chicago, 1930 .... 40.00

Plate, Martin Aviation, Vernon Kilns, brown illus of 5 aircraft, c1940, 10-1/2" d 55.00

Postcard, Friendship Airport, Baltimore, Md., textured paper, tinted art, C.T. Art-Colortone, mid-1950s, 3-1/2" x 5-1/2", unused, set of four 18.00

Program, Program of Exercises in Honor of the Bremen Fliers, 1928, 20 pgs..................................... 30.00

Souvenir book, Famous Aviators, 6-1/2" x 9-1/2", softcover, 1929, 42 pgs... 40.00

Sticker
2-1/2" x 3-3/4", National Air Races, Cleveland, 1937, gummed back 8.00
3-1/2" x 10-1/2", The Great Flying Trio, based on Atlantic flight by European aviators Von Huenefeld, Koehl, Fitzmaurice, 12 pgs of stickers, c1928 .. 25.00

Teaspoon, Aviation Building, N.Y. World's Fair, 1939................. 15.00

Windshield sticker, 5" x 7-1/2" diecut, red, white, blue, and silver, National Air Races, 1939, black and white ad on back for Bireley's beverage, unused.................. 20.00

Avon

Ding, dong…Avon calling! After years of producing fine cosmetics in interesting containers, Avon has branched out, producing a wide variety of items that collectors look for. Expect to find items that are well marked, and remember that original contents and packaging will increase values.

For additional listings, see *Warman's Americana & Collectibles*. Also see Cape Cod in this edition for information on Avon's glassware line.

Reproduction Alert.

Avon, doll, ice-skating outfit, **$5.**

After shave, figural bottle, orig contents, MIB
Big Mack, truck, Windjammer after shave.................................. 80.00
Champion Spark Plug, Wild Country after shave.......... 80.00
Chess piece, 6-1/2" h German Shepherd, Wild Country aftershave 25.00
Haynes-Apperson, 1902, Tail Winds after shave 80.00
Thunderbird, 1955, Wild Country after shave 85.00

Award, President's Club, 1993, Albee Award, MIB 125.00

Barbie, Avon Spring Blossom Barbie, first in series.......................... 40.00

Bell, frosted, orig box, 3-1/2" h .. 9.00

Bottle, figural
Boot, empty 5.00
Liberty Bell, full 10.00
Shoe, empty 5.00
Toby mug, empty...................... 5.00

Chamberstick, pewter, mkd "Avon American Heirlooms" 10.00

Collector's plate, Freedom, 1974 .... 35.00

Cologne bottle, Moodwind, dogwood flower design, paper label, 3" h 15.00

Compact, Gay Look, black faille cover, red lining, MIB 100.00

Decanter, totem pole 7.00

Goblet, Mount Vernon series, cobalt blue
George Washington **3.00**
Martha Washington................ **5.00**

Jewelry
Locket, faux pearls around edge, blue and lavender violets in center, space for two photos, 1-1/2" l............................. **12.00**
Pin, leaf shape, 50th anniversary **40.00**
Stick pin, key, goldtone, 2" l. **15.00**

Magazine tear sheet, Avon for Men, 1967 .... **5.00**

Perfume bottle
Elusive, clear, silver top, 3" h.. **9.00**
Owl, frosted glass, 4-1/2" h **9.00**

Plate
For Avon Representatives Only, 1977 .... **5.00**
Strawberry, 1978, 7-1/2" d ... **12.00**
Wildflowers of the Southern States, Wedgwood, 8" d **15.00**

Potpourri, figural pig, orig sticker **5.00**

Radio, 1-1/2" x 3" x 7-1/4", Avon Skin So Soft AM/FM, bottle shape, orig box **20.00**

Soaky
Mickey Mouse, 1969, orig bubble bath and box, 7" h............ **25.00**
Pluto, empty, 6" h **20.00**

Soap
Artistocat Kitten, 1970s, orig box **65.00**
Christmas Children, girl holds doll, boy holds toy rocking horse, 1983 .... **9.00**

Statue, Mother's Love, 1982, 6" h **15.00**

Stein, train, 1982, 8" h **25.00**

Thimble, porcelain, blue and red flowers, mkd "Avon" **6.00**

Avon, hair lotion, Indian head bottle, amber, 4 oz, original contents, **$7.50.**

Baby-Related Collectibles

Grandmas and politicians love them, and now more and more collectors are seeking items related to them. Perhaps it's nostalgia, perhaps it's the delightful colorful images. Whatever the reason, items related to babies and their care are quite popular.

Baby related, head planter, smiling baby's face, pink bonnet and shoulders, unmarked, **$30.**

Baby bank, Kewpie, Lefton China, bisque, orig foil label, 1950s, 7-1/4" h 145.00

Baby bath tub, enameled cast iron, cast iron stand, Hungarian.. 195.00

Baby bottle, emb "Baby" and emb image of infant, bottom mkd Keystone, 6-3/4" h 30.00

Baby ring, 12k yellow gold, 4mm garnet...................................... 75.00

Baby scale, metal 65.00

Baby spoon, sterling silver, monogrammed "F," marked GHF Sterling (G.H. French Co., Mass.), some wear, 3" l...................... 12.50

Bib clips, sterling silver, clothespin type 75.00

Blanket, 38" x 45", light blue and white, jointed teddy bears in various poses, 1940s............ 100.00

Bowl and spoon, sterling silver, Wm. B. Kerr & Co., early 20th C, acid-etched design of children riding different animals from seven countries, minor dents, Gorham monogrammed spoon, 5 troy oz 200.00

Calendar, 1941, Mennen, baby products illus......................... 15.00

Feeding dish, sections, little girl feeding teddy bear, 8" d......... 65.00

Pinback button, Metzer's Milk Infant Keeps Them Smiling, 1" d, c1930 .... 12.00

Push toy, plastic, yellow dog, red ears, blue wheels..................... 3.50

Rattle, Palmer Cox Brownie head with bells, sterling and mother-of-pearl, late 19th C, 3 3/4" l ... 150.00

Baby related, print, Maude Tousey Fangle, brown-eyed baby in blue bonnet, 9" x 12", c1930-40, **$25.**

Record book, pink and blue cover, 1950s, unused........................ 15.00

Sweater, hand-knitted, cream wool with satin ribbon trim, newborn to three months 35.00

Talcum tin
Bauer & Black, oval, 4-1/2" x 3-1/2" 80.00
California Perfume Co., toy soldier graphic, 2 small areas of paint loss, oval, 4" h................... 75.00
Johnson & Johnson 20.00

Baccarat Glass

This French glassware manufacturer is still producing lovely wares, and its paperweights are well known to collectors. Vintage Baccarat glass commands high prices, but contemporary pieces can be found at flea markets for reasonable amounts.

Bonbon, 5-3/4" d, amberina, swirled mold, pedestal foot, emb "Baccarat" 150.00

Box, cov, white airplane design on sides, etched mark, 2-1/4" h, 2-3/4" d 125.00

Cologne bottle, 6" h, Rose Tiente, matching stopper, price for pr 100.00

Figure
Cat, clear, sgd "Baccarat," orig box, 3-7/8" h.......................... 175.00
Porcupine, clear, trademark on base, 5" l, 3" h................. 150.00

Finger bowl, with underplate, ruby ground, gold medallions and floral decor 350.00

Ice bucket, two reeded bands, swing handle, silvered metal mounts, ball finial on lid 200.00

Baccarat, obelisk, crystal, **$45.**

Liquor set, 8-1/2" h decanter, 10 matching cordials, gilt dec Neoclassical motif 450.00

Paperweight, Virgo, sulphide, c1955 .... 150.00

Toothpick holder, Rose Tiente 115.00

Vase, colorless, swollen rectilinear vessel, dec with band of engraved water birds in stream, flowers on shore, pattern of raised curvilinear stripes, 6" h 290.00

Wash bowl and pitcher, 12-1/2" h pitcher, 16-1/2" d bowl, colorless, swirled rib design, pitcher with applied handle and polished base, ground table ring on bowl, polished chip 250.00

Badges

Nametags and identification badges have become quite popular with collectors, and each provides a brief glimpse into history. Examples found with photographs and other pertinent information about the original user are especially prized.

Badges, AAA School Safety Patrol, 1950s, each **$10.**

American Field Service, WWI volunteer organization, sterling 35.00

Captain, Boy's State, American Legion logo 38.00

Car, North Riding, metal frame, plastic front, shield dec 15.00

Chauffeur's Illinois, 1951, 1-3/4" x 1-1/4" 25.00

Oklahoma, 1938, pin-type back 35.00

Dick Tracy Detective Club, brass, Dick Tracy in center with star on each side 30.00

Employee, National Cash Register Co., Dayton, Ohio, emb metal, 1-5/8" h, 2" l 90.00

Fire Department, Inspector, U.S. Naval Air Station, fire truck in center of shield 50.00

Hopalong Cassidy, six-pointed star, silvered metal, 2-1/4" d 40.00

Junior Police, Brattleboro, Vt., 1950s 35.00

Nazi, wound type, silver 70.00

Police, "Special Officer," brasstone, 1-3/4" x 2-1/2" 30.00

Hunting, fishing, trapping license badge, New York, 1930, 1-3/4" 55.00

Service station attendant Conoco, nickel over brass, cloisonné porcelain lettering, 1-5/8" h, 2-1/4" l .... 170.00 Standard Oil, nickel over brass, cloisonné porcelain lettering, 1-5/8" h, 2-1/4" l .... 325.00 Texaco, bronze finish, cloisonné porcelain logo, 1-3/4" h, 2" l 275.00

Sons of Veterans Auxiliary, 37th National Encampment, 1923, silver text on yellow ribbon 15.00

Three Stooges, Clark Collector Cups, black and white images, red and blue lettering, Norman Maurer Productions 14.00

Bakelite

Bakelite is an early form of plastic that was first produced in 1907. A registered trade name, Bakelite was derived from the name of its inventor, Leo H. Baekeland. Items made of Bakelite were formed in molds, subjected to heat and pressure, and then cooled.

Ashtray, black and white, 8" d . 45.00

Box, cov, amber and brown swirl 20.00

Bracelet, bangle, red Carved floral, hinged, oval, c1930, 1-1/4" w .... 450.00 Green dots dec, 1/2" w 425.00

Bracelet, stretch, lemon slices, brown cylinder shapes.................... 100.00

Buckle, carved flower on each end, dark blue, rect 20.00

Button, translucent amber and brown swirl, orig card, set of five 15.00

Cake server, green handle....... 12.00

Crib toy, boy, 1930s, 6" l 295.00

Corn cob holder, diamond shape, 2 prongs, red or green, pr 15.00

Desk set, Art Deco, butterscotch, ink tray, two note pad holders... 225.00

Hair comb............................... 10.00

Napkin ring, chick.................. 30.00

Bakelite, radio, General Electric, 1941, Bakelite case, **$65.**

Pie crimper, marbleized butterscotch handle 6.50

Pin
Bellhop, articulated, 1930s 300.00

Horse head, c-clasp, 2" w, 2-1/4" l 350.00

Salt and pepper shakers, pr, gear shape, marbleized caramel, chrome lids, 2" h 85.00

Stationery box, Art Deco winged horse design, brown, American Stationery Co. 75.00

Toothpick holder, figural dachshund, green 95.00

Ballerinas

Swirling images of dancing ladies grace many types of objects, all to the delight of ballerina collectors.

Ballerina, "Tina the Ballerina," 45 rpm record, Peter Pan Players & Orchestra, **$5.**

Annalee, Tina Elephant, lace tu tu, store exclusive, orig tags, 8" h 65.00

Barbie outfit, #989, leotard, paper tiara and skirt, 1965 .... 150.00

Charm, silvertone...................... 15.00

Christmas figure, Little Miss Mistletoe, Lefton, 4-1/4" h 35.00

Doll
Effanbee, Nutcracker ballerina, 15" h 95.00
Lee Middleton, white tutu.. 185.00
Madame Alexander, Elise, 1970s, MIB 125.00

Figure, glass, Burmese, Fenton, hand dec, sgd by decorator, 6-1/4" h 125.00

Figure, porcelain
Dresden, hand painted, gold accents, layers of pink porcelain lace and porcelain roses, stamped "Large Crove D, Karl Klette"............................. 175.00
Lladro, Julia, #1361 .... 230.00
Royal Doulton, NH 2116, 1952, 7-1/2" h 400.00
Royal Dux, adjusting shoe, raised pink triangle mark, 7-1/4" h 135.00

Handkerchief, child's, printed design, pink and white............ 5.00

Lamp, bedroom type, ballerina and clown, mkd "Made in Czechoslovakia"................... 135.00

Music box, bisque figure with glass eyes, cylinder base, French, 9" h 300.00

Paper dolls, Little Ballerina, Whitman #1951, c1959, uncut 28.00

Pin, figural, rhinestones, silver setting, 2-1/2" l 95.00

Plate, Avondale, 10" d 60.00

Wall plaques, pr, 9-1/2" h, Attitude and Arabesque, Ceramic Arts Studio, name and CAS stamp on back of each......................... 135.00

Banks, Still

The golden age of still banks was ushered in with the advent of the cast-iron bank. Usually in the form of animals or humans, they were often painted to increase their appeal, and many businesses and banks used them as a means of advertising. Tin-lithographed still banks were often used as premiums, being popular from 1930 to 1955.

Still banks, as listed here, are those with no moving parts. Mechanical banks, with some type of action, are thoroughly covered in *Warman's Antiques & Collectibles.*

For additional listings, see *Warman's Antiques & Collectibles* and *Warman's Americana & Collectibles.*

Reproduction Alert.

Ahorro Bancomer, 7" d, 9" h, hard vinyl green chili pepper soccer player with sombrero, base inscribed "Mexico 86" 25.00

Amoco 586 Oil, 2-1/4" d, 2-7/8" h, tin replica can, 1950s-60s...... 15.00

Boy Scout, cast iron 175.00

Church, tin litho, U.S. Metal Co 18.00

Cities Service Station, 2-1/8" d, 3-1/4" h, tin litho oil can replica,

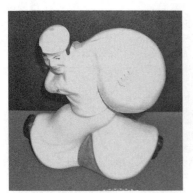

Banks, still, sailor, ceramic, figural, sack slung over back, marked "The Seaman's Bank for Savings," original tin closure, **$25.**

green and white paper label, late 1930s 48.00

Colonial Dixie, 7" h, painted composition, 2-1/2" x 2-3/4" red base with name in white and slogan "At your service, Suh," fleshtones, gray hair, red mouth, blue eyes and hat, black jacket, maroon vest, white trousers, rubber disk trap, 1960s 40.00

Copper and Brass Sales, Snappy Service, 6-1/4" h, figural plaster, smiling saluting figure, blue

uniform, white hat, red shield on chest, 1960s 65.00

Elephant, diecast pot metal, painted ivory, 6" l, 5-1/2" h 235.00

Glass, buffalo on one side, Indian on other, round, 7" h 22.50

Globe, "As you save so you prosper" on pedestal, Ohio Art Co., 4-1/2" h 35.00

Gulfpride Motor Oil, 2-1/8" d, 2-3/4" h, tin litho, quart oil can replica, white, gold trim, blue and orange text, Gulf logo, product text on back, 1950s 18.00

Jumping Jacks Shoes, 5-1/4" x 2-3/4" h, pink plastic, designed like show, name incised on each side, Nashua, NH, store, c1970 ...... 25.00

Laurel, Stan, figural painted hard vinyl, holding suitcase, © 1972 Larry Harmon Pictures, Play Pal Plastics, 5" d base, 13-1/2" h . 20.00

Official Little League Hobby Cash, 4-1/2" x 5" h, plastic baseball shape, red accents, black text on front of green base, 1970s 25.00

Oscar Mayer, weinermobile, bank, plastic...................................... 30.00

Peter Rabbit, Wedgwood, 6 sides, 3-1/2" h 30.00

Pinocchio on whale, musical, Schmid.................................... 35.00

Banks, still, pirate's treasure chest, brass, embossed pistols, sword, pirate, some wear, **$12.**

Safe, cast iron, orig paint, 3-3/4" w, 5-1/2" h 280.00

Savings Eagle, 7-1/2" h, ceramic, figural, brown and white, facing to right, three stars in relief on base, Emigrant Industrial Savings Bank, c1960...................................... 30.00

Uncle Sam, register bank, three-coin register opens at $10, will hold up to $50, Ohio Art Co. 35.00

Unisphere Savings Bank, 6" h, plastic, orange, New York World's Fair, 1964-65, orig box 45.00

Veedol 10-30 Motor Oil, 2-1/8" d, 2-7/8" h, deep blue can replica, gold and red text, early 1950s 40.00

Barber Bottles

At the turn of the century, barbershops used decorated bottles to hold oils and other liquids that were used on a daily basis. These colorful glass bottles included examples made of art glass, pattern glass, and milk glass, as well as a variety of commercially prepared and labeled bottles. Reproductions scared off many collectors in the early 1980s, but collectors have learned how to detect the fakes and are again seeking out interesting examples.

For additional listings, see *Warman's Antiques & Collectibles*.

Reproduction Alert.

Amber, Hobnail, three-ring neck, curled lip, bulbous base, 6-3/4" h 240.00

Amethyst, Hobnail, 7" h 250.00

Aqua, Inverted Thumbprint, enameled deco of 18th C gentleman, two panels satin finish, two panels clear, metal top, 9-1/2" h 280.00

Bristol glass, white, enamel and gold trim, 7" h 60.00

Clear
Hazel Atlas, double plastic cap possibly Bakelite, 7" h, pr 45.00
Paper label, Empire Quinine Hair Tonic, Empire Barber and Beauty Supply Co., screw cap, contents, one-gal, 12" h 25.00

Coin Spot, cranberry opalescent, orig stopper, 8-1/2" h 395.00

Cranberry glass, white enamel dec of young child, 8" h 175.00

Green, all-over pattern of white enameled flowers with orange centers, white stopper, 9" h . 250.00

Lime green, ribbed mold, 7-1/2" h 365.00

Milk glass
  Bay Rum, 7" h..................... **260.00**
  Witch Hazel, painted letters and
    flower dec, 9" h **115.00**
Opal glass, squatty, blue and purple
  pansies dec, Mt. Washington, 7" h
  .... **100.00**
Overshot, screw-on top, polished
  pontil, c1850...................... **150.00**
Purple, white enameled floral dec,
  missing stopper, 8-1/2" h..... **150.00**

Ruby stained, etched decoration, 6-
  1/2" h **250.00**
Satin, white, emb florals, cartouche
  for paper label, 9-3/4" h **35.00**
Vaseline, opalescent Daisy and Fern
  pattern, 7" h.......................... **360.00**

Barber bottles, Bay Rum,
milk glass, original
porcelain stopper, 9-1/2" h,
$145.

Barbershop and Beauty Shop Collectibles

Flea markets are great places to search for items related to barbershops and beauty shops. Following the decline of the barbershop as an important social institution and with the advent of uni-sex regional chains, early barbering and beauty products are becoming increasingly popular. Attractive advertising and interesting examples of barbering equipment add color and style to collections.

For additional listings, see *Warman's Americana & Collectibles* as well as Barber Bottles and Shaving Mugs in this edition.

Barber brush
  Half doll porcelain handle.... **20.00**
  Penguin handle, wood, paint
    chipped, 1940s **35.00**
Barber pole, hand turned wood,
  some wear to paint............. **350.00**
Child's barber chair, hand made,
  fiberglass speedboat body, beauty
  chair base with foot pump action
  .... **150.00**
Comb holder, Jeris Disinfecting
  System, heavy glass jar, turquoise
  plastic lid and strainer, 11-1/4" h
  .... **48.00**

Barber shop collectibles, razor sterilizer,
nickel-plated brass, 7-1/4" x 4-7/8" x
9-1/4" h, **$175.**

Counter mat, Wardonia Razor
  Blades, rubber, 9" x 8" **18.00**
Display case, West Hair Nets, tiered
  display case, tin litho picture of
  flapper in touring car inside lid,
  15" h, 6" w, 5" d..................... **60.00**
Hair net, Sensation, orig envelope
  .... **12.00**
Magazine tear sheet, adv
  Eversharp Schick Safety Razor,
    1958................................... **8.00**
  Norelco Speedshaver, 1957..... **6.00**
  Remington Rollectric, 1958 ... **8.00**
  Sunbeam Blade Electric
    Shavemaster Razor, 1957 ... **6.00**
Match book cover, Norman's
  Modern Barber Shop.............. **6.00**
Newspaper, *Barber's Journal*, 1881
  .... **12.00**
Poster, Packer's Tar Soap, scene of
  barber shaving customer, 1900, 9" x
  12"... **40.00**
Razor tin, Yankee Blades, tin litho,
  eagles and center image of man
  shaving, red ground, 1-1/4" w, 2-
  1/4" l.................................... **200.00**
Safety razor, Burham, razor with 3
  blades in orig envelope, tin litho
  safety razor tin, red ground, black
  lettering, unused **160.00**
Shaving brush, Ever Ready, black
  celluloid handle, dark bristles, orig
  box **15.00**

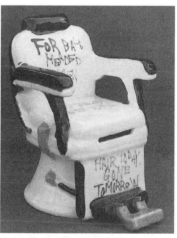

Barber shop collectibles, blade bank,
figural barber chair, "For Bald Headed
Men, Hair Today, Gone Tomorrow,"
white, black trim and lettering,
5-1/2" h, **$200.**

Shaving mirror, nickel silver, swing
  type, Geisha standing on ornate
  base, mkd "Golden Mfg Co.,
  Chicago," c1890, 19" h **165.00**
Sign
  Barber, Bastian Bros, NY, Allied
    Printing, Rochester, 15" x 6"
    .... **165.00**
  Beauty Shoppe, two-sided flange
    sign, porcelain, Art Deco lady
    with finger wave hairdo, 12" h,
    24" l **275.00**

Tin
    Bouquet Talcum Powder 25.00
    Magic Shaving Powder 25.00

Yankee Blades, eagles and center
    image of man shaving.... 200.00

Towel steamer, nickel-plated copper,
    porcelain-over-steel base..... 325.00

Barbie

Mattel patented the Barbie fashion doll in 1958, with the first versions reaching store shelves in 1959. Her friends, including Ken and Skipper, joined the ranks in subsequent years. Accessories, clothes, room settings, and all types of related merchandise soon followed. A plethora of books cover Barbie, and her life is well documented. Her appeal is widespread, and she is the most collected doll ever created.

For additional listings, see *Warman's Antiques & Collectibles* and *Warman's Americana & Collectibles*.

Accessories
    Barbie Café Today, dated 1970, NRFB, age discoloration to box, fading, slightly scuffed... 475.00
    Barbie Teen Dream Bedroom, dated 1970, MIB, discoloration to orig box................................... 65.00
    Swimming pool, inflatable, no box 20.00

Activity book, Skipper and Scott Beauty Sticker Fun, 1980 .... 5.00

Car, Hot Rod, #1460, 1963 ..... 195.00

Carrying case, Barbie and Midge, pink, 1964 .... 30.00

Catalog booklet, Barbie, Ken, Midge, wardrobe, 32 pgs, 1962, 3" x 4" 10.00

Colorforms set 15.00

Cookbook, Barbie's Easy-As-Pie Cookbook, Cynthia Lawrence, 1964, 1st printing, 114 pgs.............. 15.00

Clothing
    #790, Time for Tennis, Ken, NRFB 115.00

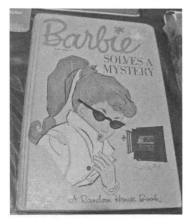

Barbie, book, *Barbie Solves a Mystery*, Random House, **$5.**

#954, Career Girl, VG 80.00
#984, American Airlines Stewardess, VG................ 90.00
#992, Golden Elegance, VG 115.00
#0874, Arabian Nights, Ken, NRFB 125.00
#1234, The Combination, Francie, NRFB 125.00
#1616, Campuss Sweetheart, NM 255.00
#1667, Benefit Performance, VG 145.00
#1935, Learning to Ride, Skipper, NRFB 155.00

Disk, I Love Barbie, flasher, full color portrait, 1970s, 2" d 3.00

Doll, Barbie
    American Girl Barbie, brunette, bendable legs, #1658 Garden Wedding, box, VG 350.00
    Bubble cut, blond, straight legs, one-pc red nylon swimsuit, red open toe shoes, orig box with gold wire stand, no box, VG 225.00
    Color Magic Barbie, lemon yellow hair, yellow metal barrette, undressed, no box, VG... 365.00
    Happy Holidays, orig box, 1988, #1, NRFB............................. 230.00
    Happy Holidays, 1989, NRFB 70.00
    Happy Holidays, 1994, NRFB, box slightly scuffed, sticker residue on plastic window............ 35.00
    Ponytail, #5, brunette, orig set, Pak outfit, no box, NM/VG... 225.00
    Ponytail, #6, blond, red nylon one-pc swimsuit, red open toe shoes, orig box with cardboard liner, black wire stand, light blue cover booklet, VG 215.00
    Russell Stover Candies, ©1966, blond, multicolored dress, MIB 30.00

Barbie, doll, Holiday Barbie, white fur trim, maroon velvet and gold gown, NRFB, **$20.**

    Sun Luvin Malibu Barbie, © 1978 Mattel, mirrored sunglasses, tan lines, MIB......................... 25.00
    Teen Talk Barbie, #1612, ©1991 Mattel, Black, NRFB......... 55.00
    Twist 'n' Turn, blond, bent legs, orig multicolored knit swimsuit, booklet, paper label, NRFB 300.00

Doll, Barbie's family and friends
    Allan, painted red hair, straight legs, blue swim trucks, wrist tag, black wire stand, booklet, orig box............................... 65.00
    Christie, Twist 'n' Turn, dark reddish-brown hair, orig swimsuit, wrist tag, clear plastic stand, NRFB 275.00
    Francie, brunette, two-pc yellow nylon swimsuit, orig clear plastic bag, cardboard hanger, NRFP, orig price sticker 250.00
    Julia, talking, gold and silver jumpsuit with belt, wrist tag, clear plastic stand, NRFB,

Barbie, plates, heart shape, plastic, price for pair, **$5.**

nonworking, box age discolored, scuffed, and worn 225.00

Ken, brunette flocked hair, red swim trunks, worn wrist tag, booklet, yellow terrycloth towel, cork sandals in cellophane bag, black white stand, orig box, VG 155.00

Ken, painted blond hair, straight legs, red swim trunks, red and white striped jacket, wrist tag, cork sandals, black wire stand, orig box, MIB 120.00

Skipper Pose'n Play, blond, blue and white outfit, wrist tag, orig clear plastic bag, cardboard hanger, NRFP 85.00

Skooter, straight legs, lavender dress, cross necklace, played-with condition 40.00

Knitting case, purple vinyl, matching lid, metal closure, dark pink braided handle, VG 60.00

Lunch box, The World of Barbie, vinyl, blue, multicolor images of Barbie, copyright 1971 Mattel, King-Seeley, used, 6-3/4" x 8-3/4" x 4" d... 50.00

Paper doll book, Whitman, uncut Barbie and Ken Cut-Outs, #1986, dated 1970, NM................ 35.00

Barbie's Boutique, #1954, dated 1973, NM........................... 85.00

Barbie Dolls and Clothes, #1976, dated 1969, NM................ 50.00

Pencil case, Skipper and Skooter, Standard Plastic, 1966........... 15.00

Poster, Peppermint Princess Barbie, Fossil Watches, © 1995 Mattel, 22" x 28" 15.00

Barbie, paint book, *Barbie Seashore Scientist*, Golden Books, unused, **$12.**

Record, 33-1/3 rpm, Sing-Along, unused, 12-1/2" x 12-1/2"........ 6.00

Screen Styler, computer program, NRFB 5.00

Stand, black wire, mid-1960s... 15.00

Bar Ware

Back in the days when recreation rooms were popular in homes, bars were often an important component of that scene. Of course, a well-equipped bar was a necessity. Novelty items and functional equipment from bars are now making their way to flea markets.

For additional listings, see Cocktail Shakers in this edition.

Bar guide, *Esquire's Liquor Intelligencer*, 1938, wear, few pages loose, 5-1/2" x 7".................... 28.00

Battery operated toy, bartender, unused, MIB 50.00

Bottle stopper, figural
Kissing Couple...................... 25.00
Man, tips hat........................ 25.00
Man, pop-up head 40.00

Cocktail napkin, San Diego All-Star Game, July 14, 1992................. 2.00

Cordial set, six glass cordials with cut floral dec, 1-1/2" x 3", matching 12" x 3-1/2" aluminum tray... 95.00

Hor d'ouevre pick
Fruit, set of 12 .... 20.00
Man, top hat 3.50

Ice bucket
Aluminum, brown Bakelite handles and knob, mkd "West Bend

Penguin Hot and Cold Server," 10" w, 8" h,........................ 45.00

Glass, hp horse and riding crops on both sides, hammered aluminum handle, gold band at top and bottom.............................. 15.00

Jewelry, pin and earrings set, large martini glass with olive, silver-tone earrings with open-work, 1960s 35.00

Barware, napkins, different recipes on each, printed in red on white, original box, **$15.**

Jigger, frosted glass, Indian motif, Canada on back, 4-oz 4.00

Liquor set
7" h golf club, shot glass on each end, one holds 1 oz, other 2 oz, golf ball cork screw, 6-1/4" bottle and can opener iron, 9" stirrer iron, orig box with red felt lining, unused............................. 20.00

14" h, marbleized plastic bowling ball container, chrome dispenser, shot glasses trimmed with red, green, or blue glass rings, gilded metal figural finial 75.00

Measuring cup, 4-1/4" d, 6" h, tin, gray, black, and red, conical, cat on front with name "Meesbecher" and "Luchs," inside mkd for measuring cocktail ingredients, in German, "Zucker, Butter, Kakao, Salz," etc. 25.00

Mixer, clear glass, black lettering, recipes on side, 5-3/4" h **14.00**

Paper napkins, Ed Nofziger's Mad-Nagerie Sip 'n Snack, different animal illus, orig box, 6-1/2" x 6-1/2" **14.00**

Recipe card, 4" x 5", orig mechanical card in full color cardboard envelope, c1920, wear **18.00**

Seltzer bottle, blue glass, "Babad's Miami Seltzer Co.," bottle made in Czechoslovakia **100.00**

Shot serving set, 2" d, 6" h painted wooden figure holding orig set of six plastic nesting shot glasses, blue, lavender, green, yellow, orange, and red, figure wearing black tuxedo and top hat, mkd "Whoopee," figure opens at waist to store glasses, late 1930s-40s **35.00**

Swizzle stick, glass

Advertising, colored 3.50
Amber 1.50
Black 2.00
Christmas, set of six 25.00
Man, top hat 3.50
Souvenir, Hotel Lexington, amethyst, 1939 World's Fair 20.00
Spatter knob, clear stirrer 1.00

Tom and Jerry set

Fostoria, American pattern, bowl and eight mugs 250.00
Hall China, black, ftd bowl, 18 five-oz cups 190.00

Tray and coasters, wood, tray shows man sleeping and "Silence, Genius at Work," coasters with humorous sayings, Canada, 1950s, tray 12" x 8", six coasters 3" d 75.00

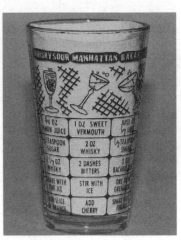
Barware, glass with directions for mixing drinks, 6" h, **$2.**

Baseball Cards

Baseball cards were first printed in the late 19th century. By 1900 the most common cards were those made by tobacco companies, including American Tobacco Company. Most of the tobacco-related cards (identified as T cards) were produced between 1909 and 1915. During the 1920s, American Caramel, National Caramel, and York Caramel candy companies issued cards identified in lists as E cards.

During the 1930s, Goudey Gum Company of Boston, and Gum, Inc., were the primary producers of baseball cards. Following World War II, Bowman Gum of Philadelphia, the successor to Gum, Inc., led the way. Topps, Inc., of Brooklyn, N.Y., bought Bowman in 1956, and Fleer of Philadelphia and Donruss of Memphis joined the competitive ranks in the early 1980s.

The following listings are merely a sampling of the thousands of baseball cards available. For detailed listings, see *2005 Standard Catalog of Baseball Cards*, 14th ed, by Bob Lemke; and *Warman's Baseball Card Field Guide*, both by KP Books.

For additional listings, see *Warman's Antiques & Collectibles* and *Warman's Americana & Collectibles*.

Reproduction Alert.

Banks, Ernie, #525, Topps, 1971 .... **35.00**

Berger, Walter, #25, Diamond Stars, National Chicle Co., 1935 ...... **12.00**

Bluege, Ossie, #71, Diamond Stars, National Chicle Co., 1935 ...... **15.00**

Bolten, Cliff, #47, Diamond Stars, National Chicle Co., 1935, crease **8.00**

Brett, George, KC Royals, Topps, rookie card, 1975 .... **20.00**

Brock, Lou, #625, Topps, 1971 .... **20.00**

Carlton, Steve, #55, Topps, 1971 .... **15.00**

Detroit Tigers 1984 World Champions, 20 circular cards, each with color photo in center, © Major League Baseball Players Assn 1985, uncut, 13" x 16-1/4" **20.00**

Dykes, Jimmy, #42, Diamond Stars, National Chicle Co., 1935 ...... **15.00**

Farrell, Rick, #48, National Chicle Co., © 1935 .... **25.00**

Garvey, Steve, #341, Topps, 1971 .... **35.00**

Gibson, Bob, #61, St. Louis Cardinals, Fleer, 1963 .... **10.00**

Jackson, Reggie, #300, Topps, 1975 .... **15.00**

Lombardi, Earnie, #36, Diamond Stars, National Chicle Co., 1935, name "Ernie" misspelled variation,

Baseball cards, Pete Rose, National League All-Star Outfield, #320, Topps, 1975, **$15.**

Baseball cards: here's a clever way to display your favorite baseball cards, each card is carefully enclosed in an archival envelope and the whole grouping is archivally matted and framed, **$150.**

Baseball cards, Carl Yastrzemski, Red Sox, A.L. All-Star, #720, Topps, 1980, **$5.**

dust soil on both sides, wear around corners 75.00

Lucas, Red, #46, Diamond Stars, National Chicle Co., 1935, tack hole 10.00

Lyons, Ted, #43, National Chicle Co., © 1935 .... 25.00

Mays, Willie and Willie McCovey, NY Giants uniforms, #423, Topps, 1967 .... 12.00

Oliver, Gene, #247, Topps, 1969, white letter variation 15.00

Palmer, Jim, #475, Baltimore Orioles, Topps, 1967 .... 30.00

Robinson, Brooks, #1, Baltimore Orioles, Topps, 1969 .... 8.00

Robinson, Frank, Hank Bauer and Brooks Robinson, Baltimore Orioles, #1, Topps, 1967 .... 10.00

Rodgers, Brooke, #10, Topps, 1961 .... 27.50

Rolfe, Robert, #29, Diamond Stars, National Chicle Co., 1935 ...... 15.00

Schmidt, Mike, #70, Topps, 1975 .... 35.00

Selkirk, Geo, #88, National Chicle Co., © 1936 .... 25.00

Urbanski, Billie, #37, Diamond Stars, National Chicle Co., 1935 ...... 12.00

Baseball Memorabilia

"Play ball!" How those words excite fans and collectors alike. America's fascination with this popular national pastime guarantees a wide range of collectibles to choose from at flea markets.

For additional listings, see *Warman's Antiques & Collectibles* and *Warman's Americana & Collectibles.*

Reproduction Alert.

Ashtray, 1" x 6" x 8" high gloss glazed ceramic, slightly raised images of batter and pitcher, background

baseball diamond and stadium seats, c1960 .... 25.00

Autograph
Aaron, Hank, baseball bat .. 135.00

A swing and a hit

Hillerich & Bradsby, Louisville Slugger Co. produces special black ebony bats to commemorate World Series games. The bats have gold facsimile signatures of the team members, and they are awarded to participating players and league dignitaries. Because they are produced in limited numbers, collector interest tends to drive the marketplace.

1965, Minnesota Twins	600.00
1992, Atlanta Braves	500.00
1993, Toronto Blue Jays	500.00

Carew, Rod, 11-1/2" x 14-1/2" four page folio from *The Sporting News,* June 29, 1974 .... 20.00
Coveleski, Stanley, Hall of Fame postcard, 1969 .... 20.00
Dawson, Andre, baseball...... 25.00
DiMaggio, Joe, black-and-white glossy photo, 11" x 14" ... 175.00
Grimes, Burleigh, Brooklyn jacket and cap, 8" x 10" glossy black and white 35.00
Herman, Billy, Brooklyn uniform, 8" x 10" glossy black and white 25.00
Lyons, Ted, 8" x 10" glossy black and white......................... 35.00
Seaver, Tom, 8-1/4" x 11" glossy paper cover from *Sport,* May 1976................................. 25.00
Snider, Duke, 3" x 5" white index card.................................... 20.00
Spahn, Warren, Milwaukee uniform, 8" x 10" glossy photo, c1953 .... 20.00
Williams, Dick, Oakland Athletics, 8" x 10" glossy photo, c1971 .... 14.00

Badge, 3-1/2", cello, red, white, and blue Luis Aparicio, Chicago White Sox, MLB, ©Major League Baseball, 1969 .... 20.00

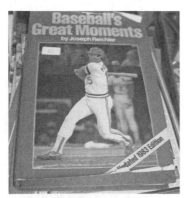
Baseball collectibles, book, *Baseball's Greatest Moments,* Joseph Reichter, 1993, original dust jacket, **$10.**

Minnesota Twins, Western Division Champions, American League, 1987 .... 8.00
Baseball card locker, 3" x 8" x 10" h, olive green plastic replica of double wall locker, left side for American League teams, right for National League teams, Lakeside Toys, ©1966 .... 10.00
Bedspread, child's, 60" x 96", stitched batter, baseball diamond, pennant, glove, and baseball, 1950s..... 35.00
Bobbing head
5-1/2" h, painted composition, blue cap, painted white "M," white shirt trimmed in blue, red sq base, mkd "Japan" 30.00
7" h, Cleveland Indians, 1962 .... 125.00
Calendar, 1983, Chicago Cubs, by Jim Langford............................ 9.50
Can, RC Cola, #18, series #2, 1978, opened 2.00
Cereal box, Kellogg's Frosted Mini-Wheats, ©1993, action photo of Reggie Jackson, NY Yankees, coupon for watch on side, flattened 14.00
Cereal box panel, Wheaties, two 6" x 8-1/4" cut panels
Bridges, Tom and Schoolboy Rowe, Detroit Tigers, 1935 .... 25.00
Medwick, Joe, #12 in series, 1937 .... 28.00
Charm bracelet, 7" l, St. Louis Cardinals, brass, Bush Memorial Stadium and Gateway Arch charms along with letters to spell "Cardinals," c1970 .... 20.00
Child's book, *Inside Baseball for Little Leaguers,* Wonder Book, © 1958, 64 pgs.......................... 12.00
Coffee mug, 4-3/4" h, KC Royals, glossy black plastic, thermal wall with full-color cameo photos of players, Fan Appreciation Day premium from Eight O'Clock Coffee, A & P Grocery, late 1970s 15.00
Exhibit card, 3-3/8" x 5-3/8", sepia tone, facsimile signature, c1960
Drysdale, Don...................... 20.00
Killebrew, Harmon 15.00
Mays, Willie......................... 20.00
Mazeroski, Bill..................... 15.00
Pierson, Albie 15.00
Gum wrapper, Double Play, 7" x 7-1/4" silver foil paper, Meadow Gold Bubble Gum Cooler, red, orange, and white designs, blue and white art portraits of Cal Ripken Jr, Ryne

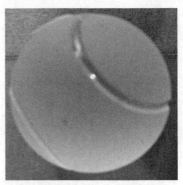
Baseball collectibles, paperweight, frosted glass, figural baseball, **$45.**

Sandberg, Dan Quisenberry, early 1990s, unused........................ 20.00
Hartland figure
7" h, Nelson Fox, Chicago White Sox..................................... 85.00
7-1/2" h, Roger Maris, 25th anniversary, © 1988, MIB 55.00
Lunch box, Toronto Blue Jays, 7" x 8-1/2" x 4", blue vinyl, plastic handle, back panel with trademark logos for sponsors Coca-Cola and Kraft Foods, late 1980s 20.00
Magazine
Baseball Monthly, Vol. 1, #4, June 1962.................................... 5.00
Sports All Stars Baseball 1960, Eddie Matthews on cover, 96 pgs 20.00
Marble game, "Action Baseball," Pressman Toy Corp., 15" x 19" wood frame, emb metal playing surface, 1950s.. 20.00
Patch, 2-1/8" d, felt, Home Run, red, white, and blue, baseball, glove at top, four diamonds at bottom, 1950s...................................... 15.00
Pennant
2-1/4" x 4-1/4", White Sox, dark blue and white, 1930s 15.00
3-3/4" x 8-1/2", Boston Braves, white on blue, yellow band, 1940s 20.00
3-3/4" x 8-1/2", Cleveland Indians, red on black, 1940s 20.00
28-1/2" l, Washington Senators, red felt, white text 30.00
Photo
Baltimore Orioles 1951 team, 10" x 12" glossy black and white, players' names below 40.00
Baseball Stars-Present and Future, Don Drysdale, Dean Chance, Willie Mays, Sandy Koufax, Jim Fregosi, Dick Radatz, Dick Farrell, Joe Pepitone, facsimile

signatures, c1961, 8-1/2" x 11" **15.00**

Feller, Bob, facsimile signature, lower right "Consultant On Youth Activities- Motorola, Inc.," 1960s **15.00**

National Girls Baseball League, Queens, 11-3/4" x 14-3/4" thin cardboard white folder, 11" x 13-7/8" black and white team photo, c1950 .... **30.00**

The Whiz Kids of 1950, The Fightin' Phillies, 10" x 35", black and white, newspaper supplement **75.00**

Place mat, 10" x 13-1/2", white paper, red art and text "Congratulations to Mgr Dick Williams and the Boston Red Sox, 1967 A. L. Champs" . **8.00**

Ribbon and pin, 3-1/2" l wooden miniature bat, stickpin fastener with 3" white fabric ribbon with Cubs emblem and "Rooter," mkd "Pat. Apld For," c1908 .... **25.00**

Sign, 10-1/2" x 13-1/2", Catfish Hunter, blue cap and windbreaker, jaw bulging as one hand delves into package of Red Man Chewing Tobacco, c1970 .... **30.00**

Team ball, 2-3/4" d, Philadelphia Phillies, facsimile signatures, 1954 .... **45.00**

Viewmaster reel set, Baseball Stars of the Major Leagues, reels #725, 726, 727, descriptive leaflet for #726, © 1953 .... **30.00**

Yearbook
Los Angeles Dodgers, 1968.. **15.00**

New York Mets, 1973............ **10.00**

Weekly chart, 19" x 25", paper, issued by Columbia Beer, for use in tavern, 1954, unused **18.00**

Wiffle ball, white plastic, orig 2" sq Trading Disk box, © 1977 .... **5.00**

World Series pins
1966, Dodgers.................... **100.00**
1974, Oakland A's **375.00**
1982, St. Louis Cardinals...... **50.00**
1984, San Diego Padres........ **75.00**
1995, Atlanta Braves........... **100.00**

World Series program
1948, Indians v Braves, no writing, some cover wear.............. **85.00**
1996, Yankees v Braves......... **10.00**

Basketball Memorabilia

Since its introduction in 1891, players and spectators have enjoyed the game of basketball. So popular is the sport that phrases such as "Hoosier Hysteria" and "March Madness" have been added to the lexicon. The NBA is working hard to promote collecting among its fans, and the WNBA has created a whole new field of collectibles.

For additional listings, see *Warman's Americana & Collectibles*.

Action figure, MOC
Barkley, Charles, Headliners NBA **10.00**
Drexler, Clyde, Rockets, Headliners NBA **5.00**
Frazier, Will, Starting Line-Up, 1997 .... **15.00**
Hill, Grant, Detroit Pistons, Headliners NBA **7.50**

Autograph
Bryant, Kobe, on jersey **340.00**
Johnson, Magic, 8" x 10" photo **36.00**
Jones, Eddie, on jersey **185.00**
Mercer, Ron, 8" x 10 photo... **15.00**
O'Brian, Larry, 3" x 5" white index card, personalized............ **10.00**
Parish, Robert, *Beckett Basketball Monthly*, August 1992, back cover with photo of Boston Celtics Larry Bird, Robert Parish, Kevin McHale, black marker signature "Robert Parish" **10.00**

Bobbing head figure, New York Nicks, smiling player holding ball, Japan sticker, 1962, 5-3/4" h **225.00**

Christmas ornament, Hallmark Treasury series, MIB
Hill, Grant, 1998, includes Fleer Skybox trading card, 4-1/4" h **12.00**
Johnson, Magic, 1997, includes Fleer Skybox trading card, 5-1/2" h............................. **14.00**
New York Nicks, 1997 .... **8.00**
Seattle Sonics, 1997............... **8.00**

Game, Cadaco, #165, 1973, unused, MIB **30.00**

Pencil holder, 4" x 5" x 5-1/2", painted bisque, hollow basketball next to figure wearing yellow and white uniform, mkd "Japan," small

Basketball memorabilia, action figure, Dennis Rodman, interchangeable head and clothes, MOC, **$12.**

Basketball memorabilia, Hallmark Magic Johnson ornament, original box, **$20.**

"Rubens Originals" foil sticker, 1970s.. 14.00

Photograph
Grove City, OH, early 1930s, 5" x 7"
.... 30.00

Petrovic Drazen, wire service photo of young Yugoslav player, 1989
.... 3.50

Plaque, David Robinson, photo of him wearing Spurs jersey, copyrighted 1990 NBA, and cards, matted, display frame, 8" x 10"
.... 35.00

Seals and diecuts, Dennison, package of four pcs, unused, orig cellophane packaging.............. 7.50

Tie tack, basketball player 12.00

Baskets

Wonderful examples of all types of baskets can be found at flea markets. Check carefully for wear and damage, and make sure they are priced accordingly.

For additional listings, see *Warman's Antiques & Collectibles*.

Baby basket, wicker, hood formed at one end, handles, some damage and splits.. 75.00

Beverage, wicker, places to hold four wine bottles, high handle........ 5.00

Cheese basket, woven splint, old patina, some damage, string wrapped repair at rims, 21" d
.... 115.00

Christmas tree, wood, painted green, white "snow" and multicolored decorations 7.50

Egg, woven splint 35.00

Gathering, rye straw, oval, wear and damage, 15" x 21" 85.00

Loom, woven splint, hanging type, natural, pink, and green, varnished, 9-1/2" w, 8-3/4" h................... 95.00

Market, woven splint handle, 16" l
.... 90.00

Melon shape, woven splint, bentwood handle, 15" d 85.00

Nantucket, oval, open, two carved handles, 10" l, 7-1/2" w, 3-3/4" h, handle repaired, late 19th/early 20th C 575.00

Peach, wide slats, wooden base, 11-1/2" h 6.00

Picnic, woven splint, two folding lids attached to sides with leather loops, c1950...................................... 25.00

Baskets, Buttocks, 4" x 11", **$95.**

Baskets, woven, red and green splint, red and green woven straw trim on handle and around rim, 12-1/4" l, **$65.**

Pumpkin shape, wooden cutout pumpkin shapes form two ends, hand painted, sgd, dated......... 7.50

Sewing, cov, round, ring-type handles, slight wear.............. 45.00

Batman

"Holy cow, Batman! Why is everyone staring at us?" This famous super hero and his cast of cohorts can be found in abundance at local flea markets. Watch for examples related to contemporary movies as well as items with tie-ins to the television series and the comic characters.

Batmobile, Corgi, #267, diecast, ©1983, MIB 190.00

Battery operated toy, Batmobile, red, orig box 275.00

Coloring book, 1963, used 20.00

Comic book, Batman Comic, #22, April-May 1944, first appearance of Alfred the butler................. 125.00

Costume, pants, shirt, cowl, and cape, heavy cotton, © NPP, c1966
.... 30.00

Desk set, calendar, stapler, and pencil sharpener, MIB.................... 150.00

Figure
Batman, Ertl, cast metal, 1990, sealed in orig blister pack with collector card, 2" h 15.00

Batman, comic book, DC, #431, **$3.25.**

Penguin, Batman Returns, Applause tag, plastic, 1992, 9" h **25.00**

Game, Batman and Robin, Hasbro, © 1965 NPP **35.00**

Inflatable figure, plastic, 1989, 13" h **40.00**

Kite, Batman & Robin, plastic, 1982, sealed in orig package **20.00**

Marionette, 15" h, painted plaster head and hands, wood body and legs, fabric costume, 1960s ... **40.00**

Notebook, spiral bound, Michael Keaton, unused........................ **1.50**

Party favor rings, black and yellow symbol, black base, eight plastic rings, Unique Industries, ©1992 DC Comics, Inc.............................. **5.00**

Party hat, thin cardboard, Batman and Robin running, ©1966 DC Comics Inc............................... **7.50**

Pen, baseball bat shape, plastic... **5.00**

Pez, Batman, #5, 1985, used **35.00**

Puzzle, Batman and Robin, 1981, 130 pcs, unused, 10-3/4" x 8-1/2" **12.00**

Robot, tin wind-up, Biliken, Japan, MIB...................................... **175.00**

Scale model, Bat Car, Valtoys, 3-3/4" l, MOC **25.00**

Schoolbook cover, 1966, 20" x 13" **15.00**

Straw, figural, 18 assorted figures in box **9.00**

Toy
Bat Cave, 1960s, orig box **85.00**
Pix-A-Go-Go, featuring the Penguin, National Periodical Publications, 1966, sealed in orig shrink wrap **75.00**

Batman, light, wristwatch form, plastic face with paper label, marked "1966 N.P.P. Inc." and "Bantamlite," face 2-1/4" diameter, strap 7-3/4" l, **$110.**

Battery-Operated Toys

Battery-operated toys have amused children for decades. Originally inexpensive, these toys were made in large quantities, and many still exist today. Values increase quickly for examples in good working condition and for those playthings with interesting actions or with the original box.

Astro Dog, Japan, orig box.... **450.00**

Big Top Champ Circus Clown, MIB.. **95.00**

BMW 3.5 CSL turbo car, tin, Dunlop and Bosch Electric advertising, MIB.................. **120.00**

Brave Eagle, beating drum, raising war hoop, MIB..................... **145.00**

Bubble Blowing Monkey, raises hand from pan on lap to mouth, MIB...................................... **195.00**

Button the Pup, MIB **375.00**

Captain Bushwell, vinyl head, Japan, 1970s, MIB **85.00**

Captain Robo and Space Transporter, 21st Century Toys, Japan, 1970s, plastic **125.00**

Battery operated, automata, Shaving man, cloth, celluloid, and litho tin, **$45.**

Carnival Choo Choo, plastic, Hong Kong, 1970s, MIB.................. **55.00**

Comical Clara, MIB.............. **195.00**

Family Panda, panda pulls baby panda on carriage, 1970s **25.00**

Fighter Plane Bombardier, orig box **395.00**

Highway Patrol Police Car, blinking red light on top, MIB **75.00**

Indian Scout AT-11, Amar Toys, Indian , 1950s........................ **95.00**

Knock-Out Boxers, orig box **295.00**

Lamborghini Contach car, red, MIB...................................... **120.00**

Loop the Loop Monkey, TN, Japan, orig box, 1970s **35.00**

Battery operated, automata, Mamma bear feeding baby bear, plush, cloth, and litho tin, **$35.**

Battery operated, automata, Maxwell Coffee Loving Bear, Rosko Tested, original box, **$45.**

Love-Love Volkswagen Beetle, blinking light in back window, tin, orange, Mobil, Champion, Goodyear sayings, VW on hubcaps, MIB 145.00

Luncheonette Bank, tin litho, plastic waitress, fabric clothing, serves coffee after coin is inserted, orig full color box, box professionally restored 500.00

Magic Snowman, white fabric, red facial accents and gloves, orig box with cellophane window, Modern Toys, Japan, c1960 .... 225.00

McGregor, Scotsman smoking cigar, moves up and down from treasure chest, MIB........................... 195.00

Musical rabbit, litho metal, beats drum, Japan, orig box 50.00

My Fair Dancer, litho tin, dancer in naval outfit, seahorse graphics on base, MIB, 11" h 225.00

Picnic Bear, orig box 125.00

Racing Camaro, Esso, Taiyo, Japan, MIB.. 50.00

Roller Coaster, plastic, Hong Kong, 1970s, MIB 55.00

Rosko, bartender, shakes, pours and drinks, smoke rises from ears, MIB 75.00

Santa Claus, orig box 225.00

School bus, tin litho, switch opens doors, headlights light 175.00

Smoking Grandpa, Japan....... 95.00

Sniffy Dog with Bee, Modern Toys, Japan, 1970s, MIB 55.00

Space Explorer, turn-over action, Gakken, Japan, MIB 100.00

Taxi Cab, Andy Gard, yellow, remote control wheel steering, dome signal light, 10" l, MIB 250.00

Tumbles the Bear, Yanoman, 1970s, MIB 85.00

Battery operated, automata, chimp drinking coke, plush, cloth, plastic bottle and glass, litho tin base, **$45.**

US Army Helicopter 90.00

Waltzing Matilda, play wear .. 75.00

Battery operated, automata, Maxwell Coffee Loving Bear, black plush bear, litho tin, MIB, **$45.**

Bavarian China

Flea markets are wonderful places to find examples of this colorful china. Several china manufacturers in the Bavarian porcelain center of southern Germany produced a wide variety of items that are collectively referred to as Bavarian china.

For additional listings, see *Warman's Antiques & Collectibles.*

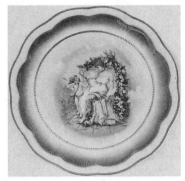

Bavarian China, plate, multicolored transfer, classical theme with woman being shot by Cupid's arrows, gold beads, dark blue scalloped border, scalloped edges, marked "Z S & C R" in shield with crown, "Bavaria" below in light red, **$24.**

Bowl, large orange poppies, green leaves 85.00

Creamer and sugar, purple and white pansy dec, mkd "Meschendorf, Bavaria" 65.00

Cup and saucer, roses and leaves, gold handle 25.00

Dinner service, King Cedric, service for eight, plus two platters .. 150.00

Hair receiver, apple blossom dec, mkd "T S. & Co." 60.00

Plate
8" d, pastel fruit, ivory ground, mkd "Sevres Bavaria" 70.00
8-1/2" d, hp bunches of white daisies, green leaves, long stems, pink to green shaded ground, gold lined rim 24.00

Portrait plate, elaborate portrait of lady, sgd "L. B. Chaffee, R. C. Bavaria" 100.00

Ramekin and underplate, ruffled, small red roses and green leaves, gold trim 45.00

Relish, 8" l, two multicolored birds on branches, blue and ochre lustered border, red mark 20.00

Bavarian China, "An Irish Jaunting Car" dish, Bavaria Schumann, 4-1/2" x 6-3/4", **$10.**

Salt and pepper shakers, pink apple blossom sprays, white ground, reticulated gold tops, pr 35.00

Shaving mug, pink carnations, mkd "Royal Bavaria" 65.00

Sugar shaker, hp, pastel pansies 60.00

Teapot, yellow, colorful iris dec 60.00

Vase, 9-1/2" h, ovoid, hp purple florals, yellow to green shaded ground, gold rim, mkd "Z S & Co. Bavaria" 80.00

Beanie Babies

The original set of nine Beanie Babies was released in 1993. The resulting collector enthusiasm and speculation quickly priced many children out of the market. Intended as simple, inexpensive playthings, these bean-stuffed personalities took on a life of their own, with some examples commanding exorbitant prices. The current market has returned to a level more consistent with the fun factor of these toys. Look for Beanie Babies issued as advertising promotions. They may have a double collector value in the future.

Advertising

A & W Rootbear Bear 18.00

Caesar's Pizza, Christmas, 1997 .... 15.00

Dairy Queen Cone 15.00

Energizer Bunny 15.00

Ernie the Keebler Elf 15.00

Harley Davidson, series II 50.00

Hawaiian Punch 15.00

M & M's, four-pc set 45.00

Mr. Peanut, Planters 10.00

NBC Studios, peacock 25.00

Pillsbury Doughboy 15.00

Travel Lodge Sleep Bear 15.00

Retired

Ally the Alligator, style #4032 .... 40.00

Baldy Eagle, orig tag 18.00

Bernie the St. Bernard 6.00

Blizzard the white tiger 6.00

Brittania the Bear, MIP 12.00

Bruno the terrier 6.00

Cassie the collie 7.50

Clubby, tag protector, plastic box 7.00

Cupid, tag protector 6.00

Daisy the cow 6.00

Ears the bunny 12.00

Erin 35.00

Fetch the golden retriever 6.00

Flip the cat 24.00

Glory The Bear, MIP 12.00

Gobbles Turkey, orig tag 18.00

Gracie the swan 7.00

Issy 6.00

Jester the clown fish 6.00

Jolly Walrus, orig tag 18.00

Beanie Babies, Congo, **$5.**

Maple The Bear, MIP 12.00

Mum, tag protector.................... 6.00

Patti the platypus 15.00

Peace, tag protector 10.00

Pinky Flamingo, orig tag........ 18.00

Pumpkin, tag protector, tag protector
.... 10.00

Quackers the duck 8.00

Rover the dog......................... 16.00

Seaweed, tag protector 10.00

Sizzle, red, red velvet neck bow, tag
protector 7.50

Sly the fox 6.00

Smooch..................................... 20.00

Spangle, pink face, plastic encased
tag 20.00

Beanie babies: dealers with large assortment of beanie babies are found at flea markets such as this one, held in Landisville, PA, Labor Day 2004. Prices ranged from a few dollars to **$25.**

Waddie the penguin 15.00

Weenie the dog 15.00

Wise 16.00

Ziggy the zebra 10.00

Beatles

The Fab Four created quite a sensation with their music during the 1960s. Beatlemania fueled the creation of a plethora of items paying tribute to the group and bearing the singers' likenesses. Record albums, concert ephemera, and even dolls can be found at local flea markets.

For additional listings, see *Warman's Americana & Collectibles*.

Reproduction Alert.

Arcade card, shows all four, black-and-white, cream reverse with write-up on the group, 1965 ... 8.00

Beach towel, terry cloth, Beatles in bathing suits, c1960, 34" x 57"
.... 115.00

Bubble gum card, Topps, 1964
#12 .... 5.00
#50 .... 9.00

Cake decorating kit, figurals, playing instruments, set of four, MIB..................................... 175.00

Collector plate, Sgt Pepper, 25th Anniversary, 1992, Delphi, orig paperwork and box 35.00

Diary, 1964, unused 15.00

Game, Flip Your Wig, Milton Bradley, 1964 .... 95.00

Glass, pictures Beatles with instruments, insulating coating around middle, 1960s, 5-1/4" h
.... 185.00

Handkerchief, 8-1/2" sq.......... 20.00

Jigsaw puzzle, official Beatles fan club puzzle, black-and-white, shows band with instruments, 1964, 8-1/4" x 10-3/4" 40.00

Lunchbox, Yellow Submarine
.... 175.00

Magazine
Accoustic Guitar, Vol. 2 #1 (July/August 1991), Beatles cover, includes transcriptions for three Beatles songs 6.00
Saturday Evening Post, Aug. 27, 1966, Beatles cover, illus six-page article on the group, loose cover, 11" x 14" 20.00
The Beatles Book Monthly #16, Nov. 1964, U.K. fan magazine, Paul and Ringo on cover, 6" x 8-1/2" 18.00
TV Guide, commemorative ed, 1995, includes story on Beatles
.... 5.00

Notebook, white, black letters, sepia-toned figures, NEMS 40.00

Pennant, 23" l, felt, white, red, and black, printed illus and facsimile

Beatles, Remco nodders, each 5" h, original box, set of four, **$500.**

signatures, ©Official Licensee, 1964 .... **40.00**

Postcard, shows Beatles with printed autographs, 1964, unused, two pinholes **10.00**

Record, LP, orig cov

Magical Mystery Tour, Capitol 2835, stereo **25.00**
Sgt Pepper, Toshiba, LF-95014 .... **35.00**

Scrapbook, NEMS, 1964.......... **20.00**

Souvenir song album, features words and music to early

recordings, biographical sketches and guitar chords, early 1960s, 32 pgs, small tears **25.00**

Sheet music, *Day Tripper*, 1964 .... **20.00**

T-Shirt, Beatles '65, size large, unused **20.00**

Beatrix Potter

Collectors are hot on the trail of this lovable English hare, and flea markets are a good place to spot him. Peter and the rest of the Beatrix Potter family are frequently sighted, since many of the items are in current production and, thus, readily available.

For additional listings, see *Warman's Antiques & Collectibles.*

Beatrix Potter, 1981 calendar, The Tales of Beatrix Potter, **$1.**

Baby cup, silver plate, "The World of Peter Rabbit by Beatrix Potter," F. Warne & Co. Ltd. **40.00**

Barbie, 2002 Peter Rabbit Centenary **29.95**

Book
Ginger and Pickles, F. Warne & Co. Ltd., copyright renewed 1937, pictorial endpapers, paste-on picture on cover, owner's name inside cover **25.00**
Histoire de Jeannot Lapin, French, translated by Victorine Ballon and Julienne Profichet, F. Warne & Co. Ltd., color illus and endpapers, hardcover, slight wear to edges.................... **50.00**
The Roly-Poly Pudding, Frederick Warne, NY, 1908 .... **80.00**

Cookie tin, Peter Rabbit, 3" h, 7-1/2" d **8.00**

Cup and saucer, Peter Rabbit, Wedgwood, 1958 .... **140.00**

Figure
Anna Maria, F. Warne & Co. Ltd., stamped "Beswick, England" and "Beatrix Potter's Anna Maria" on bottom, 3" h **350.00**
Benjamin Bunny, Beswick, 1st version gold mark BP-2 . **480.00**
Flopsy, Mopsy and Cottontail, Beswick, 1st version gold mark BP-2............................... **330.00**
Lady Mouse, Beswick, gold mark, BP-2................................... **300.00**
Little Pig Robinson, Beswick, first version, blue stripes, gold mark **375.00**
Mr. Benjamin Bunny, Beswick, 4" h, 3-7/8" l, brown mark........ **75.00**

Mrs. Rabbit and bunnies, Beswick, 3-5/8" h, brown mark....... **75.00**
Peter Rabbit, Beswick, 1st version gold mark BP-2 .... **240.00**
Timmy Willie, F. Warne & Co. Ltd., stamped "Beswick, England" on bottom, copyright 1949, 3" h **50.00**
Tommy Brock, Beswick, 1st gold mark, 3-3/8" h **450.00**

Game, Peter Rabbit's Race Game **45.00**

Pendant, F. Warne & Co. Ltd., knitting bunny in rocking chair, 3-1/4" h **30.00**

Print, Squirrel Nutkin from *Tale of Squirrel Nutkin,* published by F. Warne, 1950s **25.00**

Beatrix Potter, teapot, one cup size, Peter Rabbit, **$20.**

Belleek

There's an old Irish saying that newlyweds who receive a wedding gift of Belleek will have their marriage blessed with lasting happiness. It's a great sentiment, and Belleek certainly does make a nice wedding gift. A thin, ivory-colored porcelain with an almost iridescent look, Belleek traces its roots to Fermanagh, Ireland, in 1857. The approximate age of a piece can be determined by looking at the mark. From 1863 to 1946 black marks were used; green marks were introduced in 1946.

For additional listings, see *Warman's Antiques & Collectibles* and *Warman's English & Continental Pottery & Porcelain.*

Biscuit barrel, Basketweave pattern, cov, 6th green mark, 1965-80 .... 100.00

Bread plate, Shamrock pattern, double handle, 3rd green mark, 10-1/2" l, 9-1/4" w 80.00

Butter dish, cov, Limpet pattern, 1st black mark, 6-1/2" d top, 8-1/2" d base 475.00

Cake plate, mask with grape leaves pattern, four looped handles, pale yellow edge, 3rd black mark, 10-1/2" d 155.00

Creamer, Cleary pattern, 3rd green mark 60.00

Creamer and sugar
Clover pattern, 6th green mark, 1965-80 .... 100.00
Shamrock pattern, married pair, green marks, 1945-55 .... 120.00

Cup and saucer, Shell pattern, 2nd black mark, 1891-1926 .... 195.00

Demitasse cup and saucer, green mark on cup, gold mark on saucer, c1956 .... 50.00

Dish, Shamrock pattern, 3rd green mark 60.00

Figure
Harp, 3rd green mark, 6" h 70.00
Terrier, green mark, 3-1/2" h 45.00

Honey pot, barrel type, clover leaves dec, 7th gold-brown mark, 1980-93 .... 80.00

Mug, 4-1/2" h, pink luster and enamel dec, continuous scene of drunken taverners, artist sgd "EMS '04," printed Ceramic Art Co. mark, Trenton, New Jersey, c1904 . 150.00

Mustache cup, Tridacna pattern, first black mark 125.00

Pitcher, 9" h, Aberdeen, applied with flowers and leaves, second black mark, c1900, chips to leaves 300.00

Plate, Harp and Shamrock pattern, 5th mark, 9" d 60.00

Potpourri vase, Basketweave pattern, 6th green mark, 1965-80, 4-1/2" h 100.00

Belleek, snack set, cup and sandwich plate, shamrock decoration, **$30.**

Salt, open, star, 3rd black mark 60.00

Sugar bowl, open, yellow ribbon and box accents, green mark 45.00

Tea set, Basketweave pattern, 6th green mark, 1965-80, repair to spout 275.00

Vase, 10" h, cylindrical, hand painted, egrets in landscape, artist sgd "A.MacM.F.," printed mark, Trenton, NJ, c1900 .... 215.00

Bells

From the tinkle of a silver bell to the clanging of a ship's bell, the music of bells has enchanted collectors for decades. When considering a purchase, check for stress fractures and other signs of use, and also look to see if the clapper is original.

Ceramic
Boy and girl angels, holding green letters that spell Noel, Ucago Co. 40.00
Christmas angel, holding candle, Lefton 20.00
Hummel, 1978 .... 95.00
Mermaid, 4-1/2" h 24.00
Noel, set of mother and three children, red dresses, Napco Co., 1956 .... 60.00

Chrome, 3" h, 2" d, chrome, Bakelite finial, sgd "Chase Chrome & Brass" on int 145.00

Church, cast brass, wrought iron clapper, late 18th C, 20" h.... 990.00

Cast iron, profiles of Franklin Roosevelt, Winston Churchill, and Joseph Stalin emb on sides, large "V" emb on handle, rim emb "cast with metal from German aircraft shot down over Britain 1939-45,

R.A.F. Benevolent Fund," 6" h 145.00

Desk, bronze, iron base, ornate mechanism, Victorian, 3" w, 5" h 135.00

Door-mounted, brass, filigree mounting 45.00

Glass
Cambridge, Rose Point....... 150.00
Daisy and Button, vaseline, 6-1/2" h 75.00

Bells, school bell type, wooden handle, metal base, **$45.**

Fenton, Statue of Liberty, hand-painted dec........................ 35.00
Murano, gold wash, orig sticker, 4" h **65.00**

Bells, metal novelty, Liberty Bell, 2-1/2" h, **$2.50.**

Princess House, cut design, 6-3/4" h 10.00

Bells, hummingbird, Lenox, limited edition, **$20.**

Porcelain, Danbury Mint, Mother's Day, pink flowers................... 18.00
Sleigh, leather strap, seven graduated brass bells 75.00

Belt Buckles

A collection of belt buckles consists of items that are small and easy to store, and which represent a variety of materials. What more could one want in a collection? Some of the more ornate examples are elaborately cast or set with precious and semi-precious stones.

Reproduction Alert.

Bakelite
O-shaped, red, silvertone knobs, 2-1/2" d 60.00
Round, carved, black front, yellow back, 3" d.......................... **55.00**

Belt buckles, Chicago World's Fair, **$25.**

Boy Scouts, 1977 National Jamboree 15.00
Iron Maiden, "Number of the Beast," shows album cover, made in England................................. 40.00
Lion Oil Co., silvertone, mountain lion and company name, owner's name and 1993 on back, 2-1/4" x 3-1/4" 35.00
Marlboro, brass, oval, star and steer, copyright 1987, 2-1/2" x 3-1/2" 20.00
Masonic, emblem, 2" x 2-7/8".. 12.00

National Finals Rodeo, Hesston, 1977, bull riding 42.00
Piedmont Airlines, goldtone, orig plastic wrap and box, 2-7/8" x 2-3/8"....................................... 150.00
Popeye, US Spinach Growers, Strength through Spinach 8.00
Schlitz Light, brass and pewter, light blue enamel inlay, 1976......... 25.00
Shriner, emblem, silvertone..... 20.00
Steam shovel, brass 12.00
Western, Wil-Aren Originals, 2-1/2" h, 3-3/4" w 20.00

Bennington Pottery

Although the company has been in existence for a century and a half, only its more contemporary items are included here.

Bowl, arched emb dec, brown glaze, hairline 30.00
Bread plate, 6" d 8.00

Chamberstick, ring handle, brown Rockingham glaze................. 20.00
Cup and saucer, dark blue spattered glaze.. 15.00

Bennington Pottery, pitcher, tulips motif, medium brown glaze, 5" h, **$145.**

Custard cup, brown Rockingham glaze.. 10.00

Mug, two tone blue dip glaze, double ring handles.......................... 15.00

Plate, abstract fish dec, 10" d ... 70.00

Wall plaque, owl, 8-3/4" x 7"... 65.00

Beswick

Beswick characters are well known to collectors and include figures from children's literature as well as animals and other subjects. James Wright Beswick and his son, John, organized the firm in the 1890s. By 1969, the company was sold to Royal Doulton Tableware, Ltd., which still produces many Beswick animals.

Character jug
Midshipman, 5-1/4" h 185.00
Old Mr. Brown, 1987-1992, 3" h 200.00
Tony Weller, second version, #281, 7" h 150.00

Child's feeding dish, Mickey and Donald on bicycle................ 140.00

Decanter, monk, underplate and four mugs 250.00

Figure
Alice in Wonderland, 4-5/8" h 125.00
Cardinal, #927, pink, 6-1/4" h 160.00
Cecily Parsley, Beatrix Potter, gold mark 270.00
Cheshire Cat, 3-1/2" h 125.00
Fierce Bad Rabbit, 4-3/4" h 165.00
Foxy Whiskered Gentleman, 4-3/4" h............................. 48.00
Grooming Kittens, two tabbies 135.00
Hereford Bull, 6" h.............. 225.00
Horse, #915, 3-1/8" h........... 90.00
Jemima Puddleduck, Beatrix Potter, 1947................................. 95.00
Johnny Town Mouse, Beatrix Potter, 1954, 3-1/2" h.................. 65.00
Labrador Retriever, black, 5-3/4" h 85.00
Mr. Jeremy Fisher, Beatrix Potter, gold mark...................... 290.00
Mrs. Ribby, Beatrix Potter, 1951, 3-1/2" h................................. 75.00
Mrs. Tittlemouse, Beatrix Potter, 1st gold mark, 3-1/2" h........ 325.00
Old Mr. Brown, 3-1/4" h..... 125.00
Palamino Horse, 7-1/2" h... 200.00
Peter Rabbit, Beatrix Potter, 1st gold mark, 4-5/8" h 295.00
Scottie, white, ladybug on nose, HN804, 1940-69............. 225.00
Squirrel Nutkin, Beatrix Potter 220.00
Swish Tail Horse, #1182, orig Beswick sticker, 8-1/2" h 225.00
Timmy Tiptoes, Beatrix Potter, gold mark............................... 225.00
Tony Weller.......................... 85.00

Top Cat and Choo Choo, 4-1/2" h 160.00
Trout, #1390, 4" h 150.00

Mug
Falstaff, inscribed "Pistol with Wit or Steel, Merry Wives of Windsor," #1127, 1948-73, 4" h 85.00
Hamlet, inscribed "To Be or Not To Be," #1147, 4-1/4" h.......... 85.00

Plate, Disney characters, 7" d ... 95.00

Shoe, old woman seated inside, Beatrix Potter, gold stamped mark, 3-3/4" w, 2-1/2" h................. 175.00

Tankard, A Christmas Carol, 1971 .... 50.00

Teapot, Sairy Gump, 5-1/2" h 300.00

Tulip vase, shape #843, semi-gloss white, 1940-43, 4" h............... 50.00

Beswick China, mug, Dickens scene, marked "Beswick (logo) Collectors International John Beswick Limited Royal Doulton Group, 1974, This is Number 8927 of an Edition of 15,000," **$45.**

Bibles

Bibles are only occasionally found at flea markets, since most families either keep those that belonged to their loved ones, or donate them to a local church. From time to time, old large family bibles do surface at flea markets and book sales. Prices can range from a few dollars to several hundred, depending on the illustrations, date, type of bible, condition, etc. Potential buyers are often more interested in the genealogical information that might be contained therein. Before selling a family bible, consider sharing its historical or genealogical information with family members. Additionally, historical societies and libraries are generally grateful for such information.

Bibles, The Dore Bible Gallery, by Gustave Dore, Henry Altemus, Philadelphia, **$50.**

Family Bible, dates start 1825, many engravings, 11" x 9-1/2" **250.00**

Family Worship Edition, King James Version, 1948, many color pictures, Nashville Bible House, Nashville, Tenn., ink spots on some pages **35.00**

Gilt engraved tooled leather, 1867, American Bible Society, N.Y., trace gilt to page edges, a few minor tears, 5-3/4" x 4-1/4"............. **60.00**

New Testament Bible ABC Book, full-color illus, The Book Concern, Columbus, Ohio, name on front cover, 16 pgs, 8-1/4" x 10-1/2". **8.00**

Presentation Bible, Masonic Edition, Masonic emblem on cover, copyright 1932, never inscribed **395.00**

Service testament and prayer book, U.S. Military issue, 1943, leather case imprinted with gold

Bibles, miniature, Novum Testamentum Domini Nostri Jesu Christi, Interprete Theodore Beza, Acadmiae Typographi MDCLXVI, tooled leather cover with worn gilt trim, 4-1/2" x 2-1/4", **$195.**

name of orig owner, tear to case at snap... **80.00**

Soldier's pocket bible, New Testament and Psalms, 1862, inscribed 1864/Lowell, Mass. **275.00**

Bicentennial

Remember all that hoopla surrounding 1976? How many of you have stashed away some bit of Bicentennial memorabilia? These items are becoming more common at flea markets, and historically minded individuals are adding them to their collections. Perhaps these pieces of the past will turn into treasures.

Bowl, eagle dec, blue striped border, Mottahedeh, Chinese Export reproduction made for US State Dept use................................. **75.00**

Decanter, colorless, etched eagle, flag, 1776-96, 11" h................ **25.00**

Dolls, Campbell Soup, hard plastic, Colonial clothes, 10-1/2" h, pr **150.00**

Flag, 13 stars in circle, orig box **25.00**

Guidebook, *Washington: The Official Bicentennial Guidebook*, ed by Nancy Love, 1976, softcover, 213 pgs..................................... **5.00**

Medal, pewter, Spirit of '76 on one side, separate cardboard easel back, orig booklet **5.00**

Paperweight, rect, white lettering, rust ground............................. **6.00**

Pendant, gold filled, diecut Liberty Bell in center, circled by enameled red, white, and blue stars, 24" l chain **45.00**

Pinback button, Spirit of '76, America's Bicentennial, 1776-1976, 3-1/2" d **20.00**

Pitcher, Patriots, parian-type body, blue stripe at top, orig tag, Lenox **60.00**

Placemat, paper, unused, red, white, and blue .... **.50**

Plate
Avon, clear glass, bald eagle holding shield and arrows, "United States of America Bicentennial 1776-1976," 9-1/8" l, 6-3/4" w **5.00**
Fenton, powder blue, George Washington at Valley Forge, 3rd in a series of 4, 8-1/4" d ... **35.00**
Frankoma, Patriots/Leaders, white sand glaze, 8-1/2" d.......... **30.00**
Schmid, Mickey Mouse, orig box **45.00**

Tray, anodized aluminum, mkd "The United States of America 1776-

1976" and "Pepsi 1898-1976," 10-7/8" d 25.00

Tumbler, black and metallic gold deco, White House on one side,

Bicentennial, train set, TCA Bicentennial Special, 1976 Seaboard Coast Line locomotive, 1975 American Eagle passenger car, 1974 Stars & Stripes passenger car, MIB, **$125.**

Capitol on other, "United States Bicentennial 1776-1976" 5.00

U.S. mint set, silver, 1976, San Francisco, uncirculated 30.00

Bicentennial, magazine, *MAD*, **$15.**

Bicentennial, Indiana Glass Bicentennial plate, Liberty Bell design, original box, **$5.**

Bicycles

"Look, Ma! No hands!" Gee, haven't we all shouted that once or twice? And how many of us wish we still had those really nifty old bikes, banana seats and all? Don't overlook bicycle related memorabilia that can be found at flea markets.

For additional listings, see *Warman's Americana & Collectibles*.

Bicycle
Ace Clyde and Motor Works, metal label, as found cond 150.00
Columbia, Fire Arrow 300.00
Huffy, Radiobike.............. 2,000.00
Murry Jet X-64, girl's.......... 195.00
Roadmaster, Luxury Liner, restored 620.00
Schwinn, Corvette 300.00
Schwinn, Hornet 425.00
Schwinn, Mark II Jaguar 750.00
Sears, Elgin, Skylark, very good orig cond 2,250.00

Book, *Riding High*, A. Judson Palmer, autographed 65.00

Catalog
Eclipse, Elmira, N.Y............. 48.00
Indian Bicycle....................... 90.00

Bicycles, poster, The Sterling Bicycle, Built Like a Watch, two early bathing beauties, framed, but glass broken, **$45.**

Rollfast.................................. 70.00

Cycling and motoring guide, Southeast England, c1910, routes and mileage 5.00

Dimestore soldier, Manoil, #50, bicycle dispatch rider 50.00

Display card, Sport Shoes, Xtrulock, 1930s, 11-5/8" x 15-1/2" 30.00

Handle bar grips, wooden, for high wheeler, unused..................... 65.00

Ink blotter, Fisk Tires, 6-1/4" x 3-1/2" 15.00

License, 3-1/4" l, diecut brass, stylized "C" stamped in black, Courtland Co. Sidepath, serial number, early 1890s 85.00

Magazine, *American Bicyclist and Motorcyclist,* May, 1957........ 10.00

Magazine tear sheet
Columbia Bicycles, *Saturday Evening Post,* 1949 .... 5.00
Murray Bicycles, Strato-Flite, LeMans and Wildcat, *Boys' Life,* 1966 .... 3.00
Raleigh, Chopper, *Boys' Life,* 1970 .... 3.00
Roadmaster, half sheet, *Saturday*

Bicycles, Schwinn, blue, boy's, **$45.**

Evening Post, 1951 .... **2.00**
Schwinn Bicycles, from back cover,
reverse slightly scuffed **2.00**
Sears, The Screamer Bicycle .. **3.00**

Nameplate, Rollfast, 1-1/2" x 3",
brass, curled for attachment, 1930s
.... **15.00**

Paperweight, 2-1/2" x 4", black and
white photo of Col. Albert A. Pope,
titled "The Pioneer of the Great
Movement For Better American
Roads," Abrams Paperweight Co.,
Pittsburgh, PA, 1890s **38.00**

Pin, bicycle shape
Goldtone, front wheel turns, faux
pearls, 2-1/4" x 2-5/8" **8.50**
Silvertone, clear stones in center, 2"
x 1-1/4" **15.00**

Pinback button, Schwinn, 7/8" d
.... **28.00**

Program, Penn Wheelman Frolic,
1927, Minstrels, Orpheum Theater,
64 pgs..................................... **42.00**

Tie tac, Schwinn, gold plated, 1/2" h
.... **15.00**

Big Little Books

The Whitman Publishing Company first trademarked these books in the 1930s, but the term is also used to describe similar books published by a number of other companies. Several advertisers contracted to use Big Little Books as premiums, including Cocomalt and Kool-Aid. Television characters were introduced to the format in the 1950s.

Ace Drummond By Captain Eddie Rickenbacker, Whitman #1177, 1935 .... **30.00**

Daktari, Night of Terror **30.00**

David Copperfield, Whitman #1148, 1934, movie edition, W. C. Fields, Freddy Bartholomew........... **100.00**

Don Winslow USN, Whitman #1107, 1935 .... **50.00**

Flash Gordon and the Witch Queen of Mongo, Alex Raymond..... **75.00**

Foreign Spies, Doctor Doom and the Ghost Submarine, 1939 .... **35.00**

Hunting For Pirate Gold, Whitman #1172, 1935 .... **30.00**

Inspector Wade of Scotland Yard, Saalfield, 1940 .... **20.00**

Joe Palooka's Great Adventure, Saalfield #1168, 1949, 3-1/2" x 4-1/2" format **25.00**

Jungle Jim And The Vampire Woman, Whitman #1139, 1937 .... **35.00**

Just Kids and the Mysterious Stranger, Saalfield, 1935 .... **25.00**

Kazan in the Revenge of the North **25.00**

Little Red School House, Dickie Moore, several front pages missing **20.00**

Lone Ranger and the Black Shirt Highwayman, 1939 .... **20.00**

Major Matt Mason Movie Mission, 1968 .... **20.00**

Mickey Mouse and Pluto the Racer, 1936 .... **75.00**

Pluto the Pup, Whitman #1467, 1938 .... **65.00**

Radio Patrol, Outwitting the Gang Chief, 1939............................. **20.00**

Rex Beach's Jaragu of the Jungle, Whitman #1424..................... **20.00**

Robinson Crusoe, Whitman #719, undated, c1933, 356 pgs........ **27.50**

Skyroads With Hurricane Hawk, Whitman #1127, 1936........... **30.00**

Snow White and the Seven Dwarfs, Walt Disney Enterprises, 1938 .... **45.00**

Stan Kent, Freshman Fullback, Saalfield, 1936 .... **15.00**

State Trooper and the Kidnapped Governor, Jim Craig, 1938.... **42.50**

Sybil Jason in Little Big Shot, Whitman #1149..................... **28.00**

Terry & War in the Jungle, 1936 .... **35.00**

The Hooded Flyer, Whitman #1423, 1937 .... **35.00**

The Island In The Sky, Whitman #1110, 1936 .... **30.00**

The Lost Transport, BTLB, Whitman #1413, 1940 .... **30.00**

The Man from U.N.C.L.E., The Calcutta Affair, 1967............ **15.00**

The Story of Jackie Cooper, 1933 .... **40.00**

Tom Beatty, wear to cover **25.00**

Treasure Island, Whitman #720, 1933, 356 pgs.................................... **27.50**

Better Little Book, *Red Barry Undercover Man*, Will Gould, Whitman Publishing Co., #1426, **$12.**

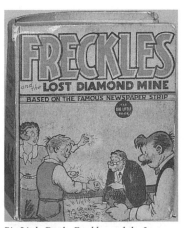

Big Little Book, *Freckles and the Lost Diamond Mine*, **$25.**

Better Little Books

Brer Rabbit from Song of the South,
Whitman #1426, 1947 .... 75.00

Bugs Bunny and the Pirate Loot,
Whitman #1403, 1947 .... 40.00

*Disney's Cinderella and the Magic
Wand,* Whitman #711-10 ..... 40.00

Disney's Thumper and the 7 Dwarfs,
Whitman #1409 .... 40.00

Gang Busters Smash Through,
Whitman #1437, 1942 .... 25.00

Ghost Avenger, Whitman #1462, 1943
.... 30.00

G-Men Breaking the Gambling Ring,
Whitman #1493, 1938 .... 40.00

Inspector Charlie Chan, Whitman
#1424, 1942 .... 60.00

Jungle Jim, Whitman #1138, dusty
covers 20.00

*King Of the Royal Mounted And The
Great Jewel Mystery,* Whitman
#1486, 1939 .... 40.00

*Mandrake The Magician The
Midnight Monster,* Whitman
#1431, 1939 .... 30.00

*Mickey Mouse In The Treasure
Hunt,* 1941, wear and soiling 45.00

Mr. District Attorney, Whitman
#1408, 1941 .... 50.00

*Steve Hunter Of The U. S. Coast
Guard Under Secret Orders,*
Whitman #1426, 1942 .... 40.00

Tailspin Tommy All-Pictures Comics,
Whitman #1410, 1941 .... 25.00

Bing and Grondahl

This Danish company has produced fine-quality Christmas plates for decades. However, many collectors have chosen to branch out and also include some of the company's other products, such as bells and figurines, in its collections.

Bell
1976, Old North Church, Boston,
Mass., 5" h 25.00
1978, Notre Dame Cathedral 50.00
1991, Independence Hall, 4" h, MIB
.... 30.00

Cake plate, ftd, sea gull dec ... 100.00

Coffeepot, cov, sea gull dec ... 200.00

Bing and Grondahl, Christmas plate, 1968, 7-1/4" d, **$30.**

Compote, sea gull dec, 9-1/2" d
.... 100.00

Cup and saucer, sea gull dec .. 85.00

Figurine
Boy with accordion, #1991, boy
seated on barrel, 9" h 195.00
English setter, #2015, 8-3/4" h
.... 350.00
Girl with doll, #1721, 8" h .. 110.00
Girl with flowers, #2298, 6" h
.... 140.00
Penguin, #1821, 3-1/8" h.... 150.00
Skier, 8-1/2" h 130.00
Youthful Boldness, #2162, 7-1/2" h
.... 175.00

Gravy boat, attached underplate,
seagull dec 130.00

Limited edition collector plate,
Christmas
1960, Danish village church . 85.00
1973, Country Christmas 20.00
1981, Christmas Peace 35.00
1999, Dancing on Christmas Eve
.... 125.00

Limited edition collector plate,
Mother's Day, 6" d
1971, hare and young 40.00
1979, fox and cubs 35.00
1980, woodpecker and young 35.00
1982, lion and cubs 45.00
1984, stork and nestling 40.00

Sugar bowl, cov, sea gull dec ... 80.00

Teapot, cov, seagull dec 190.00

Thimble, soaring seagull, mkd "B &
G 4831, Made in Denmark" .. 20.00

Bing and Grondahl, vase, 7-1/4" h, **$40.**

Bing and Grondahl, Christmas plate, 1970, wooden frame, **$35.**

Birdhouses

Due to their folk art nature, many vintage birdhouses can be found in collector's living rooms, as opposed to their usual places in pine trees and on fence posts. Vintage birdhouses in good original condition are in demand, but don't overlook some of the high-quality contemporary examples on today's market.

Metal
Contemporary, made from 5 Colorado license plates, 9" h, 5" l, 5" w 18.00
Vintage, made from two-qt tin can, orig gray paint, some rust 22.50

Pottery, cottage design in blues, greens and reds, Louisville Stoneware, 10" h 55.00

Wood
Martin house, 20-hole 60.00
Vintage, traditional form, metal roof, orig red paint, 7" h .. 65.00
Wayne Sims, contemporary, church design, rough cedar siding, 10" h 20.00
Wren house, repainted brown 20.00

Birdcage, wood, scrolled crest, wirework rests, **$20.**

Bisque

Bisque is a rather generic term used for china wares that have been fired, but that have not been glazed. Pieces usually have a slightly rough texture, and they are highly susceptible to chips.

For additional listings, see *Warman's Antiques & Collectibles*.

Ashtray, 3" d, black boy in outhouse while other boy waits, mkd "Japan" 35.00

Bank, Porky Pig, 1930s 60.00

Doll
Black, articulated arms and legs, hp facial features, new dress, 4-1/2" h 20.00
German, one-pc body and head, sleep eyes, closed mouth, glued wig, 2-1/2" h 65.00

Figure
Boy playing mandolin, mkd "Heubach" 75.00
Elephant, 4" h 9.00
Fiddler, Occupied Japan, 3" h 9.00

Piano baby
2-3/4" h, girl, lying down on tummy, looking upright, hands folded, crisp mold, Germany 75.00
3-1/2" h, Heubach, Dutch boy, sitting down, upper body lifts

Bisque, figures, matched pair, girl cradling dove, boy holding rabbit, mauve, fleshtones, white, and gold, pink and green enameled flowers, price for pair, **$245.**

off to reveal small storage compartment 135.00
4-1/2" h, Dutch boy, seated .. 75.00
6" h, 10" l, Andrea, by Sadak, 1950's crawling baby, pink bow on right arm, mkd "23/109" in red 100.00

Stopper, clown figure, removable hat, mkd "Germany 6325," 3-3/4" h 25.00

Toothbrush holder
Mickey and Minnie Mouse, copyright Walt Disney, mkd "Made in Japan," worn paint, 4-1/2" h 245.00
Moon Mullins and Kayo, 4" h 45.00

Black Memorabilia

Black memorabilia is a term used to describe a very broad field of collectibles. It encompasses Black history and ethnic issues, as well as those items that have impacted our lives from a cultural standpoint. America's flea markets are great sources for Black memorabilia now that more dealers are recognizing the increased popularity of these items.

For additional listings, see *Warman's Antiques & Collectibles* and *Warman's Americana & Collectibles.*

Reproduction Alert.

Black memorabilia, sheet music, The Banjo Picker, A Southland Intermezzo for Piano by Frederick Groton, Carl Fischer Inc., New York publisher, green on white cover, **$15.**

Advertising tin, Durham's Cocoanut 175.00

Baby rattle, 8" l, celluloid, figural, standing Black man, top hat and tails, holding bouquet of flowers, white, red, and black, mkd "Made in Japan" 45.00

Black memorabilia, print, framed, primitive funeral scene, **$120.**

Bank, Mammy, cast iron, 4-1/2" h 95.00

Bean bag game, Three Black Crows, painted wood, swing out targets 195.00

Birthday card, Black boy blowing out candles on cake, ©Hall Brothers, 1940s, 4" x 5" 25.00

Bottle opener, 7" h, figural, minstrel, painted wood......................... 42.00

Children's book, *Beloved Belindy,* Johnny Gruelle, 1926............. 25.00

Cigar box, Sir Jonathon brand 45.00

Clock, luncheon type, black women dec, 1950s 45.00

Comics page, Kemple Duke of Dahomey, 1911 .... 45.00

Cookbook, *Dixie Southern Cookbook* 50.00

Dart board, tin over cardboard, Sambo, name on straw hat, Wyandotte Toy Mfg., dents and scratch, 23" h, 14" w 80.00

Dice, multicolor, spring activated, mkd "Alco Britain HK".......... 90.00

Doll, Cream of Wheat Chef, stuffed cloth, 1960s............................. 80.00

Figure, Sambo, Brayton Laguna, 7-3/4"....................................... 115.00

Game, The Game of Hitch Hiker, Whitman, 1937...................... 75.00

Hair care product, High Life Perfume Valmor Products, 3-1/4" glass bottle, graphic label of white man in tux, black young woman with slick wavy hair, c1940 ... 25.00

Magazine, *Life,* Dec. 8, 1972, featuring Diana Ross on cover 18.00

Magic lantern slide, man playing banjo....................................... 24.00

Black memorabilia, Mammy toaster cover, cloth, 8" plus skirt, **$35.**

Needle book, Luzianne Coffee adv 22.50

Nodder, 4-1/4" h, painted metal, boy in yellow hat, smoking cigar, mkd "Occupied Japan"................... 55.00

Notepad and pencil holder, painted hard plastic, Mammy, insert pencil as broomstick in one hand, orig paper label, 1950s................ 150.00

Photograph, unidentified subject Little boy in front of train 75.00

Black memorabilia, salt and pepper shakers, pair, chefs, white aprons, gold spoon, red highlights, woman with souvenir banner for Green Lantern, WV, **$35.**

Man in formal dress, graduation, 1910 .... 45.00

Pie bird, black boy scout, yellow uniform, brown hat, mkd "England," 3-1/2" h, light stains 65.00

Pinback button
All Power to the People, portrait of Huey Newton, overprinted in dark blue, black text 35.00
I Raise You, black man in uniform holding cable with word "elevator" next to him, art by Goldberg 40.00
Ten Days-Smoke Up, caricature of black man standing before judge, art by Tep, c1912, 7/8" d .. 35.00

Pitcher, Mandy, Omnibus 160.00

Poster, 22" h, 14" w, cardboard, Ragtime Jubilee, Big Time Minstrel Review 25.00

Program, 8-3/4" x 11-1/2", The Green Pastures play, green and purple cover, band "Pulitzer Prize Play of 1930," 16 black and white pgs, 1932 .... 40.00

Ramp walker, multicolor, USA, c1920 .... 65.00

Recipe holder, Mammy, wood 45.00

Salt and pepper shakers, pr
Mammy & Chef, 5" h 55.00
Native on Hippo 215.00

Sheet music, Sam the Accordion Man 20.00

Sign, diecut cardboard
Gold Dust Washing Powder, Gold Dust Twins shown on package, large letter "L" on top, formerly part of larger hanging sign, 13-1/2" h, 9-1/2" w 60.00
Hambone Sweets, color graphics on both sides, black caricature

aviator smiling and puffing on cigar while seated in aircraft, titled "Going Over," orig string loop handle, late 1920s, 7" d 38.00

Tea towel, boy and girl eating watermelon, pr 25.00

Tin, 7-1/4" h, Sunny South Peanuts 75.00

Tip tray, 4" d, Cottolene Shortening, litho tin 65.00

Toy
Dancing Dan, in front of lamp post on stage, microphone remote attached to stage, 13" h, MIB 375.00
Trapeze Artist, squeeze type, painted wood 45.00

Wall pocket, Blackamoor, mkd "Royal Copley" 70.00

Blenko

Blenko handcrafted glass was made in Milton, W.Va. Interesting crackle glass items and a reliance on strong colors have earned the company a place in the hearts of many. Original labels read "Blenko Handcraft" and are shaped like a hand.

Blenko, compote, amberina, twisted base, original foil label, **$35.**

Barber bottle, 8" h, crackle glass, clear, hobs dec, screw-on metal cap with band of matching hops, orig label 45.00

Bottle, 13" h, #7225, tangerine, crystal stopper, orig label 140.00

Bowl
11" d, Ring, emerald green, textured, remnants of orig label, 1982-99 .... 125.00
16" d, green, ftd, orig label 145.00

Decanter
16-1/2" h, #920, crackle, amethyst, rough pontil, c1955 .... 135.00
23-1/2" h, yellow cylindrical body, deep blue round stopper, orig tag 185.00

Paperweight, 3-1/2" h, 4-1/2" d top, mushroom shape, green, yellow swirls 45.00

Pitcher
7-1/2" h, pale orchid, applied clear glass handle, ruffled edge, 2003 .... 60.00
8" h, deep blue, double sided pouring spout 45.00
9-1/2" h, tangerine, crackle, designed by Joel Meyers, pontil mark, 1940-50s 65.00

Sculpture
7" h, owl, amber, orig label 75.00
11-1/2" l, squash, hand blown, amber, teal stem, orig label 65.00

Vase
10" h, #6026 Regal, red, designed by Wayne Husted, sgd, 1960-61 .... 150.00

10" h, tumbler type, clear cracked vase, three applied teal blue leaves, 1940s-50s 145.00
11-1/2" h, topaz gold, cobalt blue spiral wrapped around mid-section, orig label, etched "Blenko 2002" on base 40.00
17" h, crackle, orange 135.00

Blenko, vase, fan shape, blue crackle, clear disk base, original label, **$95.**

Blue and White Pottery/Stoneware

Although termed blue-and-white, this category also includes blue-and-gray pottery and stoneware. Widely produced from the late 19th century through the 1930s, these items were originally marketed as inexpensive wares for everyday household use. Butter crocks, pitchers, and saltboxes are among the most commonly found pieces. Many examples feature a white or gray body with an embossed geometric, floral, or fruit pattern. The piece was then highlighted with bands and splashes of blue to accentuate the molded pattern.

Reproduction Alert.

Blue and white stoneware, spittoon, drapery motif, 7-1/2" d, 5-1/4" h, **$85.**

Bowl
Apricot pattern, milk bowl, 4" h, 9-1/2" d 80.00
Flying Birds, berry bowl..... **125.00**

Butter crock
Colonial, with lid, 4-1/4" h. 375.00
Daisy & Trellis, with lid, minor glaze flake at bail 80.00

Canister, basketweave, lid
Cereal.................................. 395.00
Coffee.................................. 375.00

Raisins 350.00
Pitcher
Cherries and leaves, 8-1/2" h 195.00
Dutch Boy & Girl, 6-1/2" h. 125.00
Swirl, relief scroll design, 11" h, short hairline.................... 90.00
Salt box, hanging, 6" d, 6" h
Good Luck pattern, orig lid present, but broken, surface chipping 50.00

Blue and white stoneware, soap dish, scrolled design, unmarked, 4-7/8" d, **$125.**

Blue and white stoneware, pitcher, man with stein, **$85.**

Honecomb pattern with relief apricot, replaced wood lid, surface chipping............... 65.00
Relief butterfly design, matching lid, base chips................. 100.00

Blue Ridge Pottery

Erwin, Tenn., was home to Southern Potteries, Inc., chartered in 1920. By 1938, the company was producing Blue Ridge dinnerware, marketing the items as "Hand Painted Under the Glaze." Most of its competitors used decals to create designs, and Southern Potteries was able to capitalize on this difference. The colorful, cheery floral patterns made Blue Ridge dinnerware a favorite with consumers. However, inexpensive imports and a move toward plastic dinnerware forced the company out of business in 1957.

For additional listings, see *Warman's Americana & Collectibles*.

Ashtray, Chintz 35.00
Bon bon
Easter Parade, flat 150.00
Nova Rose...................... 55.00

Bowl, Bluebell Bouquet, 9" d.... 24.00
Bread and butter plate, 6" d
Applejack.............................. 10.00
Crab Apple............................ 7.50

Cake plate
Fruit Fantasy.......................... 50.00
Nocturne, yellow, matching server 140.00
Verna, maple leaf shape 125.00

Blue Ridge Pottery, teapot, 7" h, 10" l, **$125.**

Cereal bowl, Dutch Bouquet, 6" d
.... 15.00

Cigarette box
Ships 100.00
Seaside 175.00

Cream and sugar, footed
Rose Marie........................... 140.00
Rose of Sharon.................... 140.00

Cup and saucer
Cock O' the Morn 25.00
Poinsettia............................. 10.00

Dinner plate
Becky, 10" d 20.00

Blue Bouquet, 9" d................ 15.00
Daffodil, 10" d 20.00
Fruit Punch, 10-1/2" d.......... 25.00

Dinnerware set
Daffodil, 45 pcs 575.00
Stanhouse Ivy, 45 pcs 425.00
Winnie, Skyline shape, 31 pcs
.... 325.00

Gravy boat, Bluebell Bouquet . 35.00

Luncheon plate, Becky, 8" d ... 12.00

Pie plate, Cassandra, maroon border
.... 25.00

Pitcher
Alice, 6" h 275.00
Helen, 4-1/2" h 120.00
Sculptured Fruit, 6-1/2" h
.... 135.00

Platter
Applejack............................. 38.00
Chrysanthemum................... 28.50

Relish tray, Iris, four sections
.... 150.00

Salad bowl, Candlewick 85.00

Salt and pepper shakers, pr, footed
Dog Tooth Violet 115.00

Blue Ridge Pottery, platter, 11-3/4" d, **$25.**

Floral Blossom..................... 125.00
Rose of Marie 95.00

Spoon rest, Apple.................... 45.00

Teapot, Chickory, crazed inside
.... 45.00

Vegetable bowl, Carol's Roses
.... 18.00

Blue Willow

This intricate pattern features a weeping willow along the banks of a river by a Japanese village. More than 200 manufacturers have produced items with variations of this pattern, generally blue on a white background. Josiah Spode first introduced the pattern in 1810, and it is still being used today.

For additional listings, see *Warman's Antiques & Collectibles*.

Blue Willow, cup and saucer, unmarked, **$5.**

Berry bowl, Homer Laughlin, small
.... 6.50

Bouillon and underplate, Ridgway
.... 85.00

Bowl, 9" d, Mason..................... 45.00

Cereal bowl, unmarked............. 8.00

Child's tea set, 14 pcs, orig box
.... 175.00

Creamer, Royal China, round handle
.... 10.00

Cup and saucer
Buffalo Pottery 25.00
Homer Laughlin 10.00
Shenango 15.00

Demitasse cup and saucer, mkd
"Allerton" 15.00

Dessert plate, unmarked........... 5.00

Dinner plate
Booth's 65.00
Buffalo Pottery 20.00
Johnson Bros 15.00
Royal China 10.00
Unmarked.............................. 8.00

Gravy boat, mkd "Willow, Woods Ware, Woods & Sons, England," 8-1/4" l..................................... 100.00

Grill plate, mkd "Moriyama," 10-1/2" d 45.00

Blue Willow, platter, large, **$175.**

Oil lamp, blue and white ceramic base, 1950s............................. 85.00

Pie plate, 10" d 50.00

Platter, unmarked, 11" x 13-1/2"
.... 165.00

Salad plate, 7-1/2" d, Made in Japan
.... 10.00

Soup bowl, unmarked 10.00

Sugar, cov
    Allerton.................................. 65.00
    Royal China 40.00
Teapot, cov, emb "Sadler, England"
    .... 165.00

Tray, metal, wear 15.00
Vegetable bowl, open, round, mkd
    "J. & G. Meakin" 65.00

Water set, 9" h pitcher, six 3-5/8" h
    tumblers, orig "Japan" paper labels
    .... 245.00

★ Bohemian Glass

The once independent country of Bohemia, now a part of the Czech Republic, produced a variety of fine glassware: etched, cut, overlay, and colored. Its glassware, which first appeared in America in the early 1820s, continues to be exported to the U.S. today. Much of what appears at flea markets are the later wares, including flashed wares in amber, green, blue, ruby, and even black. These are usually found with etched patterns.

For additional listings, see *Warman's Antiques & Collectibles* and *Warman's Glass*.

Reproduction Alert.

Bohemian glass, decanters, ruby stained cut to clear, left: pair of matching decanters with grape vine motif, one with original stopper, **$135;** right: floral and foliage decoration, **$75.**

Basket, 8" d, irid green body dec with amethyst straw marks, metal rim and handle, Wilhelm Kralik 150.00

Bell, green, gold dec, orig sticker "Handmade Bohemia Czechoslovakia," 7" h............. 85.00

Bowl, 6" d, green ground, random ruby threading, c1910 .... 175.00

Compote, 9-1/4" h, irid green, threaded glass trim on bowl, pedestal, and foot, c1900..... 175.00

Dresser bottle, 8-1/4" h, cut panel body, enameled dec, c1890 ... 90.00

Ramekin, 3" w, translucent yellow and clear, dec with red, green, yellow, and blue scrolling, white dotted and gold horizontal band, price for set of eight 100.00

Rose bowl, 5" h, optic ribbed body, applied ruffled rim, cobalt blue, Harrach............................... 110.00

Toothpick holder, 2-1/2" h, tapering body, brass rim, threaded irid body, Pallme-Koening.................. 115.00

Urn, 11" h, ftd, cranberry, medallion coat of arms, gold encrustations, polychrome floral scrolling, raised glass jewels, two jewels missing 175.00

Vase
    3-1/4" h, paneled shouldered body, irid dark olive green/brown 35.00

Bohemian glass, decanter set, four matching cordials and tray, ruby stained, etched grapes and vine decoration, **$95.**

    7-1/2" h, irid, stylized floral metal frame 125.00
    8-1/4" h, bulbous stick, quadrafold rim, deep amethyst, irid blue oil spot finish 120.00
    8-1/4" h, bulbous stick, tri-fold rim, cranberry, overall gold oil spot finish, random threading at rim 150.00

Bookends

These useful objects can be found in almost every medium and range from purely functional to extraordinarily whimsical.

For additional listings, see *Warman's Americana & Collectibles*.

Bookends, two pairs, wire-haired terriers, **$195;** labs with ivy trim, **$175.**

Bookends, cast bronze, sailing ships motif, felt bottoms, **$65.**

Anchors, brass, mounted to faux stone base, 8" h 48.00

Cocker spaniels, chalkware, 5-1/2" h 30.00

Dolphins, jumping, bronze, 7-1/2" h 80.00

Elephant, Rookwood Pottery, ivory color, 1936, 5-1/2" h, 6" l 225.00

Globes, brass, hardwood base, 7" h 115.00

Horse, rearing, L.E. Smith, emerald green glass, 8" h 55.00

Indian brave, chiseled face of native American, metal, green felt back, 6-1/2" h, 4-1/4" w, 2-1/8" d 75.00

Indian chief, bust, leather headdress 130.00

Knights, on charging horse, bronze, 1920s, 4" w, 8-1/4" h 285.00

Liberty Bell, bronze, 5" h 35.00

Lyres, enameled brass, green shading to black at edges, stamped "Made in Israel," 7" h 48.00

Puppies, bronzed pot metal, three puppies resting their heads together, felt base 70.00

Terriers, cast iron, orig paint and felt, 4-3/4" w, 2" d, 4-5/8" d 280.00

USS Constitution, chalkware, 5-1/2" h 15.00

Bookends, cast iron, Amish man and lady, some loss to paint, **$55.**

Bookends, Art Deco, bronzed nude, marked "WB" in shield, 8" h, **$300.**

Wagon train, painted cast iron, American Hardware Co., dated 1931, some loss to paint 90.00

Bookmarks

Ranging from delicate filagreed clips to intricately embroidered fabric to simple cardboard shapes, bookmarks have assisted readers for decades. Interesting examples can be found at flea markets if one looks carefully.

Bookmarks, Stevensgraph, Centennial, The Father of Our Country, George Washington, The first in peace, the first in war, the first in the hearts of his Countrymen, **$195.**

Advertising
Cruver Co., diecut thin celluloid topped by red and yellow roses, green rose bud and leafy stems, lower half black and white text, 1912 Newark Industrial Exposition 35.00
Erlanger Theatre, Chicago, showing Romeo & Juliet, with Norma Shearer and Leslie Howard, 1936, info on back regarding Chicago Public Library 20.00
Geneva National Mineral Water, celluloid, diecut water fountain, adv on back, c1905 .... 35.00
Kirk Johnson & Co., pianos and organs, Lebanon, PA, little Victorian girl in pink dress, carrying bouquet of pink roses, 2" x 6" 15.00
Poll Parrot shoes, die-cut cardboard, "They Speak for Themselves," 3-3/4" x 1-1/2" 12.00

Bookmarks, woven silk calendar, Louisiana Purchase Exposition, "St. Louis 1904," 10" x 3", **$150.**

Cross stitch, on punched paper, "Love," beige, salmon and green dec, 6-1/4" l.............................. 9.00

Easter, 2-1/2" x 7", silk ribbon, pale lavender, inscribed "An Easter Psalm" 5.00

Embroidered, "Week of Birthdays," flowers in metallic red thread, poem, 8-1/2" x 2".................. 75.00

Photograph, on paper, young woman 5.00

Plastic
Donald Duck figural, "Book Mark, Disneyland," hand-painted 26.00
Lord's Prayer, die-cut cross, page-holder type, 4-3/4" x 1-1/4" 6.00

Political
Abraham Lincoln, oval silhouette, quote from Gettysburg Address, cloth, black on cream, with orig sales card, c1935, 5-1/2" h 20.00

Our Choice 1892, diecut stiff celluloid, mounted sepia real jugate photo of Cleveland-Stevenson and Harrison-Reid, 2" x 5", price for pr 200.00

Silver plated, Apollo Silver Co., scrolling letter "A," c1900 ...... 35.00

Sterling silver, Gorham, etched "C" with floral engraving............. 25.00

World's Fair, 1964-65 New York World's Fair, celluloid............ 35.00

Books

All types of books can be found at flea markets. A book's value can be increased by a great binding, an early copyright, a first printing, interesting illustrations, an original dustjacket, or a famous author. At flea markets, prices for books can range from a quarter to thousands of dollars.

Many book collectors are turning to their computers and using the Internet to find books. There are several Web sites devoted to antique books that offer several ways to search for titles and values.

To remove a musty smell from a book, sprinkle baking soda onto several pages, close, and let it rest for a few days. When you remove the baking soda, the smell should disappear. Avoid books with mold, or you might be bringing home a big problem.

For additional listings, see *Warman's Antiques & Collectibles* and *Warman's Americana & Collectibles*.

The following listings are a mere sampling of the many books that may be found at flea markets.

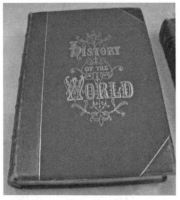

Book, *History of the World*, illustrated, ex-library copy, **$15.**

A Lovely Find, Wm Allen Knight, Wilde Co., 1943, 41 pgs......... 10.00

America's Colorful Railroads, Don Bal Jr., Bonanza Books, 1980 .... 15.00

Ancient Evenings, Norman Mailer, Little Brown, 1st ed., sgd by author 20.00

An Eye for the Dragon, Southeast Asia Observed: 1954-1970, Dennis Bloodworth, Farrar Strass & Girous, 1970, 1st ed., Book of the Month Club, 188 pgs 8.75

Aunt Emma's Cope Book, Erma Bombeck, McGraw-Hill, 1979, 1st ed., 180 pgs............................. 8.50

Authentic Life of President McKinley, The, Memorial Edition, 1901 .... 20.00

Beauties and Antiquities of Ireland, T. O. Russell, 1897, 399 pgs, gold emb front board 25.00

Bermuda Triangle-An Incredible Saga of Unexplained Disappearances, Charles Berlitz, Doubleday, 1974, 203 pgs........ 8.75

Billy, The Classic Hitter, Billy Williams, Rand McNally, 1974, 1st ed, dj....................................... 15.00

Book, *An Architectural History of Chestnut Hill*, paper covers, **$35.**

Christmas in Germany, Peter Andrews, World Book, Inc., 1974, 64 pgs...................................... 12.00

Dear Sir, Humorous Letters to Draft Boards, Juliet Lowell, Duell, Sloane, Pierce, 1944 .... 4.50

East Wind West Wind, Pearl S. Buck, 1930, 3rd printing, dj 22.50

Foil Travelers, Ballads, Tales, and Talk, Texas Folklore Society, No. 25, So Methodist Press, 1953 .... **8.00**

Good Night Sweet Prince, G. Fowler, Blakiston Co., 1944, Book of the Month Club edition, 474 pgs, dj **12.00**

Herbert Hoover-A Reminiscent Biography, Will Irwin, third printing, June, 1928 .... **20.00**

Jenny Lind's America, Frances Cavannah, Chilton Book Co., 1969 .... **7.00**

John Jay Janney's Virginia, An American Farm Lad's Life in Early 19th C, Asa Moore Janney, EPM Publications, 1978, illus, map **4.50**

John Muir's Longest Walk: John Earl, A Photographer, Traces His Journey to Florida, John Earl, Doubleday, 1971, 1st ed **15.00**

Lore of the Lakes, Told in Story & Picture, Dana Thomas Bowen, Freshwater Press, 1969, 9th printing, 314 pgs, photos **15.00**

Book, *The Calumet Baking Book,* 1929, 31 pages, **$10.**

Louisana Purchase, Robert Tallant, Random House, 1952 .... **7.00**

Moonspender, Jonathan Gash, St Martin's Press, 1987, 215 pgs, dj **22.50**

Once A Wilderness, Arthur Poiund, Reynard & Hitchcock, 1934 .... **6.00**

Our Forgotten Past-Seven Centuries of Life on the Land, Jerome Blum, Thames & Hudson, 1982, 1st ed., dj **8.75**

Plowing on Sunday, Sterling North, MacMillan, 1934, 1st ed **10.00**

Ramona, Helen Jackson, Little Brown & Co., 1916, 457 pgs **7.00**

Stillmeadow Calendar: A Countrywoman's Journal, Gladys Taber, 1967, 25 pgs, illus by Sidonie Coryn, dj **8.00**

Treasure of Christmas Crafts & Foods, Better Homes & Gardens, Meredith Corp, 1980, 384 pgs **12.00**

Twelve Brave Boys Who Became Famous Men, Esther E. Enock, Pickering & Ingils, 1940s **8.00**

Wild Bill Hickock Tames The West, Stewart H. Holbrook, Landmark/Random House, 1952 .... **7.00**

Within the Iron Gates, F. Rafer, Times Mirror, 1988, illus......... **6.50**

Bootjacks

Designed to ease the removal of boots, bootjacks were primarily made of cast iron or wood. The heel of a boot is placed in the U-shaped opening at the front of the jack, the other foot is placed on the rear of the jack, and the boot is pried off the front foot. Examples range from crude, one-of-a-kind versions to examples with elaborate, artistic castings and carvings.

In 1852, the United States Patent Office awarded its first patent for a bootjack to Saris Thomson of Hartsville, Mass.

Reproduction Alert.

Bootjacks, assorted wooden bootjacks, some home made, priced from **$5** to **$10.**

Beetle, cast iron, mkd "Depose," French, 10-1/2" l **50.00**

Lee Riders, wooden, small pc of rubber missing, 12" l **35.00**

Naughty Nellie
Antique, cast iron, 9-1/2" l **80.00**
Reproduction, cast iron, 9" l **10.00**

Scrolled design with horseshoe end, Victorian, cast iron, 11" l **195.00**

Scrolled design with V-shaped end, openwork design of intertwined stems, cast iron, 12" l **45.00**

Bootjacks, cast iron, lyre base with "Try Me" in the design, 12" l, **$35.**

Wooden, homemade
  Tiger maple, 10" l **30.00**
  Pine, oval ends, sq nails, 25" l **30.00**

Walnut, carved heart and
  openwork, 22" l **45.00**

Bottle Openers

Back in the dark ages before pull tops and twist off tops, folks actually used these wonderful bottle openers. Today collectors seek them out at flea markets. Some collectors prefer the figural types and try to find interesting examples with good paint. Other collectors concentrate on finding interesting advertising bottle openers.

Reproduction Alert.

I'll drink to that!

Raymond Brown's name might not be a familiar one, but you've probably seen one of his best-known invention—a cast-iron wall-mount bottle opener. In 1925, when soda was sold in glass bottles, Brown, the owner of several bottling plants, developed an opener that didn't damage the bottle when the cap was pried off. To make the new opener, Brown Manufacturing in Newport News, Va., was founded. Brown's opener consisted of a slanted, curved lip that attached to the wall with two screws. By adding a space for advertising, Brown greatly expanded the market for his device. The most famous advertiser was Coca-Cola.

Brown's design, the Starr "X" bottle opener, is still produced for bottlers, breweries, wholesalers, distributors, and retailers. For a list of advertising that has appeared on the openers over the years, see the Starr Web site at www.bottleopener.com.

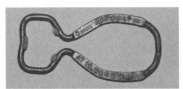

Bottle openers, Dr. Pepper, **$30.**

Benson & Hedges 100s, bottle opener and keychain, metal, 1-1/2" x 3-1/2" 10.00

Biltmore Hotel, Los Angeles, mkd "Vaughn USA" 12.00

Black boy and alligator, figural, cast iron, 2-3/4" h 145.00

Canada Dry, metal, 3-1/8" l 3.50

Coca-Cola, wall-mount, Starr X type, cast iron, some rust 22.00

Coors, America's Fine Light Beer, Ekco, Chicago, US Pat. Pending 6.00

Drunk, on a lamp post, cast iron, paint chips, 4-3/8" h 15.00

Edelweiss Beer, A Case of Good Judgment, metal, 4-3/4" l 3.00

Falstaff Beer, wall-mount, Starr X type, orig box 24.00

Heinz 57, bottle shape 18.00

Leg shape, brass, 3" l 22.00

Miller Brewing Co., metal, some rust 3.00

Old Crow, wooden figure, bottle opener under head, corkscrew hidden in leg, holding cane, 7-3/4" h, chip on hat brim 10.00

QNB, blue and white plastic 1.00

Pabst, metal, some rust 2.00

Parrot, on stand, cast iron, mkd "JW" (John Wright), 5-1/4" h 95.00

Royal Crown Cola, Best Taste Calls for RC 5.00

SAS, Scandinavian airlines, hard plastic, 3-1/2" l......................... 9.25

Singing cowboy, cast iron, 4-3/4" h 95.00

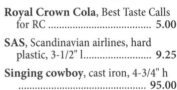

Bell Telephone, hard hat, cast iron, MIB 50.00

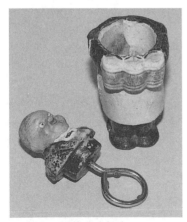

Bottle openers, figural, butler, composition, **$55.**

Bottle openers, golf club theme, combination bottle opener and cork screw, sterling silver, marked "Blackinton & Co.," 4-1/2" l, **$295.**

Bottles

Many types of bottles are found at flea markets. Prices vary according to rarity, condition, and color. Buying bottles may become even more interesting if you engage the dealer in conversation and ask where the bottle came from, was it dug, part of a collection, etc. Several excellent reference books are available to assist collectors.

For additional listings, see *Warman's Antiques & Collectibles Price Guide* and *Warman's Glass*. The following listings are a mere sampling of the bottles that may be found at flea markets.

Bottles, figural bottles, violin shape, cobalt blue, each **$25.**

Acme Nursing Bottle, clear, lay-down type, emb 70.00

Alpine Herb Bitters, amber, sq, smooth base, tooled lip, 9-5/8" h 175.00

Bull Dog Brand Liquid Glue, aqua, ring collar 6.50

Calla Nurser, oval, clear, emb, ring on neck 8.50

Carter's 1897, golden amber, cone shape, few scratches 35.00

Golden Key Ammonia, paper label, 8" h... 5.00

Herberlings, banana flavoring paper label, 8" h.............................. 10.00

Kranks Cold Cream, milk glass 6.50

Land of Lakes, honeycomb, metal cap... 8.00

Louis & Co., lemon extract 10.00

Lysol, cylindrical, amber, emb "Not to be Taken" 12.00

Mother's Comfort, clear, turtle type 25.00

Napa Soda Natural Mineral Water, sapphire blue, "W" on base, wear 140.00

Neamand's Drug Store, clear 30.00

Owl Drug Co., owl sitting on mortar, cobalt blue 70.00

Pre Cream Rye, bartender's type 35.00

Sloan's Liniment, castor oil 20.00

Standard Oil Co, colorless, orig label, 6" h 7.50

Bottles, Paine's, brown, triangular, **$125.**

Bottles, Hutchinson-type, "Jumbo Bottling Works, Cincinnati, O.," aqua, embossed letters, chipped lip, 7" h, **$65.**

Tippecanoe, Warner & Co., amber, applied mushroom lip, 9" h... 95.00

Warner's Safe Bitters, amber, applied mouth, smooth base, 8-1/2" h 265.00

Whitehouse Vinegar, jug shape, 10" h...................................... 20.00

Zingan Bitters, amber, applied mouth, smooth base, 11-7/8" h 150.00

Boxes

Collectors love boxes of all kinds. Interior decorators also scout flea markets for useful boxes. The colorful labels of these vintage packages are delightful to display. Locked boxes offer the mystery of a treasure inside, but don't be lured into paying too much.

Boxes, display, Yucatan Gum, lithographed tin, 6" h, 6-3/4" w, **$275.**

Advertising

Adams Sappota Chewing Gum, 7-1/2" x 8-1/2", two Victorian ladies, graphic labels **90.00**

Baker's Chocolate, wood, 12-lb size **25.00**

Fil Au Pierrot, 4" x 7" x 2-3/4", cardboard, multicolored, lightly emb pictorial label, late 1930s **12.00**

King Brand Rolled Oats **45.00**

Ladies Favorite Polish, paper label **10.00**

National Lead Co., paint chip samples **25.00**

Whitman's Pleasure Island Chocolates, cardboard, pirate scenes on five sides, map on bottom, 1924 .... **28.00**

Williams Brothers Valvriggans, men's long underwear **15.00**

Accessory type

Book shape, green onyx, brass and wood trim, wear and chips, 5" l **165.00**

Collar box, gold paper ground, pink, green and yellow flowers, clear celluloid overlay, pretty woman in center **175.00**

Dresser, white ground, small pink flowers and green leaves, mkd "Nippon," rect **35.00**

Heart shape, silver-plated, small gold bow trim, velvet lining **35.00**

Storage type

Apple, pine, old red paint, conical feet, 9-3/4" x 10" x 4" h .. **310.00**

Boxes, tin, An-Du-Septic Dustless Crayon, black, gold lettering, trademark in center, **$95.**

Candle, hanging, pine and hardwood, old worn gray paint, 10-1/4" w **330.00**

Dome top, cast brass, relief eagle and crowns, English, 19th C, 4" l **175.00**

Pine, worn orig brown graining, yellow ground, machine dovetails, 16-1/4" l **200.00**

Boy Scouts

The Boy Scout pledge has been recited by millions of youngsters throughout the years. Collectibles relating to scouting troops, jamborees, etc., are eagerly sought and readily found at flea markets.

For additional listings, see *Warman's Americana & Collectibles*.

Activities chart, 23" x 35-1/2", full color, 1955, folded as issued **15.00**

Award certificate, 5-1/2" x 8", buff paper certificate for waste paper

Boy Scouts, neckerchief, emblem in center, four Boy Scout activities in corners, semiphore border, brown and red, 14-5/8" square, **$20.**

collection during March-April 1945 .... **7.50**

Badge, metal bar pin overlaid by red and white striped fabric, gold luster metal pendant with Gen Eisenhower portrait in military uniform, text on reverse "Patriotic Achievement" for waste paper collection, March-April 1945 .... **15.00**

Belt, 30-1/2" l, 1-1/4" w, tooled brown leather, logo and rope design, copper accent metal buckle, 1960s **12.00**

Brochure, 1964 National Jamboree, Valley Forge, PA **2.00**

Bulletin, 8-1/2" x 11", May 1939, Scouting Central Ohio **2.50**

Calendar, 1960, 16" x 33-1/2", 50th Anniversary, Ever Onward, adv for Northampton, PA, funeral home **10.00**

Canteen, Diamond Brand, canvas cover, c1950 .... **12.00**

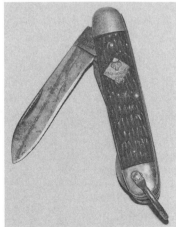

Boy Scouts, Camillus three-blade knife, Cub Scouts BSA, 6" with blade extended, **$18.**

Eagle Scout announcement, 6" x 11-1/2", black and white handbill, Sept. 26, 1938 public award presentation............................ **2.00**

First day cover, 3" x 6" envelope with stamp issued for 50th anniversary, 1960, postmarked Washington DC **5.00**

Handbook, March 1963, Norman Rockwell cover...................... **20.00**

Hat, scout master's, Boy Scouts of America insignia, felt, c1950 .... **125.00**

Jacket, Sea Explorers B.S.A., white canvas fabric naval middy blouse, rear sailor collar, stitched white fabric patch "National Standard Explorer Unit," other patches, c1950 .... **15.00**

License plate attachment, 4-1/2" x 11", diecut, Scouts-Conrad Weiser, Berks County, PA, frontiersman in white, navy blue ground, 1960s **10.00**

Patch
Diamond Jubilee, 3" d **18.00**

St.. Louis Council 1941 Camporee, 3-1/2" x 2"......................... **36.00**
York-Adams Area Council (PA), center V, 1943, 2-1/2" d, felt, unused............................... **10.00**
1974 Third Jumpin' Joe Jamboree, Eastern Arkansas Area Council, 3" d **14.00**

Program, 8-1/2" x 11", Forty-Niner Council, Stockton, CA **3.50**

Roly Poly, celluloid, saluting Boy Scout, 1920s........................... **40.00**

Boyd Crystal Art Glass

The Boyd Family of Cambridge, Ohio, has made some interesting colored glassware over the years. Many of its molds were purchased from leading glass companies, such as Imperial.

For additional listings, see *Warman's Americana & Collectibles* and *Warman's Glass*.

Animal covered dish
Frog, Columbia Green.......... 45.00
Hen, cherry red 27.00
Rabbit, scalloped nest, blue, 1983 .... 37.50
Turkey, Peacock Blue Satin .. 25.00
Turtle, Columbia Green........ 45.00

Airplane, blue carnival 25.00

Bernie the Eagle
Alexandrite............................. 9.00
Cobalt Carnival.................... 10.00
Rosie Brown 9.00

Brian the Bunny
Nutmeg Carnival 9.00
Toffee Slag 9.00

Box, cov, Candlewick, vaseline, sgd 25.00

Cat slipper, moss green........... 12.00

Fuzzy Bear
Caramel Slag........................ 17.00
Cobalt blue 55.00
Ritz Blue 15.00

Hand, rubina, 4" l 20.00

Boyd Crystal Art Glass, bird, light blue, **$10.**

Jennifer Doll
Harvest Gold.......................... 9.00
Spring Surprise.................... 10.00

Pickle dish, orange and yellow slag, yellow hob trim, sides emb "Love's request is Pickles," 9" l.......... 45.00

Pie vent, duck, blue................. 35.00

Salt
Bird, orange and gold slag, 3" l 26.00

Chick, Spring Surprise, red and gold slag, 2" 10.00

Shoe, Daisy and Button, bow on front, ribbed bottom, mkd, 5-1/2"
Light blue.............................. 40.00
Vaseline................................. 20.00

Southern Belle, Sunburst........ 26.00

Sports Car, moss green slag.... 15.00

Tomahawk, cobalt, 7" l 26.00

Toothpick holder
Bulldog head, Toffee Slag..... 17.00
Gypsy Pot, butternut 8.50

Train, six cars, 1980s
Iridescent milk glass 45.00
Lavender............................... 40.00
Purple 40.00

Willie Mouse, cobalt blue slag 9.00

Wine glass, chocolate slag, 1st logo, 4" h... 20.00

Boyd's Bears & Friends

What's better than a teddy bear? How about collectible teddy bears with personality? Plus, Boyd's bears have companion figurines, magnets, and accessories, making them a popular collectible for the new millennium.

Boyd's Bears & Friends, Christmas tree bear, tan plush bear, green velvet tree with red embroidery, gold star, **$10.**

Alica R. Angel 18.00

Bailey's Birthday, #2014, 1993
.... 20.00

Gary Bearenthal, bean bag construction, 16" h 50.00

Hemingway, fishing vest and hat, 14" h 32.00

Lincoln B. Bearrington, golden brown mohair, 16" h 85.00

Miss Prissy Fussybuns, long haired white cat, dark blue hat with flowers, 16" h 25.00

McBruin, To Serve with Honor, 1st edition 40.00

Mrs. Trumball, fully jointed, hand-knit green sweater, matching hat, 10" h 28.00

Mr. Trumball, mocha colored, dark brown sweater, plaid bowtie, 10" h 25.00

Noah 15.00

Regena Haresford, white rabbit, blue checked dress, matching bow, 13" h 25.00

Sally Quignapple & Annie, bear 10" h, doll 5" h 22.00

Boyd's Bears & Friends, Fillmore M. Bearington, red and gray sweater, pewter paw print buttons, original tags, **$20.**

Theodore 30.00

Uncle Elliot, orig box, 1996 .... 95.00

Uncle Leo, hand-knit sweater, ball cap, 10" h 32.00

Vanessa R. Angel 15.00

Brass

An alloy of copper and zinc, brass is an extremely durable yet malleable metal. It has long been favored for creating decorative and functional objects. Because it is so durable many brass items can be found at flea markets. Avoid pieces with unusual wear, those that are broken, or examples that are poorly polished.

For additional listings, see *Warman's Antiques & Collectibles*.

Reproduction Alert.

Brass, pie crimper with coggle wheel, **$10.**

Ashtray, rope design on rim, 5" d
.... 12.00

Bed warmer, pierced brass pan, long wooden handle, 40-1/2" l 150.00

Brochure holder, Elevated News-Take One, 5-1/2" sq, 15" h 35.00

Candlestick, 8-3/8" h, push-rod, round base 90.00

Chestnut roaster, heart-shaped, pierced lid, decorative handle, English, 19-1/2" l 300.00

Cigar cutter, pocket type 40.00

Desk tray, 2-1/4" x 8-1/8", red, gold, and black enamel logo for "Lehigh

and Wilkes-Barre Coal Co.," relief in center for NY state distributor Frederic A. Potts & Co., Inc.
.... 15.00

Brass, chamberstick, rectangular base, push-up, ring handle, **$150.**

Brass, vase, triangular, three handles, flared top, 8-3/4" h, **$55.**

Door slot, mkd "Letters" on hinged flap, 2-3/4" h, 6-1/2" w 25.00

Easel, desk top, ornate frame ... 35.00

Letter opener, 6-1/2" l, Union Station, St. Louis.................... 25.00

Mortar and pestle, 4-1/2" h.... 65.00

Pail, iron bail with rat-tail ends, 8" h, 12"dia...................................... 45.00

Sleigh bells, set of 6, graduated, on leather strap, 24" l................. 145.00

Steam whistle, 2-1/2" d, 12" h, single chime, lever control............. 150.00

Teapot, floral design on 1 side, Oriental lettering on other, swing handle, 9" x 7"........................ 30.00

Tray, stamped with Holland scenes, attached handles, 17" x 10" 45.00

Trump indicator, circular flat brass disk, green enamel top, celluloid rotating suit and no trumps indicator 130.00

Brastoff, Sascha

This internationally known designer and artist began producing ceramic artware in 1953. If a piece is marked with his full name, it was made by him. Pieces marked "Sascha B" indicate he supervised the production, but didn't necessarily make the item himself.

Ashtray
Igloo design, 4-1/2" h, 6" d... 55.00
Rooftops, enameled copper 150.00

Bowl
Mosaic pattern, 3 feet, minor paint chips, 14-1/2" l, 12" w 145.00
Star Steed pattern, sunfish design, three feet, 9-3/4" l, 8-1/2" w 110.00

Box, cov, mosaic, figural dog finial, 6-1/2" sq............................. 165.00

Candy box, cov, gray mottled matte finish, seated figure with turban, sgd "Sascha B" on front in gold, gold rooster mark on lid int., 5-3/4" d 150.00

Charger
11-3/4" d, Star Steed, gray ground, mkd "Sascha B" on front, rooster mark on back 150.00
14" h, lime green fading to black, colorful fruit, sgd on front 145.00

Dish
Alaska pattern, shell form, 11-1/2" l 85.00
Jewel Bird pattern, 10" d 85.00
Star Steed pattern, sq 65.00

Figure
Horse, rearing, foam green, platinum spatter glaze ... 160.00
Polar bear, 9" l 195.00

Plate, ChiChi Bird pattern, sgd, 8-1/2" d 195.00

Platter, Alaska pattern, seal on white ground with blue sky, painted by Matt Adams, 13-3/4" x 8-1/4" 130.00

Tobacco jar, Abstract pattern, stainless steel lid, rust stains, glaze flaws, 6-1/2" h.................... 65.00

Vase
8-1/2" h, 4" d, Eskimo Man, sgd "Sascha B, #047" 145.00
12" h, Orange and Gold, sgd, #V-3 .... 155.00

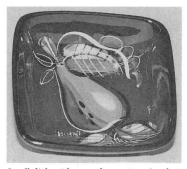

Small dish with pear decoration, Sascha B., 3-3/4" square, **$25.**

Wall plaque, stylized fish, one turquoise, one maroon, 12" l, pr 110.00

Wall pocket, Provincial Rooster pattern, 4" h, 5" w.................. 95.00

Breweriana

Collectors have always enjoyed finding new examples of breweriana at their favorite flea markets. Some specialize in items from a particular brewery, while others collect only one type of item, such as beer trays. Whatever they enjoy, their collections are bound to be colorful.

For additional listings, see *Warman's Americana & Collectibles*.

Reproduction Alert.

Ashtray, A. Coors Co., Golden CO, pottery 22.00

Bank, Pabst Blue Ribbon Beer, miniature beer can, 1936-37 patent

date, coin slot in top, 2-3/4" h 38.00

Breweriana, metal bottle opener, "Carling, Not For Sale," 3-5/8" l, **$2.**

Banner, Bud Light Beer, Welcome to the Kemper Open, red and gold, plastic, rope ties, 112" x 36" 35.00

Bar light, Schlitz, logo on front and back, gold-colored plastic, plaster goddess, glass globe, 1976, 45" h 140.00

Beer stein
Budweiser, Clydesdales, 1988, 6" h 25.00
Miller, 1988, Great American Achievements 22.50

Beer tap, Schlitz, wood and ceramic, worn.. 25.00

Bottle opener
Blatz Milwaukee Beer............. 8.00
Wylre's Holland Brand Beer ... 5.00

Coaster, Piels Beer, 3-1/4" x 3-1/2", vacu-form thin plastic, bright yellow border, full-color art of Bert & Harry and balloon text captions, Piel Bros Brooklyn ©1958, price for pr 12.00

Clock
Budweiser, pocket watch form, electric, "Budweiser 1876, King of Beers," 15-1/2" d 55.00
Pabst Blue Ribbon, plastic, 17" d 90.00

Cup, Hamm's Beer, blue and red artwork of trademark bear relaxing in back yard, beret and glasses on one side, running with tray of beer on other, Dixie, c1970, 5" h, set of four 16.00

Display figure
Don Q Rum, 12-1/2" h painted composition, mounted on 1-1/4" x 4-1/2" x 5-1/4" wooden base, Schieffelic & Co., NY, distributor for Puerto Rican distillery, 1940s 70.00

Pfeiffer's, 7-1/4" h, painted plaster, 4" sq base, Plasto Mfg Co., Chicago, stamp, 1950s 38.00
Scotch Heather, 3" x 5" x 9-1/2" h painted plaster, ivory caricature Scotsman, black base, white lettering "McRae's Scotch Heather Whiskey Punch," greeting felt skid pad, 1950s 25.00

Door push, Pabst Blue Ribbon Beer, 7-1/4" h, 4-1/4" w 125.00

Lighter, miniature Miller Beer can shape, out of butane, 1" w, 2-3/4" h 10.00

Mug
Schlitz, brewery emblem on both sides, scene of barrels brought by boat being loaded on horse-drawn cart, 7" h................. 6.00
Smith's Musty Ale, base mkd "WM Brunt Pottery Co., E. Liverpool" 26.00

Playing cards, Miller High Life, "The Champagne of Bottle Beer," Girl on

Breweriana, beer tap, Neuweiler Light Lager Beer, yellow casing, black and red lettering, **$12.**

Breweriana, suds scraper, Say Hanley's For Ale, plastic, red, gold lettering, 8-3/4" l, **$20.**

Moon logo, 1950s, orig box, used 16.50

Score pad, Falstaff Beer, for gin rummy, eight sheets, 8-3/4" x 7-5/8" 12.00

Sign
Bavarian Beer, red, white, and gold, tin over cardboard, 1950s, 6" x 10"..................................... 35.00
Budweiser, cardboard, "Custer's Last Stand," shows Battle of Little Big Horn, 20" h, 41" w ... 125.00
Genesee Beer, doubled-sided window sign, late 1950s, 11" d 18.00
O'Keefe Canadian Ale, hard plastic, wooden easel for countertop display, 16" x 11" 14.00
Pabst, red neon, blue ribbon border, plastic protector, 19" h, 21" w 90.00

Taste test kit, 2" x 2-1/4" x 4" box, pr of shot glasses mkd "Calvert Reserve" "A" or "B," four unused "Whiskey Export" cards for tasters, orig instruction pamphlet, 1940s 10.00

Tray
Budweiser, tin, "St. Louis Levee In Early Seventies," shows paddlewheeler at busy dock, 1914 copyright 140.00
Coors Light, gray and white, dated 1982, wear, 13" d 10.00
Falcon International Beer, Falcon logo, red, white, black, and gold, scratches........................... 18.00
Fitzgerald's Ale, Fitzgerald Bros. Brewing Co., Troy, T. Burgomaster Beer, 13" d, 1-1/4" h................................. 80.00
Schlitz, "The beer that made Milwaukee famous," 13" d 75.00

Breyer

Founded in 1943, the Breyer Molding Company of Chicago has created some interesting radio and television cases. However, the company is best known for its animals, which were started as a sideline but had gained great popularity by 1958. The facility continued to develop new techniques, creating interesting new figures, primarily horses. The production operation was moved to New Jersey after the firm was acquired by Reeves International.

Breyer, donkey, 8-1/2" l, **$65.**

Accessories

Bucket, MIB................................ 3.00

Crop 8.00

Horse barn, pine, MIB 270.00

Leather saddlebag, MIB......... 16.00

McClellan military saddle set, MIB
.... 30.00

Nylon halter with cotton lead rope, MIB............................. 12.00

Stable blanket, quilted, blue and yellow....................................... 5.00

Tack box, blue, MIB 10.00

Animals

Alpine Goat, 1999, MIB 6.00

Boxer, 8" h 40.00

Collie, Honey, 1995-1996, MIB 55.00

Elephant, re-release, 1992-1993, MIB
.... 45.00

Hawk, black, 1991-1992 .... 25.00

Jolly Cholly Basset Hound, tri-color, #325, 7" h..................... 35.00

Moose, 1966-1996 .... 35.00

Texas Longhorn Bull, 1963-1990
.... 30.00

Horses

Arabian foal, black, 1999, MIB
.... 15.00

Black Stallion Returns set, 1983-1993 .... 65.00

Chestnut Pinto Paint Western Prancing, chestnut and white, 9" h
.... 35.00

Chestnut Sorrel Belgian, red on yellow ribbon, #94, 9-1/2" h.. 40.00

Dan Patch, limited edition, 1990, MIB...................................... 90.00

Dapple Grey Old Timer, c1970-87, 6-3/4" h 40.00

Fighting Stallion, #31, alabaster, 1965-85, 11-1/4" h 32.00

Jack Frost Christmas Horse, #700499, 1999..................... 225.00

Little Bits scale (approx 4-1/2" to 5" h)
Appaloosa, 1985-1988.......... 15.00
Clydesdale, 1984-1988.......... 20.00

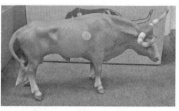

Breyer, Texas Longhorn, No. 75, original box, **$30.**

Morganglanz, picture box....... 35.00

Palomino Twin Foals, #1256, MIB
.... 28.50

Robinhood, on horse, 1950s, 8" h
.... 175.00

Seabiscuit, Dark Bay, 1979-80, 3" h
.... 35.00

Secretariat, 1987-1996, MIB ... 50.00

Shetland Pony, alabaster, 1963-1973
.... 25.00

Smart Little Lena, horse and calf, MIB...................................... 37.50

Stablemate scale (approx 2-3/4" h)
Citation, 1975-1990.............. 10.00
Thoroughbred mare, bay, 1989-1994................................. 15.00

Western Prancing, with saddle and blanket, 9" l, 8-1/2" h............. 35.00

Bride's Baskets

The term bride's basket usually refers to a decorative glass bowl in a fancy silver or silver-plate holder. This traditional gift to brides was meant as a showpiece for the young couple's sideboard. Over time, bowls would be damaged, so it is not uncommon to find a bowl that is mismatched with a base.

For additional listings, see *Warman's Antiques & Collectibles*.

Blue and white glass bowl, enameled floral dec, 6" d..... 250.00

Blue, ruffled, leaves, blossom, gold dec, no frame...................... 150.00

Cranberry, applied glass trim, SP holder, 6" d 195.00

Cranberry opalescent, no frame
.... 140.00

Fenton, maize, amber and crystal crest, hp roses on int., white ext., SP holder, 10-1/2" d................. 275.00

Hobnail, pink, blue ruffled rim, SP holder dec with leaves, 10" d, 11" h
.... 525.00

Opalescent, white, cranberry ruffled rim, applied vaseline rope handle, 9" h... 95.00

Peachblow, shiny finish bowl, applied amber rim, SP Wilcox holder, 9" d
.... 215.00

Satin glass, shaded purple, white underside, purple and white enameled flowers, lacy foliage dec,

Bride's basket, pink cased bowl with clear ruffled edge, hand painted floral decoration, ornate silver-plated frame, 11" d, 12" h, **$250.**

10-3/4" d 225.00

Silver plated, mkd "Middletown Plate Co., Quadruple Plate 1857," 9-1/2" d, 5-1/2" h excluding handle 140.00

Spiral white and turquoise dec, ruffled, colorless thorn handle, 8-1/2" d 125.00

Vasa Murrhina, outer amber layer, center layer with cream colored spots, random toffee colored spots, dark veins, gold mica flakes, mulberry pink lining, crossed thorn handles, 10" d 635.00

British Royalty

Generations of collectors have been fascinated by the British Royal family, having saved memorabilia associated with the king's clan. Quite an assortment of memorabilia survives from past, in addition to the plethora of items associated with present-day royal weddings, births, and state visits.

British Royalty, Duke & Duchess of Windsor, mug, In Memoriam, black and white portraits, birth, marriage, accession abdication, death dates, Dorincourt, 3-3/8" h, **$45.**

Badge, 3" d, black and white, photo portrait of Her Majesty Queen Elizabeth II and His Royal Highness Prince Philip, in ceremonial clothes, c1954...................................... 18.00

Book, *King Albert's Book,* 8-3/4" x 11-1/8", hardcover, 188 black and white pgs, 17 pgs with tipped-in full color plates by noted artists .. 75.00

Bottle opener and key fob, Queen Elizabeth II, color printing, 1-3/4" x 2-1/2" 7.50

Box, cov, Elizabeth the Queen Mother, 1980, 80th Birthday, color portrait, Crown Staffordshire, 4" d 75.00

Cup and saucer, Elizabeth II, portrait flanked by flags, coronation, pairs of flags inside cup and saucer.............................. 45.00

Goblet, Royal Wedding Commemorative, 6" h, MIB .. 70.00

Loving cup, Elizabeth II and Philip, 1972 Silver Wedding Anniversary, Paragon, 3" h 175.00

Magic Lantern slide, Victoria and Albert..................................... 25.00

Matchbook cover, Their Most Gracious Majesties, Canada, May 15-June 15, 1939.................... 18.00

Mug, Queen Elizabeth Coronation, 1953 .... 24.00

Pinback button
Queen Elizabeth, black and white cello, coronation portrait photo, red, white, and purple fabric ribbons, miniature gold luster finish metal replica crown pin, c1953, 1-3/4" d 15.00
Queen Elizabeth and Prince Philip, red, white, and blue cello, center black and white portraits, 1951 visit to Canada, waxed fabric red, white, and blue ribbons ... 20.00

Plate, Queen Victoria, Jubilee Year, Royal Worcester, 10-1/2" d .. 275.00

Souvenir pencil, 6-1/2" l, silver lustered wooden barrel, black portrait, and "Coronation Edward VIII 12th May 1937, God Save the King," short tribute verse, black image of Westminster Abbey 12.00

British Royalty, "Coronation, June 2nd, 1953, H.M. Queen Elizabeth II," 4-1/8" h, crazed, **$30.**

Tin, Queen Elizabeth, Coronation, June, 1953, slight discoloration top, rust inside................................ 8.00

British Royalty, Queen Elizabeth II, plate made to commemorate visit to Philadelphia, July 1976, light blue jasper ground, arches and flowers on rim, swags, ribbons and rams' heads surrounding classical figures in white, yellow, lavender, and green, central bust of Elizabeth, inscription in gold "Royal Visit to America, Philadelphia, July 1976," Wedgwood, impressed marks on back with gold inscription stating it is no. 4 of a limited edition of 12, original box and certificate of authenticity, 8-5/8" d, **$290.**

Bronze

An alloy of copper and tin, bronze is a sturdy metal that has been used to create functional and decorative objects for centuries. Collectors should be aware that some objects merely have a bronze coating and are not solid bronze. Those pieces are valued considerably less than if they were solid bronze.

For additional listings, see *Warman's Antiques & Collectibles.*

Ashtray, round, leaf form, applied salamander, c1910, 7-1/2" d 120.00

Bookends, pr, baby shoes, dated 1948 .... 25.00

Bookrack, extending, Moffat, cast ends with Indian brave, polychrome paint, emb "9964," c1928, 14" l extended, 6-1/2" h 285.00

Bronze, plaque, portrait of Monet, 8-1/2" d, **$250.**

Bust, Buddha, serene expression, draped covering, cloud tiara, verdigris finish, 9-1/2" h 195.00

Candlesticks, pr, figural
6" h, owl, granite base 225.00
10" h Don Quixote standing and holding a lance, 11" h Pancho Sanchez, riding a donkey and holding a staff, each with inverted helmet-formed sconce, both on tripod base, early 20th C 300.00

Charger, doré, deeply cast geometric designs on rim, stamped "Tiffany Studios New York #1746," 12" d, area of discoloration, minor edge dent 330.00

Figure
Dog with game, dark patina, American School, 20th C, 6" h 90.00
Mythical beast, tail raised, supporting figure sitting on its back, table form base, Southeast Asia, 18th or 19th C, 3-1/4" w, 2-

1/2" d, 5-7/8" h, one leg loose 175.00

Jose stick holder, 4-3/4" h, attendant holding cloth with censer on top, opening in censer to hold joss stick, dark brown patina, China, Ming Dynasty, several holes 200.00

Sculpture, Startled Finch on a Perch, Ferdinand Pautrot, gold-green patina, sgd on base "F. Pautrot," 5" h 260.00

Scepter, 20-1/2" l, three cast faces, paneled rod, engraved swirled designs, crown finials, Oriental 175.00

Smoking tray, 6-1/4" d, doré finish, applied scrolling on ash bowl, cigar rests, matchbox holder, unmarked, c1910 .... 70.00

Tray, 9" d, band of hammered designs, mkd "Apollo Studios, New York" c1910 .... 45.00

Wall plaque, American Telephone and Telegraph Co., 9" d 250.00

Bubblegum and Non-Sport Trading Cards

Bubblegum trading cards were big business in the late 1930s, especially for the Goudey Gum Company and National Chicle Company. They produced several series that had collectors clamoring for more. Bowman, Donruss, Topps, and Fleer eventually joined the marketplace also. Today, some companies omit the gum, concentrating solely on the trading cards.

These listings are just a sampling of the many cards available. Unless otherwise noted, prices are for complete sets in excellent condition.

Andy Griffth Show, 1990, set of 110 cards, mint 25.00

Batman, Topps, 1966, Riddle-back series, set of 38 .... 250.00

Battlestar Galactica, Topps, 132 cards and 22 stickers to set ... 30.00

Close Encounters of the Third Kind, Wonder Bread, ©1978 Columbia Pictures Industries, set of 24 .... 14.00

Combat, series 2, Donruss, 1964, set of 66 .... 250.00

DC Comics, Impel Marketing, ©1991 DC Comics, set of 180 .... 12.00

Elvis Presley, Boxcar Enterprises, Inc., 1978, complete set 135.00

Fabian, Topps, 1959, set of 115 .... 120.00

Green Hornet, #29, 1966 .... 5.00

Bubble gum cards, non-sport, Batman, 'What Tim Burton Wants," #238, Second Series, **$.25.**

Bubble gum cards, nonsport, Chester A. Arthur, #24, Bowman, 1952, US Presidents series, **$.75.**

Hopalong Cassidy, False Paradise 2.50

Marvel Universe III, Impel Marketing, © 1992 Marvel Entertainment Group, holograms, set of five 15.00

Mickey Mouse, #3 .... 30.00

Knight Rider, Donruss, © 1982 Universal City, set of 55 .... 10.00

Rock Stars, Donruss, 1979, set of 66 .... 48.00

Simpons, Radioactive Man, #412 .... 5.00

Superman the Movie, Topps, © 1978 DC Comics, set of 77 cards, 16 foil stickers 25.00

Tarzan, 1966, Philadelphia Chewing Gum Co., set of 66 .... 185.00

X-Men, ©1992 Marvel Entertainment Group, holograms, set of five 15.00

Buffalo Pottery

The Buffalo Pottery Co., Buffalo, New York, was chartered in 1901, with the kiln fired up for production in October of 1903. Early Buffalo Pottery production consisted mainly of semi-vitreous china dinner sets. Buffalo was the first pottery in the United States to successfully produce the Blue Willow pattern. From 1908 to 1909 and again from 1921 to 1923, Buffalo Pottery produced the line for which it is most famous—Deldare Ware. In 1915, the manufacturing process was modernized, giving the company the ability to produce vitrified china. Consequently, hotel and institutional ware became the main production items, with hand-decorated ware de-emphasized. In the early 1920s, fine china was made for home use.

For additional listings, see *Warman's Antiques & Collectibles*.

Buffalo Pottery, child's feeding plate, ABCs around outer rim, center with Dolly Dingle-type scene of little boy comforting little girl with doll, marked "Semivitreous, (buffalo) Buffalo Pottery," edge chip, **$25.**

Advertising plate, 7-1/2" d, dark teal, seal and buffalos, Advance Commerce Prudence Industry, We're Coming Back to Buffalo, Buffalo, NY, back mid "Made Exclusively for L. L. Millring Copyrighted" 65.00

Butter pat, 3-3/4" d, Blue Willow 38.50

Cereal bowl, restaurant ware, white, green stripes 5.00

Charger, 13-3/4" d, Deldare, Fallowfield Hunt.................. 375.00

Cup and saucer, Deldare, street scene 225.00

Gravy boat, 8" l, cream, pink flowered border, green leaves, gold trim.. 25.00

Jug, 6-1/4" h
Cinderella, 1906, restoration to spout............................... 200.00
Souvenir, blue and green transfer print, inscribed "The Whaling City Souvenir of New Bedford, Mass," whaling motifs, staining 325.00

Mug, 4-1/2" h, Calumet Club 90.00

Buffalo Pottery, plate, Fallowfield Hunt, olive green ground, maker's mark and date 1908 on back, 9-1/4"d, **$250.**

Buffalo Pottery, dinner set, Blue Willow, 52 pieces, **$125.**

Plate
9-3/8" d, Deldare, Fallowfield Hunt the Start, artist sgd "A. Delaney" 295.00
9-3/4" d, Indian Head Pontiac 55.00

Platter
9" l oval, white 85.00
13-1/2" l, US Army Medical Dept., 1943................................. 60.00

Soup bowl, 4" d, International House of Pancakes............................ 20.00

Sugar bowl, cov, Blue Willow 90.00

Bunnykins

These charming bunny characters have delighted children for many years. But, did you know that they were created by a nun? Barbara Vernon Bailey submitted her designs from the convent. Many of her designs were inspired by stories she remembered her father telling. The Bunnykins line was introduced in 1934. A new series of figures was modeled by Albert Hallam in the 1970s.

Baby plate, Letter Box, Barbara
    Vernon Bailey 75.00

Baby set, plate and two-handled mug,
    Royal Doulton........................ 55.00

Bowl, Royal Doulton, Barbara Vernon
    .... 95.00

Bunnykins, mug, Bunnykins border,
other Bunnykins playing, **$18.**

Child's cup, two handles, mkd
    "English Fine Bone China,
    Bunnykins, Royal Doulton
    Tableware Ltd, 1936"............. 55.00

Child's plate, Royal Doulton, 8" d
    Bunnykins at school 12.50
    Mother and father bunnykins 15.00

Christmas plate, 8" d 18.00

Figure, Royal Dounton
    Bridesmaid, DB173, 3-3/4" .. 40.00
    Buntie Bunnykins helping Mother,
      DB2.................................... 85.00
    Doctor Bunnykins, 4-1/2" h . 40.00
    Little Jack Horner, 3-1/2" h .. 60.00
    Mother and Baby Bunnykins,
      DB167, 1997 .... 45.00
    Mystic Bunnykins, DB197, 4-3/4" h
      .... 50.00
    Seaside, 1998 .... 55.00

Uncle Sam, brown backstamp,
    1985, 4-1/2" h 45.00

Bunnykins, child's dish, 6-1/4" d, **$40.**

Buttonhooks

Originally used for hooking tiny buttons on gloves, dresses, and shoes, these long narrow hooks are sometimes found hiding in vintage sewing baskets.

Bakelite handle, orange, 6" l... 40.00

Bone handle, folding, 3-3/4" l
    .... 20.00

Celluloid handle
    6-1/8" l, mkd "Parisian Ivory,"
      Loonen France trademark 25.00
    7-1/8" l, black etched floral design
      .... 12.50

Sterling
    3" l, folding, repoussé 50.00
    4-1/2" l, repoussé, English
      hallmarks 125.00

6-1/8" l, feather paisley design
    .... 35.00

6-1/4" l, swirling design, mkd
    "Tiffany & Co." 100.00

6-3/4" l 30.00

7-1/4" l, Art Nouveau design
    .... 45.00

7-1/4" l, shield shaped handle,
    hallmark for Birmingham,
    England, 1907 .... 25.00

Buttonhook, plastic handle with pearlized green ground, delicate etched design,
7-1/2" l, **$3.**

Buttons

Buttons are collected according to age, material, and subject matter. The National Button Society, founded in 1939, has designated 1918 as the dividing line between old and modern buttons. Shanks and backmarks are important elements to consider when determining age.

Bakelite

Log, carved, red...................... 2.50
Round, maroon, two hole sew
through, 1-1/8" d............... 7.00
Tortoiseshell, large disc, 2-1/8" d
.... 5.00

Black glass

Gold luster, fabric-look, self shank,
mkd "Le Mode," 1950s, 7/8" l
.... 4.00
Silver luster, petal look, self shank
with threaded groove, mkd "Le
Chic," 1950s, 13/16" 4.00

Brass, Picador, tinted, steel back, wire
shank, 1-1/8" d 10.00

Carnival glass, purple

Buckle & Scrolls, 5/8" d........ 10.00
Frog....................................... 12.00
Lazy Wheel, 5/8" d 12.00
Windmill, 5/8" d.................. 14.00

Celluloid

1" d, pink, cup shaped, gold painted
deer escutcheon, celluloid shank
.... 5.00
1-1/2" d, metal fox head, pink
rhinestone eyes 9.50

China

5/8" d, black and white........... 7.00
5/8" d, luster, orange rim........ 7.00
7/16" d, blue calico 8.50
1/2", luster and orange rim 7.00

Cloisonné, 1-1/2" d, mermaid, hand
made, shank 32.00

Figural, plastic
Apple, realistic coloring, metal
shank................................. 1.25
Flower basket, pastels, metal shank
.... 1.50
Mouse, small, blue, self shank 3.00

Kaleidoscope, 1/2" d, gold and silver
flecks...................................... 18.50

Lucite, clear
1-1/8" d, red pansy 25.00
1-1/2" d, carved underside color
.... 10.00

Metal

1/2" d, brass colored pointalist field,
silver eight-pointed starburst in
center, japanned, wire shank
.... 10.00
1/2" d, silvered, wreath of three
pronged leaves, small raised
center dot, two-pc construction,
japanned back, wire shank 10.00
1/2" d, steelcut center............. 4.50
1" d, shell and steelcut.......... 10.00
1-1/2" d, lady lounging, twinkle
background, metal shank
.... 19.00

Moonglow, glass
1/2" d, green flower, gold trim 2.00

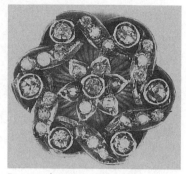

Buttons, rhinestone and enamel, central
floral decoration, shank type, **$2.50.**

1/2" d, white, gold trim, four lobed,
self shank 2.00

Pewter, stamped, 1-1/2" d, The
Trumpeter of Cracow, lead pewter
mounted over painted metal brass
back with shelf shank............ 12.50

Plastic, 1-5/8" d, metal insert of
woman's head, attached celluloid
loop shank 10.00

Rhinestone, pot metal
1/2" x 1", bug 36.00
1" d, round............................. 32.00

Byers' Choice

Joyce Byers started creating colorful singing Christmas carolers in the late 1960s. By 1978, this home occupation developed into a family business and financial success. Today Byers' Choice is located in Chalfont, PA, and visitors to the busy facility can see Carolers, Williamsburg figures, and other Byers' Choice personalities come to life. The secondary market for these figures is just starting to become established. Expect to see some fluctuation in pricing.

American Red Cross nurse, 1999
.... 90.00

Belsnickel, 1998 .... 95.00

Bob Cratchit, and Tiny Tim, 1990
.... 75.00

Boy

Holding lamb, 1996 .... 75.00
Holding skates, 1990 .... 45.00
Plaid jacket, tree, logs, 1992
.... 70.00
With goose in basket, 1995
.... 45.00

Butcher, 1995 .... 75.00

Candle seller, 1998.................. 75.00

Caroler

Man, sheet music, 1992........ 55.00
Woman, mink muff, 1991 .... 65.00

Byers' Choice, man feeding birds, sitting
on wooden bench, **$75.**

Chimney Sweep, ladder, 1991 75.00

Conductor, with stand, 1989... 75.00

Couple in sleigh, 1995.......... 160.00

Doll seller, 1995....................... 75.00

Drosselmeier, 1996 .... 50.00

Father Christmas, 1992........ 160.00

Family, three in sleigh, 1995.. 190.00

Flower seller, with basket of flowers,
1994 .... 55.00

Gingerbread maker, and cart, 1996
.... 95.00

Girl

Basket of holly, 1996............. 50.00
Tree, 1990 .... 55.00

Byers' Choice, Williamsburg man, **$50.**

Grandmother, doll and presents, 1996 .... 55.00

Lamplighter, ladder and torch, 1994 .... 70.00

Man
 Crabtree and Evelyn, 1996 ... 65.00
 Holding basket of pinecones, 1998 .... 50.00
 Holding Christmas tree and ornaments, 1996 .... 100.00
 Seated on bench, feeding birds, 1997 .... 75.00
 With toy horse, wreath, and presents, 1995 .... 140.00

Mrs. Claus, 1987 .... 65.00

Old Befana, 1992 .... 55.00

Old woman, with presents, 1992 .... 80.00

Photographer, camera on tripod, 1998 .... 95.00

Policeman, 1994 .... 50.00

Puppeteer, 1996 .... 95.00

Salvation Army
 Boy with flag, 1997 .... 45.00
 Girl, 1995 .... 65.00
 Man with drum, 1996 .... 50.00
 Man with trumpet, 1993 ...... 45.00

Man with tuba, 1998 .... 50.00
Woman with bell and kettle, 1992 .... 70.00
Woman with tambourine, 1994 .... 95.00

Santa
 With list, 1987 .... 95.00
 With reindeer treats and deer, 1997 .... 160.00

Schoolgirl, lunch pail, 1993..... 75.00

School teacher, 1992 .... 160.00

Skater
 Boy, 1995 .... 60.00
 Girl, 1994 .... 60.00

Snowman with broom, 1992. 75.00

Soloist, 1996 .... 55.00

St. Lucia, 1996 .... 60.00

St. Nicolas, gift sack, pipe, 1996 .... 60.00

Toddler and doll on sled, 1991, white snowsuit 55.00

Toy maker Santa, 1995 .... 160.00

Williamsburg
 Drummer, 1999 .... 65.00
 Fifer, 1999 .... 65.00

Byers' Choice, left: Williamsburg boy with recorder; right: girl with pickle, each **$45.**

Byers' Choice, Happy Scrooge, **$95.**

Girl with hoop, 1998 .... 50.00
Man, 1998, orig box 60.00
Woman, 1998........................ 75.00

Woman
 Crabtree & Evelyn, 1996....... 55.00
 In velvet gown, music, 1989 .... 90.00
 With basket of apples and goose, 1995 .... 130.00
 With black fur muff, 1996.... 70.00
 With gingerbread man and goose, 1995, orig box 80.00
 With toddler, 1994................ 70.00
 With white mink muff, 1990 .... 65.00

Wreath seller, wreath stand, 1997 .... 130.00

Cake Collectibles

Here's a sweet collectible for you. In our recent trips to flea markets, we've seen more and more of these items. Doesn't anyone bake anymore? It certainly seems as if there are a lot of cake pans for sale! More and more collectors are also seeking out vintage bride and groom cake toppers.

Cake cutting set, Fagley Junior Card Party Cake Cutters, deck of cards, heart, diamond, spade and club, orig 3-1/2" x 3-1/2" box **15.00**

Cake plate
China, white ground, pink roses **60.00**
Depression-era glass, colorless, block type pattern, matching aluminum cover **65.00**

Cake collectibles, icing knife, "Swans Down Cake Flour Makes Better Cakes," 12-2/3" l, **$5.**

Candle holders, for birthday cake, plastic, pink, c1950, set of 20 ... **2.00**

Cookie board, wood, metal top, 12 impressions **35.00**

Decoration, 2" h hard plastic figure of Batman or Robin, 1960s **8.00**

Pan
Bird shape, old **30.00**
Child's building block shape . **10.00**
Christmas tree shape, Wilton.. **7.50**
Garfield shape **15.00**
Santa shape **10.00**

Topper
Bells, pink satin **25.00**
Bride and Groom, tulle on base, orig flowers, c1945 .... **65.00**
Bugs Bunny, six matching birthday candle holders, Wilton, 1978 .... **24.00**

Snoopy **24.00**
Snow White **24.00**

Cake collectibles, cake plate, white ground, multicolored flowers and green luster trim, marked "Silesien (crown crossed swords) Germany," **$30.**

Cake collectibles, plate, white, gold trim, self handles, **$35.**

Calculators

What would we do without pocket calculators? Some of the first models are beginning to command steep prices; however, as with most other collectibles, condition is important. Collectors also want the original box and instruction sheet. Don't overlook examples with advertising.

Addiator Duplex, brass **25.00**

Belltown Antique Car Club Show, 30th Anniversary, Aug. 4, 1996, "A World of Thanks," 2-1/4" x 3-1/2" **5.00**

Bohn Instant **30.00**

Bowmar, 901B **70.00**

Burger King, Nickelodeon, 1999, 3-1/2" l **5.00**

Burroughs **55.00**

Casio, HL-809, 2-3/4" x 4-1/2", MIB **25.00**

Commodore, MM1 .... **75.00**

Craig, 4502 .... **55.00**

Lloyds, 303 .... **20.00**

National **25.00**

Novus, 650 Mathbox, 2-1/2" x 5" **18.00**

Political, 2" x 2" x 2-1/4", high gloss cardboard replica of matchbook cover, miniature plastic calculator, one side with gold presidential official emblem, tiny George Bush facsimile signature, simulated striker side with gold image of helicopter at White House lawn, inscribed "Presidential Helicopter Squadron-1," given to those who flew on helicopter during George H. W. Bush's presidency **40.00**

Calculators, solar powered, silvered front, black engraved plaque, "Compliments of J. P. Smalley Auction Co.," **$5.**

Radio Shack, EC 425 .... 50.00
Royal, Digital 3 .... 110.00

Wendy's, pen, pencil, and calculator set.. 6.00

Calendar Plates

Many of these interesting plates were made as giveaways for local merchants. They were often produced by popular manufacturers of the day, such as Homer Laughlin and Royal China. Many have fanciful gold trim and interesting scenes. Expect to pay more for a plate that is sold in the area where it originated.

Calendar plate, 1961, God Bless This House, zodiac signs, blue and white, marked "Alfred Meakin, Staffordshire, England," **$18.50.**

1906, compliments of A. K. Clemmer, Kulpsville, PA, scattered florals and calendar pages, crazing, stains 25.00

1906, seasonal floral sprigs, scattered calendar pages, gold lettering "Prince Furniture Co., Complete Home Furnishers, No. 502 Hamilton St., Allentown, Pa," beaded edges 90.00

1907, compliments Pownall Hardware Co. Coatsville, PA, four pretty girls, calendar in center, gold lettering 70.00

1908, compliments of A. A. Eckert, General Merchandise, Packerton, PA pretty girl, calendar pages in center, gold lettering 55.00

1909, compliments of D. H. Sharrer, Manufacturer and Dealer in Choice Flour, Feed Grain, etc., New Chester, Pa, brown striped kitten, gold lettering, calendar pages around edge............................ 45.00

1909, compliments of John U. Francis, Jr., Fancy and Staple Groceries,

Oaks, PA, Iron Stone China, with lion and shield mark 35.00

1910, W. P. Stellmach, Bottler, Schlitz Beer, Shamokin, PA, pretty lady in red touring outfit, driving early auto, seasonal floral sprigs, calendar pages, gold text 65.00

1913, Wm F. Weber, Allentown, PA holly and roses dec, gold trimmed edge... 95.00

1915, Klopp & Kalbach, North Heidelburg, PA, cobalt blue border with gold trim, flags, calendar pages, map of Panama Canal, address on front 25.00

1916, E. G. Hassler, Groceries, Dry Goods & Notions, 500 Schuykill Ave, Reading, PA, pretty girl, calendar pages, blue birds, green ribbon garland on border, gold lettering and edge................. 80. 00

1917, compliments of E. D. Reitter, Hoppenville, PA, pair of grazing deer, calendar pages on border and flags, gold lettering................ 65.00

1920, compliments of H. R. Sloan, Springfield, MO, multicolored flags of several nations, American flag in

Calendar plate, 1910, dog motif, "Compliments of the Summitville Bank," **$45.**

Calendar plate, 1909, John Kemper, Harness Maker, Butler, Pa, Mediterranean woman in center, marked "Voorey," 9" d, **$45.**

center, back mkd "D. E. McNicol, East Liverpool, O 918," crazing 60.00

1955, floral wreath, Simplicity, Canonsburg, 10" d 15.00

1960, Zodiac figures, edge chip, 9-1/2" d 6.50

1961, English cottage and bridge, "God Bless This House Through All This Year," Royal Staffordshire, 9" d 18.50

1964, montage of New Jersey map, capitol dome, state seal and Revolutionary War soldier, "The State of New Jersey 1664 Tercentenary 1964," Kettlesprings Kilns, Alliance, Ohio, 10-1/8" d 28.00

1971, cherubs playing and working, Wedgwood, 9-7/8" d............. 32.00

1974, God Bless Our House, maroon and white, mkd "Alfred Meakin Staffordshire England," 9" d 7.50

Calendars

Ever since the advent of the new millennium, calendars seem be everywhere. A stroll through your favorite flea market may not yield as many contemporary versions as a trip to the local bookstore, but some interesting vintage examples certainly await collectors. Vintage calendars often contain artwork by the best illustrators of the day, in addition to advertising, household hints, and necessary timely information.

Calendar, 1925, W. J. Keefer, Shanksville, PA, girl in pretty broad brimmed hat, full calendar pad, **$45.**

1897, pansy, each page with different litho of a pansy, scalloped edges, printed in Bavaria, designed in England, 6" x 4-1/4" **65.00**

1908, woman with red poppies, heavily emb, adv for J.I. Sawyel, General Merchandise, Smithshire, IL, full pad, 10" x 14" **270.00**

1909, American Clay Machinery Co., pocket size, bound in leather-type material, world maps, populations of US states, 2-1/2" w, 4-1/2" h **12.00**

1913, Swift's Premium, 4 pages, each with different scene, 17" x 9" **20.00**

1918, Swift's Premium, The Girl I Leave Behind Me, soldier saying goodbye, illus by Haskell Coffin, sheets for January to March, pc missing, 15" x 8-1/4" **100.00**

1924, Red Goose Shoes, Getting His Goat, mountain goat hunter, H. C. Edwards, artist, ads for Red Goose Shoes, Friedman-Shelby Shoe Co, Atlantic Shoes, Pacific Shoes, 8" x 19" wall type **25.00**

1931, Midland Wood Products, Midland, Ontario, each page is different model home with floor plan on reverse, 9-3/4" x 5-1/2" **35.00**

1935, Harmon Coal Co., Columbus, OH, weekly memo type **20.00**

1936, Seasons Greetings, Moss Grocery Store, Montpelier, MO, 8 w, 16" h, creases to cardboard **7.00**

1951, Puzzling Pups, Kinghon, 10" x 17" **60.00**

1952, Songbird Families, series 6, Betty Carnes, watercolors by Roger Tory Peterson, published by Barton-Cotton Co. **12.75**

1959, Ramco Piston Rings, tin, stand-up type **12.00**

Calendar, 1941, K & L Lumber, Quakertown, PA, shows bungalow styles, **$18.**

1960, Look for the Sign of Happy Motoring, Esso Gas, adv for R. Y. Foster, Johnson City, TN, 14-3/4" x 8-1/2" **48.00**

1963, Seattle World's Fair, linen towel, 30" x 15-1/4" **38.00**

1976, Mischief Makers, three puppies and a basket, full calendar pad, Leo's Shoe Store, Rehrersburg, Pa., 16-1/2" x 10" **12.00**

California Potteries

This catchall category includes small studio potteries located in California.

Will & George Climes
  Bluebird figurine, paper label, 3-1/4" h............................. **40.00**
  Robin figurine, paper label, 3" h **40.00**

Freeman & McFarlin, elephant figurine, orig foil sticker, chips on ear and trunk, 6" h, 7-1/2" l **55.00**

Garden City Pottery
  Flower pot, matte black, conical, 10" w, 8-3/4" h **175.00**
  Flower pot and saucer, yellow, 13" w, 11-1/8" h, 12-5/8" d saucer **160.00**

Hollydale, chop plate, gold-yellow, swirled edges, 11-1/2" d **22.00**

Madeline Original, vase......... **35.00**

California Potteries, "Artist California" Gouder vase, 5" h, 9-1/2" w, cracked, **$12.**

Maurice of California, covered cigarette and two ashtrays, white with gold trim, three pcs....... 25.00

Pierce Porcelains, Howard Pierce Bowl, 13" l, free-form, black ext., speckled black and white int., 1950s 75.00
Candleholders, pr, 2-3/4" h, comma shape, high gloss gray glaze 100.00
Jug, 5-3/4" h, bulbous, brown mottled rough textured glaze, stamp mark 110.00
Planter, 7" h, white bisque angel holding songbook 175.00

California Potteries, California Faience, vase, 1920s, 4" h, **$115.**

Santa Rosa, L.A. Potteries, plate, hp plums, 10-1/8" d 18.00

Evan K. Shaw, bud vase, Bugs Bunny, mkd "N 10," 7" h 185.00

Treasure Craft, ashtray 12.00

Cambridge Glass

Cambridge Glass Company of Cambridge, Ohio, was incorporated in 1901. Initially, the company made clear tableware, but it later expanded into colored, etched, and engraved glass. More than 40 different hues were produced in blown and pressed glass. Cambridge used five different marks, but not every piece was marked. The plant closed in 1954, with some of the molds being sold to the Imperial Glass Company in Bellaire, Ohio.

For additional listings, see *Warman's Antiques & Collectibles* and *Warman's Glass*.

Cambridge Glass Co., dinner plate, clear, etched Cleo pattern, **$45.**

Banana bowl, Inverted Thistle, 7" l, radium green, mkd "Near-cut" 95.00

Bonbon, Diane, crystal, 8-1/2". 25.00

Bookends, pr, eagle, crystal 65.00

Bowl and underplate, Wildflower, crystal, gold trim 385.00

Butter dish, cov, Gadroon, crystal 45.00

Candy dish, cov, Wildflower, crystal, three parts 20.00

Celery tray, Gloria, five-part ... 70.00

Champagne, Wildflower, crystal 24.00

Cigarette box, Caprice, blue, 3-1/2" x 4-1/2" 70.00

Claret, Wildflower, crystal, 4-1/2 oz 42.00

Cocktail
Caprice, blue 48.00
Diane, crystal 15.00

Comport, Shell Line, Crown Tuscan 55.00

Creamer and sugar
Caprice, crystal 35.00
Cascade, emerald green 35.00

Cup and saucer
Decagon, pink 10.00
Martha Washington............. 45.00

Decanter set, decanter, stopper, six handled 2-1/2 oz tumblers, Tally Ho, amethyst....................... 185.00

Finger bowl, Adam, yellow 25.00

Flower frog
Draped Lady, dark pink 185.00
Nude, crystal, 6-1/2" h.......... 95.00
Seagull, crystal..................... 85.00

Fruit bowl, Decagon, pink, 5-1/2" d 5.50

Goblet
Chantilly, crystal.................. 35.00
Rose Point, crystal, 10 oz 30.00

Ice bucket, Chrysanthemum, pink, silver handle 85.00

Iced tea tumbler, Lexington ... 18.00

Lemon plate, Caprice, blue, 5" d 15.00

Nut bowl, Diane, crystal, tab handle 58.00

Plate
Apple Blossom, pink, 8-1/2" d 20.00
Decagon, pink, 8" 8.00

Relish
Caprice, club, #170, blue 115.00
Mt. Vernon, five parts, crystal 35.00

Server, center handle, Apple Blossom, amber...................................... 30.00

Sherbet, Daffodil, crystal 27.50

Swan, crystal, sgd, 7" 35.00

Tumbler
Adam, yellow, ftd................. 25.00
Caprice, blue, 12-oz, ftd 40.00

Vase
Diane, crystal, keyhole, 12" h 110.00
Shell, #131, Crown Tuscan 175.00

Wine
Caprice, crystal 24.00
Diane, crystal, 2-1/2 oz 30.00

Cameras and Accessories

Many cameras and their accessories and ephemera find their way to flea markets. Carefully check completeness and condition. To some extent, value will be determined by the type of lens or the special features available on a particular model.

For additional listings, see *Warman's Antiques & Collectibles* and *Warman's Americana & Collectibles*.

Cameras and accessories, tripod, Folmer & Schwing Div, wood legs, large top, **$200.**

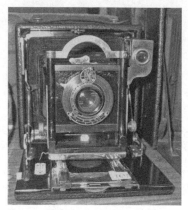

Cameras and accessories, Eastman Kodak, **$80.**

Cameras and accessories, Rolleiflex, **$75.**

Accessories, Kodak Kodachrome box, bag and metal film can, 1959 .... 12.00

Beaker, clear glass, footed, "Use Only Kodak For Photography," 4" h 20.00

Camera
Agfa Isolette 30.00
Ansco, Vest Pocket No. 1, c1915, strut-type folding camera 30.00
Argus Argoflex 75 .... 10.00
Bell & Howell, Stereo Colorist I 80.00
Canon Canonette 45.00

CMC Camera 30.00
Houghton, London, Ensign Greyhound, folding 18.00
Kodak Bantam f8, c1940, Bakelite body 25.00
Kodak Brownie Hawkeye 5.00
Kodak Duaflex 10.00
Kodak Hawkeye No. 2C 5.00
Kodak Tourist II 15.00
Minolta 16, 1960s 35.00
Pho-tak Corp., Marksman, 1950s 10.00
Polaroid 95, 1948 .... 25.00
Universal, Univex Minicam . 50.00
Voigtlander Avus 60.00

Sign, 15" x 18", Dupont Defender Photographic Products, buff gray wooden frame holding black and white semi-gloss photo enlargements of scenic mountain view and three posed young ladies, both have "Defender" name centered on bottom of frame, applied yellow blue paper sticker with Dupont slogan, 1940s, price for pr 18.00

Trimming board, Kodak, No. 1, 5-x-6 wooden base 20.00

Cameras and accessories, Cycle Poco #2, **$65.**

Campbell's Soup

Joseph Campbell and Abram Anderson started a canning plant in Camden, New Jersey, in 1869, but it wasn't until 1897 that the facility began producing soup. The red-and-white Campbell's label was introduced in 1898, and the gold medallion that graced the company's cans until just recently was awarded in 1900. The pudgy, round-faced Campbell Kids were introduced in 1904, but their contemporary physiques are slimmer and trimmer.

Baby dish, shows Campbell's Kids, 7-1/2" d 55.00

Bank, ceramic, 1970s 70.00

Book, *The Campbell's Kids at Home* by Alma S. Lach, Rand McNally Elf Book, 1954, story by Alma S. Lach, minor wear 35.00

Christmas ornament 15.00

Cookbook, *The Soup and Sandwich Handbook*, Campbell Soups, thermal mug on cover, 1971 . 12.00

Doll, boy and girl, vinyl, orig clothes, pr 115.00

Novelty radio, tomato soup can shape, orig box 45.00

Campbell's Soup collectibles, soup mug, marked "Produced for Houston Harvest Gift Products LLC, Made in China, Franklin Park, IL," copyright 1998 & trademarks licensed by Campbell Soup Company, All Rights Reserved, **$5.**

Pennants, pr, felt, "Campbell's Soups," white text, red ground, one shows child in rocker, one shows child with pail, 21" h, 8" w 200.00

Poster, Campbell's Kids behind board promoting weekly grocer's specials, can of soup in lower-left corner, tears, framed, 30" h, 23" w 90.00

Soup mug, ceramic, multicolored transfer of Campbell Kid in chef's hat 5.00

Watch, 1" goldtone case, black plastic strap, face with boy in green shorts carrying lunch box, 1982 ...... 45.00

Candlesticks

Designed to keep a burning candle upright, candlesticks can be found in all shapes and sizes at flea markets. Don't be afraid to mix and match odd ones, making for an interesting functional display. The prices listed here are for pairs of candlesticks, the most desirable way to buy them. Discount these prices by 50 to 75 percent when purchasing a single example.

Candlesticks, Romanesque, L.E. Smith Glass, 2-1/2" h, pair, **$22.**

Brass
  Queen Anne, ring-turned base, boldly turned column, orig pushup, 12" h 275.00
  Saucer base, push-ups, tooled rings around columns, 4-1/2" h 175.00
  Victorian, beehive, pushup, mkd England, 6" h 165.00

Ceramic, figural
  Angels, Holt Howard, 1960, 4" h 50.00
  Girls, Norcrest, hands in muffs, red coats, 4-1/2" h 40.00

  Mr & Mrs. Claus, unmarked, colorful, 4" h 25.00
  Reindeer, Lefton, 4-1/2" h 45.00

Glass
  Black, low, Fostoria 65.00
  Crystal, L.E. Smith, 4-1/2" h 32.50
  Milk glass, Dolphin pattern, Westmoreland, 4-1/2" h ... 45.00

Candlestick, porcelain, figural pierrot seated with legs outstretched, bowl supporting candle socket resting on legs, blue decoration on white, green anchor mark, 8" l, 6-1/2" h, **$210.**

Candlesticks, camphor glass, yellow-green, 7" h, **$70.**

Graniteware, white, saucer base, ring handle 40.00

Porcelain, ivory, gold accents, Lenox 75.00

Pottery
  Hull, Blossomtime, T11 .... 75.00
  Niloak, Mission Ware 90.00

Tin, Tindeco, orig stenciling, 6-3/4" h 65.00

Candlewick

Imperial pattern No. 400, known as Candlewick, was introduced in 1936 and was an instant hit with American consumers. The line was continuously produced until 1982. After Imperial declared bankruptcy, several of the molds were sold, and other companies began producing this pattern, often in different colors.

For additional listings, see *Warman's Americana & Collectibles, Warman's Glass* and *Warman's Depression Glass.*

Reproduction alert.

Candlewick, candleholder, two lites, **$65.**

Candlewick, relish, 400/112, 10-1/2" d, three-part, well for mayonnaise jar, **$75.**

Candlewick, relish, 400/256, two-part, 10-1/2" l, oval, two tab handles, **$25.**

After dinner cup and saucer
.... 20.00

Ashtray, 400/150, 6" d, large beads, pink... 15.00

Atomizer, 400/247 shaker, atomizer top, amethyst 150.00

Baked apple dish, 6-1/2" 25.00

Basket, turned-up sides, applied handle, 6-1/2"........................ 35.00

Bell, 400/108, four-bead handle, 4" h
.... 60.00

Bonbon, #51H, heart shape, handle, 6".. 35.00

Bowl, #106B, belled, 12" d........ 70.00

Bud vase, 400/25, 3-3/4" h, beaded foot, ball shape, crimped top 35.00

Butter dish, 1/4-pound............ 25.00

Cake plate, sterling silver pedestal
.... 65.00

Canape plate, #36.................... 12.00

Candleholder, rolled saucer, 3-1/2" h
.... 15.00

Candy dish, cov, 400/59, 5-1/2" d, two-bead finial 40.00

Celery tray, #105, 13" 40.00

Champagne, saucer................. 20.00

Cigarette holder, eagle 95.00

Coaster 12.00

Cocktail set, 6" d plate with 2-1/2" off-center indent, #111 1-bead cocktail glass.......................... 35.00

Compote, four-bead stem, 8" d
.... 65.00

Cordial, flared belled top four graduated beads in stem 48.00

Creamer and sugar, question mark handle 30.00

Cup and saucer, #37, coffee.... 14.00

Deviled egg tray, 11-1/2" d..... 95.00

Float bowl, 11" d...................... 55.00

Goblet, flared bell bowl, four graduated beads in stem, 9 oz
.... 15.00

Iced tea tumbler, 400/19, beaded base, straight sides 15.00

Jelly server, one bead stem, two-bead cover 50.00

Candlewick, nappy, sweetheart shape, **$12.**

Candlewick, oval relish dish, 4-5/8" x 8-1/2", **$15.**

Marmalade jar, cov 60.00	10-1/4" d 35.00	**Tidbit server**, two tiers 60.00
Mint dish, 5" d, applied handle 20.00	**Relish**, #55, 4 part 30.00	**Tumbler**, water, 400/19, beaded base, straight sides, 10 oz, 4-3/4" h 18.00
Pastry tray, #68D, floral cutting, 11-1/2" l 80.00	**Salt and pepper shakers**, pr, #247 .... 45.00	
Plate, beaded edge 6" d .... 8.00 8-1/2" d 12.00	**Sherbet**, low, #19, 5-oz .... 18.00 **Tea cup and saucer** 15.00	**Vase**, 400/87F, fan, 8" h .... 30.00 **Wine**, belled bowl, hollow trumpet stem with beads, 5 oz 25.00

Candy Containers

Figural glass candy containers have been a part of childhood since 1876, when they were first introduced at the Centennial Exposition in Philadelphia. These interesting glass containers often commemorated historical events. Candy containers were also made of papier-mâché, cardboard, and tin. All are highly collectible and eagerly sought at flea markets.

For additional listings, see *Warman's Antiques & Collectibles*.

Reproduction alert.

Battleship, glass, orig cardboard closure, printed "Victory Glass Inc." 48.00

Black cat, with pumpkin, papier-mâché, German 75.00

Boat, clear glass, orig label, 5-1/4" l 40.00

Boot, papier-mâché, red and white 24.00

Bulldog, clear glass, orig paint 90.00

Dog, blue glass 15.00

Duck, cardboard, nodding head 18.50

Football, tin, German 35.00

Candy containers, left: chicken with kerchief, yellow body, right: horse with chenille ears, green and pink body, composition and papier-mâché bodies, springs for necks, each **$35.**

Hen on nest, milk glass, two pcs 15.00

Irishman, top hat and pipe, papier-mâché 12.00

Lantern, large, glass and metal 35.00

Locomotive, #888, clear glass, 4" l 35.00

Model T, clear glass 24.00

Owl, glass, stylized feathers, painted, screw-on cap 90.00

Pistol, clear glass 30.00

Rabbit, papier-mache, pulling basket, pasteboard wheels 55.00

Rooster, clear glass, screw-on cap 125.00

Santa Claus, plastic, standing, opening for candy in back, Rosbro Plastics, 5" h 30.00

Suitcase, cardboard, The Leader Novelty Candy Co., 2-1/2" h, 2-3/4" w 35.00

Telephone, clear, glass, candlestick type 50.00

Truck, Cherrydale Farms, metal, movable wheels, labeled "Nobel Hall Made in China," 7" l, 3-1/2" w, 4" h 5.00

Turkey, chalk, metal feet, German 35.00

Candy containers, rabbit, pressed glass, clear, no closure, **$40.**

Candy containers, chicken on nest, pressed glass, clear, no closure, **$30.**

Cap Guns

"Bang! Bang!" was the cry of many a youngster playing Cowboys and Indians. Whether you were the good guy or the bad guy, you needed a reliable six-shooter. The first toy cap gun was produced in the 1870s and was made of cast iron. It remained the material of choice until around World War II, when paper, rubber, glass, steel, tin, wood and even zinc were used. By the 1950s, diecast metal and plastic were being used.

Cap guns, left: unmarked, black grip, played with condition, **$5;** top: Hubley, "Gold Rodeo," c1955, **$110;** right: RTS, Made in Italy, **$10;** bottom: Kilgore, "Eagle," 1950-55, **$85.**

Border Patrol, Kilgore, cast iron 70.00

Buck'n Bronc 115.00

Buffalo Bill, J.&E. Stevens, repeating, 1920s, orig box 320.00

Champion, Kilgore, brown grips, 1960s, 11" l 70.00

Cheyenne Shooter, Hamilton 70.00

Circle A, Oh Boy series 65.00

Derringer, Hubley, white plastic handle, worn, 3-1/4" l 7.50

Dynamite, MIB 85.00

Fanner 50, Mattel
Impala grips, c1962, 10-1/2" l 55.00
Stag grips, c1959, 10-1/2" l. 210.00

Flintlock, double barrel, Hubley, amber color, 9" l 25.00

Gene Autry .44, Leslie-Henry, 1950s, 11" l 165.00

Hubley, white handle, 11" l.... 125.00

Invincible, Kilgore, cast iron, c1938, 5" l 35.00

Kusan, #280 .... 15.00

Maverick
Long barrel, black and white grips, 1960s, 11" l 280.00
Short barrel, nickel finish, new white grips, 1960s, 9" l..... 55.00

Cap guns, here is an assortment of cap guns, ranging in price from **$20** to **$45.**

Pony Boy, orig black and white holster, 1950s, 9-1/2" l 45.00

Presto, 5" w, 3-1/4" h 40.00

Red Ranger, Wyandotte 175.00

Roy Rogers, double holster and gun set, Kilgore 225.00

Texan, Hubley, 1940s, black grips, 9-1/2" l 130.00

Wagon Trail, white grips, 9" l 175.00

Cape Cod by Avon

This ruby red pattern was an instant hit with Avon lovers. Today, many pieces can be found at flea markets. Remember that this is a mass-produced pattern and examples in very good condition are available.

Butter dish, cov, MIB 65.00

Candleholder, MIB 27.50

Candy dish, MIB 40.00

Coffee cup 12.00

Cape Cod, luncheon plate, red, **$10.**

Creamer, orig scented candle, MIB 37.50

Cruet 20.00

Dessert plate 8.00

Dinner plate, 11" d, 1982, MIB 37.50

Goblet 8.00

Luncheon plate 10.00

Mug, ftd, two in orig box 30.00

Napkin rings, 1-3/4" d, set of four 45.00

Platter, MIB 37.50

Salad plate 8.00

Salt and pepper shakers, pr, MIB 42.00

Saucer 6.00

Cape Cod, salt and pepper shakers, 4-1/2" h, pair, **$42.**

Tumbler 18.00	**Water pitcher**, 48-oz, 7-1/2" h 40.00	**Wine decanter** 36.00
Vase, ftd, 8" h 24.00	**Wine goblet**, MIB 18.00	

Carnival Chalkware

Brightly painted plaster-of-Paris figures given away as prizes at carnivals continue to capture the eye of collectors. Most of these figures date from the 1920s through the 1960s.

Carnival chalkware, bank, bull dog, black, white, gray, yellow, red, and blue, dark olive green collar, large, **$35.**

Carnival chalkware, figure, woman in blue dress, holding skirt up with one hand, **$35.**

Carnival chalkware, zebra, **$45.**

Ashtray
  Collie, 8-3/4" h, ashtray 3-1/2" d
  .... 22.00
  German shepherd, dated 1936,
    paint loss, 8-1/2" h 20.00

Bank, dog, long ears, yellow bow tie, wear, 12" h 32.00

Figure
  Cocker spaniel, reclining 20.00

Collie, black and white, some
  glitter, base chips, 11-1/2" h
  .... 40.00
Elephant by tree stump, three chips,
  6" h 15.00
Horse, flat back side, 5-1/2" h **15.00**
Poodle, sitting, 3-1/2" h........ 10.00
Scottie, two dogs side by side, chips,
  9-1/4" h............................. 85.00
Superman, 1940s, 15-3/8" h **165.00**
Tex, cowboy, 11" h 20.00

Carnival Glass

Carnival glass can be found in many different colors, including marigold, purples, greens, blues, reds, and pastels, all with a metallic-looking sheen or iridescence. Many different manufacturers created the hundreds of patterns.

For additional listings, see *Warman's Carnival Glass*, *Warman's Antiques & Collectibles*, *Warman's Glass*.

Reproduction alert.

Banana boat, Grape and Cable, Northwood, purple 185.00

Berry bowl, individual, Peacock at Fountain, Northwood, purple, 5" d 35.00

Berry bowl, master, Grape and Cable, Northwood, emerald green . 145.00

Bonbon, Grape and Cable, Northwood, two handles, marigold 50.00

Bowl
  Fan Tail, Fenton, blue 20.00
  Fruits & Flowers, amethyst, 7-1/4" d
  .... 70.00

Holly Whirl, marigold, radium
  .... 85.00
Kittens, six ruffles, marigold
  .... 135.00
Orange Tree, tree trunk center,
  white, 9" d 90.00
Peacock & Grape, marigold, 9" d
  .... 50.00

Carnival glass, bowl, Blackberry Wreath, 7" d, **$80.**

Peacock at Urn, green, 10-1/2" d 250.00
Raindrops, peach opalescent, 8-3/4" d............................ 85.00
Stag & Holly, ruffled, powder blue, marigold overlay 200.00
Strawberry, pie crust edge, purple, 8" d 90.00
Vintage Leaf, green, 7-1/2" d 72.00

Bushel basket, white, Northwood 120.00

Butter dish, cov, Grape and Cable, Northwood, green 175.00

Calling card tray, Pond Lily, white 25.00

Candy dish, Drapery, white... 125.00

Compote, Wild Flower, light marigold 65.00

Hat, Blackberry Spray, green, two sides up, 6-1/2" h.................... 95.00

Hatpin holder, Grape and Cable, Northwood, purple.............. 175.00

Ice cream bowl, Daisy Wreath, Westmoreland, moonstone, 8-1/2" d 110.00

Mug, 3-1/2" h
Orange Tree, aqua 60.00
Singing Birds, amethyst 215.00

Nappy, Heavy Grape, electric purple 110.00

Pickle dish, Poppy, blue........... 45.00

Pitcher, 9" h, Butterfly & Berry, marigold 265.00

Plate, Adam & Eve, Fenton, blue 10.00

Punch cup
Hobstar & Feather 25.00
Wreath of Roses, Vintage int., blue 40.00

Punch set, Grape, Imperial, marigold 300.00

Rose bowl
Double Stem, domed foot, peach opalescent...................... 160.00
Fine Cut & Roses, purple ... 135.00
Frosted Block, deep marigold 30.00

Sweetmeat compote, cov, Grape and Cable, Northwood, purple... 170.00

Tankard pitcher, Paneled Dandelion, marigold 400.00

Toothpick holder, Kittens, ruffled, marigold, radium finish...... 115.00

Tumble-up, Smooth Rays, marigold 60.00

Tumbler
Butterfly & Berry, marigold . 30.00

Carnival glass, rose bowl, Swirled Hobnail, Millersburg, **$165.**

Concave Diamond, Celeste blue 30.00
Peacock at Fountain, amethyst 25.00
Tiger Lily, marigold.............. 75.00

Vase
Morning Glory, 6-1/2" h, olive green, 6-1/2" h.................. 60.00
Ripple, amethyst, 11" h 110.00
Thin Rib, 10" h, blue, 10" h.. 60.00

Water pitcher
Grape, Imperial, electric purple 600.00
Peacock at Fountain, Northwood, amethyst......................... 250.00

Water set, Cardinal, Westmoreland, white, hp red birds, seven pcs 125.00

Wine set, Golden Harvest, purple, seven pcs................................. 75.00

Cartoon Characters

They've entertained generations for decades and now collectors seek them out at flea markets. The charm and humor of cartoon characters light up collections across the country.

Bank, The Jetsons, spaceship, licensed by Hanna Barbera 375.00

Big little book
Ella Cinders and the Mysterious House, Whitman #1106, 1934 .... 55.00
Smitty In Going Native, Whitman #1477, wear 20.00
Tom and Jerry Meet Mr. Fingers 20.00

Birthday card, Ziggy, unused ... 1.00

Bubble gum wrapper, Popeye, 1981, 5-1/2" x 5-1/2" 45.00

Charm, Shmoo, bright silver-colored plastic, 1940s 18.00

Colorforms, Huckleberry Hound, 1960, MIB 75.00

Coloring book
Mr. Peabody, Whitman #1034, ©1977 .... 15.00
Tommy Tortoise and Moe Hare, Saalfield, ©1961 .... 24.00
Yogi Bear, Whitman, ©1963 . 8.00

Comic book, *Felix the Cat*, All Pictures Comics, 1945........... 50.00

Cookie jar
Bugs Bunny 40.00

Cartoon characters, Little Lulu, bank, figural, vinyl, red, black, white, and blue, **$18.**

Cartoon characters, comic book, *Ritchie Rich, the Poor Little Rich Poor and Casper the Friendly Ghost*, Harvey World, No. 42, Jan, **$15.**

Felix the Cat........................... 50.00

Costume, Top Cat, Ben Cooper, #848, ©Barbera-Hanna Pictures, c1970, orig box.................................. 25.00

Counter display, Sunoco promotion, six different 3" to 4" rubber Looney Tunes figures, 1989, 17" x 15" 60.00

Doll
Archie, cloth, 16" h............... 30.00
Felix the Cat........................... 8.00

Drinking glass
Foghorn Leghorn, ©1976....... 8.00
Pepsi, Go-Go Gophers, 1970s 12.00
Pepsi, Warner Brothers Looney Tunes, copyright 1966........ 8.00
Welch's, 1971, Hot Dog Goes to School................................. 5.00

Egg cup, Betty Boop, figural, glazed ceramic, stamped "Made in Japan," 1930s, 1-5/8" d, 2-3/8" h...... 250.00

Figure
Archie, Sirocco, painted brown military uniform and hat, 1944 .... 24.00
Li'l Abner, plastic, hp, Marx, 1950s, 2-1/2" h............................. 12.00

Mammy and Pappy Yokum, plastic, hp, Marx, 1950s, 2" h, 1-1/2" h 20.00
Popeye, jointed wood, 4-1/2" h, copyright K.F.S. 145.00

Game
Barney Google an' Snuffy Smith, Milton Bradley, 1963, orig box 42.00
Underdog, 1964, missing one decal 65.00
Yogi Bear Rummy Game, Ed-U-Cards, ©1961 .... 10.00

Gum pack, Magoo Tatoo, 1" x 1-3/4" packet, neatly opened wrapper, ©1967 .... 12.00

Hand puppet, plush, tag "Bugs Bunny 50th Birthday Celebration," 1990, 14" h............................ 12.00

Lunch box, Woody Woodpecker and Buzz Buzzard, dark green leather, multicolored image of Woody stitched on front, holding hammer, copyright Walter Lantz Productions, c1970.............. 175.00

Mug, Woody & Friends, white hard plastic, full color images, 1960s, 3" h.. 10.00

Music box, Betty Boop, cowgirl 45.00

Napkin holder, Popeye, ceramic 15.00

Patch, Daffy Duck, 1960s, 3" d... 5.00

Perfume set, Little Lulu........... 85.00

Pinback button
Betty Boop for President, 1-3/4" d 5.00
High Admiral Cigarettes, Yellow Kid.................................... 35.00
Member Archie Club, 1-1/2" d 20.00

Record, Huckleberry Hound with stories and songs of Uncle Remus, 33-1/3 rpm, CBS Records, ©1977 .... 12.00

Ring, Betty Rubble, off-white plastic, expansion band, diecut portrait, c1960..................................... 25.00

Salt and pepper shakers, pr Bugs Bunny and Taz............. 15.00

Cartoon characters, plastic mug, Bugs Bunny, **$12.50.**

Felix the Cat........................... 20.00

Sandals, pr, Underdog, 7-1/2" x 11-1/4" diecut card, 6-1/2" l orange and yellow sandals, ©Leonardo TTV 1978............................... 20.00

Sheet music, *Woody Woodpecker*, ©1947, red and white cover 4.00

String holder, Betty Boop, hp, figural, plaster, 5-3/4" l........ 295.00

Sunday comic cut-out supplement, Foxy Grandpa's loop-the-loop, New York American and Journal Sunday, May 10, 1903, 10" x 14" stiff paper, full color artwork, unused 45.00

Target set, Felix the Cat, 2-in-1, gun and orig stoppers, orig box . 175.00

Thermos, Casper the Friendly Ghost 75.00

Tru-Vue card, Huck Hound, Pop Goes Yogi Bear, ©1960, 4" x 6", unopened.................................. 5.00

Vase, Betty Boop 30.00

Word Search puzzle book, The Jetsons, 1978, unused............ 10.00

Wristwatch, Smitty, gray aged dial, black, white, red and green figure, New Haven Clock Co., orig case, c1935.................................... 250.00

Cash Registers

One of the necessities of any store is a good cash register. However, with today's electronic gadgets, the large styles of yesterday have been cast aside. Collectors gather up these units, restore them, and then enjoy their purchase.

National
Candy store size, ornate cast detail, milk glass shelf on front, 21-1/4" x 10-1/4" x 16" 675.00
Model 313, small, emb brass, marble ledge, 17" h, missing "Amount Purchased" marquee, restored 750.00

Model 317, emb brass, 1914 .... 1,300.00
Wooden, loose money in back 125.00

Cash register, National, 1914,

Cassidy, Hopalong

Hopalong Cassidy was a cowboy hero who successfully made the leap from movies to radio to television. Hoppy was also a master at self- promotion and did a lot of advertising, as did many other early cowboy heroes.

Hopalong Cassidy, vinyl saddlebags, **$1,300.**

Autograph book, 4-3/4" x 5-3/4" x 1", zippered leather, photo of Hoppy and Topper, facsimile signature, 17 pgs with autographs, 1950s 75.00

Badge, teller's, 3" black and white celluloid, red, white, and black text "Ask Me About The Hopalong Cassidy Savings Club" 50.00

Bedroom slippers, child's, 5-1/2" l, black and white felt, imprint of Hoppy and name on each, black vinyl soles, c1950 95.00

Binoculars, 4-1/2" x 5-1/8", painted black metal, plastic eyecups, decal, c1950 .... 45.00

Birthday card, Hopalong Cassidy's Bar-20 Ranch, little girl in Hoppy outfit feeding apple to white pony, c1950 .... 45.00

Box, 7-7/8" x 9-5/8" x 2", Hopalong Cassidy Socks, c1950 .... 125.00

Bubble gum card, False Paradise 2.50

Calendar, 1952, Mobil gas station, Portland, OR, ©Brown & Bigelow 145.00

Comic book, Fawcett Vol 5, #28, 1949 .... 30.00

Crayon and stencil set, orig diecut insert, 18 crayons, three coloring sheets, orig box, Transgram ©1950 William Boyd 100.00

Cup, 2-3/4" d, 3" h, ceramic, white, green art and text, c1950 .... 30.00

Dixie picture, 8" x 10", full color, brown cowboy outfit, holding Topper's reins, green margin band with Paramount text 45.00

Dominos, Milton Bradley #4104, ©1950, 9-1/2" x 12-1/4" x 1-1/4" box 120.00

Figure set, hard plastic, Hoppy, removable hat, horses, Ideal Toy Corp, c1950 .... 45.00

Milk bottle cap, 4" d, Superior Dairies, Statesville, NC, white waxed stiff paper, red images, flattened 18.00

Pennant, 27" l, black felt, name in white rope lettering, white felt band, 1950s 40.00

Paint book, 10-7/8" x 14-7/8", full color front and back covers, ©1950 Doubleday & Co. 75.00

Premium game, Hopalong Tag, 4-1/4" x 5-1/2" brown on white folder, back cover ad for Butter-Nut Bread and Hoppy TV show, KGO-TV, San Francisco, ©1949 William Boyd Ltd. 85.00

Premium picture, 7" x 8-1/2" black and white photo, facsimile signature, Good Luck Your Friend Hoppy, ©1949 William Boyd Ltd., Barclay Knitwear Co. 25.00

Pressbook, 11-1/2" x 14-3/4" black and white thin paper folder, Mystery Man, United Artists, 1944 .... 18.00

Hopalong Cassidy, comic book, *Hopalong Cassidy*, DC Comics, **$75.**

Pulp, *Triple Western*, Vol 1, #3, Fall 1947, The Bar 20 Rides Again 12.00

Ruler, 12" l, yellow, wood, black text on one side, "Drink Northland

Milk-Hoppy's Favorite," c1950 .... 40.00

School book cover, 9" x 12", brown paper folder, black printing, "Eat

Bond Bread-Hoppy's Favorite," c1950 .... 25.00

Thermos, 6-1/4" h, metal, Hoppy on Topper, with gun, ©Aladdin 1954 .... 65.00

Cast Iron

Cast iron has long been a favorite metal for creating durable goods, such as cooking utensils, farm implements, and tools.

Buyer beware!

A lot of people are seeing stars these days, reproduction stars that is. That's not a good thing!

It seems these architectural minatures are everywhere. It only took a few showing up in illustrations in decorator magazines for people to go crazy for the things. Trouble is, many are being offered on the secondary market, where they're being represented as old. Your socks are probably older than these things.

The original building stars were used on the outside of 19th-century structures, tying off the ends of metal supports that helped stabilize the structure.

There's nothing wrong with buying the newer versions, providing you know what you're getting and the price is reasonable. How do you tell the new from the old? Most of the contemporary examples have been intentionally rusted. New rust has a bright-orange color, compared to the darker rust found on an object that has aged slowly over a long period of time.

Andirons, pr, faceted ball finials, knife blade, arched bases, penny feet, 20" h, rusted surface.... 325.00

Boot scraper, scroll ends, green granite base 110.00

Broiler, 16" w, 15" h, three heart dec, short splayed feet, hinged support in back, shallow shelf between two feet broken off, Scottish 125.00

Christmas tree stand, openwork base with trees and stars, orig green paint, 2-1/2" h, 7-3/4" sq 75.00

Crucifix, 52" h, cast, log shaped cross cov with ivy, later added small spelter figure of Jesus, wear to old silver paint 175.00

Dutch oven, #8, Griswold, painted black 55.00

Egg beater, Dover, wooden knob, 10-1/4" l.. 25.00

Game rack, 12-1/2" w, 15" h, ring with eight hooks, tapered top straps, look hanger, one hook replaced 115.00

Hitching post, jockey, yellow, red, green, black, and white painted detail, wired for lantern, 31" h 275.00

Cast iron, door knocker, kissing couple, painted white ground, fleshtone faces, blond and brown hair, heart outlined in pink, 5-1/2" h, **$95.**

Cast iron, skeleton key, 5-1/2" l, **$20.**

Mirror, gilt, rococo scrolled acanthus frame, oval beveled mirror, Victorian, 22" h 75.00

Muffin tin, hearts motif, eight cups 110.00

Match safe, double holders, 4" h, 4" w 125.00

Sieve, 9-3/8" l, punched, flattened handle, rattail hanging hook 165.00

Skillet, #8, Griswold 38.00

Snow bird, 6" wingspan........... 40.00

Spatula, 10" l, 2" w, flattened handle, hanging hook, wear............. 115.00

Trivet, horseshoe shape, "Good Luck To All Who Use This Stand," 1870 patent date, repainted, 8" l, 4-1/2" w 20.00

Catalogs

Old trade and merchandise catalogs are sought by collectors. They are sometimes the best source of information about what a company produced.

For additional listings, see *Warman's Antiques & Collectibles* and *Warman's Americana & Collectibles*.

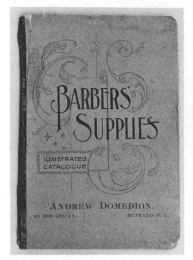

Catalog, Barber Supplies, Andrew Domedion, Buffalo, NY, 140 pgs, 7" x 10-1/4", **$65.**

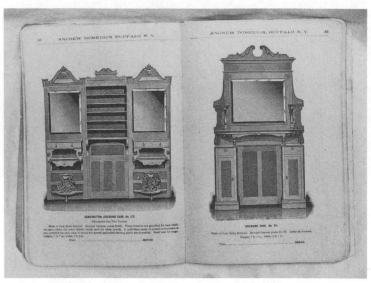

Interior view of Andrew Domedion catalog, showing detailed illustrations.

Arkansas Nursery Co., Fayetteville, AR, 1921, 34 pgs, 6" x 9", Catalog No. 43 .... **10.00**

Baraca & Philathea Supply Co., Syracuse, NY, 1923, 32 pgs, 3-1/2" x 6" **21.00**

Bausch & Lomb Optical Co., Rochester, N.Y., 122 pgs, 1919 .... **55.00**

Big Gem Art Advertising Calendars, US, 1936, 10" x 16-1/2", salesman's demo kit, 10" x 16-1/2" folder with two 14" x 8-1/2" calendars laid down, green folder wraps, gold lettering.............. **30.00**

Burgess Plant & Seed Co., Galesburg, Wis., 82 pgs, 1944 **10.00**

Butler Brothers, St. Louis, 50th anniversary catalog, May 1927, 420 pgs **40.00**

Century Furniture Co., Grand Rapids, Mich., 40 pgs, 1931 .. **50.00**

Choice-Vend, Inc., Windsor Locks, CT, 1974, 35 pgs, 8-1/2" x 11", three-ring binder, color **22.00**

Chrysler Sales Division, Detroit, MI, 1950, 18 pgs, 8" x 10", 24" x 30" sheet folded as issued, color, shows 19 models **24.00**

Detroit Dental Mfg Co., Detroit, MI, c1924, 11 pgs, 5-14" x 8-1/4", Gilmore Adjustable Attachments **15.00**

Eugene Dietzgen Co., Anabasis, NY, c1939, 56 pgs, 5-3/4" x 8-3/4" **22.00**

Frank & Son, Inc., New York, NY, c19128, eight pgs, 3" x 6" **10.00**

Geneva Wagon Co., Geneva, N.Y., 44 pgs, 1905, worn **75.00**

Gretsch, Cincinnati, OH, 1975, 12 pgs, 8-1/2" x 11", color **15.00**

Hartz Mountain Products, 32 pgs, 1933 .... **18.00**

Holtzman-Cabot Electric, Boston, MA, 1905, 4 pgs, 6-3/4" x 9-1/2" **15.00**

Howard Tresses, New York, NY, c1935, 30 pgs, 5-3/4" x 9" **16.00**

Jordan, Marsh & Co., Boston, Mass., 254 pgs, 1895 .... **35.00**

Kirsch Manufacturing Co., Diturgis, Mich., 18 pgs, 1922 **12.00**

Milton Bradley Co., Boston, Mass., 124 pgs, 1923 .... **22.00**

Montgomery Ward & Co., Fall & Winter, 1,144 pgs, 1956 .... **32.00**

National Lumber Mfgrs, Washington, DC, 1929, 30 pgs, 8-1/4" x 11" **20.00**

Norlin Music Inc., Lincolnwood, IL, c1975, 12 pgs, 7-1/2" x 11" **15.00**

Oakes Poultry and Hog Equipment, Tipton, Ind., 60 pgs, 1957 .... **7.50**

Pass & Seymour, Inc., Syracuse, NY, 1919, 137 pgs, 7-1/2" x 10-3/4", Catalog No. 25 .... **26.00**

Reliable Incubators, Quincy, Ill., 1896 .... **28.00**

Safe Cabinet Co., Chicago, IL, c1931, 40 pgs, 6" x 9" **15.00**

Schenfeld & Sons, New York, NY, no date, 1970s, 24 pgs, 6-3/4" x 9-1/2", 58 material swatches tipped in **24.00**

United States Rubber Co., New Orleans, LA, c1940, 12 pgs, 9" x 12", Keds Footwear **32.00**

Wanamaker, John, New York, NY, 1920s, eight pgs, 4-3/4" x 6", March is the Month of China **36.00**

Whitemore Associates, Inc., Boston, MA, 1950, 160 pgs, 6" x 9" **30.00**

Catalog, Chicago Bridge & Iron Works: Water Towers, 1912, **$20.**

Cat Collectibles

It's purrfectly obvious: cat collectors love their cats, whether they are live and furry or an inanimate collectible. More often than not, collectors purchase objects that resemble their favorite furry friends.

For additional listings, see *Warman's Americana & Collectibles*.

Reproduction alert.

Avon bottle, Kitten's Hideaway, white kitten in brown basket, 1974... **8.00**

Bookends, pr, ceramic, one with black and white cat stretching his paw through to other bookend, second bookend has gray mouse with mallet, ready to strike extended cat's paw, incised "©1983" and ceramist's initials **35.00**

Bookmark, figural cat face, celluloid, reverse mkd "don't kiss me," 22" l green cord, c1920, 1-3/4" w x 1-3/4" h **65.00**

Clock, 9" h, ceramic, Sessions, white cat holding clock, 1950s **50.00**

Comic book
  Black Cat Comics, Harvey Publications, June 1946, #12 .... **200.00**
  Cosmos Cat, Fox Features Syndicate, 1946, #4 .... **40.00**

Cup and saucer, child size, cat on pussy willow twig, mkd "Made in Japan"..................................... **12.00**

Figure
  Siamese, ceramic, model #4693, paper label "Lefton Japan," 8" h **28.00**
  Three pink kittens, attached and seated on blue Victorian-style sofa with gold trim, stamped

Cat collectibles, M.A. Hadley pottery cat, 5" h, **$25.**

Cat collectibles, children's book, *The Tale of Pierrot and His Cat*, Florence Evans, watercolor illustrations by Albertine Randall Wheelan, **$65.**

"©1959 Bradley Onimco," 4" h **25.00**

Handkerchief, embroidered **5.00**

Mug, 3-1/4" h, ceramic, cat face, white, dark blue floral collar and handle, incised "Avon"........... **18.00**

Nodder, 4-1/4" h, yellow, black stripes, fuzzy, blue rhinestone eyes, paper label "Made in Hong Kong" **8.50**

Paperweight, Glass, rect, multicolored scene of cats playing with yarn **25.00**

Pitcher, figural, tail forms handle, clear glass, incised "WMF Germany," 8-1/4" h **25.00**

Planter, brown and white cat, blue bow, standing upright, one paw raised **12.00**

Puzzle, 10-1/2" x 14", cardboard, yellow cat in blue pants and white sailor hat, playing concertino **10.00**

Salt and pepper shakers, pr
  Hello Kitty, matching undertray **60.00**
  Mr & Mrs Black Cat, stamped "Japan"............................. **15.00**
  Thai and Thai-Thai, Siamese cats, Ceramic Arts Studio **135.00**

Serving tray, 15" x 21", metal, painted gold, aqua border, two Siamese cats in center, sgd "Alexander"............................. **65.00**

Tape measure, celluloid case, pictures of playing cats, tape mkd "Made in U.S.A." **35.00**

Teapot, figural, Norcrest **10.00**

Tea towel, linen **10.00**

Toy, cat with shoe, celluloid, orange accents, red neck bow, tin litho shoe, mkd "Made in Japan," 1950s **65.00**

Wall plaque, chalkware, Tabby cat face, red ears and big bow, green eyes, 6-1/2" h **45.00**

Cat collectibles, doorstop, white, green eyes, long torso, original paint, **$95.**

Celluloid

The first commercially successful form of plastic, celluloid has been a part of our world since the 1870s. Modern plastics have proved to be safer and easier to manufacture, so items made from celluloid are becoming quite collectible.

For additional information, see *Warman's Antiques & Collectibles*, and *Warman's Americana & Collectibles*.

Animal
Bear, cream, pink and gray highlights, VCO/USA, 5" w **20.00**

Donkey, molded harnesses and saddle, grayish brown, red, and orange, VCO/USA **35.00**

Horse, 7" l, cream, brown highlights, hp eyes, marked with VCO intertwined mark, 7" l **48.00**

Hound dog, long tail, peach celluloid, gray highlights, crossed circle Japan mark, 5" l...... **20.00**

Bar pin, ivory-grained, orange and brown layered pearlescence, hp rose motif **28.00**

Blotter pad, 3" x 7-1/2", Exchange Buffet, three cardboard ink blotter sheets bound by cello cap rivet, 1905 Whitehead & Hoag patent **15.00**

Bookmark, cream colored, diecut, poinsettia motif, Psalm 22 printed on front................................. **15.00**

Brush and comb set, child's, orig box **20.00**

Clothing brush, 3-1/2" d, graphic red, white, and blue eagle, gold and

Celluloid items, candlesticks, 5-1/2" h, pair, **$75.**

navy blue borders, "Eagle White Lead, Old Dutch Process," Parisian Novelty, 1924 patent on curl, black bristles **40.00**

Cuff links, pr, matching stickpin, lever back links of silver tone metal, octagonal framework with circular imitation ivory set with rhinestone **75.00**

Doll, blue glass eyes, moveable arms and legs, dressed in fabric skirt, crochet top, bandana around head, earrings, 9" h **90.00**

Dresser tray, imitation tortoiseshell rim, glass and lace center...... **30.00**

Hat pin, conical, imitation tortoiseshell, 12" l.................. **20.00**

Gauge, 3" x 3", Standard Roller Bearing Co., diecut openings, 1920s **15.00**

Ink blotter, 2" x 6-1/4", tinted color real oval photo, titled "Lake View, Siloam Springs, Ark," brass fasteners, unused blue blotter sheets, Cruver Mfg Co., Chicago, c1915..................................... **25.00**

Napkin ring, 1" w, basketweave strips **15.00**

Pocket mirror, oval, woman with long red hair, teal blue dress and cloche, holding bouquet of roses, 2-1/4" l................................... **45.00**

Pocket scale, 2-3/4" x 5-1/4" cream colored diecut sleeve with two

small windows and removable inside card for figuring prices of coal by the ton, C. B. Lang Fuel Co., International Falls, Minn **20.00**

Rattle, blue and white, egg shape, white handle **18.50**

Ribbon badge, 1-3/4" celluloid in brass frame, real photo sepia image of John Stetson, red, white, and blue fabric rosette attached to 8-1/2" h ribbon badge, brass hanger with cello insert reading "Aide," gold text on green, white, red, and blue ribbons "Dedication and Flag Raising Jon B. Stetson Public School May 5, 1917," bar pin **40.00**

Vanity set, amber, teal-green pearlescent laminate surface with hp rose dec, dresser tray, hair receiver, nail butter, scissors, button hook, c1930 .... **45.00**

Vase, 7" h, yellow, fluted top, painted pink and blue floral motif..... **30.00**

Watch holder, 6-1/2" l, wall hanging, figural banjo-clock style, pearlescent blue, green, and amber, Wilcox trademark, late 1920s **25.00**

Celluloid items, mustache comb, leg shape, stained gray on leg, black high button boot, 5-3/4" h, **$50.**

Celluloid items, dresser set, 10 "French Ivory" items in original case, **$35.**

Cereal Boxes

Cereal boxes have incorporated clever advertising, premiums, and activities for years. Early boxes were designed to appeal to the cook in the household, but as children began requesting their favorite brands and saving box tops to get a specific premium, the whole industry refocused on that group. By the 1970s, special promotional boxes were created, giving collectors even more opportunities to expand their collections.

Cereal box, Post, Hulk, limited edition cereal, empty, **$5.**

Batman, Ralston, hologram T-shirt offer, 1989 .... 9.00

Corn Kix, Rocket Space O-Gauge, 1950s 80.00

Corn Pops, Kellogg's, Batman Forever with Batman, #1 in series of 4, copyright 1995 .... 10.00

Froot Loops, Kellogg's, Mattel Fun on Wheels contest, 1970 .... 30.00

Kellogg's Frosted Mini-Wheats, 1992 Olympics, basketball, flattened 8.00

Post Toasties Corn Flakes, sample, Mickey and Pluto on back panel, 5-5/8" h 195.00

Rice Chex, red check design, 1950s 65.00

Sugar Smacks, seal balancing bowl of cereal on nose, Exploding Battleship offer on back, 1958, 9-oz, hole in bottom front, 7-1/2" x 9-1/2" 36.00

Wheaties
Muhammad Ali, 1960s picture, 1998 .... 20.00

Cereal box, Wheaties, 30th Super Bowl, 1967-1996, empty, **$2.**

Lou Gehrig, flat 8.50
Babe Ruth, flat 8.50

Cereal Premiums

This category includes all of those fun things we saved after eating all that cereal. Sometimes these goodies were tucked into the box. Other premiums were things that you earned, through saving box tops, coupons, etc. Whatever the method, the treasure was the premium, and, at today's prices, collectors are having the most fun now.

Booklet, Kellogg's Funny Jungleland Moving Pictures, 6" x 7-1/4", full color, ©1932 .... 20.00

Bowl sitter, pencil topper, Pinocchio 10.00

Cereal bowl, Tom Mix, "Hot Ralston Cereal for Straight Shooters," white china, illus, Ralston Purina... 35.00

Cereal box ad, Post Sugar Crisp, three bears with baseball equipment, billboard with Ted Williams in background, 1955 6.00

Christmas ornament
Detroit Tigers, Sports Collectors Series, Topperscot, Inc., MIB 8.00

Sugar Bear, spins inside glow-in-the-dark holder, MIP, 4" h, 2" w 10.00

Comic book, *Dick Tracy Comic Book,* Popped Wheat, 1947..... 6.00

Delivery truck, 1921 Model T, Matchbox, copyright 1989, Kellogg's Apple Jacks 8.00

Figures, Snap, Crackle, and Pop, wood and fabric, mkd, dated, Kellogg's 1972 .... 55.00

Flashlight, Lurch, attached by cellophane to box of Addams Family Cereal, Ralston, copyright 1991 .... 8.00

Cereal premium, Kellogg's Story Book of Games, Kellogg Co., 1931, #190, eight pages, original spinner, **$25.**

Flicker ring, Frankenberry playing drums, early 1970s 100.00

Magnet, Trix, Arjon Manufacturing Corp., MOC 8.00

Military insignia button, Kellogg's Pep, complete set of 36, litho tin, insignia of US Army, Air Force, Navy, or Marine unit, 1943 .... 375.00

Newspaper ad, 10-1/2" x 15-1/2", full color, lower half of Sunday comic strip, 1934, Quaker Wheat Crackers offer for premium physical development set endorsed by Max Baer... 5.00

Premium button, Kellogg's Pep, litho tin, character portrait and name on front, "Kellogg's Pep" in blue on reverse
B. O. Plenty 100.00
Felix 110.00
Foxy Grandpa 30.00
Lil Abner.............................. 25.00
The Phantom....................... 100.00

Signal Light, Jack Armstrong Safety Signal-Light Kit, Wheaties, 1-5/8" x 2-1/4" cardboard box, orig bicycle light....................................... 195.00

Spoon, silver plated, emb "Kellogg's" 10.00

Wacky Wobbler, Count Chocula, bobbing head, made by Funko Inc., orig box, 7" h 10.00

Weather forecast ring, Howie Wing, Kellogg's, 1930s 250.00

Character and Promotional Drinking Glasses

Our favorite cartoon characters, superheroes, and sports characters can be found parading around clear glass drinking glasses and mugs. Many have an advertiser, such as Pepsi or McDonald's behind them. Dedicated collectors of these cheerful creations can tell you all about the variations, who made what glass in what year, how many in each series, etc. They prefer glasses that have never been used, and certainly favor those glasses who have never seen the insides of a modern dishwasher.

Amazing Spiderman, Marvel Comics, 1977 .... 5.00

Animal Crackers, Lyle, 1978 .... 9.00

Aquaman, DC Comics, Pepsi, 1978 .... 17.50

Archie, takes The Gang For A Ride 4.50

Batman, Pepsi, 16-oz, 1978...... 18.00

BC Ice Age, riding on wheel, Arby's, 1981 .... 9.00

Beaky Buzzard, Warner Bros., Pepsi, 1973 .... 17.50

Big Mac, McVote, McDonald's, 1986 .... 5.00

Bugs Bunny, Pepsi, 1973, copyright Warner Bros. Inc. 9.00

Bullwinkle, Crossing the Delaware, Arby's, 1976 .... 12.00

Charlie Chaplin, Arby's............ 7.50

Daffy Duck, Pepsi, Warner Bros., 1976 .... 18.00

Dinosaurs, Triceratops, Coca-Cola, European, 6-7/8" h 12.00

Disney on Parade, Coca-Cola .. 5.00

Empire Strikes Back, Luke Skywalker, Burger King, 1980 .... 17.50

Endangered Species, Bengal Tiger, Burger Chef, 1978.................... 7.50

Flash, Pepsi, 1976 .... 18.00

Have It Your Way, two drummers, piper, Burger King, 1976 .... 10.00

Hot Air Balloon, Dr. Pepper 9.00

Hot Dog Goes to School, 1971 4.50

Howard the Duck, Marvel Comics, 1977 .... 4.00

Hulkamania, WWF, Swarts Peanut Butter, orig lid 9.00

Little Bamm-Bamm, Flintstones, Hardee's, 1991.......................... 6.00

Mayor McCheese taking pictures, McDonald's.............................. 5.00

Noid, beach chair, Domino's Pizza, 1988 .... 2.50

Peter Pan, McDonald's, Disney movie series, Canadian 20.00

Popeye, Coca-Cola, Kollect-A-Set 6.00

Road Runner, Pepsi 3.00

Santa and Elves, Coca-Cola 7.50

Seattle Seahawks, Beeson Eller, Beamon, McDonald's 10.00

Search for Spock, Enterprise Destroyed, Star Trek III, Taco Bell 15.00

Superman, Pepsi, 1975 .... 18.00

Taz and Bugs, Warner Bros, Pepsi 10.00

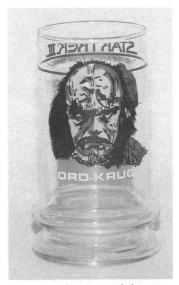

Character and promotional glass, Lord-Kruge, Star Trek III, Taco Bell, 5-3/4" h, **$4.**

Character and promotional glass, mug, Odie and Garfield, paddling canoe, McDonald's, ©1978 United Features Syndicate, **$5.**

That's All Folks, Elmer, Welch's, 1974 .... 6.00

Underdog, Brockway Glass Co., Pepsi, 16-oz, small logo 25.00

United Oil Baseball, Babe Ruth, Pepsi 15.00

Utah, State collectors series, David Keith Mansion, Pizza Hut 5.00

Washington, Burger Chef 7.00

Wonder Woman, National Periodical Pub... 10.00

World on Ice, Snow White and Dopey 14.00

Character Clocks

Telling time is more fun when your favorite character gives you a hand. Condition is important when collecting clocks and watches. Examples with original bands, boxes, stands, and works will bring a higher price.

Character watch, Shirley Temple, pocket-watch style, **$30.**

Batman, Janex, talking alarm clock, 1975, MIB 50.00

Betty Boop 45.00

Davy Crockett, wall, pendulum 75.00

Flintstones, wall clock, battery op 15.00

Hello Kitty, alarm, MIB 65.00

Howdy Doody, talking............ 65.00

Mickey Mouse, Bradley animated hands 45.00

Pluto, Allied, alarm, 1955 .... 60.00

Roy Rogers, alarm clock, color dial, c1970.................................... 30.00

Sesame Street, schoolhouse shape 25.00

Trix The Rabbit, alarm, c1960 .... 15.00

Sleeping Beauty, Phinney-Walker, alarm, 1950s 50.00

Snoopy, alarm clock............... 30.00

Star Wars, alarm clock, talking 35.00

Woody Woodpecker, Columbia Time, Woody's Café, 1959 ..... 75.00

Character clock, Pickaninny, alarm clock, advertising Louisiana Molasses, D. B. Scully Co. Syrup Co., Chicago, Ill, green "moving eyes," yellow and red bow tie, copyright 1938, **$125.**

Character Collectibles

Some characters got their start on early radio programs, some were popular advertising spokesmen, and some were permanent fixtures on the newspaper comic page. As collectors become younger and younger, so do the ages of the characters they search for. Foxy Grandpa is giving way to Gumby and now even Rugrats.

For additional listings, see *Warman's Antiques & Collectibles* and *Warman's Americana & Collectibles,* as well as specific categories in this edition.

Abbott & Costello, ring photo sheet, 1" x 1-7/8" high gloss black and white paper, two miniature photos, c1940...................................... 20.00

Al Capp, record album, Al Capp on Campus, Jubilee Records, 1970s 18.00

Andy Gump, brush and mirror 20.00

Barney Google, pep pin, Kellogg's, 1946 .... 18.00

Blondie and Dagwood
Blondie paint set, American Crayon, 1946 .... 75.00

Blondie's peg board set, King Features, 1934 .... 90.00

Dagwood, marionette, 1945 100.00

Bugs Bunny, cookie jar 40.00

Charlie Chaplin
Doll, fabric........................... 175.00
Figure, lead, 2-1/2" h............ 40.00

Character collectibles, Bing Crosby, record duster, photo and facsimile signature, yellow celluloid top, advertising for Decca Records, Bond's Electric, Trenton, NJ, 3-1/2" d, **$12.**

Chester Gump, nodder, ceramic 75.00

Daffy Duck, character drinking glass, Pepsi, Warner Brothers Looney Tunes, copyright 1980 8.00

Dennis the Menace
Book, *Dennis The Menace*, Hank Ketchum, Holt & Co., 1952, 1st ed, hardcover 35.00
Lamp, figural 50.00

Dick Tracy
Badge, Secret Service Patrol, Quaker, 1938 .... 50.00
Candy bar wrapper, premium offer, 1950s 10.00
Christmas tree light bulb, 1930s 40.00
Toy, two-way radio set, 1950, MIB 40.00

Flintstones, playset, #4672, copyright 1961, 15" x 24" x 4" orig box, played-with condition 165.00

Flipper, puzzle, Whitman, 1960 .... 12.00

Ken Griffin, poster, 14" x 22", magic show, c1955 .... 15.00

Heckle and Jeckle, premium ring, thin copper luster metal band, circular copper luster frame with

Character collectibles, Humpty Dumpty character bank, pottery, 3-5/8" h, **$65.**

convex metal insert, color image, mkd "Copyright Terrytoons," c1977, set of three 18.00

Humpty Dumpty, potato chip tin, 1990s... 7.00

Jetsons
Colorforms Set, ©Colorforms and Hanna-Barbera, 1963....... 40.00
Record, "The Jetsons, First Family on the Moon," 33 RPM, 1977 .... 60.00

Kayo and Moon Mullins, pinback button, black and white, *Los Angeles Evening Express* contest, 1-1/4" d 45.00

James Bond
Board game, James Bond Secret Service Game, Spears, 1965 .... 60.00
Diecast set, Spy Who Loved Me Jr., Corgi.................................. 15.00

Jerry Lewis, ruler, The Nutty Professor, 12" l, white plastic, 1963 .... 18.00

Character collectibles, Borden ceramic mugs, Elsie and Elmer, Universal Pottery, 3-1/8" h, each **$5.**

Harold Lloyd, doll fabric, oilcloth-like fabric, printed doll, 1930s 48.00

Pink Panther
Music box, Royal Orleans, Christmas, 1984 .... 30.00
Sticker book, Pink Panther at the Circus, Golden, 1963........ 10.00

Pixie and Dixie, magic slate, 1959 .... 15.00

Popeye
Beach set, Peer Products, King Features, 1950s................. 15.00
Candy cigarettes, Primrose Confectionery, England, 1959 .... 15.00
Flashlight, figural, King Features 30.00
Pencil sharpener, figural, Bakelite, copyright 1929 King Features Syndicate, 1-3/4" h 75.00

Steve Canyon, costume, Halco, 1959 .... 25.00

Tom and Jerry
Go kart, Marx, 1973, plastic, friction 30.00
Puzzle, child's, ©1954........... 12.00
Pinback button, Tom and Jerry Go For Stroehmann's Bread, black, red and white litho, 1950s 25.00

Uncle Walt and Skeezix, pencil holder, F.A.S., bisque, 5" h..... 75.00

Yogi Bear
Coat rack, Wolverine, 1979 .. 40.00
Doll, Knickerbocker, 1959, plush, vinyl face 75.00

Chase Chrome and Brass

This American firm produced many interesting chrome and brass items. Their pieces are well marked and quite stylish.

Ashtray, 4-3/8" d, golf clubs and balls as cigarette rests, mkd........... 45.00

Bell, 3" h, 2" d, chrome, Bakelite finial, sgd on int. 145.00

Bud vase, 9" h, chrome, holds four stems, mkd 75.00

Cordial, chrome, ftd................. 85.00

Gravy boat, ladle, underplate, Lotus pattern, chrome, mkd 75.00

Ice bucket, tongs, 7-1/4" d, 7" h, Antarctica pattern, Russel Wright design **175.00**

Salad set, 11" l, serving fork and spoon, teak handles, mkd **45.00**

Salt and pepper shakers, pr, 1-1/4" h, Skyway, polished chromium, centaur logo........ **35.00**

Sauce boat, ladle, underplate, Lotus pattern, chrome, mkd **65.00**

Server, 9" w, 7" h, Pretzel Man, copper, centaur logo on support post **140.00**

Chase Chrome & Brass Co., chambersticks, pair, thumb holder, brass, column shaped cut design on chimneys, marked, 7-1/4" h, price for pair, **$115.**

Tray
Triple, yellow Bakelite handle, emb dec, designed by Harry Laylon, orig box and gift card, centaur logo, 6-3/4" w, 10-3/4" l, 1-3/4" h folded **60.00**
Two tiers, #17077, two 8" trays, ridged orange Bakelite handle, mkd, 10" h........................ **50.00**

Chein Toys

An American toy company, Chein produced quality toys from the 1930s through the 1950s. Many of its playthings were lithographed on tin, and they are clearly marked.

Bank, litho tin
Cash register, mechanical, records dimes................................. **15.00**
Clown, mechanical, 1940s, 5" h, coin trap missing **145.00**
Happy Days, 1930s, scratches **20.00**

Cookie jar, 6-7/8" d, 9" h, Disney **75.00**

Easter basket, 7-3/4" d, 7-3/4" h, nursery rhyme, tin litho, minor rust **85.00**

Globe, 6" d, 9-3/4" h, litho tin, early 1930s...................................... **75.00**

Sand pail
Circus theme, 5" h **165.00**
Fish at sea, 8" h, some rust. **150.00**

Sand pail shovel, 14" l, tiger face, tail on handle, some play wear.... **55.00**

Tea set, Snoopy, metal, 1970 .... **50.00**

Chein Toys, piano Ladeon, litho tin, paper player piano-type rolls, **$275.**

Top
Donald Duck being tied up by Huey and Dewey, Mickey and Pluto driving in convertible, Mickey

riding on Goofy, red wood handle, 7-1/2" d, 6" h, ... **95.00**
Snoopy, Charlie Brown, Lucy, and Linus, Model #263, 1960s **32.00**

Toy, litho tin wind-up, some play wear
Bear, 5" h **50.00**
Boat, Peggy Jane, 13" l.......... **55.00**
Duck, long bill, c1955, 4" h **145.00**
Twisting bear, 4-3/4" h, blue cap, yellow shirt, blue pants, red suspenders, 1930s, not working **27.50**

Toy, push type, some play wear
Popper, wooden handle, popping plastic balls, tin litho base, yellow plastic wheels, c1960 .... **35.00**
Rotor Mower, lawn mower, litho tin **95.00**

Chess Sets

This game of kings has been played for centuries. Be certain that all of the playing pieces are present and that the age of the board matches the age of the pieces.

Bakelite, 1930s-1940s, box rough and hinge damaged **380.00**

Carved marble pieces, fitted case, no playing board **40.00**

Civil War, Franklin Mint....... **365.00**

Football, hard plastic figures, green and white board, 1967, with *Official Football Chess Rule Book*, 22 pgs, unplayed, figures 3" h, box 24" x 19"................................ **78.00**

Lord of the Rings **240.00**

Plastic, molded, black and white, cardboard board.................... **20.00**

Porcelain, blue and white, bases mkd "Royal Dux, Made in Czechoslovakia," early 20th C **995.00**

Chess set, Replica 11th Century Figures, white and red imitation ivory figures, original box, **$65.**

The box exterior of the chess set at left.

Revolutionary War, Franklin Mint, issued 1986 .... 280.00

Star Trek, 25th Anniversary Edition, authorized by Paramount Pictures 300.00

Wood, hand carved, c1920 .... 80.00

Children's Collectibles

This category is a bit of a catchall, including things that children played with, as well as articles they used in their rooms.

Children's collectibles, storybook character, Curious George, stuffed plush, red shirt with yellow stitching, **$15.**

Alarm clock, Mickey Mouse, House Martin, 1988 .... 12.00

Baking set, Pillsbury, cookie cutter, six press-out sheets, pictures of Dick Tracy and pals, 1937 ..... 50.00

Bib clips, sterling silver, clothespin type 75.00

Blocks, wood, bright colors, c1950, some wear.............................. 20.00

Cloth book, handmade, buttons, zipper, etc. to teach children hand skills 10.00

Crayon box, tin, Transogram, Donald and Mickey, 1946 ...... 30.00

Crib, tapered high posts with incised line beading along edges, urn shaped supports on all sides, refinished, 38-3/4" d, 69-1/2" h, orig 48" l rails 250.00

Crib toy, Humpty Dumpty, Fisher-Price, 1970s 5.00

Christening outfit, gown, slip, and cap, white cotton, c1920 .... 85.00

Cup, Felix sip-a-drink, 5" h 15.00

Diaper holder, fabric, clown face, striped body 10.00

Hot water bottle, Olive Oyl and Swee' Pea, Duarry, 1970 .... 30.00

Jack-in-the-box, Cat in the Hat, Mattel, 1969 .... 90.00

Kite, Sky Floater, Spectra Star 5.00

Lamp, Donald Duck in tug boat, Dolly Toy, 1970s 80.00

Manicure set, Mary Poppins, Tre-Jur, 1964 .... 20.00

Mug, white glass, red animal characters, Hazel Atlas, 1930-40, 3" h.. 25.00

Night light, Goofy, Horsman, green, 1973 .... 16.00

Pastry set, Little Orphan Annie, Transogram, 1950s 20.00

Pencil case, Willie Whopper, 1930s 45.00

Piano, "Concert," baby grand 110.00

Print, Asleep & Awake, Bessie Gutmann, double matted, orig frame 150.00

Rattle, Popeye, Cribmates, 1979 .... 8.00

Sand pail, Donald Duck, Ohio Art, 1950s...................................... 40.00

Scooter, Bonzo, 7" h scooter, 6" Bonzo, litho tin wind-up..... 130.00

Sewing machine, Singer, cast iron and nickeled steel, 6-3/4" h. 150.00

Snow shovel, Donald Duck, Ohio Art, wood, tin litho 60.00

Squeak toy, Felix, 1930s, 6" h.. 35.00

Stove, Little Orphan Annie, electric, gold metal, litho plates, 1930s 100.00

Tiddly Winks, Ludwig Von Drake, Whitman, 1961 .... 10.00

Toothbrush, Goofy, Pepsodent, 1970s... 5.00

Wagon, Roller Bearing Coaster, wood, metal fittings, black stenciled label, old red and brown paint, some touch-up to paint................. 385.00

Walker, primitive, wood ring top, wood seat, replacement wrought iron ring base with wheels 145.00

Wall plaques, plaster of Paris, Jack and Jill on one, Humpty Dumpty other, self-framed, pr 20.00

Wastebasket, tin, Mickey and Minnie, Chein........................ 25.00

Children's collectibles, two handmade calico animals, left: red and white polka dot cat, white string eye, **$4;** faded blue floral print elephant, buttons hold on movable legs, button eye, **$5.**

Children's Dishes

We've all made mud pies and other goodies. And, what better way to serve them to our dolls and teddies than on pretty, child-size dishes?

Children's dishes, Doric & Pansy pattern, Depression glass, ultramarine, cup, **$40**; saucer, **$8.50**, and plate, **$12.50**, creamer, **$50**.

Baking set, tin, cookie tin, canister, bowl, pie pan, cake pans, angel food pan, muffin pan, etc. **25.00**

Bundt pan, aluminum, 3-3/4" w **4.00**

Candleholders, pr, Swirl pattern, opaque green milk glass **65.00**

Cereal bowl, Popeye, National Home Products, 1979 .... **8.00**

Chocolate pot, china, decal with Model T and passengers **90.00**

Cup
Mickey Mouse, silver plated, Cavalier, 3" h **25.00**
Olive Oyl, Coke, Kollcct-A-Set, 1977 .... **4.00**

Cup and saucer
Blue Willow pattern **15.00**
Holly, Napco, Japan, 2-1/4" d saucer **7.00**
Luster ware, Japan, floral dec. **4.50**
Peach Luster, Fire-King **25.00**

Dinnerware set
China, pink transferware Punch dec, mkd "Allerton & Sons," cup, saucer and three 5-1/2" d plates **150.00**
Depression glass, My Little Hostess, orig box **175.00**
Plastic, Tinkerbell, Walt Disney, nine pcs **25.00**

Mug
Little Bo Peep, 3-1/2" h **22.00**
Little Orphan Annie, Ovaltine, Beetleware, 1933 .... **25.00**
Popeye, KFS, ceramic, musical, 1982 .... **10.00**

Party set, Flintstones, Reed, tablecloth, napkins, plates, cups, 1969 .... **10.00**

Plate, Hey Diddle Diddle, blue and white, 6-1/2" d **30.00**

Silverware set, aluminum, four spoons, four forks, knife, and pie server **15.00**

Strainer and meat grinder, Little Homemaker, Wirecraft Corp., NYC, MOC **18.00**

Children's dishes, play tea set, Cabbage Patch, plastic, 26 pieces, NRFB, **$20**.

Sugar bowl, luster ware, Japan, 1-1/2" h **3.00**

Teapot
Aluminum, black wood knob, swing handle **25.00**
Plastic, mkd "Eagle Toys, Made in Canada," 4" x 6" **3.00**

Tea set
Akro Agate, orig box mkd "The Little American Maid, No. 3000" **300.00**
China, Victorian children playing, Germany **285.00**
Tin, Mary Poppins, J. Chein, 1964 .... **45.00**
Tin, Pinocchio, Ohio Art, 1939 .... **75.00**

Chintz Ware

Chintz ware is the general term for brightly colored, multi-flower china patterns made primarily in England. These popular patterns resemble chintz fabrics and were produced by many manufacturers. After declining in popularity for years following World War II, chintz has enjoyed a lively comeback over the past several years.

For additional listings, see *Warman's Antiques & Collectibles* and *Warman's English & Continental Pottery & Porcelain.*

Reproduction alert.

Chintz ware, handled dish, Japan, 5-5/8" square, **$25.**

Basket, Summertime pattern, Rowsley shape, Grimwades, Royal Winton.................................. 165.00

Bowl, Marguerite, Royal Winton, 9-1/2" x 10" 265.00

Bread tray, Old Cottage, Royal Winton.................................. 200.00

Breakfast set, Rosebud Iridescent, green 250.00

Bud vase, Old Cottage Chintz pattern, Grimwades, Royal Winton, 5" h
.... 85.00

Butter dish, Pink Chintz pattern, A. G. Richardson, Crown Ducal
.... 125.00

Cake plate, Sweet Pea pattern, Grimwades, Royal Winton . 150.00

Comport, Spring Blossom, A. G. Richardson, 7" d 195.00

Creamer and sugar, Queen Anne, Royal Winton....................... 285.00

Cup and saucer

Marina pattern, Elijah Cotton
.... 50.00
Primrose, Oleander shape, Shelley
.... 195.00
Rosalynde pattern, James Kent Ltd
.... 75.00

Demitasse cup and saucer, Esther pattern, Grimwades, Royal Winton
.... 79.00

Eggcup, Hazel pattern, ftd, Grimwades, Royal Winton . 100.00

Mustard pot, cov, underplate, Rosetime, Lord Nelson.......... 85.00

Pin dish, Melody, Shelley, 4-1/2" l
.... 85.00

Plate
Ascot, Majestic, Grimwades, Royal Winton, 6" d 75.00

Chintz ware, pitcher, Chinese Rose, James Kent, **$120.**

Chintz ware, creamer and sugar on tray, Empire, Delphi pattern, **$235.**

Melody, Royal Crown, 9" d
.... 195.00
Old Cottage, Royal Winton, 8" d
.... 50.00
Rosalynde pattern, James Kent, 9" d
.... 75.00
Sweet Pea, Royal Winton, 5" sq
.... 100.00

Salt and pepper shakers, pr, tray, Du Barry, James Kent 95.00

Sandwich tray, Crocus, Grimwades, Royal Winton 125.00

Soup bowl, two handles, underplate, Old Cottage, Royal Winton . 145.00

Sugar shaker, Du Barry, James Kent
.... 125.00

Teapot, cov
Marina, Lord Nelson 325.00
Primula, A. G. Richardson   275.00

Tray, Old Cottage, Royal Winton
.... 150.00

Vase, Bedale pattern, Gem shape, Grimwades, Royal Winton .. 125.00

Chocolate Related

Many collectors suffer from a sweet tooth. Happily there are wonderful examples of items relating to chocolate that can satisfy those cravings.

Advertising logo watch, M & Ms, Mars Candy
Canadian, Minis, blue and yellow sports style, black plastic strap, 1998, mint 25.00
50th Birthday, yellow case, red and green strap, party hat on face, Birthday Club package, 9" x 12" printed envelope, mint..... 20.00
Millenium, silvertone case, emb black leather strap, "The Official Candy of the Millenium" on crystal, red M&M on face, 1998, mint.................................. 18.00

Autograph, Vernon L. Heath, Pres of Heath Bar Co., typed letter sgd,

Chocolate related, Hershey's Sweet Milk Chocolate box, worn, **$15.**

L. S. Heath & Son letterhead, dated Oct 21, 1957, blue ink signature
.... 5.00

Box, Mint Ju-ju-bees.................. 5.00

Box wrapper, 8" x 12", Crispettes Delicious Popcorn Confection, red and blue glassine wrapper, repeating design, ©1926 .... 20.00

Calendar, wall, 1917, Nevins Candy, 3-1/4" x 6-1/4", two-ply cardboard, color portrait of young lady .. 15.00

Camera, pocket, Hershey's Milk Chocolate, 1-1/4" x 2-1/2" x 5" chocolate brown and silver box, 110 film, orig instructions, China, 1980s **10.00**

Dealer award, 11" h, shield, brown wood, brushed white metal plaque, Jolly Time logo at top, two cans of popcorn "Presented in Sincere Appreciation Of The Loyal and Devoted Corporation In The Promotion of Jolly Time Volumized Pop Corn A Product of the American Pop Corn Company Sioux City Iowa During The Company's 25th Anniversary Year 1939 to P. K. Branthoover" **65.00**

Doll, 12-1/2" h, Little Hans, Nestle Chocolate premium, ©1969 .. **60.00**

Game, 2" x 9-1/2" x 18-1/2", Hershey Land Game, ©1983 CBS Toys and Hershey Foods **10.00**

Invoice, 8-1/4" x 8-3/4", Pittsburgh company, dated Dec. 8, 1926, to Brockmeyer Cigar Co St. Louis, for 48 cartons of Clark Bars **25.00**

Jar, cov, 7-1/2" x 8" x 9-1/2" h, ceramic, Nerd figure, orig sticker "Nerds, United Silver & Cutlery Corp, ©1984, Willy Wonka Brands" **24.00**

Kit, 9-1/2" x 12-1/2" mailer, Hershey's Certified Chocolate Lovers Club,

8-1/2" x 11" paper certificate with "kiss paper" seal, membership card, 1-3/4" celluloid pinback, unused **15.00**

Mask, 6-1/4" h black on red thin cardboard, smiling monster with long nose and one sharp tooth, Shotwell Confections premium, 1930s **40.00**

Pail
5" d top, 5" h, Hershey's, litho tin, montage of bite sized candy wrappers around perimeter, Ohio Art Co. **20.00**
7-1/4" x 7", Riley's Rum & Butter Toffee, Halifax, England, emb name, silhouettes of children playing with kite, slip lid . **50.00**

Planter, 5-1/2" x 7" h, snow covered brown chimney, red M & M character dressed as Santa, brown sack on back standing on shoulders of yellow M & M character, © Mars Inc., 1996-97 .... **20.00**

Postal cover, Hershey Chocolate Corporation, 4" x 9-1/2" white paper business envelope, black return address and pictorial trademark of toddler holding cocoa cup while emerging from cocoa bean, mimeographed address, early 1900s **15.00**

Chocolate related, candy mold, bust of Admiral Dewey, shield and "Dewey" on chest, pewter, marked "#254, T. Mills & Bro., Philadelphia," 6-1/4" w, 2-3/4" h open, **$300.**

Ribbon badge, 1-3/4" d black and white celluloid, Milton S. Hershey 81st Birthday Party, attached red, white, and blue ribbon, Keystone Badge Co. paper on back, 1938 .... **35.00**

Tin, 2" x 4" x 7-1/2", Whitman's, litho tin, hinged, Salmugundi, gold mosaic pattern, ©S. F. W & S. Inc., c1920-30 .... **15.00**

Christmas and Easter Seals

The National Tuberculosis Association issued seals, pinback buttons, and other items in order to educate the public and raise funds for their work. The American Lung Association also issued seals.

Christmas and Easter Seals, 1996, American Lung Association, full sheet of various multicolored children's Christmas drawings, unused, **$4.50.**

Booklet, Christmas Seals, 200, thin paper between each sheet, 1939 .... **22.00**

Bottle, commemorative, Coca-Cola, Easter Seals, 1997 .... **11.50**

Figurine, girl holding potted flower, "His Love will Shine on You," Easter Seals Limited Edition **11.50**

Gummed sticker
1913, 1" x 1-1/2", red, green, and white **3.50**
1940, 7/8" x 1", TB Assn **2.00**
1942, 7/8" x 1", TB Assn **2.00**

Poster
Fight the Big Bad Wolf 'Tuberculosis,' Buy Christmas Seals, paper, shows wolf and pigs, 1934, pinholes, 1" tear, 15" x 10-1/2" **160.00**
Holiday Greetings, Sold Here, Christmas Seals, Protect your Home from Tuberculosis, hardstock, Santa Claus art by Walter Sasse, Official Post Office

Dept. stamps, 1936, some soiling, 11" x 14" **45.00**

Christmas and Easter Seals, uncut sheet of 1977 Christmas Seals, **$3.**

Christmas

One of the most celebrated holidays of the year has provided us with many collectibles. Some collectors specialize in only one type of object or one character, such as Santa. Others just love Christmas and collect a wide variety of objects.

For additional listings, see *Warman's Antiques & Collectibles* and *Warman's Americana & Collectibles*, as well as *Vintage Christmas Ceramic Collectibles* by Walter Dworkin, KP Books.

Bank, 5" h, snowman, white, black bowler hat, red scarf, orig box 15.00

Book
A Christmas Carol, Dickens, Dana Estes & Co., 1902, five full-color illus 28.00
Christmas in Mexico, Jadwigo Lopez, World Book, 1976, 80 pgs 8.00
Felicity's Surprise, A Christmas Story, Valerie Tripp, Pleasant Co., 1st ed 7.00
Murder for Christmas, Thomas Godfrey, Wings Books, 1989, 1st ed., 465 pgs 12.00
The Real Christmas, Pat Boone, Fleming M. Revell Co., 1961, 62 pgs 15.00

Candleholder
Angels, pair playing violins, Holt-Howard Co., 1963, 4-1/2" h 18.00

Christmas items, diecuts, four different images of children, carefully cut out and pasted to gold foil backings, each **$20.**

Choir kid angels, white gowns, each holding letter to spell Noel, 3-3/4" h, set of four 28.00
Santa King, Holt-Howard Co., 1960, 4-3/4" h 40.00
Two girls in red pajamas, one holding wreath letters "NO," other with "EL," Commodore Co., 4-1/2" h 25.00
Wee Three Kings, Holt-Howard Co., 1960, 4-1/2" h, set of three 60.00

Candy box, cardboard, string handle, Merry Christmas, Happy New Year, carolers in village, 1920s, 4-1/2" l 8.00

Candy cane, 6" l, chenille, red and white 4.00

Candy container
Belsnickle style, faded felt outfit, 7" h 275.00
Santa wearing snow shoes and holding Christmas tree, hard plastic, sack with opening for candy, Rosbro Plastics, 4-1/2" h 40.00

Figure, ceramic
Boy pushing girl in sleigh, Lefton Co., pr 25.00
Christmas girls, Norcrest, 4" h 45.00
Girl in sleigh, 5-1/4" h 60.00
Kissing couple, 3-3/4" h, pr .. 15.00
Pixies holding gift 15.00

Hors d'oeurve holder, Snow lady, Poinsettia Studios, 7-3/4" h ... 40.00

Icicles, metal, twisted, color or silver, 4" h 1.00

Ink blotter, booklet of blotters with holiday lantern motif, "May this be your Merriest Christmas and 1929 your Happiest Year," The Charis Corp of Allentown, PA, 2-1/2" x 6" 45.00

Light bulb, figural
Cluster of grapes, purple, mkd "15V Japan" on cap, 2-3/4" h..... 12.00
Lantern, hp, late 1940s-early 1950s, 2-1/2" x 4-1/2" 22.50
Snowman, milk glass, mkd "120V Japan" on cap, 3-1/2" h..... 12.50

Napkin holder, ceramic, Santa, Josef Originals, 4-3/4" h 24.00

Christmas items, Santa, skiing, faded red jacket, blue pants, white "fur" trim, pack on back with small green tree and boxes, holding ski poles in each hand, **$35.**

Christmas items, Santa, full size, store display type, moves and gives Christmas greetings when activated, **$75.**

Christmas items, Santa Claus rubber squeak toy, Sanitoy, 9" h, **$15.**

Nativity set, Precious Moments, "Prepare Ye The Way Of The Lord," #E-0508, angels preparing manger, 1983, from 1" to 6 1/2" h, six pcs 120.00

Oil and vinegar cruets, ceramic, Santa, Napco, 5-1/2" h, pr 30.00

Ornament
Angel, chromolithograph, tinsel trim, German 7" h............ 20.00
Campbell Soup Kids, 1988, MIB 12.50
Heart, glass, red, 3-1/2" h..... 15.00
Mickey Mouse's 50th Birthday, Schmid, limited edition, 1978, orig box 15.00

Santa Claus, red plastic, painted white trim, black eyes, 1940s-1950s, 3-1/4" h 18.00
Turkey, Great Gobbles, Christopher Radko, retired, hang tag attached, 6" h 60.00

Pinback button, celluloid cover, metal back, Santa, "Merry Christmas & Happy New Year," 1-1/4" d 35.00

Planter, figural lady
Holding gift, white hooded cloak, red dress, Brinns, 6" h...... 35.00
Holding gifts, red coat, green skirt, Napco, 7-1/4" h 45.00
Holding green gift and muff, Relpo, 7-1/2" h............................ 45.00
Holding two gifts, red hat and coat, ruffled white skirt, Inarco, 1963, 6" h 35.00
Holding wreath, red jacket, white skirt, poinsettia in hair, Napco, 7" h 45.00

Plate, Cherubs surrounding Nativity scene, Wedgwood, 1997 .... 15.00

Postcard, A Hearty Christmas Greeting, sledding Victorian children.................................... 4.00

Record, Little Drummer Boy, Abbey Choir, Diplomat...................... 5.00

Salt and pepper shakers, pr, figural Christmas trees, Lefton, 4" h 12.00
Cloud Santas, Holt-Howard Co., 3-1/2" h............................ 30.00
Reindeer salt, Santa in sleigh pepper, 3-1/2" h................ 28.00
Santa, stacking, Holt-Howard Co., 1959, 5-1/2" h.................. 30.00
Snowman, stacking, Napco, 4-1/4" h 15.00
Snowmen waving, 4" h......... 15.00

Christmas items, ornaments, contemporary, **$2** each.

Sheet music, *Rudolph the Red-Nosed Reindeer* by Johnny Mark, copyright 1949, with lyrics and music as recorded by Gene Autry 6.00

Snow dome, Nativity scene, #833, made in Hong Kong, 2-1/4" h 10.00

Stocking, red flannel
Mr. & Mrs. Frosty, white flannel top cuff, name written in glitter box on cuff, 1950s................... 12.00
Santa, stenciled Santa and sleigh, 12" l 15.00

Tag, 2-3/4" l, Christmas Greetings, dog in wrapped box, made in USA 2.00

Tree
3" h, brush, green, mica trim, red wood base........................... 5.00
12" h, feather, white sq red base, mkd "West Germany"...... 72.00

Tree stand, cast iron, Christmas scenes, three diamond-shape screws, sgd "Gesetzl-Gesch," 6" h, 11-1/2" sq............................. 100.00

Tree topper, silvered glass, multicolored, 9" h................. 20.00

Cigar Collectibles

The fine art of cigar smoking has been revived, and, along with this newfound interest, collectors are enjoying an increase in the number cigar-related collectibles to add to their collections.

Ashtray, made with orig cigar wrappers including King Edwards S&S, Dutch Masters and Robt. Burns de Luxe, wrappers under clear glass, three cigar slots, 4-1/4" d.. 35.00

Can, El Paxo, litho tin, Indian princess, 5" d 185.00

Cigar band, 3" l, foil, World's Fair 1939, blue and orange against gold, Trylon and Perisphere in center with "Memories Special" and "Memories Remembrance," unused 5.00

Cigar box, White Owl, New York World Fair 1939 exhibit building, 5/8" x 3-5/8 x 5-1/8" 25.00

Cigar box label
American Belle, 6" x 9", young lady flanked by flowers, herald crest, medallions, harbor scene, early 1900s 30.00
Blue Ribbon, litho, blue ribbon against blue sunburst, c1900 .... 1.50
Flor De Bouquet, color litho of pretty woman in garden setting,

Cigar collectibles, War Eagles Cigar tin, 5-1/4" h, 5" d, **$130.**

copyright June 12, 1874, unused 5.00
Nov. 11th Victory Day, 6" x 8-3/4", State of Liberty illus, emb gold and black 18.00
Pedro Perez, 2-1/4" x 3" oval, early 1900s 5.00
Round-Up, 2-1/4" x 3" oval, early 1900s 6.50
Wizard, 4" x 4-1/2", early 1900s 6.00

Cigar case, silver color, holds three cigars, 5-1/2" 12.00

Counter display, litho tin, "Kennebec" in silver oval over portrait of Indian flanked by tomahawks, image repeated inside lid, 2-1/4" h, 8-1/2" w, 5" d 32.00

Jar, amber glass, fired-on text, tin lid, "Mercantile Cigars, 5 Cents," 5-1/2" h, 4-1/2" d 16.50

Pinback button
Dutch Masters, blue lettering, white ground, "President" in red letters, 1950s 8.00
Enjoy A Cigar, brown on yellow, slogan "Join The Cigar Enjoyment Parade," c1930 **30.00**

Premium coupon, United Cigar Stores Company of America, set of four 8.00

Sign, cardboard
Orange Flower, string hanger, green border, orange ground, white lettering outlined in black, flower sprig, c1930, 6-1/2" x 11". 20.00
"Smoke Jennie Lind, Hand Made Havana, 5 Cents," 8-1/4" x 14-1/2" 132.00

Cigar collectibles, cigar cutter, pocket type, sterling silver, embossed Indian head, 1-1/2" l, **$75.**

Sign, paper, Golden's Blue Ribbon Cigars, blue and white, 5-1/2" x 10" 8.00

Sign, tin, Charles The Great Cigars, tin, shows full box of cigars, ashtray, fancy match safe, c1910, framed, 17-1/2" l 275.00

Tin
Old Abe Cigars, round, paper label 65.00
Reichard's Cadet Cigar 85.00

Cigarette Collectibles

Lately, the cigarette industry has taken a beating in regards to its product and its advertising methods. However, collecting interest in the topic is hot! Whether this politically incorrect habit will be snuffed out is anyone's guess.

Ashtray, metal, figural, Mt. Rushmore, made in Japan 17.50

Banner, Old Gold Cigarettes, Not A Cough In The Car Load, 42" x 120" 95.00

Box, cardboard, flat 50, cardboard case shows three guards holding

Cigarette items, tin, Murad The Turkish Cigarette, S. Anargyros, faded, C.5, **$15.**

cards saying "Season's Greetings" 85.00

Cigarette cards
British Consuls, Canadian issue, set of eight 8.00
Wings, c1940, set of 50 .... 60.00

Cigarette case, enameled, woman's, black, envelope style, red stone dec, 3" x 4" 35.00

Cigarette holder, aluminum top, brown Bakelite mouth piece, stamped "Denicotea Cunni," 4" l 55.00

Cigarette silk
Duckbill, New South Wales, yellowed, 2" x 3" 7.50
Goat, Italy, slight fraying, 2" x 3" 9.00
Gorilla, French Congo, 2" x 3" 9.00

Display, litho tin, "They're so Refreshing! Kool Cigarettes," 8" h, 7 1/8" w, 4-1/8" d 25.00

Game, Camels, The Game, MIB, 1992 .... 10.00

Cigarette items, sign, Fatima, A Sensible Cigarette, green ground, red lettering, litho tin, C.8, **$85.**

Cigarette items, counter mat, Smoke Kool Cigarettes, white lettering on green, **$35.**

Matchbook cover, Topps Gum, O. Soglow art, flattened, WWII era 10.00

Money clip, Chesterfield Cigarettes, white enamel and chrome, Liggit & Myers Tobacco Co., made by Robbins Co., c1950 .... 20.00

Pin set, Smokin' Joe's Racing, 4" x 7" colorful cardboard folder with set of six driver pins, licensed for Winston Cup by Sports Marketing Enterprises, 1994 .... 15.00

Pinback button
Perfection Cigarettes, multicolored image of lady, back paper with list of tobacco products.... 20.00
Philip Morris Cigarettes, black, white, and fleshtones, c1930 .... 50.00

Sign, paper, model in negligee, glamour pose, Brown & Williamson Co., c1940s, 12" x 18", two archival tape repairs on back 65.00

Sign, tin, Smoke Kools, emb penguin with pack of Kools, 16-3/4" x 8-1/2" 80.00

Thermometer, litho tin, "Chesterfield, More Than Ever, They Satisfy," emb cigarette pack, 13-1/2" h, 5-3/4" w 95.00

Tin, vertical, litho tin
Ardath Cigarettes Splendo, Mild Natural Egyptian Blend ... 37.50
Pall Mall, Christmas dec 18.00

Circus Collectibles

Whether it's the allure of the big tent or the dazzling acts, circuses have delighted kids of all ages since the 18th century. Of course this has helped to generate lots of collectibles, advertising, schedules, etc.

Circus items, tickets, each **$5.**

Christmas card, Clyde Beatty-Cole Bros, 8" x 9-1/2", multicolored, 1959 .... 8.00

Circus pass, Circus Hall of Fame, Sarasota, Fla. 3.50

Clown, celluloid figure riding fuzzy horse, mkd "M. M.," orig box 75.00

Figurine, circus elephant, sitting, Wade, 1-1/4" h 8.00

Lid, Animal Heroes of Dixie's Circus Radio Stories, 2-1/4" d 3.00

Little Golden Book, *Howdy Doody's Circus*, 1st ed, 1950 .... 16.00

Magazine/program, Ringling Bros. and Barnum & Bailey Circus, 1949, cover illus by E. McKnight Kauffer 32.00

Pinback button, Souvenir of the Circus, clown, 1-3/4" d 9.50

Pop-up book, *Circus*, 1979 ..... 15.00

Poster
Al G. Kelly & Miller Bros. giraffe, 28" h, 21" w 60.00
Hunt Bros. Circus, shows saber tooth tiger 95.00
Tom Mix Circus and Wild West, white linen backing, professional mounted paper poster, 28" x 42" 115.00

Circus items, poster, Ringling Bros, Barnum & Bailey, menagerie, black and white, matted and framed, **$35.**

Press-out book, *Tiny Circus*, Whitman, 1972, 8" x 11-1/2"... 9.00

Ring, gray metal, circus giant Al Tomaini................................. 35.00

Stuffed toy, elephant, King Tusk, gold blanket with silver trim, 5" l plastic tusks, Ringling Bros. Barnum and Bailey Combined Shows, made in Korea, 11" h, 21" l 48.00

Circus items, magazine-program, Clyde Beatty-Cole Bros, Dale Hoover in Person, **$15.**

Civil War

This sad time in American history has led to an interesting range of collectibles, including weapons, uniforms, flags, and ephemera. Ask about the provenance when purchasing this type of material as that adds to the value and helps assure you're not buying a fake.

Reproduction alert.

Civil War, belt buckle, early puppy paw type, 1862-65, **$165.**

Badge, Delegate, G.A.R., Indiana, metal hanger bar, cello pendant joined by red, white, and blue striped ribbon, inscribed in gold, dark bronze luster hanger with IN state seal, view of "Entrance to Soldier's Home, Marion, Ind.," 36th annual encampment, May 1915, ribbon worn............................ 25.00

Belt, enlisted man's, black leather, brass retaining clips, oval brass "U.S." buckle 175.00

Book
Confederate General Robt. E. Lee & His Campaigns in Virginia, 1906, 300 pgs, fold-out maps 45.00
Life of Lincoln, Herndon/Welk, c1889, 500 pgs................. 19.95
Personal Memoir of General Sheridan, 1889, limited edition, two volumes, faux leather, fold-out maps........................... 45.00

Button, brass, U. S. eagle imprint 10.00

Fife, 17-1/2" l, rosewood, nickel silver ends, 8 bands, orig dark finish, faint signature "W. Crosby, Boston" 125.00

Newspaper, Cincinnati Gazette, for year of 1863, fold lines and minor damage, group of 19 newspapers 150.00

Picture card, 2-5/8" x 3-7/8", black and white illus of *Monitor & Merrimack,* titled below....... 25.00

Civil War, jewelry, watch fob, bone, carved by prisoner, 10-1/2" l, **$200.**

Print, *Battles of the Rebellion, 1863,* Charles Magnus lithographer, hand-colored, framed 400.00

Ribbon, 2" x 3-1/2", white silk, center red, white, and blue image of US flag with 20 stars, blue image of bugle and saber sword crossed over flag pole, blue lettering "Union and Democracy"............................ 65.00

Tintype, unidentified Union soldier 30.00

Clarice Cliff

To some collectors the name Clarice Cliff means Art Deco. To others, it's the bright ceramics created by this talented English woman. Cliff's work is becoming very popular and very expensive. Look for patterns created by Cliff for many different English manufacturers.

Reproduction alert.

Biscuit barrel, Celtic Harvest, hp floral dec, 6-1/2" h............... 395.00

Bowl, lotus pattern, matte white, Newport Pottery, England, 8-3/4" d 120.00

Cup and saucer
Bizarre, conical shape, Orange Autumn, printed factory marks 425.00
Florals, molded swirls, Royal Staffordshire..................... 60.00

Fruit bowl, Lily Pad, blues and greens, 5" h, 8" l................... 300.00

Honey pot, Beehive, Crocus, printed factory marks, 4" h.............. 595.00

Plate
Crocus, 8-3/4" d.................. 200.00
Lodore, 1931, 6" d 110.00

Platter
Harvest pattern, mulberry transfer ware, A. J. Wilkinson & Son, Ltd., England, 11-3/4" l.... 90.00
Lodore, 1930, 12-1/4" 110.00

Salt and pepper shakers, pr, Bizarre, Blue Chintz 550.00

Sugar sifter, conical, Autumn Crocus, 5-1/2" h................... 600.00

Clarice Cliff, teapot, Bizarre Ware, 5" h, **$245.**

Tea cup and saucer, Queen Elizabeth II coronation, registry date 1952 .... 70.00

Teapot, Cotswold, 5" h 245.00

Trio, 3" h teacup, 5-1/4" d saucer, 6" plate, Springtime pattern 50.00

Vegetable dish, cov, Duvivier 115.00

Wall vase, cloud shape with flying swallow 200.00

Clickers

These little giveaways were popular with early advertisers and children, too.

Advertising
Buster Brown 225.00
Columbus Buggy Co., 1-1/4" d 185.00
Endicott-Johnson 35.00
Fort Pitt, 1-7/8" l 55.00
OshKosh, Clicks Everywhere with Everyone, Buy 'em at Armstrong's 65.00

Pillsbury's Best, Minneapolis, MN, 1-1/4" d 145.00
Poll Parrot Shoes, 4-1/4" 90.00
Purity Ice Cream, York Sanitary Milk Co., celluloid 195.00
Quaker State, 1-7/8" l 68.00
Red Goose Shoes, standing goose 110.00
Saplio, Clean Up, 1-1/4" d 120.00
Sohio, 2-3/8" l 65.00
Weather Bird Shoes 65.00

Halloween, frog-shaped, shows witch on broom, haunted house and flying bats, T. Cohn, 1940s, tin, 3" l 30.00

Kirchhof, litho tin
Frog, Life of the Party Products, 3" l 38.00
Joker and lady, 1920s.............. 8.00

Japanese, litho tin
Alligator................................. 20.00
Western theme 20.00

Clickers, Halloween, Kirchhof, Newark, N.J., 1-3/4" l, **$17.50.**

Clickers, Buster Brown Shoes, lithographed tin, **$10.**

Clocks

Tick-tock. Most clock collectors specialize and seek particular manufacturers or certain types of clocks. Buyers should carefully examine a clock to determine if it's in working order. Missing parts may result in considerable expense after the sale when it's time to pay for repairs.

For additional listings, see *Warman's Antiques & Collectibles* and *Warman's Americana & Collectibles*.

Advertising

Hire's Root Beer, "Drink Hires Root Beer with Root Barks, Herbs," 15" d 250.00

Nestle Cookie Mix, 4" d, 5-1/2" h, silvered metal bell chimes,

enameled high gloss chocolate brown metal case, Lafayette Watch Co., late 1940s...................... 35.00

None Such Mincemeat, pumpkin face, 8-1/2" w, some wear 300.00

Alarm

Football, 7" h painted composition football player, 2-1/2" x 7-1/2" grass green base, white helmet, trousers striped in blue, red jersey with white "32" decal, red

Clock, TV type, ceramic, black panther holding clock, gold highlights, unmarked, **$65.**

and blue stockings, white shoes, ©1975 Sears 14.00
Soccer, 4" d, wind-up, ivory white metal case, convex plexiglass, scene of soccer players in colorful uniforms 20.00

Animated
Ballerina, music box, United 150.00
Fireplace, Mastercrafter's ... 125.00
Grandmother, rocking chair, Haddon............................ 190.00
Spinning Wheel, Lux 85.00

Clock, shelf, New England Clock Co., pendulum, contemporary version of earlier style, **$15.**

Clock, wall, Howard Miller, battery operated, wood grained case, 24" round, **$95.**

Ansonia
China, white scrolled case, painted cherry blossom design, paw feet, works mkd "June 14, '81, Ansonia Clock Co., New York," 10-1/4" w, 11-1/2" h, minor imperfections on case 350.00
Shelf, gingerbread, carved and pressed walnut case, paper on zinc dial, silver dec glass, 8-day time and strike movement with pendulum, 22" h 185.00

Carriage, New Haven Clock Co., gilded brass case, beveled glass, gold repaint to case, orig pendulum and key, 11-1/2" h................ 315.00

Desk, American, shaped rect, brass case, white enamel bordering cobalt blue, stylized applied monogram, decorative brass corners, central dial with Arabic numerals, 4-3/4" h 150.00

Germany, mantel, white onyx, amber and brown striations, ormolu mounts with shells, paw feet, porcelain dial with chased ormolu center with rampant lions, works mkd "Germany," no key, dial damaged, 13" l, 10-3/4" h 275.00

Clock, mantel, Waterbury, original key and pendulum, **$125.**

Seth Thomas, Cambridge, textured oak case, 8-day movement, 23-3/4" h, 15" w 315.00

Wall, Have A Happy Day, Smiley face, electric, mkd "Robertshaw Controls Co. of Lux Time Division," early 1970s, 7" d 10.00

Weather station, L.L. Bean, clock, thermometer, hygrometer and moonphase, oak jointed round case, 11-3/4" d, bezel...................... 75.00

Clock, shelf, Eli Terry & Sons, Plymouth, CT, 8 day, stencil decoration, claw feet, **$465.**

Cloisonné

Cloisonné is an interesting decorative technique in which small wires are adhered to a metal surface, and then the design is filled in with enamel, creating a very colorful pattern. The more intricate the design and the enameling, or the older the piece, the higher the price can be.

For additional listings, see *Warman's Antiques & Collectibles Price Guide.*

Reproduction alert.

Cloisonné, powder box, covered, yellow background, multicolored floral designs, 3-3/4" d, **$80.**

Box, cov, 2" x 3" 100.00

Candlesticks, pr, figural, blue mythical animals seated on round dark red base with open work sides, three feet, each animal holds flower in mouth, red candle socket on back, 7-1/8" h 200.00

Charger, roosters and floral dec, black ground, Chinese, late 19th C, surface scratches, 14" d 190.00

Cigarette case, green, 3 dragons, Chinese 175.00

Cross pendant, blue ground, rose and white dec, Russian hallmarks 150.00

Desk set, brush pot, pen, pen tray, blotter and paper holder, Japan 130.00

Jardinière, bronze, bands of cloisonné designs, golden yellow and blue triangles, polychrome geometric designs on dark blue, chrysanthemums on light blue, cast relief scene of water lily, turtle, and flowering branches on int., 13" d, 10" h, soldered repair at foot 220.00

Planter, classical symbol and scroll dec, blue ground, Chinese, 11" d 100.00

Cloisonné, plate, multicolored, Japanese, 5" d, **$75.**

Tea kettle, multicolor scrolling lotus flowers, medium blue ground, double handles, Chinese, 19th C 690.00

Vase, 3" h, animal head handles, gilt rims and bases, China, 19th C, pr 375.00

Clothes Sprinklers

Here's a part of the flea market world that has taken off. Who would have ever thought that Grandma's way of preparing to iron would become so popular with collectors? Because many of these handy sprinklers are figural, they make great display pieces.

Ceramic
Chinese man, Cleminson, 8" h 80.00
Dutch boy, 8-1/4" h 295.00
Elephant, pink and gray 165.00
Elephant, white................... 110.00
Iron shape, white, green ivy dec 125.00
Kate, Cleminson, 6-1/2" h 40.00

Mammy, white dress, 7" h .. 495.00
Rooster, 10" h 175.00
Siamese cat, 8-1/4" h 195.00
Sprinkle Plenty, 8" h............. 85.00

Glass, clear recycled bottle, black rubber and tin stopper top...... 5.00

Plastic, Merry Maid, mkd "Made in USA".. 15.00

Clothes sprinklers, ceramic, Sprinkles Plenty, yellow and green, **$85.**

Clothing

As fashions change from year to year, collecting vintage clothing never seems to go out of style. Many clothing collectors look for prestigious labels as well as garments that are in good condition.

For additional listings, see *Warman's Antiques & Collectibles* and *Warman's Americana & Collectibles,* as well as specific topics in this edition.

Bathing suit, girl's, cotton print, ruffles, 1950s 15.00

Bed jacket, satin, pink, ecru lace trim, labeled "B. Altman & Co. NY," 1930s.. 35.00

Bloomers, wool, cream 25.00

Blouse
Chiffon, green, child's multiple rows of ruffles 15.00

Cotton, white, cutwork, Victorian 20.00
Lace, ecru, evening style, gathered waist, 1950s 18.00

Clothing, man's, bathing suit, black wool, **$30.**

Dress, girl's
Georgette and chiffon, pink, c1920 .... 75.00
Gingham, blue and white, hand and machine sewn, white embroidery trim, 25" h 50.00
Knit, two pcs, 1930 .... 25.00

Dress, lady's
Beige lace, light tan silk crepe, lace belt with brass buckle, pleated lace skirt, lace tunic with ruffles at neckline, three-quarter length lace jacket with long sleeves, pin tucks, collar, c1925, some damage to dress shoulder 65.00
Chiffon, blue, edges trimmed with braided fabric, 1925 .... 40.00
Crochet, navy blue cotton, long fringe, deep scoop neckline, satin fringe hem, mid 1940s 35.00
Pale lilac silk, sq cut steel buttons, cream lace collar, bubble-effect skirt, draped back, c1900, wear 60.00
Wool jersey, black, long sleeves, wrap style hem trimmed with red wool jersey, patch pocket, black silk lining, labeled "Bill Blass, Made in U.S.A," late 1970s 40.00

Evening gown, lady's
Crepe, brown, matching velvet capelet with feather trim, c1930 .... 40.00
Net and taffeta, black, lace flowers, c1940 .... 48.00
Organza, white, shirred, rhinestones, c1940 .... 45.00
Silk, black, embroidered all over with black glass beads, halter style neckline, single strap on low back, labeled "Lillie Rubin, 100% silk, Made in China," 1970s 60.00

Nightgown, white cotton, elaborate yoke of ruched white lawn alternating with lace, long lace trimmed sleeves, placket with lace trim, c1910 .... 20.00

Clothing, child's, dress, matching cape, white cotton, 1890s, **$90.**

Pajama's
Girl's, baby doll style, cotton, pink hearts, 1960s 7.00
Lady's, silk, red, 1920s 75.00

Pant suit, top and palazzo pants, Andrea Gayle, bright green, orange, yellow, pink, gray and purple satiny material, two pcs 65.00

Petticoat, cream organdy, pin tucks, lace, ruffles at hem, train, c1890 .... 35.00

Robe, printed green, tan, gray, yellow, and ivory silk, swirls, floral, and feather shapes, c1945 .... 60.00

Skirt, lady's, black wool, Victorian 45.00

Sport coat, men's, green, purple, blue, and white floral print on mustard yellow ground, mkd "Camelot Brothers Co.," mid-1960s 35.00

Suit
Boy's, navy wool blazer, short pants, orig Tom Sawyer brand.... 45.00
Lady's, linen, straight skirt, jacket with shoulder pads and fitted waist, English 70.00
Man's, black gabardine, jacket, vest, trousers, size 42, c1940 .... 50.00

Teddy, yellow, pink emb trim on bodice, 1920s 25.00

Wedding gown, satin, ivory, padded shoulders, sweetheart neckline, waist swag, self train, c1945 150.00

Poplin, white, middy style, c1910 .... 15.00
Silk, cream, embroidered, 1900s 65.00

Bridesmaid's gown, pink chiffon, satin ribbon trim, size 10 ...... 50.00

Cape
Girl's, flannel wool, ivory, silk cord embroidery...................... 45.00
Lady's, mohair, black, ankle length, c1930 .... 75.00

Chemise, linen, ruffles and lace at cuffs, late 18th/early 19th C.. 25.00

Christening gown, cotton, white, lace trim, matching bonnet, 47" l 115.00

Coat
Boy's, linen, hand stitched, dec cuffs.................................. 35.00
Lady's, Persian lamb, black, matching hat and muff 95.00

Clothing Accessories

Clothing accents and accessories are even more collectible than vintage clothing. Perhaps this is because many of these accessories are just as fun to use today as when they were originally created. And, as with vintage clothing, with proper care and handling, it's perfectly acceptable to use these collectibles.

For additional listings, see *Warman's Antiques & Collectibles* and *Warman's Americana & Collectibles*, as well as specific topics in this edition.

Apron
Gingham, green, embroidered
design, pockets................. **10.00**
Printed cotton, Christmas, patch
pockets **15.00**

Baby bonnet, white cotton, pink
ribbon ties, c1960.................. **10.00**

Bonnet
Beaded, jet beads, 19th C..... **95.00**
Silk, hand crocheted lace **36.00**

Collar
Beaded and fur, white, early 1950s
.... **10.00**
Black silk and velvet, steel beading,
c1890 .... **25.00**

Gloves, pr
Girl's, white nylon, ruffled cuff
.... **10.00**
Lady's, satin, long, white **20.00**

Handbag,
Alligator, brown, brass clasp, brown
leather lining, c1945 .... **45.00**
Black velvet, lined with cream
silk with rosettes, pierced ivory
frame, c1930..................... **45.00**
Floral tapestry, rose, green, and
blue on cream ground, black
border, brass frame with chain
handle, c1940, 8-1/2" x 5-1/2"
.... **30.00**

Handkerchief, printed
Christmas poinsettia design, red
stitched edge **10.00**
Valentine's Day motif, red and
white................................ **5.00**

Hat
Beanie (Beanie & Cecil), propeller
top **55.00**
Indiana Jones, "Official," size XL
.... **50.00**

Muff
Child's, white rabbit fur **25.00**
Lady's, mink **45.00**

Necktie, men's
Bow-tie, white polka dots on black
.... **10.00**
Fish, 1940s........................... **5.00**
Striped, rayon, 1930s.............. **3.00**

Scarf, Maggie Rouff, Paris, black,
fuchsia, rose, pink, and off-white,
black borders with geometric-style
flowers, 1930s, 30" sq **30.00**

Shawl
Paisley, dark ground, long fringe,
small holes **70.00**
Silk, floral ivory satin embroidery
on ivory background, knotted
satin fringe, Spanish, c1900, 44"
sq **75.00**

Shoes, children's
Faux crocodile and suede, side
buckle, rust, 1930s **36.00**
Leather, Oxford, black kid, Buster
Brown brand, 1930s......... **40.00**
Leather, T-strap style, brown
leather, black, rust, and tan
suede, Red Goose brand. 1930s
.... **40.00**

Shoes, lady's
Leather, brown, high button top
.... **40.00**
Low heels, black kid, black patent
toes, Buster Brown brand **145.00**

Shoes, men's
Boots, work type, leather, early,
11" h, pr........................... **25.00**
Dress, brown, c1950 .... **20.00**

Socks, men's, rayon and silk, cotton
toe and heel, black, colored arrow,
1950s...................................... **5.00**

Stole, marabou, white.............. **50.00**

Sweater
Child's, hand-knit, train on back
.... **30.00**
Lady's, cashmere, cream, fur collar,
embroidered silk lining, labeled
"Hadley Cashmere," crocheted
buttons at cuffs, late 1950s **65.00**

Vest, white cotton, mother-of-pearl
buttons, c1910 .... **65.00**

Coca-Cola

An Atlanta pharmacist, John S Pemberton, is credited with first developing the syrup base used for Coca-Cola. He was attempting to formulate a patent medicine for those experiencing headaches, nervousness, or stomach upsets. In 1887, Willis E. Venable mixed the syrup with carbonated water, and the rest was history. The *Atlanta Journal* carried the first print ad for Coca-Cola on May 29, 1886. In 1893, a trademark was granted for Coca-Cola written in script, and in 1945, the term Coke was registered.

For additional listings, see *Warman's Advertising*, *Warman's Antiques & Collectibles* and *Warman's Americana & Collectibles*.

Reproduction alert.

Coca-Cola items, tray, Coke Refreshes You, hand pouring from Coke bottle into glass, garden setting, **$28.**

Banner, silk, white with gold fringe, "things go better with Coke" in red text, 1960s, light soiling, 46" h, 23-1/2" w **55.00**

Binder cover, 13" x 15-1/2", rigid cardboard under textured red oilcloth cover, inner spine of four ring metal binder for adv sales sheets, 1950s.......................... **40.00**

Bingo card, 8-1/2" x 9", cardboard, red and black printing, 25 diecut windows, bottom text

"Compliments Coca-Cola Bottling Co.," Kemper-Thomas Cincinnati, OH, 1940s **25.00**

Bottle, 9-1/2" h, Penn State Championship Season, 1986-87 .... **12.00**

Calendar, 1958........................ **95.00**

Card table, 1930s, bottle logos in corners, Coke tag on back..... **55.00**

Grading

Coca-cola items are often sold with a condition grade designation, like C 8.5. This coding gives collectors valuable information. Of course, the higher the grade, the higher the price.

10 = mint, unused, no wear or fading
9.5 = near mint, very minor imperfections
8.5 = outstanding, few minor imperfections
8 = excellent, light scratches, minor dents, light edge wear
7.5 = fine-plus, some scratches, fading
7 = fine, noticeable scratches, light dents
6.5 = fine-minus (good), noticeable slight damage, slight rust
6 = poor, noticeable damage, discoloration

Carrier, six-pack
  Aluminum, 1940s, embossed "Coca-Cola" 72.00
  Wooden, early 1940s, lift handle, "Drink Coca-Cola in Bottles, Pause...Go refreshed" logo with wings, mkd "new consumer case," red on yellow ground 245.00

Change tray
  1914, Betty.......................... 150.00
  1941, girl with skates............ 48.00

Clock, light-up, metal and glass, rectangular, "Drink Coca-Cola," clock face over red text, white ground, 11" h, 12" w 165.00

Coasters, colored aluminum, 1950s, boxed set of eight, orig box... 65.00

Cooler, Cavalier picnic cooler, 1950s, "Drink Coca-Cola in Bottles," orig box, 18" h, 18" w, 13" d........ 440.00

Dispenser, syrup, countertop, metal, 1940s, "Drink Coca-Cola, Ice Cold" in oval, end has "Have A Coke" in circle, with glass stand/mounting hardware, 14" h, 8" w, 18" d 110.00

Doll, Santa Claus, 1950s-1960s, stuffed body, black boots, 18" h 110.00

Door pull, 8" h, plastic and metal, bottle shape, orig instructions and screws, C-9.3-9.5 .... 275.00

Game board, 11-1/4" x 26-1/2", Steps to Health, prepared and distributed by Coca-Cola Co. of Canada, Ltd., copyright 1938, orig unmarked brown paper envelope........... 60.00

Letterhead, 8-1/2" x 11" stationery, Coca-Cola Bottling Co., Macon, GA, c1914.. 5.00

Magazine advertisement
  1914, "Delicious Coca-Cola, Pure and Wholesome," portrait of woman drinking glass of Coke, back cover of The National Sunday Magazine, framed 38.50
  1936, "Thru 50 Years...the pause that refreshes," color image of two women in bathing suits 44.00

Menu sign, tin, 1960s, "Enjoy Coca-Cola" in red circle logo beside "things go better with Coke" slogan, red/white top over green board, 28" h, 20" w.......................... 330.00

Paperweight, girl in white swimsuit 80.00

Prize chance card, 7" x 8-1/4", red and black printing on white, listing of 70 lady first names and corresponding number of red dots to be punched out, 1940s, unused 5.00

Service pin, 10 Years, 10k gold, raised image of bottle, c1930 .... 65.00

Sign, cardboard cutout, 1951, "Be refreshed" in banner by button

Coca-Cola items, music box, Seasons Greetings, Santa, revolving train, original box, **$25.**

Coca-Cola items, Barbie, red and white polka dot dress, holds glass of Coke in one hand, parasol in other, original box, **$20.**

sign, three women at table drinking glasses of Coke 16" h, 24" w 165.00

Sign, paper, "Take Along Coke in 12 oz. Cans, Buy a Case," large-diamond can and dock scene, framed, 20" h, 36" w 365.00

Sign, tin, embossed, 1961, "Drink Coca-Cola, Enjoy That Refreshing New Feeling," white text on red fish tail ground on white, clean-cut ends, rolled top/bottom border, 24" h, 36" w.......................... 150.00

Thermometer, tin, 5" x 17" diecut emb tin, figural Pat'd Dec 25, 1923 bottle, 1930s 150.00

Toy
  Car, litho tin, Ford taxi, friction, made by Taiyo, 1960s, orig box 315.00
  Truck, Buddy L, model 5426, pressed steel, yellow with five cases and two hand trucks, orig box, truck C.9................. 550.00
  Van, Corgi, 5" l diecast metal and plastic replica, copyright 1978, color box with display window 35.00

Trade publication, *The Coca-Cola Bottler*, 8-1/2" x 11", 60 pgs, March, 1946 .... 25.00

Tray
  1935, Madge Evans, C-7.5 .. 165.00
  1940, sailor girl, girl in sailor outfit sitting on dock 615.00
  1941, skater girl, woman in skates sitting on log 425.00
  1950, menu girl 95.00
  1958, picnic basket............ 120.00

Uniform patch, Enjoy Coke...... 3.00

Cocktail Shakers

"Make mine a dry martini" was the plea of many well-heeled party guests we gazed at in the movies. To make that perfect drink, a clever device called the cocktail shaker was used. Today these shakers are finding their way to flea markets and collectors.

Aluminum, gold color, shaker top has insert with holes, Mirro, 1950s,

Cocktail shakers, chromed metal, black wood handle, coffeepot shape, **$35.**

8-1/2" h 18.00

Chrome
Farberware, 1950s, 12" h...... 30.00
Mr Bartender, measuring jigger, glass insert, 8" h 25.00

Farber Bros., Bakelite handle, 12-1/2" h 85.00

Glass
Cobalt blue, barbell, three-pc chrome top 495.00
Clear, silver-plate top, 9" h ... 48.00
Clear with recipes, metal lid, 1950s, 8-1/4" h............................ 35.00
Clear with yellow circles of varying sizes, chrome pour top with removable lid, 11-1/4" h .. 22.00
Ruby, gold rooster on side, two gold bands, chrome strainer and top, bands worn, dent in lid, 11" h 85.00

Plastic and metal, traffic light shape, battery op, orig swizzle stick, 1950s 50.00

Cocktail shakers, aluminum, two parts, marked "Stainless Steel, Made in USA," **$15.**

Silver, repoussé, scenes of woman, cottage, windmill, scrolled shield, hallmarks, wear, 12" h 195.00

Coffee Mills

The secret to a really great cup of coffee has always been freshly ground coffee beans. Today's collectors are discovering this is still the case. With the current popularity of coffee, perhaps we'll see an increase in coffee mills.

Arcade, wall style, top jar emb "Crystal," tin twist lid mkd Arcade, lower glass container on adjustable platform, overall 17" h......... 185.00

Crown Coffee Mill, cast iron, mounted on wood base, decal "Crown Coffee Mill Made By Landers, Frary, & Clark, New

Coffee mills, wall type, cast iron top, grinder, and handle, Golden Rule, Columbus, Ohio, ornate plaque with name, cup missing, **$200.**

Britain, Conn, U.S.A.," number 11 emb on top lid 525.00

Enterprise
#0 .... 100.00
#00, two wheel, store type, orig paint, orig decals, 12-1/2" x 7-1/2" x 8-3/4", C 8+ ... 1,450.00
#9, orig dec and decals, bright orange/red paint, blue on top of base and edges of wheels, gold detailed lettering, drawer in base stenciled "No. 9," eagle finial, white porcelain knob, minor wear, restored break on lid, 28-1/2" h..................... 1,200.00

Imperial No. 705, long cast iron crank handle, domed cast iron top, molded scrolls above dovetailed case, small drawers, remnants of label above drawer, 11" h 65.00

Kitchen Aid, electric, white metal

Coffee mills, counter top, cast iron, remnants of decorative decals at top, base embossed "Enterprise Mfg Co., Philadelphia, PA," **$200.**

base with glass jar, 14" h **145.00**

Olde Thompson, wooden, drawer, handle with wooden knob, 6-3/4" sq **95.00**

Parker's Union Coffee Mill, wood, label on front, 9-1/4" h **145.00**

Rossenhaus, wooden, German or Dutch, 3-3/4" x 4-1/4", 8" h ... **48.00**

Sun Manufacturing, Greenfield, Ohio, worn orig label, round wooden sides, cast iron hardware, 12" h...................................... **300.00**

Wood, drawer, metal cup to hold beans, iron handle, 7-1/4" sq **125.00**

Coffee Tins

Here's an advertising category that has only gotten hotter over the past few years. Collected for their colorful labels, these tins are found in many sizes and shapes.

Coffee tin, Old Reliable Coffee, one-pound, keywind, **$20.**

Anchor Coffee, 1-lb **25.00**

Blanke's Portonilla Coffee, green and gold, bail handle, dome lid, c1900, 10" h **80.00**

Comrade, 1-lb, orig lid, key wind **170.00**

Dining Car, 1-lb, orig lid, key wind **95.00**

Eight O'Clock Coffee, 1-lb, orig lid, key wind **40.00**

Folger's Coffee, 5-lb, keywind **50.00**

Gold Bond Coffee, 1-lb, screw top **35.00**

Gold Metal Coffee, 1-lb, orig lid 1930s...................................... **45.00**

Hatchet Brand Coffee, 1-lb, orig lid **40.00**

Hills Bros Vacuum Packed Coffee, 1-lb, orig lid, 1930s................ **45.00**

Honeymoon Coffee, paper label over tin, 1-lb, C.8+ **275.00**

King Cole, 1-lb, orig lid **300.00**

Luzianne Coffee, small size, Mammy illus.......................... **95.00**

Mammy Coffee, 4-lb size, Mammy illus **500.00**

National's Best Blend, 1-lb, screw top.. **60.00**

Red Rose, 1-lb, keywind **45.00**

Sears Coffee Pail................... **200.00**

Universal, 1-lb, E. B. Miller & Co., Uncle Sam image, knob top .. **50.00**

Wedding Breakfast, 1-lb, keywind **50.00**

Coffee tin, Campbell's Brand Coffee, four pounds, **$120.**

Zat Zit Brand Steel Cut Coffee Sells Like Lightning, 1-lb, 1920s **35.00**

College Collectibles

Flea markets are great places to look for college items. Most collectors concentrate on memorabilia from their alma mater.

Ashtray, Harvard University, glass, 3-1/2" sq.................................... **3.00**

Book, *The University of Minnesota 1851-1951*, Minnesota Press, sgd by author, 609 pgs, maps....... **10.00**

Coloring book, Univ. of Florida Gators, 1982, unused............. **15.00**

Compact, Roanoke Univ, gold tone **28.00**

Cuff links, pr, Vassar College, gold tone **25.00**

Final exam, science, Yale, 1905, folded.................................... **25.00**

Handbook, Harbrace College, 1951, hardcover................................ **4.00**

Lunch box, oval, graphics of colorful college pennants.................... **16.00**

Mascot, Baylor Univ., bear, hard rubber, 1950s......................... **20.00**

Pennant, Iowa State, maroon and gold felt, 23" l......................... **12.00**

Photograph, Colorado Agricultural College, black-and-white photo of track team, 1904................... **65.00**

Pinback button, Texas Bowl, 1960s, red and white.......................... **4.00**

Plate

Alma College, Alma, Mich., Vernon
Kilns 30.00
Robinson Hall, Albion College,
Albion, Mich., Wedgwood,
10-1/4" d 45.00

Postcard, unused

A and M College, campus scene
.... 1.00
Campus, Univ. of Chicago, Ill., 1926
.... 2.50
Main Hall, Rutgers Univ., N.J., 1946
.... 2.00
Meridian Senior High School-
Junior College, Meridian, Miss
.... 4.00

College collectibles, Vassar College,
Taylor Hall, plate, blue and white
transfer, identification on back, plus
retailer's mark, and "Wedgwood, Made
in England," **$45.**

Record, College Marching Songs,
Russ Morgan & His Band, 45 rpm,
Decca, four-record set 65.00

Ring, man's, Lafayette Univ, PA
.... 200.00

Souvenir spoon, St. Mary's College
.... 35.00

Yearbook, Oregon Agricultural
College, 1920 .... 50.00

Coloring and Activity Books

Remember how much fun it was to color and paint? Today's collectors are still trying to "stay in the lines" as they accumulate interesting coloring books. Coloring and paint books were introduced in the early 1900s, but they didn't really catch on until the 1930s, when manufacturers began printing coloring books based on child stars, such as Shirley Temple. Most collectors look for uncolored books, but some will buy books with neatly executed work.

Prices listed are for unused books, unless otherwise noted.

Coloring books, *Lots to Color,*
©MCMLXXIII The Saalfield Publishing
Co., Akron, Ohio, some pages neatly
colored, **$8.50.**

*Alice in Wonderland Big Coloring
Book*, Whitman #301 Big Golden,
1951 .... 50.00

Banana Splits 48.00

Bullwinkle & Dudley Do Right,
Saalfield, 1971 .... 30.00

Bunny, Southfield Publishing, 7" x
8-1/4", 1950 .... 10.00

*Christmas Cut-Out and Coloring
Book*, illus by Florence Sarah
Winship, flocked hat on cover
Santa, 1954 .... 35.00

*Crusader Rabbit Trace and Color
Book*, Whitman, 1959 .... 50.00

Elsie's My Family and Friends, 10
pgs, 4" x 6" 22.00

E. T. Coloring Book, Wanderer
Book, Simon & Schuster, Universal
Studios, 1982 .... 15.00

GI Joe, 1982, few pages colored
.... 10.00

Coloring books, *Indian Fighter Color
Book*, Stephens Publishing Co., 13" x
10-3/4", unused, **$15.**

Coloring books, *Coronation Coloring
Book*, Queen Elizabeth, **$20.**

*Lady and the Tramp Sticker Activity
Book* 6.00

Lester Lightbulb Safety First,
Massachusetts Electric Co., ©1977
.... 15.00

Lone Ranger, 1959 .... 50.00

Mister Magoo, Whitman, 1965, few
pages colored 45.00

Mr. T, #2814, green cover 8.50

Pink Panther Coloring Book,
Whitman, 1976 .... 10.00

Popeye and Swee' Pea Coloring Book, Whitman, 1056-31, 1970 .... 7.00

Raggedy Ann Coloring Book, 1968 .... 6.00

School Days Coloring Book, 1956, six pgs colored 9.50

Trace and Color Book, Roger Rabbit, Golden, #2355 .... 5.00

Thundercats, red cover, 1989 ... 15.00

Wizard of Oz, Waldman Publishing Corp., N.Y., 1966 .... 10.00

Comedian Collectibles

Those who can make us laugh seem to find their way into our hearts. Some collectors are now choosing to concentrate on these folks and are having a great time doing it.

Also see Autographs, Character Collectibles, and Movie Collectibles in this edition.

Book, *Don't Shoot, It's Only Me: Bob Hope's Comedy History of the United States,* Bob Hope, Putnam, 1990, 315 pgs, used 7.50

Colorforms, Three Stooges, 1959, MIB 270.00

Coloring book, unused
Bob Hope, Saalfield 18.00
Dick Van Dyke Show 75.00
Laugh-in 20.00
Sgt Bilko 60.00

Comic book
Get Smart, #5 .... 5.00
Jackie Gleason & The Honeymooners, #2 .... 35.00
Laurel & Hardy 3-D Comic Book, #2, 1987 .... 7.00

Cookie jar, I Love Lucy 100.00

Game, Laurel and Hardy, Transogram, 1962 copyright . 42.50

Magazine
Life, Feb. 4, 1946, Bob Hope and Bing Crosby cover 10.00
Pet Milk Magazine, 1958, Red Skelton cover 15.00

Comedian collectibles, comic book, *Bob Hope,* Superman DC National Comics, No. 40, September, **$65.**

Time, April 7, 1947, Fred Allen cover story 25.00
TV Guide, Feb. 25-March 3, 1967, Phyllis Diller cover 15.00

Matchbook, Comedian Series, 1975
Fields, W.C. 5.00
Lewis, Jerry 5.00
Marx, Groucho 21.00

Notebook binder, Laugh-In, 1969 .... 20.00

Photo, sgd, 8" x 10"
Hope, Bob 35.00
Jones, Spike 25.00
Seinfeld, Jerry 20.00
Skelton, Red 45.00

Press kit, George Carlin, 1977 .... 10.00

Puppet, Jerry Lewis, 9" h, fabric, soft vinyl head, c1950 .... 55.00

Salt and pepper shakers, pr, Three Stooges 20.00

Tobacco card, Jimmy Durante, 1930s 10.00

T-shirt, Carrot Top, black, XL .. 10.00

Waste basket, Laugh-In, litho show characters 45.00

Comic Books

Comic books date back to the 1890s when newspapers started to print their popular funny-strips in book form. By the late 1930s, comic book manufacturers were producing all kinds of tales to delight young readers. Through the years, the artwork found in comic books has gotten more and more sophisticated, and many collectors now specialize in a particular artist or maker. Don't overlook the comic books that were printed as give-aways and premiums.

This is one of those areas in which collectors have learned to rely on good reference books. Collectors have their favorite one. Proper storage of comic books is vital. Check out the supplies offered at many comic book stores and consider them an important tool in your long term collecting future investment.

For additional listings, see *Warman's Antiques & Collectibles* and *Warman's Americana & Collectibles,* as well as specific topics in this edition.

Reproduction alert.

Action Comics, #35, April 1941 **95.00**

Atom, #35 .... **26.00**

Battlestar Galactica, 1978, 10" x 13-1/2" **15.00**

Blondie, 1972, 14" x 11" **15.00**

Blue Beetle, #26, Oct, 1943 ..... **145.00**

Boy Who Never Heard of Captain Marvel, Bond Bread, 1940s .. **40.00**

Crime Reporter, #2 .... **68.00**

Daredevil, Oct, #114 .... **10.00**

DC Super Spectacular, #20 ...... **80.00**

Detective Comics, #105, Nov, 1945 .... **155.00**

Dick Tracy in 3-D, Blackthorne, 1986 .... **4.00**

Famous Crimes, #4 .... **100.00**

Fightin' Marines, #15 .... **5.00**

Flash Gordon, #16 .... **18.00**

GI Joe I Battle, #1 .... **60.00**

Giveway Comics #3, Captain Marvel and the Lt. Of Safety, 1951 .... **250.00**

Jungle Adventures, #3 .... **2.00**

Katy Keene, #45 .... **12.50**

Major Inapak Space Ace, #1, 1951, Magazine Enterprises, N.Y., giveaway for "Inapak-The Best Chocolate Drink in the World" **10.00**

Mister Miracle, June, #2 .... **9.00**

Moon Girl Fights Crime, EC Comic, #7 .... **150.00**

Oliver Twist, Classics Illustrated, #17 .... **2.00**

Red Ryder, Frame-Up, Dell, #133, August, 1954 .... **18.00**

Comic book, *Beetle Bailey*, Dell, May, **$25.**

Sherlock Holmes, Classics Illustrated, #2 .... **40.00**

Six Gun Heroes, #81 .... **12.00**

Sleeping Beauty, Walt Disney, #1 .... **20.00**

Spiderman, 1974, 14" x 11" **15.00**

Strange Adventures, #7 .... **45.00**

Super Heroes, #4 .... **2.50**

Tales of the Wizard of Oz, Dell, #1306, 1962 .... **10.00**

Unexpected, #143 .... **7.00**

Wacky Racers, #2 .... **10.00**

War Stories, #2 .... **6.00**

X-Force, #8 .... **12.00**

Compacts and Purse Accessories

Ladies have been powdering their noses for years and using interesting compacts to perform this task. Today's collectors have a variety of shapes, materials, and makers to search for at flea markets.

For additional listings, see *Warman's Antiques & Collectibles* and *Warman's Americana & Collectibles*.

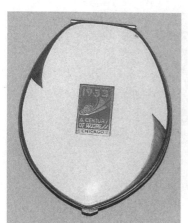

Compacts, 1933 Chicago World's Fair, **$65.**

Avon

Oval, lid dec with blue and green checkerboard pattern....... 35.00
Owl, solid perfume, rhinestone eyes, orig box, 1-1/4" x 2"
.... 60.00

Celluloid, orange compact studded with floral rhinestone motif, 3" d
.... 45.00

BOAC, British Overseas Airways Corp, 3" d, gold, black leatherette, gold metal logo, framed mirror, BOAC puff, royal blue felt cover
.... 70.00

Coty, #405, envelope box.......... 65.00

Daniel, black leather, portrait of lady encased in plastic dome, Paris
.... 90.00

Djer Kiss, with fairy................. 95.00

Dorset, 3-1/8" sq, white, gold birds, flowers, and leaves, mkd "Dorset, Fifth Avenue," slight discoloration around edges 15.00

Dunhill, Mary, rouge 28.00

Elgin, I Love You in different languages, cupids and hearts on front 48.00

Estee Lauder, compact necklace, oval silvertone engraved pendant suspended from ornate silvertone ball and tube chain, orig solid fragrance............................... 55.00

Evans, goldtone and mother-of-pearl, compact and lipstick combination
.... 45.00

German, 2-7/8" d, double mirror, couple in colonial dress, mkd "Made in West Germany," slight discoloration.......................... 10.00

Halston, silver plated, name on puff, used 150.00

K & K, brass, colored engine tooled dec basket compact, multicolored silk flowers enclosed in plastic dome lid, emb swinging handle
.... 125.00

Kigu, lady swinging.................. 45.00

Lampi, light blue enamel, five colorful three-dimensional scenes from *Alice in Wonderland* enclosed in plastic domes on lid
.... 180.00

Mondane Beauty Box, goldtone, rhinestone basket, three reservoirs
.... 125.00

Petit Point, 2-1/4" x 2-3/4", gold metal edge, red and yellow roses, blue flowers, green leaves, plain black petit point on back....... 15.00

Princess Pat, rouge and large puff, orig package 20.00

Rowanta, brown enamel, oval petit-point compact........................ 65.00

Schildraut, seed-pearl design.. 55.00

Compacts, souvenir, 1937 Great Lakes Expo, Cleveland Centennial, metal, black and silver, raised sailboats, powder and rouge compartments, 2-1/2" d, **$45.**

Timepact, enamel, black, elongated horseshoe shape, case and watch
.... 190.00

Unknown Maker
Goldtone, heart shape, brocade lid
.... 50.00
Plastic, red, white, and blue, Naval Officer's cap shape 85.00

Volupt, USA, Adam and Eve, under apple tree 50.00

Whiting & Davis, vanity bag, silvered mesh, etched and engraved lid, braided carrying chain, 1920s
.... 425.00

Woolworth, Karess, polished goldtone, corset shaped, vanity case, powder and rouge compartments 45.00

Yardley, goldtone, vanity case, red, white, and blue emb design no lid, powder and rouge compartments
.... 75.00

Computers and Computer Games

Technology is improving so rapidly that your computer is almost outdated before you've even had a chance to remove it from the box. With our increasing reliance on computers and our continual quest for the biggest and the fastest, it's a sure bet that more computers will find their way to flea markets. Make sure you've got all the parts and as many original documents as possible when buying a computer on the secondary market. Because this is a relatively new segment of the flea market scene for many dealers, firm pricing is not yet established.

AOL giveaway disk, Windows Version 3.0, Canadian, 1998, MSP
.... 8.00

Apple
Macintosh, 128K, 1st ed, standard keyboard and mouse...... 225.00

Macintosh Plus, 1MB, beige
.... 50.00

Computers and computer games, America Online 4.0 disk, mint in package, **$1.**

Computers and computer games: quite a selection of Play Station games were offered by two young dealers at the Landisville Flea Market, September 2004.

IIc, 128K RAM, 1st "portable" computer made by Apple, includes power supply **50.00**

Atari, XL 800, additional modem **95.00**

Compaq, typical PC, heavily used **20.00**

Epson, HX-40, laptop, 4MB RAM, 1987 .... **75.00**

Fujitshu, laptop, 1989 .... 25.00

Game
Bugs and Loops, Creative Specialities, 1970.............. **30.00**
Chess, Atari 2.00
Dark Legions, Strategy Simulations Inc., 1996......................... **15.00**
James Bond, The Stealth Affair, 1990................................. **15.00**
Joint Strike Fighter, Eidos, 1998, user manual, MIB **25.00**

Karate, Froggo Games, Atari.. 2.00

IBM, typical PC, 5-1/4" floppy drive 25.00

Packard Bell, typical PC, 3-1/4" disc drive, moderate use.............. 25.00

Zenith, PC, 5-1/4" floppy drive, 28K hard drive, working condition 25.00

Construction Toys

Building toys have delighted children for many years. Today's collectors look for sets in original boxes with all the tools, vehicles, instructions, etc.

A. C. Gilbert
Chemistry Experiment Lab, three-pc metal box..................... **35.00**
Erector Set, No. 4, complete, orig instructions................... **285.00**
Erector set, No. 8-1/2, All Electric Set, MIB **110.00**
Erector Set No. 10181, Action Helicopter........................ **80.00**

American National Building Box, The White House, wood pieces, landscaping, orig wood box **120.00**

Auburn Rubber, Building Bricks, 1940s..................................... **25.00**

Embossing Company, No. 408, Jonnyville Blocks, deluxe edition, blocks, trees, hook and ladder, village plan **65.00**

Construction toy, Erector Set, red metal box, No. 10051, original contents, **$85.**

Halsman
American Plastic Bricks, #717 .... **45.00**
Early settlers log set, based on Disneyland's Tom Sawyer's Island, 1960s 25.00

Lego, Main Street Set, orig box and pcs, unused.......................... 120.00

Lincoln Logs, #25.................... 75.00

Tinkertoy, box with odd parts and pieces 10.00

Cookbooks and Recipe Leaflets

What's for supper? The answer to this perplexing question might be as close as your nearest flea market—perhaps you might want to try something daring and different—something that catches your eye while browsing through a nifty cookbook. Collectors have long treasured these books and leaflets promoting different household products. Collectors are eager to find those with advertising or displays that show vintage china patterns, accessories, etc.

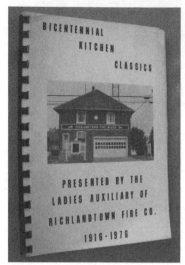

Cookbooks and recipe books, *Bicentennial Kitchen Classics*, Presented by the Ladies Auxiliary of Richlandtown Fire Co., 1916-1976, black and white photo on cover, black spiral binding, **$2.50.**

Any One Can Bake, Royal Baking Powder, 1929, 100 pgs 10.00

Arm & Hammer Good Things to Eat, Church & Dwight Co., 3" x 5", 1925, 32 pgs 5.00

Armour's Star Ham, Armour & Co., Chicago, IL, c1933, 28 pgs, 5" x 6-1/2" 10.00

Baker's Chocolate Cookbook, 1926, 64 pgs 15.00

Betty Crocker Do-Ahead Cookbook, Golden Press, 1974, 4th printing, spiral bound 10.00

Carnation Cookbook, Mary Blake, 1943, softcover 10.00

Classic Cooking with Coca-Cola 5.00

Favorite Recipes From Our Best Cooks Cookbook, Women's Club of Batavia, Ohio, Circulation Service, 1981 .... 4.00

From Amish and Mennonite Kitchens, Phyllis Pell, Good &

Rachel Pellman, 1984, 420 pgs 10.00

Game Cookery, E. N. & Edith Sturdivant, Outdoor Life, 1967, 166 pgs 6.00

Green on Greens, Vegetable Cookbook, Bert Greene, Workmans, NY, 1984, paperback, 432 pgs, 450 recipes, illus 9.00

Hershey's Index Recipe Book, 1934 .... 12.00

Holiday Food Fun: Creative Ideas for Halloween, Thanksgiving, Christmas, and More, Pub. Int., Ltd., 1993, 4th ed, 96 pgs 8.00

Julia Child, The Way to Cook, 1989, hardcover 25.00

Knox Gelatine Cookbook, 1933, 71 pgs 12.00

Kraft Mini Marshallows, mini booklet 3.00

Louisiana Kitchen, Chef Paul Prudhomme, 1984, 351 pgs .. 12.00

Magic in Herbs, Leonie de Sounin, Gramercy, 1941 .... 9.50

Martha Washington Log Cabin Cookbook, Philadelphia, 1924, 132 pgs 38.00

McCormack Cookbook, 1924, 32 pgs 34.00

McNess Cookbook, 1933 .... 35.00

Cookbooks and recipe books, *Knox Quickies*, 1938, 23 pages, **$10.**

Cookbooks and recipe books, *The Great 20th Century Cook Book*, by Maud C. Cooke, The L.W. Walter Co., Chicago, 1902, worn, **$12.**

Meta Given's Modern Encyclopedia of Cooking, 1959, hardcover 45.00

Metropolitan Cook Book, February 1948, red, white, and blue cover 12.00

Monarch Range Cook Book, shows gas and electric ranges, 72 pgs 10.00

My Better Homes & Gardens Cook Book, Meredith Publishing, 1935, 10th printing, tabs 18.00

New Ideas For Kraft Oil, mini booklet 3.00

Pillsbury Family Cookbook, 1863 .... 12.00

Rawleigh's Good Health Guide Almanac Cookbook, 1951, 31 pgs 12.00

Robertson Cookbook, Elizabeth Gray, Robert Shaw Thermostat Co., Youngwood, PA, 1940 .... 18.00

Royal Cookbook, 1939, 64 pgs . 10.00

Ryzon Baking Powder Cookbook, Marion Harris Neil, 1916, hardcover, 81 pgs 25.00

Shumway's Canning Recipes, booklet form 5.00

Southern Sideboards Recipe Book, Junior League of Jackson, MS, 1980, 5th printing, spiral bound, 414 pgs 9.00

The Cookbook of the Stars, 1941, hardcover, 394 pgs 35.00

The Cookie Cookbook, Deloris K Clem, Castle Books, 1966, slight edge wear 11.50

The Vegetarian Cook Book, E. P. Dutton, Pacific Press, 1914, 271 pgs 50.00

Your Frigidaire Recipes, 1937 .... 3.50

Cookie Cutters

Cookie cutters are found in various metals and plastics. Look for cutters in good condition and that are free of rust and crumbs.

The following are tin or aluminum figural cookie cutters.

Cookie cutters, tin, hand made, left: turkey; right: woman, each **$28.**

Bird, hand-made, 3-1/2" x 4".... 15.00

Biscuit, red wood handle, 2-3/4" d 8.00

Bunny, rolled edge, 5" h 3.50

Chicken, 2" w, 2" h, 1920s 22.50

Club, green wood handle 7.50

Cowboy, gingerbread type, 6" h, stamped design, aluminum .. 15.00

Flower, red wood handle, 2-1/2" d 8.00

Gingerbread man, rolled edge, spot soldered, 5" h 4.00

Horse, 1-3/4" 5.00

Lion, 1-3/4" 5.00

Rabbit, green wood handle, 4" l 12.50

Reindeer, tin, 3" 12.00

Santa 6.00

Squirrel, soldered handle, used 10.00

Cookie cutters, tin, horse head, **$15.**

Star, 2" 6.50

Turkey, 2" 8.50

Cookie Jars

Cookie jars have been a highly desirable collectible for years. Today more and more cookie jars are appearing at flea markets, some new, some vintage. If you're looking for new jars, check for a signature by the artist or company's mark and the original box will add to the value. If vintage jars are more your style, check carefully for signs of use and damage.

For additional listings, see *Warman's Antiques & Collectibles* and *Warman's Americana & Collectibles.*

Apple Barrel, Metlox 75.00

Ballerina Bear, Metlox 90.00

Bear, Avon, California Originals, 1979 .... 70.00

Bird House, Treasure Craft 45.00

Blue Bonnet Sue 40.00

Bugs Bunny 40.00

Cactus, wearing bandana and cowboy hat, Treasure Craft 50.00

Cat in a Basket, American Bisque 50.00

Chef, American Bisque 70.00

Clock, Brush 145.00

Cookie Jug, brown stoneware, 11" h 30.00

Curious George 50.00

Elvis, in car 60.00

Felix 50.00

Flintstones 50.00

Friendship Space Ship, McCoy 115.00

I Love Lucy 80.00

Maxine 65.00

Mr. Rabbit, American Bisque 145.00

Nightmare before Christmas, Jack on tombstone, Treasure Craft 75.00

Cookie jar, McCoy, Indian, 10-3/8" h, **$400.**

Olympics, Warner Bros., 1996. 75.00

Cookie jar, Gingerbread boy, brown, white drip glaze, **$20.**

Quaker Oats, 120th Anniversary 70.00

Pillsbury Funfetti 45.00

Pink Panther, Treasure Craft .. 95.00

Popeye, McCoy, white suit, 1965 .... 100.00

Rocking Horse, Fitz & Floyd 165.00

Santa's Magic Workshop ... 115.00

Smokey Bear, 50th Anniversary 225.00

Sugar Town General Store .. 60.00

Superman 85.00

Cookie jar, McCoy, coffee grinder, 10" h, **$48.**

Sylvester and Tweety, Applause 55.00

Television Set, young Indian and teepee image on front 120.00

Tony the Tiger, Kellogg's, 1960s, plastic.................................... 25.00

Troll, Norlin 55.00

Uncle Sam, American Cookie Jar Co 110.00

Yosemite Sam 40.00

Wizard of Oz, Clay Art, white, relief figures, 1990 .... 30.00

Cookie jar, Old Woman in a Shoe, green roof, **$68.**

Copper

Copper has long been a favored metal with craftsmen as it is relatively easy to work with and is durable. Copper culinary items are lined with a thin protective coating of tin to prevent poisoning. It is not uncommon to find these items relined. Care should be taken to make sure the protective lining is intact before using any copper pots, etc. for domestic use.

Ashtray, sombrero shape, painted design of trees and water, 4" d 12.00

Blowtorch, Bernz, red wood handle, 10" h.. 30.00

Breadbox, 12" l, 7-1/2" w, 11" h, chamfered oblong rect form, hinged cov, paneled domical form, brass finial raising from lozenge-shaped plaque over brass ring handles, brass bottom, Neoclassical, possibly Dutch, c1800........................ 165.00

Copper, pan with wooden handle, **$10.**

Carpenter's pot, 11" l, 8" h, globular, dovetailed body, raised on three plain strap work iron legs, conforming handle................ **70.00**

Colander, punched star design, 10-3/4" d **80.00**

Funnel, 4" h **12.00**

Ladle, 6" d copper bowl with rounded bottom, wrought-iron handle, 20-3/8" l **45.00**

Measure, round with flat bottom, straight sides, broad flared tapering spout, C-shaped handle, wear, dents, 10" h, 6-5/8" d **25.00**

Pan
Frying, metal handle, 5-1/4" d, 9-1/4" l.............................. **35.00**

I. Young & Co., East Boston, Mass., brass handle, copper pan 1-3/4" h, 3-1/4" d............. **25.00**

Copper, wash boiler, tin lid, wood handles, **$95.**

Teakettle, dovetailed, hinged cover on spout, scrolled finial, stamped initials, 10" h........................ **165.00**

Teapot, Paul Revereware, wooden grip on handle **30.00**

Wash tub **75.00**

Water urn, 14" h, copper body, int. with capped warming tube, applied brass ram's head handles, urn finial, brass spout, sq base with four ball feet, unmarked, repairs to lid **125.00**

Corporate Collectibles

The year 2004 is going to be remembered for when the stock market reacted negatively to many corporate scandals and the subsequent publicity that surrounded their trials, etc. As soon as some of the big corporations filed for bankruptcy, collectibles bearing their logos began to appear at flea markets. When the big "E" from in front of the former Enron building was sold, it made the evening news. More and more companies are issuing items imprinted with their logo. Many of these items are finding their way to local flea markets.

Corporate, bear, advertising give-away by Summit Bank, original Vermont Teddy Bear hang tags, outfitted in hiking gear, flag reads "Reach Higher, Summit Bank," **$20.**

Ashtray, Xerox........................... **1.00**

Cap, khaki, Enron.................... **10.00**

Cigarette lighter, Seagrams...... **2.00**

Cufflinks, Enron, gold plated.. **15.00**

Door mat, rubber, white lettering "Bucks County Bank & Trust" **10.00**

Golf ball, Enron **1.00**

Golf tee, Philip Morris, three in orig package **3.00**

Magazine, *Martha Stewart Living* .... **.50**

Mouse pad, Enron **2.00**

Mug, Bell Telephone **4.00**

Pen, Worldcom........................... **1.00**

Pocket knife, Enron.................. **8.00**

Sign, big "E" from Enron headquarters................. **44,000.00**

Stock certificate, Enron........... **2.00**

Tie tac, Champion Spark Plugs, silver tone.. **5.00**

Travel mug, Mobil Oil **4.00**

Corporate, sign, Hess', green cloth, white lettering, from former Allentown, PA, department store, **$65.**

Costumes

Playing dress-up has always been fun for children. Collectors today enjoy finding vintage Halloween and other type of costumes. It's possible to find some very interesting costumes and accessories at flea markets. Value depends on the costume being in very good condition, the mask in the same condition, and both present in the original box.

Costume, Ben Cooper, left: witch; right: Blue Fairy, medium, both Magic-Glo, each **$35.**

Alice in Wonderland, Ben Cooper, 1950-70s 40.00

Aquaman, Ben Cooper, 1967 ... 20.00

Archies, Ben Cooper, 1969 .... 30.00

Banana Splits 80.00

Bat Masterson 140.00

Batman, display bag, vinyl cape, mask, cuffs and badge, ©1966 National Periodical Publications 120.00

Captain Action, cloth outfit, mask, knife, two pistols, skull, brass knuckles, holster, belt, rifle and boots, ©1966 Ideal Toy Corp, MIB 225.00

Captain Kangaroo 90.00

Casper, Ghostland, Collegeville, #216 .... 30.00

Captain American, Ben Cooper, 1967 .... 80.00

Cowardly Lion, Ben Cooper, 1975 .... 15.00

Cowboy, child size
Boots, Acme 85.00
Chaps 90.00
Outfit, four pcs, 1960s 200.00
Vest and chaps, hide rosettes 150.00

E. T. 15.00

Flipper, Collegeville, 1964 .... 20.00

Fred Flintstone, Ben Cooper, ©1973 Hanna-Barbera 40.00

Green Lantern, Ben Cooper, 1967 .... 80.00

Mad Hatter, Ben Cooper, 1950-70s 25.00

Matador, adult size, heavily embroidered, sequins and gold metallic thread, minor wear 120.00

Miss Piggy 15.00

Moonraker, Roger Moore mask, space suit, 1979 .... 20.00

Phantom, Character Costumes, 1989 .... 40.00

Costume, theatrical, angel, white gown, separate feathered wings, **$45.**

Red Riding Hood, home made, c1950 .... 35.00

Rosey the Robot 350.00

Star Wars, R2D2, Ben Cooper, ©1977 .... 40.00

Steve Canyon, Halco, 1959 ...... 25.00

Superman, Ben Cooper 50.00

Winky Dink 200.00

Zorro 90.00

Country Store Collectibles

Today we tend to think of old-time store items as "Country Store." In reality, much of the memorabilia we collect was from small stores located in cities as well as country locales. These stores offered people a place to meet, stock up on supplies, and catch up on the latest gossip. They were filled with advertising, cases, cabinets, and all kinds of consumer goods.

Broom display, hanging, metal, round with ring for holding brooms by handles 100.00

Coffee barrel, BAR Special Blend, R.A. Railton Co., Chicago, 75 lbs, 25-1/2" h, 17-1/2" d 175.00

Coffee grinder, double wheel, Enterprise, cast iron, old red and blue repaint, yellow details, finial replaced 357.50

Counter display, Sir Walter Raleigh Tin, six orig pocket tins 130.00

Counter jar
Lance Crackers, clear, red tin lid 20.00
Necco Candies, clear, orig lid, 10-1/2" h........................... 65.00
Planters Peanuts, 7" d glass jar with lid, yellow and blue Mr. Peanut image, orig 8" x 8" x 9-1/2"

corrugated cardboard shipping carton 90.00

Cracker box lid, tin with glass insert Purity Pretzel Co., Stuber & Kuck Co., Peoria, Ill.................. 30.00
Uneeda Bakers..................... 30.00

Crate, Rumford Baking Powder, held 1 dozen cans, 5-3/4" h, 13" w, 10" d 25.00

Country store, potbelly stove, cast iron, UMCO, No. 212, original top plate lifter, **$125.**

Display, Beechnut Gum, tin, 27-1/2" x 15-1/2", c1950, 3 tiers **130.00**

Scoop, 5", tin, wood handle **28.00**

Seed box
Choice Flower Seeds From D.M. Ferry & Co., Detroit, Mich.,
shows 3 children in flower garden, oak, litho paper label under lid, 6-3/4" h, 11-1/2" w, 9-3/4" d **440.00**
Reliable Seeds, From the Sioux City Nursery & Seed Co. Sioux City, Iowa, wood, machine dovetails, paper labels on front and inside lid, chipping to labels **200.00**

Seed packet, Ruppert's Seeds, Washington, D.C., orig 10 cents, color picture of the vegetable or fruit **2.00**

Spool cabinet, Clark's Mile-End Spool, wood, five drawers with reverse-painted glass fronts advertising product, paint loss to glass, 19" h, 30" w **495.00**

String holder, cast iron
Beehive form, 6" h, 7-1/4 dia **150.00**
Inverted J-shaped arm, 11" h **45.00**

Tobacco cutter, cast iron, "Griffin Goodner Grocer Co., Tulsa, Okla," 1914 patent date, 8-1/2" h, 12-3/4" l **195.00**

Country store, cigar cutter, Arora Cigar, E. Kleener & Co., NY, store type, **$175.**

Cowan Pottery

Cowan Pottery encompasses both utilitarian ware and artistic ware. R. Guy Cowan began making pottery in Ohio around 1915 and continued until 1931. Most pieces are marked with an incised name. Later a black stamp mark and initials were used.

Bookends, pr, Sunbonnet Girl, antique green crystalline glaze **375.00**

Bowl, irid blue luster glaze, ink mark, 12" d **70.00**

Candleholders, pr, 8-1/2" h, Ming Green glaze, c1928 .... **80.00**

Card holder, green, chip, 3-1/2" h **50.00**

Cigarette holder, sea horse, aqua **42.00**

Cowan Pottery, centerpiece vase, flat semi-circle on base, green tones, semi-crystalline glaze, 8-1/4" w, 5-1/4" h, **$80.**

Compote, diamond shape, tan ext., green int., 2" h **38.00**

Console set, oval bowl, 2 short candlesticks, white **200.00**

Demitasse cup and saucer, 2-1/2" h cup, 4" saucer, block letter logo **35.00**

Flower frog, 7" h, figural nude, #698, orig ivory glaze **275.00**

Lamp base, molded leaves, gray and ivory semi-gloss glaze, orig fittings, 19" h **100.00**

Match holder, cream color, 3-1/2" h **65.00**

Snack set, hexagon-shaped plate, solid light blue **115.00**

Vase
5" h, shouldered form, pink and maroon high glaze, imp mark **70.00**
10-3/4" h, irid blue, c1925 .... **90.00**

Cowan Pottery, bud vase, figural seahorse base, blue iridescent glaze, 7-1/4" h, **$35.**

Cowboy Heroes

Although most cowboy heroes were matinee idols, there were some cowboy heroes who were popular radio and/or television personalities. Many of today's collectors specialize in one character or show, but some are fascinated with all kinds of cowboy memorabilia.

For additional listings, see *Warman's Americana & Collectibles* and categories covering specific cowboys in this edition.

Cowboy heroes, photograph, black and white, autographed in pencil, "To Calvin from Roy," early, **$250.**

Arcade card
Bob Baker, on rearing horse, black-and-white 12.00
John Mack Brown, green tones 12.00
Sunset Carson, red tones...... 12.00
Charles Starrett, full color.... 15.00

Autograph, 8" x 10" photo, personalized inscription
Conners, Chuck.................... 35.00
McCoy, Time........................ 75.00

Better Little Book, *Buck Jones and The Two-Gun Kid*, Whitman, #1404, 1937 .... 30.00

Big little book
Bobby Benson On The H-Bar O Ranch, Whitman #1108, 1934, wear................................... 20.00
Buffalo Bill Plays a Long Hand, 1939................................. 25.00

Cowboy heroes, Red Ryder Lucky Coin, **$10.**

Lone Ranger and the Menace of Murder Valley, 1938......... 30.00
Rin Tin Tin & The Hidden Treasure 18.00

Book, Songs of the Western Trails, 60 pgs, 1940................................ 40.00

Bookends, pr, End of the Trail, cast iron 115.00

Box, Annie Oakley holster set, Daisy, 10-1/2" x 12-1/2" 175.00

BB gun, Daisy, Red Ryder 50th Anniversary........................... 90.00

Calendar, 1952, Myers Truck Lines, Knox City, Mo., cowgirl and horse, unused, 20-3/4" x 12" 22.50

Chaps and vest, Tom Mix Ralston Straight Shooters, Ralston premium, 11" x 24" pr brown suede chaps, nickel accents, red, white, and blue cloth patch, 14" x 16" brown suede vest with matching patch, c1935........................ 200.00

Coloring book, Bonanza 30.00

Comic book, Cowgirl Romances, Fiction House Magazine, 1952, #11 .... 90.00

Dixie Cup picture, color
Elliott, Bill, and Gabby Hayes 50.00
Maynard, Ken, In Old Santa Fe 30.00
McCoy, Tim........................ 15.00
Stanwyck, Barbara................ 50.00

Figure, Buffalo Bill, metal, Blenheim 20.00

Game, board, Annie Oakley, Milton Bradley.................................... 45.00

Guitar, Buck Jones, 37" l........ 250.00

Magazine, *Parade*, cover and story about Bonanza...................... 25.00

Membership card, Straight Arrow, ©1949 National Biscuit Co., sign language................................ 35.00

Movie, *Zane Gray Adventure Stories Action-Packed Thrillers*, 16mm, orig box.................................. 40.00

Cowboy heroes, Ranger Joe cereal bowl and mug, blue decoration, white ground, **$45.**

Photograph, William S. Hart, 1980s re-release 5.50

Playing cards, Bonanza, 1970s 18.00

Poster, Ponderosa, c1967, facsimile autographs of cast, 22-1/2" x 17" 18.00

Puzzle, frame tray, Fess Parker 35.00

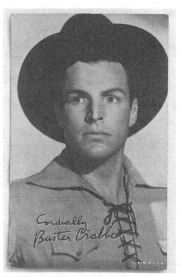

Cowboy heroes, Arcade card, Buster Crabbe, facsimile signature, greentone, **$15.**

Record, Bobby Benson's B-Bar-B Riders, 10-1/8" x 10-1/8" illus picture sleeve, 78 rpm record, white and white label, "The Story of the Golden Palomino," Decca #88036, copyright 1950...................... **12.00**

Sheet music, *You Two-Timed Me One Time Too Often* by Jenny Lou Carson, recorded by Tex Ritter, 1945, Ritter on cover **15.00**

Snack set, plate and mug, Cisco Kid **50.00**

Target game, Straight Arrow, litho tin board, three magnetic feather-tipped arrows, National Biscuit Co., c1950...................................... **75.00**

Cow Collectibles

Cows have been a part of the folk art and country decorating schemes for years. Dedicated cow collectors will be the first to tell you that they are also popular themes for advertising and even children's items.

Cow collectibles, advertising mirror, Horlick's Malted Milk, woman in rural garb holding can of malted milk, standing beside cow, farmer plowing in background, multicolored image, gold border with blue lettering, 2-1/8" d, **$65.**

Souvenir of Washington, D.C., mkd "Hand Painted, Japan," 1940s, 3-1/4" h, 5-1/4" l............... **45.00**

Doll, Moo Cow, Cloverland Dairy, cow, stuffed plush, collar ribbon, copper luster metal cow bell . **15.00**

Pinback button, Guernsey-The Only Breed Increasing in Every State, multicolored portrait of cow's head, blue award ribbon, c1930...... **18.00**

Poster, Evaporated Milk-Pure Cow's Milk, black and white illus of cows, green ground, c1940.............. **25.00**

Sugar, cov, figural, Elmer, c1940 .... **40.00**

Toy, ramp walker, plastic, brown and white, 1950s, mkd "Made in Hong Kong," orig sealed cellophane **18.00**

Cow collectibles, M.A. Hadley pottery cow plate, 11" h, **$20.**

Bank, Nestle Nespray, figural, vinyl **40.00**

Beanie baby, Bessie the cow.... **60.00**

Blotter, Cow Brand Baking Soda, 4" x 9-1/4" **15.00**

Butter crock, stoneware, blue and white, cows dec.................... **250.00**

Butter stamp, one-pc, cow with tree, 3-5/8" d **170.00**

Charm, 1" d, Swift's Brookfield, brass, emb cow on award base, inscribed "June Dairy Month Award," early 1900s...................................... **17.50**

Comic book, *Cow Puncher*, Avon Periodicals, 1947, #7 .... **200.00**

Cookie jar
Brush-McCoy, mouse on cow, early 1950s **200.00**
Elsie the Cow in barrel, 11-1/2" h **400.00**

Creamer
Fairway, Made in Japan, 1950s, 4-1/2" h, 6-1/2" l............... **38.00**

Cow collectibles, planter, ivory colored calf with black trim, unmarked, **$9.**

Cracker Jack

When Frederick William Rueckheim added molasses to popcorn in1896, the concoction became known as Cracker Jack. Beginning in 1910, each box contained a coupon that could be redeemed for a prize. It wasn't until 1912 that the prizes themselves were placed in the boxes.

The Cracker Jack sailor boy and his little dog Bingo first appeared in the company's advertisements in 1916 and debuted on the boxes in 1919. Early toy prizes were made of paper, wood, and even lead, with plastic toys introduced after 1948.

Cracker Jack, prize, boxcar, red plastic, **$7.50.**

Activity book, *Cracker Jack Painting & Drawing Book*, Saalfield, 1917, 24 pgs 35.00

Business card, 3" x 4-7/8", red, white, and blue, F. W. Rueckheim & Bro. Manufacturing Confectioners, Chicago address, late 1800s .. 75.00

Charm, owl, 1920s, 7/8" h.......... 9.00

Doll, Cracker Jack boy, fabric, 8" h 16.00

Mechanical card, 3-3/8" h, diecut, boy holding box of Cracker Jack, slotted for movement, c1910 .... 125.00

Premium booklet, 1-3/4" x 2-1/8", *The Baby Bears and Elly El,* eight black and white pgs, story told in prose, art by Grace Grayton, copyright 1913, 1914, 1920, 1922 .... 75.00

Prize
Auto Race spin toy 15.00
Chair, 1920s 12.00
Fire truck, tin litho, 1930s, 1-3/4" l 45.00
Horse and wagon, tin, red, white and blue, 1930s, 2-1/4" l .. 65.00
Magnet, horseshoe, orig paper wrapper 15.00
Pocket watch, dark silver luster white metal 30.00
Rocking horse, 1920s, 11/16" 12.00
Spoon and fork, tin, 1930s, 2" l 12.00
Telescope, 1920s, 1-1/16" l... 12.00

Puzzle, Coney Island, 2-1/2" x 5-3/4" diecut stiff paper, laughing boy and girl riding roller coaster, 1930s 115.00

Cracker Jack, three prizes, blue parader, red elephant, red cowgirl, each **$3.50.**

Top, 1-1/2" d, tin, pointed wooden peg through center, yellow, blue, and orange, c1940 .... 24.00

Transfer, 2-1/2" x 5-1/4", rd and blue on white transfer paper, "The More You Eat The More You Want," c1920 .... 35.00

Whistle, mkd "Close Ends with Fingers," 1930s, 1-15/16"....... 10.00

Crackle Glass

Crackle glass can be identified by the web-like system of light cracks that cover the surface of the glass. These cracks are an intentional part of the design, but since they are random, no two pieces are alike. From the late 1930s to the early 1970s, crackle glass was quite popular in the West Virginia glass houses, including Pilgrim, Blenko, Kanawha, and Viking.

For additional listings, see *Warman's Glass.*

Bottle, stopper, 16" h, clear, sgd, Blenko Glass, 16" h 175.00

Bowl, clear bowl, amethyst foot, Blenko Glass, 5-1/4" d, 8-1/4" h 85.00

Brandy snifter, clear, turquoise foot, Blenko Glass, 8" h 35.00

Bud vase, amberina, Kanawha, orig label, 7-1/4" h 60.00

Candy dish, cov, amberina, Kanawha, 3" h....................... 45.00

Creamer, emerald green body, clear handle, Pilgrim..................... 35.00

Nappy, heart shaped, amberina, hand-blown, pontil scar, Blenko Glass, 5" x 5-1/4" x 2" h 65.00

Paperweight, apple, red, applied clear stem and leaf, Blenko Glass, 6" h... 55.00

Crackle glass, creamer, amberina, pinched at waist, applied clear handle, **$20.**

Pitcher
4" h, blue, applied reeded handle
.... 20.00
5-1/4" h, blue, applied clear handle,
mold blown, Kanawha 30.00
5-1/4" h, green, applied green
handle, mold blown, Kanawha
.... 25.00

6" h, blue, applied clear handle,
Blenko Glass.................... 40.00
Punch cup, emerald green body,
clear handle, Pilgrim............ 20.00
Rose bowl, reddish-orange, pinched
top, hand blown, pontil mark,
Pilgrim............................ 60.00

Tankard, 12" h, clear, applied clear
handle.................................... 35.00
Vase
4" h, 4" w, double neck, Blenko
Glass 35.00
5-1/2" h, smoke gray 65.00
9" h, blue, Blenko Glass........ 55.00

Cranberry Glass

When a glassmaker mixes a small amount of powdered gold in a warm blob of molten glass, the glass changes to a rich cranberry color, hence the name. Because glassmakers used slightly different formulas, there are slight differences in shade between examples of cranberry glass.

For additional listings, see *Warman's Antiques & Collectibles* and *Warman's Glass*.

Reproduction alert.

Basket, 8" h, 5" w, deep color, ruffled
edge, applied colorless handle,
Victorian................................ 90.00

Bottle, 7-3/4" h, 4" d, flattened
bulbous, frosted, gold church scene,
small boats on back, gold around
top.. 135.00

Brandy jug, 8" h, Inverted
Thumbprint pattern, applied
colorless handle, colorless hollow
stopper, pontil 90.00

Butter dish, cov, round, Hobnail
pattern 125.00

Candlesticks, pr, 10-5/8" h, heavily
encrusted gold and polychrome dec
.... 190.00

Cologne bottle, 2-3/8" d, 8-5/8" h,
gold scrolls, small gold flowers,
matching sq cranberry bubble
stopper................................ 185.00

Creamer, Optic pattern, fluted top,
applied clear handle 90.00

Finger bowl, scalloped, matching
underplate 145.00

Jack-in-the-pulpit vase, 6" h, tulip
form, orig Pilgrim Glass label
.... 35.00

Muffineer, Parian Swirl pattern
.... 125.00

Mug, 4" h, 2-3/4" d, Baby Inverted
Thumbprint pattern, applied
colorless handle and pedestal foot
.... 65.00

Perfume bottle, 3-1/2" h, ball form
body, white enamel floral dec, orig
clear ball stopper 80.00

Pitcher, 6-1/2" h, Ripple and
Thumbprint pattern, bulbous,
round mouth, applied clear handle
.... 125.00

Rose bowl, 3-3/4" h, six-crimp top,
worn gold rim........................ 95.00

Sauce dish, Hobb's Hobnail pattern
.... 45.00

Spooner, Paneled Sprig pattern
.... 125.00

Toothpick holder, crystal prunts
.... 48.00

Tumble-up, Inverted Thumbprint
pattern 75.00

Vase
7-1/2" h, emb ribs, applied colorless
feet, three swirled applied
colorless leaves around base
.... 110.00

Cranberry glass, sugar shaker, paneled body, gold washed pierced top, **$95.**

8" h, vertical bands of ribbed
thumbprints cut to colorless,
ground pontil 110.00
8-7/8" h, bulbous, white enameled
lilies of the valley dec, cylinder
neck 115.00

Cuff Links

Certain fashion styles dictated long sleeves that needed to be fastened with a decorative cuff link. These little jewelry treasures have been making colorful statements for years. Look for backs and closures in different styles.

Brushed and textured gold-tone metal, smoky black center stone, 1970s.. 6.00

Cameo, Simmons, green and white, toggle type, orig box.............. 50.00

Coral, red cabochon, gold plated surround, chain and bar back 125.00

Gold filled, Christian Dior, textured ovals, orig box, c1960 .... 40.00

Gold, 10k yellow, hexagon shape, engine turned engraved design on front, sgd "NJSC" in four leaf clover, c1920.................................... 125.00

Gold, 14k rose, cushion shape top, inlaid turquoise, crescent shape back, late 19th C, wear and some cracking to turquoise 175.00

Goldtone, Retro, opposed goldtone swirls set with colorless

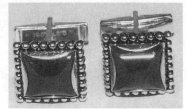

Green stones, gold finish, pair, **$1.**

rhinestones, sgd "Coro Duette," 1931 patent no., 2-1/2" w x 1-1/2" 75.00

Kiwanis, enameled, round, medium blue ground, white K, 1" w.... 28.00

Mexican silver
Rect, onyx and abalone mosaic pattern, shaped rim, mkd "PGC," 1940s 70.00

Square, green stone, mask design, Taxco maker's marks........ 40.00

Silver colored, prong-set yellow stones..................................... 12.00

Silvertone
Knight riding horse................ 8.00
Mother-of-pearl disks 10.00

Snappers, enameled black and white, 1/2" d 15.00

Sterling silver
DaVinci, blue cut glass border 40.00
Polish, nugget type, European style toggle back, mkd "M1" 75.00

Swank, cocktail watch, c1960 .... 125.00

Cupids

Cute little cupids have been charming our hearts since Victorian times. They can be found on many types of objects, just watch out for those arrows. They might be pointing at you.

Cupids, shelf, oak, scene of five cupids pulling and pushing large dog, 16" l, 10" h, **$125.**

Box, cov, porcelain, yellow glazed ground, cupids on base and top, flower finial, green "Hand Painted, Made in Japan" mark, 4-1/4" l 30.00

Brooch, cameo style resin, round, cream ground, raised cupids, fairy, flowers, scalloped bezel with gold-tone beads, 2-1/8" d.............. 45.00

Button, two cupids climbing over brick wall, 1-1/2" d................ 45.00

Dish, heart shape, figural cupid mounted on one side, Avon, MIB 10.00

Dresser box, ceramic, heart shaped, cupids on top, bow pattern on base 35.00

Dresser set, beveled mirror with red cupids, brass handles with filigree 250.00

Easter postcard, pair of Cupids with Easter egg, unused 5.00

Figure, bisque, 4-1/2" h 20.00

Jar, cov, porcelain, orange and gold, center scene of Victorian woman and cupid, 4-1/2" d................ 35.00

Leather postcard, cupid with heart in wheelbarrow, "It's all for You," postmarked Indianapolis 6.00

Limited edition plate, Wedgwood, Mother's Day, 1984, musical cupids under tree.............................. 40.00

Cupids, valentine, "Cupids Court, You Stole My Heart, And I Sentence You to Be My Valentine," fold out type, multicolored boys and girls as judge, policeman, etc., marked "Made in USA," **$15.**

Pin, shooting arrow
Brass, Coro, lavender and white rhinestones, c1940, 2" x 2" 42.00

Sterling silver, intent expression, stamped "Sterling" on back, c1940, 2" l, 2-1/2" w 110.00

Postcard, Cupid sharpening arrow, holding bow, unused 5.00

Print, Cupid Asleep or Cupid Awake, orig frame 115.00

Trinket box, cov, metal, oval, ftd, emb cupids, floral swags, and cornucopia, two goldtone cupids on lavender-pink lid, red felt lining, emb "Japan," 2-1/2" l 12.50

Tumbler, etched wrap-around design, 1870s, 3-3/4" h...................... 35.00

Valentine
Biplane with cupid, "To My Valentine, Cupid's stolen my heart which he is bringing to you" 15.00
Man and woman in floral heart wreath with cupid, "A Token of My True Love".................... 7.50

Cups and Saucers

Cup and saucer collecting is a hobby that many different generations have enjoyed. Some porcelain makers have created special cups and saucers for collectors. Other collectors prefer collecting cups and saucers that were made as dinnerware or even Depression glass patterns.

Cups and saucers, Haviland, **$30.**

Adderley, bone china
Coronation, George and Elizabeth, sepia portraits, multicolor royal crest on saucer, gold trim 95.00
Pink, blue, and yellow flowers, mkd 10.00

Bavaria, Alice pattern, white gold trim, mkd 15.00

Bridgewater, Emma, England, blackberries pattern 80.00

Carlsbad, Austria, lavender coneflowers, mkd "LS&S, Carlsbad, Austria".................................. 27.50

English, Tuscan pattern, bone china, mkd....................................... 15.00

Flow blue
Hamilton pattern.................. 45.00
Indian pattern, Pratt.......... 135.00

Germany, roses dec, gold handle, mkd....................................... 30.00

Japanese
Anniversary, colorful florals, gold trim, paper label 20.00
Southwicke pattern, white, silver trim, mkd 12.50

Johnson Bros, Albany pattern, flow blue 85.00

Limoges, Moss Rose pattern, gold trim, mkd "H & Co. Limoges" 30.00

Quimper, hex shape, male peasant on panel, scattered red and blue florals, blue outlined rims, gold outlined wishbone handle with blue dashes, "HenRiot Quimper France" marks...................................... 50.00

Remember Me, brown and pink flowers, scalloped saucer, mustache guard in cup 35.00

Cups and saucers, mustache cups and saucers, left: white ironstone type, worn gold decoration, **$20**; German, transfer decoration of pink rose, gold border, **$25**; French, pink band on cup and saucer, delicate handle with gold trim, **$35.**

Souvenir, Washington DC, man courting woman in 18th C style clothes, gold trim, 1950s 35.00

Woods, handleless, Woods Rose 65.00

Cuspidors

Called cuspidors or spittoons, these functional items can be found in metal or ceramic. They were common elements in bars, on trains, and even in homes.

Brass, small dents 95.00

Cast iron, turtle form, copper shell and bowl, mkd "Golden Novelty Co., Chicago, Ill.," 1901 patent date, orig paint, 13-1/2" l 485.00

Graniteware, cobalt/white swirl, white int., 4-1/4" h, 7-1/2" d 300.00

Ironstone, warrior and lion transfer, copper luster....................... 265.00

Pewter, bulbous body, flared rim, handle, 4-3/4" h..................... 85.00

Spongeware, circular sponged dabs around body, blue bands at rim and shoulder, 4-1/2" h 120.00

Staffordshire, blue transfer, molded basketweave pattern............ 260.00

Cuspidors, carnival glass, soda gold, Imperial Glass, 7" d, **$42.**

Stoneware

Albany glaze, incised "L.J. Underwood. Barberton, Ohio. July 24, '09" and "L.J.U., 7-24-1909" 95.00

Blue and white, butterfly and shield pattern 85.00

Brown glaze, embossed vines 35.00

Yellowware, green, blue and tan sponging, 7-1/2" d 85.00

Cuspidors, Bennington Pottery, yellow ware ground, brown glaze, 7-1/4" d, 3-3/4" h, **$90.**

Cut Glass

Cut glass should sparkle and feel sharp to the touch. It has been made by American and European companies for many years. Most companies didn't sign their work, but collectors can identify different makers by their intricate patterns. Minor flakes can be ground away and such small repairs do not affect the value negatively.

For additional listings, see *Warman's Antiques & Collectibles* and *Warman's Glass.*

Cut glass, vase, Durand, original paper label. Often pressed glass looks like cut glass. This example is pressed to imitate fine cut crystal. It still retains its original paper label, **$25.**

Banana bowl, 11" d, 6-1/2" d, Harvard pattern, hobstar bottom 210.00

Basket, diamond miters, diamond points, small stars, 6" x 4-1/4" x 6" h, pinhead nick 55.00

Bowl

8" d, brilliant cut pinwheels, hobstars, and miters 145.00

8-1/4" d, heavy blank, serrated rim, two rows of vertical rays, star bottom 45.00

9" d, deep cut, medallions, large pointed ovals, arches, and base 110.00

Butter dish, cov, hobstar 250.00

Candlesticks, pr, hobstars, teardrop stem, hobstar base, 9-1/2" h 250.00

Carafe, 2-1/2" floral leaf band, star, file, fan, and criss-cross cutting, molded neck, 8" h.................. 70.00

Champagne, Kalana Lily, pattern, Dorflinger 75.00

Cider pitcher, 7" h, hobstars, zippers, fine diamonds, honeycomb cut handle, 7" h 175.00

Compote, hobstar and arches, flared pedestal, 6" h 150.00

Creamer and sugar, hobstar, American Brilliant Period, 3" h 50.00

Cut glass, left: bowl, serrated edge, one tip smoothed, **$35;** center: vase with cupped in-rim, **$40;** right: bowl, small, **$30;** all with rayed hobstars and diamonds.

Decanter, stopper, large hobstars, deep miters, fan, file, hallmarked silver neck and rim, 11" h, 3" sq 130.00

Dish, heart shaped, handle, American Brilliant Period, 5" 45.00

Ice bucket, Harvard pattern, floral cutting, eight sided form, 6-1/2" h, minor edge flaking on handles 100.00

Knife rest................................. 95.00

Nappy, 9" d, deep cut arches, pointed sunbursts and medallions ... 135.00

Perfume bottle, six-sided, alternating panels of Harvard

pattern and engraved florals, rayed base, matching faceted stopper, American Brilliant Period... 175.00

Pickle tray, checkerboard, hobstar, 7" x 3".. 45.00

Plate, alternating hobstars and, large graduated circles and fans, notched miters, hobstars, 15-3/4" h, Higgins & Seiter 250.00

Punch ladle, 11-1/2" l, silver plated emb shell bowl, cut and notched prism handle 165.00

Relish, two handles, divided, Jupiter pattern, Meriden, 8" l 120.00

Salt shaker, Notched prism columns 30.00

Tumbler, hobstars.................... 40.00

Vase
12" h, three cartouches of roses, star and hobstar cut ground 225.00
12" h, 5-1/2" w, triangular, three large and three small hobstars, double notched pedestal and flaring base 150.00

Water pitcher, Keystone Rose pattern, 10" h...................... 190.00

Water set, Daisy & Button pattern, 10" h pitcher, eleven water tumblers 250.00

Czechoslovakian Collectibles

Finding an object marked "Made in Czechoslovakia" assures you that it was made after 1918, when the country proclaimed its independence. Marks that also include other names, such as Bohemia or Austria, indicate that the piece pre-dates the country's independence. Expect to find good quality workmanship and bright colors.

Czechoslovakian, tea set, pink ground, medallion with black ground, multicolored flowers, teapot, creamer, covered sugar, six plates, six cups and saucers, **$200.**

Belt buckle, metal, four amber rhinestones, mkd "Czechoslovakia 81-Ges Gesch"........................ 18.00

Bowl, brightly colored dec, incised mark, 9" d 60.00

Box, cov, blue glass, sterling rosary 120.00

Cologne bottle, 4" h, porcelain, glossy blue, bow front 40.00

Container, cov, 10-1/2" h, egg-shaped ribbed body, transparent green glass, hinged brass mount, gilded int., late 19th/early 20th C, some flaking to gilt 185.00

Flower frog, bird on stump, pottery 35.00

Necklace
Fringed, multicolor, 2 baroque pearls, 4" w, 20" l............ 110.00
Glass, red center pendant, brass setting, red glass and brass filigree beads, 13" l, mkd 95.00
Marbleized green stone, set in brass, small green spacer beads, clear rhinestones set at top 80.00

Perfume bottle, small, heavily cut Amethyst 125.00
Crystal, large faceted stopper 60.00

Pitcher, crackled, irid marigold flashing, hp underwater scene of fish and coral, polished pontil, 6" h 150.00

Place card holders, glass, set of six, orig box................................. 40.00

Powder box, cov, yellow glass, black knob finial on lid.................. 75.00

Vase
6-1/4" h, glass, cylindrical, mottled white and purple, cased to clear, enameled stylized vignette of woman fishing, silver mounted rim with English hallmarks, c1930 .... 275.00
10" h, pottery, brightly painted, incised numbers.............. 90.00

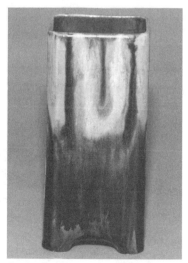

Czechoslovakian, multi-color square vase, 4-5/8" h, **$14.**

Dairy Collectibles

Collecting items pertaining to dairies is a popular segment of the antiques and collectibles marketplace. Some collectors specialize in examples from local dairies, while others concentrate on specific items such as milk bottles or milk bottle caps.

Cookbook
1001 Dairy Dishes from the Sealtest Kitchens, softcover, 1963, 288 pgs 5.00
Dairy-Best Desserts, softcover, 1960s, 18 pgs, 5-1/4" x 7-1/2" 2.00

Drinking glass
King Quality Dairy, St. Louis, red text, 5-1/4" h..................... 45.00
Little pig playing fiddle, red image, copyright Walt Disney, 2nd Dairy Series, 1936-37, 4-1/4" h 70.00

Milk box, galvanized
Property of Homestead Dairy, painted white, insulated, 10" x 11" x 13-1/2".................... 20.00
Hedlins Richer Milk, 10" x 10" x 12-1/2"............................. 45.00

Model train car, HO scale, Dairymen's League billboard refrigerator car, missing brake wheel....................................... 10.00

Dairy collectibles, advertising match safe, De Laval Cream Separator, litho on tin, original box, **$90.**

Paperweight, white-veined marble, embedded emblem, Dixie Dairy 75th Anniversary.................. **25.00**

Pinback, 3" d, Mr. Quality, Lassos Your Milk Mark, Inter-State Milk Producers Cooperative, maroon and blue on white, western character throwing rope around slogan, 1970s 12.00

Spinner, plastic with paper inlay, Dellwood Milk & Dairy Products 30.00

Thermometer, silhouette image of baby in highchair, "Compliments of Barry's Dairy Products, Phone 1062, New Ulm, Minn.," 4" x 5" 45.00

Trade card, diecut, Borden milk wagon pulled by horse 25.00

Wall plaque, 11" h, Miss Dairylea, molded vinyl, hp, young blond girl, red dress and bonnet, 1960s 115.00

Whistle, plastic, bugle shape, red and white, Foremost Dairy, 1950s, 5" l 32.00

Decorative Accessories

Call it "kitsch" or "bric-a-brac," but decorative accessories make a statement about who we are as we decorate our living spaces. Decorators have been using objects d'art for years. Now that many of these objects are coming onto the flea market scene, collectors get a second chance to add some of these decorative objects to their domain.

Decorative accessories, wall decorations, two gold and green fish, both with white and black accents, matching "bubbles" to also mount on wall, painted plaster, 1950s, **$15.**

Bird house, snow covered, DeForest 110.00

Carousel horse, Allen Herschell, metal, restored..................... 800.00

Compote, alabaster, four white birds perched on edge 10.00

Cricket cage, brass 35.00

Crocus pot, ceramic, white ground, purple floral design 2.00

Figure
Cat, 3-1/4" h, glass, blue, sgd "Daum France," 20th C .. 185.00
Dog, 7-1/2" h, seated, hand modeled, tooled fur and facial features, mat glaze with metallic

Decorative accessories, framed wall art, Blue Rocks Stadium, Wilmington, DE, one of a kind composite featuring mementos and trivia related to baseball team and stadium, **$60.**

speckles, traces of white paint 110.00

Lamb, 3-1/2" l, 2-1/4" h, pearlware, reclining, white, brown legs, ears, tail, and facial features, light green base, hairlines in base 165.00

Man riding white horse, 18" l, 20" h, colonial uniform, horse, porcelain 290.00

Fruit, alabaster, apple, pear or orange, each......................... 45.00

Immigrants totem, 2-1/2" w, 3" d, 26" h, attributed to Canada, late 19th/early 20th C, polychrome, carved pine, four seated male figures all wearing hats, one cross-legged, one in kilt, lowest with head of dog at his feet, stand 815.00

Inkwell, 4-1/4" d, 4-5/8" h, brass, orb inkwell opening to glass liner, raised on three silvered seated hound figures joined by chains at collars, set with marcasite eyes, round socle base, French, late 19th C.. 375.00

Jar, cov, 6" d, 6-1/2" h, stoneware, figure of pig eating from trough on lid, German, some damage to base 115.00

Lamp, traffic meter base, cloth shade 50.00

Magnifier, 8" l, silver-plated bronze, Faux Bamboo, c1960-65, made for and retailed by Bonwit Teller, N.Y., mkd as such, also "Made in Italy" 100.00

Mantel ornaments, 12-1/2" h, fruit and foliage design, chalkware, American, made in 19th C, some paint wear, pr...................... 475.00

Schierschnitt, 12-7/8" x 13-7/8", bouquet in vase, bright green, c1840, framed...................... 350.00

Sculpture, 15-1/2" wingspan, 20" h, eagle, carved wood, standing, spread wings........................ 395.00

Stamp box, 4-3/4" l, carved fruitwood, figural cat lying inside shoe, glass eyes, hinged lid, early 20th C 225.00

Theorem, watercolor on velvet, basket of fruit, unidentified maker, framed 200.00

Wall plaque, Masks, Comedy and Tragedy, white ceramic.......... 70.00

Watch holder, 10" h, 5-3/8" d, figural, silver plated metal, detailed jockey and race horse figure, mkd

Decorative accessories, baptismal certificate, 1894, Pennsylvania, pre-printed form with name of child, parents, place of birth, baptism, etc. Many folks like to frame these as family remembrances; this unframed one would be valued at **$20**.

"Reed & Barton," loss to orig silver plate 525.00

Decoys

Designed to coax waterfowl into target range, decoys have been made of wood, papier-mâché, canvas, and metal. These hand-carved and even machine made decoys have been recognized as an indigenous American art form. Signed examples are quite desirable, as are decoys made by noted regional artists.

For additional listings, see *Warman's Antiques & Collectibles*.

Reproduction alert.

Decoys, three ducks, some wear, each **$75-$125.**

Black Bellied Bustard, miniature, H. Gills, initialed "H. G. 1957," identified in pencil, natural wood base, 3-1/2" x 4".................. 230.00

Black duck, sleeper, old black paint, tan feather detail, green, black, and white lines on wings, later paint on eyes and bill, age splits in base, 11-1/2" l 195.00

Bluebill hen, Irving Miller, Monroe, MI, carved wood, glass eyes, orig paint, 11-1/2" l..................... 165.00

Canada goose, folding, waterproof wax-coated graphics, W.R. Johnson Co., Seattle, WA, 1940s.......... 75.00

Canvasback drake, Charles Bean, c1980, orig red, white, black, and gray paint, red glass eyes, minor crazing and chips, 15" l 110.00

Canvasback hen, unsigned, by Charles Bean, c1980, brown, black, and gray paint, glass eyes, 14-1/2" l, 6-1/4" h 110.00

Dove, papier-mâché, clothespin on bottom to hold decoy in place, 9" l 35.00

Ear of corn
Papier-mâché, Carry-Lite Decoy Co., Milwaukee, Wisc., 1940s, unused.............................. 45.00
Wooden, painted yellow, 9" l 25.00

Fish, 13-1/4" l, orig mustard paint, black stripes, tin fins, red faceted bead eyes, 13-1/4" l.............. 360.00

Goldeneye drake, tack eyes, lead weight inset in bottom, hollow construction held together with pegs, by Stanley Grant, Barnegat Bay, New Jersey, c1880, old repaint, bill repaired 225.00

Hooded Merganser Drake, miniature, H. Gibbs, 1965, sgd in pencil on base, 2-1/2" x 2-3/4" 290.00

Mallard drake, Delaware River, PA, c1920, flocked, old dark gray and green paint, blue green head, green bill, carved eyes, lead keel weight, slightly raised carved wings, some wear, 15-3/4" l....................... 200.00

Merganser, red breast, carved late 20th C, Maine or Nova Scotia, 19" l 335.00

Pintail drake, Zeke McDonald, MI, high head, hollow body, glass eyes, orig paint, c1910................. 550.00

Red Head, Eastern Shore of Maryland, 13" l.................... 135.00

Ruddy Duck Drake, Len Carmeghi, Mt Clemens, MI, hollow body, glass eyes, orig paint, sgd and dated, 10-3/4" l..................................... 250.00

Sickle Bill Curlew, unknown maker, carved wood, glass eyes, pitchfork tine beak, orig paint, 22" l... 150.00

Degenhart Glass

Operating from 1947 until 1978, John and Elizabeth Degenhart created glass novelties under the name of Crystal Art Glass. They created some unusual colors. When Crystal Art Glass went out of business, many of the molds were purchased by Boyd Crystal Art Glass, also located in Cambridge, Ohio.

Reproduction alert.

Degenhart Glass, owl, jade, **$42.**

Animal covered dish
Hen, mint green, 3"............. 22.00
Robin, blue, 5-1/2" w............. 40.00
Turkey, custard 60.00

Bell, Bicentennial, vaseline....... 15.50

Boot, 2-1/2" h, black slag, "D" in heart mark............................. 25.00

Candy jar, cov, amberina......... 24.00

Child's mug, Stork and Peacock 27.50

Coaster, intro 1974, mkd 1975, crystal 9.00

Creamer and sugar, Daisy and Button, carnival..................... 45.00

Cup plate, heart and lyre, mulberry 15.00

Figure, Bernard and Eldena, "D" in heart mark on base, 2-3/4" h
Amethyst carnival 18.00
Cranberry ice........................ 15.00

Hand, pink................................. 25.00

Hat, Daisy and button, milk blue 10.00

Jewel box, heart shape, blue 38.00

Owl
Chad's blue........................... 45.00
Cobalt blue 35.00
Emerald green 45.00
Midnight sun........................ 30.00
Purple slag........................... 35.00
Rose Marie........................... 45.00
Vaseline............................... 30.00

Pooch
Amethyst 40.00
Bittersweet 15.50
Brown 15.00
Cobalt blue 28.00
Fawn 17.50
Henri Blue 15.50

Salt, bird, amber 12.00

Degenhart Glass, cup plate, Elizabeth Degenhart, blue, 5-1/2" d, **$55.**

Tomahawk, 2" w, 3-3/4" l, "D" in heart mark
Amethyst carnival 18.00
Chocolate slag....................... 15.00
Cobalt blue carnival 15.00

Toothpick holder
Basket, milk white................ 20.00
Elephant's head, jade 24.00
Forget-Me-Not, Bloody Mary 24.00

Wine glass, Buzz Saw
Cobalt blue 20.00
Milk glass, blue..................... 22.00

Delftware

Traditional Dutch motifs of windmills and tulips often decorate these wares, which are white with blue decorations.

For additional listings, see *Warman's Antiques & Collectibles* and *Warman's English & Continental Pottery & Porcelain*.

Reproduction alert.

Ashtray, windmill scene, applied Dutch shoes on rim, mkd, 4-1/4" d 15.00

Charger, blue and white, floral rim, landscape, 12" d, edge chips 200.00

Coffee grinder, wall mount, orig decal "Made in Holland, DEVE, 1921," 13" l 300.00

Creamer, cow shape, windmill on one side, floral deco on the other, 3-1/4" h, 5-1/2" l 25.00

Decanter, windmill scene, bottom mkd "Delft, Blauw, Ram, made in Holland," missing cork 45.00

Figure, Dutch girl, Japan, 4-1/4" h 18.00

Fruit basket, blue and white center plate, wirework sides and handle 225.00

Pin, floral, sterling framing and clasp, mkd, 1-1/8" d 40.00

Plate
7-7/8" d, tin glazed earthenware, central blue rosette, England, 18th C, chips 125.00
8-7/8" d, tin glazed earthenware, flowers, bird in birdbath in center, minor damage 150.00
9-1/8" d, white tin glazed earthenware, two-tone blue flowers, wavy border, "6" mark, edge flakes, old repairs 115.00

Urn, 3-1/4" h, windmill on front, bottom mkd "4107, Delft Blue, Holland" 25.00

Vase, 18" h, ftd, cherub framed with applied fruit wreath, two figure centaurs on each side, mkd with hand painted rooster and "22" 350.00

Wall pocket, Dutch shoe, windmill scene, mkd, hole in heel to hang, 8" l 20.00

Delftware, coffee grinder, blue and white decoration with windmill scene, original cast iron crank and grinder, glass cup, 14-1/2" l, **$90.**

Department 56®

One of the fastest growing areas of collectibles are those wonderful buildings known as Department 56®. The strange name is derived from the fact that in 1976, a retail floral company, Bachmans, located in Eden Prairie, Minnesota, introduced a group of ceramic lighted buildings. Bachman's used a numbering system to identify each of its departments and this name stuck like the glitter on the roofs of the buildings that collectors began to notice. The first set of glazed, lighted, ceramic buildings was titled The Original Snow Village®.

In 1979, 12 new pieces for The Original Snow Village were introduced along with the first village accessory. The first collection of The Original Snow Village was then retired. The Heritage Village Collection® was developed as it introduced a Dickens Village Series® in 1984 with seven shops and village church. Within two years, the Heritage Village series was expanded by adding the New England Village Series® as well as the Alpine Village Series®. In 1987, the Christmas in the City® series and the Little Town of Bethlehem were added, with the North Pole Series coming into production in 1990. In 1992, Forstmann Little of New York purchased the Department 56 series. The Home of the Holidays series was begun in 1995 with a set of 13 items and more accessories such as trees, snow and even a cobblestone road; 1998 saw the introduction of the first year-round village, based on a 19th C American resort.

Many collectors remain true to their preferred series, while others like to expand their lighted Christmas villages by incorporating pieces from many of the series.

The secondary market for Department 56® items is just becoming established as more pieces are finding their way to flea markets and auction. Like most modern day collectibles, having the original box adds to the value.

Department 56®, Leacock Poulterer, retired, **$35.**

Dickens Village

1984
Bean and Son Smithy Shop 135.00
Candle Shop........................ 145.00
Green Grocer 115.00
Jones & Co. Brush/Basket Shop
.... 125.00

1985
Thatched Cottage 300.00
Tudor Cottage.................... 200.00
Village Church................... 100.00

Department 56®, carriage house, retired, **$30.**

Department 56®, train station, Weston Station, 1987, **$95.**

1986
Cottage of Bob Cratchit and Tiny
  Tim 45.00
Fezziwig's Warehouse........... 20.00
Scrooge & Marley Counting House
.... 80.00

1987
Dickens Village sign 10.00
Old Curiosity Shop 30.00

1988
Booter and Cobbler.............. 60.00
George Weeton Watchmaker
.... 65.00
Ivy Glen Church 75.00
Nicholas Nickleby Cottage ... 45.00

1989
Kings Road Cab.................... 30.00
Peggotty's Seaside Cottage, tan
.... 90.00
Ruth Marion 175.00
Victoria Station 90.00

1990
King's Road.......................... 30.00
Tutbury Printer 35.00

Department 56®, Village Ice Crystal gate and walls, retired, MIB, **$30.**

1991
Ashbury Inn 35.00
Fagin's Hide-A-Way 30.00

1992
King's Road Post Office 15.00
Lionhead Bridge................... 15.00

1993
Dashing through the Snow .. 40.00
Pump Lane Shoppes............. 90.00

1994
Boarding & Lodging School
.... 40.00
Chelsea Market Mistletoe..... 30.00
Mr. & Mrs. Pickle 40.00
Whittlesbourne Church 75.00

Department 56®, Chelsea Market Curiosities Monger & cart, retired, **$20.**

Depression Glass

Depression glass was made from 1920 to 1940. It was inexpensive machine-made glass and was produced by numerous companies in various patterns and colors.

For additional listings, see *Warman's Depression Glass.*

The following listings are a mere sampling of the current Depression glass market.

Reproduction alert.

Ashtray
Adam, green, 4-1/2" d 25.00
Diana, pink 4.00
Early American Prescut, crystal
.... 4.00
Forest Green, 4-5/8" sq 5.50
Manhattan, 4" d 11.00
Moderntone, cobalt blue 235.00
Moroccan Amethyst, 3-1/2" d 5.75
National, crystal 4.50
Windsor, pink, 5-3/4" d 35.00

Berry bowl, individual
Anniversary, irid 4.50
Bowknot, green 16.00
Bubble, blue 30.00
Dewdrop, crystal 9.00
Fortune, pink 6.00
Iris, crystal, ruffled 11.00
National, crystal 4.00
Normandie, irid 5.00
Old Cafe, ruby 6.00
Patrician, amber 12.00
Sharon, pink 10.00

Bowl
American Pioneer, crystal, 9" d
.... 24.00
Early American Prescut, crystal,
8-3/4" d 9.00
Iris, irid, 9-1/2" d 10.00
Roxana, golden topaz 12.00

Bread and butter plate
American Pioneer, crystal, 6" d
.... 12.50
Bubble, crystal, 6-3/4" d 3.50
Cloverleaf, green, 6" d 32.00
Doric, green or pink, 6" d 6.50

Butter dish, cov
Anniversary, pink 60.00
Block Optic green 50.00
Cameo, green 250.00
Dewdrop, crystal 32.00
Doric, green 90.00
Lace Edge 85.00
Madrid, amber 80.00
Moderntone, cobalt, metal cov
.... 100.00
Royal Lace, pink 150.00
Windsor pink 60.00

Cake plate
Adam, green 32.00
American Sweetheart, monax
.... 24.00
Anniversary, crystal, round 7.50
Block Optic, crystal 18.00
Cameo, green, 10" d 27.00
Cherry Blossom, green 38.00
Holiday, pink, 10-1/2" d 100.00
Miss America 25.00
Thistle, Macbeth-Evans, green
.... 150.00

Cake stand, Harp, crystal 25.00

Candleholders, pr
Iris, crystal 42.00
National, crystal 30.00

Candy dish, cov
Cloverleaf, green 45.00
Dewdrop 30.00
Floragold, irid 15.00
Moroccan Amethyst 32.00
Ribbon, black 38.00

Casserole, cov, Dewdrop, crystal
.... 27.50

Celery tray, Pretzel, crystal 8.00

Cereal bowl
Bubble, green 19.00
Dogwood, pink 32.00
Horseshoe, green or yellow .. 25.00
Old Cafe, crystal or pink 8.00
Ribbon, green 25.00
Royal Ruby 12.00

Chop plate, American Sweetheart,
monax 24.00

Cigarette box, National, crystal
.... 15.00

Coaster
Adam, pink 32.00
Cherry Blossom, pink 15.00
Manhattan, crystal 18.00

Cocktail
Iris, crystal 25.00
Manhattan, crystal 4.00
Royal Ruby 8.50

Comport
Anniversary, crystal 6.50

Depression glass, Royal Lace, dinner plate, pink, **$27.50.**

Windsor, crystal 6.00

Cookie jar, cov
Mayfair, green 575.00
Princess, blue 875.00

Creamer
Adam, green 22.00
Bamboo Optic, Liberty, ftd, green
.... 10.00
Bubble, green 14.00
Colonial Knife & Fork, crystal
.... 18.00
Cube, green 10.00
Dewdrop 8.50
Holiday, pink 12.50
National, crystal 6.50
Newport, cobalt 20.00
Ovide, Hazel Atlas, black 7.00
Royal Ruby, flat 8.00
Sunflower, green or pink 20.00

Cup and saucer
American Sweetheart, red .. 160.00
Bubble, red 15.00
Cameo, crystal 14.00
Cherry Blossom, pink 34.00
Dogwood, pink, thin 20.00
Lorain, crystal or green 15.00
Miss America, pink 36.00
Parrot green 55.00

Dinner plate
Cherry Blossom, pink 35.00
Doric & Pansy, ultramarine . 35.00
Early American Prescut, crystal
.... 15.00

Floragold, irid........................ 35.00
Florentine No. 1, green, 10" d 16.00
Florentine No. 2, yellow, 10" d
.... 15.00
Homespun, crystal or pink, 9-1/2" d
.... 17.00
Iris, irid, 9" d 45.00
Lace Edge, blue, 10" d 90.00
Lorain, yellow...................... 90.00
Manhattan, crystal, 10-1/4" d 23.00
Miss America, crystal........... 15.00
Moroccan Amethyst, amethyst,
9-3/4" d............................. 7.00
Newport, fired-on color, 8-1/2" d
.... 15.00
Parrot, green, 9" d 38.00
Petalware, monax, 9" d 10.00
Pretzel, crystal, 9-3/4" d 10.00
Primo, green, 10" d.............. 22.50
Rosemary, green, 9-1/2" d.... 15.00
Ships, cobalt, 9" d 32.00
Sierra Pinwheel, green, 9" d . 18.00
Starlight, crystal, 9-1/2" d 7.00
Waterford, crystal 10.00
Windsor, green or pink, 9" d 25.00

Juice tumbler, ftd
Cameo, green...................... 42.00
Madrid, amber 15.00
Old Cafe, crystal or pink 10.00
Royal Ruby, ruby 5.00

Luncheon plate
American Sweetheart, monax, 9" d
.... 10.00
Circle, green or pink, 8-1/4" d
.... 11.00
Columbia, pink, 9-1/2" d...... 32.00
Dogwood, pink, 9-1/4" d 36.00
Egg Harbor, green or pink 9.00
Floral, green, 9" d 30.00
Floral and Diamond Band, green or
pink, 8" d 40.00
Fortune, crystal or pink, 8" d 17.50
Georgian, green, 8" d 10.00
Madrid, amber, 8-7/8" d......... 8.00
Mayfair, pink, 8-1/2" d 25.00
National, crystal, 8" d 6.50
Patrick, pink, 8" d................. 45.00
Peanut Butter, crystal, 8" d..... 5.00
Romansque, octagonal, gold, 8" d
.... 8.00
Roulette, crystal, 8-1/2" d........ 7.00
Royal Lace, cobalt, 8-1/2" d.. 30.00
Tea Room, green, 8-1/4" d ... 37.50
Thistle, green, 8" d 22.00
Vernon, green or yellow, 8" d 10.00

Mayonnaise set, underplate, orig
ladle
Diamond Quilted, blue......... 65.00
Patrick, yellow 80.00

Mug
Block Optic, green................ 35.00
Moderntone, white................. 8.50

Pitcher
Adam, pink, 32-oz.............. 125.00
Floragold, irid....................... 40.00

Depression glass, Aurora, breakfast
plate, 6-1/2" d, cobalt blue, quite a buy at
$5; most Depression glass dealers would
have marked it **$12.50.**

Forest Green, 22-oz 22.50
Fruits, green 85.00
Ring, decorated or green, 60-oz
.... 25.00
Royal Lace, green 160.00

Platter
Cherry Blossom, green......... 48.00
Lace Edge, blue, 13" l 165.00
Royal Lace, pink 40.00
Windsor, green, oval, 11-1/2" l
.... 25.00

Punch bowl set, Royal Ruby, bowl,
12 cups.............................. 110.00

Punch cup, National, crystal 3.50

Relish
Doric, green......................... 32.00
Early American Prescut, crystal,
three-part 6.50
Lorain, four-part, crystal or green,
8" d 17.50
Miss America, four-part, crystal
.... 11.00
Pretzel, three-part, crystal 9.00
Princess, four-part, apricot 100.00
Tea Room, divided, green 30.00

Salad plate
Adam, pink, 7-3/4" d............ 18.00
Bowknot, green, 7" d............ 12.50
Moderntone, Hazel Atlas, cobalt,
7-3/4" d............................ 12.50
Patrician, amber, 7-1/2" d 15.00
Rose Cameo, green, 7" d....... 16.00

Salt and pepper shakers, pr
Adam, green 100.00
American Sweetheart, monax
.... 325.00
Florentine No. 2, Hazel Atlas, green
.... 40.00
Hex Optic, green or pink...... 30.00
National, crystal 10.00
Ribbon, green 25.00
Waterford, crystal 7.00

Sandwich server, center handle
Landrum, topaz.................... 55.00
Old English, amber............... 60.00

Spiral, green.......................... 30.00
Twisted Optic, canary........... 35.00

Sherbet
Adam, green 40.00
April, ftd, pink, 4" h 15.00
Cameo, green........................ 35.00
Cherry Blossom, pink 19.50
Daisy, amber.......................... 7.00
Florentine No. 2, yellow 8.00
Forest Green, Boopie, green... 7.00
Hex Optic, green or pink........ 5.00
Old English, green................ 20.00
Parrot, cone shape, green..... 24.00
Raindrops, crystal 4.50
Sunflower, green................... 13.50
Thumbprint, green................. 7.00
Windsor, pink....................... 13.00

Sugar, cov
Adam, pink........................... 45.00
Bamboo Optic, ftd, green..... 10.00
Holiday, pink 25.00
Madrid, amber 7.00
Ring, dec 10.00
Sierra Pinwheel, pink 20.00
Tulip, blue............................ 20.00

Tray, National, crystal 17.50

Tumbler
Bamboo Optic, ftd, pink....... 15.00
Bubble, crystal 5.00
Cloverleaf, green, ftd 50.00
Dogwood, pink...................... 45.00
Fortune, pink........................ 10.00
Hex Optic, green or pink........ 8.00
Horseshoe, green, ftd 22.00
Mayfair, ftd, pink.................. 40.00
Manhattan, ftd...................... 19.00
Moderntone, cone, white 4.00
Peanut Butter, crystal 7.00
Princess, green 28.00
Pyramid, ftd, crystal or pink 50.00
Rose Cameo, green............... 22.50
Ships, cobalt 14.00
Vernon, yellow...................... 35.00

Vase
Cameo, green, 8" h 70.00
Iris, crystal........................... 32.00
National, crystal, 9" h........... 20.00

Vegetable, open
Cameo, green........................ 30.00
Daisy, amber......................... 13.00
Florentine No. 2, cov, yellow 55.00
Sharon, oval, amber 20.00
Star, amber 10.00
Tea Room, green 75.00

Wall vase, Anniversary, pink ... 90.00

Whiskey
Diamond Quilted, pink 12.00
Hex Optic, green or pink........ 8.50
Hobnail, crystal 5.00

Wine
Manhattan 5.00
Miss America, pink 115.00

Desert Storm

Collectibles from this historical event are making their way to flea markets. Because these items are relatively new, expect to find them in very good condition.

Commemorative plate, Hamilton Collection, 8-1/2" d, MIB **38.00**

Comic book, Desert Storm Journal, #7 .... **8.00**

Flag, white, yellow center ribbon, slight fading from use **5.00**

Key chain, "Operation Desert Storm, Come Home," with yellow ribbon, 2" **8.00**

Lighter, butane, "Desert Storm" **5.00**

Medallion, ceramic, "Protecting World Peace," 1991, MIB **12.00**

Pin, Support Our Troops, Desert Storm **3.00**

Pinback button
Operation Desert Storm, Support Our Troops **7.50**
Support Desert Storm, Free Kuwait, US and Kuwait flags.......... **8.50**

Soda bottle, Jolt, painted, 12 oz **5.00**

Desert Storm, helmet, camouflage, name stenciled on front, original liner, **$25.**

Dexterity Puzzles

Small enough to hold in the palm of your hand, these little puzzles have provided hours of enjoyment for kids and collectors alike. From inauspicious beginnings as premiums or giveaways, these tiny playthings have certainly increased in value over the years.

Dexterity puzzles, Santa Claus, 2-1/4" d, **$30.**

Indian, tin and glass, "Nabisco Shredded Wheat Juniors" on back, 1-1/4" d **15.00**

Lone Ranger, 5" x 3-1/2" **60.00**

Lucky Horseshoe, cardboard and glass, A.C. Gilbert Co., c1940, 3 1/4" x 4 1/4" **40.00**

Miller High Life, can-shape, in orig plastic wrapper, 5" h **20.00**

New York-Paris Aero Race .. **65.00**

Pin U Ring It, cardboard, paper and glass, by Journet, directions on bottom, 3-1/4" x 4-1/4".......... **20.00**

Reddy Killowatt...................... **15.00**

Sgt. Biff O'Hara, Nabisco Shredded Wheat Juniors, 1-1/4" d......... **30.00**

Turnstyle Puzzle, cardboard, paper and glass, by Journet, directions on bottom, 5" x 4"...................... **25.00**

Voslu, aircraft in flight, silvered rim, plastic cover, full color paper playing surface, inscription "1908 80 Kahen/Frankreich, German, c1970...................................... **35.00**

Witch, flying on broomstick, orange background, round, early...... **45.00**

Camel Lights, clear styrene plastic key chain case, miniature replica of cigarette pack, small square opening in top to capture nine miniature filter tip cigarettes in filter ends up, c1980 .... **25.00**

Felix, German, metal, 1920s, 2" d **80.00**

Harlequin Puzzle, cardboard, paper and glass, by Journet, directions on bottom, 3-1/4" x 4-1/4".......... **30.00**

Hungry Pup, cardboard and glass, A.C. Gilbert Co., c1940, 3-1/4" x 4-1/4" **40.00**

Dexterity puzzles, Gilbert Puzzle Parties, set of dexterity puzzles, The A. C. Gilbert Co., New Haven, Conn, MIB, **$45.**

Dick Tracy

Here's a comic strip character that made it to the big-time—movies! And, he and his pals generated some great collectibles along the way.

Dick Tracy, Aladdin plastic lunch box and thermos, **$20.**

Dick Tracy, toy, Dick Tracy's Police Squad Car, Playmates, NRFB, **$15.**

Air Detective cap, Quaker, 1938 .... 150.00

Badge, Detective Club Crime Stoppers, Guild, 1940s........... 30.00

Big Little Book, Whitman, hardcover
Dick Tracy and the Racketeer Gang, 1936...................... 25.00
Dick Tracy Encounters Facey, 1967.............................. 10.00

Book, *Ace Detective*, Whitman, 1943 .... 30.00

Camera, 127mnm, 1950s, 5-1/2" l, 2-1/4" w, 3" h 75.00

Cereal premium, *Secret Detective Methods and Magic Tricks Book*, Quaker, 1939........................... 35.00

Colorforms, 1962 .... 20.00

Comic book
Dick Tracy Comic Book, Popped Wheat Cereal, 1947 .... 6.00
Motorola Presents Dick Tracy Comics, 1953 .... 15.00

Crimestopper Club kit, Chicago Tribune premium, 1961 .... 35.00

Film, 8mm, "Brain Game," black-and-white, silent, Republic Pictures, orig box 5-1/4" sq.......................... 22.00

Game, Dick Tracy, Selchow & Righter, 1961 .... 25.00

Little Golden Book, *Dick Tracy*, 1962 .... 18.00

Magazine ad, Kraft caramels, 1958, 10" x 13"................................. 16.00

Marbles, Dick Tracy Straight Shooters, orig bag.................. 15.00

Play set, Hubley, cap gun, holster, handcuffs, wallet, flashlight, badge, magnifying glass, 1970s 35.00

Pop gun, paper, Tip Top Bread premium................................ 35.00

Puzzle, The Bank Holdup, Jaymar, interlocking pcs, 1960s.......... 20.00

Radio, two-way electronic wrist, Remco, plastic, battery operated, 1950s, pr 60.00

Ring, enameled portrait, Miller Bros., 1940s...................................... 60.00

Toy car
Dick Tracy car, Marx, 1950s 125.00
Get away car, Playmates, 1990 .... 15.00
Squad car, convertible, Marx, friction, 1948.................. 200.00

Trading cards, Willard's Chocolates, 56 cards, 1930s, complete set 90.00

Transfer, Official Member Dick Tracy Crime Stoppers, blue and red graphics, 1940s, 10" x 8"........ 15.00

Water pistol, Luger style, 1971 .... 40.00

Whistle, Police No. 64, Marx, tin 20.00

Disneyana

Walt Disney was the impetus for a wonderful cast of characters that still delights children of all ages. Through the many Disney movies and television shows, many collectibles are available. Check for the official "Walt Disney Enterprises" logo.

Activity book, *Toby Tyler Circus Playbook,* Whitman, 1959.... **25.00**

Bank
Mickey Mouse Club, vinyl, Play Pal Plastics, 1970s **15.00**
Pinocchio, Crown Toy, wood compsition, metal trap door, 1939 .... **80.00**

Bell, Tinkerbell handle, bronze colored metal, emb "Copyright Walt Disney Productions," 3-1/4" h **55.00**

Big little book, *Mickey Mouse Presents A Silly Symphony,* Whitman, 1934 .... **35.00**

Bean bag game, Mickey Mouse, 1930s.................................... **100.00**

Better little book
Disney's Donald Duck, Ghost Morgan's Treasure, Whitman #1411 .... **50.00**
Disney's Mickey Mouse on Haunted Island, Whitman #708-10.. **50.00**
Disney's Silly Symphony Presents Donald Duck, Whitman #1169 .... **25.00**
Robin Hood of the Range, Whitman, 1942 .... **20.00**

Book
Donald Duck Sees South America, D. C. Heath & Co., Walt Disney Storybooks, hardcover, 6-1/4" x 5-1/2" **40.00**
Pinocchio, Grosset and Dunlap, laminated cover............... **30.00**
Thumper, Grosset & Dunlap, 1942, 32 pgs **30.00**

Bookends, pr, Donald Duck carrying school books, chalkware **25.00**

Calculator, Happy Birthday Donald Duck, 1934-84, Bradley Quartz Calculator, clock, 12" ruler, made in Hong King, mint in orig mailing box **35.00**

Card game, Pluto, Whitman, 1939 copyright, black, white, and red illus, 35 playing cards............ **50.00**

Crayons, Mickey Mouse, Transogram, 1946 .... **20.00**

Cup and saucer, Fantasia, Vernon Kilns, 1940............................. **70.00**

Dinner set, Mickey Mouse, Empresa Electro, china, 2" h creamer, six plates, two oval platters, divided dish, 1930s.......................... **200.00**

Doll, Pollyanna, 30" h............. **100.00**

Drinking glass, Donald Duck, "Full, Going, Going, Gone!," 1940s, 4-3/4" h **40.00**

Earrings, clip-on, Mickey Mouse **35.00**

Figure
Alice, plastic, hp, Marx, 1950s, 2-1/2" h............................... **10.00**
Daisy, plastic, hp, Marx, 1950s, 2-1/2" h............................... **12.00**
Donald Duck, accordian, bisque, 1930s, 4" h **195.00**
Dumbo.................................. **35.00**
Goofy, Marx, Snap-Eeze **12.00**
Mickey Mouse, Fun-E-Flex, bendy, 1930s **130.00**
Minnie Mouse, plastic, hp, Marx, 1950s, 2-1/2" h **12.00**
Pinocchio, bisque, 1940s, 3" h **110.00**
Thumper, painted and glazed ceramic, tan, brown and pink, Hagen-Renaker, 1940s **50.00**

Greeting card, get well, diecut Mickey, Hallmark, 1930s **35.00**

Disneyana, Mickey Mouse, doorstop, cast iron, yellow gloves, red shorts, white accents, gold shoes, **$185.**

Hair brush, Mickey Mouse, Walt Disney Enterprises, 1930, orig box **45.00**

Hand puppet, Horace Horsecollar, Gund, 1950s............................ **30.00**

Jewelry box, Fantasia, Schmid, musical, 1990......................... **30.00**

Magazine
Mickey Mouse Magazine, Vol. 2, #1, October 1936, Kay Kamen Ltd., 36 pgs **195.00**
Newsweek, February 13, 1950, three-pg article about Cinderella, color cover................... **25.00**

Mask, diecut stiff paper, Doc, premium from Stroehmann's Bread, ad for Snow White Cake, marked "Part-T-Mask/Eison-Freeman Co, Inc.," poem on back, ©1937 .... **25.00**

Mousketeer ears, Mickey Mouse Club, Kohner **15.00**

Music box, Happy, figural........ **30.00**

Night light, Goofy, Horsman, green, 1973 .... **16.00**

Nodder, Donald Duck, 1960s .. **50.00**

Paint book, Pinocchio, 1939 ... **60.00**

Paper dolls, *Mary Poppins Cut-Out Book*, Watkins-Strathmore Co., 1964, uncut............................ **40.00**

Pencil, 5-1/2" l, red, white, and blue, Donald Duck Bread, Ungles Baking Co, 1950s **25.00**

Disneyana, Donald Duck, Nu-Blue Sunoco, ink blotter, unused, **$35.**

Pencil box, Dixon, Donald Ducky flying plane, holding tomahawk 50.00

Pinback button
Donald Duck, Wanna Fight, 1930s 40.00
Mickey Mouse Club, copyright 1928, 1-1/4" 42.00

Print shop kit, Mickey Mouse, Fulton Specialty, 1930s.......... 80.00

Puzzle, Black Hole, Whitman, 1979 .... 15.00

Radio, Mickey Mouse, Philgee, 1970s 20.00

Record, Mickey Mouse Club March, 7" x 7" colorful stiff paper sleeve, 45 rpm record, Disneyland label, ©1962 .... 20.00

Ring, brass, thin expansion band, diecut brass figure of black, white, and red Mickey in Santa suit, green gloves, ©Walt Disney Productions, 1970s...................................... 12.00

Disneyana, Seven Dwarfs, set of soft vinyl figures, original packaging, **$45.**

Disneyana, book, *Walt Disney's Mickey Mouse Book*, A Golden Shape Book, **$5.**

Rug, Uncle Scrooge McDuck, woven, 1950s, 34" x 21" 175.00

Salt and pepper shakers, pr
Ludwig Von Drake, 1961, MIP 285.00
Mickey and Minnie, glazed ceramic, cork stoppers ... 375.00
Pluto, glazed white china, over glaze black and red paint dec, Leeds China, 1947............ 30.00

Snow shovel, Donald Duck, Ohio Art, litho tin, wood handle ... 60.00

Soaky, Donald Duck, 1950s...... 15.00

Teapot, cov, large, Mickey Mouse 95.00

Television, Build Your Own TV, six Walt Disney full-color films, punched out parts, Tower Press Product, Made in England, 1950s, 9-1/2" x 7" 125.00

Thermometer, 6" x 6" ceramic Sportsman plaque, Donald as bowler, black text, Kemper-Thomas Co., 1940s 35.00

Toothbrush, Mickey Mouse Club, Pepsodent, 1970s..................... 4.00

Toy
Donald Duck, litho tin wind-up, Schuco, 5-1/2" h 350.00
Mickey Mouse, squeeze, Dell, rubber, hitchhiking hobo, 1950s 35.00
Mickey Mouse tractor, Sun Rubber, rubber, 5" l....................... 50.00
Mickey Mouse, wind-up, Gabriel, transparent plastic, visible gears, 1978................................... 10.00

Tray, Mickey and Minnie, Ohio Art, 1930s, tin, 7-1/2" l 95.00

Valentine, Jiminy Cricket, diecut, movable arms, 1939 .... 27.50

Wall plaque, Mickey Mouse as band leader, mkd "Ceramica De Cuernavaca," 1970s................ 95.00

Wristwatch, silvered metal case, white dial, Mickey with red gloves, c1970, working 50.00

Disneyland and Disney World

From celebrities to kids of all ages, lots of folks enjoy Disneyland and Disney World. Collectibles from these wonderful amusement parks are eagerly sought.

Ashtray, Disneyland, mkd "Walt Disney Productions Japan," some fading, 5" 8.00

Book, *Disneyland The First Quarter Century*, hardcover.............. 45.00

Bottle opener, Walt Disney World, 4-1/2" l..................................... 5.00

Box, cov, porcelain, Castle, white, mkd "Disneyland ©Walt Disney Productions," 4-5/8" l, 3-1/4" w, 2" h 40.00

Charm bracelet, Disneyland, six charms, ©Walt Disney Productions, MIB... 40.00

Coke cans, Toon Town, six-pack, Mickey, Roger Rabbit, Donald, Goofy 20.00

Flasher pin, I Like Disneyland/ Mickey Mouse, 1950s 40.00

Game, Adventures in Costumeland Game, Walt Disney World, 1980s 75.00

Disney World, tin tray, 10-3/4" d, **$7.50.**

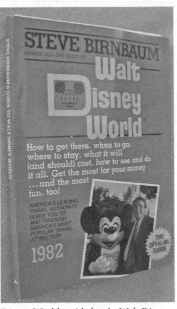

Disney World, guide book, *Walt Disney World*, Steve Birnbaum, 1982, red cover, **$15.**

Invitation, 25th Anniversary, cast members open house, 1-5/8" d silver medallion attached **30.00**

Little Golden Book, *Donald Duck in Disneyland*, 1955 .... **15.00**

Locket, brass, heart shape, raised castle on front, pink and blue accents, late 1950s **28.00**

Map, Welcome to Disneyland, fold-out, 1958, 12" x 8-1/2" **80.00**

Pin, Tokyo, "First Day Last Day," Mickey **30.00**

Pinback button, Main Street Commemorative, blue text, 3,000th Performance, Sept. 4, 1991, color photo...................................... **37.50**

Plate, Disneyland, Mark Twain, palette mark with "Eleanore Welborn Art Productions, Monterey, California," 1950s, 6" d **85.00**

Poster, Family Fun Night, 1971, ©Walt Disney Productions, 9" x 12" **45.00**

Puzzle, Tea Party, Tower Press, copyright 1960 Walt Disney Productions **30.00**

Record story book, Disneyland Davy Crockett, 1971, 7-1/4" sq **35.00**

Salt and pepper shakers, pr, one shows Main Street, other shows Sleeping Beauty castle **30.00**

Sign, Studio One and Tavern Guild Private Party, May 25, 1978... **35.00**

Thermos, Disney's Wonderful World, Aladdin, 6-1/2" h **10.00**

Tray, metal, white designs around rim, 1960s............................. **15.00**

Wrist watch, 35 Years of Magic-Disneyland, Mickey's face, band with relief of Fantasy Land Castle, the Matterhorn and Ferris wheel, Japan, MIB............................. **25.00**

Dog Collectibles

Collecting dog-related items is a fun sport for many collectors. Some specialize in collectibles showing a certain breed; others look for items with canines that resemble a favorite pet. Those who are celebrity-minded search for famous dog characters, such as Tige, Rin Tin Tin, and Lassie.

Badge, 3" red, white, and blue litho pinback, "Kids Ken-L-Klub" ... **7.50**

Big little book, *Lassie, Adventure In Alaska*, 1967 .... **12.00**

Book
Huskies in Action, The Fascination of Sled Dog Racing, Rico Pfirstinger, 1995, color photos **15.00**
Lassie & The Mystery of Blackberry Bog, Dorothea Snow, Whitman, illus by Ken Sawyer, 1946 .. **5.00**
The Rin Tin Tin Book of Dog Care, Lee Duncan, Prentice Hall, 1958, dj....................................... **40.00**

Bottle opener, wall-mount, cast iron, bulldog, 4" h, 3-1/2" w........... **75.00**

Calendar plate, 1910, black and white Bulldog, white china, gold trim.. **45.00**

Cookie jar, McCoy, Mac Dog, mkd "208 USA" **160.00**

Costume jewelry, pin, begging poodle pin, Trifari, goldtone, gray rhinestone accents, mother-of-pearl body, red cabachon eye **45.00**

Dresser jar, cov, satin glass, dog finial...................................... **45.00**

Dog collectibles, anyone looking for a specific breed figurine might have been in luck with this nice assortment found at the Landisville Flea Market in September of 2004.

Figure

Beagle, #1072, Llardo 140.00

Bonzo Dog, 3" h, bisque, mkd "Germany," c1920 .... 45.00

Collie, bisque, black and brown 40.00

Dachshund, Beswick, #1469 50.00

Pointer hound dog, hydrant, burgundy glazed pottery, wood base, mkd "Souvenir of Lawton, Okla," Camark Pottery 75.00

Folder, 8-1/2" x 11" paper folder for retailers of Ken-L-Ration dog food 12.50

Magazine ad, Gaines dog food, Rin Tin Tin, 1947 .... 9.00

Pinback button, Duke the Peters Dog, multicolored, black Labrador clenching Peters shotgun shell carton in mouth, white lettering on black rim 12.00

Ramp walker, 3-1/2" l dachshund, brown hard plastic, black and yellow accents, Marx, 1950s.. 15.00

Salt and pepper shakers, pr

Poodle, heads, Rosemeade 165.00

RCA Nipper, Lenox.............. 75.00

Stuffed toy, Lassie, vinyl collar 75.00

Toothbrush holder, dog holds toothbrush in mouth, Japan, 5-1/8" h 95.00

Wall plaque, Collie, Mortens Studio 24.00

Dog collectibles, print, titled "Only a Dog," Victorian children playing dress-up with dog, matted and framed, **$35.**

Dog collectibles, doorstop, wired hair terrier, cast iron, some loss to paint, **$145.**

Dog collectibles, doorstop, Scottie, black, cast iron, **$165.**

Dollhouse Furniture

Dollhouse furnishings are those tiny articles used to finish and accessorize a dollhouse. Materials and methods of production range from fine handmade wooden pieces to molded plastic items. Several toy manufacturers, such as Tootsietoy, Petite Princess, and Renwal, made dollhouse furnishings.

Arm chair, Petite Princess, matching ottoman 27.50

Bathroom set, Tootsietoy, 10 pcs, orig box................................... 85.00

Doll house furnishings, exterior accessories, picnic table, round table with umbrella, deck chairs, fountain, lawnmower, etc., all plastic, price for grouping, **$25.**

Bear rug, white, purple velvet lining, glass eyes 35.00

Bed, Renwal, twin size............... 9.00

Bedroom suite, Tootsietoy, six pcs, orig box.................................. 65.00

Bird cage, brass, floor stand 12.00

Bunk beds, plastic...................... 5.00

Canopy bed, wood, hand made quilt and bed hangings 45.00

Candelabra, Petite Princess, MOC 12.00

Chaise lounge, Petite Princess 10.00

Chest of drawers, walnut, handmade 65.00

Cradle, Renwal, turquoise........ 16.00

Desk, maple, hinged front, royal blue and black int......................... 115.00

Fireplace, Renwal, brown plastic 37.50

Doll house furnishings, living room suite, two sectional upholstered sofas, three upholstered wing chairs, upholstered swivel barrel back chair, pair of modern high back upholstered chairs with matching ottomans, set of eight red and white upholstered Petit Princess chairs, price for grouping, **$60.**

Garbage can, lid lifts with foot pedal, red body, yellow pedal and lid, Renwal 15.00

Kitchen set, Allied, hard plastic, orig box 30.00

Living room suite
Arcade, cast iron, sofa and chair 185.00

Tootsietoy, sofa, two chairs, library table, two lamps, phonograph stand, seven pcs 90.00

Painting, oil on canvas, portrait of gentleman, framed 45.00

Patio set, plastic, picnic table, chaise lounge, two chairs, umbrella and stand 5.00

Piano, Ideal, plastic, litho, mirror 30.00

Plant stand, Petite Princess 1.00

Server, woodtone plastic, Renwal 5.00

Wing chair, Petite Princess, MIB 15.00

Dollhouses

Early dollhouses were reserved for the wealthy and were designed primarily as display cabinets for collections of valuable miniatures rather than as playthings for children. The first American doll houses were made in the late 18th century, but it wasn't until 1860, with the development of chromolithography, that they were mass-produced.

Bing, Germany, garage, litho tin, double doors, complete with two orig cars 600.00

Bliss, chromolithograph on wood
Stable, two-story, red shingle roof, painted green and red cupola, painted red base, single opening door on 2nd floor, brown papier-mache horse, mkd "R. Bliss" 900.00
Victorian, two rooms, two-story, high steeple roof, dormer windows, spindled porch railing, second floor balcony 1,400.00

Converse, cottage, red and green litho on redwood, printed bay windows, roof dormer 550.00

Ideal
Colonial style, three rooms up, three rooms down, balcony, back open 300.00

Fantasy Room, Petite Princess, red, MIB 45.00

Marx, litho tin, two-story house, detailed living room with fireplace, kitchen cupboard with dishes, toy soldier motif in nursery, 19" l, 8" d, 16" h, front door missing, some rust damage, some play wear 45.00

McLoughlin, folding, two rooms, dec int, orig box 825.00

Tootsietoy, printed Masonite, half timbered style, four rooms, removable roof 200.00

Unknown American maker, hand crafted, 20th C
Cape Cod, 1950s style, two floors, red hearts on white shutters, one-pc tin litho roof, white porch posts and railing 125.00
Colonial style, three stories, white clapboards, blue shutters, red roof and clear plastic windows, electrified, as-found with

Doll house, interior view showing two bedrooms and living room, attic space, **$95.**

contents including wooden furniture, accessories, rugs, 1970s, 36" w, 18" d, 24" h 45.00
Colonial style, two stories, white clapboards, copper gutters, wall papered int. walls, detailed trim, two floors, two story side porch, hand cut shingles 400.00
Victorian type two story house, wrap-a-round front porch on two sides, dormers, several pieces of window trim missing and glass replaced, electrified, 24" w, 25" d, 24" h 350.00

Wolverine, litho tin, two-story house, five rooms, bay windows, 10 pcs of period plastic furniture, 22" l, 12" deep, 15" h, chimney missing, some play wear.................................. 45.00

Doll house, custom made, shingle roof, clapboard siding, two stories, blue shutters, **$95.**

Doll Accessories

Collectors are just finding out what little girls have always known—you can't really play dolls unless you also have the beds, cribs, bassinets, and other necessary items found in a real nursery. Barbie has her own furniture and accessories, plus an extensive wardrobe. But, she wasn't the first doll to be so fortunate. Many early dolls came complete with trunks of clothes, shoes, and other fine accessories.

Doll accessories, doll sized chairs, cane seats, saber legs, price for pr, **$100.**

Baby bottle, glass, black plastic top, rubber nipple 5.00

Baby bottle, plastic, "milk" disappears 8.00

Bassinet, fold-up type, holds water 65.00

Blanket chest, pine, old worn repaint, six-board type 450.00

Bottle sterlizer, granitewate ... 35.00

Bunk beds, wood, orig bedding, c1960 .... 80.00

Carpet sweeper, Minnie Mouse and Donald Duck, Ohio Art, 1930s, wooden handle 50.00

Chair, Queen Anne style, upholstered seat 90.00

Chest of drawers, Empire style, mahogany and mahogany veneer, three dovetailed drawers, scrolled feet, some veneer damage ... 500.00

Clothespins, plastic, set of 20.... 5.00

Cradle, pine, bell rings when rocked back and forth 45.00

Crib, light oak, movable side rails, orig hand made bedding, c1955 .... 70.00

Doll bed, high scrolled Victorian-style headboard, matching footboard, mahogany, new quilt and bedding......................... 250.00

Fainting couch, professionally restored................................ 130.00

Kitchen set, metal, sink, stove and refrigerator, colorful litho dec 175.00

Rocker, pierced pressed board back and seat, scrolled arms........ 125.00

Snow shovel, litho tin, wood handle, Donald Duck, Ohio Art......... 60.00

Doll accessories, doll bottle equipment, sterilizer, rack fitted with five bottles, funnel, etc., American Metal Specialties, wear to original box, **$45.**

Stroller, red plaid seat, white metal frame, c1960, played-with condition 20.00

Throw rug, Mickey and Minnie in airplane, Donald parachuting, 26" x 41".. 60.00

Trash can, Mickey and Minnie, tin litho, Chein 25.00

Trunk, dome-top, lined with wallpaper, orig handles 75.00

Wash tub, aluminum, 5" d 15.00

Watering can, Minnie Mouse, Ohio Art... 20.00

Dolls

Made from a wide variety of materials, dolls have always been favorite playthings of the young and the young at heart. Doll collectors are a very dedicated group. Some specialize in a particular style of doll or company, while others simply love them all. There are hundreds of examples for collectors to consider. Condition, age, markings, and original clothing all help to determine a doll's value.

Many good doll reference books exist. A favorite for any flea market shopper should be Dawn Herlocher's *Antique Trader's Doll Makers & Marks;* and *200 Years of Dolls.*

Artist type
Dianna Effner, Sweetness, christening dress, 1988 .... 125.00
Lee Middleton, Alexis, skating outfit.............................. 350.00

Boudoir type, French, cloth face 160.00

Celebrity or character
Bert, Sesame Street, Knickerbocker, 1981, MIB......................... 25.00
Brooke Shields, MIB............. 30.00
Captain Caveman, stuffed, 30" h 65.00
Charlie McCarthy, composition, movable mouth, 1930s... 185.00

Cher, ©1975 Mego, MIB....... 50.00
Cinderella, holding Little Golden Book 20.00
Deputy Dawg, Ideal, 1960s... 60.00
Gizmo, squeaker.................. 30.00
Kate Jackson, Mattel, 12" h .. 70.00
Little Debbie, mail-in premium, 1985, 12" h........................ 50.00

Dolls, Sauerkraut Bunch, Zapf Creation, MIB, **$20.**

Mary Poppins, Horsman, 1964 .... 55.00
Spiderman, Mego, NRFP, orig price sticker 85.00

Cloth
Baby, composition head, stuffed body and limbs, American Character 125.00
Heather, Knickerbocker, painted features, calico dress and hat, MIB 20.00
Raggedy Ann, Christmas box 35.00

Composition
Alice in Wonderland, Horsman, MIB 95.00

Dolls, Ideal, yellow bonnet and dress, MIB, **$24.**

Anne Shirley, Effanbee, orig clothes, 18" h 195.00
Baby Dear, Vogue, bent baby limbs, 1961, 12" h 40.00
Barbara Lou, Effanbee, orig clothes, 21" h 350.00
Bottle Tot, American Character, orig clothes, 13" h 175.00
Deanna Durbin, orig box, 15" h 245.00
Dream Baby, Arranbee, redressed, 20" h 115.00
Giggle Doll, Cameo Doll Co., orig box, 12" h 375.00
Joyce, Horsman, 18" h 50.00
Judy Garland, Wizard of Oz costume, Ideal, 18" h...... 675.00
Nancy, Arranbee, orig outfit, 21" h 410.00
Sparkle Plenty, Ideal, 1947. 125.00
Toni, American Character, redressed 45.00

Plastic
Betsy McCall, jointed knees, brunette rooted hair, orig red and white striped skirt, white organdy top, c1960, 8" h .. 45.00
Bonnie Braids, walking, 6" h 30.00
Karne Ballerina, Eegee, jointed at knees, ankles, neck, shoulders, and hips, ballet shoes, satin and net ballet dress, c1958, 21" h, MIB 45.00
Mary Ellen, Madame Alexander, orig clothes, 31" h 225.00
Merri, Cosmopolitan Doll Co., 14" h 20.00
Penny Brite, orig clothes 45.00
Sweet Sue, blond wig, blue sleep eyes, rose dec white taffeta dress, pearl pin, 15" h............... 200.00
Tammy, Ideal, orig clothes ... 45.00
Tiny Terri Lee, Terri Lee Dolls, trunk with six orig outfits, 10" h 450.00

Rubber, 11" h, Sun Rubber Co., molded features
Betty Bows, drinks and wets, c1953 .... 35.00
Gerber Baby, open nurser mouth, dimples, crossed baby legs 45.00

Vinyl
Baby Linda, Terri Lee, molded painted hair, black eyes, c1951, 9" h 95.00
Bobbsey Twins, Stratemeyer Syndicate, MIB................. 50.00
Butterball, Effanbee, all orig 65.00
Cheerful Tearful, Mattel, orig clothes, 1966, 12" h 35.00
Dale, Negro, Topper Corp 12.00
Dawn, Topper Corp.............. 15.00
Dimples, vinyl head, cloth bean bag body, Eegee 24.00
Ginny, Girl Scout outfit, 8" h 115.00

Dolls, Jan Hagara, Effanbee, Laurel's Toy Cat, small stuffed fabric cat, pink dress and bonnet, blond curly hair, MIB, **$60.**

Little Dear, Arranbee, c1956, 8" h 80.00

Dolls, Dynasty Doll, clown, **$10.**

Warman's Flea Market

Mary Poppins, Horsman **70.00**
Ruthie, Horsman, 12-1/2" h . **30.00**

Dolls, Nancy Ann Storybook, pair, both played-with condition, each **$15.**

Shirley Temple, Ideal, c1962, orig
box, 15" h **275.00**
Truly Scrumptious, Mattel,
11-1/2" h........................... **95.00**

Vinyl and hard plastic
Andy, Eegee, 12" h................ **25.00**
Baby Party, vinyl head and arms,
hard plastic body and legs,
Topper **35.00**
Chatty Cathy, Mattel, talking, MIB
.... **85.00**
Littlest Angel, Arranbee, 11" h
.... **45.00**

Dolls, Suzanne Gibson, Reeves International, Grandma and Red Riding Hood, limited edition, 1983, MIB, **$65.**

Doorknobs

If a man's home is his castle, it's no wonder that collectors have latched on to the idea of collecting ornamental doorknobs and other types of hardware. A special doorknob can give a house personality and a bit of pizzazz.

Doorknob
Arts and Crafts, stamped metal,
rose motif, one nickel-plated,
one copper-plated, knobs 2" d,
matching plates 9" h x 1-1/2" w,
pr **50.00**
Brass, emb, with plate, pr..... **45.00**
Eastlake style, brass.............. **40.00**
Glass, clear, pr **25.00**

Glass, mercury, 2-1/4" d, pr . **80.00**
Porcelain, Limoges, floral deco,
gold accents, pr **150.00**

Doorknob plate, china, oval, rose
pattern, 6-3/8" h, 3-1/2" w, set of
four **55.00**

Door knocker, dog, cast iron, old tan
paint...................................... **235.00**

Mail slot cover, brass, emb "Letters,"
Victorian................................. **48.00**

Doorknockers, cast iron, oval, painted, multicolored, floral basket with bow, 4" l, **$35.**

Doorknob, brass Victorian set, **$22.50.**

Doorknockers, brass, urn shape, 7" l,
$45.

Doorstops

Functional figural doorstops became popular in the late 19th century. Examples could be either flat-backed or three-dimensional. The doorstop's condition is critical to determining value, and collectors prefer doorstops with as much original paint as possible. The following listings are for examples that retain at least 80% of their original paint.

Reproduction alert.

Note: All listings are cast iron unless otherwise noted.

Doorstop, cast iron, flower basket, multicolored flowers, **$75.**

Bellhop, blue uniform, with orange markings, brown base, 8-7/8" h 300.00

Boston terrier, 9-1/2" h 85.00

Bowl, green-blue, natural colored fruit, sgd "Hubley 456" 125.00

Cat, black, red ribbon and bow around neck, on pillow, 8" h 155.00

Clipper ship, mkd "Copyright Creation Co. 1930, 10-1/2" h, 11-1/4" w 75.00

Cottage, cape cod type, blue roof, flowers, fenced garden, bath, sgd

"Eastern Specialty Mfg Co. 14," 8-5/8" l, 5-3/4" h...................... 150.00

Drum Major, ivory uniform, red hat with feather, yellow baton, left hand on waist, sq base, 12-5/8" h. 225.00

Duck, white, green bush and grass 335.00

Flower basket
Marigolds, Hubley, mkd "Made in USA and 315, 7-1/2" x 8" 175.00
Petunias & Daisies, Hubley 115.00

Frog, sitting, yellow and green, 3" h 50.00

Golfer, 10" h 475.00

Little Miss Muffett, sitting on mushroom, blue dress, blond hair 175.00

Mammy, full figure, Hubley, red dress, white apron, polka-dot bandanna on head............... 225.00

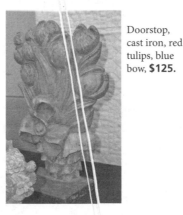

Doorstop, cast iron, red tulips, blue bow, **$125.**

Doorstop, cast iron, peacock, some loss to original paint, **$225.**

Monkey, wrap-around tail, full figure, brown and tan.......... 250.00

Owl, sitting on books, sgd "Eastern Spec Co.," 9-1/2" h 285.00

Pan, sitting on mushroom, green outfit, red hat and sleeves, flute, green grass base, 7" h 165.00

Peasant woman, blue dress, black hair, fruit basket on head 250.00

Pointer dog, 8" h, 14" w......... 495.00

Show horse, Chestnut, Hubley, slight retouch to nose.................... 150.00

Squirrel, sitting on stump, brown and tan.. 275.00

Windmill, ivory, red roof, house at side, green base, 6-3/4" h 115.00

Dr. Seuss

Remember reading *Green Eggs and Ham* and *The Cat In The Hat*? Both of those titles are dear to Dr. Seuss collectors. This is a field in which collectors are still establishing fair market values, primarily because so many of the items are just now entering the secondary market. Adding to the thrill of the hunt is the fact that this favorite author also wrote under several pseudonyms.

Book

Dr. Seuss's ABC, Beginner Book, hard cover, 1963, book club edition 10.00
Green Eggs and Ham, 1966.. 2.00
Happy Birthday To You!, 1959 .... 26.00
The Cat in the Hat, Random House, 1957 .... 7.50
The Hat Comes Back, Random House, 1958........................ 7.50
You're Only Old Once, 1986 12.00

Cereal bowl, plastic, "The Wubbulous World of Dr. Seuss" 6.00

Christmas decoration, Dept 56. How The Grinch Stole Christmas series
Christmas countdown tree, 24 resin ornaments 50.00
Cindy Lou Who's House 75.00
Musical Sleigh 45.00
Town Hall 75.00

Dr. Seuss, Coleco Thidwick the Moose, original box, **$110.**

Dr. Seuss, Welch's Cat in the Hat jelly glass, **$4.**

Christmas ornament, Horton Hatches the Egg, Hallmark, MIB 14.00

Doll

Cat in the Hat, Coleco, 1983. 40.00
Grinch, Coleco, 1983 .... 55.00
Horton the Elephant, Coleco, 1983 .... 25.00
Lorax, Coleco, 1983 .... 25.00
Talking Cat in the Hat, Mattel, 1970 .... 60.00
Thidwick the Moose, Coleco, 1983 .... 15.00
Yertle the Turtle, Coleco, 1983 .... 15.00

Figure, Horton the Elephant, china, 4" l, 5-1/4" h........................... 55.00

Growth chart, The Cat in the Hat Growth Chart, paper, orig packaging............................... 17.50

Jelly glass, No. 1, The Cat In The Hat and the Zubbie Wump, "The Wubbulous World of Dr Seuss," 1996, 4" h................................. 2.00

Lunchbox, metal, Aladdin, 1970, matching plastic thermos.... 200.00

Pin, pewter, figural, Cat in the Hat 12.00

Puppet, Cat in the Hat, talking, Mattel, 1970........................... 50.00

Toy

Jack-in-the-box, Mattel, 1969 **90.00**
Mattel-O-Phone, 1970.......... 40.00
Riding toy, Coleco, 1983....... 25.00

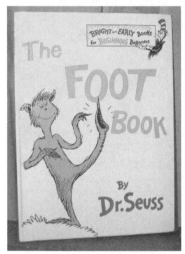

Dr. Seuss, book, *The Foot Book,* Bright & Early Beginner Books series, **$1.**

Drinking Glasses

Many drinking glasses start out life as part of a set, but due to breakage and other tragedies, they are sometimes orphaned and end up at flea markets, just waiting for a new home.

Bohemian glass, ruby flashed, cut design, gold dec, four-pc set 150.00

Carnival glass
Acorn Burrs, marigold 60.00
Orange Tree, blue 60.00
Peacock at Fountain, amethyst 25.00

Cut glass
Clear Button Russian pattern 95.00

Hobstars............ .... 40.00

Depression era
Flowers, yellow and green.... 12.00
Madrid, amber 9.00
Princess, yellow, ftd.............. 30.00
Stars, white 10.00
Sunbonnet Girl, red, white and blue 15.00

Fostoria
American, ftd 11.00
Colony, flat 27.00

Drinking glasses, Libbey, red, yellow and blue tulips, 6-1/2" h, **$150.**

Heisey, Rose Etch, 12-oz., ftd.... 50.00

Libbey Glass, green, slight swirl pattern, mkd, set of five 72.00

Northwood, blue, 1" opalescent white band at top, mkd 10.00

Pattern glass
Broken Column, ruby trim .. 65.00
Bull's Eye and Diamond Panels 50.00
Cherry and Cable, color trim 20.00
Cranes and Herons, etched .. 30.00
Croesus, amethyst 90.00

Dakota, etched fern and berry dec 35.00
Esther, green, gold trim 45.00
Festoon 20.00
Yale 25.00

Drug Store Collectibles

Aacchhoo! Here is another collecting field where the collectors are beginning to really specialize. Whether they collect paper epherma relating to drug stores, or perhaps collect items related to a favorite local drug store, or perhaps bottles or old packaging, this is a fun category. However, please don't try any of the remedies you might find. Those old compounds might not be stable any more.

For additional listings, see *Warman's Americana & Collectibles*.

Drugstore collectibles, box, Deer Skin Prophylactic Rubbers, silver and black box, 2-1/4" x 2" x 1/2", **$20.**

Almanac, 1937, *The Ladies Birthday Almanac*, Medlock's Drug Store, Roscoe, Texas......................... 12.00

Book, *Yellow Magic, The Story of Penicillin*, J. D. Ratcliff, Random House, 1945, 1st ed. 8.50

Bottle
Bromo-Seltzer, The Emerson Company, Baltimore cobalt, 2-1/2" d............................ 10.00
Leitsch's Drugstore, light aqua 20.00
Sodium Phosphate, United Drug Company, corked, aluminum screw-top, 4-oz................. 30.00

Calendar, 1901, Colgate, miniature, flower...................................... 20.00

Charm, 1-1/4" h, Boyd's Battery, narrow silver metal ring surrounds larger central metal segment with text surrounded by 12 individual circles in brass, silver, or copper luster, opposite side with inscription "Patented Jan 17, 1878," small brass loop on top 24.00

Display, *Blue-Jay Corn Plasters*, cardboard, two drawers, "Make hard roads easy," displays two hobos walking along railroad tracks while passing billboard for Blue-Jay Plasters, ©1903, 6-1/2" h, 9-1/4" l, 10-1/4" d 50.00

Fan, cardboard with wooden handle "666 Quartette" laxative, Hill's Pharmacy, Tampa, Fla., cardboard, chipped wooden handle, creases, 11-1/4" h 16.00
Tums for the Tummy, hand screen type, young boy beckons to girl leaving drugstore 35.00

Glass, ice cream soda
Clear, ribbed stems, 8" h, set of five 30.00
Light amber, 7" h, set of six.. 55.00

Jar, glass, Ramon's, countertop, blue metal lid, Ramon's character in two places 150.00

Matchbook, Humphrey Drug Store, Home Store of Vice President Hubert H. Humprey, Liberty Bell 7.50

Needle book, Rexall - Make A Point of Saving At Our Rexall Drug Store, three needle packets and threader 16.00

Ornament, Hallmark, Neighborhood Drugstore, Nostalgic Houses and Shops series, MIB, 1994 .... 25.00

Pinback button, Fox Drug Co. Business is Good, dark blue on white, bright red running fox in center "Follow the Fox!," St. Louis back paper, 1940s 12.00

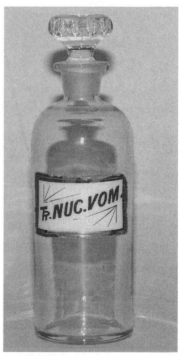

Drugstore collectibles, apothecary jar, Tr. Nuc. Vom., glass stopper, 9-1/4" h, **$65.**

Postcard, interior of Harry Neamand's drugstore, Perkasie, PA, c1940..................................... 20.00

Scale, chemist's, General Scientific Co., milk glass platforms, two weights, 8" h, 13" w 150.00

Stamp case, book shape, By-Lo Breath Perfume, black, white, and red celluloid, spine lettered "Stamp

And Court Plaster Edition," early 1900s....................................... 55.00

Tin

ADS Apsirin Highest Purity, green, red, and white 7.50

Babcock's Corylopsis of Japan Talcum Powder, 4-1/2" h, full, c1920 .... 18.00

BC Headache Neuralgia, blue and white.................................. 6.00

DeWitt's Throat Lozenges, blue, white, and black, 60 orig lozenges............................. 5.00

Doan's, tin and cardboard, 40-count 7.00

Dream Girl Talcum Powder, 2" x 6", black and white on red 25.00

Dr. Scholl's Foot Powder, cylindrical, green, black and gold, 6-1/4" h.................... 20.00

Huyler's Glycerine Tablets 5.00

Men-Tho-Lo, Leighton Supply Co., orig box and instruction sheet, 2-1/2" d............................ 12.50

Nebs Pain Reliever, light blue, black, and white 7.50

Nyal Cold Capsules, Nyal Co., Detroit, black and orange, 3" x 2" x 1/2" 12.50

Toy, Nature's Remedy Tablets, celluloid, center wooden spinner dowel, brown and white, c1920 .... 20.00

Trade card, Hood's Latest Tooth Powder, Emlet's Drug Store, Havover, Pa., shows woman's face breaking through newspaper 15.00

Duncan and Miller Glassware

The glass company known as Duncan & Sons and, later, Duncan and Miller, was founded in 1865 and continued through 1956. Their slogan was "The Loveliest Glassware in America," and many collectors will certainly agree with that sentiment.

For additional listings, see *Warman's Antiques & Collectibles*, *Warman's Glass*, and *Warman's Depression Glass*.

Duncan and Miller Glass, cornucopia, opalescent white and pale blue, small feet, **$35.**

Ale glass, Teardrop, crystal...... 18.50

Almond bowl, Sandwich, crystal 12.00

Animal
Heron................................. 100.00
Swan, red bowl, 7-1/2" h 45.00

Ashtray, Terrace, red, sq 35.00

Basket, Sandwich, crystal....... 135.00

Bowl, First Love, crystal, 9" d... 75.00

Butter, cov, Sandwich, crystal, quarter pound 40.00

Cake stand, Sandwich, crystal, 11-1/2" d 95.00

Candlesticks, pr, Sandwich, crystal 30.00

Candy jar, cov, Sandwich, chartreuse, 8-1/2" h 95.00

Champagne, Tear Drop, 5 oz .. 10.00

Coaster, Sandwich, crystal....... 12.00

Cocktail glass, Caribbean, blue, 3-3/4 oz.................................. 48.00

Console bowl, 11" d, Rose etch, crystal 37.50

Creamer, Teardrop, 5 oz 9.00

Cup and saucer, Radiance, light blue 24.00

Demitasse cup and saucer, Teardrop, crystal.................... 12.00

Goblet
Caribbean, blue 40.00
Festival of Flowers, crystal ... 30.00
Plaza, cobalt.......................... 40.00
Teardrop, crystal.................... 15.00

Ice cream dish, Sandwich, crystal, ftd 12.00

Juice tumbler, Sandwich, crystal, 3-3/4" h, ftd 12.00

Nappy, Sandwich, crystal, two parts, divided, handle...................... 15.00

Oyster cocktail
First Love, crystal 24.00
Teardrop, crystal.................... 9.00

Plate
Canterbury, crystal, 8" d......... 8.00
Radiance, light blue, 8-1/2" d 12.00
Spiral Flute, crystal, 10-3/8" d 15.00

Relish dish
Caribbean, blue, divided 30.00
Terrace, five-part, hammered aluminum center lid, 12" w 50.00

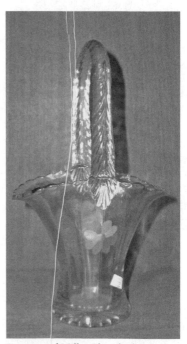

Duncan and Miller Glass, basket, green, etched floral design, **$65.**

Sugar, Caribbean, crystal 12.00

Tumbler, Terrace, red 40.00

Whiskey, Seahorse, etch #502, red and crystal 48.00

Wine glass, Sandwich, crystal 24.00

Earp, Wyatt

Hugh O'Brian starred when Wyatt Earp's character got his own television show. Western collectors search for this cowboy hero at many flea markets.

Big little book, *Hugh O'Brian's TV's Wyatt Earp*, Whitman #1644, ©1958 .... **10.00**

Cereal bowl, Hazel Atlas **30.00**

Calendar plate, 1982, Wild West, Wedgwood, 10-1/8" d **60.00**

Color and stencil set, Hugh O'Brian, MIB **145.00**

Comic book, *Wyatt Earp*, #21, 1958 .... **10.00**

Holster set, 29" l, sand colored, dark brown tooling, Esquire Novelty Co., late 1950s **60.00**

Magazine, *Look,* Hugh O'Brien **15.00**

Mug, Wild West Collection, mkd "D6711," 1985-89, handle is a gun and sheriff's badge, 5-1/2" h **200.00**

Puzzle, frame tray, full-color portrait, Whitman, 1958 .... **25.00**

Record, The Legend of Wyatt Earp, RCA Victor, TV theme song on one side, Jesse James song on other side **12.00**

Statue, Hartland **125.00**

Easter Collectibles

Here's a holiday that's always hoppy to be collected. From chicks to bunnies, this one is fun and whimsical, in addition to having a serious, religious side.

Book, *The Easter Story*, 1904.. **32.50**

Bookmark, 2-1/2" x 7", ribbon, pale pink, inscribed Easter religious passage................................... **10.00**

Candle, rabbit, sitting, off-white, mkd "Tavern Novelty Co.," 5" h, 4" d **10.00**

Candy container
Easter Bunny dressed like cowboy, hard plastic, pulling "wood-look" cart, 1950s, yellow and blue, 13" l **22.00**
Rabbit, crouching on all fours, papier-mâché, removable head for storage of candy, mkd "Made in Germany, U.S. Zone, 4" x 4" **45.00**

Decoration, cardboard and tissue paper honeycomb, unfolds to set-up, rabbit sitting among lilacs, surrounded by honeycomb eggs and basket, USA, 8-1/2" l **20.00**

Easter egg
Milk glass, white, gilded lettering "Easter Greetings," painted purple spring flowers, 6"... **45.00**
Papier-mâché, two baby chicks on front, Easter basket filled with lily of the valley flowers, flowered paper int., 3" w, 4-1/2" l **75.00**

Figure
1-1/2" x 3" x 2-1/2" h, yellow painted chick standing next to woven basket, wood base, stamped "Germany," c1930 .... **35.00**
2-1/2" x 4" x 3-1/4" h, celluloid, rabbit pushes egg-shaped buggy with chick inside, red and blue highlights, c1920 .... **35.00**

Greeting card, stand-up, girl, "To Wish you a Happy Easter," yellow tissue paper honeycomb skirt, USA, 7" h.. **5.00**

Easter collectibles, back row, two papier-mâché rabbit candy containers with oversized ears, German, each **$90;** white papier-mâché stork figure, metal legs, **$65;** white papier-mâché duck figure with real feathers, **$50;** papier-mâché rabbit pulling cart with movable head, possibly replaced cart, **$25;** papier-mâché sitting rabbit, **$45;** green papier-mâché pig candy container, **$35;** plaster of Paris hen on nest, some losses, **$30.**

Easter collectibles, egg, milk glass, decorated with yellow and maroon pansies, wear to gold "Easter Greetings," **$45.**

Plate

Ceramic, Easter Morning Visitor, Recco, from the "Hearts & Flowers" collection by Sandra Kuck, two girls with bunny and basket of flowers, #2474A, 7th in series, 1992, 8-1/2" d........ **25.00**

Paper, Easter bunny, eggs, and spring flowers, 8-3/4" sq **4.00**

Sterling silver, "Easter Christ," Salvador Dali, Lincoln Mint, 1972, 1st ed, orig box, 9" d **225.00**

Postcard, 3-1/2" x 5-1/2", color, lightly embossed

Angel with lamb, 1910 .... **3.00**

Baby chicks, early 1900s......... **3.00**

Chickens with eggs in floral basket, 1906..................................... **4.00**

Cross, German publisher, 1910 .... **3.00**

Picnic scene, German publisher, early 1900s **3.50**

Rattle, dancing rabbit, pink, blue jacket and holding a blue carrot, dancing, hard plastic, mkd "Irwin" 4" h... **4.00**

Sheet music, *Easter Dawn*, by A. Fieldhouse, 1904.................... **15.00**

Snowbunnies figures, Dept. 56
Counting the Days Til Easter, 1997, MIB **24.00**
I'll Color the Easter Egg, MIB **18.00**
Wishing You a Happy Easter, MIB **32.50**

Easter collectibles, candelabra, three bunnies, each with candle socket, Holt Howard, **$85.**

Toy, musical Easter basket, cardboard, plastic handle, orig box, mkd "Mattel, 1952," 4" x 6"........... **65.00**

Eggbeaters

Before modern kitchens were outfitted with electric appliances, eggbeaters were powered by hand. More than 1,000 patents were issued for items designed to beat eggs, and most of them were granted prior to the 1900s.

A & J, center drive, blue and white painted wood handle, 1923... **30.00**

Aluminum Beauty, Made in USA, Pat. April 20, 1920................. **12.00**

Baby Bingo, tin, 5-1/2" l............ **8.00**

Dover, cast iron, 1904 .... **35.00**

Ekco

A & J High Speed Beater, red Bakelite handle, wooden knob, 12" l **40.00**
Best, two arrowheads mark, turquoise plastic handle and knob, 12" l **8.00**

H-L Beater, Tarrytown, NY, No. 0, cast wheel, gears, loop type handle,

wood knob, wavy beaters, 9" l **40.00**

Ladd Beater, No. 1, United Royalties Corp, NY, patent July 7, 1908, Feb. 24, 1915, coiled wire knob, 11" l **35.00**

Taplin Light Running Eggbeater, metal, 1908 patent date, 10-1/2" l **35.00**

Turbine Egg Beater, metal, wooden knob, Cassady-Fairbank Mfg. Co., Chicago, 1912 patent date, 10-1/2" l **32.50**

Ullman, wooden handle, 11" l **18.00**

Eggbeaters, Keystone Egg and Cream Beater, metal top, **$75.**

Unmarked, child-size, red wooden handle, 4-1/4" l **9.50**

Eggcups

Delicate eggcups make a wonderful collection, both useful and pretty to look at. Some were made as part of dinner services, and others were simply novelty items.

Advertising, Fanny Farmer, rabbit standing nest to egg shell, 2-1/2" h **65.00**

Ceramic or porcelain

Child's, Indian motif, gold trim, blue Japan stamp, 2-1/4" h **18.00**

Chintz, Rosalynde pattern, James Kent, double..................... **80.00**

Figural, lady with hat, salt shaker in red hat, mkd "Italy C22," 5-1/2" h **65.00**

Hand-painted, mkd "Japan," 1950s, 4" h **12.00**

Hen on nest, mkd "Worcester Royal Porcelain Co., Ltd., Worcester, England," 4-5/8" h **30.00**

Limoges, white, gold trim **30.00**

Mickey Mouse, mkd "Walt Disney Productions," 3-3/4" h....... **85.00**

Organdie, Vernon Kilns **15.00**

Popeye sitting at table, spinach, Japan, 1940s 30.00
Rabbit with cane, incised "Germany 6450" on back, red stamped "76"

Eggcups, Stangl, 3-1/4" h, **$25.**

on base, 3-1/4" h, 2-1/2" w 50.00
Rooster, mkd "Made in Japan," 2-1/4" h............................. 15.00
Swee' Pea, Vandor, 1980 .... 10.00

Glass, figural
Bunny with eggcup on back, hp, Fenton, sgd by artist, orig box, 3-1/2" h............................. 28.00
Chick, white milk glass, mkd "Made in France/Opalex" 18.00
Hand holding cup, blue milk glass 25.00

Jasper, blue, white dec, Wedgwood, Portland base mark, 1910 ..... 85.00

Silverplate, holds 4 eggs, ftd base with swags, mkd "C & Co, E.P.," castle mark 235.00

Sterling silver, hallmarked Chester, 1911-12, maker SB 35.00

Wood
Chick, bright yellow, child size, 1-3/4" d, 2-3/4" h.............. 25.00

Little boy's head, hp, mkd "Made in Italy"................................. 20.00

Eggcups, Blue Willow, border at base, marked "England," 2-1/4" h, **$18.**

Elephant Collectibles

Many folks consider elephants to be a symbol of luck. Particularly lucky are those elephants with their trunks raised. Whether due to their size or the fact that they are exotic, people just seem to enjoy them.

Advertising trade card, 4-7/8" x 3", Clark's Spool Cotton, Jumbo's

Elephants, whiskey decanter, Ski Country, **$15.**

Arrival, sepia, white, adv on back 7.50

Bank, chalk, orig paint, c1930, 12" h 125.00

Book, Edward Allen, *Fun By The Ton*... 20.00

Bookends, pr, Ronson, sgd "L. V. Aronson, copyright 1923"
Elephant Country, black painted metal, elephant against landscape, back emb with design, 4-3/4" w, 4" h 195.00
Howdah, black finish, verdigris accents, ivory painted tusks, orig felt, 4-1/2" h 160.00

Bottle opener, figural, cast iron, sitting, trunk raised
Brown, pink eyes and tongue, 3-1/2" h............................. 55.00
Pink, "GOP" on base, 3-1/4" h 55.00

Christmas ornament, blown glass, gray body, red blanket, 3-1/2" l 95.00

Cigarette dispenser, cast iron 95.00

Clothes sprinkler bottle...... 165.00

Elephants, cast-iron cigarette dispenser, decal for 1933 Chicago World's Fair, 5" h, 8" l, **$165.**

Creamer and sugar, lusterware, red blankets, black riding on sugar, mkd "Made in Japan," c1940 .... 195.00

Figure
Brass, bronze finish, trunk in air, 29" h, 30" l 300.00
Glass, trunk raised, 2-1/2" l, 3" h 12.00
Porcelain, Armani 280.00
Teak, carved adult and baby, 20th C, one tusk missing, 23-1/2" h 140.00

Lamp, elephant with girl, hand painted, Japan, 14" h 45.00

Letter opener, celluloid, marked "Depose-Germany," c1900..... 40.00

Mug, Frankoma, 1970s............ 20.00

Napkin ring, Bakelite, navy blue, c1940..................................... 65.00

Pie bird, dark gray, mkd "Nutbrown Pie Funnel, Made in England," c1940.................................. 195.00

Pin, 2" l, 1-1/2" h, rhinestones, pink tusks, black enamel trim, trunk up 95.00

Pitcher
2-1/2" h, white, orange and blue trim, tail forms handle..... 20.00
6-1/2" h, figural, black man as handle, incised "5020"... 185.00

Planter, figural, pottery
5" h, glossy finish 18.00
8" x 5-1/2"............................. 20.00

Postcard, Elephant Hotel, Margate City, N.J., 1953 .... 7.50

Salt and pepper shakers, pr, figural, mkd "Japan"............................. 24.00

Toothbrush holder, 5" h, mkd "Made in Japan," 1940s-50s 165.00

Toy, Jumbo, litho tin wind, mkd "U. S. Zone Germany," 3-1/2" h 85.00

Enesco

Enesco has made quality limited editions for years. Some are marked with a stamp, while others have foil labels or paper tags. The company's Precious Moments line is a favorite of collectors.

Also see Precious Moments in this edition.

Bank, Garfield, arms folded, 6" h 60.00

Christmas ornament, John Deere, Model B, Mrs. Claus driving, 1998, MIB....................................... 60.00

Cookie jar
Garfield................................. 90.00
Sugar Town General Store.... 60.00

Dealer sign, "The Rose O'Neill Kewpie Collection by Enesco," 3-3/4" h, 1991 .... 45.00

Egg timer, Prayer Lady, pink, 6" h 125.00

Figure
Athena, mermaid, 6" h 70.00
Betsy Ross and Friend, 4-1/2" h 18.00
Birthstone mermaid, September, Shimmer Stone, Coral Kingdom, holding clamshell with sapphire-colored stone, 1994 .... 85.00
Irish Mouse, hard plastic, 2-1/2" h 5.00
Mermaid, Sabrina, Shimmer Stone, mkd "Coral Kingdom ®," Sabrina ©1993 Enesco Corp, #, star mark, orig tag and box, 6" h 110.00

Pluto, 1960s, copyright Walt Disney Productions, 6-1/4" h....... 60.00
Shaggy Dog, copyright Walt Disney Productions, orig paper tag, foil sticker, 5" h...................... 65.00
Tigger and Winnie the Pooh, Friends Together Forever, orig 14k gold-plated pewter charm, 5-1/2" h, MIB 50.00

Enesco, "Pals" figurine, circa 1982, with box (not shown), 3-3/4" h, **$10.**

Halloween light, Cherished Teddies, Stacy, ghost costume, vinyl, 17" h 100.00

Lady head vase, 8" h, orig foil label 380.00

Mug, Mouseketeers, emb Mickey Mouse face, foil label, c1960 . 50.00

Music box, Love Story, Mickey and Minnie Mouse, plays "Love Makes The World Go Round," 6" h, orig paper label 75.00

Planter, Viennese Waltz, ruffled gown, gold trim, 8" h............. 60.00

Powder shaker, winking cat.... 15.00

Salt and pepper shakers, pr
Blue Birds, orig paper labels, 4" h 24.00
Christmas Presents, white, green dots, red ribbon, paper label, 2-1/2" h........................... 16.00
Colonial America, orig box, 4" h 24.00
Piggy Chef, yellow base, clear plastic pig, white plastic chef hat, paper label, orig box 18.00
Squirrels, holding large green acorn, orig gold foil labels 22.00

Ertl

Although Ertl has produced a wide range of toys and figures, the company is perhaps best known as a manufacturer of farm toys. Ertl also specializes in promotional and commemorative trucks and banks, the sale of which has most certainly assisted a number of volunteer fire companies and other civic groups.

Ertl, diecast cars, Replica series, each **$5.**

Airplane
American Airlines 40.00
Shell Oil, tri-motor 50.00
US Navy Air Express 30.00

American Muscle Street Rods series
American Graffiti, 1932 Ford Duece Coupe, 1999, MIB 40.00
Chevy 3100 Stepside, 1955, white, red bed liner, 1994, MIB .. 35.00
Cobra 427 Roadster, 1957, 1999, yellow, black stripes, MIB 30.00
Corvette Stingray, 1963, black, 1993, MIB 35.00
Ford Newstalgia, 1939, 1998, canary yellow, MIB 25.00
Ford Street Rod, 1940, 1998, blue, orange and red flames on hood, broken bumpers, orig box 15.00

Bank
Dodge Airflow, 1939, Texaco on sides, bank, MIB 15.00

Ford Van, 1932, Anheuser Busch logo, 1991, 6-1/2" l 40.00
Jewel Tea, 1905 truck, MIB .. 65.00
Kodak, replica of Ford's first delivery car, MIB 75.00

Car
Batmobile, 1989, paint worn, 3-3/4" l 5.00
Cale Yarborough, Nascar stock car, Pow-R-Pull, 3" l, MOC 30.00
Dick Tracy, Microsize set, 1990, crayons and cars, MIB 8.50
Ken Schrader Budweiser Monte Carlo, 1995, MIB 75.00

Combine, International Harvester, 1974 .... 110.00

Ertl, diecast cars, top: Camaro, **$15;** bottom: Corvette, **$15.**

Ertl, diecast cars, top: The Fall Guy, **$25;** bottom: A Team Corvette, **$25.**

Figure, diecast
Daffy Duck, driving fire engine, Looney Tunes, 1980s, MOC 40.00
Wondergirl, 1990, MOC, 2" l 15.00

Semi-trailer
John Deere, 1980s, MIB 75.00
US Express, 1986, MIB 75.00

Tractor
International, play wear, 9-1/2" l 35.00
John Deere, utility tractor, 1993, 1/16th scale 36.00

Trailer, farm, movable tailgate, paint chips, 3-3/4" h, 12" l 12.00

Watch, service premium for Ertl employees, orig box............... 75.00

Eyeglasses

Some collectors are always on the lookout for vintage eyeglasses. Spectacles are great decorator accents. Other flea market buyers look for period eyeglasses that they can use for theatrical purposes or that can be worn during historical reenactments.

Aviator frames, dark brown prescription lenses, mkd "Luxottica Lance 135," 1970s 20.00

Bakelite, honey colored, round lenses, 1940s 12.00

Cat's eye style, lady's, 1950s
Cocoa brown, rhinestone trim, mkd "L. Errard" 50.00

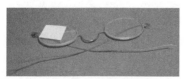

Eyeglasses, pewter frames, oval lenses, late 19th C, original case, **$65.**

Gold tone frame, mkd "Ful Vue," orig case mkd "Geden Colitz Opticians, Boston" 80.00
Pewter look, black trim, etched silver at corners, plastic ear pcs, 5-1/2" w 35.00

Colonial style, silver brass frames, sliding adjustable flat brass rim, oval lenses, stamped "Botian," on rim, c1770-1810 .... 150.00

Folding, imitation tortoiseshell cat's eye style frame and handles, aurora borealis rhinestone trim, 4-1/2" w, 3-1/2" handle 30.00

Gold, 12k, scrolled dec, small MOP nose pcs, 4-1/4" w................. 25.00

Lorgnette
Cream-colored cat's eye plastic, rhinestone dec, side handle 55.00
Spring loaded, gunmetal colored steel, hidden spring, 6" l, suspended from 1" d metal

Eyeglasses, gold-rimmed spectacles, **$20.**

brooch, retractable fine chain
.... 110.00

Lucite, brown, white, and translucent
speckles, mkd "Christian Frame
Italy 1635, 5-1/4-50-2-FILOS"
.... 10.00

Monocle, gold frame................ 25.00

Plastic
Eight-sided lenses................. 20.00
Harry Potter style, child's, 1930s
.... 75.00
Mauritius, red with rhinestones and
leopard 32.00
Swank, black with glitter...... 32.00
Vogue, cat's-eye, gold and taupe,
silver and gold accents..... 32.00

Safety, Bausch and Lomb, steel
frames, plastic nose pads, wrap
around earwings with rubber
protectors, orig prescription lenses,
mkd "BB&L Ful-Vue 23," case
stamped "Wm H Price, Opticians,
Bethlehem, PA," c1930 .... 45.00

Tortoiseshell, oval lenses, 1900s
.... 75.00

Wire rim, gold, case mkd
"Henderson Jeweler and
Optometrist, Delhi, N.Y.'....... 35.00

Eyeglasses, assortment of old eyeglasses, some gold frames, some pewter, few with original cases, late 19th C, ranging in price from **$45** to **$100.**

Fans, Hand-Held, Advertising

Today we tend to think of fans as decorative accessories, but for our ancestors, they were the primary means of cooling themselves. Collectors can find a wide range of advertising fans, usually with a decorative image on one side and advertising on the back. The highest value usually is achieved when the fan is sold near where the original advertiser was located.

For additional listings, see *Warman's American & Collectibles*.

Alka Seltz, 8-1/2" x 9-1/2", 4-1/2" wooden rod handle, cartoon ad, late 1930s-40s, creased **25.00**

Bradley Knit Wear, 7" x 8" cardboard, 5-1/2" wood handle, multicolored images of swimsuits, customer text on back, late 1920s-early 1930s **20.00**

Garrett's Snuff, 7-1/2" x 9" cardboard, 4" l bamboo loop, multicolored image of hunters and hunting dog relaxing at fireplace, puppies pulling at hunting jacket, caption "There Goes Your Old Hunting Coat," black and white illus of Memphis factory, monthly calendars for April 1937 through July 1938 .... **20.00**

Independent Life and Accident Insurance Co., Jacksonville, Fla., Cooling Off, naked child walking toward river, Scheer, #3183, cardboard, wooden handle ... **18.00**

New Home Sewing Machine, 8-1/2" x 10" diecut cardboard, 3-3/4" wooden rod handle, full color portrait of young lady and sponsor name, black and white pictures of sewing machines on back, early 1900s-20s **15.00**

Reddy Kilowatt, 8-1/4" x 9" diecut cardboard, 4" l thin balsa wood handle, dark pink image, red facial markings, slogans, 1980s **20.00**

666 Laxative-Tonic, 7" x 7-1/2" diecut cardboard, 4" l thin balsa

Fan, advertising, paper, Charles Twelvetrees illustration, 7" h, 10" w, **$15.**

wood handle, full-color image of youngster and birds singing "666 Carol" from sheet music, 1936 .... **15.00**

The Valley of Fair Play, 9-1/2" x 10-1/2" diecut cardboard, white ground, aerial black and white photo view of show manufacturing community, Endicott-Johnson Shoes, Feb 1923 patent date .. **18.00**

Tip-Top Bread, diecut cardboard, full color stars artwork, reverse with six red, white, and blue illus of suggested snacks using bread, c1930, 7-1/4" x 9-1/4" **25.00**

Fan, framed silk fan, white, hand embroidered silver bead work, **$75.**

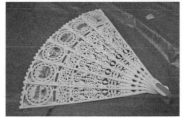

Fan, souvenir, ivory colored plastic, decals with French scenes, red ribbon, **$5.**

Farm Collectibles

Farm collectors are saving an important part of our American heritage. Collecting and protecting the items related to or used on a farm will give future generations insights into the amount of work farming entailed.

Warman's Flea Market

Farm collectibles, barn with cupola, silo, and shed, ceramic, with light, red, tan, gray, and white, snowy base, **$9.**

Advertisement, 1948 Oliver Model 88 industrial tractor, black-and-white, 10-1/4" x 7-1/2" **20.00**

Book, *Farm Life on The South Plains Of Texas* **18.50**

Booklet, International Harvester, *Make Soil Productive*, 64 pgs, 1931 .... **8.50**

Bridle rosette, heart shape...... **38.50**

Catalog, John Deere Co., Chicago, Ill., 24 pgs, 1970 .... **14.00**

Cider press, oak and other hardwoods, old refinish, mortised and pegged, base with four legs, threaded wooden shaft missing its handle, 44" h, 26" w, 15" d... **220.00**

Farm collectibles, wagon wheels, wood and iron, repainted, price for pair, **$250.**

Fan, hand, Wallace's Farmer and Iowa Homestead Newspaper, little girl standing in front of school, holding book and blue metal lunch box, 1955, 10" w, 10-1/2" h............ **35.00**

Feed sack, printed cloth
Advertising type **18.00**
All over floral dec **15.00**

Feed chest, smoke-decor, white ground with black smoke, slant-lid, 3 interior compartments, turned legs with ball feet, wear, mouse holes, 35-1/2" h, 53-1/4" w, 24" d **375.00**

Flour sack, printed paper, Harvest Queen Improved Roller Flour, Red Mills, shows woman in bonnet, Centre Hill, Pa., framed, soiled, stains, 20" h, 14" w **50.00**

Goat yoke, single, wood, bentwood bow **60.00**

Hay fork, wooden, four-prong, three wooden prongs on front with 4th mounted on handle with iron bracket, 84" l........................... **60.00**

Hay hook, cast iron with wood handle, 14" l........................... **15.00**

Magazine, *Farm Journal*, Feb. 1963, chickens on cover **4.00**

Medallion, John Deere, front shows bust of John Deere and "He gave the world the steel plow," back shows wagon train and plow with "John Deere Quality Farm Equipment, since 1837" **35.00**

Memo book, Agrico Fertilizer, 1947 calendar **3.50**

Milking stool, wooden, crescent-shaped seat, three round splayed stake legs, primitive, refinished, 8" h, 17" w, 7" d **35.00**

Operator's manual
Allis-Chalmers, model B front-mounted planter, 600 series, soiling................................. **8.25**
Ford, model 8N tractor, 1948 **50.00**

Farm collectibles, chicken feeders, tin, each **$17.**

John Deere, horse-drawn cultivator, seven pgs, stains, folds..... **40.00**
John Deere, sweep-type planting and fertilizing attachments for tractor cultivators, light soiling **5.25**

Pinback button, celluloid, Purina Chicken Chowder, red and white checkered feed sack, blue ground, white slogan "If Chicken Chowder Won't Make Your Hens Lay They Must Be Roosters," 1920s **10.00**

Sickle, 21" l, wooden frame, iron blade **25.00**

Sign, Slow, Cattle Crossing, porcelain, two-sided, flange, 18" h, 14" w **115.00**

Tape measure, metal, Kent Feeds, Nichols (Iowa) Grain and Feed, two-digit phone number, 2" d **25.00**

Farm collectibles, tin sign, "Ford Farming," 11" x 22", **$30.**

Fast Food Collectibles

The hamburger has long been a popular American food, and fast food restaurants have certainly done their best to convince us that they hold the secret to the perfect sandwich. And, in an effort to increase sales and generate future purchases, they've added toys and premiums. These special extras have become an interesting part of the collectibles marketplace.

For additional listings, see *Warman's Americana & Collectibles* and McDonald's in this edition.

Fast food collectibles, Big Boy, bank, red and white checked overalls, brown hair, blue and white eyes, **$20.**

Ashtray, Big Boy, heavy glass, orange image and inscription "Frisch's Big Boy," 1968, 3-1/2" d 12.00

Bank, 3-1/2" x 3-1/2" x 5", Howard Johnson's Restaurants, white hard plastic, building shape........... 20.00

Booklet, 5-1/2" x 7-1/2", Burger King Draw & Color, ©1979 .... 24.00

Bucket lid, Colonel Sanders, 8-1/2" d cardboard, brown on white, 1960s 5.00

Building
Bob's Big Boy Restaurant, Lefton, NRFB 45.00
McDonald's, Dept 56 .... 55.00

Calendar, Burger King, Olympic games theme, 1980.................. 4.00

Coloring book, *Sambo's Restaurant Family Funbook Activity Book*, 1978, unused 42.00

Doll, Burger King, molded plastic head and hands, 1980, 22" h . 35.00

Employee badge, 3-1/2" d
Big Boy, Manners, black and white, cartoon art, early 1960s ... 25.00
KFC, Take Home A Colonel's Dozen 15 Melt In Your Mouth Biscuits, white, red and brown text, 1960s 20.00

Glider, King Glider, Burger King, Styrofoam, 1978 .... 2.50

Hand puppet, 10" h, Burger Chef, flannel felt, soft vinyl head, early 1970s..................................... 35.00

Hat, 8-1/2" x 15", Captain Crook, McDonald's, thin cardboard, ©1978 .... 8.00

Iron-on, 5" x 8-1/2" white tissue sheet with 4-1/2" x 6" black, white, red, and yellow picture of Ronald McDonald and porpoise, early 1970s..................................... 10.00

Magic pipe, 6" l, red hard plastic, white Styrofoam ball, Burger King, 1980s... 1.00

Menu, Denny's, plastic coated, c1960 .... 2.50

Mug, Hardees Breakfast Club, 1993 .... 3.00

Night light, Big Boy, 2" d, hard plastic, brass prongs, 1960s... 18.00

Paperweight, Wendy's, "Decade II," metal and celluloid 30.00

Patch, employee, stitched fabric
2-1/2" x 3-3/4", McDonald's, c1960 .... 10.00
2-3/4" x 4-1/4" Big Boy, black and white figure, red stripe accents, 1950-60........................... 15.00

Photo, 8-1/2" x 10-1/2" full color, banded in yellow across bottom, blue McDonald's ad text, facsimile signatures of Schmid Franz,

Fast food collectibles, Dairy Queen whistle, 3-1/8" h, **$10.**

Woodrow Barnaby, Captain Penny, early 1960s............................ 15.00

Pinback, Big Boy, 3" d, black and white face, red inscription "Should He Stay Or Go!," 1980s 18.00

Puzzle, 6-1/4" x 9-1/4" frame tray puzzle, Big Boy, orig manila envelope, c1960 .... 35.00

Salt and pepper shakers, pr, Col. Harland Sanders, 4-1/2" h, hard white plastic figures, Canadian, 1960s...................................... 20.00

Teddy bear, Burger King, Crayola blue bear, 1986, 7" h 8.00

Toy
Ball, 2" x 4" x 1" h ball launching catapult, Burger King, red plastic, ©1980 .... 1.00
Saucer launcher, Burger King, blue plastic, ©1979 .... 2.00

Tumbler, 3-1/2" h, Miss Dairylea, maroon images on clear.......... 8.00

Watch, Burger King, 1970s, silvertone case, blue suede strap, blue background on face 50.00

Whistle, Dairy Queen, white plastic ice cream on tan cone 4.00

Fenton Glass

Founded by Frank L. Fenton in 1905 in Martin's Ferry, Ohio, Fenton first decorated glassware for other makers. By 1907, the company was making its own glass and had relocated to Williamstown, West Virginia. Today the company is still producing quality glass, and collectors are encouraged to visit the factory site and museum in Williamstown. Fenton family members and their decorators frequently sign pieces.

For additional listings see *Warman's Antiques & Collectibles* and *Warman's Glass.*

Fenton Glass, collector plate, Bicentennial, 1776-1976, Patrick Henry, original box, **$20.**

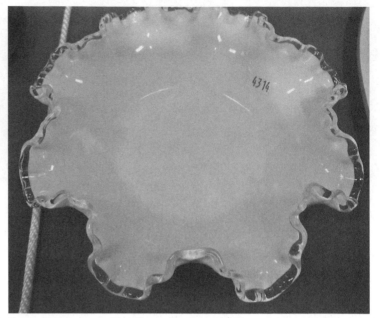

Fenton Glass, compote, Silver Crest, white opaque, **$65.**

Ashtray, Hobnail, topaz opalescent, fan shape.............................. 15.00

Banana bowl, Silver Crest, low, ftd 50.00

Basket, Silver Crest, crystal handle 45.00

Bell, modern carnival
Inverted Strawberry, purple. 15.00
Mother & Child, red............. 30.00

Bicentennial plate, white milk glass, orig box.................................. 20.00

Bonbon
Dolphin, handle, green......... 32.50
Rosalene Butterfly, two handles 35.00

Bowl, modern carnival
Fan Tail, blue 20.00
Fan Tail, red.......................... 25.00
Grape & Cable, ice blue........ 35.00

Cake dish, Pink Pastel, ftd, 12-1/2" d 65.00

Candlesticks, pr
Ming, cornucopia, 5" h, pr ... 50.00

Silvertone, Sheffield, blue..... 24.00

Candy dish, cov
Cherry Chain, Fenton, candy dish, purple 30.00
Teardrop, white 55.00

Cocktail shaker, #6120 Plymouth, Crystal 55.00

Compote, modern carnival
Inverted Strawberry, aqua opalescent......................... 60.00
Persian Medallion, purple.... 25.00
Roses, purple 30.00
Whirling Star, purple 30.00

Creamer
Coin Dot, Cranberry Opalescent, 4" 65.00
Diamond Optic, ruby 30.00

Epergne, Petite French Opal, 4" h 40.00

Fairy light, Colonial Amber, Hobnail, three pcs 25.00

Float bowl, Silver Crest, 13" d 45.00

Flower frog, Nymph, blue opalescent, 6-3/4" h, 2-3/4" w 48.00

Goblet, Lincoln Inn, red 24.00

Hat, Coin Dot, French Opal...... 45.00

Hurricane lamp, five petal blue dogwood dec 75.00

Jack-in-the-pulpit, Silver Crest 45.00

Nut bowl, Fenton Flower, aqua opalescent 30.00

Perfume bottle, Peach Crest, DeVilbiss.............................. 75.00

Pitcher, Grape & Cable, modern carnival, purple 30.00

Plate
Adam & Eve, blue, 8" d 10.00
Fan Tail, lavender 20.00

Rose bowl, Black Rose, 6-1/2" d 40.00

Salt and pepper shakers, pr, Hobnail, cranberry opalescent, #3806 .... 50.00

Sherbet, Plymouth, amber 15.00

Spittoon, Grape & Cable, modern carnival, purple 25.00

Vase
Grape & Cable, modern carnival, ice blue 30.00
Rose Crest, triangle, 5" h...... 55.00

Fenton Glass, vase, white hobnail, ruffled lip, paper label, 10-1/2" **$55.**

Fenton Glass, cake plate, opaque white, hobnails, original label, **$35.**

Fiesta

Frederick Rhead designed this popular Homer Laughlin pattern. It was first introduced in 1936 and became a real hit after a vigorous marketing campaign in the early 1940s. Original colors were red, dark blue, light green, brilliant yellow, and ivory. Turquoise was added in 1937. Red was removed in 1943, but brought back in 1959. Light green, dark blue, and ivory were retired in 1951 and replaced by forest green, rose, chartreuse, and gray. Medium green was added in the late 1950s. By 1969, the popular pattern was redesigned and finally discontinued in 1972. However, by 1986, Homer Laughlin had reintroduced the pattern, but in a new formula and with new colors, including a darker blue, black, white, apricot, rose, and even pastels some years later.

For additional listings, see *Warman's Antiques & Collectibles*, *Warman's Americana & Collectibles*, and *Warman's American Pottery & Porcelain*.

Reproduction alert.

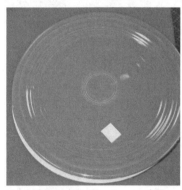

Fiesta, dinner plate, forest green, **$40.**

Bud vase, ivory, 6-1/2" h 65.00

Candleholders, pr
   Bulb, turquoise 115.00
   Bulb, yellow 110.00
   Tripod, light green 330.00

Carafe
   Light green 185.00
   Red....................................... 275.00

Casserole, ivory........................ 88.00

Chop plate, 14-1/4" d
   Chartreuse 65.00
   Gray 70.00

Coffeepot, cov
   Green 225.00
   Ivory.................................... 245.00

Creamer
   Chartreuse 40.00
   Cobalt blue, stick handle...... 50.00
   Medium Green 80.00
   Rose 35.00

Cup and saucer
   Cobalt blue 155.00
   Medium green 255.00
   Red...................................... 100.00

   Turquoise............................ 155.00
Juice tumbler, 4-1/2" h
   Cobalt blue 45.00
   Light green 55.00
   Rose 60.00

Mixing bowl
   #1, red................................ 180.00
   #2, cobalt blue 200.00
   #3, ivory.............................. 80.00
   #4, light green..................... 85.00
   #5, turquoise....................... 85.00
   #6, light green................... 110.00
   #7, cobalt blue 160.00

Mug
   Chartreuse 80.00
   Cobalt blue 55.00
   Gray 72.00
   Ivory..................................... 72.00
   Medium green 140.00
   Red....................................... 75.00

Plate, 7" d
   Green 6.50
   Turquoise............................... 7.50

Plate, 9" d
   Gray 35.00
   Medium green 100.00
   Red....................................... 55.00
   Turquoise.............................. 60.00
   Yellow 45.00

Platter
   Medium green 165.00
   Turquoise.............................. 24.00
   Red....................................... 50.00
   Rose 40.00

Relish, yellow base, cobalt blue center, four yellow inserts, gold trim................................... 135.00

Salad bowl, 9-3/8" d, yellow .. 100.00

Salt and pepper shakers, pr
   Cobalt blue 24.00
   Yellow 40.00

Fiesta, teapot, turquoise, **$65.**

Stack set, cobalt and green bowls,
   orange lid............................ 140.00

Sugar bowl, cov
   Gray 80.00
   Rose 70.00

Teapot, medium
   Cobalt blue 145.00
   Red....................................... 100.00
   Yellow 100.00

Teapot, large
   Light green 180.00
   Red....................................... 195.00

Utility tray
   Cobalt blue 17.50
   Light green 25.00
   Red....................................... 70.00
   Turquoise.............................. 20.00

Vase, 8" h
   Ivory.................................... 440.00
   Light green 475.00
   Turquoise............................ 415.00
   Yellow 420.00

Water tumbler
   Cobalt blue 80.00
   Ivory..................................... 72.00
   Red....................................... 75.00

Fifties Collectibles

Collectors are now beginning to collect things based on the decade when they were popular. This new collecting trend is showing up at most flea markets and major antiques shows. The decade that seems the most popular with collectors at the moment is the 1950s. Many collectors start with the furniture of the era and then add decorative accessories to complete the look.

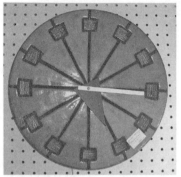

Fifties collectibles, clock, wall, "Meriden," black, orange, and burnt-orange, electric, **$250.**

Fifties collectibles, canister set, teak, original lids, **$350.**

Ashtray, glass, free-form, heavy orange body, controlled bubbles 30.00

Canisters, cov, set of four, aqua plastic, white dec 65.00

Clock, wall, battery operated, round center, black and white sunburst spokes with numbers 115.00

Highwayman art, oil painting, typical 16" x 20" 300.00

Lamp, floor, brushed aluminum, adjustable white shades......... 95.00

Lamp, table
Ceramic, bulbous base, bright colors, orig shade 55.00
Lava, working condition 45.00

Magazine tear sheet, furniture store ad, framed 35.00

Mug, ceramic, yellow Smiley face 5.00

Pin, artist's palette shape, copper, enamel dec............................. 35.00

Toy
Dump truck, yellow and red metal body, some play wear....... 65.00
Suzy washing machine, tin litho, some play wear................. 45.00

Wallpaper, unused roll, bright tropical print 25.00

Wall plaques, mosaic on board, dancing figures, bright colors, pr 225.00

Fifties collectibles, lamp, classic "S" shape, black and white stripes shades, **$850.**

Fifties collectibles, chair, Paul McCobb, **$150.**

Figurines

Collectors will usually find an assortment of figurines to pick from while browsing at their favorite flea market. Some specialize in certain types of figurines, while others concentrate on specific makers.

Aloha, Treasure Craft, 1959 ..... 45.00

August angel, Band Creations, 1995 .... 5.00

Buffalo, Crystal World 200.00

Cat and mouse, T. Suzuki 20.00

Cheeser Snowman, C. Thammer Vongsa 4.00

Cherished Teddy, In Grandmother's Attic, Enesco 30.00

Dove, Artesania Rinconada, retired 1987 .... 90.00

Dreamsicles, K. Haynes
Here's Looking at You 24.00
Santa's Elf, ... 30.00
Wildflower 20.00

Figurines, chickadee perched on holly, Lenox, limited edition, original certificate, **$25.**

Figurine, moose, brown, shaded green and white base, unmarked, **$10.**

Duckling, glass, Fenton 125.00

Friar, holding sausages, pewter and ceramic, 3-1/4" h 50.00

Gepetto, the Toymaker, Kurt Adler 60.00

Girl with watering can, Japan 35.00

Graduate, Pen Delflin, hp stonecraft 85.00

Man, glass, blue head, hands, and shows, applied bushy hair, 4" h 12.00

Munchkins, R. Olszewski 45.00

Oriental girl, 6" h 15.00

Polar Pal, paddling kayak, with Malamute puppy, icy blue pool

base, Westland Resin, retired 35.00

Skating bear, Ringling Bros 20.00

Snowbunny, "I'll Love You Forever," Dept 56, 4-3/4" h 15.00

Sweet shop and bakery, J. Berg Victor 15.00

Whale watch, Noah's Ark, Harmony Kingdom 15.00

Wild Rabbit, Artesania Rinconada, retired 1995 .... 100.00

Wolfe's Pride, Hamilton Gifts . 25.00

Woman, wearing evening gown, holding feather fan 12.00

Zack, Miss Martha Originals 15.00

Figurines, left: bunny playing drum; right: bunny pulling chick, both Goebel, **$20.**

Firefighters

Hats off to firefighters, those brave men and women who help others in time of need. Many of them also collect fire memorabilia.

Advertising button, Knox's Gelatine Running Team, Johnstown, text around bottom "Compliments of Tryon Hook & Ladder Co.," Johnstown, NY, young Black cook, large bowl of gelatin, and cookbook, blue text letters "Taint

Firefighters, toy, Texaco Fire Chief, fire truck, original box, **$55.**

Nun Too Much Cos It's Knox's," orig back Pulver paper, 2" d 250.00

Badge, Mineola Fire Dept, relief image of fire hydrant on 1 side, hook and ladder on other, c1950, 2" x 2" 10.00

Battery operated toy, Fireman, multicolored litho tin, three small ladder sections, Sonsco, Japan, c1950 .... 195.00

Bucket, galvanized tin, red lettering, "Fire Only" 35.00

Business card, Duluth Fire Appliance Co., Chas T Abbott, Manager, c1895, 3" x 5" 18.00

Commemorative mug, glass, Roslyn Fire Company, Roslyn, PA, May 21, 1983, Mack Aerialscope Fire Truck 15.00

Dress hat, Fire Dept Chicago, black, red piping 25.00

Firefighters, fire mark, painted cast iron, William Penn in oval center, marked "Leader," **$225.**

Firefighters, toy, Fire Chief car, battery operated, marked "Made in China," MIB, **$45.**

Figurine, Real Heroes Top Jake Firefighter, firefighter in full gear, Ertl, 1998, 12" h, NRFB 35.00

Fire engine nameplate
Ahrens-Fox 15.00
LaFrance 17.50
Mack Trucks, bulldog........... 25.00

Fire extinguisher, Fyr Fyter Fire Fighter Model A, brass 45.00

Helmet, Quakertown Fire Dept, No. 1, black, leather shield, orig liner 75.00

Hose nozzle, brass.................. 50.00

Liquor decanter, Fireman's Thirst Extinguisher 20.00

Patch, Texas State Fireman's Assoc, 3-7/8" d 7.50

Pinback button, celluloid, "Firemen's Celebration," on ribbon, shows fireman, 1958, 1-1/4" d, 3-3/4" l 18.00

Postcard, real photo, unused
Firemen searching for victims of 1906 fire 10.00
Main Fire Station, Water Street, Piqua, OH........................... 5.00
Quakertown, PA, firehouse and borough hall...................... 8.00

Ribbon, 1958, Firemen's Celebration, multicolored pinback, 3-3/4" l ribbon 18.00

Stein, Tribute to American Firefighters, Avon, 1989, 8" h 40.00

Tie tac, 1/2" d, Member, County Firemen's Ass'n, 10k gold mounting, keystone shape, blue and rust colored enamel, center white enamel "6" 30.00

Toy
Chief's car, litho tin, battery op, Linemar, Japan, 1950s, MIB 225.00
Fire pumper, Fisher-Price, Model #336, 1983, play wear....... 15.00
Fire station, Fisher-Price, Model #928, MIB......................... 80.00
Helmet, Emergency 51 .... 40.00

Firefighters, helmet, Asst. chief engineer, red and white paint, wear, **$185.**

Ramp walker, fireman with hose, Marx 110.00

Watch fob, 1-1/4" d, aluminum, accepted by small red fire helmet, New Kensington, PA, firehouse, inscription "1928 Wet Penna. Volunteer Fireman's Assn," back reads "33rd Annual Convention/ The Aluminum City/Aug 1926," black leather strap 15.00

Wrench, brass, seven-function, polished, lacquered, 12-3/4" x 3-1/4" 95.00

Fire-King

Made by Anchor Hocking Glass Co., production of ovenproof Fire-King glass began in 1942 and continued until 1972. Dinnerware was made in several patterns, and a variety of colors, including azurite, forest green, gray, ivory, jade-ite, peach luster, pink, ruby red, sapphire blue, opaque turquoise, and white. Some pieces were also decorated with decals. Jade-ite items, a light green opaque color, are currently the most popular and command high prices. Fire-King also manufactured utilitarian kitchenware that is also quite popular with collectors.

For additional listings, see *Warman's Americana & Collectibles*, *Warman's Glass*, and *Warman's Depression Glass*.

Dinnerware

Alice, Jade-ite
Cup and saucer.................... 12.00
Dinner plate......................... 25.00
Salad plate 14.00

Charm, Azurite
Bowl, 4-3/4" d...................... 5.00
Cereal bowl, 6" d 18.00
Cup and saucer...................... 4.00
Luncheon plate...................... 5.00
Salad plate 15.00

Golden Anniversary, white

Bowl, 8" d 6.00
Creamer 3.50
Cup and saucer....................... 5.00
Dinner plate........................... 3.00
Fruit bowl, 4-7/8" d 4.00
Plate, 7-1/2" d 2.00
Platter, oval.......................... 10.00
Soup bowl 7.50
Sugar, open 3.50

Jane Ray
Berry bowl, ivory.................. 35.00
Cup and saucer..................... 15.00
Dinner plate, 9" d, ivory....... 25.00
Soup bowl, 7-5/8" d 30.00

Fire-King, Jade-ite ball jug, **$550.**

Laurel Gray
Bowl, 4-1/2" d........................ 6.00
Creamer and sugar................. 7.00
Cup and saucer...................... 5.00
Dinner plate........................... 8.00
Serving plate, 11"................. 40.00

Peach Luster
Bowl, 4-7/8" d........................ 4.50
Creamer................................. 4.50
Cup and saucer...................... 6.00
Custard cup, ruffled 1.00
Dessert bowl, 4-7/8" d........... 4.00
Dinner plate, 9" d 6.50
Salad plate, 7-1/2" d 3.00
Serving plate, 11" d 14.00
Soup bowl, 7-5/8" d.............. 9.50
Sugar, cov............................ 10.00

Restaurant ware, Jade-ite, heavy
Bowl, 4-3/4" d...................... 15.00
Cereal bowl, 5" d 35.00
Chili bowl 15.00
Creamer and sugar, cov........ 35.00
Cup and saucer..................... 18.00
Dinner plate, 9" d 32.00
Grill plate............................. 35.00
Luncheon plate..................... 85.00
Mug...................................... 15.00
Platter, 9-1/4" l..................... 60.00
Platter, 11-1/2" l................... 65.00
Salad plate 15.00

Swirl, Azurite
Cup and saucer...................... 8.00
Dinner plate........................... 8.50

Platter, oval.......................... 20.00
Salad plate 7.00

Kitchenware

Red Dots
Grease jar, white 35.00
Mixing bowl set, white, 7", 8" and
  9" d 70.00
Salt and pepper shakers, white, pr
  .... 45.00

Stripes
Grease jar............................. 35.00
Salt and pepper shakers, pr
  .... 37.50

Swirl
Pie pan, orig label................ 15.00
Range shaker, orig tulip top. 24.00

Tulip
Bowl, 9-1/2" d...................... 35.00
Grease jar, ivory................... 35.00
Grease jar, white 35.00

Turquoise, bowl, splashproof, three-
  qt.. 25.00

Ovenware

Baker, Sapphire Blue, individual
  serving size 4.50

Casserole, cov, Sapphire Blue, one-
  pint 14.00

Custard cup, crystal, orig label. 3.00

Loaf pan, Sapphire Blue........... 17.50

Pie plate, crystal, 10-oz............. 4.00

Utility bowl, Sapphire Blue, 7" d
  .... 14.00

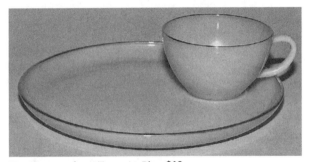

Fire-King, snack set, Turquoise Blue, **$10.**

Fireplace Collectibles

In addition to providing a place to hang your stocking at Christmas, fireplaces also serve as important decorative and functional elements. And, as such, they need to be accessorized. Flea markets are wonderful places to find interesting objects to accomplish this goal.

Fireplace, bellows, left: wood panels, make-do tin nozzle, worn leather, **$25;** right: small size, wood panels, embossed brass nozzle, worn leather, **$35.**

Andirons, pr
8" w, 27" d, 14-3/4" h, brass and iron, belted ball tops, baluster ring-turned shaft, sq stepped base, conforming log stops on curved log supports, America, mid-19th C, dents 500.00
8-3/4" w, 16" d, 12" h, brass, round ball finials, scrolled spur legs, ball feet........................... 385.00
9-1/2" w, 16-1/2" d, 21-1/2" h, America, last quarter 18th C, brass urn-tops over iron knife-blade shaft, lower brass shield, arched legs over penny feet
  .... 650.00

Bellows, fruit and foliage decor, yellow paint, green banding, 18" l
  .... 330.00

Broom, wooden handle, 49-1/4" l
  .... 35.00

Coal hood, hammered brass, emb tavern scenes, 25" h............... 90.00

Fender, brass, reticulated front
  .... 245.00

Fireback, cast iron, figures in relief, floral garland border, floral basket cartouche flanked by sphinx, dated 1663, cracked, 26" x 16-1/2"
  .... 110.00

Fire lighter, gun shape, Dunhill
  .... 90.00

Fireplace, artificial, cast iron, electric, Arts & Crafts style, two bulbs with porcelain sockets, 21" w 375.00

Fire screen

Bamboo, brass mounted, foliate painted panel, turned supports and trestle base, Victorian, 31" w, 40" h 150.00

Oak, medallion decor, beadwork molding, 27" h, 20" w 90.00

Walnut, openwork cresting, revolving screen painted with dec scenes, trestle base, Renaissance Revival, American, 26-1/2" w, 44" h, ... 300.00

Hearth trivet, wrought iron

15-1/2" l, 6-1/4" d, round, flattened handle, hanger hook, three-legged base, rust............. 220.00

23-1/2" l, 11-1/2" w, sq, square grilling surface, flattened handle, circular end, four sun-like stamps 250.00

Kettle stand, 10-3/4" h, brass and wrought iron, tripod base, round column, painted black, circular brass top with pierced designs, scalloped edges.................... 100.00

Log fork, wrought iron, long round handle, cast-brass ovoid finial, some rust, 44" l...................... 25.00

Mantle

Cast iron, late 19th C., 40" h, 43" w 1,200.00

Oak, full columns, beveled mirror, 82" h, 60" w 1,400.00

Shovel and tongs, wrought iron, brass finials, 30" l 55.00

Fireplace, tool set, chrome, Art Deco, 12-1/2" h, **$145.**

Fishbowl Ornaments

Perhaps you want to give your very own Nemo a little company or a place to play hide and seek with her friends. Imaginative collectors can find an interesting assortment of aquatic ornaments to brighten their aquariums. Check that the paint is non-toxic and the item is waterproof.

Aquarium background panel, blues, greens............................ 2.00

Castle, ceramic

4" h, 3-3/4" w, white and brown 16.00

4" h, 4-1/4" w, mkd Zenith, 1968 .... 12.00

Ferns, flowers, vines, plastic, each .... .50

Figure

Deep Sea Diver 2.00

Goldfish, ceramic, 3-1/2" l, pr 22.00

Mermaid, seated.................... 3.00

Pagoda, ceramic, blue, yellow, burgundy and green, 3-1/4" h, 3-1/2" w, Japan...................... 16.00

Fishbowl ornament, Redware aquarium castle, greenish glaze, 3-1/2" h, **$15.**

Fisher-Price Toys

What kid didn't play with Fisher-Price toys as a child? Founded in East Aurora, New York, in 1930, the company eventually became one of the leading producers of children's toys. Collectors still search for, and sometimes play with, all types of Fisher-Price items. Flea markets are prime hunting ground in the hunt for both old and new examples.

Airport crew, 1983, MIP......... 15.00

Bouncy racer........................... 40.00

Bunny Cart, #311 .... 100.00

Circus train set, four pcs, 30" l 48.00

Cotton Tail cart 150.00

Crazy clown brigade, 1983.... 35.00

Cruise boat, *SS Tadpole,* 1988 15.00

Dinky engine, 1959................. 35.00

Doggy racer, 1942 .... 150.00

Dollhouse, furniture, 1969, orig box 225.00

Donald Duck Xylophone 65.00

Dr. Doodle, #132, 1940, 10" h. 95.00

Express train, three cars, 1987 10.00

Fisher-Price, doll, Puffalump, limited edition dress-up kid, pink dress and bonnet, MIB, **$15.**

Fun Jet, 1970 .... 25.00

Garage, two stories, 1970......... **25.00**

Fisher-Price, busy box, baby crib toy, some play wear, **$3.**

Hickory Dickory Dock, radio and clock.................................... 30.00

Jingle Giraffe........................ 150.00

Jumbo Jitterbug..................... 65.00

Little Mart, 1987, MIP............. 50.00

Little People Farm Play Set, #2501, 1986, played-with cond, orig box 55.00

Little Snoopy, wood and plastic 18.50

Lacing shoe, Play Family, 1965 35.00

Magic Key Mansion, six rooms, furnishings, 125-pc set........ 245.00

Mickey Mouse Drummer 60.00

Molly Mop, #190.................... 250.00

Music Box, #795 .... 10.00

Playground, 1986 .... 10.00

Pluto, push toy, 1936, 8" l......... 80.00

Safety school bus, 1962 .... 80.00

Sesame Street clubhouse, 1977, played-with cond.................. 45.00

Talk back telephone, 1961 ..... 75.00

Timber toter, model #810....... 50.00

Waggy Woofy, model #437... 100.00

Windup Clock, #998, played-with cond 75.00

Woodsey Squirrel.................. 50.00

Ziggy Zilo, model #737, 1958 . 50.00

Fisher-Price, Family Play School, plastic, **$15.**

Fisher-Price, Donald Duck, No. 400, litho paper, green wooden base with red wheels, play wear, **$45.**

Fishing

Perhaps the only thing better than meandering through a flea market on a lazy summer afternoon is going to the waterhole to do a little fishing. Several auction houses have established record-setting prices for lures, ephemera, and other related fishing items, look for their catalogs while browsing at flea markets.

For additional listings, see *Warman's Antiques & Collectibles*, and *Warman's Americana & Collectibles*.

Badge, 1-3/4" d, Fishing, Trapping, Hunting License, NY, 1930.... 55.00

Bobber
Panfish float, hp, black, red and white stripes, 5" l.............. 12.00
Pike float, hp, yellow, green and red stripes, 12" l...................... 27.50

Book
Lures: The Guide to Sport Fishing, Keith C. Schuyler, 1955, dj 20.00

Practical Black Bass Fishing, Mark Sosin and Bill Dance, 1977, illus 10.00

Creel, wicker, rear hinged door, 9-1/2" w, 8" d, 8" h, repairs 110.00

Decoy, Ice King, perch, wood, painted, Bear Creek Co., 7" l . 70.00

Fishing license
California, encased in slotted metal frame, 1935 .... 5.00

Connecticut, 1935, for resident use, yellow, black, and white... 65.00
Pennsylvania, 1945, blue and white, black serial number 18.00

Lure
Carters Bestever, 3" l, white and red, pressed eyes 9.00
Creek Chub Co., Baby Beetle, yellow and green wings............... 40.00
Heddon, King Bassor, red, gold spot, glass eyes 35.00

Fishing collectibles, lure, Creek Chub Bait Co., Garrett, IN, Baby Pikie Minnow, glass eyes, white, yellow, red, and silver-blue body, trademark rainbow, series 907, 3-1/4" l, original box, **$30.**

Meadow Brook, rainbow, 1-1/4" l, orig box 120.00
Paw Paw, underwater minnow, green, and black, tack eyes, three hooks 18.00
Pfleuger, polished nickel minnow, glass eyes, five hooks, 3-5/8" l 250.00
Shakespeare, mouse, white and red, thin body, glass eyes, 3-5/8" l 30.00
South Bend, Panatella, green crackleback finish, glass eyes, orig box 50.00

Souvenir, Lucky Lure, Souv of Indian Lake, OH, 3-1/2" l, nude black female, MOC 130.00

Reel
Ambassador 5500C Silver, counter balance, handle, high speed gear rates 120.00
Hardy, Perfect Fly Reel, English, 3-3/8" x 1-1/4" 150.00
Horton, #3, suede bag 425.00
Meek 33, Bluegrass, suede bag 425.00
Penn-Jic Master No. 500, 3" d 65.00
Pflueger 1420 templar, lightly scratched owner's name . 175.00
Shakespeare, tournament... 110.00
Union Hardware Co., raised pillar type, nickel and brass 30.00

Rod
Bamboo, fly fishing, orig reel, wear 125.00
Hardy, split-bamboo fly, English, two-pc, one tip, 7' l 250.00
Heddon Co., casting, nickel silver fittings, split-bamboo fly, fish decal brown wraps, bag and tube, 5-1/2' l 50.00

Fishing, tin, Weber Floataline, 2-1/2" square, **$5.**

Montaque, bamboo, two tips, orig case 135.00
Shakespeare Co., premier model, three-pc, two tips, split-bamboo fly, dark brown wraps, 7-1/2' l 35.00

Tackle box, leather 470.00

Trophy, large mouth bass, mounted on 13" x 9" wood.................. 115.00

Flag-Related

It's a grand old flag, indeed. Not only are flags collectible, but so are countless items having a flag motif. Don't throw out that old worn flag, give it to your local VFW or Boy Scouts for proper disposal.

Flag collectibles, framed lithograph, Lady Liberty holding flag, tramp art type frame, **$45.**

Antenna flag, 4" x 9-1/2", red, white, and blue, two-sided, plastic, tension spring, 4-1/4" x 10" cardboard folder with Nixon/Lodge 18.00

Booklet, *Our Flag*, Department of Defense, 1960, 24 pgs 7.50

Calendar, 1932, image of Betsy Ross sewing flag, George Washington looking on, full calendar pad, large size 35.00

Cigar felt, American flag, 48 stars, 10-1/2" x 8-1/2" 4.00

Flag
36-star, 1908-12, stars sewn on, 4" x 5" 70.00
38-star, coarse muslin, mounted on stick, 12-1/2" x 22" 50.00

Flag collectibles, envelope, printed semblances of stars and stripes, 45 stars, **$9.**

44-star, tacked to 50" wooden pole, stains, tears, 19-3/4" x 34-1/2" 145.00

Flag collectibles, costume jewelry flag pin, 1-7/8" h, **$5.**

45-star, painted stars, tear, 11" x 16"
.... 85.00

Flag pole stand, lion-paw feet, mkd "Loyalty," "Fraternity," "Charity" and "1883," 3-1/2" h, 8" sq... 175.00

Jewelry, costume, flag pin
Ciner, enameled stripes, raised gold lines, 50 stars, 1-1/2" x 1-3/4"
.... 32.00

Coro, red, white and blue enameling, clear rhinestones, 1-1/4" x 1-1/2" 88.00
Unmarked, rhinestones, 2" h
.... 18.00

Pinback button, celluloid, American flag, 7/8" d 18.00

Postcard, flag and poem, Our country stands for Humanity..., unused, 1920s......................... 8.00

Poster, "Give It Your Best, World War II, shows 48-star flag, 1942 office of War Information, fold lines, 28-1/2" x 20"...................................... 60.00

Trivet, Frankoma, sand glaze, America's Stars & Stripes, Flag of Freedom, 1776-1976, commemorative backstamp, 6-1/2" d 20.00

Flashlights

Shall we shed a little light on an interesting collectible topic? Flashlights actually evolved from early bicycle lights. Conrad Hubert invented the first tubular hand-held flashlight in 1899.

Candle, Eveready, #1643, cast metal base, cream-colored painted candle, 1932 .... 40.00

Lantern
Delta Lantern, Buddy model, 1919
.... 15.00
Eveready, #4707, nickel-plated case, large bull's eye lens, 1912
.... 25.00

Novelty
Felix the Cat, with whistle, 1960s
.... 50.00
Flintstones, 1975, MOC, 3" h
.... 15.00
Frankenstein, c1960, 9-1/2" l............................ 48.00
Hopalong Cassidy, 6-1/2" l, signal siren, metal, ©Wm Boyd 1950
.... 125.00
Hulk Hogan, WWF Wrestling, 1991
.... 12.00

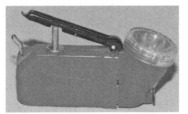

Flashlights, Daco-Lite, Dayton Acme Co., hand powered, red plastic case, black metal pump handle, 5-3/4" l, **$10.**

Peter Pan, McDonald's premium, MIB 4.00
Reddy Kilowatt, 3" l red and white plastic, brass key chain, orig unopened clear cellophane pack, 1950s-60s 24.00
Schlitz, 10" h hard plastic brown glass bottle, replica paper stickers, gray plastic cap, orig

2-1/2" x 2-1/2" x 10" box, c1970
.... 20.00

Railroad, Jenks, brass, patent July 25, 1911 .... 90.00

Tubular
Aurora, all nickel case 20.00
Bond Electric Co., Jersey City, N.J., 1940s, 5-1/4" l 10.00
Homart, all metal, 1930s, 10-1/2" l
.... 35.00
Ray-O-Vac, Space Patrol....... 40.00
Winchester, marble lens, gold-colored body, 1919-26, 5-1/2" l
.... 100.00
Yale, #3302, double-ended, flood lens and spot lens............. 30.00

Vest pocket
Eveready, Masterlight, #6662, nickel-plated, ruby push-button switch, 1904 .... 30.00
Franco, glass button switch
.... 25.00

Flatware

Whether you're setting an elegant table or striving for an informal look, great looking flatware is a must. There are many patterns to choose from, and the price range reflects the age, maker, and composition of the service being considered. In addition to a number of excellent reference books, there are many matching services that can help you complete a flatware set. Many of us enjoy the hunt and prefer to scout flea markets for those additional place settings and unique serving pieces.

Bacon server, Old Maryland, Kirk-

Steiff....................................... 90.00

Bonbon, Princess Patricia, Gorham
.... 18.50

Bouillon spoon, Georgian Maid, International........................... 16.00

Butter knife
Bridal Rose, Alvin 30.00
Celeste, Gorham 12.00

Flatware, sterling silver knife, English hallmarks, grapes pattern, **$10.**

Federal Cotillion, Frank Smith
.... 24.00
Gadroon, International 15.00
Silver Wheat, Reed & Barton 15.00

Cake server, Early American, Lunt
.... 25.00

Cheese knife, Allure, Rogers, 1939
.... 8.00

Citrus spoon, Georgian Maid,
International.......................... 15.00

Cocktail fork
Contour, Towle 24.00
Early American, Lunt........... 24.00
Empress, International......... 10.00

Coffee spoon, Georgian Maid,
International.......................... 15.00

Cold meat fork
Moselle, American Silver Co. 60.00
Silver Spray, Towle............... 32.00
Woodwind, Reed & Barton .. 53.00

Cream soup spoon
Bridal Rose, Alvin 65.00
Castle Rose, Royal Crest....... 15.00
Fleetwood, Manchester........ 30.00
Gadroon, International 24.00
Pointed Antique, Reed & Barton
.... 24.00

Demitasse spoon
Early American, Lunt........... 15.00
Virginia Carvel, Towle.......... 12.00

Dessert spoon, Bridal Rose, Alvin
.... 60.00

Dinner fork
Bridal Rose, Alvin 55.00
Celeste, Gorham 22.00
Concord, Whiting................. 25.00
Federal Cotillion, Frank Smith
.... 38.00
Fleetwood, Manchester 30.00

Dinner knife
Colonial Fiddle, Tuttle.......... 25.00
King George, Gorham 40.00
Lily of the Valley, Gorham ... 27.50

Fish knife, Acorn, Jensen........ 38.00

Fish set, Early American, Lunt 40.00

Grapefruit spoon
Fleetwood, Manchester 20.00
Orange Blossom, Rogers 5.00

Gravy ladle
Continental, Tuttle 70.00
Early American, Lunt........... 45.00

Federal Cotillion, Frank Smith
.... 95.00
Horizon, Easterling 40.00
Silver Wheat, Reed & Barton 40.00

Ice cream fork
Gadroon, International 20.00
Gainsborough, Alvin, monogram
.... 12.00

Iced tea spoon
Bamboo, Tiffany & Co., set of four
in orig box...................... 175.00
Federal Cotillion, Frank Smith
.... 35.00
Lily of the Valley, Gorham ... 30.00
Romansque, Alvin................ 20.00

Lemon fork
Celeste, Gorham 13.00
Silver Spray, Towle............... 16.00

Letter opener, King Edward,
Gorham................................. 25.00

Luncheon fork
Gainsborough, Alvin 20.00
King Albert, Whiting 20.00
King Edward, Gorham 27.00
Pointed Antique, Reed & Barton,
engraved........................... 24.00

Luncheon knife
Georgian Maid, International 35.00

Flatware, Gorham Chantilly pattern,
sterling silver, 12 each: 9-1/8" l knives,
7-1/8" l tablespoons, 6-1/2" l salad forks,
7-5/8" l dinner forks, 6-1/4" l butter
spreaders; 24 5-7/8" l teaspoons; two
8-1/2" l serving tablespoons; salad set,
6-3/4" l master butter knife, 7-1/8" l
gravy ladle, all pieces marked "Gorham
Sterling," fitted walnut case, some pieces
in original wrappings, **$1,200.**

King Edward, Gorham 24.00
King George, Gorham 35.00

Meat fork, DuBarry, International
.... 90.00

Olive fork, Chippendale, Alvin 25.00

Pasta scoop, Beauvoir, Tuttle .. 25.00

Pickle fork, Celeste, Gorham... 14.00

Pie server, Acorn, Jensen....... 135.00

Place setting
Contour, Towle 95.00
Prelude, International 60.00

Salad fork
Castle Rose, Royal Crest....... 20.00
Chapel Bells, Alvin 20.00
Early American, Lunt........... 15.00

Salad serving fork and spoon,
Chambord, Reed & Barton . 200.00

Salt spoon, Old Master, Towle. 11.00

Sardine fork, Cambridge, Gorham
.... 50.00

Soup spoon, oval
Celeste, Gorham 17.00
Elegante, Reed & Barton 21.00

Strawberry fork, King Edward,
Gorham................................. 21.00

Sugar shell, Federal Cotillion, Frank
Smith 40.00

Sugar spoon
Copenhagen, Manchester..... 24.00
Fairfax, Dugan...................... 28.00
Tara, Reed & Barton............. 21.00
Windsor, Towle..................... 12.00

Sugar tongs, Bridal Rose, Alvin, large
.... 90.00

Tablespoon
Colonial Fiddle, Tuttle, pierced
.... 55.00
Elegante, Reed & Barton 21.00
King Albert, Whiting 30.00
Rambler Rose, Towle............ 30.00

Teaspoon
Bridal Rose, Alvin 24.00
Castle Rose, Royal Crest....... 12.00
Celeste, Gorham 11.00
Fairfax, Dugan...................... 18.00
Old Master, Towle................ 17.00
Rambler Rose, Towle............ 15.00
Rose Solitaire, Towle 10.00
Wildflower, Royal Crest........ 10.00

Tomato server, King Edward,
Gorham................................. 68.00

Florence Ceramics

Florence Ward began producing decorative ceramic items in her Pasadena, California, workshop in 1939. By 1946, her business had grown to the point that it occupied a full-size plant, and her husband and son joined the company to help keep up with demand. Semi-porcelain figurines and other decorative accessories were produced until 1977 when operations ceased.

Bust, white, choir boy, 9-1/2" h 75.00

Cigarette box, cov, winter 245.00

Dealer sign............................. 395.00

Figure
Abigail................................. 165.00
Bea 150.00
Blue Boy, 12" h 295.00
Delia.................................... 135.00
Douglas............................... 240.00
Irene.................................... 55.00
Marie Antoinette, 10" h...... 245.00
Matilda, 8-1/2" h 145.00

Melanie, gray dress, red trim
.... 120.00
Pinkie, 11-1/2" h................. 295.00
Rhett, white, 9" h................ 385.00
Scarlett, beige dress............ 180.00
Sue Ellen, 8-1/4" h 150.00
Suzette, 6" h 85.00
Vivian, 10" h 245.00

Flower frog, Oriental boy and girl, c1950, pr 125.00

Wall plaque, figural lady in center, 6" w, 7" h 100.00

Florence Ceramics, Mickey and Minnie, Florence/Guiseppe Armani, original box, each **$95.**

Flow Blue

The name of this pretty china is derived from the blue design that is flowed or blurred on a white background to create a distinctive look. Flow blue china was first produced in 1830 in the Staffordshire district of England. Many potteries manufactured flow blue, including some American firms.

For additional listings, see *Warman's Antiques & Collectibles*, *Warman's Americana & Collectibles*, and *Warman's English & Continental Pottery & Porcelain*.

Reproduction alert.

Ashtray, cherub decal in center, Sebring China, 4-1/2" d 95.00

Bacon platter, Touraine, 10" l
.... 245.00

Flow blue china, Persian Moss pattern, creamer, marked "Made in Germany," 4-1/8" h, **$55.**

Flow blue china, Chapoo pattern, plate, marked "Ironstone, J. Wedgwood," 9-1/2" d, **$150.**

Bone dish, Argyle, J & E Mayer
.... 55.00

Butter dish, cov, insert
Chapoo, Wedgwood 525.00

La Francaise, gold tracing.... 45.00

Butter pat, 3" d
Argyle, J & E Mayer.............. 40.00
Delph, Sebring...................... 35.00
Paisley, Mercer Pottery......... 65.00
Windmill, The French China Co
.... 40.00

Flow blue china, soup bowl, Watteau pattern, Doulton, 9-1/2" d, **$50.**

Cake plate, Cracked Ice,
International Pottery........... 120.00

Calendar plate, 1910, La Francaise,
9" d.. 50.00

Coffee cup and saucer, Arcadia,
large 85.00

Creamer
Calico, Warwick.................. 250.00
Fairy Villas, 5" h 275.00
La Francaise, gold tracing.... 85.00

Cup, handleless, Amoy 250.00

Cup and saucer
Colonial, Homer Laughlin ... 85.00
Touraine............................... 90.00
Winona, French China Co.... 65.00

Dessert bowl, Poppy, Warwick 30.00

Gravy boat, Chapoo, Wedgwood
.... 275.00

Jardiniere, Autumn Leaves, Warwick,
8" x 7-1/2"............................. 550.00

Milk pitcher, Argyle, J & E Mayer,
7" h.. 150.00

Plate
Argyle, J & E Mayer, 8" d...... 60.00
Autumn Leaves, Warwick, 10-1/2" d
.... 135.00
Colonial, Homer Laughlin, 10" d
.... 65.00
Eclipse, Johnson Bros., 7" d.. 65.00
La Francaise, gold tracing, 9" d
.... 40.00
Luzerne, Mercer Pottery, 10" d
.... 110.00
Royal Blue, Burgess & Campbell,
9-7/8" d............................. 75.00
Snowflake, Knowles, Taylor,
Knowles, 9" d 65.00
Touraine, Stanley Pottery, 8-3/4" d
.... 60.00

Platter, Windmill, The French China
Co., 13" l 125.00

Relish
Autumn Leaves, Warwick, 8" l
.... 110.00
Windmill, The French China Co.,
oval, 10" l.......................... 55.00

Serving bowl, Conway, 9" d .. 135.00

Soup plate
Alaska, Grindley................... 75.00
Paisley, Mercer Pottery......... 75.00
Royal Blue, Burgess & Campbell
.... 55.00
Touraine, Stanley Pottery, 7-1/2" d
.... 75.00
Windmill, The French China Co.,
8" d 45.00

Syrup pitcher, Autumn Leaves,
Warwick, silver plate lid...... 275.00

Tea cup and saucer
La Francaise, gold tracing.... 85.00
Winona, The French China Co.
.... 65.00

Teapot, cov, Strawberry.......... 200.00

Toothbrush holder, Alaska,
Grindley................................ 145.00

Tray, Thistle, Burroughs &
Mountford, 6" sq, handles..... 95.00

Vegetable bowl, open, Windmill,
The French China Co., 9" d
.... 95.00

Flower Frogs

Flower frogs are those neat holders that were sometimes designed to complement a bowl or vase. Others were made to be purely functional and had holes to insert flower stems, making flower arranging a little easier.

Flower frogs, Art Deco white ceramic, girl with edge of drape in hand, **$85.**

Art Deco lady
6" h, white porcelain, dancing nude
.... 90.00
7-1/2" h, mkd "3941 Germany,"
c1930 .... 195.00

Bird, figural, bright colors, Made in
Japan 50.00

California Pottery, candle holder
type, made to hold fresh flowers
around candle, mkd "Calif USA
V17," 3-1/2" h, 4" w 20.00

Cambridge Glass
Draped Lady, amber, 8-1/2" h
.... 200.00
Rose Lady, green 250.00
Two Kids, crystal................ 155.00

Florence Ceramics, Oriental boy
and girl, c1950, pr 125.00

German, nude, lavender scarf,
porcelain, 9-1/2" h............... 135.00

Rookwood, figural nude, porcelain
glaze, c1930 .... 325.00

Silver deposit glass, clear glass frog
with candleholder, 4" d 45.00

Van Briggle, light blue, mkd "Van
Briggle/Colo. Spgs," 4-1/2" d
.... 85.00

Weller, Brighton Woodpecker, 6" h,
3-1/2" w, 3" l 520.00

★ Flue Covers

There was a time when flue covers weren't too highly thought of; they were stuck in front of the stove pipe opening to do a job, but as with many other collectibles, now folks are starting to really look at some of the scenes and respect the artistry that they represent. Today many of them are getting a whole new lease on life, now hanging to brighten up a wall, and they probably make the new owners smile as much as they did Grandma in her day.

Reproduction alert.

Flue covers, two children in woodland setting, little girl in long white dress, black cape, holding hand of taller boy in white shirt, green knickers, brown hat and stockings, signed and dated "1908" on back, **$24.**

Baby, smiling face, wearing lacy bonnet, c1890-1930 .... 175.00

Basket with cherries, green ground, orig hanging chain 20.00

Courting couple, metal frame and chain, brown paper backing, 10-1/4" d 110.00

Lighthouse, print sealed under glass, aluminum cover with slot to hold dried flowers, creating landscape around lighthouse, 7" d 25.00

Little girl
Big blue hat, matching blue dress, gold border, orig hanging chain 30.00
Purple hooded cape, holding pansies, metal frame and chain, 7-3/4" d 100.00
White dress, gray bonnet with daisies, metal frame and chain, 7-3/4" d 100.00

Pair of birds, artist sgd " Maville," c1900, 13" w 48.00

Pair of ducks in flight, border of ferns and flowers, gilt scalloped border, artist sgd "Maville," ©1898 Ketterlings Litho, Phila, NY, and Chicago 40.00

Silhouette type portrait, lady in center holding lilies, black-mirrored border, orig hanging chain 20.00

Flue covers, little girl in big blue hat, matching blue dress, gold border, original hanging chain, **$30.**

Woodland setting, little girl in long white dress, black cape, holding hand of taller boy in white shirt, green knickers, brown hat and stockings, sgd and dated "1908" on back 24.00

Flue covers, basket with cherries, green ground, original hanging chain, **$20.**

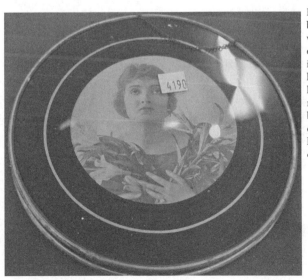

Flue covers, black and white portrait of lady in center holding lilies, black mirrored border, original hanging chain, **$20.**

Folk Art

Folk art remains one area of collecting that doesn't have clearly defined boundaries. Some people confine folk art to non-academic, handmade objects. Others include manufactured material. It's definitely an area where the "beauty is in the eye of the beholder" as each collector sees things just a little differently. The following listings illustrate the diversity of this category. It's also a collecting area that tends to be costly to the pocket book. Many collectors like to patronize contemporary folk artists in their areas and include their works in their collections.

Folk art, bar of Proctor and Gamble soup carved into the shape of a rabbit, 4-3/8" x 2-3/4", **$20.**

Bank, 3-1/4" h, gourd form, paint decorated with face 115.00

Bookends, pr, sculpted sandstone, seated figures of Adam and Eve, mkd "E. Reed 1976 A.D.," 11" h, pr 495.00

Candle stand, laminated hardwoods, sq top with egg and dart molding, four ladies legs shaped supports with turned drop, old mellow finish, 16" w, 15-1/2" d, 30-1/4" h, repairs.................................. 375.00

Cane, wooden
Dog handle, dark-brown paint, root-carved, worn 165.00
Lion's head, glass eyes, gold metal band with presentation engraving dated 1924, Malacca shaft, horn ferrule.......... 485.00
Snake, one spiraling snake, black bead eyes, salmon repair, mushroom cap handle, 31-1/2" l 375.00

Face jug
Abraham Lincoln, green running glaze, incised inscription on back "Abraham Lincoln, Shyster Lawyer from Illonois (sic) Also Was President Of The North," sgd "Cleater Meaders, 1993," 12-1/2" h........................ 475.00
Burlon Craig, glossy black-brown Albany slip, large ears, pop-eyed, one-pc eyebrow, china plate teeth, pierced nostrils, mkd "B.B Craig, Vale, N.C.," c1980-82, 6" h 275.00
Marie Rogers, glossy Albany slip with multicolor drippings, tongue sticking out, white teeth, blue pupils, incised beard and eyelashes, script and impressed marks, early 1980s, 9-1/8" h 165.00

Figure, carved and painted wood
Man with drum, Alabama, late 19th/early 20th C, 5" h 360.00
Snake, old dark red paint, yellow polka dots, black, white, and blue eyes, early 20th C, old chip on tail, 25-1/2" l.................... 575.00
Woman, standing, applied extended arms, metal tack eyes and buttons, alligatored surface, America, late 19th C, 6-1/2" h 600.00

Frame, 19-1/4" x 23-1/4", cross corner, applied leaves, rosettes, and fish, chip carved edges, alligatored black paint........................... 200.00

Indian club, red and black grained, 18" h, pr 185.00

Model, Chinese style sidewheel paddle boat, small horse drawn cart, two horses powering wheels, carved man, 29" l, 11-1/4" d, 8" h, minor breaks 115.00

Sculpture, limestone
Bust, Indian, mkd "E.R." (Popeye Reed), 9-1/2" h 275.00
Indian in canoe, mkd "E. Reed 1976 A.D.," 5-1/2" h, 7-3/4" l .. 660.00

Settee, Windsor, continuous arm, by Steve Deen, painted by Peter Deen, cherry, scrolled arms, spindle back, turned legs, stretchers, distressed green paint, 56-1/2" l, 17-1/2" d 17-1/2" h seat, 29" h back **2,475.00**

Theorem, watercolor on velvet, American School, early 19th C, unsigned
Flowers, shades of blue, gold, green, and brown, ivory ground, period gilt frame, 6" x 6-1/2", toning, losses to frame 440.00
Freehand peaches, grapes, and cherries, gilt frame, 13-1/2" x 11", minor surface wear and stains 450.00

Tinsel picture, flower arrangement, reverse-painted glass backed with foil and paper, American School, late 19th C, Victorian frame, 22" x 17", repaired 180.00

Watercolor drawing, on paper, framed
Bird, flower and star, green, red, and yellow, painted on lined paper, 7-1/2" w, 7-1/2" h 550.00
Birds on branches, yellow, red, blue, and green, sgd in blue ink "Catharine E. Habecker 1844," molded frames with minor wear, 6-1/4" w, 7" h, price for pr 990.00
Flowers and heart, yellow roses and snowdrops in corners, heart formed of multicolor vining flowers, "Forget Me Not" with verse, name and 1866, molded wooden frame, glued down, foxing, edge damage, 11" h, 12-1/4" w 110.00
Naïve painting of a woman, long orange and blue striped dress, blue gloves, holding tulip and flower, bird above her head, 6-1/4" w, 7-3/4" h 470.00

Food Molds

Flea markets are great places to find food molds. Originally intended for creating cakes, ice cream, chocolate, etc. in interesting shapes, many of these molds are now collected for their decorative appeal.

Food molds, pewter, ice cream mold, figural standing Uncle Sam, marked "E & Co. 1073," **$295.**

Food molds, Stangl, embossed purple grapes, green leaves, marked, **$35.**

Cast iron
Lamb, seated......................... 95.00
Rabbit, Griswold................. 225.00

Graniteware
Strawberry, gray, 1-3/4" h, 5" l, 4" w
.... 235.00
Turk's head, blue/white swirl
.... 115.00

Ironstone
Corn, mkd "Made in USA," chips, hairline 35.00
Grapes, oval with flat bottom, rounded fluted sides 175.00

Pewter, ice cream mold
Christmas tree, E. & Co. 1154
.... 85.00
Floral wreath, E. & Co., 1142, 3-3/4" d........................... 40.00
Heart, E. & Co., N.Y., 902, 4-1/8" h
.... 38.50

Redware, Turk's head, scalloped and fluted, hairlines, 8" d 85.00

Tin
Fish 45.00
Melon, two mark, marked "Kraemer" 48.00
Pear, oval, deep ruffled sides, 3-1/2" x 5-1/2" 90.00

Tinned cast steel, three rows of eight acorns, for maple candy, stamped "Handle & Smith Birmingham"
.... 45.00

Food molds, pewter ice cream mold, stork with bag, marked "E.&Co. N.Y. 1151," 5-1/4" h, **$85.**

Yellowware, pudding mold
Bunch of grapes.................. 125.00
Ear of corn, scalloped designs on interior sides, simple gallery-like foot, oval, 4-3/8" h, 7-3/8" x 9-1/4"............................. 170.00
Pear, dark-brown glaze, roughness on rim, hairline, 4" h, 7" d 50.00
Sheath of wheat, minor rim chips, 3-1/4" h, 7-5/8" l............. 110.00

Wood, carved fruitwood, cookie mold, floral and foliate carved design in heart shape, 19th C, minor wear, 6-5/8" x 7" 355.00

Football Memorabilia

Every collector has a favorite team or player. Most can tell you more about their collection and the game of football than you'll ever need to know. This dedicated fan truly enjoys the sport and the collectibles it generates every year.

Action figure, Starting Lineup, Hirschel Walker, Dallas Cowboy, ©1988, 8" x 9", MOC 8.00

Autographed NFL football
Allen, Marcus 190.00
Culpepper, Daunte.............. 180.00
Dent, Richard, Super Bowl 20
.... 200.00
Elway, John 250.00
Favre, Brett 200.00

Autographed jersey
Aikman, Troy, pro-cut, Nike
.... 285.00
Csonka, Larry, Dolphins, aqua, Wilson 250.00
Farve, Brett, Packers, green, Nike
.... 300.00
Griese, Bob, Dolphins, Champion
.... 250.00

Autographed photo, 8" x 10"
Crockett, Ray, Detroit............ 5.00
Eliss, Luther, Detroit 5.00

Football collectibles, plastic cup, Hardee's ABC Monday Night Football, 7" h, **$1.**

Howard, Desmond, Washington
.... **10.00**

Bank, 4-1/2" h, ceramic, helmet,
high gloss black finish, orange
helmet stripe, white face guard
bands, orange and black decal
"Northampton Area Senior High
School/Konkreet Kids," First
National Bank of Bath, 1960s, orig
box **14.00**

Bobbing head
6-1/4" h, Baltimore Colts, MIB,
1961-63............................. **48.00**
6-1/2" h, Cardinals, 1960s **25.00**

Book, *The Big One, Michigan vs
Ohio State, A History of America's
Greatest Football Rivalry*, Bill
Cromartie, Rutledge Press,
Nashville, 1988, 399 pgs, dj... **10.00**

Bumper sticker, 3" x 12", New York
Giants Championship, red, white,
and blue, Jan. 25, 1987 Super Bowl
XXI... **3.00**

Cereal trading card, Bob St. Clair,
#103, Post Cereal **3.00**

Drinking glass, clear glass
4-1/2" h, Michigan State Spartans,
green and white art and
inscriptions **5.00**
5" h, Baltimore Colts, blue and
white image of passer and
punter, repeated white Colt
horseshoe symbol, 1950s, set of
six **25.00**

Football, 6-1/2" x 11", brown pebble-
grained leather, Wilson, inscribed
facsimile signature "O. J. Simpson,"
late 1970s, deflated................ **15.00**

Game, 8-3/4" x 11-1/2" green thin
cardboard board, silhouette of
cheering crowd at bottom, metal
spinner, instruction sheet, score
sheets, three wooden playing pcs,
1930s.................................... **15.00**

Hartland figure
Browns, orig box **95.00**
Giants, orig box **150.00**

Media guide, *Philadelphia Stars*,
1984, 124 pgs........................... **8.00**

Pennant
Chicago Bears, black ground,
orange "Bears," orange, green
and red football art, orange felt
trim, late 1940s **25.00**
Cincinnati Bengal's Super Bowl 16
AFC Champions, orange
.... **65.00**
Denver Broncos World
Championship, 1977 .... **45.00**
New York Giants Championship,
12" x 30", red, white, and blue,
1986 .... **4.00**
Philadelphia Eagles, 1940s-1950s,
28" l **35.00**

Pinback button, 1-3/4" x 2-3/4" oval,
Penn State, blue and white...... **2.50**

Pin-up, Topps, Merlin Olsen, Los
Angeles Rams, #25 uniform.... **5.00**

Playing cards, Philadelphia Eagles,
two complete 52 card decks, orig
slipcase, 1970s **15.00**

Program
New York Giants Game Day, Official
Publication of the National
Football League, Dec. 6, 1981
.... **1.00**
Super Bowl XXII, 1988......... **20.00**

Football collectibles,
Christmas ornament,
celluloid, orange and
gray uniform, mkd
"T. Japan," 4-1/2" h,
$90.

Salt and pepper shakers, pr, 3" l
brown grained football, 2" x 2" x
1-1/2" tan football player head with
black eye slits, red mouth, Elbee
Art, Cleveland, 1950s **12.00**

Sleeping bag, 32" x 64", National
Football League Players, players
and facsimile signatures, c1980
.... **20.00**

Ticket, 2-1/2" x 4-1/8", 35th Annual
Orange Bowl Classic, color photo
of trophy with oranges and football
player statue on top, 1969 ..... **12.00**

TV Guide, Super Bowl Preview, Jan.
28-Feb. 3, 1995 .... **6.00**

Yearbook, Green Bay Packers, 1974,
autographed by coaches and players
.... **40.00**

Fossils

Want to collect the oldest thing at any flea market? Head for the dealers selling fossils. Collecting these treasures created by Mother Nature has long been popular. Expect unique, one-of-a-kind items, as the search continues for dinosaur footprints or bugs captured in amber. Pricing is determined by the detail of the fossil, as well as the material containing it.

Amber, unmounted, with visible
inclusion
Large..................................... **90.00**
Medium **50.00**
Small..................................... **20.00**

Crystal, polished
Large..................................... **25.00**
Medium **15.00**
Small....................................... **5.00**

Geode
Large..................................... **20.00**
Medium **15.00**
Small..................................... **12.00**

Mineral specimen, identified
Large..................................... **12.00**
Medium **8.00**
Small....................................... **3.00**

Specimen box, 35 identified mineral
samples, divided wooden box

Fossils, assorted geodes, prices range
from **$12** to **$20.**

.... 60.00 | **Slate fragment**, with visible fossil
Large...................................... 65.00

Fossils, specimen box with 35 various identified mineral samples, divided wooden box, **$60.**

Fossils, assorted mineral specimens, prices range from **$3** to **$12.**

Fostoria Glass

The Fostoria Glass Company was initially located in Fostoria, Ohio, but in 1891 it was relocated to Moundsville, West Virginia. Its fine glass tableware included delicate engraved patterns and also pressed patterns. Like many other American glass manufacturers of that era, several of its lines were also produced in various colors.

For additional listings see *Warman's Antiques & Collectibles*, *Warman's Depression Glass*, and *Warman's Glass*.

Reproduction alert.

Note: Prices listed are for clear, unless another color is indicated.

Ashtray, Century, individual size
.... 12.00
Berry bowl, June, blue............ 50.00
Bonbon, Raleigh 15.00
Bookends, pr, Lyre 145.00
Bowl
Coronet, handle, 11" d 60.00

Flame, oval, 12-1/2" l, oval... 45.00
Butter, cov, America, round... 125.00
Cake plate
Baroque, crystal, handle....... 65.00
Fern, ebony, gold trim, two handles,
10" d 85.00
Candelabra, pr, Baroque, crystal, 2-lite, #2484 .... 295.00
Candlesticks, pr, Randolph, 6" h
.... 45.00
Candy dish, cov, Coin, amber, round
.... 35.00
Celery vase, Double Greek Key
.... 140.00
Champagne
Distinction, red 14.00
Fern, #5298, pink 55.00
Heraldry, #6012.................... 10.00
Rambler.............................. 30.00
Cheese and cracker, Chintz ... 70.00
Cigarette holder, ashtray, Two Tone, #5092, amethyst and crystal.. 75.00
Claret, June, blue...................... 95.00

Comport, Baroque, flared, gold tint
.... 68.00
Creamer and sugar
Alexis, hotel size, cut dec ... 115.00
Fairfax, green, ftd................ 35.00
Cream soup, American 47.50
Cruet, Coin, olive green 50.00

Fostoria, American pattern, water pitcher, ice lip, **$165.**

Fostoria, American pattern, sherbets, each **$9,** and water goblets, **$17.50.**

Cup and saucer
Century................................ 22.00
Raleigh................................ 12.50

Demitasse cup and saucer, June,
topaz 60.00

Dinner plate
Century................................ 60.00
Colony.................................. 35.00

Egg cup, Randolph.................. 15.00

Goblet, water
American, 7" h...................... 17.50
Baroque, blue........................ 25.00
Chintz 25.00
Colonial Dame, 11-oz............ 15.00

Ice tub, American, 6-1/2" d...... 60.00

Jug, Baroque, crystal 225.00

Juice tumbler, Navarre............ 24.00

Luncheon plate, Lafayette 24.00

Mayonnaise, divided, two ladles,
Century.................................. 42.50

Nut bowl, Baroque, three toes, topaz
yellow..................................... 35.00

Pitcher
Beverly, amber.................... 125.00
Jamestown, green 115.00
Meadow Rose 195.00

Platter, American, 12" l............ 60.00

Relish
American, two-part.............. 18.00
Chintz, two-part................... 30.00
Silver Spruce, three-part 35.00

Salad bowl, Fairfax, green....... 27.50

Salad plate
Baroque, blue........................ 14.00
Fairfax, green......................... 6.50

Sherbet
Colonial Dame...................... 10.00
Fairfax, yellow 12.00
Jamestown, medium blue..... 15.00
Versailles, topaz................... 18.00

Sugar, cov, Coin, olive green 30.00

Syrup, glass lid, American 135.00

Top hat, American, 4" h 50.00

Torte plate, Century, lacy leaf etch,
14" d....................................... 48.00

Tumbler
Chintz, ftd............................. 24.00
Vernon, etched 17.50

Vase
American, flared, 9-1/2" h . 200.00
Two Tone, #2470, red and crystal,
10" h 150.00

Water pitcher, Coin, olive green
.... 55.00

Wedding bowl, Coin, red........ 65.00

Whiskey, American.................. 17.50

Wine
American 15.00
Argus, ruby.......................... 25.00
Chintz.................................. 38.00
Laurel.................................. 35.00
Jamestown, green 20.00
Oriental................................ 25.00

Franciscan Ware

Gladding, McBean and Co., of Los Angeles, California, first produced this popular dinnerware around 1934. Its use of primary colors and simple shapes was met with much enthusiasm. Production was finally halted in 1986.

For additional listings, see *Warman's Americana & Collectibles* and *Warman's American Pottery & Porcelain*.

Franciscan dinnerware, Desert Rose pattern, vegetable bowls, **$90;** teapot, **$150;** soup bowls, **$20;** creamer, **$30.**

Ashtray, Starburst 25.00

Bowl
Apple, ftd............................. 22.00
Coronado, turquoise............. 17.50

Bread and butter plate
Coronado, turquoise.............. 4.25
Hacienda.............................. 8.00
Ivy 15.00
Larkspur 6.00

Butter dish, cov, Starburst....... 42.00

Casserole, cov
Ivy, 1-1/2 qt........................ 350.00
October.............................. 420.00
Starburst, 9-5/8" d 365.00

Cereal bowl
Indian Summer 4.50
Meadow Rose 22.00

Coffeepot
Denmark, blue.................... 100.00
Heritage 80.00

Franciscan dinnerware, salt and pepper shakers, pair, rosebuds, pink, green foliage, **$65.**

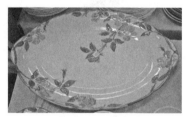

Franciscan dinnerware, Desert Rose pattern, large platter, pink flowers, **$115.**

Chop plate
Apple, 14" d 195.00
Starburst 62.00

Creamer and sugar
Apple................................... 60.00
Magnolia.............................. 75.00

Cup and saucer
Apple.................................... 9.50
Hacienda.............................. 20.00
Poppy 32.00

Demitasse cup and saucer
Coronado, white 37.50
Desert Rose 48.00
Rosemore 45.00

Dinner plate
Apple 20.00
Coronado, coral 9.50
Larkspur 12.00
Poppy 37.50

Eggcup, Desert Rose 35.00

Fruit bowl
Poppy 30.00
Starburst 12.00

Gravy boat
Arcadia, green, gold trim ... 145.00
Fremont 145.00
Granville 120.00
Huntingdon, attached underplate
.... 450.00
Mesa, gold trim 110.00
Woodside 140.00

Grill plate, Apple 140.00

Jam jar, Apple 135.00

Luncheon plate, Meadow Rose
.... 14.00

Mixing bowls, nested three-pc set,
Apple 400.00

Oil and vinegar cruet set, Starburst
.... 335.00

Pepper mill, Starburst 350.00

Platter
Fremont, large 175.00
Olympic, large 165.00
Renaissance, medium 150.00

Relish
Coronado, 12" l 70.00
Ivy, 11" l 60.00

Salad plate, Apple 18.00

Salt and pepper shakers, pr
Apple, small 36.00
Mariposa 98.00

Side salad plate, Starburst, crescent
shape 27.50

Soup bowl, Desert Rose 20.00

Sugar bowl, cov
Canton 75.00
Del Monte 82.00
Olympic 90.00

Teapot, cov
Ivy 430.00
Mariposa 165.00
Meadow Rose 200.00

Tile, Fresh Fruit 50.00

Tray, three tiers, Starburst 335.00

Turkey platter, Apple 320.00

Vegetable bowl, cov, Palomar, Jasper
.... 190.00

Vegetable bowl, oval
Carmel 80.00
Daisy 40.00
Fremont 95.00
Woodside 90.00

Frankart

Frankart is the name used by artist Arthur Von Frankenberg, who achieved his goal of mass-producing "art objects" in the mid-1920s. Most of his creations were stylized forms, particularly ashtrays, bookends, lamps, vases, etc. The pieces were cast in white metal, and one of several popular metallic finishes was then applied. Finishes ranged in color from copper to gold to gunmetal gray, in addition to several iridescent pastel colors.

Note: The following listings have a bronzoid finish (bronze colored).

Ashtray
Duck, outstretched wings support
green glass ash receiver . 145.00
Nude, kneeling on cushions,
holding 3" d removable pottery
ashtray 250.00
Scottie and frog, 8-3/4" l, 5-1/2" h,
paint loss 65.00

Bookends, pr
Cocker Spaniels, c1934, 6-1/4" h
.... 165.00
Gazelles, 7-1/4" l, 6-1/4" h
.... 225.00
Owls, 6" h 225.00

Scotties, 5" l, 5" h 250.00

Cigarette box, back-to-back nudes
supporting green glass box
.... 475.00

Lamp, standing nude holding 6"
round crackle glass globe shade
.... 450.00

Vase, No. F603, seated figure
mounted on wrought iron stand,
removable green Steuben vase,
12" h 150.00

Frankart, vase, No. F603, seated figure mounted on wrought iron stand, removable green Steuben vase, 12" h, **$150.**

Frankoma Pottery

John N. Frank founded Frankoma Pottery in Oklahoma in 1933. Prior to 1954, the pottery used a honey-tan colored clay from Ada, Oklahoma. Brick-red clay from Sapulpa has also been used, and pink clay is in use currently. The plant has suffered several disastrous fires over the years, including one that destroyed all of the molds that had been used prior to 1983.

For additional listings, see *Warman's Americana & Collectibles* and *Warman's American Pottery & Porcelain*.

Frankoma, yellow GOP elephant mug, **$20.**

Ashtray, Texas shape, pink, mkd 459, 6-1/4" l 17.50

Batter pitcher, Mayan-Aztec, Desert gold glaze, two qts 70.00

Bookends, pr, horses, black glaze, leopard mark 385.00

Bowl, 11" d, 3-1/2" h, blue with green, mkd "Frankoma 202" 95.00

Butter dish, cov, Aztec, green .. 25.00

Canister set, Desert Gold, Ring Band design, flour, sugar, coffee, and tea, four pcs 110.00

Casserole, Aztec, #7W, 10" w ... 40.00

Christmas plate, 8-1/2" d
1967, Gifts for the Christ Child 65.00
1970, Joy to the World 80.00

Cornucopia, Desert gold glaze, #222, 12" l.. 60.00

Creamer and sugar, Ada clay 35.00

Crocus vase, Ada clay, Brown Satin glaze, mold #43, 8" h 60.00

Deviled egg tray, green glaze, mkd "Frankoma #819, 12" d 35.00

Dish, leaf-shape, green and brown, mkd 225, 9-1/4" x 4 1/2"........ 18.00

Figure
Garden Girl, #700, Prairie green glaze 165.00
Indian maiden, brown glaze, 12-1/2" h.......................... 75.00
Woman, brown, 14-1/2" h 45.00

Masks, pr, black glaze, 6-3/4" h happy face, 8-3/4" sad face............. 130.00

Mug
Republican elephant, maroon, 1984, 4" h 20.00
U.S. Postal Service, "National Maintenance Training Center, Norman, Okla., black, 4" h 24.00

Pitcher, ice lip, green and brown, 6" d, 8" h 85.00

Planter
Cactus, Ada clay 65.00
Duck, brown 40.00

Frankoma, Indian figure, brown matte glaze, 8" h, **$65.**

Frankoma pottery, bowl, green, marked "5XL Frankoma," **$20.**

Plate
1974 Battles for Independence, 3rd in series of five, sand color, 8-1/4" d............................. 40.00
Kansas Centennial, 1861-1961, 9" d 25.00

Soup tureen, cov, Plainsman Gold, orig ladle................................. 65.00

Teapot, brown glaze, 6-3/4" h .. 50.00

Trivet
Two birds in a tree, brown, leaf pattern around edge......... 25.00
Oklahoma, Prairie Green, 6-1/2" d 28.00

Vase, Wagon Wheels, Prarie green glaze, Ada white clay, 8" h 65.00

Wall pocket
Boot, brown, mkd 133, slight chip, 7" h 35.00
Phoebe head, white, 1973-1975 re-issue, 7" h, 5" w 75.00

Fraternal and Service Collectibles

Folks have often saved family items relating to benevolent societies and service clubs. Today, many of these articles are entering the flea market scene. These items tell interesting stories about how past generations spent some of their leisure time.

Fraternal and service, Knights Templer, pin tray, Alleghany Commandery, Alleghany, Penn, tan ground, red and gold highlights, **$20.**

Attendee pin, Lion, 1954-55 ..... 7.00

Belt buckle, Rotary Club, cog emblem, silvertone, 2-1/2" d. 20.00

Cream and sugar, Eastern Star, Lefton 50.00

Cufflinks, pr
Kiwanis, enameled, round, medium blue ground, white K, 1" w 28.00
Lions 30.00

Cufflinks and tie clip, Masonic, cameo-type carving............. 150.00

Fez, Knights of Columbus......... 20.00

Letter opener, Masonic, "Jordan Lodge No. 247, F&AM, Robert Rogove-WN. 1967," in plastic case, worn lettering........................ 20.00

Medal
Loyal Order of Moose, heavily oxidized, 3-1/2" d............. 12.00
Salvation Army, "With Heart to God and Hand to Man 1880-1955," 1-1/4" d.................. 18.00
Shriner, Amarillo, Texas....... 90.00

Mug, Rotary Club, Tulsa, OK, mkd "Frankoma Pottery," 3" d....... 10.00

Paperweight, Lions International, brass, figural lion, 2" w, 3" l... 15.00

Pinback button, BPOE, celluloid, "Dedication, New Home, Dunellen Lodge No. 1488, October 27, 1927" on torn ribbon, 1-1/2" d, 2-1/2" l 38.00

Plate, Masonic, Shenango China 85.00

Ribbon badge, 2 1/2" x 9", top layers of black mesh fabric with silver star, metallic red center, red, white, and blue ribbons, white ribbon, silver image for Junior Order of United American Mechanics, black "Harris Council No. 174 Harrisburg, Pa" cardboard on reverse mkd "Manufactured by Whitehead & Clark Ribbon Badge Makers," early 1890s..................................... 50.00

Ring, Osiris, sterling silver, synthetic ruby, sides show horses and chariot, Chicago 75.00

Salt and pepper shakers, pr, Lions International, "Iowa" in blue, Milford Pottery by KlayKraft, 1-3/4" h 12.00

Fraternal and service, ewer, blue and white, black lettering "Commemorating 125th Anniversary of the Grand Lodge of Pennsylvania, 1786-1911," Trenton Pottery, gold handle, **$125.**

Fraternal and service, International Order of Odd Fellows ribbon and badge, Salina, Kansas, **$30.**

Service pin, 50 Years, Lions....... 7.00

Shaving mug, Odd Fellows, traditional IOOF symbols, with owner's name, 3-3/4" h.......... 80.00

Sign, Lions International, round, enameled metal, 30" d........... 50.00

Vest, Cousin Jacks Lions Breakfast Club, Grass Valley, 1970s....... 15.00

Watch fob, Osiris, sterling silver, enameled in red-brown, green and yellow, "Osiris Temple Boosters Club," back mkd "Robbins Co., Attleboro, Mass.," 1-3/8" d 75.00

Frog Collectibles

Ribbit, ribbit! From Kermit to Frogger, frogs have been popular advertising characters in our culture.

Advertising trade card, Pond's Extract 7.50

Band, Lefton Pottery trio, saxophone, accordion and banjo players, 3" h 75.00

Beanie Baby
Legs the Frog, retired October 97, protector........................... 55.00
Smoochy the Frog, protector 16.00

Candy mold, tin 48.00

Clicker, Life of the Party Products, Kirchhof, Newark, N.J. 18.00

Condiment set, figural salt and pepper shakers on tray, stamped

Frogs, toy, litho tin wind-up, green felt, yellow butterfly, marked "Made in Japan," 4-3/4" l, **$48.**

"Hand Decorated, Shafford, Japan"
.... 48.00

Cookie jar, green frog with yellow bow tie 55.00

Figure
Bisque, German, 1" h 15.00
Ceramic, Josef, 5-3/4" x 4".... 40.00

Netsuke, ivory, sgd, silver stand with turquoise lady bug, 1-1/4" h 145.00

Pin, figural
Enamel, black, green eyes, Ciner, 1-1/2" x 2" 200.00
Goldtone, clear rhinestones, emerald green cabochon eyes, 2" h 45.00
Rhinestones, 43 clear stones, green stones for eyes, 3" l 50.00
Sterling silver, amethyst colored glass eyes, Taxco, 1-1/2" h 45.00

Planter, Niloak, dark brown swirls, 4-1/2" h 55.00

Sculpture, The Frog Prince, Franklin Mint, 1986 .... 40.00

Stein, Budweiser, frog posing with bottle, another on handle, mkd "Handcrafted by Ceramate," 6" h
.... 28.00

Frogs, fishing lure, Paw Paw, Wotterfrog, three treble, hair covered hooks, painted eyes, yellow with black speckles, 3-1/2" l, **$20.**

Toothbrush holder, frog playing mandolin, mkd "Goldcastle, Made in Japan," 6" h 145.00

Viewmaster reel, Scenes from the Muppet Movie, blister pack, MIP
.... 8.00

Fruit Jars

People in some areas of the country refer to these utilitarian glass jars as "canning jars," while others refer to them as "fruit jars" or "preserving jars." In any event, the first machine-made jar of this type was promoted by Thomas W. Dyott in 1829, and the screw-lid jar was patented in November of 1858.

Fruit jars, Crown Imperial, quart, aqua, glass insert top with zinc screw band, **$18.**

Amazon Swift Seal, clear, glass lid, wire bail, quart 6.00

Atlas E-Z Seal, green, pint 15.00

Atlas Mason's Patent, apple green, pint 25.00

Ball Ideal, aqua, pint, glass lid, wire bail 3.00

Ball Mason, apple green, 1/2-gal
.... 30.00

Bloeser, aqua, quart, ground rim, glass lid mkd "Pat Sept 27, 1887,"

orig wire and metal clamp with neck tie wire 90.00

Eagle, aqua, quart, applied smooth lip, fabricated closure 90.00

Everlasting Jar, light green, quart
.... 30.00

Fruit Keeper, GCC Co. monogram, aqua, quart 50.00

Griffen's, Patent Oct 7 1862, amber, quart, ground lip, glass lid with cage like clam 70.00

Lafayette (in script, underlined), aqua, quart, base mkd "2," stopper neck finish three-pc glass and metal stopper, mkd "Patented Sept. 2 1884 Aug. 4 1885" 110.00

Mansfield Improved Mason, lavender tint, quart, glass insert, screw band............................. 60.00

Mason Improved, two dots below Mason, apple green, quart 30.00

Mason's Patent, teal, 1/2-gal... 25.00

Mason's 20 Patent, Nov. 30th 1858, aqua, quart 30.00

Millville Atmospheric Fruit Jar, aqua, 56 oz, reverse mkd "Whitall's Patent June 18th 1861," glass lid,

Fruit jars, Atlas E-Z Seal, quart, bail top, **$5.**

squared iron yoke clamp with thumbscrew........................... 45.00

Presto Wide Mouth, clear, glass lid, wire bail, 1/2-pint.................. 3.50

Safety Valve Patd May 21 1895 HC, dark aqua, half gallon, Greek Key design around shoulder and base, glass lid mkd "1," ground lip, metal band clamp with bail handle
.... 55.00

The Empire, aqua, quart, base mkd "Pat Feb 13 1866," ground rim, glass lid 80.00

The Hero, aqua, quart, ground lip, glass insert with "WHA" monogram

on interior center, series of patent dates on exterior, screw band, rim roughness 25.00

Trade Marks Mason's CFJCO Improved, aqua, midget pint 25.00

Fulper

Fulper Pottery, located in Flemington, New Jersey, manufactured stoneware and pottery from the early 1800s until 1935. Its pieces are usually well marked.

For additional listings, see *Warman's Antiques & Collectibles* and *Warman's American Pottery & Porcelain*.

Fulper Pottery, mug, mottled oil glaze, light green ground, stamped mark, 4-3/4" d, 3-3/4" h, **$75.**

Bowl, scalloped rim, shades of tan, green, gray, blue and rust, 3-1/2" h, 8" d 345.00

Bud vase, baluster, butterscotch flambé glaze, ink racetrack mark, 9" h 275.00

Console set, 7-3/4" d floriform bowl, pr 4-1/4" h candlesticks, cov in turquoise and clear crystalline flambé glaze, ink racetrack mark, touch-up on one candlestick rim 100.00

Doorstop, 8" x 10", figural bulldog, amber, blue, purple crystalline glaze, unmarked, restoration to tip of ear and one toe................ 600.00

Flower frog
Lily pad, matte green, 4" d . 135.00

Mushroom form, wisteria, 1-1/2" h, 2-1/2" d............................. 75.00

Low bowl, blue with brown drip glaze, 11" d 250.00

Mug, Prang, green crystalline over brown, 4" x 5" 225.00

Pitcher, blended, ringed, 6-1/2" h, 5-1/2" w 135.00

Plate, Oriental style, oatmeal color with blue freckles, 9-1/8" d 185.00

Trivet, lavender blue, 6-1/2" d 145.00

Vase
Blue and green mirror glaze, bulbous, flaring rim, raised racetrack mark, 7" h....... 290.00
Cat's Eye flambé glaze, pillow, ink racetrack mark, 6-1/4" h 175.00
Chinese Blue flambé glaze, speckled blue glaze, rect ink mark, 5" h 230.00

Vessel
Frothy blue flambé glaze, squatty, two angular handles, ink racetrack mark, 6" d, 5" h, restoration to one handle 195.00
Mirrored Cat's Eye flambé glaze, spherical, two buttressed handles, ink racetrack mark, 7-1/2" d, 6-1/4" h............ 435.00

Fulper Pottery, bud vase, flambé with crystalline glaze, c1918, 9" h, **$145.**

Funeral

Morbid as it may seem, death- and funeral-related items are popular collectibles with some people. Postmortem photographs and casket hardware are a few of the items they look for.

Funeral, pin, daguerreotype, hair stored on back, gold filled frame, 1-1/2" x 1-1/8", **$85.**

Bottle, Frigid embalming fluid, emb, full, 8-1/2" h........................... 90.00

Cane, 4-1/2" l x 1-1/2" h staghorn handle, 1/2" dec gold filled collar, opens with straight pull to reveal long brass internal measuring stick, when locked in place graduated inches allow undertaker to measure deceased for coffin, briarwood shaft, 1" brass ferrule, English, c1890, 35" l 1,350.00

Casket, child's, cypress, Birmingham Casket Co., Birmingham, Ala., 1930s, 46" l 115.00

Casket plate, "Our Darling" in banner over lamb, Victorian 20.00

Casket stands, sawhorse-type, turned wood, painted black, pr 70.00

Fan, cardboard, three-section, shows family in church, "Presented for your comfort by Wm. J. Schlup Funeral Home, The Home of Sincerity in Service, Akron, Ohio" 15.00

Hand truck, used for moving caskets, brass plate for "C.W. Price, Greenfield, Ohio," 1897 patent, brass-plated steel, spoked wheels in two sizes, rubber tires, 19-1/2" h, 45" l, 20-1/2" w, collapses to 8" h 200.00

Funeral, child's wooden coffin, 43" l, 14" w, **$200.**

Photograph
Cabinet card, memorial floral arrangements, imprint of Clifford & Son, Muscatine, Iowa 6.00
Memorial, 1890s, man's portrait in gilded frame sitting on a stool surrounded by funeral sprays, mounted, image size 7-1/2" x 9-1/2"................................ 18.50
Military funeral, postcard size 12.00

Furniture

Flea markets are great places to look for furniture. And, you can expect to find furniture from almost every time period and in all kinds of condition. When shopping for furniture, make sure you take a measuring tape, know your room sizes, and have a way to get your treasures home.

For additional listings and a detailed list of reference books, see *Warman's American Furniture* and *Warman's Antiques & Collectible.*

Furniture, blanket chest, Lane, cedar lined, pre-World War II, applied moldings, turned ball feet with scrolled returns, **$125.**

Bed, high headboard, walnut, plain, Victorian, 52" w, 50" h......... 250.00

Bed, rope
Federal, wear to blue paint. 215.00
Jenny Lind, stripped........... 100.00

Blanket chest
New England, pine, lift top, two drawers........................... 300.00
Oriental carving, brass lock plate 150.00

Bookcase, barrister type, stacking, glass front, four sections, removable top and base 395.00

Book stand, Arts & Crafts, oak, four open shelves with cutout sides and through tenons, 45-3/4" h ... 500.00

Bureau, molded crest over rect mirror, candle holders at side, two lidded boxes, three drawers, orig dark brown paint, gold striping, floral dec.............................. 500.00

Butler's tray table, mahogany 125.00

Furniture, rocker, pressed back, oak, face on back, **$195.**

Furniture, cottage dresser, painted tan, brown trim, multicolored florals, **$185.**

Chair
Chippendale, English or Irish, walnut, pierced Gothic back splat, scrolled handholds, slip

Furniture, detail photo of mirror decoration of vanity mirror, part of suite, **$500;** also shown is Chinese export blue and white porcelain beaker-form lamp, c1790-1810, **$200.**

seat cov in cream-colored silk upholstery, sq legs, small scalloped returns on front apron, refinished, one foot ended out, 19" h seat, 37" h back..... 400.00
Queen Anne, ladderback, five back slats, rush seat............... 200.00
Oak, pressed back.............. 100.00
Windsor, high comb back, 1920s 95.00

Chest of drawers
Country style, solid cherry, four large drawers, scrolled front piece, scrolled feet, refinished, old glass knobs............... 750.00
Eastlake, mahogany, five full drawers, two half drawers, carved leaf and branch dec, 38" w, 55" h...................... 300.00
Hendreon, dark brown, gold sponge dec finish simulating tortoise shell, four drawers, short block feet, flush mounted brass handles on drawers and sides of case, branded signature inside drawers, 28" w, 12-1/2" d, 28-1/4" h......................... 250.00
Victorian, walnut, white marble top, three drawers, one hidden drawer in base, carved fruit and nut pulls, 39" w, 32" h 700.00

Church bench
23" l, oak............................. 135.00
61" l, primitive, solid ends . 165.00

Clothes tree, oak, sq center posts, all orig hooks........................... 150.00

Corner chair, New England, maple, turned stretcher base 175.00

Cupboard, step back, painted blue-gray, 19th C......................... 500.00

Day bed, country, birch, old red paint, tapered supports on head and footboards, tapered legs, raised turned feet, casters, contemporary blue and white upholstery, 74" l, 25-1/2" d, 27-1/4" h 400.00

Desk, 36" x 72-1/2" x 29-1/2" h, oak, light natural finish, traces of white, carved horseshoe detail, plate glass top, matching desk chair with cowhide back, Brandt Company 500.00

Desk chair, Arts & Crafts, Charles Limbert, horizontal H-back, orig leather seat, branded mark, c1912, 35" h..................................... 550.00

Dining room chairs
Chippendale-style, one arm chair, five side chairs, veneered, pierced splat, slip seat, cabriole legs, paw feet.................. 950.00
Sheraton, one armchair, five side chairs, walnut and mahogany,

Furniture, armoire, cedar lining in hanging section, Bakelite accents at handles, part of bedroom suite, bed, dresser and vanity with engraved mirrors, Depression-era, **$500.**

mahogany flame veneer panels, rect crests with brass line inlay, rope twist carving on back crosspieces, reeded serpentine rear stiles, ring turned front legs, old refinishing, contemporary burgundy upholstered seats, restorations, 17" h seats, 31" h backs........................... 1,150.00

Easel, Aesthetic Movement, 19th C, ash, cresting with stylized scroll, rod and ball design, straight legs and spindle-inset supports, 64" h 275.00

Furniture, chair, Quaint Furniture, Stickley Bros. Co., Grand Rapids, Mich., oak, **$300.**

Filing cabinet, oak, four drawers, worn finish 400.00

Glider, metal, repainted turquoise, working condition 500.00

Hall bench, Colonial Revival, Baroque-style, cherry, shell carved crest over cartouche and griffin carved panel back, lift seat, high arms, mask carved base, paw feet, c1910, 51" h 700.00

Highboy, Chippendale style, Philadelphia, some period elements, some hardware missing 650.00

High chair, Shaker-style, ladder back, woven splint seat, turned finials, foot rest, mustard paint, 24" h seat, 38" h back................. 880.00

Jelly cupboard, two doors, stripped 350.00

Kitchen cabinet, painted surface, agateware sliding work surface, some wear........................... 350.00

Loveseat, Sheraton style, mahogany, reupholstered in dusty rose and tan stripe fabric 200.00

Morris chair, as found cond, very worn orig cushions.............. 200.00

Music cabinet, Art Nouveau, hardwood, cherry finish, crest with beveled glass, paneled door, applied dec, 49" h 200.00

Night stand, sq top, slightly splayed legs, small drawer, refinished 200.00

Pie safe, poplar and white pine, light brown paint dec, two drawers over two paneled doors, two circular vents on each side, 54-1/2" h 600.00

Plant stand, cast iron, worn orig gilding with red and green dec, onyx inset top, bottom shelf, 14" x 14" x 30" h........................... 165.00

Quilt rack, Renaissance Revival, American, walnut, faceted turned rods on trestle base, 27" w, 35" h 200.00

Rocking chair
Boston style, maple seat, worn 250.00
Cane seat and back, newly caned 300.00
Wicker, painted, upholstered seat 215.00

Shelf
Empire, oak, beveled mirror 125.00
Shaker style, cherry, double row of pegs, 84" l 95.00

Sideboard, Art Deco, France, c1928, walnut and burl book-matched veneer, Bakelite cabinet doors and drawer pulls, 76" l, 19-1/2" d, 50-5/8" h 900.00

Stool, primitive, pine, stretcher base 95.00

Table
Coffee table, blue glass top, curving sides, lower shelf 120.00
Dining, rect, extra leaves, mahogany colored, c1940 .... 115.00
Drop leaf, cherry, refinished, burn mark on one leaf 400.00
Kitchen, oak, drop leaf, some wear, c1890 .... 200.00

Lamp, Kittinger, mahogany, concave shaped top, one drawer, shelf in base, branded and metal labels inside dovetailed drawer, tapered legs, casters, 19" w, 18" d, 26" h 250.00
Side, half moon top painted yellow, natural straight legs 200.00
Tilt top, painted blue, Chinoiserie dec top............................ 425.00
Trestle base, three board top, 64" l 425.00

Wash stand
Federal, painted, wear to paint 285.00
Hepplewhite, painted pine, one board top painted yellow 195.00
Sheraton, mahogany........... 210.00

Furniture, recliner, modern, leather covering, **$100.**

Games

Kids of all ages have enjoyed games for decades. Some played hard, but today's collectors love those who carefully preserved the pieces and instructions, and who took good care of the box. Flea markets are great sources for vintage games as well as for those that feature popular television and movie characters.

Games, Bumpa, Milton Bradley, stand-up colored letters, with original rack, 36 pieces, **$15.**

Acquire, Avalon 25.00

All Star Hockey, metal figures, 1960s 90.00

Ally Oop Game, cylinder-shaped container 75.00

Anagrams Game, Milton Bradley, 1930s 35.00

Apple's Way, Milton Bradley, 1974 .... 25.00

Beetle Bailey 25.00

Bozo the Clown Circus Game, Transogram 15.00

Candyland, Milton Bradley, 1960s 10.00

Captain Video 125.00

Charge Account, Lowell, 1961 12.00

Clue, Parker Bros., 1949, 1st ed. 35.00

Dick Tracy Crime Stopper Game, Ideal, 1963 .... 40.00

Dream House 25.00

Dukes of Hazzard, Ideal, 1981 .... 10.00

Easy Money, Milton Bradley 7.50

Family Ties 20.00

Finance and Fortune, Parker Bros., 1930s 45.00

General Hospital, Cardinal, 1982 .... 18.00

Giggles Game, Rosebud Art Co., 1950s 45.00

Hardy Boys, 1959 .... 35.00

Huckleberry Hound Bumps, Transogram, 1961 .... 50.00

I Spy 50.00

Knight Rider 25.00

Little House on the Prairie .. 25.00

Mystery Date 75.00

Games, The Color Kittens, Golden Book Game, **$8.**

Games, Krokay and 5 Other Games, No. 3378, Transogram, copyright, MCMXXXVII, **$20.**

Name That Tune, Milton Bradley, 1959 .... 20.00

Password, Milton Bradley, 1963 .... 15.00

Readers Digest Computer Game, Selchow & Righter, 1980, used 9-volt battery 25.00

Ruff and Ready, Transogram, 1962 .... 35.00

Silly Sidney, Transogram, 1963 .... 55.00

Terry Toons, Ideal 45.00

Twilight Zone 195.00

Who Framed Roger Rabbit, Milton Bradley, 1988 .... 35.00

World's Fair Game, New York, 1964-65, Milton Bradley, 20" x 22" vinyl playing sheet, orig box 30.00

You're Out, Corey Game Co., 1941 .... 40.00

Zorro, Whitman, 1958 .... 30.00

Gardening

There's something therapeutic about gardening. And, when the weather is bad, why not collect gardening items to soothe your spirit? Many landscapers use antique elements to enhance garden areas, so dig around flea markets for interesting gates, garden benches, etc. Some decorators also like to use garden themed items to add a focal point to a room.

Autograph, Eula Whitehouse, book, *Texas Flowers in Natural Colors*, 1st ed., 1936 .... 48.00

Bird bath
Cast iron, some rust 95.00
Concrete, two-pc 35.00

Book
Crockett's Tool Shed, Gardening Equipment, James Crockett, photos by Lou Jones, 1989 . 7.00

Daylilies and How to Grow Them, Ben Arthur Davis, 1954, 1st ed, some wear to dj 8.00
Successful Gardening with Perennials, Helen Van Pelt

Gardening collectibles, fountain with bronze nymph figure, 30" x 26", green stained-glass surround, copper base, **$1,800.**

Garden bench, precast concrete 45.00

Gardening gloves, well worn ... 2.00

Harvester, R.C. Kingmaker, Carlisle, Ky., orig red and black paint, handle shows some wear, 16" h, 10-1/2" w 165.00

Harvesting basket, woven splint 65.00

Hoe, heart shaped blade, worn wooden handle 20.00

Panel, wrought iron, climbing vine dec, some orig gilt dec, slight rust 300.00

Planter, cement, painted green, white Viking ship and lion dec, 1930s, 15" sq, 10" h, pr 155.00

Seed box, litho label, wooden box with lid 30.00

Seedling bell, glass dome, knob top 35.00

Seed packet
Shaker 7.50
Typical 3.00

Shears, wooden handles 25.00

Shovel, worn wood handle 15.00

Sprayer, Gulf Space, small dent in tank, 18" l 65.00

Sundial, brass, mounted on marble base 125.00

Gardening collectibles, planter, cast iron, painted white, grapes and leaves, some rust, **$65.**

Trellis, three shaped wood stripes, old white paint 45.00

Urns, pr, concrete 85.00

Watering can
Brass, 9-1/2" l, 4-3/8" h, few small dents 8.00
Metal, painted black, orig sprinkler attachment, 12" h 25.00
Porcelain, painted flowers, 8-1/2" h 17.50
Tin, wide brass head 25.00

Watering pot, patent April 17, 1894, mkd "Imported for R & J Farquatlar & Co., Boston, Reliable Seeds, Market Street," 22" l, 9" w, 9-1/4" h 225.00

Wheel barrow, wood wheel and body, removable sides, old green paint, 62" l, 27" h, 23" w 225.00

Wilson, 1976, 1st edition, worn dj 12.00
Taylor's Guide to Gardening, Techniques, Planning, Planting & Caring For Your Garden, Houghton Mifflin Co., 1991, 1st ed. 7.00

Brooch, 1-3/8" h, watering can, goldtone watering can, flowers, faux pearls on handle 22.00

Child's watering can, Mistress Mary, Cohn Toys, Brooklyn, NY, 8" w, 6-1/2" h, wear 115.00

Drying rack, primitive, hand made 20.00

Flowerpot, clay, typical 1.00

Garfield

Who's the coolest cat around the cartoon pages these days? Garfield! Flea markets are favorite hangouts for this lasagna-loving feline and his buddies.

Alarm clock, Sunbeam, 1978 .... 115.00

Bank
Ceramic, bowling, mkd "Garfield Copyright 1981, United Feature Syndicate, Inc.," orig stopper 60.00
Ceramic, wearing graduation gown and cap, 5-1/2" h, mkd "Enesco" 60.00
Plastic, gum ball type, "Can I Borrow A Penny," orig plastic key, 6-1/2" h 20.00

Beach towel, Franco design, 28" x 51" 18.00

Bookends, pr, lounging Garfield, white base, Enesco, 1981, 4-1/2" w, 5-1/2" h 50.00

Clock, battery operated, 1978, 6-1/2" h 32.00

Lunch box, plastic 5.00

Mug
Ceramic, "I am A Redskins Fanatic" 15.00
Glass, McDonald's 10.00

Nodder, MIB, 7-1/2" h 27.00

Pencil holder, plastic, figural, Garfield 2.00

PEZ 6.50

Statue, boxing, United Feature Syndicate, Inc., 1981, 4-1/4" h 35.00

Telephone, figural 48.00

Garfield, mug, Garfield paddling canoe, "I'm easy to get along with when things go my way," Jim Davis facsimile signature McDonald's, multicolored decoration on clear glass, ©1978 United Features Syndicate, **$5.**

Thimble, dressed as Santa 14.00

Tie, blue background 12.00

Trophy, Garfield leaning towards Arlene, captioned "Where have you been all my life?" 4-1/4" h..... 25.00

Window sticker, stuffed figure, four suction cups, faded body, 6-1/2" h
.... 4.00

Gas Station Collectibles

Whether you refer to this category as Gas Station Collectibles, Service Station Memorabilia, or Petroliana isn't important. What does matter is that there are plenty of advertising items, premiums, and related materials from those places that sell us gas so we can drive to flea markets!

Gas station collectibles, sign, metal, green and white, "Ask for Quaker State Motor Oil," **$175.**

Gas station collectibles, tin, Gulf Lustertone Car Wax, **$15.**

Gas station collectibles, sign, double sided, Gulf, **$145.**

Award patch, 3" x 4-1/2", stitched fabric, Shell Oil Safe Driver..... 4.00

Badge, 2" x 3" diecut litho tin, 1" tab hinge extension at top, Amoco, Border Patrol, Junion Patrol Inspector, 1960s..................... 12.00

Banner, Texaco Havoline, plastic, 8" l
.... 65.00

Blotter, 3-1/4" x 6", Socony Motor Oil, Skippy in winter clothes, "Brrr An' Me Forgettin' to Change My Oil," ©Standard Oil Co. of NY, late 1920s, unused....................... 25.00

Calendar
1924, Pennsylvania Independent Oil Company, 20" x 27-1/2"
.... 20.00
1951, Coronet Kiddies, Butler's Sunoco adv...................... 10.00

1966 Texaco station, "girlie" type, unsigned............................ 15.00

Calendar card, 2-1/4" x 3-3/4", calendar on back
Gulf Oil Corp, 1947-48 calendar
.... 4.00
Socony Gasoline/Motor Oils, 1927 calendar............................ 35.00

Car attachment, Shell Oil, 3-3/4" x 5-1/2" metal domed image of Shell symbol, three colorful International Code Flags, late 1930s 190.00

Coaster/ashtray, Mobil Safe Driving Award, 1953, metal, shield logo, 4" d... 25.00

Coloring book, Esso Happy Motoring, unused.................. 25.00

Credit card, 1-3/4" x 3-1/2", plastic, Union Oil Co., CA, 1960.......... 4.00

Dashboard memo, Harry's Auto Service, Auto Repairing of All Kinds, Bernard, OH, use to record dates, car servicing info 55.00

Display, 8-1/2" h, Humble Oil, figural tiger, 1960s 45.00

Drinking glass, Phillips 66, Deem Oil Co., St. Louis, 5-1/4" h..... 48.00

Fan, 10-1/2" l, 7-5/8" w, Sinclair Opaline Motor Oil, adv on back
.... 75.00

Game, Champion Spark Plugs Road Race, 9" x 12" stiff paper, blue, white, and green folder cover, 1935
.... 50.00

Gas station collectibles, Esso paper sign, **$145.**

Gas station collectibles, gas globe, Shell, milk glass, 19" h, **$400.**

Gas pump, electric, orig hose, nozzle missing, 16" w, 10" d, 36" h 325.00

Handbook, 5" x 8", *Blue Sunoco Citizens Handbook for 1932, What Every Voter Should Know,* 32 pgs, page and photo for each candidate 10.00

Jacket, AC Spark Plug, white, black collar, red and white "AC S.N.A.R.T." patches, Great Lakes Sportswear Mfg Co., orig mailer, 1972 .... 20.00

Key chain, flicker, Amoco, As You Travel Ask Us, back side has place for name and address with please return to 12.00

Measuring can, Be-Sure Gasoline, side pouring spout................. 12.00

Mechanical pencil, BP Maximum Energy Gasolines, floating race car, 1960s..................................... 25.00

Oil can, D-A Speed Sport Oil, yellow full quart with old cars, checkered flags logo, "Racing Division, D-A Lubricant, Indianapolis, Indiana," C9+ 50.00

Pencil, lead, Gulf Oil, unused..... 5.00

Pinback button
2-1/4" d, RPM Motor Oil, red, white letters outlined in blue, early 1960s 5.00
3-1/2" h, Drain and Refill Mobiloil Today, red, white, and blue, 1930s 35.00
3-1/2" d, Standard Gasoline Unsurpassed, black rim, red, white, and blue, 1930s 35.00

Poster
11" x 22", Hey Kids Bardahl, black and red text, c1955........... 45.00
12" x 18", Gulf Refining Company Charg-A-Plates, 1932, thin cardboard......................... 35.00

Puzzle, Sohio Ethyl Gasoline, Mickey Mouse, plastic, 1950s, adv on back 72.00

Service cap, Quaker State Motor Oil, garrison-style, green oilcloth, white lettering and fabric piping, 1930s, soiled from use 20.00

Sign
Fisk Tires, porcelain, 1930s 425.00
Sinclair Gas, porcelain 100.00

Stamp album, 3-1/4" x 6" booklet, Sinclair Customers Premium Plan, ©1936, unused 12.00

Thermometer, Shell Anti-Freeze 85.00

Uniform patch, 2" x 3-1/2", Esso, red, white, and blue, 1970s 3.50

GI Joe

Billed as "A Real American Hero," Hasbro's GI Joe has been a favorite for years. Collectors search for GI Joe action figures, accessories, vehicles, etc. Over the years, GI Joe has undergone changes in size and even attitude, resulting in a variety of items to collect.

For additional listings, see *Warman's Americana & Collectibles* and *Toys & Prices,* 12th edition, edited by Karen O'Brien, KP Books.

GI Joe collectibles, doll, GI Jane, Classic 1997 Limited Edition, MIB, **$35.**

Accessories
Ammo belt............................ 18.00
Bullet proof vest, secret agent 8.00
Heavy Artillery Laser, MIB .. 45.00
Goggles, orange 14.00

Jet pack, Jump 25.00
Life ring 1.00
Machine gun, played-with, orig box 20.00
Marine bunk bed set, Hasbro, Model #7722..................... 55.00
Marine first aid set, Hasbro, 1964 .... 45.00
Paratropper parachute pack, Hasbro #7709, 1964 .... 30.00
Navy flag............................... 28.00
Sand bag 5.00
Ski Patrol Set 95.00
Snowshoes 15.00
Sleeping bag......................... 24.00
Tent, poles missing.............. 20.00

Action figure, 3-3/4"
Armadillo, 1988, loose 12.00
Blizzard, 1988, MOC 35.00
Breaker, 1982, loose.............. 20.00
Buzzer, 1985, MOC............... 45.00
Clutch, 1982, loose 15.00
Cobra, 1982, loose 40.00
Crystal Ball, 1987, loose 12.00
Dee-Jay, 1985, MOC 12.00
Desert Camo Savage, 1994, mail-in, loose 6.00
Grunt, 1982, loose 22.00

GI Joe collectibles, figure, Adventure Team, 12" h, **$75.**

Iceberg, 1986, loose 10.00
Muskrat, 1988, loose 12.00
Snow Job, 1983, loose........... 25.00
Torch, 1985, MOC 60.00
Torpedo, 1983, MOC............ 50.00
Wild Bill, 1991, MOC 50.00
Windmill, 1988, loose 7.00

G

Zandor, 1986, Canadian, MOC
.... 25.00

Action figure, posable, Hall of Fame, Hasbro, 12" h, NRFB

Combat Camo Duke, 1993 ... 40.00

Rapid Deployment Force, Marine, 1994.................................. 45.00

Rapid-Fire Ultimate Commano, 1993.................................. 45.00

Surveillance Specialist, 1995 40.00

Clothing

Beret, green 85.00

Boots, short, black................. 4.00

Boots, tall, brown 8.00

Combat fatigue pants set, model #7504, 1964 .... 15.00

Communications poncho, model #7702................................ 35.00

Hat, Army 28.00

Helmet, dark blue................. 18.00

Jacket, dress, Marine 30.00

Jacket, Russian...................... 12.00

Navy attack work pants set, model #7609................................ 25.00

Pants, dress, Marine 6.00

Pants, ski patrol.................... 22.00

Set, secret agent, trench coat, bullet proof vest.......................... 28.00

Shirt, Navy, one pocket 4.00

Shirt, soldier, no pockets........ 8.00

Coloring book, 48 pgs, Spanish text, 1989 .... 15.00

Set

Atomic Man Secret Outpost, good box...................................... 85.00

Dragon Fortress, Hasbro, Ken Masters and Ryu, 1993..... 10.00

Payload, #7a, Hasbro, Astro pilot, black suit, green and silver accents 4.00

Surveillance Specialist, Hasbro, Kay Bee Exclusive, 1995.......... 10.00

35th anniversary gift set, Hasbro, Then and Now, 1999, MIP 75.00

Vehicle

Amphibious Personnel Carrier, MIB 150.00

Armored car, Irwin, friction, 1968 .... 150.00

Armored Missile Vehicle Wolverine, orig, box, card missing 90.00

Flying Submarine, orig box, card missing............................. 40.00

Jet fighter plane, Irwin, friction, 1967 .... 225.00

Military staff car, Irwin, friction, 1967 .... 200.00

Rocket command center, Hasbro, model #7571.................... 60.00

Tank Car, motorized, MOC.. 12.00

Weapon

Bayonet................................. 15.00

Flare pistol 2.00

GI Joe collectibles, comic book, *GI Joe, Order of Battle*, Marvel, No. 4 of four issue series, May, No. 02576, **$4.**

High caliber weapons arsenal, 1994, MIP.................................... 10.00

M-16 .... 30.00

Mountain assault mission gear, 1993, MIP........................ 12.00

Night stick 20.00

Smart gun blaster, 1993.......... 3.00

Swamp fighter mission gear, 1994, MIP.................................... 12.00

Glass Knives

Most glass knives date to the Depression, produced by many of the glass manufacturers who dominated the market at that period. They vary in color and design, and, as with most collectibles, a premium is paid for examples with the original box.

Block pattern, pink 45.00

Flower handle, pink, inscribed "Nettie," mkd "Made in USA" 40.00

Plain, green, 9-1/8" l................. 42.00

Three Leaf pattern, crystal 18.00

Three Star pattern, Barry Importing Co., Broadway, N.Y.

Blue...................................... 42.00

Crystal, orig box 40.00

Pink....................................... 38.00

Vitex, crystal, orig box, 9" l 40.00

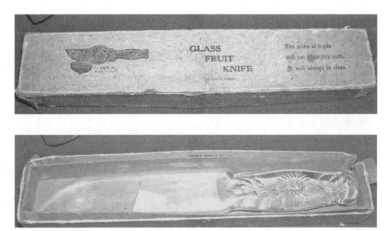

Glass knives, green, Dur-X, single flower handle, original box (shown above), **$35.**

Goebel

Many dealers and collectors associate the name "Goebel" with Hummels, but the company has also produced many other figures, animals, and accessories. Look for Hummel-type markings and well-made porcelain.

Goebel, plate, marked "Frauenkirche" with city hall and cathedral, St. Peter in Munich, made by W. Goebel, Bavaria, L Mün 47, ©Goebel trademark with bee in V, W Germany, **$40.**

Animal figure
Buffalo, 6" h 70.00
Fish, incised mark, 3" 45.00
Irish Setter, 10" h 90.00

Spaniel Dog, 8" h 80.00
Bank, Squirrel 35.00
Decanter, Friar Tuck, large
.... 130.00
Figure
Bellhop, Sheraton, orig suitcases
.... 425.00
Betsey Clark 100.00
Eleanor, mkd "Made in West Germany," incised numbers, 8-3/4" h 75.00
Elisabeth, gold trim, mkd "Made in West Germany," incised numbers, 8-3/4" h 75.00
Flower pot, Oriental man attached to side, crown mark 90.00
Perfume lamp, Bambi, stylized bee mark, foil paper label, 6-1/2" h
.... 275.00
Salt and pepper shakers, pr
Friar Tuck, full bee mark, "Made in West Germany," 4" h 145.00
Frog and toadstool 35.00

Goebel, plate, Collectors' Club Member, Goebel, Hummel type girl sitting under umbrella in center, **$20.**

Peppers, one red, other green, full bee mark, black "Germany" stamp, 2" w 30.00
Vase, Figaro the Cat 90.00

Golf Collectibles

"Fore!" When you consider that the game of golf has been played since the 15th century, you begin to understand how many golf collectibles are available to collectors. Flea markets are great sources for interesting clubs, paper ephemera, and other related items.

Ashtray, Senior PGA Golf Tour, ceramic, figural sand trap, green golf flag missing 7.00
Autograph
Elkington, Steve, U.S. Open golf cap
.... 35.00
Lafleur, Guy, 8" x 10-3/4" *Sports Illustration* cover with full color action photo, 1977 .... 20.00
Woods, Tiger, black-and-white photo, 8" x 10" 65.00
Badge
Bob Hope Desert Classic, 1980
.... 3.50
Henredon Classic, 1987 .... 7.50
Senior PGA Tour 3.50
Ball
Gutta percha, made in Great Britain, c1895, 60% to 70% paint, numerous iron marks 440.00

Lynx, rubber core 18.00
Book
Golf My Way, Jack Nicklaus with Ken Bowden, Simon & Schuster, 1974, softcover, 265 pgs 8.00
The Golfers Companion, Peter Lawless, 1st ed, 1937, 512 pgs
.... 150.00
Cigarette card, A. Padgham, British Sporting Personalities series, issued by W.D. & H.O. Wills, 1937, photo of 1936 British Open champion, 3" x 2" 5.00
Club
Fleetwood, Draper Maynard Co., Plymouth, NH, #10 .... 25.00
Hagen, iron-man sand wedge, wood shaft 170.00
Lady Diana, Mashie 5 iron ... 50.00

Wilson, wedge, staff model, 1959, steel shaft 60.00

Golf collectibles, limited edition figure, golfer, Straight & True, Lenox, MIB, **$45.**

Instruction package, 9-1/2" x 11" blister card, Lear Jet Stereo 78-tape cartridge, 24-pg Step by Step booklet, 1970s **18.00**

Martini pitcher, sterling silver overlay of golfer on both sides **100.00**

Medallion, 14k yg, inscribed "G. V. C. Golf Chairman 1973," intaglio snowflake design, 1" d **75.00**

Paperweight, US Open, 1980 .... **32.00**

Plate, crossed golf clubs under "D," Syracuse China, scalloped edge, 9-3/4" d **35.00**

Program, Bob Hope Desert Classic, 1967 .... **20.00**

Putter, The Spaulding, gooseneck blade, period replacement grip, 32-3/4" l **140.00**

Tees, James Bond, six tees and pencil in leather pouch, English, 1987 .... **8.00**

Whiskey bottle, 12-1/2" h, Beam, glazed figural china, Menehune native, white plastic flowers lei, paper tropical skirt, gold and aircraft symbols, holding golf ball, base inscribed "1975 Tenth Anniversary Hawaiian Open," with United Airlines emblem, front with complete Jim Beam Whiskey foil paper sticker **20.00**

Graniteware

Graniteware is the name given to metal kitchen and dinnerwares that have an interesting speckled or swirled paint decoration. The first graniteware was made in Germany in the 1830s. By World War I, American manufacturers were taking over the market. Common colors include gray and white, but savvy collectors will tell you that graniteware comes in a variety of colors. Graniteware is still being produced.

Adhering single or multiple layers of enamel to metal items through the use of high temperatures resulted in a product with a glass-like finish that was referred to as graniteware. Although such pieces were advertised as quite durable, they do in fact chip rather easily. Pattern and color are extremely important when determining value.

Reproduction alert:

Contemporary makers of graniteware produce some of the same forms and colors as those used for vintage pieces. In addition, individual pieces of vintage graniteware have been reglazed in highly desirable patterns, including Red Swirl.

Graniteware, gill measures, gray, 1/8 quart, **$500**; 1/4 quart, **$165**.

Baking pan, white, black trim, 9" x 13" x 2-1/2" h, some wear...... **15.00**

Berry bucket, brown mottled, tin lid, wooden knob, bail handle, 4-1/4" h, 6-1/4" d **85.00**

Bowl
Blue and white, medium swirl, black trim, c1960, 6-1/8" d **35.00**
Red and white stripes, 8" d, 3-1/4" h **32.00**

Bread box, white, lavender tulip dec, brass handle and latch, 13" l, 6" h **95.00**

Candlestick, gray, finger hold **115.00**

Coffeepot
Blue and white swirl, black handle and finial, 10-1/8" h **140.00**
Gray, gooseneck spout, pewter-decor engraved Victorian design, 9-3/4" h........................... **150.00**

Colander, gray **35.00**

Cookie sheet, mottled blue and white **225.00**

Cream can, gray, tin lid, wire bail, 4-1/2" h **225.00**

Cup, cream and green, rolled rim **48.00**

Dipper, gray **40.00**

Dustpan, gray mottled............ **35.00**

Food mold, blue and white swirl, turk's head **115.00**

Funnel, white, cobalt blue trim, 4" l **25.00**

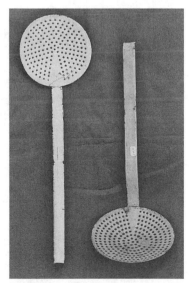

Graniteware, skimmers, left, white, 16" l, **$24**; right: tan, 13-1/2" l, **$20**.

Frying pan, blue and white speckled, 7-1/4" w 45.00

Ladle, white, 14" l 12.00

Match safe, gray, double pockets, 5-1/8" h 225.00

Mending kit, Mendets 19.50

Milk pail, orange, blue, black, and white Art Deco design, 8" h 70.00

Mixing bowl, green, black trim, 11" d 32.00

Muffin pan, eight-hole, gray 40.00

Mug, white, black trim, 2-1/4" h 12.50

Pie pan, cobalt blue and white swirl 45.00

Pitcher, blue and white, swirl dec, French, 1920s, 15" h 225.00

Plate, gray and white, 9" d 20.00

Roaster, gray mottled, metal rack, indented handle, 17" l 35.00

Sauce pan, gray mottled, 8-1/4" d 20.00

Strainer, blue and white, double handles 50.00

Teapot, solid blue, chrome lid with clear glass insert knob, 10" h 130.00

Tray, blue and white swirl, white back, 17" x 13-1/2" 90.00

Utensils on rack, hanging
Green, three utensils, emb diamond design, 18" l 250.00
Red shading to orange, four utensils, 12" h 280.00

Gray's Pottery

This Stoke-on-Trent English pottery is starting to catch on with collectors. Many pieces have luster trim or gold, silver, or copper banding. Look for the distinctive sailing ship mark.

Creamer, copper luster, floral trim, 3-1/4" h 40.00

Cup and saucer
Copper fluster, pink floral dec, sailing ship mark 22.00
Purple luster, Dickens ware dec 30.00

Jar, cov, turquoise blue ext., white int 20.00

Jewel box, cov, copper luster, hand painted sailing ship on lid, Sailor's Poem inside, 1934-61, 4" x 5" 45.00

Pin dish, 4" w
Isle of Amble souvenir 12.00
MBG 18.50

Pitcher
Gaudy Welsh type floral dec, pink and green, pink band 35.00
Mariner's Compass, multicolored compass on one side, poem on other 45.00
Silver luster trim, silver band, grapes dec 40.00

Tobacco jar, copper luster dec, hunting scene 175.00

Gray's Pottery, ashtray, Queen Elizabeth II, June 1953, 4-1/2" l, **$15.**

Gray's Pottery, pitcher, Sunderland luster type pink decorated body, titled "Ye Old Jug Inn" below multicolored transfer of thatched roof inn, verse on reverse, 5" h, **$65.**

Gray's Pottery, reverse of pitcher, verse reads "Women make men love, Love makes them sad, Sadness makes them drink, And drinking makes them mad."

Greeting Cards

From "Merry Christmas" to "Happy Birthday," we've grown up sending and receiving greeting cards. Some folks save these remembrances, and many find their way to flea markets. Some collectors look for examples with colorful images or witty sayings, while others search for interesting autographs. This is one area in which prices for the secondary market are still being established.

Greeting cards, birthday, 1930s, **$1.**

Birthday

Amos & Andy, brown portraits, message includes song title "Check and Double Check," Rust Craft, inked birthday note **28.00**

Ballerina, A Birthday Message, Sunshine Card **2.00**

Blondie, Dagwood illus, full color, Hallmark, ©1939 .... **20.00**

Boy Scout, Happy Scout Birthday, recruitment nature, c1960, unused with orig mailing envelope, card 5-3/8" x 4-1/4" **5.00**

First Lady, card sgd "Mrs. Eisenhower, Nov. 14, 1965, Dear Delores, May we celebrate many more mutual birthdays together," orig envelope **70.00**

Golliwogg, "Say! What's Cookin?," mammy with young boy and pie **28.00**

Christmas

A Christmas Wish for Someone Very Nice!, little girl playing toy piano, Christmas tree, wrapped presents, Pollyanna Cards, 1950s **3.00**

Christmas Cheer, red poinsettias with glitter trim, mkd "Made in U.S.A.," late 1940s **2.50**

Delta Airlines, Midnight Clear, Delta DC-4, 1950s, used .. **14.00**

Hello There! Merry Christmas, diecut Santa, toys in pack on back, Rust Craft, 1950s **3.00**

Hi! It's Christmas, triangular shaped card, Norcross, New York, 1950s **3.50**

Seasons Greetings The Detroit Tigers, 5-1/2" x 7-3/4" card

Greeting cards, framed Christmas cards, the mat has been cut out to highlight the bell shape of the cards, **$15.**

Greeting cards, Sincere congratulations, peach colored ground, white roses, green leaves, verse, **$1.**

with red, white, and blue tigers in baseball uniforms, white snowflakes against green background, white envelope, 1970s **20.00**

Snow people, Best wishes for Christmas and the New Year, Plastichrome, Made in USA **1.50**

Superman Brings You Christmas Greetings, 1940s............... **50.00**

Get Well, Amos n' Andy, black-and-white photo, Hall Bros., ©1951 .... **30.00**

⭐ ## Mary Gregory-type Glass

For generations, there have been rumors of a glass decorator by the name of Mary Gregory that worked at the Sandwich Glass Factory, Sandwich, MA. Mary's favorite thing to paint were white enamel figures of children, often playing, chasing butterflies, etc. Well, researchers today have decided Miss Gregory probably didn't do all that painting in her two years at the factory and many of the pieces attributed to her are actually of Bohemian origin.

If you find these children with eyes that are slanted, you've got a fake in your hands and you should be paying for a reproduction, not an original late 19th C piece of glass.

For additional examples, see *Warman's Glass.*

Reproduction alert.

Ale glass, 6" h, green, ribbed optic, white enameled dec of children, flakes...................................... **60.00**

Barber bottle, 7-1/2" h, cobalt blue ground, white enameled boy and girl playing badminton **135.00**

Bowl, 5-1/2" w, 2" h, sq, turned edges, cranberry, multicolored enamel dec of child, polished pontil **70.00**

Champagne tumbler, 5" h, green, white enamel dec of girl........ **70.00**

Cologne bottle, sapphire blue, white enameled child **155.00**

Cruet, orig stopper, 8" h, clear, ribbed optic, white enameled boy, chips on stopper **50.00**

Decanter, stopper, 12" h, clear, white enameled woman with basket **175.00**

Ewer, 8" h, blue, ribbed optic, white enamel dec of young boy holding flowers, applied clear handle **130.00**

Mary Gregory-type glassware, water set, colorless body, water pitcher and six tumblers, white enameled children, schoolmaster on pitcher, **$195.**

Milk pitcher, 6" h, cranberry ground, white enameled girl, clear applied handle 50.00

Miniature, stein, 1-5/8" d, 4" h, green, Inverted Baby Thumbprint, multicolored enamel dec of child, hinged pewter lid with cranberry insert, chip on int. rim 70.00

Mug
    3" h, 2-1/8" d, cranberry ground, white enameled boy, applied clear handle 85.00
    4-1/2" h, amber ground, ribbed, white enameled girl praying 65.00

Perfume bottle, 4-5/8" h, 2" d, cranberry ground, white enameled little girl dec, clear bubble stopper 165.00

Pitcher
    6-1/2" h, blue ground, white enameled boy with boat. 150.00
    6-5/8" h, 4-1/4" d, lime green ground, bulbous, optic effect, round mouth, white enameled boy, applied green handle 145.00
    9-1/4" h, clear ground, white and flesh enamel dec of boy in tree, girl below 150.00

Plate, 6-1/4" d, cobalt blue ground, white enameled girl with butterfly net 125.00

Salt shaker, 5" h, blue ground, paneled, white enameled girl in garden, brass top 190.00

Stein, 5-5/8" h, 2-1/4" d, blue, Inverted Thumbprint, white enamel dec of boy, hinged pewter lid with opal blue insert, thumb tab off 90.00

Tumbler, 3-1/2" h, 2-1/8" d, green, heavy white enamel, cowboy on horse, titled "Bronco Buster," polished table rim 30.00

Vase
    4" h, cranberry ground, white enameled boy and wagon 95.00
    5-1/2" h, cranberry, white enameled girl 100.00
    6-1/2" h, green ground, white enameled young man 90.00
    8" h, double ring shape, sapphire blue ground, young boy dec 195.00
    9" h, 4" d, frosted emerald green ground, white enameled girl holds flowers in her apron and hand 165.00

Griswold

Here's a name that evokes thoughts of cast-iron skillets and kitchen implements. Griswold items are frequently found at flea markets. The company based in Erie, Pennsylvania, originally produced hardware. By 1914, it had begun making the cast-iron cookware that many people associate with its name. In 1946, the company was sold to a group of New York investors, and in the late 1950s the trade name Griswold was sold to its major competitor, the Wagner Manufacturing Co. Wagner continued operations, but dropped the words "Erie, Pa" from the trademark.

Griswold, No. 50 Hearts Star muffin tin, **$2,000.**

Ashtray, round, match holder . 25.00

Bread stick pan
    #21 .... 85.00
    #23 .... 90.00

Corn stick pan
    #28, Wheat and Corn 175.00
    #262 .... 50.00
    #273 .... 25.00

Dutch oven, #8 .... 80.00

Famous Patty Molds, orig box
    .... 30.00

Food mold
    Lamb.................................... 125.00
    Rabbit 200.00

Popover pan, #10.................... 30.00

Skillet
    #3, small logo 10.00
    #5, block, smooth bottom 40.00
    #6, block, heat ring.............. 50.00
    #7, block, smooth bottom 25.00
    #8, small logo 15.00
    #10, block logo, heat ring..... 60.00

Waffle iron
    #8 .... 40.00
    #9 .... 60.00

Griswold, parlor stove, cast iron body, embossed "Home Stove Co., Indianapolis," painted gold top, finial, foot rail, and legs, lift-out disk embossed "Griswold, Erie, PA, U.S.A., American, 6 in," **$150.**

Haeger Potteries

Haeger Pottery has an interesting history. Established as a brickyard in Dundee, Illinois, in 1871, the company began producing an art pottery line in 1914. Its high quality luster glazes and soft pastels met with success. A line named "Royal Haeger" was introduced in 1938. Members of the Haeger family are still involved with the pottery.

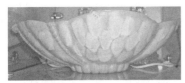

Haeger Pottery, centerpiece bowl, pink ground, blue and white highlights, beaded trim, **$35.**

Basket, yellow and green, 8-1/2" h 60.00

Bird house, pink, #287, two wrens 35.00

Haeger Pottery, gazelle, pink high-gloss glaze, paper tag, 1968, 21-1/2" h, **$125.**

Bowl, shell form, 18" l 18.00

Candy dish, cov, textured white, sgd "Royal Haeger" 12.00

Console set, Persian Blue, #316-H, foil labels 35.00

Ewer, long thin neck, 18-1/2" h 70.00

Figure
Bird, yellow, mauve, blue, R124 .... 30.00
Cat, orange, #1792, 21" h ... 190.00
Cocker spaniel puppy, reclining, 2-3/4" h 25.00
Garden Girl, #R995 .... 35.00
Hound, brown, 4" h 40.00
Ram, maroon, 8-1/2" h 130.00
Swan with uplifted wings, light gray and brown, 9" l 50.00
Warlord, pink, 12" h, 12" w 125.00

Flower pot, 4-1/4" h, 5-1/2" d 20.00

Lavabo, white, light blue, 19" h top, 7" h base 75.00

Pitcher, #408, blended agate glaze, 18-1/2" h 55.00

Planter
Bassinet, blue, 5" h, 7" l 12.00
It's A Boy, light blue, 3-3/4" h, 4-1/4" sq 16.00
Madonna with Cherub, blue, 11" h 35.00
Wheelbarrow, 7" l 15.00

Vase
R446, lily, blue, green and pink, 1930-40s, 14" h 100.00
R670, cylinder, white, 9" h ... 12.00

Haeger Pottery, vases, gazelles, gold-mustard ground, green highlights, price for pair, **$90.**

R1919, white, concentric black, green, and orchid rings around base, 10" h 25.00

Wall pocket, fish, blue............. 40.00

Haeger Pottery, candleholders, pair, boat shaped, green, yellow, brown, and black, original foil label "Handcrafted Haeger," $20.

Hair Related

Today we've got a commodity the Victorians couldn't get enough of—hair. And to think that we pay barbers and beauticians to cut it off! During the Victorian era, people saved every loose strand of hair in dresser jars called hair receivers. When enough hair had been accumulated, it was used to make jewelry and ornate flower wreaths. Of course, all of the voluminous hair that was so popular during that time had to be brushed and tucked in place with hair combs, barrettes, etc.

Hair brush, sterling silver, Art Nouveau style 125.00

Hair comb
Celluloid, engraved grapes, tortoise shell look 12.00
Celluloid, rhinestone trim.... 45.00
Gutta percha, French jet, Victorian 95.00
Mexican silver, mkd "Made en Mexico, 925" 15.00
Sterling silver, three turquoise stones, wave shape 45.00

Hair pick, single-prong hair ornament, imitation ivory, gracefully twisted top, diecut filigree, 7" l 35.00

Hair pin, silver twisted work, two-pronged comb, Victorian, c1890,

Hair related, hair receiver, two-piece, top with yellow and white roses, green leaves, yellow ground, **$85.**

5" l... 75.00

Hair receiver, top with center hole, porcelain, roses dec 85.00

Jewelry
Brooch, central oval glazed compartment with braided light brown hair, scrolled frame, convex back, 10k yg, c1840 .... 195.00
Locket, oval, beveled-edge glass front and back, braided knot of gray hair, plain gold filled frame, c1850 .... 200.00

Wreath, ornate flowers made from hair, paper leaves, other period decorations, 19" x 23" shadow box 145.00

Hall China

Hall China Company was located in East Liverpool, Ohio, and produced semi-porcelain dinnerware. By 1911, Robert T. Hall had perfected a non-crazing vitrified china, allowing the body and the glaze to be fired at one time. Initially, Hall's basic product was dinnerware for hotels and restaurants. Eventually, the line was extended to include premiums and retail wares, such as Autumn Leaf for the Jewel Tea. An extensive line of teapots was introduced around 1920, and kitchenware was introduced in 1931. The company is still in business today.

For additional listings, see *Warman's Antiques & Collectible*, *Warman's Americana & Collectibles*, *Warman's American Pottery & Porcelain*, and Autumn Leaf in this edition.

Ashtray, Chinese Red............... 30.00

Bean pot, Orange Poppy........ 115.00

Bowl, Crocus, 9" d 45.00

Bread and butter plate
Crocus................................... 12.00
Pastel Morning Glory 6.00

Cake plate, Orange Poppy 20.00

Casserole, cov, Rose White 30.00

Cereal bowl, Pastel Morning Glory 17.50

Coffeepot, Orange Poppy, Great American 85.00

Creamer, Lazy Daisies, Kraft... 15.00

Cup and saucer
Blue Bouquet 25.00
Red Poppy............................. 15.00
Taverne 20.00

Custard cup, Orange Poppy 6.50

Dinner plate
Crocus................................... 38.50
Pastel Morning Glory 25.00

Drip jar, Red Poppy 30.00

French baker, Taverne............. 30.00

Gravy boat, Serenade 40.00

Jug
Radiance 48.00
Rose White, 7-3/4" h 48.00

Luncheon plate
Crocus................................... 15.00
Pastel Morning Glory 12.00

Mixing bowl, Crocus, 7-1/2" d 55.00

Onion soup, cov, Red Dot 48.00

Pie baker, Pastel Morning Glory 30.00

Platter, Cameo Rose, medium . 40.00

Pretzel jar, cov, Taverne......... 195.00

Refrigerator container, Hotpoint, yellow, 4-1/4" h 80.00

Refrigerator jug, Hotpoint, Chinese blue, 7" h................................. 70.00

Salad plate
Crocus................................... 12.00

Hall China, teapot, Globe, no-drip, Addison gray, standard gold decoration, six-cup, **$60.**

Hall china, milk pitcher, teal blue, gold laurel wreath with name "M. Francis," marked "Hall 625," **$35.**

Pastel Morning Glory 9.00

Silverware caddy, Red Poppy, 1940s, 9" l 75.00

Sugar bowl, cov, Mount Vernon 20.00

Sugar shaker, handle, Crocus 150.00

Stack set, Red Poppy 75.00

Teapot
Airflow, cobalt blue 200.00
Crocus................................. 175.00
Morning, Chinese Red 200.00
Radiance and Wheat 390.00
Ribbed Rutherford, Chinese Red 390.00

Twin Spout, emerald green .. 80.00
Windshield, gold dot dec, gold label 65.00

Tom and Jerry set, bowl, 12 mugs, black, gold lettering............... 65.00

Vegetable bowl
Cameo Rose 30.00
Red Poppy............................ 25.00

Hallmark

Hallmark is an American success story. In 1913, brothers Joyce and Rollie Hall established their company to sell Christmas cards. Through purchases of printing and engraving plants, they developed into a nationwide company. After World War II, they expanded and attracted famous artists to the company. One of Hallmark's most popular lines, the Keepsake Ornament series, was started in 1973.

Cookie cutter, Peanuts, Lucy holding package, Snoopy in a Santa hat, Linus holding lights and Charlie Brown holding ornament, set of 4 .... 100.00

Figure, Scribbles, painted plaster, blond hair, country boy outfit, broad brim hat, bib overalls, c1940, 4-3/4" h 25.00

Greeting card, birthday, black characters, copyright Hall Brothers, Inc., c1940s, 4" x 5" 25.00

Jewelry, Valentine pin 10.00

Magazine advertisement, Thanksgiving cards adv, 1959. 5.00

Ornament
Barbie, 1993, 1st in series, orig box 125.00
Calico Mouse, Merry Miniatures, 1977, 2-1/4" h................. 100.00
Enterprise, 1991, MIB 225.00

From Our House To Yours, 1992 .... 10.00
Frosty Friends, Eskimo and Husky in igloo, 2nd in series, 1981, no box, 2" h 350.00
Heavenly Angel, 1992, MIB, 3" h 32.00
Mustang, Classic Car series, 1992, MIB 48.00

Hallmark, Rocking Horse ornament, 1981, MIB, **$40.**

Noel Railroad, Coal Car, miniature, 1990, 2nd in series 24.50
Puppy's Best Friend, 1986, worn orig box 28.00
Snowman, Merry Miniatures, 1976, 2-1/4" h............................. 70.00
Superman lunchbox, 1998, tin, 3-1/4" x 2-1/2" 13.50
World-Class Teacher, 1992, 3-1/4" h, MIB 9.00

Hallmark, 1957 Corvette ornament, first in Classic American Cars series, 1991, MIB, **$100.**

Hallmark, Barbie Christmas ornaments, all MIB, left: Chinese Barbie, Dolls of the World series, **$4;** right: Cheer for Fun, **$7.50;** bottom: Hatbox Doll Case, 1962, **$9.**

Halloween

Among holiday collectibles, Halloween is second only to Christmas. Early Halloween items have a distinctive look that appeal to many collectors.

Reproduction alert.

Halloween, cookie cutters, Trick or Treat, six original metal cutters, colorful original box, **$18.**

Candle, jack-o-lantern, 4" h..... **15.00**

Cookie cutter
Aluminum, startled cat, 3-1/4" w
.... **7.00**
Tin, witch on broom, Foose. **15.00**

Costume, child's
Dr. Kildare **45.00**
Fred Flintstone **25.00**
Howard the Duck, Collegeville, 1986, orig box **60.00**
I Dream of Jeannie, 1960s.. **125.00**
Indiana Jones........................ **80.00**
Pac Man **40.00**
The Fonz, Happy Days, Ben Cooper, 1976, orig box **35.00**

Cup, paper with handle, orange with black cats, bats, trees and full moon, C.A. Reed & Co., Williamsport, Pa., 3-3/4" h...... **5.00**

Hat, 7-1/2" x 12", diecut tissue paper, orange and black, German, 1930s, very slight use
Headband with black cat and jack-o-lantern images **10.00**
Headband with orange running cat and geometric designs **8.00**

Horn, litho tin with plastic end, witch on broom, spider webs and stars, Kirchhof, 6-1/2" l................... **20.00**

Jack-o-lantern
Black cat, cardboard, mouth insert with small tear, Western Germany......................... **475.00**
Devil, compressed paper, face restored, 6-3/4" h **500.00**

Pumpkin, cardboard, worn paper inserts in eyes and mouth, Germany, 3-1/2" h.......... **225.00**
Pumpkin, tin, nose doubles as a horn, U.S. Metal Toy Co., wear, 5" h, 6" d........................ **155.00**

Mask
Deputy Dawg, 1960s............. **32.00**
Esso Tiger, 1960s **16.00**
I Dream of Jeannie, 1970s...... **3.00**
Mork from Ork...................... **3.00**
Rabbit, 1960s....................... **10.00**
Smiling devil, red and black, Shotwell Confections premium, 1930s, 9-1/4" h **45.00**
Yogi Bear, 1950s **15.00**
Zorro, large brim, 1960s....... **35.00**

Napkin, shows black cat, jack-o-lantern man & woman, bats and moon.. **5.00**

Nodder, skeleton, papier-mâché, gray with black, green and white accents, 1930s-1940s, Japan, 5-3/4" h. **90.00**

Noisemaker
Skillet-shape, litho tin with wooden clappers, shows witches, cats,

Halloween, postcard, **$30.**

Halloween, pumpkin, fold-out type, green and orange curved stem, **$12.**

skeletons, etc., U.S. Metal Toys, 8" l, 4" w **45.00**
Twirl-type, litho tin with wooden handle, shows witch, black cat and owl, scratches, 5" l..... **45.00**

Party favor, cardboard paper face, plastic disc, eyes move, Japan
.... **45.00**

Pinback button, 3" d litho, Beningan's Tavern, black and white witch, yellow highlights, text "I Stayed For A Spell," 1970s..... **20.00**

Table decoration, black cat, tissue-paper construction, H.E. Luhr, 9-1/4" h, 6" w **32.00**

Tambourine, litho tin
Black cat motif, 7-1/4" d..... **195.00**
Jack-o-lantern motif, 6-1/4" d
.... **175.00**

Toothpick holder, papier-mâché, 1940s, Japan, 1" x 1-1/2"
Jack-o-lantern....................... **20.00**
Skull...................................... **18.00**
Witch **24.00**

Trick-or-Treat bag, cloth, orange with black ghost chasing man and woman, black vinyl handles
.... **16.00**

Handkerchiefs

Aaacchhooo! Today we grab for a box of disposable tissues, but that's not what our grandmothers did. Vintage etiquette called for well-dressed folks to carry a well-pressed handkerchief, just in case a sneeze was waiting. Remember those gallant gestures in the movies where the gent would whip out his handkerchief for the damsel in distress?

Handkerchief, St Patrick's Day motif, green and white, **$5.**

Appliquéd
Cocktail, 5" l embroidered orange flowers, cutwork, orig label "Cocktail Sixe, 100% Cotton Made in Switzerland," 12" sq **9.00**
Flowers, scalloped edge, orig label "Made in Switzerland, All Cotton," 12-1/2" sq **10.00**

Child's
Donald Duck, 8-1/4" sq, cotton, ©W.D.P. **30.00**
Valentine, 6" sq, cotton, red and white hearts........................ **6.00**

Embroidered, "A" monogram,
crocheted edges, 11" sq **12.00**

Florals
Bouquet of flowers, white waffle border, hand-rolled hem, 13" sq **12.50**

Chrysanthemums, deep rust blossoms, dark brown ground, polished cotton, machine hem, 13" sq **10.00**
Gladiolas, scalloped hem, cotton, 15-1/2" sq **15.00**
Gray flowers, orange background, scalloped hem, 13" sq **10.00**
Morning glories, red flowers on white background, black border, machine hem, 11-1/2" sq **11.50**
Pink roses, black ground, hand-rolled hem, 13-1/2" sq...... **12.50**
Poppies, red and white flowers, blue background, hand-rolled hem, 12-1/2" sq **10.00**
Roses, white and deep brown petals, medium brown shading

Handkerchief, embroidered flowers, hand crocheted edging, **$2.50.**

Handkerchief, embroidered, **$2.**

to darker brown border, machine hem, 13-1/2" sq **12.50**

Souvenir type
London, rayon, 13-1/2" sq.... **17.50**
Montana, scalloped edge, cotton, 14" sq................................. **22.00**
Niagara Falls, 10-1/2" sq, six views of falls, red and yellow roses border................................... **3.75**
Texas, hand-rolled hem, cotton, some fading, 13" sq.......... **15.00**
The Cascades St. Louis 1904, 6-1/4" x 6-1/2" folded white fabric, embroidered fair building and floral accents **25.00**

Hand-Painted China

A china painting movement in America began in 1876 and remained popular over the next 50 years. Thousands of artists, both professionals and amateur, decorated tablewares, desk accessories, many other items with florals, fruits, and conventional geometric designs and occasionally with portraits, birds, and landscapes. The porcelain blanks they painted on were often imported from manufacturers in France, Germany, Austria, Czechoslovakia, and Japan, as well as American makers such as Lenox and Willetts. Not all blanks were marked with a manufacturer and many were also not signed by the artist who created the piece, although some pieces were signed and even dated by their creators.

For additional listings, see *Warman's Antiques & Collectibles*.

Cake plate, 7" d, double handles, central conventional floral bouquet, artist sgd "IFP," marked "Schumann, Bavaria" **20.00**

Celery dish, 11-1/2" l, 5" w, yellow and pink peace rose, green leaves **45.00**

Charger, 12-1/2" d, clusters of berries, leaves, vines, and blossoms, soft colors, gold edge............. **70.00**

Cream soup cup, 4-3/8" d, double burnished gold handles and rim, conventional border, marked "Bavaria," c1900-1915 .... **25.00**

Creamer and sugar, blue and soft green floral border design on burnished gold band, ivory ground, burnished gold lids, spout, rims, and handles, sgd by artist Helen Hurley **55.00**

Cup and saucer, celadon Celtic border design, light blue border, ivory ground, burnished gold rims and handle, artist sgd "L.E.S.," marked with crown in double circle, "Victoria, Austria," 1900-20 .... **30.00**

Dish, 8-1/2" w, 2" h, handle, grape motif, gold trim, scrolled crimped border, sgd by artist H. Niemann **50.00**

Plate
6" d, pale florals, gold edge, sgd by artist T. Tanalie **15.00**
9" d, embossed trellis lace, white daisies, gold trim, sgd by artist Dorothy Riley.................. **32.00**

Rose bowl, 2-7/8" h, band of violets and burnished gold, marked "O. & E.G., Royal, Austria," c1898-1918 .... **30.00**

Serving bowl, cov, 10" l, gold and rust colored Arts & Crafts design, sgd by Mrs. E. N. Ewin, 1909, Limoges, France blank **65.00**

Hanna-Barbera

The partnership of William Denby Hanna and Joseph Roland Barbera developed slowly. They both worked for MGM, and, when a new cartoon division was started in 1937, they were teamed together. For 20 years they worked under this arrangement, creating such classics as Tom and Jerry. After striking out on their own, they began producing cartoons for television and created such great characters as Huckleberry Hound and the Flintstones. In 1966, Taft Communications purchased the company.

Hanna Barbera, toy, litho tin wind-up, Barney Rubble riding Dino, **$35.**

Coloring book, *Flintstones Color by Number,* Whitman................ **24.00**

Comic book
The Flintstones at the New York World's Fair, official fair souvenir............................ **25.00**
Space Ghost, Comico, 1987, 48 pgs **7.00**

Cookie jar, Barney Rubble, Certified International Corp, 12" h **60.00**

Hanna Barbera, toy, Rubbles Wreck, Fred Flintstone driving stylized car, **$40.**

Animation cel, Yogi Bear, late 1970s/early 1980s, single 5-1/2" image of Yogi on laser background, 13" x 11" **85.00**

Ashtray, Barney bowling, pottery, Arrow Houseware Products, Chicago, 5-14" x 8" **90.00**

Bank, Huckleberry Hound, Knickerbocker, hard plastic, 10" h **25.00**

Book, *Jetsons' Word Search Puzzles*, 1978, 64 pgs, unused............. **10.00**

Camera, Fred Flintstone, 1976, 3-1/4" x 3-3/4" **20.00**

Charm bracelet, Huckleberry Hound, Pixie, Dixie, Boo Boo, Huck, Yogi, Mr. Jims, Tom Tom, 1959, orig card....................... **80.00**

Hanna Barbera, comic book, March of Comics, The Flintstones, **$24.**

Doll, plush
Barney Rubble, Nanco, 1989, 14" h **22.00**
Yogi Bear, Knickerbocker, 1960s, 19" h **75.00**

Figure
Hokey Wolf, Marx **15.00**
Huckleberry Hound, glazed china, 6" h **20.00**
Quick Draw McGraw.......... **100.00**

Flashlight, interchangeable faces, Fred Flintstone, Huckleberry Hound and Yogi Bear, 1975, MOC **15.00**

Game
Dino the Dinosaur Game, Transogram, 1961 .... **45.00**
Huckleberry Hound Tiddly Winks, Milton Bradley, 1959........ **15.00**

Quick Draw McGraw Game, Milton Bradley, 1981...................... 5.00

Hot water bottle, Yogi Bear, 1966 .... 25.00

Lamp, Quick Draw McGraw, plastic, 22" h............................... 20.00

Lunchbox
Flintstones, Aladdin, metal, 1971 .... 95.00
Sky Commanders, plastic, 1987 .... 25.00

Mug, Fred Flintstone, Flintstone Multiple brand Vitamins, 1968, 3 1/4" h 8.00

Pinback button, Tom and Jerry Go For Stroehmann's Bread, 1950s, 1-1/8" d 27.50

Soaky, Barney Rubble, 7-3/4" h 30.00

Sticker book, Snagglepuss, Whitman, 1963 .... 15.00

Hardware

Decorative and ornate hardware has graced our homes for decades. Vintage hardware items are popular with those who are restoring antique homes, those who want to add a unique touch to a newer home, or collectors who simply appreciate the beauty of the object. Some collectors have discovered that mounting these vintage hardware beauties on a wall or board creates a neat place to hang their hat as well as an interesting display of their collection.

For additional listings, also see Doorknobs in this edition.

Catalog, Corbin Cabinet Lock Co., New Britain, CT, 1922, 483 pgs, 8-1/2" x 11", hard cover, illus.. 125.00

Door knocker
Cast iron, figural fox head.... 85.00
Wrought and hammered copper, tulip shape, monogrammed "IGW," orig dark patina, 11-1/4" h........................ 175.00

Door pull, brass, Arts & Crafts, round, grimacing figure wearing head covering, holding ring in its mouth, 8" d.......................... 270.00

Door push plate, bronze, Windsor pattern, Sargent, c1885, 16" h 150.00

Hinges, pr, wrought iron, barn type 95.00

Knob
Agateware, brown pottery, 2-1/8" d, pr 90.00
Black glass, 6-sided, 1" h, 1" d 12.50

Clear glass, 6-sided, 1" h, 1" d 7.50

Mailbox cover, vinyl, snowman 3.00

Mail slot and receiver, "Letters"
Cast iron, Gothic pattern, 2-1/2" h, 8" w.................................. 195.00
Nickel-plated cast brass, 2-1/2" h, 7" w.................................. 195.00

Outlet plate, copper, ivy design, 4-3/4" h, 3-1/4" w 30.00

Shelf bracket, wrought iron, ornate scrolling pattern, pr............... 20.00

Switch plate
Brass, for double pushbuttons 32.00
Copper, gingko design, 5" h, 3" w 30.00

Hardware, furniture drawer pulls, Victorian, embossed brass, wood drop, c1850, set of four, **$60.**

Harker Pottery

The Harker Company was one of several East Liverpool, Ohio, firms. Founded by Benjamin Harker around 1840, the company produced yellow ware items using the natural clay deposits from the surrounding area. White ware was first made about 1879. Dinnerware and table accessories were the order of the day until the plant was destroyed by fired in 1975.

For additional listings, see *Warman's Americana & Collectibles* and *Warman's American Pottery & Porcelain.*

Batter bowl, Petit Point Rose .. 60.00

Bowl, Cameo, Zephyr, blue....... 18.00

Cake server
Fruit 35.00
Petit Point Rose 20.00

Casserole, cov
Cameo, Zephyr, blue............. 50.00
Petit Point Rose 65.00

Cheese plate, Cactus Blooms, 11" d
.... 60.00

Cookie jar, cov, Modern Tulip. 85.00

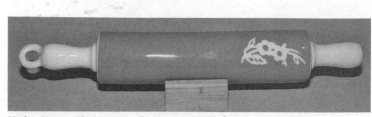

Harker Pottery, Blue Cameo rolling pin, 14-3/4" l, **$100.**

Harker Pottery, cake plate, white magnolia blossom, gray border, self handles, **$40.**

Creamer
Gem, blue 35.00
Kriebel's Dairy, Hereford, Pa
.... 50.00

Cup and saucer
Cameo, Shell Ware, blue....... 17.50
Country Charm 12.00

Dinner plate, Petit Point Rose 15.00

Mixing bowl, Red Apple, 9" d . 30.00

Pie plate, Cameo, Dainty Flower, blue
.... 75.00

Pitcher, Tulip 95.00

Platter
Colonial Lady, 12" 30.00
Ivy Vine, large...................... 75.00

Range drip jar, Ivy Vine 47.50

Rolling pin
Petit Point Rose 140.00
Tulip.................................... 150.00

Salad bowl, Red Apple............. 27.50

Scoop, Amy............................... 65.00

Snack set, Petit Point Rose....... 48.00

Spoon and fork
Kelvinator 160.00
Petit Point Rose 140.00
Silhouette, platinum trim... 170.00

Teapot, cov
Cameo 65.00
Ivy Vine 200.00

Utility tray, Red Apple 24.00

Vegetable bowl, Red Apple 32.00

Hatpin Holders and Hatpins

Hatpins are coming back into vogue with collectors. Perhaps it's the renaissance of large hats, or maybe it's the romance that hatpins evoke. Whatever the reason, more and more hatpins are entering the flea market scene, and prices are rising. Of course, if you're going to collect hatpins, you've got to have a few hatpin holders to display your treasures.

For additional listings, see *Warman's Antiques & Collectibles* and *Warman's Jewelry*.

Reproduction alert.

Doll, porcelain half doll, arms folded, satin dress as cushion for hatpins, 9" h.. 125.00

Hatpins, group of brass hatpins, all embossed with a portrait, prices range from **$35** to **$55** each.

Hatpin
Ball, rhinestones, 8-1/4" l..... 48.00
Beaded and sequined head, black, 2-3/8" x 1-1/4" d, 6-1/4" l
.... 75.00
Embossed copper top, bezel set coral colored stone, 8" l.... 95.00
Faceted glass, black, 2-1/4" x 1-1/4" d, 5-5/8" l............. 150.00
Filigree, teardrop, 3/4" l head, 7-5/8" l............................... 65.00
Iridized metal head, faceted dome, 1-3/4" d, 11-1/4" l........... 125.00
Military insignia, 2" d, 9-1/2" l
.... 125.00
Souvenir, 1607 1907 Jamestown Exposition text, silver luster metal, ornate border, Whitehead & Hoag, 1-1/4" d, 3-3/4" l 25.00

Hatpin holder, carnival glass, Grape & Cable pattern, marigold, **$200.**

Wood, black ebonized head, metal
separator, 11-1/2" l......... **100.00**

Hatpin holder, porcelain
Austrian, hp blue flowers, 5" h
.... **45.00**

Bavarian, hexagonal, pastel florals,
mkd "Z. S. & Co.," 4-3/4" h **45.00**
Germany, yellow roses, 6-1/2" h
.... **90.00**
Nippon, pink roses, green leaves,
gold trim, 4" h **100.00**

Souvenir, Capitol Building,
Washington, D.C., 4-1/2" h
.... **125.00**

Hats

A well-groomed lady used her hat to complete her ensemble. Some vintage hats are large and colorful, while others are a little more demure. There has been a resurgence of hat collecting, perhaps due to popular movies featuring stars in large bonnets. Whatever the reason, our hats are off to those who enjoy this field of collecting.

Hats, child's, Hopalong Cassidy, black felt, white name and decoration, **$150.**

Beaded, black, evening type, orig
Hess Bros label **35.00**

Boy scout, Stetson, mkd "John B.
Stetson Co. #1," leather chin strap,
c1930s **65.00**

Felt
Black, small bowl crown, short back
brim, trimmed in black ostrich
feathers, black ribbon with bow
in back, orig label "Yowell Drew
Ivey Co., Daytona Beach" **125.00**
Brown, wide brim, beige feathers,
green netting, 1930s....... **125.00**
Sapphire blue, Art-Deco style, small
matching bow and netting **40.00**

Fur
Fox, dyed black, Winkelman's label,
1950s **125.00**
Natural mink, pillbox style .. **40.00**
Wide brim, white feather dec, pink
rose, Victorian................ **175.00**

Political, 5-1/2" x 11", Experience
Counts, Vote Nixon Lodge, paper,
red, white, and blue, two-sided
adjustable telescoping paper hat,
unused **20.00**

Sport, rose colored silk flowers on
top, horsehair brim, 1920s, 10"
from front to back, 4-1/2" h **225.00**

Straw
Black, large brim, fabric crown, orig
label "Schiparallei Jr. Paris"
.... **70.00**
Navy, feathers and veil, small
turned up brim, orig label "Gage
Brothers & Co., Chicago, New
York, Since 1856" **70.00**

Velvet, black, red poppies, fully lined,
wire in brim, narrow back brim
.... **60.00**

Wool, black, close fitting, orig label
.... **45.00**

Hats, uniform hat, black patent leather covering, black plume, gold colored insignia on front with shield and plumed helmet, **$5.**

World's Fair, New York, 1964-65,
8" h, cotton twill, applied fabric
silver, orange, and blue label, woven
name "Ruth" in orange thread
.... **20.00**

Haviland China

Haviland China has an interesting history in that it was founded in America by importer David Haviland, who then moved to Limoges, France, to begin manufacturing. He was quite successful. His sons, Charles and Theodore, split the company in 1892. Theodore went on to open an American division in 1936 and continued to make produce dinnerware. The Haviland family sold the firm in 1981.

For additional listings, see *Warman's Antiques & Collectibles* and *Warman's American Pottery & Porcelain*.

Haviland China, Limoges bowl with flowers, 8-1/8" x 9-9/16", **$45.**

Bone dish, crab dec.................. 60.00

Bowl, hp yellow roses, 8" d....... 35.00

Butter dish, cov, Gold Band, mkd "Theo Haviland".................... 48.00

Butter pat, sq, rounded corners, gold trim.. 12.00

Cake plate, 10" d, gold handles and border 35.00

Celery dish, scalloped edge, green flowers, pale pink scroll 45.00

Chop plate, Chrysanthemum, #88, 11" d.. 80.00

Coffee cup, Marseille.............. 25.00

Compote, ftd, reticulated, gold trim 175.00

Cream soup, underplate, cranberry and blue scroll border 30.00

Creamer and sugar, small pink flowers, scalloped, gold trim. 65.00

Cup and saucer, deep pink flowers, scalloped gold edge 30.00

Demitasse cup and saucer, 1885 .... 30.00

Dinner plate
Crowning Fashion, tan........... 8.00
Princess 24.00

Haviland China, gravy boat and underplate, small pink and blue florals, red mark "Theodore Haviland, Limoges, France," 8" l, **$48.**

Oyster plate, blue and pink flowers, mkd "Haviland & Co.," 9" d. 120.00

Platter, Athena pattern, 14" l . 195.00

Relish dish, blue and pink flowers 25.00

Tea cup and saucer, small blue flowers, green leaves 28.00

Teapot, Baltimore Rose, #1151, #1 blank.................................... 215.00

Hawaiiana

Aloha. Some collectors are just naturally drawn to colorful Hawaiian objects. Perhaps it's the smiles of the hula girls or their alluring dance. Prices are beginning to escalate for items in this category. Be aware that objects actually made in Hawaii tend to cost more than items imported from Japan.

Ashtray, Aloha Hawaii, pot metal, emb, 1939 .... 20.00

Bell, Hula Girl, ceramic, "Hawaii" written across skirt, "Made in Japan" sticker, 4-1/2" h 36.00

Dress, lounging, 1960s, Honolulu designer Pomare Tahiti 60.00

Hawaiian, national park brochure, **$3.**

Figure, hula girl, Josef Originals, International Series, orig Hawaii Poem string tag, 4" h 80.00

Handkerchief, Aloha Hawaii, embroidered hula girl, MIB, set of four 30.00

Magazine ad, Take A Trip, Hawaii Tourist Bureau, 1934, from *Fortune Magazine* 8.00

Menu
Metropolitan Hotel, four pgs, c1974 .... 35.00
S.S. Lurline, Matson Lines, "Hawaii's Decisive Hour" print by Savage, 1956, 21" x 13-1/2" 60.00

Pillow cover, Honolulu, tropic themes and poem to mother, 17-1/4" sq plus fringe 50.00

Plate, Aloha from Hawaii, Hula maids and other colorful scenes, gold trim, 8" d 25.00

Postcard, real-photo, unused
Mauna Kea........................... 12.00
Pineapples at Harvest Time-Hawaiian Islands.............. 12.00

Hawaiian, stereograph, The Capitol Building for the Territory of Hawaii, Honolulu, history on back, Keystone View Company, #1047, **$12.**

Record, Hawaii, Melodies from Paradise, Longines Symphonetee Recording Society, presentation set 15.00

Salt and pepper shakers, pr, figural, suitcases................................. 24.00

Sheet music, *Hawaii Will Be Paradise Once More*, 1947..... 5.00

Scarf, Hawaiian Hula, silk, 35" sq 24.00

Shirt, man's
1960s, Islander 45.00
1970s, Royal Hawaiian 40.00

Stereoview, *Royal School, Honolulu, Hawaii*, Keystone View Co., #10161 .... 12.00

Swizzle stick
Hale Koa Hotel on the Beach, Waikiki, 6" l 1.00

Kahala Hilton, Honolulu, 6" l. 1.00
Spencecliff Restaurant's, 5-1/2" l 1.00

Tin, Hawaiian Coconut Snow, Lihue Kauai, Hawaii, 10-oz 35.00

Travel brochure, Hawaii Tourist Bureau, Honolulu, 1942, wear, 11" x 8-1/2" 15.50

View-Master reel, Hawaii Five-O, 1973, pack of three reels, booklet 22.00

Hazel Atlas

Hazel Glass Company merged with the Atlas Glass & Metal Company in 1902 to form Hazel Atlas. The company, based in Washington, Pennsylvania, aggressively developed ways to automate the glassware industry. Its primary output consisted of tableware, kitchen items, and tumblers.

Berry bowl, mkd "Hazel Atlas," 4-1/4" d 4.50

Bowl, cobalt blue, 7-1/2" d 45.00

Butter dish, cov, Hazel Atlas, iridescent, round 25.00

Cereal bowl, white opaque glass, black cowboy scenes............. 25.00

Custard cup, green 5.00

Child's mug, animal characters, bottom mkd "H/A," 3" h........ 20.00

Creamer, Aurora, blue, 4-1/4" h 25.00

Dinner plate, Moderntone, pink, 1940s, 9" d 7.50

Drinking glass, frosted, Florida souvenir, yellow state image, sailfish, alligator, palm tree and flamingo, 5" h 12.00

Egg cup, green........................... 7.00

Gravy boat, Florentine #2, yellow 65.00

Measuring cup, 8 oz, green 32.00

Mixing bowl
Cobalt blue, 7-1/2" d 45.00
Crystal, 6" d 12.00
Ivy dec on white, nested set of 4 .... 80.00

Old fashioned tumbler, Moroccan Amethyst, 3-1/4" h 15.00

Orange reamer, Criss-Cross, pink 295.00

Platter, Royal Lace, pink 40.00

Salad plate, Moderntone, mint green, 1940s, 6-3/4" d........................ 5.50

Salt and pepper shakers, pr, grapes, mkd.. 15.00

Sherbet, Moderntone, pink, early 1950s...................................... 5.00

Snack set
Capri Seashell, light blue...... 18.00

Hazel Atlas, drinking glass, red and blue decoration of lady watering garden flowers, **$20.**

Seashell, crystal 22.50

Sugar bowl, cov, Ovide, black, two handles 5.00

Syrup pitcher, green, tin lid, 6" h 70.00

Tom and Jerry set, two-qt punchbowl, six 6-oz mugs..... 75.00

Heisey Glass

Heisey Glass is a name most collectors recognize. That H in a diamond logo is easy to spot. But did you know that Heisey didn't mark any glass until 1901 and then used paper labels for years before starting to use the diamond mark? The Heisey Glass Company was known for its brilliant colors and excellent quality crystal.

For additional listings, see *Warman's Antiques & Collectibles* and *Warman's Glass*.

Reproduction alert.

Note: Prices listed below are for crystal unless otherwise indicated.

Heisey Glass, pitcher, 7" h, **$95.**

Heisey Glass, New Era pattern, sugar and creamer, "H" in diamond mark, **$65.**

Animal
Goose, wings half up 90.00
Plug horse, Oscar................ 115.00
Sparrow................................. 140.00

Ashtray, Empress, Sahara yellow
.... 90.00

Basket
Bow Tie, flamingo 125.00
Crystolite, 6" h 175.00
Daisy 140.00

Berry bowl, Beaded Swag, opalescent, metal foot 25.00

Cake plate
Crystolite 325.00
Rose, pedestal 325.00

Candelabra, Ridgleigh, bobeches and prisms, 7" h, pr 140.00

Candle Block, Crystolite, sq.... 20.00

Candlesticks, pr
Cascade, #142, 3-lite, crystal
.... 75.00
Tea Rose, 2-lite, fern blank
.... 120.00
Thumbprint and Panel, #1433
.... 140.00

Candy dish, cov, Empress, silver overlay, ftd 75.00

Card box, cov, Windsor, Royal Sensation cutting................. 125.00

Celery tray, Empress, Sahara yellow, 13" l.. 25.00

Champagne
Minuet 35.00
Orchid etch 55.00

Tudor 20.00

Cheese plate, Crystolite, two handles, 8" d.. 45.00

Coaster, Crystolite, Zircon....... 45.00

Cocktail, Rosalie 12.00

Cocktail shaker, Cobel, two quart
.... 55.00

Creamer, Crystolite.................. 25.00

Cream soup, Empress, Sahara yellow
.... 25.00

Cruet
Crystolite 55.00
Old Sandwich 60.00
Pleat and Panel, flamingo 65.00

Cup and saucer, Empress, Sahara yellow................................... 42.00

Floater bowl, Crystolite, 12" l, oval
.... 48.00

Floral bowl, Tear Drop, pink... 90.00

Goblet
Galaxy................................... 25.00
Narrow Flute......................... 30.00
Tudor 19.50

Iced tea tumbler, ftd
Orchid etch 65.00
Plantation 75.00

Jelly compote, Empress, Sahara yellow................................... 35.00

Jug, Queen Anne, dolphin ftd, silver overlay 125.00

Heisey Glass, milk pitcher, clear body, green angular handle, "H" in diamond mark, **$75.**

Lamp, Dolphin, candlestick type
.... 180.00

Madonna, 9" h, frosted 110.00

Mustard, cov, Flat Panel, #352 . 48.50

Nappy, Prison Stripe, #357, 4-1/2" d
.... 22.00

Nut dish, Empress, Sahara yellow
.... 20.00

Parfait, Orchid etch.................. 80.00

Punch cup, Crystolite 10.00

Salad plate, Impromptu, 7" d .. 12.00

Sandwich plate, center handle, Rose
.... 225.00

Sherbet, Orchid etch 24.00

Sherry, Renaissance, Old Glory stem, 2 oz 24.00

Soda tumbler
Coronation, #4054, 10 oz 9.50
Gascony, #3397 line, Ambassador, #452, etching, 12 oz, 5-1/2" h
.... 35.00

Sugar cube tray, Narrow Flute, flower and leaf cutting 45.00

Tankard, Greek Key 265.00

Toothpick holder, Waldorf Astoria
.... 115.00

Torte plate, Orchid etch, 14" d 90.00

Tumbler, ftd, Rose etch............ 50.00

Vase, Pineapple and Fan, green, 6" h
.... 40.00

Wine
Gascony, 2 oz, Sportsman etch
.... 60.00
Orchid etch 75.00

Hess Trucks and Oil Company Promos

We've got Hess Gas to thank for starting a wonderful line of collectible gas-related vehicles; 2004 marks the 40th Anniversary of Hess Trucks. Remember to save the original boxes and packaging for these collectible toys, along with any special promotional materials about the anniversary.

1971, Hess 800.00
1980, Hess 300.00
1984, 1986, and 1987, Hess 150.00
1990, Hess 55.00
1992, BP Oil, tanker................. 30.00
1992, Exxon, tanker................. 95.00
1993, BP Oil, car carrier 30.00
1993, Exxon, Mack truck......... 25.00
1993, Phillips 66, Marx tanker bank
.... 30.00
1993, Sunoco, Marx tanker bank
.... 40.00
1994, Citgo, tanker, orig card . 150.00
1994, Mobil, Marx tanker bank 45.00
1994, Texaco, tanker 50.00
1995, BP Oil, transporter and cars
.... 35.00

1995, Exxon, transporter and cars
.... 45.00
1995, Hess, MIB....................... 65.00
1995, Texaco, tanker 30.00
1996, Crown Petroleum, fire truck
.... 25.00
1996, Texaco, tanker, Olympics 30.00
1997, Exxon, tanker, chrome.... 25.00
1997, Gate, wrecker 25.00
1997, Texaco, 95th Anniversary train
set....................................... 300.00
1998, Crown Petroleum, tanker 30.00
1998, Marathon, tractor trailer. 45.00
1998, Texaco, Fire Chief Tank... 55.00
1999, Exxon, wrecker, gold....... 35.00
1999, Hess 40.00

Hess Trucks, atrol car, original batteries, MIB, **$20.**

1999, Texaco, Millennium Tanker
.... 40.00
2000, Hess 35.00
2000, Mobil, car carrier 40.00
2000, Texaco, Center Tanker 40.00
2001, Hess 20.00
2002, Hess, airplane transporter
.... 40.00

Hobby Horses

Children love hobby horses. From primitive homemade wooden creations to exquisite professionally made examples, these stick-and-head toys were loved and ridden for hours.

Cisco Kid, played with cond ... 30.00
Colt 45, vinyl head, wood stick,
played-with cond.................... 5.00
Mobo, c1920 .... 175.00
Rich Toys, played-with cond ... 15.00
Snoopy, vinyl head, 36" l wood stick,
played-with cond.................... 5.00
Zebra, stuffed white and black striped plush fur head, white mane, plastic eyes, red cord, wood stick, played-with cond................................. 7.50

Hobby horses, rocking horse, wood head, red burlap covering, straw fill, wood legs and rockers, red felt and leather saddle, hair name, marked "Cebasco, made in Germany," **$950.**

Hockey Memorabilia

Whether you're into field hockey or ice hockey, flea markets are a great place to score a goal with this collectible.

Autograph
Esposito, Phil, 8-1/4" x 10-7/8" color photo clipped from magazine, 1970s............... 15.00

Howe, Gordie, 8-3/8" x 11" front cover from *Sports Illustration*, March 11, 1974 issue 20.00
Hull, Bobby, 5" x 7" color photo card, 1987......................... 25.00

Trottier, Bryan, 8" x 10-3/4" front cover from *Sports Illustration*, Dec. 12, 1977 issue........... 18.00
Belt buckle, brass.................... 10.00

Hockey memorabilia, Starting Lineup Timeless Legends, Tony Esposito, **$10.**

Book, *Hockey's Great Rivalries*, Stan Fischler, Random House, 1974, hardcover, 151 pgs.................. **6.00**

Drinking glass, 3" d, 5-3/4" h, clear glass, Philadelphia Flyers-Stanley Cup Champions, redtone photo of posed team, 1974-75 .... **12.00**

Figure, Rod Gilbert, by Sports Impressions, 1994, limited edition of 3,950 pcs, NRFB, 6" h........ 35.00

Hockey puck, autographed
Belfour, Ed, Chicago............. 12.00
Burr, Shawn 3.00
Draper, Kris 15.00
Gadsby, Bill.......................... 10.00

Jersey, game-worn, NHL
Bouchard, Joel, Calgary Flames, #6, red, 96-97 .... 250.00
Cirella, Joe, Florida Panthes, #2, white, 94-95.................... 375.00
Crowder, Troy, Vancouver Vanucks, #18, white, 96-97............. 200.00
Holzinger, Brian, Tampa Bay Lighting, #9, black, 99-00 475.00
Laflamme, Christian, Chicago Blackhawks, #3, red, 98-99 .... 350.00

Mask, PCI, autographed by Patrick Roy... 70.00

Patch, 2"
Detroit Red Wings.................. 5.00
Montreal Canadiens 5.00
New York Rangers 6.00
Oilers 4.50
Quebec Nordiques.................. 5.00

Hockey memorabilia, National Hockey League puck, Art Ross Tyler, **$15.**

Starting Linuep figure
Ed Belfour, 1998 .... 12.50
Dominik Hasek, 1998........... 16.50
Gordie Howe, 1995, Timeless Legends 10.00
Brian Leetch, 1994................ 15.00
Mark Messier, 1996 .... 12.50
Felix Potvin, 1998................. 12.50
Joe Sakic, 1996...................... 17.50
Brendan Shanahan, 1996 ..... 10.00

Holiday Collectibles

Holidays have long been commemorated through a variety of collectibles, from postcards to cookie cutters. Today collectors enjoy searching through their favorite flea markets for more interesting items and then incorporating them with their décor. Here's a sampling of what's available.

For additional listings, see Christmas, Easter, and Halloween in this edition.

Holiday collectibles, Thanksgiving, postcard, two turkeys in dirigible, embossed, **$7.50.**

Bank, turkey, chalkware, tan, red and yellow, 1950s, USA, 11" h...... 85.00

Calendar, framed, November, 1933, from *St. Nicholas Magazine*, 8" x 12"... 25.00

Candles, pr, figural boy and girl pilgrims 5.00

Candy box, shamrock shape, cardboard, green, litho shamrocks on top, 8-1/2" h...................... 17.50

Candy container
Hat, green and gold cardboard hat, base label "Loft Candy Corp" 25.00
Turkey, wax, white, Fanny Farmer Candy, orig box 25.00

Decoration, honeycomb tissue paper, table top decoration, two-sided lithographed cardboard turkey, mkd USA, 8-1/2" h 15.00

Holiday collectibles, Valentine's Day, figure, girl with hearts on broad rimmed hat, red and pink layered hearts on her white skirt, gold trim, holding gold and blue parasol, marked "Samson," **$30.**

Holiday collectibles, Thanksgiving, postcard, "Wishing You A Happy Thanksgiving" on card among autumn leaves, **$5.**

Greeting card, The Mayflower, With Joyful Thanksgiving Wishes.... 8.00

Magazine cover, *Life,* March 15, 1923, cherub wearing Irish hat, playing harp 8.00

Noisemaker, crepe paper and cardboard 10.00

Pinback button, 1-1/2" d, Tournament of Roses, 1906, cream colored, red text, 3-1/4" diecut wood designed like float, hp pin flowers, green leaves, brown wooden wheel with text "Tournament of Roses, Pasadena, Cal" 30.00

Place card holder, 2-1/2" h, standing celluloid turkey, holder at base of metal spring legs 20.00

Plate, Fourth of July, Americana Holidays Collection, 1st in series, 1978, Edwin M. Knowles China Co., Bradford Exchange, 8-1/2" d. **20.00**

Postcard
Fourth of July, 3-1/4" x 5-3/4", black and white, emb image of American flag on gold pole, gold braids, text "You Are Invited To Attend Old Home Day and Carnival at Lehighton, Pa, July 4th, 1908, Thousands Are Coming, Will You Be One?" 12.00
New Year, 3-1/2" x 5-1/2", full color, lightly emb, 1907, European publisher 2.00

Holiday collectibles, Easter, figural diecut, rabbit holding three fold-out eggs, fold-out yellow tissue basket, **$45.**

Holiday collectibles, St. Patrick's Day, hats with green cellophane covering, each **$3,** porcelain leprechaun, **$7.50.**

St. Patrick's, 3-1/2" x 5-3/8", full color, red haired boy tipping hat, International Art Pub. 3.50
Thanksgiving, Pilgrim child, by Whitney, 1919 postmark ... 6.00

Puzzle, First Thanksgiving, Big Star Picture Puzzle, orig box, 10" x 13-1/2" 15.00

Tip tray, litho tin, Thanksgiving motif of boy with turkey, C.D. Kenny, Baltimore................... 90.00

Holly Hobbie

This cute country gal first appeared on the scene in the late 1970s, spreading her special brand of sunshine for several years thereafter. Holly Hobbie and her friends often had inspirational messages.

Bell, annual, bisque................. 40.00

Brunch bag, vinyl, zipper closure, Aladdin Industries, 1978, orig thermos 65.00

Holly Hobbie, doll, stuffed, printed facial features, yarn braids, blue calico hat, blue, white, and yellow calico patchwork dress, blue calico pantaloons, white socks, black strap shoes, some play wear, **$5.**

Children's play dishes, plastic, large plate, seven smaller plates, two mugs, mkd "Aluminum Specialty, Chilton Toys, Manitowoc, Wis.," 10 pcs.. 25.00

Christmas plate, 1972............. 15.00

Holly Hobbie, doll, Holiday Wishes, limited edition, MIB, **$20.**

Coffeepot, 1973, 8" h 60.00

Cradle, doll size........................ 40.00

Holly Hobbie, Coca-Cola glass, "Friendship makes the rough road smooth," 6" h, **$3.**

Creamer 25.00

Doll, Amy, 15" h........................ 30.00

Figure
Holly's Little Friend, 1971, MIB
.... 50.00
Robbie, seated with toy train
.... 25.00

Halloween costume, Ben Cooper,
American Greetings, small child
size, worn.............................. 15.00

Limited edition plate, Mother's Day,
10-1/2" d 20.00

Lunch box, metal, several different
scenes, 1979.......................... 40.00

Plaque, Love is a Way of Smiling with
Your Heart, ceramic, 1973
.... 18.00

Sugar bowl, cov 35.00

Teapot, white porcelain, green trim,
green and brown Holly, Tea for two
is twice as nice, 5-3/4" h........ 32.00

Wristwatch, Bradley, 1982......... 5.00

Holt-Howard

The partnership of brothers John and Robert J. Howard with A. Grant Holt created an import company in 1948 in Stamford, Connecticut. Robert designed some novelty ceramic containers that proved to be very successful.

Air freshner, Girl Christmas Tree
.... 65.00

Ashtray
Li'l Old Lace 50.00
Snow Baby 35.00

Bank, bobbing
Coin Clown........................ 135.00
Dandy Lion......................... 135.00

Bells, Elf Girls, pr.................... 55.00

Bud vase, Daisy Dorable.......... 70.00

Butter dish, cov, Red Rooster.. 65.00

Candelabra, Li'l Old Lace, spiral
.... 50.00

Candle climbers, set
Feathered Chicks, cracked egg floral
frog bases 78.00
Honey Bunnies 85.00
Ole Snowy............................ 48.00

Candleholders, pr
Ermine Angels with snowflake
rings 48.00
Green Holly Elf.................... 35.00
Madonna and Child 25.00
Red Rooster 30.00
Reindeer 38.00

Cereal bowl, Red Rooster........ 15.00

Coffee server, Red Rooster 65.00

Condiment jar, Pixieware, 1958
Cherries 120.00
Cocktail Cherries................ 135.00

Holt Howard, Pixiewares, condiment jars, mustard, ketchup, jam 'n' jelly, 5-1/2" h, each **$75.**

Cocktail Olives.................... 130.00
Cocktail Onions.................. 155.00

Cookie jar
Clown, pop-up.................... 225.00
Red Rooster 100.00

Cotton ball dispenser, Minnie
.... 75.00

Creamer and sugar
Red Rooster 55.00
Winking Santas 55.00

Crock, Merry Mouse, Stinky Cheese
.... 50.00

Dinner plate, Red Rooster 18.00

Egg cup, Red Rooster.............. 20.00

Head vase, My Fair Lady 75.00

Letter and pen holder, Santa. 55.00

Mug, Cozy Kittens 35.00

Napkin holder, Santa, 4"......... 25.00

Oil and vinegar, Cozy Kittens
.... 175.00

Salad dressing jar, Pixieware, 1959
Flat head, French, Italian, or
Russian Pixie.................. 140.00
Round head, French, Italian or
Russian Pixie.................. 125.00

Salt and pepper shakers, pr
Bell Bottom Gobs (sailors)... 50.00
Bunnies in baskets............... 32.00
Chattercoons, Peppy and Salty
.... 38.00
Cloud Santa 38.00
Holly Girls 20.00
Rock 'N' Roll Santas, on springs
.... 75.00
Snow Babies......................... 35.00

Home Front Collectibles

While the "boys" were off to World War II, there was a real effort here at home to influence those left behind to contribute to the war effort. Today, these items and their powerful messages are becoming choice collectibles.

Bookmark, Prevent Forest Fires, stiff orange paper, Hitler and Hirohito at top with blazing forest fire in background, US Dept of Agriculture, black and white reverse with text, 2-1/2" x 7"............. **45.00**

Game, V for Victory **40.00**

Jewelry
V-shaped victory pin, sterling silver with 30 rhinestones, 1-1/2" h, 1-1/4"............................... **60.00**
Sweetheart in script, sterling silver, gold-plated and red/white/blue Bakelite, orig box, 1-1/2" sq **95.00**

Matchbook, V for Victory, War Bond promotion, Diamond Match Co., unused, 1-1/2" x 3-3/4" **12.00**

Poster, You buy 'em, we'll fly 'em, Wilkinsons, US Government Printing Office, smiling pilot in open cockpit, khaki brown and green flight jacket and helmet, 27-7/8" x 20-1/4" **350.00**

Puzzle, Keep 'Em Flying, fighter planes, Perfect Picture Puzzle, For Victory Buy United States Savings Bonds and Stamps logo, 19-1/2" x 15-1/2" **50.00**

Sticker, Salvage Will Win The War, cartoon image of Japanese soldier choking on "v" of word "salvage," 1-1/2" x 2"............................. **25.00**

Window banner, fabric panel, printed in red, white, blue and bright gold, loop for hanging, 8-1/2" x 12"............................ **35.00**

Home front collectibles, picture frame, In Our Country's Service, That Free People Shall Not Perish From the Earth, red, white, and blue flags, eagle, composite photo of three servicemen, 16" x 20", **$20.**

Homer Laughlin

The Homer Laughlin Company is another dinnerware manufacturer that helped make East Liverpool, Ohio, a busy place. This company was producing white ware by the late 1880s. When the firm was sold to a group of investors from Pittsburgh, expansion soon followed. New plants were built in Ohio and West Virginia, and the dinnerware lines increased. Besides giving us such interesting patterns as Fiesta, and Harlequin, the firm also designed Kitchen Kraft and Riviera, plus thousands of others designs.

For additional listings, see *Warman's Americana & Collectibles* and *Warman's American Pottery & Porcelain*.

Baker, Mexicana, oval **25.00**

Berry bowl, American Provincial, Rhythm shape........................... **4.00**

Bowl, Cavalier, egg shell, numbered, set of four............................... **20.00**

Bread and butter plate
American Provincial, Rhythm shape **5.00**
Best China **4.50**

Butter, cov, Virginia Rose, jade **80.00**

Casserole, cov, large
Conchita **125.00**
Mexicana **145.00**

Cereal bowl, American Provincial, Rhythm shape.......................... **8.00**

Coffee mug, Best China **5.00**

Homer Laughlin, dinnerware set, Georgian, eggshell, multicolored floral decoration, silver trim, 56 pcs, **$45.**

Homer Laughlin, creamer, Century shape, silver decoration on ivory, **$8.50.**

Cup
Best China 3.50
Rhythm, forest green or gray
.... 7.00

Deep plate, Mexicana 45.00

Dessert bowl, Rhythm, yellow,
5-1/4" d 3.00

Dinner plate, Best China........... 3.25

Fruit bowl, Mexicana............... 15.00

Luncheon plate, American
Provincial, 8" d 8.00

Nappy, Rhythm, yellow, 8-3/4" d
.... 18.00

Pie baker, Mexicana................. 37.50

Plate, Virginia Rose, 9" d 7.50

Platter
American Provincial, Rhythm
shape 16.00
Best China, 11-1/2" l............... 5.00

Saucer
Best China 4.00
International House of Pancakes,
5-3/8" d............................. 20.00

Soup bowl, Rhythm, yellow....... 9.00

Tea service, Riviera, red, yellow,
mauve, green, and ivory cups and
saucers, yellow tea pot......... 500.00

Homer Laughlin, saucer, Century shape, multicolored floral decoration, **$2.50.**

Hooked Rugs

Once thought only as something to put on the floor, hooked rugs are now gaining folk art status. Collectors recognize the interesting designs and colors, plus the many hours of artistry involved in each piece. When cleaned and put on a stretcher frame, a vintage hooked rug can make a lovely decorating statement.

Baskets of colorful flowers, black, dark brown, and gray ground, flower and leaves in each corner divided by multicolored borders, 37" x 19-1/2", light overall wear 990.00

Chickens, central reserve with eight black and gray chickens surrounded by red and pink flower blossoms on top sides, brown and black horse below, 36" x 27-1/2", stretched on wooden frame, fading, wear 690.00

Country village, train in center, church and houses on the green, horse drawn carriages, people, and farm animals, flowering trees and shrubs, blue and purple border, 35" x 75", losses to center and border 1,530.00

Deer, running, multicolored scalloped border, blue edge binding, 34" x 21-1/2" 75.00

Dog, oblong central panel, surrounded by line and floral borders, dark orange, tan, dark purple, red, green, and blue-gray, Frost, 37" x 19-1/2", minor edge wear 275.00

Eagle motif, rope border, 54" x 37" 1,000.00

Geometric, multicolored, 40" x 25", some edge fraying 65.00

Hearts, two center hearts, star in each corner, multicolored striped field, mounted on cotton backing, stretched onto wood frame, 30-3/4" x 40-1/8", minor losses 2,115.00

Horse
Black horse on blue oval medallion, four lions and four red flowers spaced evenly around outside, dark gray braid border, hooked by PA woman, c1940-50, 42" x 46" 975.00
Horse head in center, multicolored angled line borders, olive green corner blocks, horse's head center, burgundy, red, and brown center ground, 26" x 44-1/2", mounted to stretcher, areas of loss and wear................. 260.00
Red horse, black bridle, striped mane and tail, tan medallion, two tone brown with gold background, blue and ivory corner leaves, wreath around medallion with red berries, black cloth binding, minor wear and small hole at horse's back, 24-1/2" x 41".................. 315.00

House, flanked by two trees, worked in shades of green, blue, red, and brown, mottled blue and tan ground, 16-1/2" x 26-1/2", mounted on wood frame 725.00

Hooked rugs, multicolored brick pattern, black edging, **$85.**

Lighthouse, red and white striped lighthouse in coastal setting, light blue sky with clouds, 22" x 34-1/2" 200.00

Owl, full moon, oval, late 19th C 950.00

Parcheesi board design, multicolored, 37-1/2" x 24" ... 50.00

Rabbit, gray, flanked by red tulips in each corner on dark background, scalloped pink-lavender fabric border, 25" x 18" 690.00

Welcome, semi-circle, Cape Cod origin 1,750.00

Horse Collectibles

Some collectors specialize in items related to the care of horses, others search for items used for riding, and some prefer items with images of horses.

Horse collectibles, valentine, early airplane over heart with little girl feeding horse, fold-down type, **$30.**

Bank, Beauty, cast iron, 4-1/2" h 300.00

Bells, worn leather strap with over 40 nickel bells, tug hook 225.00

Bit, eagle, mkd "G. S. Garcia" . 775.00

Book
Horse Power-A History of the Horse and Donkey in Human Societies, Brock 38.00
The Black Stallion, Walter Farley, 1st ed., dust jacket 25.00

Bridle, Calvary, mule bridle, brass "US" spots 225.00

Bridle rosette, glass with rose motif inside, mkd "Chapman" 40.00

Clock, brass horse standing next to western saddle, wood base, United 170.00

Contest flyer, Dan Patch, illus 28.00

Cookie jar, McCoy, Circus Horse, McCoy 50.00

Curry comb, tin back, leather handle, early 1900s 45.00

Decanter, Man O'War, Ezra Brooks 25.00

Fruit crate label, Bronco, bucking horse 25.00

Game, Pony Express, cast-metal horses, 1940s 85.00

Lasso, horsehair 135.00

Magazine, *Western Horseman*, Vol 1, #1, 1935 .... 30.00

Men's brush, horse head figural handle 10.00

Mug, Clydesdales, Budweiser, Christmas, Ceramarte, 1985 . 50.00

Newspaper, Horse & Stable Weekly, Boston, Jan. 2, 1891 .... 35.00

Horse collectibles, Black Beauty game, Milton Bradley Co., **$65.**

Horse collectibles, prize ribbons, assorted events, assorted shapes and colors, each **$3** to **$5.**

Postcard, bucking bronco, cowboy flying off, rodeo in Prescott, Ariz., 1920s 15.00

Saddle, McClellan type, large fenders for leg protection, early 1900s 900.00

Snow dome, Budweiser Clydesdales, 1988 limited edition 75.00

Sign, 14" x 20", The Stewart Clipping Machine, colorful image of horses in court room jury box, machine in center, cardboard litho, C.8.5 .... 475.00

Toy, Arabian Trotter, tin and composition wind-up, orig key, orig box 130.00

Tray, Genessee Twelve Horse Ale, horse team illus, 12" d 115.00

Horse Racing

Man's love for competition has long been reflected in horse racing. Smarty Jones caught the attention of many folks this past season, who will be his successor? Here's a sample of some collectibles on today's market.

Also see Kentucky Derby Glasses in this edition.

Horse racing, tile, "Favonius, Derby Winner 1871," ATCO, 6-1/8" square, **$30.**

Ashtray
Count Fleet, sgd by Lynn Bogue Hunt, ceramic, 5-1/4" sq 30.00
Kentucky Derby, 1976, Galt House, Louisville, smoke glass, 7" d 30.00

Autograph, Eddie Arcaro, 3" x 5" white chard, blue ballpoint autograph............................... 15.00

Badge
2-1/4" x 3", brightly silvered, slightly convex brass shield, Pocono Downs Security, 1950s 30.00
3" d, celluloid, full color, inscribed "Budweiser Million, Second Running/August 29, 1982," Arlington Park 2.50

Festival pin, Kentucky Derby
1974, blue and silver 85.00
1976, blue and silver 65.00
1977, green and gold............ 65.00
1978, red and gold................ 65.00
1992, gold tone 85.00
1993, gold tone 85.00

Game, Suffolk Downs, Corey Game Co., © 1938, 16" x 16-1/2" box 25.00

Gambling device, chrome stop watch case, glass cover, diecut celluloid grandstand in center, surrounded by eight openings, each with numbered running horse, early 1900s, 1-5/8" d 150.00

Pegasus parade pin, 1997 ...... 85.00

Pinback button
Silky Sullivan Winner, multicolor, white ground, blue letters, c1950 .... 20.00
Topeka Derby Day, Sept. 13, 1904, sepia 20.00

Print, Currier & Ives, "The Grand Racer Kington, by Spendthrift," 1891, unmatted, unframed . 475.00

Horse racing, Stevensgraph of Fred Archer, woven silk portrait with Prince of Wales colors, blue jacket with red sleeves, mounted in original mat, **$145.**

Sheet music, *Dan Patch March* 40.00

Soup cup, china, Beautiful Wheeling Downs, mkd "Shenango Restaurant China Soup Cup," 3-1/2" h, 3-1/4" d 30.00

Souvenir book, 1941, 67th running, 12-3/4" x 9-3/4" 85.00

Souvenir plate, Jorge Velasquez, Meadowlands jockey, Belcrest Fine China, ©1983 by Daily Racing Form, Inc, 8-1/2" d 25.00

Tray, Reynolds Aluminum, 1956, 14" x 18", some wear.................. 225.00

Trophy, silver, typical............... 50.00

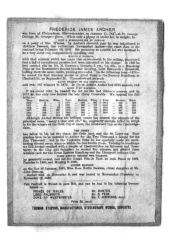

Reverse of Stevensgraph giving bio information about Fred Archer, including races won, famous horses, etc.

Hot Wheels

Harry Bradley, an automotive designer; Howard Newman, a Mattel designer; Elliot Handler, chairman of Mattel; and Jack Ryan, also of Mattel, joined forces to produce the first diecast Hot Wheels cars in 1968.

Accessories
Case, Sizzlers Race..................... 75.00
Full Curve Accessory Pak..... 12.00
Gas Pumper, Mattel 12.00
Snake Mountain Challenge . 20.00

Cars and trucks
Ambulance, #71......................... 5.00

American Tipper, redline, 1976 .... 65.00
Assault Crawler, #624 .... 5.00
Auburn 852, #94...................... 20.00
Baja Bruiser, #8258, orange, 1974 .... 75.00
Beach Bomb, green 75.00
Boss Hoss, #6406, 1971 .... 75.00

Hot Wheels, 1993 McDonald's race car, **$3.**

Carnival, #328, trademark 6 80.00
Doll Mother, stylized bee mark
.... 135.00
Friend or Foe, #434 .... 245.00
Happy Birthday, #176/0, 6" h
.... 215.00
Just Resting........................ 175.00

Little girl, #475 .... 45.00
Mischief Maker 200.00
Sensitive Hunter 210.00
She Loves Me, She Loves Me Not
.... 215.00
Tuneful Angel, #359, trademark 6
.... 45.00

Village Boy, #51/2/0, trademark 1
.... 115.00
Waiter, #154/0, trademark
2 .... 130.00

Hummel items, doll, girl, **$45.**

Hummel items, Chick Girl, full bee mark, 57/I, **$155.**

Hummel items, wall pocket, Birdwatcher, imp 360/C, Goebel, W. Germany, 1958, **$70.**

Hunting

Flea markets make great hunting, whether you're looking for big game or small treasures. Substitute a camera for the usual rifle or trap, and bring along a bag to tote your catch in.

Book
Handling Your Hunting Dog, 3rd ed, by J. Earl Bufkin, Purina Mills, 1942, 64 pgs **15.00**
The Sportsman's Almanac: A Guide to the Recreational Uses of America's Public Lands, with Special Emphasis on Hunting and Fishing, Carley Farquhar, 1963, 1st ed., 453 pgs, small tear to dj 9.50
Broadside, litho, DuPont Powders, two anxious duck hunters peeking out of camp, "Just look at 'em," image by Edmund Osthaus, c1910, 12" w, 14-1/2" h 50.00
Calendar, 1977, hunting scenes, advertises Weaver & Son Food Market, Merriam, Kansas, unused 12.00

Call
Duck, Herter's orig box 40.00
Turkey, orig box.................... 35.00
Catalog
Kirtland Bros Sporting Goods, 16 pgs, 1924 .... 15.00
National Target & Supply, Washington, DC, 1930s, 131 pgs, 8-1/2" x 11", Handbook & Catalog, cuts of targets..... 40.00
Old Town Canoe Co., Old Town, ME, 1956, 48 pgs, 6" x 8" 75.00
Weber Lifelike Fly Co., Stevens Point WI, 1938, 96 pgs, 6-1/4" x 9", No. 19 .... 60.00
Winchester Rifle, John Wayne cover, 16 pgs, 1982 .... 8.50
Counter felt, Dead Shot Powder, "Kill Your Bird Not Your Shoulder," multicolored on black, trimmed 90.00
Handbook, Winchester Ammunition, 112 pgs, 1951 .... 13.50
License
Deer, New York State, 1936, pinback style 35.00
Game, California, encased in slotted metal frame, 1941 .... 5.00
Game, New York State, 1918, red and white, serial number in blue, brass lapel stud fastener, 1-1/2" d 75.00

Game, Pennsylvania, 1949, simulated red leather case 20.00
Guide, Ontario, 1935, black and white, red numerals, worn 20.00

Magazine, *Hunting and Fishing,* April 1935 .... 24.00
Photograph
Hunter with ducks, hand-tinted, dated 1930, framed, 12-1/8" x 19-1/4" 20.00
Hunting club members posing with shotguns, 6" x 8" 145.00
Pinback button
Dupont Smokeless Powder, multicolored, fall hunting scene, pair of black and white pointer dogs, black lettering Dupont Smokeless-The Champion's Powder 100.00

Hunting collectibles, calendar plate, 1912, Winchester, rifle with grouse, autumn scene, **$75.**

Hunting collectibles, license, Penna 1939 Hunter, Resident, red and white enameled metal, **$30.**

Hot Wheels, Key Force, Swingshot Dune Buggy, #1862, MIB, **$20.**

Buzz Off, #6976, blue, 1974..... 90.00
Bywayman, #220, pearl white . 12.00
Cadillac '59, #154 .... 6.00
Camaro Z28, #33, red, chrome base 46.00
Captain America, #2879, white, 1979 .... 175.00
Cement Mixer, #6452, 1970 ... 60.00
Chevy, '57, Ultra Hots, #47 .... 110.00
Circus Cats, #3303, white, 1975 .... 75.00
Corvette, billionth.................... 10.00
Custom Firebird, blue 40.00
Custom VW Bug, redline, 1968 .... 125.00
Datsun 200XS, #3255, maroon, Canada, 1982 .... 175.00
Delivery Truck, #52 .... 32.00
Designer Dreams................. 17.50
Digger, #643 .... 5.00
Dump Truck, #38, steel bed...... 7.00
Dune Daddy, #6967, light green, 1975 .... 75.00
Earthmover, #16..................... 85.00
Emergency Squad, #7650, red, 1975 .... 65.00

Evil Weevil, #485 .... 3.00
Express Lane, #1067, orange, "Floyd's Market" 3.00
Fat Fendered '40, #216, purple 20.00
Ferrari, #312, red enamel......... 50.00
Fire Truck, 1980 .... 2.00
Fireworks 20.00
Fleetside, purple 35.00
Ford Bronco, #56, turquoise ... 18.00
Golden Knights VW Bug 20.00
GT Racer, #598, 1995 .... 3.00
Hard Rock Café I.................... 25.00
Hot Heap, #6219, 1968 .... 65.00
Jet Threat, #6179, 1976........... 60.00
Jiffy Lube, milk truck, red....... 10.00
Marrow Foundation 30.00
McDonald's, Tattoo Machine, 1993 .... 3.00
Mercedes 500 SL, 1997 .... 26.00
Motorcross Team Van, #2853, red, 1979 .... 125.00
Neet Streeter, #9510, chrome, 1976 .... 40.00
Penske 70 Mustang Mach 1 . 15.00
Penske S'Cool bus, silver........ 13.00
Poison Pinto, #9240, green, blackwall, 1977 .... 30.00
Porsche 911, #6972, orange, 1975 .... 65.00
Race Ace, #2620, white, 1968 .... 75.00
Red Baron, #6963, red, blackwall, 1977 .... 25.00
Rock Buster, #9088, yellow, blackwall, 1977 .... 15.00

Sand Crab, #6403, 1970
.... 60.00
Silhouette, #6209, 1979 .... 90.00
Super Van, #9205, chrome, 1976
.... 40.00
Swingfire, #214 .... 6.00
Tail Gunner, #29 .... 75.00
Toyota MR2 Rally, #122......... 20.00
Tractor, #145, yellow.............. 10.00
Tractor Trailer, 1979 .... 1.00
Van de Kamps, mail in premium, Hiway Hauler Truck, 1996 .... 24.00
Vega Bomb, redline, 1975 .... 85.00
VW Golf, #106, white 50.00
Waste Wagon, redline, 1971
.... 325.00
Wheel Loader, #641, orange and black 4.00
Whip Creamer, redline, #1870
.... 60.00
Zender Fact 4, #125 .... 15.00

Sets
25th anniversary, 1993, five cars
.... 38.00
30th anniversary, 30 cars 150.00
Christmas, 1999.................... 55.00
Christmas, 2000.................... 55.00
Drive-In, three cars................ 30.00
Holiday, 1995 .... 80.00
Lowrider 25.00
Muscle Cars, Set #1, two cars.. 15.00
Night at the Races 18.00

Howdy Doody

"What time is it kids? Howdy Doody Time!" Every Howdy Doody Show started with Buffalo Bob Smith asking the Peanut Gallery that question. It was a great kids show, and today's collectors are happily searching for items relating to Howdy, Mr. Bluster, Clarabelle, and the other characters.

Comic book, *Howdy Doody,* #3 1950 .... 10.00
Cup, yellow plastic, Howdy Doody's face at top, Gotham Ware...... 30.00

Fork and spoon, Kagran, Crown Silverplate, 4-1/2" l 95.00
Game, Howdy Doody Card Game, Russell Mfg. Co., orig box 75.00
Jelly glass, "Here Comes Music for Doodyville Circus," Welch's,

variation with no animals in circus wagon, early 1950s 35.00
Key chain, three-dimensional, NRFP 4.50

Howdy Doody, bank, Howdy Doody and pig, 7" h, **$35.**

Little Golden Book
Howdy Doody's Circus Book, 1950
.... 35.00
Howdy Doody & Santa Claus,
1955, 1st ed 38.00

Marionette
Howdy Doody, composition, 14" h
.... 475.00
Clarabelle, new strings, 14" h
.... 300.00
Princess Winter, Spring, Summer,
Fall, composition, cracked, 14"
.... 500.00

Night light, head moves, 6" h
.... 275.00

Pinback button, It's Howdy Doody
Time!, orange and white 18.00

Record spindle spinner, 4" h
.... 275.00

Ring, Poll Parrot, adjustable... 125.00

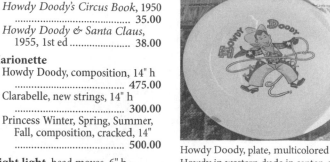

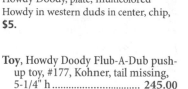

Howdy Doody, plate, multicolored
Howdy in western duds in center, chip,
$5.

Toy, Howdy Doody Flub-A-Dub push-
up toy, #177, Kohner, tail missing,
5-1/4" h 245.00

Ventriloquist dummy, composition
and cloth, Reliable, Canada, 1950s,
21" h 450.00

Hubley Toys

Hubley Manufacturing was founded in Lancaster, Pennsylvania, in 1894. The company's first toys were made of cast iron. By 1940, cast iron had been phased out and replaced with other metals and plastic.

Bookends, pr, Hunting Dog, bronze,
orig paint, c1925, 4-1/2" h... 195.00

Cap gun
Army .45-caliber pistol, nickel-
plated, brown checkered grips,
finish, 1945, 6-1/2" l 75.00
Hawk .45-caliber automatic, plastic
pearlized grip, 5-1/4" l 45.00
Pet 15.00

Doorstop
Dolly, 9-1/2" h, pink bow in blond
hair, holding doll in blue dress,
white apron, yellow dress **365.00**
Lilies of the Valley, cast iron, mkd
146, 10-1/2" h, 7-1/2" w
.... 250.00
Sealyham, full figure, cream and
tan dog, red collar 675.00

Toy, airplane
Single prop, die-cast, orange
and yellow, folding wings, 11"
wingspan 145.00

Hubley Toys, airplane, P-40, diecast,
yellow wings, orange body, rubber
wheels, 8-1/4" wingspan, 7-3/4" l, **$24.**

U.S. Army, retractable wheels,
paint chips, tires cracked, 7-1/2"
wingspan, 6" l 75.00
P-38, paint chips, 7-1/2" x 8 1/2"
.... 50.00

Toy, cars and trucks
Coupe, very worn orig paint,
deteriorated white rubber tires,
6-1/4" l 300.00

Delivery truck, worn old
repaint, label on side of panel,
deteriorated white rubber tires,
4-3/4" l 100.00
Fire truck, ladder wagon, worn old
paint, some touch-up repair,
mismatched driver, accessories
missing, 13-1/2" l 80.00
Kiddie toy race car, metal, nickel
plated driver, red, black rubber
tires, 1950s, 7" l 30.00
Milk cream truck, 1930s, one tire
missing, paint chips, 3-3/4" l
.... 365.00
Racer, driver, old worn paint, some
rust, labeled inside body, 7" l
.... 165.00
Surf 'n' Sand, jeep and boat with
trailer, blue and white, orig
window box, 15" l 95.00

Toy, motorcycle
Cast iron, replaced handle bars,
60% orig paint 200.00
Police Department Motorcycle,
Kiddietoy, 5" l, 1950s 165.00

Hull Pottery

In 1905, Addis E. Hull purchased the Acme Pottery Company in Crooksville, Ohio. In 1917, the A. E. Hull Pottery Company commenced producing art pottery, novelties, stoneware and kitchenware, including the Little Red Riding Hood line that would become one of their best sellers. Most items had a matte finish with shades of pink and blue or brown as the dominant colors.

Following a disastrous flood and fire in 1950, J. Brandon Hull reopened the factory in 1952 as the Hull Pottery Company. These newer pieces usually have a glossy finish and tend to have a more modern look. The company currently produces items for florists, e.g. the Regal and Floraline lines.

For additional listings, also see *Warman's Americana & Collectibles*.

Coaster/ashtray, gingerbread man
.... 20.00

Cornucopia
Blossom Flite, pink and black, 12" l
.... 115.00
Ebbtide, Mermaid on Shell, rose
and turquoise glaze, 7-1/2" h,
9" w 200.00

Creamer, Waterlily, L-19, 5" h
.... 75.00

Head vase, Newborn, #92, 5-3/4" h
.... 65.00

Hull pottery, vase,
pink, birds, white
interior, marked
"Hull USA,
©1957," 10-7/8" h,
$40.

Hull pottery, vases, pair, **$60.**

Pitcher, Magnolia, yellow matte glaze,
#5, 7" h 185.00

Planter, Parrot 60.00

Salt and pepper shakers, pr
Apple 25.00
Mushroom, 3-3/4" h 20.00

Tea set, Blossom Flite, teapot with lid,
creamer, sugar with lid 200.00

Teapot
Dogwood, 507, 5-1/2" h 350.00
Waterlily, L-18, 6" h 225.00

Tray, gingerbread man, brown
.... 65.00

Vase
Bow-Knot, B10, 10-1/2" h .. 495.00
Dogwood, 504, 8-1/2" h 150.00
Magnolia, H17, 12-1/2" h ... 250.00
Waterlily, L-8, 8-1/4" h 165.00

Wall pocket, cup and saucer, yellow
background, pink flower 40.00

Window box, Woodland Gloss, rose
shading to lime-green, W14, 4" h,
10" l 80.00

Hull pottery, wall pocket, pitcher shape,
floral decoration, **$135.**

Hummels

Based on original drawings by Berta Hummel, these charming children have delighted collectors for generations. Production of her figurines started in 1935.

Annual plate, Singing Lesson, 1979
.... 50.00

Annual bell, bas relief, 3rd ed, 1980,
MIB 70.00

Ashtray
Happy Pastime, #62, full bee mark,
c1950-57 .... 245.00
Joyful, #33, stylized bee mark,
c1958-64 .... 220.00

Singing Lesson, #34, full bee mark,
c1950-57 .... 285.00

Bank, Little Thrifty, #118, stylized
bee, 1958-64 .... 230.00

Bell, 1975, orig box 65.00

Bookends, pr, Apple Tree, trademark
5, 1972-79 .... 320.00

Calendar, 1955, 12 illus 15.00

Candleholder, Herald Angels, #37,
full bee mark, c1950-57 ...... 300.00

Christmas plate, 1974, orig box
.... 55.00

Figure
Apple Tree Girl, #141/I, 6" h **290.00**
Artist, #304, trademark 6..... 90.00
Barnyard Hero, #195/2/0,
trademark 2 .... 115.00
Builder, #305, trademark 4 .. 80.00

Cigarette collectibles, Winston sign, tin, **$40.**

Bottle opener, Starr "X" Coca-Cola opener with original box, **$22.50.**

Pepsi-Cola, "Bigger Better" Pepsi thermometer, tin, 16" h, **$250.**

Doll, Cabbage Patch Kids, **$35.**

Breweriana, Schlitz glass, 5-1/4" h, **$3.**

Still bank, Conoco Super Motor Oil, **$20.**

Batman, Thermos brand plastic lunch box and thermos, **$20.**

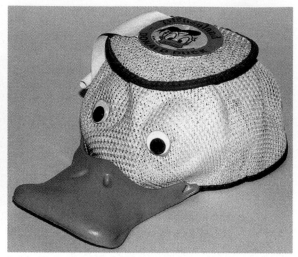

Disneyland and Disney World, Donald Duck Disneyland hat, Walt Disney Productions label, 9-1/2" l, **$20.**

Battery-operated toy, red Volkswagen Beetle, metal, 10" l, **$40.**

Bakelite, poker chip set, **$395.**

Bookends, brass squirrel, one shown, 5-1/4" h, pair, **$45.**

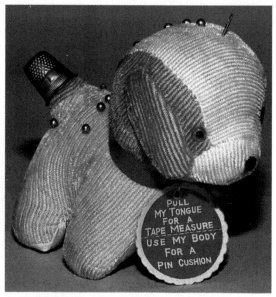

Dog collectible, pincushion with tape measure (tongue) and thimble holder (tail), 4" h, **$25.**

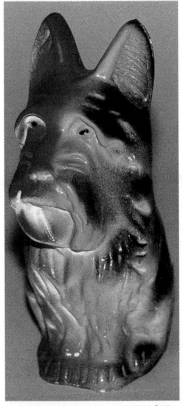

Carnival chalkware, dog, 6-1/2" h, **$15.**

Christmas collectible, "Twas the Night Before Christmas" tin with Santa on rooftop, 2-1/4" h (excluding handle), 4-3/4" l, **$358.**

Christmas collectible, postcard,
St. Nicholas in green robe, **$10.**

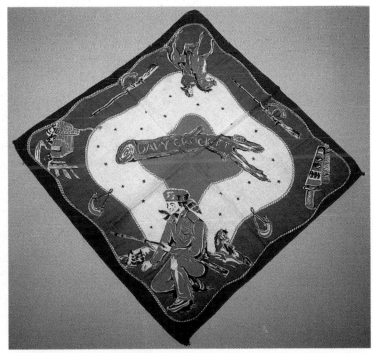

Davy Crockett, handkerchief, **$40.**

Dr. Seuss, Cat in the Hat centerpiece, Hallmark, original envelope, **$45.**

Lone Ranger gun and holster set, holster only, original box, **$500.**

Calendar plate, 1961, Royal China, **$15.**

Clock, celluloid, 3" h, **$30.**

Geisha girl, salt shaker, 3-1/4" h, **$15.**

Blue and white pottery/stoneware, pitcher, Iris design, rim chip, 8-3/4" h, **$220.**

Flow Blue, Copeland, covered soup tureen, **$650.**

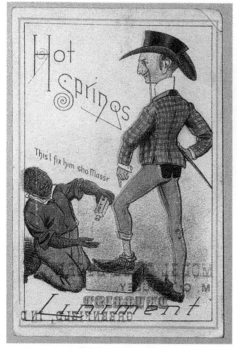

Black memorabilia, Hot Springs Liniment trade card, **$30.**

Hallmark, 1993 Holiday Barbie ornament, 1st in a series, MIB, **$55.**

Hummel, Telling Her Secret, full bee mark, 6-3/4" h, **$170.**

Lefton China, bisque figurine, girl with cat, 6" h, **$8.**

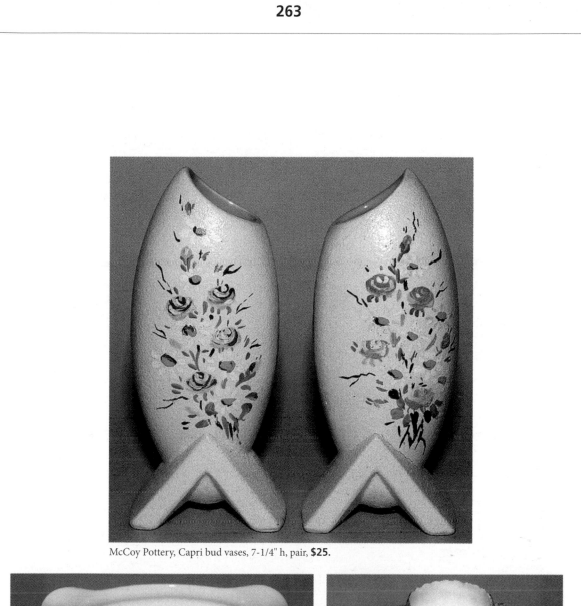

McCoy Pottery, Capri bud vases, 7-1/4" h, pair, **$25.**

Noritake China, Azalea pattern, gravy boat and attached underplate, **$50.**

Cup and saucer, demitasse cup with petal-shaped saucer, pink, gold and white, unmarked, 2-1/8" h, **$5.**

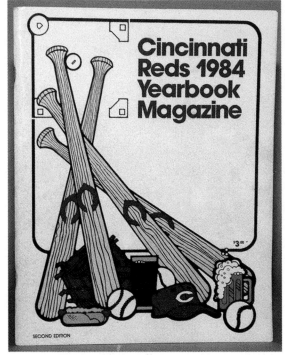

Baseball memorabilia , *Cincinnati Reds 1984 Yearbook Magazine,* 56 pages, 10-7/8" x 8-1/2", **$15.**

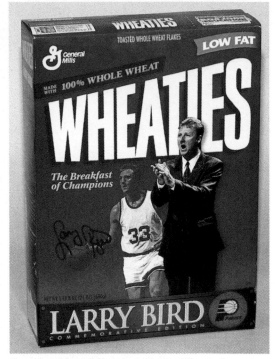

Cereal box, Larry Bird commemorative Wheaties box, unopened, **$6.50.**

Baseball memorabilia, Wilson professional softball, original box, **$25.**

Postcard, flag motif, Dexter Press, **25 cents.**

Ice Cream Collectibles

Cold and creamy, ice cream can be the perfect accompaniment to a few hours at the flea market. But, if your tastes run to ice cream collectibles instead, some great examples may be waiting for you, too.

For additional listings, see *Warman's Americana & Collectibles* and *Warman's Advertising*.

Ice cream collectibles, box, Hoffman's Ice Cream, pint, Manufactured by Hoffman-Minick Co., Chambersburg, PA, cream colored ground, green lettering, **$35.**

Advertising trade card, The Crown Ice Cream Freezer, shows cherubs, American Machine Co., Philadelphia, 2-7/8" x 4-3/8" . **15.00**

Ashtray
Castles National Dairy Ice Cream, True-Flavor, pale creamy white china, red, yellow, and black oval decal logo, 1940s, 4-1/2" d **12.00**
Carnation Ice Cream, glass **5.00**

Book cover, 11-1/2" x 18", Breyers, red, green, and yellow space rocket and related motifs, galaxy background, early 1960s, unused **15.00**

Box, Sclater's Superior Ice Cream, Marion Drug Co., Marion, Va. **12.00**

Cone holder, Sealtest Ice Cream, "Get the best - Get Sealtest," red with white lettering, paper with a metal rim, 5" h **12.00**

Mold
Flag on a shield, E. & Co., N.Y., 3-1/2" x 4"...................... **195.00**

Liberty Bell, mkd 605, 3-1/2" x 4"
.... **65.00**
Wishbone, mkd 322, 5-1/2" x 4"
.... **145.00**

Pinback
3-1/2" h, Cherry-Ripe Ice Cream, two dark red cherries on green stems and leaves, white ground, black lettering, bar pin fastener, 1940s **20.00**
3-1/2" h, National Ice Cream Week, white lettering on orange ground, bar pin fastener, 1950s **12.00**

Salt and pepper shakers, pr, Safe-T Cup ice cream cone, 3-1/2" h **35.00**

Scoop
Gilchrist #12, 11" l **55.00**
Gilchrist #31, wooden handle, 10-1/2" l........................... **60.00**

Sheet music, 9-1/4" x 12", folder and insert sheet of words and music for *I Scream-You Scream-We All Scream for Ice Cream*, ©1927 .... **25.00**

Spoon, red plastic, long handle, ice cream cone top **1.00**

Top, litho tin with wooden shaft, "Ask for Jersey Maid Milk and Ice Cream" and "Can You Spin It-80 Seconds," red on cream ground, 1915 patent date **20.00**

Towel, linen, embroidered ice cream sundae, 15" x 26" **12.00**

Ice cream collectibles, bag, unused, Frozen Drumstick, copyright I. C. Parker, 1946, list of ingredients, orange and brown printing on tan, **$10.**

Toy, ice cream truck, tin, friction, Japan, 1960 on license plate, 3-1/2" h, 8" l.......................... **85.00**

Tray, Southern Dairies, Sealtest Ice Cream **115.00**

Whistle, plastic, Dairy Queen, ice cream cone shape, 3-1/4" h **5.00**

Wrapper, Huskey Ice Cream Bar, snow dog................................ **15.00**

Ice cream collectibles, ice cream scoop, green handle, squeeze type, **$25.**

Ice Skating

Ice skating is actually an old past time, going back to a time when skates were hand made and much cruder than today's finely shaped skates. Collecting ephemera related to skating is also quite popular with today's generation.

Bobbing head, 6" h, Inky Dinky, bear, gray painted composition, ice skates, white scarf, name in black, Ice Follies Shipstand and Johnson, head professionally restored, 1960s 40.00

Christmas ornament, Hallmark, Kristi Yamaguchi, 2000, MIB 12.50

Costume, girl's, So-Fine label, 1950s Green wool, white rayon lining, white criss-cross lacing in front 35.00
Navy wool, embroidered flower trim 35.00

Doll
Ideal, Dorothy Hamill, 1970s, MIB 35.00
Mattel, Skipper, red skating outfit, 1963, MIB 95.00

Figure, Precious Moments, Dropping In For Christmas, boy skating, 1982, 5-1/2" h, MIB 45.00

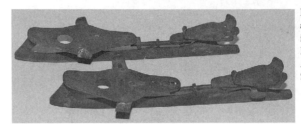

Ice skating, adjustable cast iron skates, Peck & Snyder's American Club, **$20.**

Ice skates
Child's, aluminum, leather straps, beginner's type, double runners, c1950 .... 20.00
Figure, white leather uppers, metal blades, worn, c1960 .... 10.00
Hockey, brown leather uppers, wide blades, c1960 .... 25.00

Patch
Mineola Skating Rink, Long Island, NY, 1940s 7.50
Planert Skate Club, 1930s 5.00

Pin, skater, enamel sweater, pearl fringed skirt, pearl on hat, 1-3/4" h 15.00

Program
Holiday On Ice, 30th anniversary, 1975 .... 20.00
Ice Follies, Philadelphia, 1960 .... 5.00

Tray, Coca-Cola, 1941, woman with skates 185.00

Illustrators

Many flea market adventurers are starting to specialize in one or more specific illustrators. You'll see them scouring through magazines for illustrations and advertisements by their favorites. Other collectors of illustrated items devote their search to prints, calendars, books, and other types of ephemera.

Book
Bye, Randolph, *Disappearing Depots* 85.00

Illustrators, Fern Bisel Peat, Birds, softcover, The Saalfeld Publishing Co., 1943, **$15.**

Chandler, Howard, *An Old Sweetheart of Mine* by James Whitcomb Riley, 1903 ...... 65.00
Fisher, Harrison, *Love Finds the Way* by Paul Leicester Ford, Dodd Mead & Co., 1904 .. 75.00
Peat, Fern Bisel, *The Sugar-Plum Tree and Other Verses* by Eugene Field 45.00

Magazine cover, matted and framed
Fisher, Harrison, *Saturday Evening Post*, May 18, 1907, The Man Hunt 80.00
Fisher, Harrison, *Saturday Evening Post*, June 19, 1915, Horse Woman 75.00
Fisher, Harrison, *Ladies Home Journal*, September 1909. 50.00

Postcard
Atwell, Mabel Lucie 12.00
Clapsaddle, Ellen Hattie 25.00
Outcault, R 17.50

Illustrators, Grace Drayton, postcard, "Could You Love A Little Girl Like Me," artist signed, **$15.**

Print
Smith, Jessee Wilcox, Goldilocks
and the Three Bears, © 1907, 16"
x 10-3/4" 90.00

Leyendecker, J.C., Pay Day, ©1906,
P.F. Collier and Son, 16" x 10-3/4"
.... 80.00
Remington, Frederic, Shadows
at the Water Hole, © 1907, P.F.
Collier and Son, 16" x 10-3/4"
.... 70.00

Imari

Imari is a Japanese porcelain that dates back to the late 1770s. Early Imari has a simple decoration, unlike later renditions that are also known as Imari. As the Chinese and, later, the English copied and interpreted this pattern, it developed into a rich brocade design.

For additional listings, see *Warman's Antiques & Collectibles*.

Bowl, 9" w, sq form with ribs, design of various flowers, Wan Li six-character mark on base, 19th C
.... 120.00

Charger, underglaze blue and enamel dec, central reserve of planter with flowers, grape and brocade borders, late 19th/early 20th C, 14-1/2" d
.... 250.00

Dish, shaped rim, all-over flowering vine dec, gilt highlights, 9-1/2" d
.... 150.00

Jardiniere, hexagonal, bulbous, short flared foot, alternating figures and symbols, stylized ground, 10" h
.... 265.00

Plate, Brocade pattern, 19th C, 9" d, set of nine 470.00

Sauce tureen, Boston retailer's mark, imp "Ashworth Real Ironstone," 6-1/8" h, 5-1/4" w, 9-1/4" l... 325.00

Tea bowl and saucer, floral spray dec 215.00

Urn, all over hexagonal panels with gold pheasants and orange drawings, flowers, and plant, orange, tomato red, yellow, green, and cobalt blue, old shield shaped "U.S. Customs" label underneath, 25" h 550.00

Imari, platter, iron red and cobalt blue ground border, c1875, 12-3/8" l, **$115.**

Imperial Glass

Bellaire, Ohio, was the home of Imperial Glass Company, founded in 1901. Through the years it has produced pressed glass in patterns that imitate cut glass, art glass, and animals figures, as well as elegant tableware.

For additional listings, see *Warman's Antiques & Collectibles, Warman's Depression Glass*, and Candlewick in this edition.

Imperial Glass, leaf-shaped dish with grapes, milk glass, 4-3/4" l, **$6.**

Ashtray, mkd "Nuart" 20.00

Baked apple, Cape Cod, 6" d 9.00

Bowl, Diamond Quilted, black, crimped, 7" d 20.00

Bread and butter plate, Cape Cod
.... 7.00

Bud vase, cylindrical, emerald green, orange irid int., 8-1/2" h...... 100.00

Cake stand, pressed imitation cut glass pattern, orig label 35.00

Candlesticks, pr, Amelia, 7" h. 35.00

Candy box, cov, ftd, Grape, milk glass, satin finish 40.00

Celery tray, 11" l, mkd "Nucut"
.... 18.00

Cocktail, Cape Cod 12.00

Console set, Diamond Quilted, 10-1/2" d bowl, pr candlesticks, green
.... 55.00

Coaster, Cape Cod, No. 160/76
.... 10.00

Cracker jar, cov, Americana, milk glass 60.00

Creamer and sugar, Cape Cod
.... 15.00

Cup and saucer, Cape Cod 7.50

Figure, pony stallion, caramel, c1970
.... 65.00

Goblet, Traditional 15.00

Juice tumbler, Cape Cod, 6 oz 10.00

Jug, Doeskin, milk glass, 36-oz, 8" h
.... 50.00

Nappy, Quilted Diamond, marigold,
ring handle 35.00

Parfait, Cape Cod 12.00

Plate
Cape Cod, Verdi, 8" d 15.00
Diamond Quilted, black, 8" d 15.00

Punch bowl set, Mount Vernon, 15
pcs.. 90.00

Relish
Candlewick, two-part, 6-1/2" 25.00
Cape Cod, three-part............ 35.00

Rose bowl, Molly, black, silver
deposit floral dec, 5" h 45.00

Tankard, Design No. 110, flowers,
foliage, and butterfly cutting
.... 60.00

Tea cup, #400/35 .... 8.00

Tray, Cape Cod, 12" l, 7" w 75.00

Vase
Bulbous, mustard yellow, orange
irid int., shape #1690, 6-1/2" h
.... 100.00
Cylindrical, irid marigold, wear at
collar, 11" h 75.00

Imperial Glass, cruet, purple slag, pressed cut-glass type pattern, 7" h, **$48.**

Indiana Glass

The good news is that Indiana Glass Company has a colorful history, dating back to 1907, when it was founded in Dunkirk, Ind. The bad news is that some of the company's more popular patterns have been reproduced over the years. Flea market shoppers can distinguish vintage Indiana Glass from newer pieces by examining color and the detail of the pattern.

For additional listings, see *Warman's Depression Glass.*

Indiana Glass, goblets, King's Crown pattern, cobalt blue, each **$5.**

Bowl, Daisy, amber, 9-1/4" d 35.00

Bread and butter plate, No. 620,
amber, 6" d............................... 3.00

Butter dish, cov, Sandwich, amber
dome, crystal base................. 55.00

Candlesticks, pr, Tea Room, green
.... 48.00

Cereal bowl, Horseshoe, green or
yellow..................................... 25.00

Cup
No. 618, amber or red 10.00
No. 622, crystal...................... 6.00

Dinner plate
No. 612, green, 9-3/8" d........ 12.00
No. 624, crystal, 9-5/8" d...... 12.00

Fairy lamp, Sandwich pattern,
amber, 7" h 20.00

Luncheon plate, No. 616, green or
yellow, 8" d............................ 10.00

Mayonnaise set, underplate, No. 624,
crystal, orig ladle.................. 24.00

Pitcher, Pear pattern, amber, Tiara,
c1970, 9-1/4" h....................... 75.00

Platter, Indiana Custard, French
Ivory....................................... 30.00

Sherbet, clear, 3-1/2" h.............. 9.00

Tumbler, Lorain, yellow, c1929, 5" h
.... 38.00

Indian Jewelry

Indian jewelry is abundant at most flea markets. Bargains can be found in collectible Indian jewelry, but vintage Indian jewelry is getting quite pricey.

Buy pieces because they appeal to you. Make sure the craftsmanship is good, and the stones are secure in the settings. Watch for signs of heat-stabilized turquoise when considering collectible Indian jewelry.

Indian jewelry, Indian-style, coral-colored glass beads, black glass, plastic, and silver beads, oval tan agate medallion, **$5.** This is not genuine American Indian.

Barette, silver............................ 45.00

Beads, turquoise, from Sleeping Beauty mine, graduated disks, 2-1/2" l leaf design pendant, 20" l 225.00

Bolo tie, Navajo, hand made, woven leather tie, tipped in sterling silver, sgd "Sterling," mkd by artist 112.00

Bracelet
Navajo, silver leaf design on matte black ground, 10 Kingman turquoise stones, engraved "D" on back, by J. Delgarito.. 200.00
Squash blossom design, Morenci turquoise nugget and coral accent, silver, drop style, stamped "MLS," attributed to Loren Begay 55.00
Zuni, inlaid, oval, katsina case mask, 2-1/8" w 125.00

Earrings, pr, stylized two-pc, turquoise settings 95.00

Fetish necklace
Santo Domingo, shell, turquoise, and coral triangle pieces, bird pendant with upraised wings, c1940, shortened.............. 55.00
Zuni, single strand, silver, birds, bears, frogs, and turtles, tubular silver rain spacers, 28" l. 250.00

Necklace
Heishi, 38 turquoise nuggets, silver beads and cones, 26-1/2" l 90.00
Nugget, turquoise, silver catch, Morenci, 15" l................. 200.00

Indian jewelry, bracelet, Navajo-style, sterling silver, three oval turquoise cabochons, eagle, double arrow and sun god motif, crafted by Maisel, c1940, **$125.**

Santo Domingo, five strands of graduated red coral beads, 12" l 300.00

Pin, silver and stone, inlaid Rainbow man, Zuni, 2nd quarter 20th C, stone loss, 2-1/2" h 150.00

Ring, man's, Navajo
Silver and turquoise, feathers around cabochon 120.00
Silver, coral, and turquoise 110.00

Squash blossom necklace, silver
Hopi, shadowbox style, silver, fifteen blue diamond turquoise stones, 13" l 275.00
Navajo, stamped silver with inlaid turquoise chips, stamped artist's mark for Carlos Singer on back, 13-1/4" l.......................... 275.00

Inkwells

Small receptacles designed to hold ink were a necessity in the days of quill pens and steel dip pens. Inkwells were most commonly made of glass and pottery, because the ink would not adversely affect those substances. Inkwells have become quite popular with collectors, who search for examples made of glass, bronze, pewter, pottery, and even wood. Particularly fascinating are the miniature wells designed for children's desks.

For additional listings, see *Warman's Antiques & Collectibles*.

Brass, embossed, double, two porcelain inserts, late 19th/early 20th C, 10-1/2" l, 6-1/2" w 150.00

Delft, square with round lid, c1910 .... 295.00

Glass
Clear, 2" h, 1-7/8" d 25.00
Freeblown, sq, opaque electric blue, flared mouth, pontil scar, attributed to America, 1840-60, 1-3/4" h.......................... 120.00

House, aquamarine, domed roof, rounded top windows, squared lip and plain base, c1850, 2-1/2" h............................. 50.00
Snail, clear, ground mouth, 1830-70 .... 160.00
Teakettle, glass, brick red and burgundy slag, ground mouth, brass cap, 1830-60......... 145.00

Hoof, animal hoof, English, Birmingham hallmarks on silver fitting................................... 295.00

Inkwells, cast iron, cast embossed decoration, pen rest on back, pressed vaseline glass insert, c1900, **$90.**

Paperweight, multicolored concentric millefiori, base with 1848 date canes, Whitefriars, 6-1/4" h 175.00

Porcelain, three figural crested birds, magenta, gilding, white band painted with polychrome flowers, insert and lid, underglaze blue crossed arrows, French........ 200.00

Treen, sponge-decor, brown and yellow, gilt stenciling, glass insert, Manufactured by S. Silliman & Co...Conn., 2-1/2" h............ 185.00

Insulators

Insulators date to 1837, when the telegraph was developed. Styles have been modified over the years, and collectors have a wide variety of shapes and colors to choose from.

Armstrong, clear 2.00

Brookfield
No. 20, emerald green 20.00
W. Brookfield B., aqua............ 2.00

B.T.C., aqua 5.00

Ceramic, 3-1/2" h..................... 10.00

Harlow Trade Mark, aqua 4.00

Hemingray
No. 4, 1893 patent, aqua......... 8.00
No. 12, aqua............................ 8.25
No. 53B, clear 2.00

H. G. Co., aqua 12.00

Gayner, No. 90, aqua................. 7.00

Lynchburg, No. 31, aqua 7.00

McLaughlin, No. 9, aqua.......... 2.00

Pyrex, double threaded, clear, 4" h
.... 7.50

Star, aqua 15.00

Whitall Tatum, #1, light aqua
.... 7.50

Insulators, Hemingray, No. 16, aqua, 3-3/4" d, 4-1/4" h, **$12.**

Insulators, Brookfield No. 20, emerald green glass, 4" h, **$20.**

Insulators, Hemingray No. 40, aqua, 3-3/4" d, 4-1/4" h, **$5.**

Irons

Folks have been trying to keep their clothes pressed neatly since the 12th century. Of course, irons from those days are vastly different than the streamlined appliances we use today.

For additional listings, see *Warman's Antiques & Collectibles, and Warman's Americana & Collectibles.*

Electric
American Beauty No. 66A, American Electrical Heater Co., Detroit 10.00
Singer model 820476, Singer Sewing Machine Co. 40.00

Flat iron
Dover, cold handle................ 40.00
Enterprise, Star, holes in handle
.... 40.00
Griswold #2, wooden handle
.... 120.00
Simmons Special, detachable handle............................... 90.00

Wapak #4 .... 35.00

Fluter, American Machine, wood handle, roller type 125.00

Gasoline, Coleman, Model 4A, blue
.... 100.00

Natural gas, Central Flat Iron Mfg
  Co.. 100.00

Slug
  Bless-Drake, salamander box iron
  .... 160.00
  French, "S" posts 250.00

Travel, Universal, electric, cloth cord,
  wooden handle, made by Landers,
  Frary & Clark, New Britain, 7-3/4" l
  .... 35.00

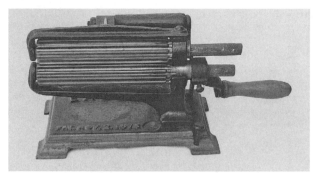

Irons, fluting machine, Eagle, mid "Pat Nov 2, 1875," cast iron and brass, original inserts, **$225.**

Ironstone

Charles Mason first patented ironstone in England in 1813. The dense, durable, white stoneware was named "Mason's Patent Ironstone China," even though the reference to china was misleading since the items were actually earthenware. Ironstone derives its name from the fact that iron slag was mixed with the clay used to produce dinnerware and the like. Manufactured throughout the 19th century, ironstone was available in plain white as well as decorated versions.

For additional listings, see *Warman's Antiques & Collectibles*, and *Warman's English and Continental Pottery & Porcelain*.

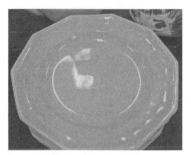

Ironstone, soup plate, 10-sided, unmarked, **$20.**

Bowl, Tamerlane pattern, Oriental
  design, J.& M.P. Bell, 9-3/4" d
  .... 165.00

Butter pat, 2-3/4" x 2-1/2", emb
  ridges along slanted sides, mkd
  "Charles Meakin England, Royal
  Ironstone China" with coat of arms
  .... 20.00

Dessert set, 12" d cake plate, eight
  7-3/4" d plates, white ground,
  decals representing different
  countries, mkd "Kaysons Fine
  Ironstone China, Japan, 1966"
  .... 36.00

Egg cup, 2-1/2" d, 3-3/4" h, raised
  grape and leaf dec 35.00

Gravy boat, underplate, mkd "Royal
  Ironstone China, Johnson Bros,
  England" 45.00

Jug, white, Strathmore, #30, mkd
  "Mason's," 5-1/4" h 100.00

Ladle, white
  Flower and fern dec, gray transfer,
    worn gold edging, 6" l...... 45.00
  Lavender daisies, gold trim, c1895
  .... 50.00
  Plain, crazed, 10-1/2" l 48.00

Pitcher, Wheat, Furnival, 12" h
  .... 165.00

Ironstone, wash bowl and pitcher set, large pitcher, bowl, small pitcher, shaving mug, covered soap dish, covered chamber pot, blue band with thin gold bands, marked "Ironstone China, W. & E. Corn, Burslem," embossed English registration mark, **$350.**

Ironstone, coffeepot, paneled body, fruit finial on domed lid, scrolling leaf dec on handle and shoulder, **$175.**

Place setting, Royal Mail, brown
  and white, mkd "Fine Staffordshire
  Ironstone...Made in England"
  .... 25.00

Plate
  Corn & Oats, mkd "J. Wedgwood,"
    c1841, 8-3/4" d 45.00
  Forget-Me-Not, mkd "E&C
    Challinor," c1862, 8-3/4" d
  .... 45.00
  Stratford Stage, mkd "Royal
    Staffordshire Ironstone"... 10.00

Platter, white, 14" x 10", mkd "Royal Ironstone China, Alfred Meakin, England" 65.00

Salad plate, Stratford Stage, mkd "Royal Staffordshire Ironstone" 4.00

Shaving mug, 3-1/2" d, 3-3/4" h, emb, gold accents, mkd "VPCO Admiral 21" 20.00

Soup tureen, cov, underplate, mkd "Bridgewood Porcelaine Opaque" 300.00

Teapot, Mason's Ironstone, Vista pattern, red and white scenic dec, matching trivet 195.00

Tea set, child's, painted pansies, faded gold trim, worn paint, 15 pcs 75.00

Toothbrush holder, mulberry variant, c1890, 5-1/2" h 75.00

Vegetable bowl, American Hurrah, mkd "J&G Meakin," 8-1/2" l 45.00

Italian Glass

Italian glassblowers have been crafting functional items and whimsical glass novelties for generations. There is strong interest in modern Italian glass. Look for bright colors and flowing forms.

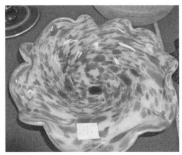

Italian glass, dish, yellow ground, multicolored spatter, undulating rim, 8" d, **$25.**

Ashtray, freeform, swirling blues, reds, and purple 20.00

Basket, Hobnail, blue, applied handle 32.00

Bottle, clear, silver overlay, orig sticker, 6" h 32.00

Bowl, freeform, crystal, cranberry veins form points at top 25.00

Cordials, etched vining leaves, blue, pink, yellow and green, set of four 50.00

Decanter set, green, gold floral dec, decanter 10" h, four glasses 3" h, set 40.00

Earrings, pr, clip, millefiori 28.00

Figure
Donald Duck, made by Cristallerie Antonio Imperatore, copyright Walt Disney Productions, MIB, 4-3/4" h............................. 50.00
Fish, multicolored, bulging eyes 25.00

Vase
5-1/2" h, irid, green waves 125.00

Italian glass, vase, blue, green and clear, 4" h, **$48.**

8" h, orange, white swirls 95.00

Ivory

Ivory is derived from the teeth or tusks of animals. Yellow-white in color, the substance is quite durable and lends itself to carving. Some ivory objects have been highlighted with ink, metal, or stones.

For additional listings, see *Warman's Antiques & Collectibles*.

Ball, carved, 2" d, three boys forming circle, clothes with traces of paint, China, 19th C, 3-3/4" with base, age cracks 115.00

Box, cov, 4-1/2" h, cylindrical, carved scene of figures in landscape, screw-on lid, China, 19th C 220.00

Cane, hand around face of young woman, curly tresses, lace collar, ebony shaft, 2/3" horn ferrule, English, c1885 .... 900.00

Earrings, pr, pierced, hand carved, drops suspended from gold filled leaves, c1910, 1-1/4" l.......... 180.00

Figure
Eagle attacking monkey, Japan, 3" h 475.00
Laughing monk, carrying turtle, staff with palm frond, bat on head, dark yellow stain, sgd, 6-1/4" h........................... 200.00
Woman, western attire, carrying purse and umbrella, China, 8-3/8" h........................... 300.00

Ivory, cane handle, carved figural dog's head, metal screw, **$95.**

Letter opener, oblong blade carved to end with writhing dragon, Chinese, early 20th C, 9-3/4" l 115.00

Necklace, hand-carved beads, c1910, 1-1/4" pendant, 15" l 165.00

Netsuke, boy holding rooster, stained details, himotoshi carved on back, Japan, c1900, 1-1/2" h 200.00

Okimono, figure of young boy and dog, sgd on bottom, Japan, Meiji period, 2-1/8" h, crack on boy's face 200.00

Snuff bottle, elephant ivory, carved bird on one side, carved rose on other, gold-tone neck chain, sgd "LRS," orig wand 125.00

Top, carved, sealing wax inlaid scribed lines, 19th C, minor cracks and chips, 2 7/8" l................ 365.00

Tusk, 18-1/4" l, carved marine tusk, line of eight buffalo in diminishing size, carved wooden stand, China, early 20th C, age cracks....... 200.00

Ivory, puzzle ball, pedestal base with carved figure of pheasant, original fitted box, **$95.**

Jade-ite Glassware

The name "jade-ite" is derived from the pale green jade-like hue of the glass, with the color varying from manufacturer to manufacturer. Anchor-Hocking and McKee are perhaps the best known makers of jade-ite. First produced around 1920, jade-ite items are still being made today.

For additional listings, see *Warman's Antiques & Collectibles, Warman's Glass,* and *Warman's Depression Glass.*

Jade-ite, triple-bar towel holder, 10" l, **$240.**

Bowl, 4-1/2" d 20.00

Bud vase, Jeannette 20.00

Butter dish, cov, 1-lb size 90.00

Canister, dark, Jeannette 80.00

Chili bowl 12.00

Coffee mug, 7 oz 12.00

Cup and saucer, Charm 15.00

Egg cup, double 20.00

Measuring cup, Jeannette, 2-oz
.... 50.00

Pitcher, sunflower in base 60.00

Platter, oval, partitioned 20.00

Range shaker, sq, mkd "Flour,"
Jeannette 45.00

Reamer 60.00

Refrigerator dish, 4" x 4", clear top
.... 18.00

Salt and pepper shakers, pr,
Ribbed, Jeannette, 4-1/2" h
.... 140.00

Tea canister, sq, light jade-ite, 48-oz
.... 145.00

Water dispenser, metal spigot
.... 150.00

Jade-ite glassware, cereal canister, silver and black diagonal label, **$40.**

Japanese Toys

Some of our favorite childhood toys were inexpensive imports from Japan. We loved the colors, the action, and the fact that we could afford them on our pitiful allowances. Now that we're all grown up, many collectors are busy buying back their happy childhood memories. Before making a purchase, check for the original box and make sure all the accessories are present. Top dollar is often paid for toys in excellent working order, especially when a maker's mark and box are included.

Japanese toys, top: Sedan, friction, MF 743, MIB, **$40.**

Boat, Great Swanee Paddle Wheeler,
friction powered tinplate, whistle
mechanism, TN, orig box 175.00

Car, tin friction, 6" l 45.00

Circus parade, tin litho wind-up,
clowns and elephants, TPS, orig
box, 11" l, C.9 .... 275.00

Crazy Clown in Crazy Car, litho
tin wind-up, MIB 175.00

Douglas Sky Rocket, 20" l
.... 140.00

Dump truck, friction powered
tinplate, red and cream, automatic
side dump action, TN, orig box
.... 150.00

Happy n' sad magic face clown,
battery operated, Yonezawa, orig
box, 10-1/2" h, C.9 .... 150.00

Harley Davidson, TN, 1950s, 9" l
.... 170.00

Jeep and trailer, battery operated,
Bandai, 1970s, MIB 45.00

Jet racer, friction, red 95.00

Mercedes Convertible 300, friction
.... 75.00

Missle launching tank, litho tin,
battery operated, four targets,
Yonezawa, orig box, 6" l, C.10
.... 125.00

Moon patrol, litho tin, battery
operated, tin astronaut driver,
plastic dome, bump and go action,
TPS, 8" l, C.9 .... 350.00

Planet Explorer, battery operated,
Modern Toys, 1960s, 9-1/2" l
.... 160.00

Reading Bear, turns page of tin book, MIB............................ 145.00

Speed Race Car #20, lavender, Modern Toys, 1950s, 6-1/2" l 155.00

Telephone Bear, litho tin, wind-up, MIB....................................... 145.00

Tugboat, 12-1/2" l, battery operated tinplate, red, cream, yellow, and blue, smoking mechanism, San, orig box................................ 200.00

Jelly Glasses

The concept of putting jelly into a glass container with colorful or whimsical decorations no doubt helped boost sales. Collectors today eagerly look for vintage and contemporary jelly glasses.

Archie, Hot Dog Goes to School, Welch's, 1971............................ 6.50

Flintstones, Fred And His Pals At Work, Welch's, 4-1/2" h 10.00

Howdy Doody, Dilly Dally is Circus Big Shot, Welch's, 4-1/4" h..... 18.00

Jack & Jill, nursery rhyme, 4-3/4" h 8.00

Pooh's Grand Adventure, The Search for Christopher Robin, 4" h 3.00

Spacemen, two yellow spacemen, planets, rockets, 1960s, 5" h 18.00

Speedy Gonzales, Speedy Snaps Up the Cheese, 1974...................... 3.00

Tom and Jerry, Tom roller skating toward open manhole 10.00

Jelly glasses, Welch's Looney Tunes Collector Series, 4" h, **$3.50.**

Jensen, Georg

This designer hailed from Denmark, but he is known worldwide for his jewelry, flatware, and decorative accessories. Most of his creations were produced in sterling silver. Expect to find pieces that are well marked.

Bar pin, sterling silver, mkd "GI #136 Sterling, Denmark," 3-3/4" x 1-1/4" 775.00

Berry spoon, Acanthus, 8-7/8" l 350.00

Bread knife, Bernadotte pattern, stainless steel blade 650.00

Brooch, sterling silver, tulips, post-1945 mark, 1-7/8" x 1-1/4" 400.00

Carving knife and fork, Acanthus, stainless blades, 11-1/4" l and 12-1/2" l 325.00

Cuff links, pr, oval, design #75A, post-1945 mark, mkd "Sterling, Made in Denmark".............. 300.00

Earrings, pr, 18k yg, circle mark, screw backs.......................... 550.00

Key ring, design #208, pineapple decorative ends, sgd "Sterling, Denmark, Georg Jensen" in dotted circle, 1-7/16" d 225.00

Meat fork, Acanthus, two tines, 8-1/8" l................................. 250.00

Ring, sterling silver, mkd #130 925 Denmark," c1915-27, size 6 .... 775.00

Serving fork and spoon, Pattern 83, hand hammered, floral engraving, openwork handles, floral ends, mark used after 1945, Danish hallmarks, "Denmark, Sterling," 9-3/8" and 10-1/4" l 1,035.00

Soup spoon, Acanthus, 6-7/8" l 95.00

Sugar tongs, mkd "925 Sterling," 4-1/4" h 175.00

Tie bar, design #64, post-1945 mark 125.00

Youth knife and fork, Acanthus, 6-3/4" l and 5-5/8" l 180.00

Jewel Tea Company

Most flea market browsers picture the Autumn Leaf pattern when they hear the name Jewel Tea, but the company was actually responsible for a diverse selection of products. The Jewel Tea Company, headquartered in Barrington, Illinois, has been supplying household necessities for years.

Bank, 1905 truck, Ertl, orig box 55.00

Beverage coaster set, Autumn Leaf pattern, orig box, 9 pcs 235.00

Christmas ornament, pewter, Oh Come All Ye Faithful, 1980s, orig box 12.00

Cookbook, *476 Tested Recipes* 5.00

Flour canister, tin body, white plastic lid, Autumn Leaf dec, 5-3/4" h, 5" d........................... 10.00

Laundry soap, Jewel T Jetco Bead Bluing, 8-3/4" x 5-3/4" 85.00

Jar, peanut butter, 3-3/4" h 45.00

Soap, Shure, three bars in box.. 85.00

Tin
  Fruitcake, 1981 .... 20.00
  Ginger, 2-oz, 3" x 2-1/4" 95.00

Truck, 1926 delivery truck, 100th anniversary, Tootsietoy, MIB 15.00

Urn, Jewel Best Coffee, made by West Bend, orig box 525.00

Jewelry, Costume

Jewelry with faux stones became fashionable in the 1920s, thanks to Coco Chanel. Initially, designers were copying real gemstone jewelry, but soon they began creating their own exciting pieces.

For additional listings, see *Warman's Americana & Collectibles* and *Warman's Jewelry*.

Reproduction alert.

Jewelry, costume, Weiss butterfly pin, 2-1/8" h, 2-5/8" w, **$45.**

Bracelet
  Ciner, rhinestones, panther, black enamel trim, sgd 215.00
  Corocraft, eight charms, gold-tone links, sgd 40.00
  Eisenberg, linked clusters of marquise-cut colorless rhinestones, v-spring and box clasp, block letters mark, safety chain, c1950, 7-1/2" l 70.00

Brooch
  Avon, acorn, gold wash, pearl trim, sgd, 1-1/2" x 1-1/2" 20.00
  B.S.K., sunflowers, pale yellow double layer flower petals, amber colored faceted stones in center, green enameled leaf, gold washed metal, 2-1/2" x 2-1/2" 45.00
  Coro, initial "M," gold tone 9.00
  Florenza, starfish, gold-tone, green, brown and gold rhinestones, Florenza........................... 65.00

Haskell, fan, Oriental design, gold-tone, bamboo handle, sgd "Haskell" 50.00
Hollycraft, floral wreath design, large center circ red rhinestone encircled by goldtone floral and foliate motifs set with small red rhinestones, sgd "Hollycraft, Copr 1954," 1-1/2" w x 3/8" 40.00
Kramer of New York, rhodium, bar pin with criss-cross clear rhinestone dangles ending in emerald stones, 2-3/4" w, 1" h 95.00
Kenneth Jay Lane, Maltese cross of large green oval cabochons and circ green rhinestones around center circ blue rhinestone, outlined in marquise and sq-cut colorless rhinestones, sgd "KJL," c1965, 3" x 3".................... 35.00
Mamsell, brown topaz colored rhinestone floral accents, gold tone stems and leaves, sgd, 2-1/8" h............................... 14.00
Rosenthal China, orange, aqua, lavender, and white, gold accents,

Jewelry, costume, pin, fish, wood, plastic eye, **$3.50.**

sgd by artist and stamped logo 35.00
Sarah Coventry, floral, textured gold tone, green rhinestone stamen center with faux pearl, 1-3/4" w 16.00
Unmarked, butterfly, silver rhinestones, 1-3/4" w 25.00
Weiss, bow, two layers, rhinestones prong set in large and small marquise, round, and baguette shaped stones, imp mark, 2-3/8" w, 1-1/2" h 175.00

Jewelry, costume, pin, pair of earrings, 6-1/2" l bracelet, light blue colored rhinestones, **$45.**

Weiss, triangle, three layers, rhinestones prong set in sq, small round, large round, baguette, and teardrop shaped stones, sgd, 2-1/2" w, 2-1/4" l 175.00

Cameo, faux carnelian surrounded by clear rhinestones, scrolled mounting, Coro 32.00

Charm bracelet
Bicentennial, red, white, and blue enamel shield charm, silver tone lantern, clipper ship, Liberty Bell, and cannon charms, 7" l 24.00

Tops, 21 weight loss related charms, silver tone, 1980s 18.00

Choker, pearls, center rect amethyst colored stone, Kenneth Lane 25.00

Clip
Eisenberg Original, Retro Modern, goldtone floral spray with large emerald-cut green rhinestone at base, smaller emerald-cut green rhinestone encircled by circ-cut green rhinestones forming flowerhead, marquise-cut green rhinestones in center of second flowerhead, sgd "Eisenberg Original," c1940-45, 3-1/4" w x 2-1/2" 155.00

Trifari, painted enamel floral spray, red flowers, colorless rhinestone centers and accents, green leaves, brown stems on rhodium plated white metal, c1935-40, sgd "Trifari," 1-1/2" w x 2-1/2" 90.00

Cross, cut crystal and sterling silver, mkd "MC, Sterling," 1-1/2" x 1" 35.00

Cuff links and tie clip set
LaMode Originals, black stone and goldtone, orig box 25.00
Mask shape, unmkd 12.00
Square, gold-plated, inset MOP disk 18.00
Swank, gold- and silver-plated, orig box 25.00

Earrings, pr, clip
Carnegie, Dangling, chandelier type, crystal and rhinestone, Carnegie 60.00
Ciner, textured goldtone circ domes, small faux pearls in star-cut settings, c1960, sgd "Ciner," 1" d 32.50
Eisenberg, clusters of prong-set cobalt blue marquise and circ rhinestones, small colorless rhinestone accents, c1950, block letter mark, 3/4" x 1-1/4 55.00
Kramer, Turquoise egg-shaped glass dangles, gold tops, mkd "Kramer" 35.00

Necklace
Carnegie, Hattie, goldtone, double strand, peridot green aurora borealis crystals, 20" l 40.00
Caslecliff, three strands, red glass beads, goldtone leaf closure, 22" l 45.00
Coro, heat style links, small spacers, gold tone, Francois, Coro, 15" l, 1937 .... 27.50
Coventry, Sarah, goldtone links, 11 faceted aurora borealis crystals, 16" l 18.00
Monet, silver tone boomerang links, extension chain, 18-1/2" l 25.00
Trifari, X" design with rhinestones, Crown Trifari, 14" l 65.00

Pendant
Sarah Coventry, teardrop, polished faux coral, plastic, gold trimmed open center, Sarah Coventry, gold-tone chain 28" l 20.00
Joseff of Hollywood, stamped gold-plated brass in a design of three overlapping circ disks with open scroll and geometric motif, suspending by two outside and two inside crossing chains a large circ disk with geo design, c1950, hook and ring clasp on gold-plated brass foxtail chain, pendant 3" w x 5", chain 16" l 200.00
Rivers, Joan, ivory colored heart shaped pendant, gold chain, orig box 20.00

Unknown maker, lucite "ice cube" held by rhodium-plated tongs on matching large curb link chain, pendant 1-3/4" w x 4", chain 30" l 75.00

Ring, Vogue, triangular cluster, one large half-round faux pearl, two flowerheads, each center set with five colorless rhinestones encircled by glass cabs, one streaked turquoise colored and other mottled green, c1960, mkd "vogue," adjustable shank, 1-7/8" w x 1-5/8" 50.00

Stickpin, Anson, owl, sterling, white opal cabochon, 2-1/2" l 25.00

Suite (Parure)
Hattie Carnegie, 17-1/2" l necklace, 1-3/4" chip earrings, goldtone, leaf design, white dangling beads and cabs, snake chain, hook and chain closure, all signed 195.00
Hobe, 15-1/4" necklace, simulated pearls and coral, each prong set into goldtone metal, decorative gold link chains applied to top row of beads, set in three graduating strands, 1" d round earrings, hallmark.......... 185.00
NYE, pin and screw back earrings, sterling silver dogwood blossoms, sgd and mkd "Sterling" 30.00
Selro, 18" l necklace, 1" w x 7" l bracelet, and 1-1/2" earrings, silvertone, marquise shaped blue Lucite transparent cabs, with marquis shaped settings of prong set light blue rhinestones, all signed 250.00
Weiss, pin and clip earrings, prong set rhinestones, sgd.......... 85.00

Tie bar, gold-plated, abstract design 2.00

Tie tack
Car, gold-plated, Sarah Coventry 4.00
Initial, "G," silver-plated 2.00

Johnson Brothers

Three English brothers founded Johnson Brothers in 1883. Their dinnerware business flourished, and a fourth brother joined the firm in 1896. He was charged with establishing a stronghold in the American market. Ultimately, this venture was so successful that additional factories were established in England, Canada, and Australia. By 1968, Johnson Brothers had become part of the Wedgwood Group.

Johnson Brothers, drinking monk plate, basket over arm, burgundy border with gold trim, **$20.**

Bread and butter plate, English Chippendale, red 30.00

Breakfast set, Lily of the Valley, five pcs... 155.00

Butter dish, cov, Eternal Beau 65.00

Cereal bowl, Old Britain Castles, blue 18.00

Coffeepot, Hearts & Flowers 200.00

Creamer and sugar, Friendly Village 35.00

Cup and saucer
Brooklyn pattern, flow blue, mkd "Royal Semi Porcelain, Johnson Brothers, England," c1900 .... 100.00
Countryside 55.00
Harvest Time 55.00
Old Britain Castles, blue....... 20.00

Dinner plate
Brooklyn pattern, flow blue, mkd "Royal Semi Porcelain, Johnson Brothers, England," c1900, 8-3/4" d.......................... 100.00
Old Britain Castles, blue....... 22.00

Fruit bowl, Old Britain Castles, blue 10.00

Gravy boat, Snow White Regency, Swirl pattern......................... 15.00

Platter
Albany, 12-3/4" l................. 225.00
Hearts & Flowers, 14" l....... 200.00
Historic America, large 265.00
Lindsey, small.................... 250.00
Old Britain Castles, brown, 12" l 165.00

Relish, Friendly Village, three-part 38.50

Salad plate, Staffordshire Bouquet, multicolored floral print 15.00

Saucer, Cherry Thieves, mkd "Staffordshire Old Granite Made in England by Johnson Brothers" 5.00

Serving bowl, Snow White Regency, Swirl pattern......................... 18.00

Soup bowl, Old Britain Castles, blue 22.00

Johnson Brothers, drinking monk plate, maroon border with gold trim, **$20.**

Soup tureen, Friendly Village, 10" x 7-1/2" 235.00

Souvenir plate, Mt. Rushmore, imported for Sunset Supply, Keystone, 10-3/4" d 15.00

Teapot
Hearts & Flowers, five-cup 270.00
Old Britain Castles, pink.... 250.00

Turkey platter, Friendly Village, 20" l 190.00

Vegetable, cov, Hearts & Flowers 185.00

Kaleidoscopes

Changing colors and patterns as they turn, kaleidoscopes date to a time when entertainment didn't involve a remote or a computer screen. Scottish scientist David Brewster is created with inventing the first kaleidoscope in 1816. The name is taken from Greek *kalos* (beautiful) and *eidos* (form) and *scopos* (viewer). Look for examples with interesting designs and colorful elements.

Kaleidoscopes, Woody Woodpecker, 8-1/4" h, 1971, **$13.**

Brass case, multicolor crystals, leather carrying case, English, c1910 .... 400.00

Paper case
Corning Glass Museum, multicolored bits of glass, c1980, 8-3/4" l 15.00
Hallmark, decorated with Peanuts characters, rainbow colors on turning cylinder, 9" l 10.00

Nightmare before Christmas, C. Bennet Scopes 20.00
Unknown maker, multicolor bits of paper, c1950 .... 5.00
Tin case, tin screw caps for ends, multicolor crystals 200.00
Von Cort, 12 gauge, 2-1/2" l 65.00

Kanawha

West Virginia was home to this glass company that produced colored glass and crackle glass. Kanawha Glass marked its wares with paper labels.

Basket, amberina crackle, 5-1/4" h 35.00
Candy dish, cov, amberina crackle, 3" h 45.00
Creamer, amberina crackle, milk white int., ruffled spout, amber glass handle, 4" h 30.00
Pitcher, crackle
Amberina, long neck, applied amber handle, 8-1/4" h 70.00

Blue, applied clear handle, 5-1/4" h 30.00
Orange, elongated spout, applied handle, 14-1/2" h 75.00
Shoe, Colonial Slipper, white milk glass, 1968, 6" l, 2-1/2" h 35.00
Syrup pitcher, ruby crackle, applied amber handle, cork stopper, stainless steel top, 6-3/4" h.... 65.00
Vase
Aqua blue, crackle, orig paper sticker, 3-1/2" h 27.50
White, blue hand painted flowers, cornflower blue satin in., orig label, 5" h 45.00
White, diamond and dot pressed pattern, red int., ruffled, 5-1/2" h 50.00
White, hand painted roses and green leaves, red satin int., ruffled, orig label, 5-1/2" h 45.00

White, raised grapevine dec, mint green int., ruffled rim, 9" h 60.00
Vinegar cruet, red crackle, applied yellow handle, 6" h 48.00

Kanawha Glass, left: ewer, gold crackle glass, applied gold handle, original foil label, **$15;** right: cruet, amberina crackle cruet, elongated tear drop-shaped stopper, applied clear handle, original foil label, **$20.**

Kanawha Glass, decanter, red, depression in original stopper and also in body, original foil label, **$45.**

Kennedy, John F.

Many people were fascinated with John F. Kennedy and his family during his life as the president. Since his tragic death, collectors have continued to keep his memory alive.

Bookmark, 2-1/4" x 8", silk, 1962 calendar, "Ask Not" phrase below illus of JFK **25.00**

Brochure
3-1/4" x 9" folded, US Senate re-election, 1958 .... **70.00**
3-3/4" x 8-1/4", red, white and blue, California Needs Kennedy, 1960 .... **60.00**

Figure, 2" x 2" x 3" h, colorful plastic, seated in gold plastic rocking chair, Mego, 3" x 7" card titled "Hush Up Toys-Rock Chair," c1963, sealed in plastic..................................... **24.00**

Lapel dec, Massachusetts Own for President, 9" l pink ribbon stapled to 2-1/2" cardboard circle, black and white photo **75.00**

Magazine
Berliner Illustrirte, 10" x 13", 84 pgs, full-color cover of JFK in front of Brandenburg Gate silhouette, 1961 .... **5.00**
Photoplay, 8-1/2" x 11", 104 pgs, March, 1964, full-color cover of JFK and Jackie.................. **12.00**

Newspaper supplement, 10" x 14", Sunday Bulletin, Philadelphia, Dec. 22, 1963, glossy **10.00**

Pennant, 12" x 29-1/2" red, white, and blue felt, shield design at left,

6" d stiff paper color photo of JFK looking at viewer, facsimile signature in white, Our 35th President John F. Kennedy.... **18.00**

Pinback button, 3-1/2" d, black and white photos, names on central gold ground, blue letters "New Frontier," gold replica of official inauguration seal, three gold stars **125.00**

Postcard, 6" x 9", color, "President and Mrs. Kennedy," c1961..... **12.00**

Sheet music, *Massachusetts My Home State, Special Kennedy Version*, blue and white, 9" x 12" **35.00**

Souvenir tray, 7" d full color painted glass tray, black and white photos of John and Robert Kennedy in center, full color painted scenes of Washington, gold and black painted rim on ribbon glass tray, House Art, 1968, orig box........................ **12.00**

Tapestry, 19" x 37", color portraits of JFK and RFK, White House scene, Belgium, 1968........................ **25.00**

Wall plaque, 7" x 11", plaster, detailed likeness, finished in gold, green felt on back, c1964 ...... **20.00**

Window adv card, 10" x 13-1/2", Unfinished Book, black and white photo, text in red and blue, adv Oct. 3, 1964 issue of *Saturday Evening Post*, featuring excerpt from book *A Nation of Immigrants* **28.00**

Kennedy. John F., framed photograph, the Kennedys, Karsh of Ottowa, 10" x 8", **$10.**

Kentucky Derby Glasses

The Run for the Roses is perhaps the best-known horse race in the world. Collectors are equally excited about the fact that this event signals the arrival of a new commemorative drinking glass each year. Examples from the 1940s through the 1960s are comparatively scarce at flea markets, but Derby glasses from later decades are available and affordable.

1945... 500.00
1948...220.00
1951.. 600.00
1959.. 120.00
1970.. 45.00
1973.. 40.00
1975, yellow and black title band, 5-1/4" h 7.50

1976, red, white, and blue, 5-1/4" h 8.50
1977, ivory accents, brown and burnt orange art, 5-1/4" h 8.00
1978, white accents, red, brown, pale green, and yellow art, 5-1/4" h 8.00
1983..15.00
1985.. 14.00
1990.. 20.00

Kentucky Derby glasses, 1979, **$10.**

Key Chains

Everybody has a couple of key chains saved, whether in a desk drawer, a pocket, or even a collection. Key chains are wonderful collectibles for children—relatively easy to find and usually inexpensive.

Key chains, left: circular bronze key fob with laurel wreath border, bronze key, **$15;** right: bronze key chain with monogram "W" in square with daggers, numbered cast metal key, **$10.**

Ballantine, Light Lager Beer, three ring motif, plastic, red and white, 3" h.. 10.00

Batman, PVC head, Funatics, MOC 2.00

Coca-Cola, Spanish version, 1960s, 1-1/2" d 8.00

Curious George, pewter, Danforth 16.00

Disney, Jack Skellington's Tombstone, brass... 3.00

Duquesne Brewing Co., Pittsburgh, PA, aluminum, penny, 1948.. 12.00

Eastern Star, enameled star 18.00

Elephant, wood, 3" l................... 3.00

Flicker, pinup, 1-1/4" x 2" 6.00

Ford, metal, mkd "Karriers USA" 4.00

Good Luck Penny, circular, "Keep me and never go broke," penny dated 1957 .... 12.00

Horse, key chain in mouth, 5" h 30.00

Johnson Feed Service, Feeding Grinding & Mixing On Your Farm, Griffin, Ga., flicker 12.00

License plate, Missouri, 1968.. 10.00

Minnie Mouse, plastic, 4" l 5.00

Old Crow Distillery, plastic, figural crow 12.00

Key chains, GE Plastics, back marked "25 Years, 1960, 1985, Reaching for the horizon…and beyond!," pewter, 1-1/2" d, **$13.50.**

Puzzle, two sided, plastic 6.00

Super Bowl XXX, 1996, NRFP. 6.00

Vincent System, Exterminators - Fumigators, Tampa, Florida, flicker 12.00

Western Auto, Over 50 Years of Service, metal 15.00

Kitchen Collectibles

The kitchen is probably the one room in the house that generates more collectibles than any other. When one considers all the equipment needed to prepare food and the dishes required to serve and store food, it isn't surprising. Somehow, many gadgets make their way to the back of the cupboard when the latest and greatest contraption arrives on the scene. Often, it's those old timers that become the basis for a collection of kitchen items.

For additional listings, see *Warman's Antiques & Collectible* and *Warman's Americana & Collectibles*.

Apple slicer-corer, Ludwig Mfg, Co., Racine, WI, copyright 1960, stainless steel blades, mint on card 12.00

Basting spoon, graniteware, cobalt blue handle 15.00

Biscuit cutter, 1-12" d, tin, bail 10.00

Bundt pan, iron, scalloped, 4-1/2 x 10-1/2" 45.00

Cake carrier, aluminum, copper brushed color 27.50

Canister, Wear-Ever, copper, 13-pc, orig lids with some touch-up to black paint 60.00

Can opener, metal, red wood handle 15.00

Cheese crock, Kraft, ceramic, name emb on top, 3-1/2" d, 2-3/4" h 15.00

Chopping knife, Henry Disston & Sons, curved steel blade, wood handle, 6-1/2" l 20.00

Double boiler, cov, Porcelier, Sprig, pink, orange, and blue flowers, white ground 40.00

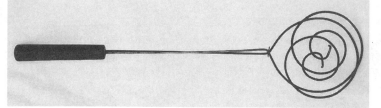

Kitchen collectibles, toaster, wire, wood handle, swivel base, sliding ring, 19-1/4" l, **$20.**

Dutch oven, enameled cast iron, aqua, mkd "DRU Made in Holland #82".................................... 165.00

Egg poacher, red enamel, gray enamel insert, 3-3/4" x 8"...... 24.00

Egg separator, aluminum, 9" l 7.00

Flour sifter, Bromweld's, side crank, red wood knob 15.00

Food chopper, aluminum shaft and blades, red wooden handle, Hazel Atlas measuring cup base 20.00

Hot pad holder, black boy, chalkware, 1940s, chips, 8" h 55.00

Lemon squeezer, tin-plated iron, 6-1/2" l 20.00

Mayonnaise maker, 8-1/4" h, Wesson, glass base, aluminum top and mixer, orig directions..... 60.00

Measuring spoon holder, ceramic sailboat and lighthouse, four slots for spoons, NJ souvenir 50.00

Meat grinder, Universal, bolts onto table, name and "Made in the USA" on side, wooden handle, used 15.00

Platter, Kraft, ceramic, 10" x 12-3/4" 18.00

Potato masher, 9" h, zig zag wire end, red catalin handle.......... 10.00

Pot scraper, Nye's Bread, black and white 275.00

Rolling pin, 10" l, 3-1/2" handles, aluminum 40.00

Set, cookie cutter, biscuit cutter, donut cutter and pastry cutter, mkd "Calumet," Wear-Ever Aluminum, made in USA, set of 4............ 14.00

Spoon rest, pear shape, red plastic, mkd "Fuller Brush Co." 5.00

Strawberry huller, Nip-It, 1906 .... 4.00

Kitchen collectibles, pie crimper, brass, 5-1/4" l, **$24.**

Tap-Icer, 9" l flexible hand held ice crusher, Williamsport, PA, maker, orig box.................................... 5.00

Tin, rect, Krispy Crackers......... 35.00

Vegetable slicer, Morris Metric, adjusting knob on side, metal, MIB 8.00

Waf-L-Ette and Patty Shell Molds, Handi Hostess Kit, Bonley Products, 1950s, orig box........ 5.00

Wall plaque
Fruit, 1950s............................. 8.00
Parrot, chalkware, 10" x 6" 18.00

Kitchen collectibles, tea kettle, black wooden knob on whistling cap, curved black metal handle, arched decoration on sides, some wear, **$5.**

Kitchen collectibles, grinder, Harras, No. 52, cast metal, side painted white, white enameled body, wood plunger and handle, **$45.**

Kitchen collectibles, chafing dish, chromed, Bakelite scroll handles, open diamond patterned cover, **$20.**

Kitchen Glassware

One area of kitchen collection that is brightly colored and durable is kitchen glassware. What started as a few manufacturers who were determined to create glass ware that could go from the stove to the table to the refrigerator has given us products few of us could live without, such as Pyrex and Corningware.

For additional listings, see *Warman's Americana & Collectibles* and *Warman's Glass*.

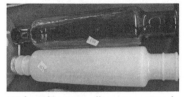

Kitchen glassware, rolling pins, original metal tops, top: cobalt blue, **$195**; bottom, opaque pale jadeite, **$225**.

Banana split dish, Jeannette, oval, crystal 5.00

Batter bowl
Anchor Hocking, set of 7", 8", 9", and 10" d, rimmed, transparent green................................. 95.00
Pyrex, nested set of three, farm motif dec 40.00

Beverage set, pitcher and six tumblers, Barlett-Collins, pastels, white loop dec 20.00

Bowl
6" d, jade-ite, Jeannette 18.00
7-1/2" d, cobalt blue, Hazel Atlas 45.00
8" d, green, Hocking............. 15.00
8" d, Orange Dot, custard..... 32.00

Butter dish, cov, one-pound size
Criss Cross, crystal 24.00
Federal, amber...................... 35.00

Cake plate, Snowflake, pink 35.00

Canister, cov, round, Seville Yellow, coffee, sugar or tea, 48-oz ... 135.00

Casserole, cov, Pyrex, one quart, divided, chartreuse, milk glass white cover with green gooseberry dec, MIB 25.00

Cheese dish, cov, slicer, opaque white 90.00

Chip and dip set, aquamarine, Anchor Hocking, orig foil label 30.00

Coffee measuring cup, Kitchen Aid advertisement, coffee measurement indicators, red and black, 4-3/8" h 18.00

Custard cup, green, Tufglas 6.50

Flour shaker
Deco, ivory, black lettering .. 45.00
Roman Arch, ivory.............. 45.00

Fruit bowl, Sunkist, pink....... 335.00

Grease jar
Red Dots, white 30.00
Seville Yellow, black trim 35.00

Iced tea spoons, colored handles, set of 12....................................... 60.00

Kitchen cabinet coffee Jar, 4" wide, 7" h, clear body, orig tin lid with minor dents, "S" in circle on bottom 48.00

Mayonnaise ladle
Amber, flat............................. 9.75
Pink, transparent 20.00

Measuring cup
2 oz, 1/4 cup, jade-ite, Jeannette 40.00
8 oz, Fire-King, one spout.... 18.50
8 oz, green, transparent 18.00
16 oz, green, regular handle 24.00

Mixing bowl
6-1/2" d, Federal, amber....... 10.00
7-1/4" d, Pyrex, yellow banded dots 10.00
7-1/2" d, Criss-Cross, blue.... 85.00
8-1/2" d, Criss-Cross, blue.. 100.00
11" d, Vitrock, white............. 15.00

Refrigerator bowl, cov, round, Jennyware, pink, 16-oz.......... 48.00

Refrigerator dish, cov
4" x 4", Criss-Cross, blue 35.00
4" x 8", Criss-Cross, blue 100.00

Kitchen glassware, reamer, Sunkist, green, marked "Made in USA, Pat No. 68764," **$45.**

6 x 3", transparent green, Tufglass 45.00
6-1/2" sq, Poppy Cocklebur, transparent green, US Glass 55.00
8" x 8", sq, amber, Federal.... 25.00

Rolling pin, dark amber, white speckles, small button knop ends, imperfections 225.00

Salt and pepper shakers, pr
Jennyware, ftd, pink 55.00
Ships, red trim, red lids........ 55.00

Salt box, crystal, 4-1/2" x 3-3/4" 25.00

Spice shaker, Genuine Three Crow Brand Warranted Pure Mace, Atlantic Spice Co. 28.00

Sugar bowl, Roman Arch, custard, red dot 60.00

Sundae, ftd, pink, Federal........ 12.00

Syrup pitcher
Crystal, gold catalin handle . 12.00
Crystal, flower etch 35.00

Tom & Jerry set, custard, bowl and 12 mugs 135.00

Towel bar, 24" l, crystal, orig hardware............................... 15.00

Tray, sq, Jeannette, handle, pink 18.00

Trivet, 9" d, round, Pyrex, crystal 12.00

Kitchen Prayer Ladies

These pretty ladies entered the kitchen scene in the 1970s and gently reminded us of the power of prayer as we bustled about.

Bank, pink.............................. 275.00

Bud vase 160.00

Canister, Instant Coffee
    Blue...................................... 175.00
    Pink....................................... 130.00

Cookie jar
    Blue...................................... 250.00
    Pink...................................... 250.00

Crumb pan 60.00

Napkin holder, pink 40.00

Salt and pepper shakers, pr, blue or
    pink.................................... 40.00

String holder, pink............... 350.00

Teapot, pink............................ 230.00

Kitchen Prayer Ladies, napkin holder, Enesco, 6-1/4" h, **$30.**

Knowles, Edwin M. China Company

Some collectors associate the name Edwin M. Knowles China Co. with fine dinnerware. Others correlate it with limited edition collector plates. The firm was founded in West Virginia in 1900 and continued producing quality wares until 1963. The company used several different marks, and should not be confused with Knowles, Taylor, & Knowles, another manufacturer of fine dinnerware.

Berry bowl, Yorktown, wheat dec
    .... 8.00

Bread and butter plate
    Accent Solid Color, dark brown
    .... 7.00
    Beverly.................................... 4.00
    Chalet..................................... 3.00
    Golden Wheat......................... 3.00

Bowl, Mexican motif 35.00

Cake plate, Yorktown, white ground,
    blue daisies 7.50

Chop plate, Petit Point Pastel
    Bouquet 27.50

Cookie jar, Tulip pattern, 7-1/2" h
    .... 65.00

Creamer, Chalet....................... 10.00

Cup and saucer
    Accent Solid Color, chartreuse
    .... 12.00
    Golden Wheat......................... 6.00
    Orange Poppy 20.00
    Rhondo 12.00

Dessert bowl, Forsythia 10.00

Dinner plate
    Deanna 10.00
    Forsythia................................ 12.00
    Golden Wheat......................... 5.00
    Petit Point Pastel Bouquet.... 12.00

Doll, Little Red Riding Hood, MIB
    .... 30.00

Fruit bowl
    Accent Solid Color, gray....... 12.00
    Orange Poppy 9.00

Gravy boat, attached underplate,
    Williamsburg......................... 40.00

Mixing bowls, nesting, white, tulip
    design 125.00

Mother's Day plate, Norman
    Rockwell, 1988 .... 15.00

Platter
    Carlton.................................. 38.00
    Carolina 45.00
    Deanna 15.00
    Rhondo 16.00

Sauceboat, stand, Mayflower... 35.00

Soup bowl
    Orange Poppy 16.00
    Yorktown, floral dec.............. 8.50

Souvenir plate, San Francisco Bay,
    Alcatraz, Treasure Island, 10" d
    .... 75.00

Sugar bowl, cov, Chalet 14.00

Vegetable bowl
    Forsythia............................... 30.00
    Rhondo 15.00

Water pitcher, Tulip pattern, ice lip
    .... 60.00

Edwin M. Knowles, cake plate, Yorktown pattern, maroon, 11-1/4" d, **$10.**

Knowles, Taylor & Knowles

Knowles, Taylor & Knowles was located in East Liverpool, Ohio. In business from 1854 to 1931, its production included ironstone, yellowware, and fine dinnerware, as well as translucent china known as Lotus Ware. Knowles, Taylor & Knowles used as many as nine different marks.

Baker, Victory, rose medallion, c1925, 9-1/2" l **20.00**

Butter dish, cov, round, gold band, orig drainer insert **45.00**

Casserole, cov, Victory, 10" l.... **35.00**

Chamber pot, white ground, gold medallions and dec **45.00**

Chamber set, blue floral transfer print, gold trim, five pcs **130.00**

Dinner plate
Ebonette................................. **38.00**
Grapevine, 10-1/4" d **10.00**

Milk pitcher, white, 1891-93 mark, 7" h....................................... **250.00**

Platter
Bittersweet, 15" l................... **25.00**
Coronado, 14-3/4" l **20.00**
Plymouth, 13" l..................... **20.00**

Tier, Ebonnette, three snack plates, black and white **12.00**

Knowles, Taylor & Knowles, Bluebird oval dish, 5-1/8" x 9-3/8", **$40.**

Vegetable bowl, roosters in center, hens around edge **15.00**

Wash bowl and pitcher set, large bowl and pitcher, small pitcher, soap dish, toothbrush holder, white, blue floral transfer............... **250.00**

Lady's Head Vases

Planters and vases in the shape of a lady's head are common sights at any flea market. But, did you ever notice how many variations and styles there are? These holders were popular with florists from the 1940s through the early 1960s.

For additional listings, see *Warman's Americana & Collectibles*.

Lady's head vases, from left: blond with upswept hairdo, one hand raised, dangling pearl earrings, Parma, #A-174, original foil label, **$40;** Christmas motif, fur trimmed red hat with holly trim, blond hair, pearl necklace, fur trimmed red dress, **$45;** blond, side curls and blue flowers in hair, slightly tilted head, pearl necklace, orange dress with white panel with matching blue flowers, Relpo, **$30;** lady in white hat and suit, blond, eyes closed, pearl necklace, unmarked, **$25.**

Unmarked
Baby, blond hair, open mouth, pink ruffled bonnet tied under chin, pink dress, 5-3/4" h **24.00**
Blue bows, pearls, head tilted to right **40.00**
Cowboy, brown hair, blue eyes, yellow hat and neckerchief, yellow star-shaped badge, unmarked, 6" h **35.00**
Green dress, gold trim **25.00**
Older face, small, white, gold trim **15.00**
White hat, purple flower and trim **20.00**
White hat, yellow flower and trim **20.00**

Ardco, blond, green dress, 7-1/2" h **265.00**

Japan
German Shepherd, 6" h **125.00**
Hair in upswept style, red bow **45.00**
Teenager, long straight blond hair, green dress **95.00**

Napcoware
#C3307, red hat and dress, orig foil label, 6" h **185.00**
#C6428, blue dress, orig paper sticker, 6" h **195.00**
#C6429, blue dress, white collar, 7-1/2" h **215.00**
#X7639, holly trim, red cap and dress **185.00**

National Potteries Co., #C5047, wide brimmed hat, orig foil label, 6-1/2" h **250.00**

Relpo, Japan, #K1633, green dress with white trim, 7-1/4" h..... **290.00**

Lady's head vase, Napcoware, 5-3/4" h, **$95.**

Lady's head vase, blue tinted hair and matching shoulders, gold trim, applied red roses and green leaves in hair and at neck, unmarked, **$20.**

Lamps

Flea markets are great places to find all kind of lamps and replacement parts. When considering a purchase, check to see that all necessary parts are included. As a precautionary measure, any vintage lamp should be rewired before placed into service.

For additional listings, see *Warman's Antiques & Collectibles, Warman's Americana & Collectibles*, and *Warman's Glass.*

Lamps, table, classic '50s style, white and black stripes shades, **$600.**

Bedroom, Southern Belle, blue, orig shade... 80.00

Lamps, chandelier, three tiers of clear icicle-like cylinders, chrome fixtures, **$195.**

Character
Casper, Archlamp, 1950, 17" h
.... 75.00
Donald Duck, china, Donald holding axe to tree trunk, 1940s
.... 150.00
Popeye, Alan Jay, 1959 .... 50.00
Woody Woodpecker, 1971.... 15.00

Children's
ABC blocks, wood and plastic, linen-over-cardboard shade
.... 25.00
Sesame Street characters, plastic and wood.......................... 15.00

Dresser, Porcelair, black cameo, silhouette of young woman, surrounded by ribbon 48.00

Floor, brass, adjustable arm..... 25.00

Headboard, pink shade, chrome
.... 65.00

Lava, red flakes move when heated
.... 70.00

Motion
Antique cars, Econolite, 1957, 11" h
.... 150.00
Fountain of Youth.............. 130.00
Niagara Falls, Goodman, extra wide style 150.00
Snow scene, bridge, Econolite
.... 175.00

Table
Milk can, metal base, repainted, decals added, no shade 10.00
Porcelain, white, baluster shaped base, painted floral dec, orig silk shade 40.00
Small stoneware crock, brown-and-white linen shade 35.00

Television
Gondola, ceramic, brown with gold trim, marked "Copyright Premco Mfg Co, Chicago, IL, 1954," 16" w, 7" h............................... 45.00
Horse Head, ceramic, 12 x 10-3/4"
.... 25.00
Panther, black, 8-1/2 x 6-1/2" 35.00

Lamps, ceramic, pony, 8" h (excluding fixture), **$15.**

Wall, tole, peach ground, white floral trim.. 10.00

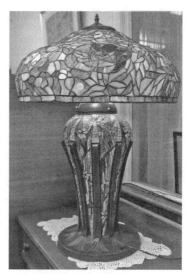

Lamps, table, stained glass, contemporary, **$200.**

Lap Desks

Because they were portable, lap desks (or folding desks as they were sometimes called) were the laptop computers of the 18th and 19th centuries. They also provided a firm writing surface as well as a place to store papers and writing instruments. Some examples are quite ornate, having locks, drawers, and even secret compartments.

Black lacquer, mother of pearl inlay of flowers, leaves and grape clusters, 4" h, 14" w, 10" d ... **600.00**

Cherry, replaced felt writing surface, ink stains in base **75.00**

Mahogany, brass bands, green leather writing surface, 6-1/2" h, 17" w, 9-3/8" d **650.00**

Mahogany, satinwood inlay, Victorian, replaced leather writing surface, repairs to underlying wood **395.00**

Rosewood, mother-of-pearl inlay, velvet writing surface, 4-1/2" h, 13" w, 10-1/4" d **700.00**

Walnut, velvet writing surface, 8-1/2" d x 12" x 5-1/2" **295.00**

Lap desk, mixed hardwoods, shown open, 15-3/4" w, 10-1/2" deep, 11-3/4" h, **$195.**

Lefton China

Founded by George Zoltan Lefton, this company has created china, porcelain, and ceramic tableware, animals, and figurines. Lefton wares are well marked, and some also include a Japanese factory mark.

For additional listings, see *Warman's Antiques & Collectibles*.

Bank, Hubert the Lion.............. **40.00**

Bookends, pr, white ceramic, gold and brown dec, football and baseball motif, gold and red foil label, 1950s **40.00**

Cake plate, Hollyberry, matching server **45.00**

Candy box, cov, heart-shaped, red and white, doves, #5597 .... **22.00**

Cigarette set, Elegant Rose, five pcs **200.00**

Cup and saucer
Christmas Cardinal **25.00**
Roses..................................... **45.00**

Decanter, figural, monk **85.00**

Dish, green holly leaf shape **12.00**

Egg, roosters and chick on lid, paper label, #3429............................ **25.00**

Figure
Birthday Boys **30.00**
Dachsund............................... **35.00**
Kewpie, orig foil label, 1950s, 7-1/4" h............................. **145.00**
Madonna and Child, #543.... **75.00**
January Angel, #3332 .... **22.00**
Pixie on mushroom watching frog, 4" h **20.00**
Rock A Bye Baby in the Treetop, 8" h **100.00**
Swan, white, gold dec........... **45.00**

Mug
Elf handle, green, #4284....... **15.00**
Grant..................................... **35.00**
Jackson.................................. **35.00**

Music box, Birthday Girl, February, 1983 .... **30.00**

Planter
Angel, on cloud **40.00**
Calico Donkey **35.00**

Lady, applied flowers on dress and lapel, holding umbrella, gold trim, 8-1/2" h **60.00**

Salt and pepper shakers, pr, fruit baskets, 2-3/4" **24.00**

Snack set, Fleur de Lis **50.00**

Teapot, To A Wild Rose, #2561 .... **165.00**

Wall plaque, mermaids, three-pc set **150.00**

Lefton China, figure, woodcock, original foil label, **$20.**

Lefton China, figure, Koala bear and cub, original foil label, **$30.**

Lenox

Walter Scott Lenox opened his porcelain factory in 1906, employing potters and decorators, whom he lured from Belleek. Fine Lenox is almost translucent in appearance. The firm is still in business and many factory outlet stores sell its products.

For additional listings, see *Warman's Antiques & Collectible* and *Warman's American Pottery & Porcelain*.

Lenox, limited edition figure, A Cherished Gift, 2004, MIB, **$65.**

Lenox, Christmas plate, 1985, original box, **$15.**

Ashtray with match holder, white, pink rose dec 45.00

Bowl, two handles, etched gold trim, M-139, pre-1930 .... 45.00

Candleholder, white, pink rose dec, 3-1/2" d 10.00

Christmas ornament, inn, gold trim, orig box 35.00

Cigarette box, white apple blossoms, green ground, wreath mark .. 40.00

Coffeepot, Cretan #0316 .... 165.00

Compote, Summer Terrace, 13" d 65.00

Cup and saucer
    Alden 25.00
    Fairfield 35.00
    Golden Wheat 35.00

Figure
    Snow Queen 70.00
    Stardust 70.00

Fruit basket, 5th anniversary plate, metal handle 10.00

Honey pot, 5" h, 6-1/4" d underplate, ivory beehive, gold bee and trim 85.00

Platter, Oak Leaf, platinum trim, 13-1/2" l 75.00

Salt, molded seashells and coral, green wreath mark, 3" d 35.00

Tea strainer, hp small pink flowers 72.00

Vase, ivory ground, pale pink roses dec, gold trim, gold mark 55.00

Lenox, vase, modern production type, **$45.**

Lenox, chop plate, Charleston pattern, **$65.**

Letter Openers

These knife-like collectibles are also handy little desk accessories. Constructed of almost any type of material, early manufacturers found them to be wonderful tools for advertising.

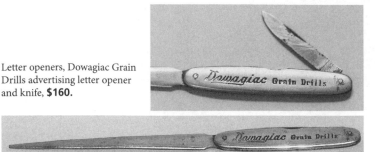

Letter openers, Dowagiac Grain Drills advertising letter opener and knife, **$160.**

metal, 7/8" applied medallion near top with text and image of race car, late 1930s 40.00

Political, Republican Convention 1976 Kansas City, Missouri, black plastic...................................... 22.00

Silver, monogrammed, English hallmarks............................. 125.00

Silver plated, horse head, Reed & Barton 95.00

Souvenir
Chicago's World's Fair, Federal Building, marble handle, metal blade 95.00
Florida, alligator shape, celluloid 10.00
Toledo, brass-colored cross, 6-5/8" l 10.00

Advertising

The Empire Varnish Co., Cleveland, Ohio, metal, 8" l 7.00
Fuller Brush Man, plastic 8.00
Martin Mfg. Co., Pick Up Beaner, Keck-Gonnerman's Bean Thresher, Phone 325, Bad Axe, Mich., celluloid handle, 8-1/2" l 20.00
Meyers Engel Co. Insurance, Harrison, 6" l copper ruler 6.00
Pennsylvania Independent Telephone Association, 50th Anniversary, 1902-1952, plastic handle, 8-1/8" l 10.00

Brass, emb florals on handle 15.00

Celluloid, metal blade, 6-1/2" l 28.00

Motor Speedway Indinapolis, Ind., 6-1/4" l, copper luster over white

Letter openers, souvenir plank, plaque reads "From the teak of H. M. S. Ironduke, Admirial Tellice's Flagship, Jutland, 1916," 10" l, **$65.**

Liberty Blue Dinnerware

Flea markets are buzzing with this blue and white dinnerware. Nicknamed Liberty Blue by dealers and collectors, the correct name is "Staffordshire Liberty Blue." Enoch Wedgwood in the Staffordshire district in England made it in 1976. The style is based on the traditional blue and white designs made in the Staffordshire district in the 19th century. The scenes reflect important times in Colonial history. Used as a promotional premium, it was eagerly acquired as a tie in to the American Bicentennial. Many mint examples are appearing on flea market tables, so collectors can afford to be choosy about condition as they build their collections of this interesting pattern.

Baker, Minute Men, oval 50.00

Berry bowl, Betsy Ross, 5-1/2" d 14.00

Bread and butter plate, Monticello, 6" d... 8.00

Cereal bowl, Mount Vernon, 6-1/2" d 22.00

Cream pitcher, Paul Revere 35.00

Cup and saucer, Paul Revere and Old North Church 17.50

Dinner plate, Independence Hall, 10" d....................................... 30.00

Gravy boat underplate, Governors House, Williamsburg............. 14.00

Pie plate, Washington Leaving Christ Church, 7" d........................... 20.00

Platter
Governor's Palace, Williamsburg, 12" l 65.00

Washington crossing Delaware, 14" l 85.00

Liberty Blue dinnerware, platter, oval, Governor's Palace, Williamsburg, 12" l, **$65.**

Liberty Blue dinnerware, dinner plate, Independence Hall, 10" d, **$30.**

Soup plate, flat rim, North Church, 8-1/2" d 30.00

Sugar bowl, cov, Betsy Ross 40.00

Teapot, cov, Minute Men, 8-7/8" w, 6-1/2" h 170.00

Tureen, cov, Boston tea party 250.00

Vegetable bowl, Fraunces Tavern, round 50.00

Lighters

Cigarette lighters have attracted collectors for years. Watch for examples with figural forms or with interesting advertising. Look for examples in good condition, but exercise caution when trying to determine if a lighter is in working order.

Advertising
Amoco, Barlow 50.00
CBC Radio, Bowers, Canada, 3-5/8" h 85.00
Loretto Casket Co., enameled on both sides, Japan 85.00
Marlboro Country Store, Zippo 40.00
Mutual Metal Products, Zippo, orig box 75.00
Sarah Coventry, silver lettering on black, Japan 25.00
Winchester Inn, Long Beach, CA, Scripto Vu 55.00

Alligator, ceramic, made in Japan, 1-3/4" h, 5" l 28.00

Boat, Occupied Japan, Bakelite and chrome 140.00

Bowling, Zippo 85.00

Donkey, ceramic, "Japan" on side, Amico, 2" h 35.00

Lantern, hp floral dec, mkd "Weston, USA" 30.00

Lenox, table model, goblet shape, Ronson 20.00

Lucite, dark pink, 1940s, 4" h 85.00

Royal Crown Derby, Imari pattern, Ronson 100.00

Scripto Vu, Ski-Doo snowmobile, 1960s 45.00

Space Needle, chrome 180.00

Spaniel, ceramic, 4-3/4" l 25.00

Stein, nautical motif, pewter, made in Japan, 5" h 20.00

Trichette Rhinestones, Wiesner, faceted prong set rhinestones 85.00

Wedgwood, jasper, light blue, white classical design 65.00

Zippo
Brushed chrome 18.00
Fishing lure, MIB 130.00
Ship and a lighthouse design, white on chrome 15.00

Limited Edition Collectibles

You're guaranteed to find limited edition collectibles at any flea market you visit. This multi-million dollar market includes many types of objects, with some very dedicated artists and companies offering their wares. Please remember that much of the value of a limited edition object lies with the original box, packaging, etc.

For additional listings, see *Warman's Americana & Collectibles.* Also see specific makers, such as Bing & Grondahl in this edition.

Bell
Bleeding Heart, Fenton, 1998 **60.00**
Christmas, Bing & Grondahl, 1983 .... 25.00
Christmas Angel, Kaiser, 1977 .... 20.00
Hummel, Schmid, 1979........ 20.00
O Come All Ye Faithful, Anri, 1978 .... 35.00

Christmas ornament
Angel, Danbury Mint, 4" h... 48.00
Angel Bear, Enesco, 1992 .... 6.00
Bailey and Matthew, Boyds, 1996 .... 10.00
Camille, Christopher Radko, 1994 .... 20.00

Candy cane, Wallace Silversmiths, 1986 .... 35.00
Choir Boy, Christopher Radko, 1992 .... 12.00
Christmas Castle, Reed & Barton, 1980 .... 60.00
Christmas is Love, Coca-Coloa, 1995 .... 5.00
Hearts & Flowers, Christopher Radko, 1990 .... 10.00
Holly Ball, Christopher Radko, 1991 .... 12.00
Holy Family, Hallmark, 1998 12.00
Sleigh bell, silver-plated, Wallace Silversmiths, 1992............ 30.00
Snowflake, sterling silver, Gorham, 1973 .... 95.00

Stewart at Play, Charming Tails, 1995 .... 5.00
Twelve Days of Christmas, sterling silver ingots, Franklin Mint 90.00

Cottage
Aurora Rainbow Row, Shelia's Collectibles, 1993 .... 10.00
Cockington Forge, Lilliput Lane 65.00
Conway Scenic Railroad Station, Shelia's Collectibles, 1994 18.00
Granny's Bonnet, Lilliput Lane 25.00
Green Gables, Anne, Hawthorne 40.00

Portland Head Lighthouse, Spencer
Collins, 1984 .... **60.00**
Rose Cottage, David Winter, 1980
.... **60.00**
Willow Wisp, David Winter, 1991
.... **90.00**

Figure
Bedtime, Sarah Kay, 1983 .... **20.00**
Budweiser Frogs, 1996 .... **20.00**
Can I Help Too?, Dept 56
Snowbaby, 1991................ **30.00**
Chocolate Factory, Dave Grossman,
1999...................................... **15.00**
Circus Serenade, Anri **85.00**
For My Sweetheart, Anri, 1987
.... **70.00**
Ivory Debutante Ball, Lenox **80.00**
Good Friends are Forever, Enesco,
1989................................... **15.00**
Our Puppy, Anri, 1985 .... **60.00**
Out of Step, Schmid, 1985.... **25.00**
Sagebrush Kids, Leading the Way,
G. Perillo, 1987................. **25.00**
Small Talk, Anri **60.00**
The Bride, Maud Humphrey
.... **40.00**

Plate
A Christmas Welcome, T. Kinkade,
Bradford Exchange, 1997. **15.00**
Ashley, Gone with the Wind Series,
Edwin M. Knowles, MIB
.... **80.00**
Cardinal, Audubon Society, 1973
.... **50.00**
Caroling, Disney, Schmid, 1975
.... **15.00**
Christmas in Mexico, Royal
Doulton, 1973 .... **10.00**
Down the Alps, Schmid, 1987
.... **60.00**
Easter, 1980, Edwin M. Knowles,
MIB **30.00**
Flowers for Mother, Schmid, 1974
.... **85.00**
Good Catch, Hamilton, 1992 **15.00**
Hopes and Dreams, Edwin M.
Knowles, 1987, MIB......... **20.00**
Just Married, Franklin Mint, 1994
.... **15.00**
Sunday Best, Reco, 1983 ...... **50.00**
The Honeymooners, Hamilton,
1987.................................... **15.00**
Toby Fillpot, Davenport Pottery
.... **20.00**

Limited editions, figure, The Legendary
Princess, Indian maiden, Lenox, MIB,
$45.

Valentine's Day, Edwin M. Knowles,
1981, MIB......................... **20.00**

Limoges

Limoges porcelain has been produced in Limoges, France, for more than a century by numerous factories, in addition to the famed Haviland. One of the most frequently encountered marks is "T. & V. Limoges," on the wares made by Tressman and Vought. Other identifiable Limoges marks are "A. L." (A. Lanternier), "J. P. L." (J. Pouyat, Limoges), "M. R." (M. Reddon), "Elite," and "Coronet."

Bowl, 4-1/2" h, ftd, hp, wild roses and
leaves, sgd "J. E. Dodge, 1892"
.... **85.00**

Box, cov, 4-1/4" sq, cobalt blue and
white ground, cupids on lid, pate-
sur-pate dec **195.00**

Cache pot, 7-1/2" w, 9" h, male
and female pheasants on front,

Limoges, oyster plate, white background,
mauve decoration, six oyster shell-
shaped depressions, center shell shaped
reserve, **$175.**

mountain scene on obverse, gold
handles and four ball feet
.... **225.00**

Cake plate, 11-1/2" d, ivory ground,
brushed gold scalloped rim, gold
medallion, marked "Limoges T &
V".. **75.00**

Candy dish, 6-1/2" d, ftd, two
handles, silver overlay, white
ground, c1920....................... **95.00**

Chocolate pot, 13" h, purple violets
and green leaves, cream-colored
ground, gold handle, spout, and
base, sgd "Kelly JPL/France"
.... **350.00**

Creamer and sugar, cov, 3-1/4" h,
purple flowers, white ground, gold
handle and trim................... **100.00**

Cup and saucer, hp, roses, gold trim,
artist sgd **75.00**

Dessert plates, 8-1/4" d, Laviolette,
gilt scalloped rim, printed green
husk trim, center violet and grape
sprays, retailed by Lewis Straus

& Sons, New York, late 19th/early
20th C, price for 12-pc set
.... **220.00**

Dresser set, pink flowers, pastel blue,
green, and yellow ground, large
tray, cov powder, cov rouge, pin
tray, talc jar, pr candlesticks, seven-
pc set.................................... **425.00**

Limoges, cake plate, Old Abbey pattern,
$45.

Figure, 25" h, 13" w, three girls, arms entwined, holding basket of flowers, books, and purse, marked "C & V" and "L & L" 460.00

Fish service, 22-3/4" platter, ten 9-1/4" plates, sgd "A. R. Bullock 1894" 1,555.00

Hair receiver, blue flowers and white butterflies, ivory ground, gold trim, marked "JPL" 80.00

Lemonade pitcher, matching tray, water lily dec, sgd "Vignard Limoges" 350.00

Nappy, 6" d, curved gold handle, gold scalloped edges, soft pink blossoms, blue-green ground................ 35.00

Oyster plate, 9-1/4" d, molded, scalloped edge, gilt rim, enamel dec of poppy sprays, raised gilt detailing, marked "A. Lanternier &

Co., Limoges," early 20th C, price for set of eight 1,500.00

Panel, 4-1/2" x 3-3/8", enameled, Christ with crown of thorns, framed 250.00

Pitcher, 6" h, 5-1/8" d, platinum handle, platinum mistletoe berries and leaves, gray and pink ground, Art Deco style, marked "J. P. Limoges, Pouyat"................. 155.00

Plaque, 7-5/8" x 4-1/2", enameled, cavalier, after Meissonier, multicolored garb and banner, late 19th C 460.00

Plate
8" d, transfer scene of peacocks and flowers, hp border.......... 290.00
9-1/2" d, Cavalier smoking pipe, marked "Coronet"............ 90.00

Punch bowl, 14" d, hand painted grapes, marked "T& V Limoges France Depose," minor repairs 320.00

Snuff box, cov, hp, wildflowers and gold tracery, pink ground, artist sgd, dated 1800................... 200.00

Tankard set, 14" h tankard, four mugs, hp, grape dec, gold and green ground, five-pc set............... 450.00

Tea set, 9-1/2" h cov teapot, two 3" h cups, two 4-1/2" d saucers, 15" d tray, cream ground, floral dec, gold trim, red stamp "L. S. & S. Limoges France," green stamp "Limoges France" on two saucers, slight wear
.... 500.00

Vase, 15" h, hand painted, sgd "Florence Sladnick" 350.00

Lincoln, Abraham

This famous American president is a favorite among collectors. Lincoln memorabilia is also a favorite with many museums, and genuine vintage articles can be prohibitively expensive. Contemporary items bearing Lincoln's likeness are more reasonably priced, however.

Abraham Lincoln, souvenir china tumbler, "Abraham Lincoln's Old Home, Springfield, Illinois," made in Germany, 3-3/4" h, **$40.**

Bank, cast metal, bronze finish, 5-1/2" h 75.00

Bust, bronze, c1900, 15" h 95.00

Calendar plate, 1911, Lincoln portrait, "Compliments of Chas. Seepe & Sons, Peru, Ill.," 9" d 95.00

Face jug, green running glaze, incised inscription on back "Abraham Lincoln, Shyster Lawyer from Illonois (sic) Also Was President Of The North," sgd "Cleater Meaders, 1993," 12-1/2" h 475.00

Newspaper, *Harper's Weekly*, March 2, 1861, Abraham Lincoln, the President-Elect, addressing the people from the Astor House balcony 40.00

Plate, commemorative, 150th anniversary of Lincoln's birth, Lincoln image, floral border, Enoch & Ralph Woods, 1959, 10" d 40.00

Tobacco silk, image of Lincoln with facsimile signature, black on white, 3" h....................................... 100.00

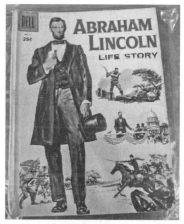

Abraham Lincoln, comic book, *Abraham Lincoln*, Dell, No. 1, **$15.**

Lindbergh, Charles

Collectors are fascinated with this early aviator and his adventures. Look for printed items, commemorative pieces, and even textiles that pertain to his many flights.

Book

The Lone Eagle: Lindbergh, Blakely Printing Co., Chicago, 1929, color portrait photo, 20 pgs, stiff paper 8" x 9" 35.00

War Within and Without, diaries and letters of Anne Morrow Lindbergh, Harcourt Brace Jovanovich, 1980, dj 8.50

Bookends, pr, 5-1/2" h, cast iron, Charles Lindbergh, wearing helmet, emb, 1929 .... 115.00

Booklet, 4" x 4-1/2", 34 pgs, *America in the Air,* sponsored by Dr. Pierce medical firm and hospital, c1927 .... 12.00

Children's book, *Boy's Story of Lindbergh, Lone Eagle*, by Richard J. Beamish, hardcover 35.00

Commemorative coin, issued for golden anniversary of flight, bust portrait, bronze 25.00

Commemorative glass, 2-3/4" x 3-3/4" h, white glass, frosted arm and text with Spirit of St. Louis flying between Statue of Liberty and Eiffel Tower, text "New York 33 Hrs-30 Mins. Paris, May 21-27" 50.00

Charles Lindbergh, poster about baby kidnapping, copies of related items, modern black frame, **$35.**

First day cover 2.25

Magazine, *Time*, June 13, 1938, color cover of Lindbergh and scientist working on Fountain of Age, 76 black-and-white pages, 8-1/2" x 11" 15.00

Newspaper, Nebraska State Journal, May 1927, covering Atlantic flight 55.00

Pin, Lucky Lindbergh 22.00

Plate, yellow glazed china, color graphics of smiling Lindy, plane over ocean between Statue of Liberty and Eiffel Tower, First To Navigate The Air In Continuous Flight From New York To Paris-1927, Limoges China Co., 8-1/2" d 24.00

Postcard, 3-1/2" x 5-1/2"

Red-tinted, Lindbergh in cockpit of Spirit of St. Louis.............. 15.00

Sepia-tone photo of Lindbergh with unidentified gentleman on ornate balcony, Underwood copyright, unused 25.00

Publicity photo, glossy sepiatone, smiling Lindbergh flanked by American and French flags, ©P & A, archivally matted and framed 40.00

Sheet music, *Lucky Lindy!,* 1927 .... 20.00

Tablet, 5-1/2" x 9", Colonel Charles A. Lindbergh Trans-Oceanic Flights, softcover 75.00

Tapestry, New York to Paris 115.00

Linemar Toys

This Japanese toy company made some of the most endearing character toys, plus other toys that captured the amusement of many souls, both young and old.

Cabin cruiser, litho tin, battery operated, detailed interior, fabric covered seats, orig box, 12" l 250.00

Clarabell Clown, tin mechanical action, 6-1/2" h 210.00

Donald Duck, Huey, Louey, and Dewey Marching Soldiers, clockwork motor, rubber titles, 11-1/4" l, scratches 375.00

Feeding birdwatcher, litho tin and plush, battery operated, orig box, 7-1/2" h 365.00

Gym toy, Donald Duck, clockwork motor, celluloid figure, red bar, doing acrobatics, 4-1/2" h ... 245.00

Linemar Toys, Popeye lantern, "One of the Many Linemar Toys, Do You Have Them All," wear to original box, **$85.**

Mickey Mouse

Moving van, litho tin friction, wear, 1950s, 13" l 300.00

Rocking on Pluto, litho tin wind-up, replaced ears and tail, 5-1/2" h 850.00

Roller skating, litho tin wind-up, pants faded, orig ears, 5-1/2" h 525.00

Xylophone, litho, clockwork motor, black, red, and yellow, orig box lid, 7" h, chips, tears to lid 750.00

Music box, cowboy dancing to music, tin and plastic, battery operated, orig box, 5" h 175.00

Pinocchio, litho tin wind-up, 6" h 100.00

Pluto the Acrobat Trapeze, celluloid, wind-up, 10" h 80.00

Prehistoric animal, T-Rex, litho tin wind-up, 9" l, 6" h, orig box 230.00

Rocket express, litho tin wind-up, train and space ship, orig box, 5-1/2" sq............................... 575.00

Walt Disney's mechanical tricycle, celluloid Donald Duck riding tin wind-up, box with illus of Mickey riding tricycle, 3-3/4" x 4" x 2-1/2" box 325.00

Linens

No dining room or bedroom is properly dressed without an assortment of linens. Today's collectors treasure these textiles. Some pieces were hand-made and exhibit exquisite craftsmanship, although machine-made examples have a beauty all their own. Enjoy them, but use them with care.

Linens, doily, crocheted, pansy border, 30 weight multicolored cotton, 9-1/2" d, **$9.**

Doily
Crocheted, pink and cream, 7" sq 5.00
Embroidered, oval, shaped scalloped edge, scrolled design, 10" x 7" 6.50
Embroidered, round, holly dec, scalloped edge.................. 18.00

Doily press, floral printed cotton, shades of rose, green, and cream, lace edging, 1920s 45.00

Dresser scarf
Beige linen, cross-stitched red ivy motif, fringed.................. 20.00
White cotton, flower basket embroidered in bright colors, white crochet edging, c1930, 24" x 38"................................. 12.00

Handkerchief
Oriental motif, orig silver tag "Hermann Irish Linen," 15" sq 17.50
Purple petunias and green crocuses, orig label ""Pure Linen, Hand Rolled," 12" sq 17.50

Napkin
Cotton, polished, peach, edged in blue and gold grosgrain ribbon, 1930s, dinner size, set of 18 .... 40.00
Linen, 25" sq, set of 6 .... 20.00
Voile, white, orange, pink, green, and yellow floral pattern, pink border, luncheon size, set of 12, 1940s 36.00

Pillowcases, pr
Cotton, embroidered multicolored flower-basket design, crochet edge, c1930...................... 15.00
Maderia, white cotton, flower silhouetted in cutwork, embroidered with satin stitch 18.00

Placemat
Cotton, woven, rect, fringe, orange and brown, mid 1940s, set of six 35.00
Linen, white, embroidered edge, early 1940s, set of 16, some stains 48.00
Linen, white, lace edge, early 1940s, set of six 36.00

Tablecloth and napkins
Damask, light blue, some minor stains, 79-1/2" x 60", four napkins 15-1/2" sq 50.00

Linens, embroidered table scarf, 10" x 15", **$2.50.**

Irish linen, four matching napkins, orig box, never used, 54" sq 30.00

Table runner
Blue and white weave, winter cabin scene at each end 5.00
Dark green tapestry type, rabbit in garden setting, with fancy script alphabet, solid dark green cotton back 12.00

Teapot cozy, blue, tan, and ivory cotton floral and pineapple print, padded, blue linen lining, early 1900s...................................... 20.00

Tea towel, printed, unused mint condition
Calendar, 1972........................ 5.00
Cats 7.50
State birds................................ 6.50
Teapots, teacups and saucers 10.00

Little Golden Books

Read me a story! From the time Simon & Schuster published the first Little Golden Book in 1942 until today, millions of stories have been read. Collectors have many fun titles to choose from, and everyone is sure to have a childhood favorite. Collectors generally will pay a little more for earlier editions, identified with an alphabetical system, with A being the most desirable.

For additional listings, see *Warman's Americana & Collectibles.*

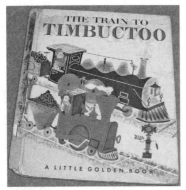

Little Golden Books, *The Train to Timbuctoo,* **$35.**

Animal Daddies and My Daddy,
#576, 1968, A............................ 5.00

Bambi, #B20, 1973 .... 12.00

Bozo the Clown, 2nd ed. **8.00**

Bugs Bunny's Birthday, 1st ed., 1950,
fair condition............................. 7.00

Cars and Trucks, 5th printing, 1971
.... 14.00

Chitty Chitty Bang Bang........ **20.00**

Christmas Carols, 1946, Connie
Malvern 10.00

Cinderella's Friends, #D115, 1950, F
edition....................................... 7.50

Colors Are Nice, #496, 1962, A
.... 6.00

*Donny and Marie: The Top Secret
Project.....................................* 5.00

Dumbo's Book of Colors, #1015-23
.... 5.00

Exploring Space, 1958 .... **20.00**

Four Little Kittens, #322, 1973, 6th
printing..................................... 4.00

Frosty the Snow Man, 1951 ..... 18.00

Gene Autry and Champion, 1956
.... 25.00

Hansel and Gretel, 1945........... 10.00

Home for a Bunny, 1979............ 4.00

Hop, Little Kangaroo, #558........ 5.00

Heidi, 1st ed., 1954..................... 6.00

Hush, Hush, It's Sleepytime, #577,
1968, A..................................... 6.50

I Have A Secret, #495, 1962, A... 8.50

Lady and the Tramp, #2082..... 15.00

Lassie and the Big Clean-Up Day,
#572, 1971, A............................ 6.00

Little Golden Book of Holidays 3.00

Little Golden Book of Wild Animals,
#499, 1960 .... 3.00

My Little Dinosaur, #571, 1971, A
.... 6.00

My Little Golden Calendar for 1961,
illus by Richard Scarry.......... 10.00

*Pluto And The Adventure of the
Golden Scepter,* #D124, 1972, A
.... 6.50

Prayers for Children, 1942, 9th
printing.................................. 10.00

Rudolph the Red Nosed Reindeer,
1958 .... 18.00

So Big, #574, 1968, red spine, A 15.00

Supercar, #492, 1962, A 25.00

Tawny Scrawny Lion, 1991, with orig
plush lion............................... 40.00

The Christmas Donkey, 1984 .... 3.00

The Christmas Story, 1952 .... 6.00

The Fuzzy Duckling, 1949 .... 10.00

The Gingerbread Man, 6th ed.
.... 5.00

Little Golden Books, *Hansel and Gretel,* **$10.**

The Golden Egg, #486, illus by Lillian
Obligado 7.50

The Happy Golden ABC's, 1979
.... 4.00

The Happy Little Whale, 3rd ed
.... 5.00

The Little Red Caboose, 13th ed.
.... 5.00

*Twelve Days of Christmas, A
Christmas Carol,* 1983 .... 8.00

Tweety Plays Catch The Puddy Kat,
1975 .... 4.00

Underdog.................................. 20.00

Walt Disney's Old Yeller, 3rd ed.,
1950s....................................... 12.00

Wheels, 1st ed., 1952.................. 8.00

When I Grow Up, #578, 1968, A
.... 5.00

Where is the Bear? #568, 1967, 3rd
ed. 6.00

Little Orphan Annie

Little Orphan Annie has been the subject of comic strips, books, radio shows, and even a modern musical.

Little Orphan Annie, Big Little Book, Little Orphan Annie and The Ghost Gang, worn, **$25.**

Little Orphan Annie, action dolls from movie release, each **$5.**

Big little book, *Little Orphan Annie in the Den of the Thieves,* 1948 .... 25.00

Colorforms, 1970s.................. 10.00

Doll, plastic, Knickerbocker, 1982 .... 15.00

Figure, lead, 1940s
  Little Orphan Annie............. 20.00
  Sandy 20.00

Game, Little Orphan Annie Light Up the Candles, Ovaltine premium
  .... 80.00

Glass, Sunday Funnies, 1976, 5-1/2" h
  .... 15.00

Mug, Bettleware, Ovaltine, 1933
  .... 25.00

Pin, secret compartment decoder, Ovaltine, 1936 .... 20.00

Plate, Daddy Warbucks, Knowles
  .... 17.50

Shaker with lid, plastic, Ovaltine
  .... 80.00

Toothbrush holder, bisque, mkd "Japan," 4" h 145.00

Toy stove, orig green paint, 1930s, 4-1/2" x 5" 125.00

Little Red Riding Hood

This storybook character has been portrayed on all manner of items, the most popular of which are the pottery pieces sold by Hull. Some people feel that Hull manufactured the blanks and sent them to Royal China and Novelty Company in Chicago for decorating. Others think that Hull contracted with Royal China for both production and decoration. In any event, prices have escalated for these charming figures.

Reproduction alert.

Little Red Riding Hood, salt and pepper shakers, one with damage, 3" h, pair, **$75.**

Allspice jar............................. 375.00

Bank, standing....................... 575.00

Canister
  Cereal................................. 950.00

  Coffee................................... 750.00
  Flour 375.00
  Sugar.................................... 600.00
  Tea 750.00

Cookie jar
  Gold stars, red shoes 300.00
  Poinsettia trim.................... 300.00

Creamer, tab handle 275.00

Match holder, Little Red Riding Hood and Wolf, striker, Staffordshire 75.00

Milk pitcher.......................... 400.00

Mustard, orig spoon.............. 250.00

Salt and pepper shakers, pr
  3-1/4" h, incised "135889," gold trim 140.00
  5-1/2" h 150.00

Teapot, cov............................. 325.00

Little Red Riding Hood, cookie jar, Hull, multicolored and gold floral trim, **$375.**

Little Tikes

When it comes to toys, many surges in collectibility begin as adults start buying back the items they remember from their childhoods. With that being the case, expect Little Likes items to continue to grow in popularity. Flea markets are excellent sources for these plastic playthings. Because the items were mass-produced, look for examples in prime condition.

Doll house, family, furniture, horse and car, blue roof, 21" h, 28" w, 17" d....................................... **95.00**

Grandma's House, grandma, girl and accessories **32.00**

Mansion dollhouse, three-story, 32" h, 44" w, 18"d................... **65.00**

Noah's Ark, Noah, lion, giraffe and sheep.. **8.00**

Pirate, 4" h **4.00**

Roadway set, 68 pcs, with train, people, station, bridge and accessories **26.50**

School bus, nine figures **9.00**

Stable set, swinging doors, fence, horses and accessories........... **70.00**

Little Tikes, nesting farm animals, plastic, discontinued set of five, 5-1/8" to 1-5/8", **$10.**

Lladro Porcelain

Brothers José, Juan, and Vincente Lladro established this Spanish ceramics business in 1951. The company produces ceramic figurines and flowers. This segment of the collectibles market underwent a period of speculation several years ago. It remains to be seen whether the high prices realized at that time will remain in place when those items return to the marketplace.

For additional listings, see *Warman's Antiques & Collectibles*.

Llardo Porcelain, five assorted child figures, prices range from **$45** to **$75.**

Girl with lamb, 10-3/4" h 65.00

Heavenly cellist..................... 200.00

Kitty Patrol............................ 185.00

New Beginning, 1999 .... 200.00

Painter, 1969 .... 40.00

Pepita, sombrero 175.00

Puppy, butterfly on tail, 4" h 250.00

Riding the Waves, 1997........ 300.00

Sewing Circle, 1986 .... 200.00

Spanish Policeman.............. 100.00

Today's Lesson, 2000 .... 250.00

Watching the Pigs, 1974....... 150.00

Wedding Couple..................... 45.00

Woman, umbrella..................... 90.00

Angel's wish............................ 95.00

August Moon, 1982.............. 175.00

Boy with lamps, 1989 .... 30.00

Breezy Afternoon................. 180.00

Girl in nightgown, pigtails, puppy on lap, 7" h........................... 125.00

Lone Ranger

The Lone Ranger and his Indian pal Tonto rode into our lives on the silver screen, over the radio waves, and through the television. For those wishing to collect, there is a plethora of items from which to choose.

Lone Ranger, radio with original box, **$2,800.**

Badge, masked cowboy, sheriff and gun, metal, orig package, 1960s, mkd "Made in Japan" **8.00**

Big little book, *Lone Ranger and the Black Shirt Highwayman*, 1939 .... **20.00**

Biscuit tin, Huntley & Palmers, color photo of Clayton Moore on Silver, ©1961 .... **125.00**

Book, *The Lone Ranger and the Warhorse*, 1951 .... **30.00**

Bread wrapper, Weber's White Bread, red, white, and blue waxed paper **40.00**

Cereal premium, National Defenders Club, Kix Cereal, danger warning siren, 7-1/8" l plastic tube,

wooden mouthpiece, slight wear **195.00**

Club button and card, Lone Ranger Safety Club, WFIL Radio and Philadelphia Daily News, 2-3/4" x 4-1/2" membership card, 1-1/4" celluloid pinback button, late 1930s **145.00**

Coloring book, 1959 .... **50.00**

Comic book, *Lone Ranger and Silver*, #369, Dell, 1951 .... **22.00**

Hair brush, wooden **25.00**

Halloween mask, 1960s **30.00**

Holster, two-gun set, no guns, 1976, Gabriel **45.00**

Member card, Treasury Department Peace Patrol, issued for US Savings Bond Peace , Patrol, black and white photo, facsimile signature, 1950s **28.00**

Pencil case, cardboard, hinged lid, brass snap fastener, green, silver and black illus, American Lead Pencil Co., 1938 .... **45.00**

Squirt gun, plastic, figural **50.00**

Lone Ranger, comic book, *The Lone Ranger*, Dell, May, **$30.**

Toy, Lone Ranger Hi-Yo Silver, tin windup, Marx, 8" h **295.00**

Longaberger Baskets

Made in Dresden, Ohio, these baskets attract a lot of attention and have a huge following. Sold mostly through home shows, baskets have begun entering the secondary market. To achieve high prices, baskets must be in mint condition. Liners and protectors add to the value, as does a maker's signature.

Longaberger baskets, Christmas Collection, 1987 Edition Mistletoe Basket, 7-1/2" h, **$75.**

All-American
2001, strawberry, liner, protector, tie-on **35.00**
2002, casserole, liner, protector **90.00**
2002, Hostess Block Party, liner, protector **180.00**

Baking dish, 2003, liner, protector **35.00**

Back porch, 2002, liner, protector, insert, and handle gripper **60.00**

Bagel, 2002, Longaberger divided container **65.00**

Barbeque buddy, 2000, small, Century Celebration **35.00**

Longaberger baskets, Generosity, 1999, green plaid liner, protector, lid, **$190.**

Basket of Love, 1995, liner, protector **35.00**

Longaberger baskets, October Fields, 2000, protector and lid, **$90.**

Bayberry, 1993, green, liner, protector 45.00

Berry, medium
1995, non-Longaberger salt, pepper & napkins lid.................... 30.00
1996, green, liner, protector 35.00

Blue Ribbon Bread, 1999, liner, protector 40.00

Boardwalk, 2002, small 65.00

Booking
Ambrosia, 1993, liner, protector, extra liner 35.00
Chives, 1996, protector 30.00
Ivy, 1992, protector............. 30.00
Laurel, 1992, protector, Longaberger Wish List..... 30.00
Lavender, 1994, booking, liner, protector........................... 45.00
Oregano, 2000, non-Longaberger lid 25.00
Parsley, 1998, protector........ 30.00

Building Tomorrow Together Bee, 1999, with liner, protector..... 35.00

Candy Cane, 1986, green 75.00

Century Celebration
Cheers, 2000, liner, protector, lid, and tie-on........................ 45.00
Hostess appreciation, liner, protector, and tine-on...... 45.00

Cheers, 2000, with protector.... 45.00

Collector's Club
Century Celebration 2000, liner, protector, lid and tie-on... 75.00
Collector's Edition, 2004, liner, protector........................... 45.00
Five Year Anniversary purse, 2001, liner, protector 60.00
Homestead, 1999, liner, protector and tine-on...................... 80.00
Membership basket, 2000, liner, protector........................... 60.00
Renewal, 1997, liner, protector 30.00
Renewal, 2002, liner, protector 20.00
25th Anniversary, l998, protector 65.00

Daisy, 1999, protector and tie-on 55.00

Darning, 2004, protector 35.00

Deck the Halls, 2000, green, liner, protector 55.00

Dresden, 2002, liner, protector, tie-on 45.00

Father's Day Pocket Change, 2002, liner, protector, lid, and tie-on 40.00

Fellowship, 1997, liner, protector, and handle gripper................ 70.00

Generosity, 1999, liner, protector, lid 190.00

Gingerbread, 1990, green 65.00

Glad Tidings, 1998, green, liner, protector 80.00

Harvest Blessing, 2000, small, liner, protector 35.00

Hostess Appreciation
1994, sgd by Bonnie, Judy, Jeff, Wendy and Ginny Longaberger, and "Fall in Dresden" pin 55.00
1998, liner, protector............ 30.00
2000, Century Celebration, liner, protector........................... 50.00

Lilac, 1994, liner, protector 45.00

Little Boardwalk, 2003, liner, protector 55.00

Little Pumpkin, 1997, liner, protector 35.00

Little Star, 2001, red, protector and lid... 40.00

Longaberger baskets, Cherished Memories, 1998, red and white striped fabric liner and ties, lid, pewter picture frame tie-on, **$100.**

October Fields, 2000, liner, protector, lid 90.00

Peg, medium, 1992, protector 30.00

Peony, 2001, liner, protector, tie-on 45.00

Petunia, 1997, liner, protector, tie-on 45.00

Proudly Longaberger Bee, 2002, liner, protector....................... 45.00

Pumpkin Patch, 2001, liner, protector, lid 55.00

Rings & Things, 1998, liner, protector, insert, jewelry pouch 40.00

Santa's Little Helper, 1999, liner, protector, and runners 55.00

Snapdragon, 1998, liner, protector 55.00

Snowflake, 1997, green, liner, protector 55.00

Spoon, 1994, small, liner, lid.... 45.00

Tissue, 1999, lid...................... 45.00

Twelve Days of Christmas, 2000, liner, protector, lid, tie-on ... 170.00

Wildflower, 1993, liner, protector 55.00

Window box, 2001, liner, protector, insert..................................... 70.00

Woven Memories, 2002, protector, lid... 45.00

Luggage

Interior decorators have been known to frequent flea markets looking for interesting old suitcases and other travel bags. What they have discovered is that luggage can serve as a wonderful storage container at the same time that it is decorative.

Child's, round, pink vinyl, black and white poodle dec, zipper closure,

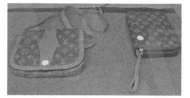

Luggage, Louis Vuitton is known for his luggage and handbags, all with his distinctive designed leather. Make sure you know your dealer if investing in this type of merchandise as fakes abound. These two were offered for **$50** each, but the buyer must decide if they are vintage or not.

pink carrying loop, wear 20.00

Hatbox, Hess's, name repeated all over box, paper and wood, string closure 25.00

Suitcase
Belber, gray, shows black porter, 6"h, 20-3/4" w, 16" d......... 35.00
Samsonite #4635, scorch marks, 6-1/2" h, 24" w, 17-1/4" d . 40.00

Tag, 1-1/2" x 2-1/2", United States Lines, America-Europe, celluloid, yellow, black, white, blue, red graphic of three-stack steamer, 1930s...................................... 40.00

Train case, brown, light beige stripes, fitted int. with mirror, molded plastic handle, 1940s 35.00

Luggage, 1930s leather suitcase, Indian profile on both sides, **$150.**

Valise, dark brown leather, padded leather handles, some wear 150.00

Lunch Boxes

As a kid, it was always easier to remember your lunch if it was packed in a brightly colored lunch box. And, although the term conjures up images of a plastic container with cartoon characters on the sides, lunch boxes or kits have been around since the mid-1930s.

Note: Prices include lunch box and thermos.

Lunch boxes, thermos, Campbell Soup, red and white, original red cap, **$30.**

Lunch boxes, Gunsmoke, metal, **$180;** Bullwinkle, vinyl, **$450.**

Plastic
Beetlejuice, 1980, Thermos.. 14.00
Ewoks, 1983, Thermos 25.00
Hot Wheels, 1984, Thermos. 70.00
Los Angeles Olympics, 1984, Thermos.......................... 25.00
Mr. T, 1984, Aladdin 30.00
Rocketeer, 1990, Aladdin 15.00
Scooby Doo, 1984, Aladdin.. 60.00
Smurfs Fishing, 1984, Thermos 20.00

Steel
Bionic Woman, with car, 1977 .... 55.00
Boston Red Sox, 6-1/2" x 8-1/2" x 3-1/2", Ardee, 1960s......... 48.00

Lunch boxes, Barbie Rockers, pink plastic, Thermos Brand, some wear, **$15.**

Care Bear Cousins, 1985, Aladdin
.... 25.00
Happy Days, 1977, Thermos
.... 60.00
Indiana Jones, 1984, King Seeley
Thermos............................. 35.00
Jonathan Livingston Seagull, 1973,
Aladdin.............................. 75.00
Muppet Babies, 1985, King Seeley
Thermos............................. 20.00

Space Shuttle Orbiter Enterprise,
6-3/4" x 8-3/4" x 4", metal, King-
Seeley thermos ©1977 ..... 48.00
Supercar, 1960s...................... 15.00
U.S. Mail, dome-top, 1969, Aladdin
.... 85.00

Vinyl
Deputy Dawg, Deputy reading book
in front of hen house, Thermos,

1961 Terrytoons copyright
.... 195.00
Peanuts, 1965, Charles Schultz,
King Seeley Thermos 35.00
Sesame Street, 1977, Aladdin,
orange............................... 45.00
Yogi Bear, Aladdin, Hanna Barbera
copyright 250.00

Lu-Ray Dinnerware

This pretty pattern was introduced by Taylor, Smith, & Taylor in the late 1930s, and production continued until the early 1950s. The pastel shades were made in Chatham Gray, Pesian Cream, Sharon Pink, Surf Green, and Windsor Blue.

Bowl
Fruit, green, 5-1/2" d............ 10.00
Vegetable, pink, 9" d............ 22.50

Calendar plate, 1951.............. 50.00

Casserole, cov, pink 155.00

Creamer, yellow 22.50

Cream soup, underplate, pink
.... 135.00

Cup, green, 2-1/2" h................... 8.00

Demittasse set, pot, cups and
saucers, pink and blue......... 185.00

Eggcup, blue 20.00

Fruit bowl, 5-1/2" d 2.00

Gravy boat, attached undertray,
yellow..................................... 25.00

Plate
Blue, 10" d............................. 28.00
Yellow, 9" d 10.00

Platter, pink, 9-1/2" x 13-1/2"
.... 22.50

Salt shaker, yellow 12.00

Teapot, pink............................. 65.00

Lu-Ray Dinnerware, blue cup, **$5.**

Lu-Ray Dinnerware, dinnerware set, pastels, some wear, 51 pieces, **$35.**

MAD Collectibles

Look for Alfred E. Neuman's smug mug on any number of items, from games to timepieces.

Bookends, pr, Alfred E. Neuman, gold plastic, black relief......... **35.00**

Card game, Parker Brothers, 1980, boxed **3.50**

Game, Screwball, The MAD MAD MAD Game, 1960, Transogram **75.00**

Magazine
MAD Magazine, December 1973 .... **3.00**

Mad Star Wars Spectacular, 1996 .... **2.00**

Model, Alfred E. Neuman, Aurora, 1965, unassembled, orig box, complete **145.00**

Paperback book, *The Bedside Mad* by William M. Gaines, 1959, 21st printing.................................. **1.50**

Skateboard, Alfred E. Neuman **120.00**

MAD collectibles, paperback book, *A MAD Look at Old Movies*, 1973, **$4.**

Maddux of California

Maddux of California was founded in 1938 in Los Angeles. The company produced and distributed novelties, figurines, planters, lamps, and other decorative accessories until 1974.

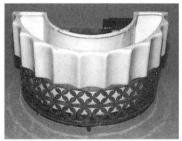

Maddux of California, TV lamp and planter, 6" h, 10" w, **$25.**

Ashtray, #731, triangular, gunmetal gray, 10-1/2" l **20.00**

Bowl, #3093, off-white, squares and circles on rim, mkd "Maddux of Calif. 3093 USA," 5 1/2" d **16.00**

Candelabra, #1036, candle holders on each end, center oval dish, 14-1/2" l **25.00**

Cookie jar, #3112, grapes........ **50.00**

Dish, divided, green, ridged borders, oval, 11" x 6" **12.00**

Figure
Bull, blue and white 110.00
Flamingo, 6-1/2" h................ **40.00**

Low bowl, 6" h figural flamingo, head down, pink and green, 13" l, 6-1/4" w, 2" h **195.00**

Planter
#107, light pink glossy int., matte light turquoise ext. with allover gold swirling, 4-5/8" d, 3-3/4" h **24.00**
#445, flamingo, mkd "Maddux of Calif, #445, copyright 1959, Made in USA," 6" h **165.00**
#518, deer leaping over log, 8-1/2" h **25.00**
#528, pheasant, white, 11-1/4" h, 7-1/4" w **38.00**

Television lamp, #828, swan, planter back, white, 9" w, 12" h **50.00**

Vegetable bowl, cov, white and turquoise, mkd "Maddux of California, 3066B USA," 7-3/4" w, 4-1/2" h **25.00**

Magazines

Magazine collecting offers a unique perspective on American life. By reading the old issues, you can get a clearer idea of what life was like, what products were being advertised, who was making news, etc. Some collectors buy magazines that they can take apart and sell as individual advertisements or articles.

Amateur Photographer's Weekly, June 6, 1919 .... **3.00**

American Heritage, Oct. 1958, Pocahontas cover.................... **6.00**

American Legion Weekly, 8-1/4" x 11-1/2", black and white, pulp, 24

pgs, Oct. 1, 1920, articles about Harding and Cox **20.00**

Better Homes and Gardens, Dec. 1942 .... **6.00**

Car Toons, Dec. 1969.................. **3.00**

Child's Life, 1930 .... **4.00**

Delineator, 1904........................ **20.00**

Ellery Queen Mystery Magazine, 1950s.. **5.00**

Family Health, September 1976, John Wayne cover and article........ **10.00**

Farm Life, 1923 .... **6.00**

Magazines, *Woman's Home Companion*, January 1949, Harry Anders' cover illustration of children sledding, **$25.**

Fortune, March 1974.................... 3.00

Fra, The, 9" x 14", Oct. 1915, published by Elbert Hubbard, 176 pgs, pulp 30.00

Good Housekeeping, 1965.......... 4.00

Horticulture, Dec. 1959, poinsettia cover 3.50

Humpty Dumpty, 1960s............. 3.00

Iron Man, Dec. 1962 .... 7.50

Jack & Jill, 1961 .... 10.00

Life
Dec. 8, 1941, Douglas MacArthur 9.00

July 7, 1961, Ike Down on the Farm cover 10.00
March 13, 1964, series on World War I................................... 7.00
March 11, 1966, Adam West as Batman on cover 30.00

Look, Gary Cooper as Lou Gehrig cover 45.00

McCall's, 1961, Christmas Make-It Ideas.. 5.00

Magazines, *Woman's Home Companion*, Easter issue, April 1913, Marion Powers' cover, **$15.**

Magazines, *Good Housekeeping*, Sept. 1916, Coles Phillips' cover, **$35**

National Geographic
1923, 12 issues...................... 55.00
1958, 12 issues...................... 12.00

Popular Sports, Fall 1943 .... 4.00

Quick Magazine, April 13, 1953, Lucille Ball cover 32.50

Redbook, June 1925 .... 5.00

Seventeen Magazine, June, 1970, Susan Dey cover 45.00

Time, June 19, 1944, Eisenhower cover 8.00

Wee Wisdom, July 1939.............. 7.50

Magnifying Glasses

Did you ever play detective and scour the house with a magnifying glass in your hand? Most of us did at one time or another. And, as baby boomers age, perhaps a few of us will be looking for them to help read that fine print in the local newspaper.

Brass and rosewood, matching letter opener, 10" l 50.00

Cracker Jack prize.................. 10.00

Ivory handle, large round glass lens 125.00

Jade handle, large oval glass lens 35.00

Plastic handle, rect lens 10.00

Porcelain handle, floral dec, large round glass lens..................... 75.00

Sterling silver, emb floral dec, large round glass lens..................... 95.00

Wood handle, large round glass lens 27.50

Magnifying glass, black plastic frame, 10X magnification, **$3.**

Majolica

Majolica is defined as an opaque tin glazed pottery. Made for centuries, most majolica pieces consist of designs with naturalistic elements such as flowers, leaves, insects, and shells. Few majolica pieces are marked. Many pieces show wear, chips, repairs, or some sort of damage. Take any defects into consideration, remembering that a damaged piece will always bring a lower price than a perfect one.

For additional listings, see *Warman's Antiques & Collectible, Warman's American Pottery & Porcelain*, and *Warman's English & Continental Pottery & Porcelain*.

Reproduction alert.

Majolica, plate with parrots, **$85.**

Basket, bird on branch, pink ribbon on handle, 10" x 6-1/2" 250.00

Bread tray, floral, butterflies, pastel colors, "Waste Not Want Not" 250.00

Butter pat
Butterfly, Fielding, stains ... 220.00
Grape, Clifton, rim nick 145.00

Cake stand
Etruscan, morning glory, 8-1/4" 175.00
Wedgwood, green leaf, green ground, 8" d, 2-1/2" h 125.00

Candlestick, water lily form, all green, Wardle 125.00

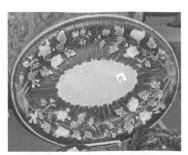

Majolica, bread plate, cobalt blue ground, pink flowers, green leaves, brown twigs as handles, turquoise center, **$175.**

Cheese keeper, Raspberry pattern, unmarked, pink raspberries, foliate, mottled green, gold, and brown ground, 11-3/4" d, 9" h, hairline on lid, chips on base plate 425.00

Creamer, Shell and Seaweed pattern, Griffin, Smith & Hill, 5-1/2" h, rim roughness 200.00

Cup and saucer
Etruscan, bamboo 125.00
Lovebirds on branch, green and tan 75.00

Humidor, cov, figural
Clown head, yellow hat and collar, 6" h 75.00
Man, night cape and pipe, 4-1/2" h 75.00

Match striker, Continental
Lady with tambourine, 10-1/2" 100.00
Man with violin, 12" 125.00

Oyster plate
French Orchies, blue and beige, 10" d 150.00
Seaweed and Shell, cobalt blue center, 10" d.................... 375.00

Pitcher
Gnarled tree truck and florals, 8" h 150.00
Robin, mottled, 9-1/4" h 100.00

Plate
Bird in flight, fern and cattail, white ground, 8-1/2" d 125.00
Blackberry and basketweave, brown, 9" d 125.00

Sugar, open, Shell and Seaweed pattern, Griffin, Smith & Hill, 3-1/2" h, rim roughness 125.00

Teapot, cov
Bird and Bird's Nest, figural, brown and green, 9" 225.00
Fan and Scroll, Fielding, insect, pebble ground, cream and purple, 7" 275.00

Tea trivet, round, multicolor . 155.00

Majolica, butter dish, covered, yellow water lilies, green leaves, turquoise blue ground, brown border, chips, **$40.**

Tile, red rose center, shaded blue ground, mkd "Made in England, H & R Johnson, Ltd.," 6" sq 45.00

Vase, applied duck, full-relief bamboo and water plants, cream glossy cylinder, gold trim, 11" h 270.00

Waste bowl, 5" d, 3" h, Shell and Seaweed pattern, Griffin, Smith & Hill, in-the-making flake 175.00

Majolica, leaf form plate, dark green glaze, Wedgwood, 8-1/2" l, **$35.**

Marx Toys

Louis Marx founded the Marx Toy Co. in 1921. He stressed high quality at the lowest possible price. Marx toys tend to be very colorful, and many can be found with their original box, which greatly enhances the price.

Marx Toys, Moon Mullins and Kayo, mechanical handcar with track, original box with blue lettering, wear, **$90.**

Army car, battery operated 65.00

Astronaut, figure, white plastic, 5-1/2" h 10.00

Bagatelle
Combat, 1950s, NMIB.......... 50.00
Pop A Puppet, 1950s, orig box 25.00

Bop-A-Bear, battery operated, orig box 265.00

Falcon, plastic bubble top, black rubber tires........................... 50.00

Fred Flintstone and Dino, litho tin windup, 1962 .... 50.00

Gravel Gertie, figure, white plastic, 2" h.. 12.00

Jalopy pickup, litho tin wind-up, 7" l 60.00

Midget Road Building Set, litho tin wind-up, 1939, 5-1/2" l tractor 30.00

Model, Wells Fargo Stagecoach, 1953, MIB 295.00

Pinocchio, walker, 1939, 9" h 225.00

Pluto Rolykin, 1-1/2" h 15.00

Royal Bus Lines, litho tin wind-up, 1930s, 10-1/4" l.................... 135.00

Stake bed truck, pressed steel, wooden wheels, 1936, 7" l..... 65.00

Marx Toys, playset, The White House, original box with some shelf wear, **$75.**

Marx Toys, Donald the Demon plastic Nutty Mads figure, Marx, 1963, 5" h, **$15.**

Train set, #532, 4 cars, 10 pcs of track 200.00

Tricky Taxi, tin windup, 4-1/2" l 85.00

Zippo, climbing monkey, multicolored litho tinplate, pull-string mechanism, 10" l 60.00

Matchbox Toys

Matchbox toys were developed by Lesney in 1953. The name reflected the idea that there was a miniature toy packed in a box that resembled a matchbox. The toys were first exported to America from England in 1958 and were an instant success.

Atlantic Trailer, tan body, six metal

Matchbox Toys, Caterpillar bulldozer, No. 64, 1979, **$3.**

wheels, 1956 .... 15.00

Big Tipper, MIB...................... 24.00

Brady Bunch, station wagon, 1997 .... 4.00

Case Tractor bulldozer, red body, yellow base, 1969.................... 5.00

CJB Jeep, #53, 1971................. 18.00

Commer, ice cream canteen truck 10.00

Dodge Daytona turbo, 1994 ... 1.50

Excavator, red, #32, MOC........ 18.00

Ford
Customline Station Wagon, yellow body, 1957 .... 20.00
Escort..................................... 2.00

GMC, tipper truck.................... 10.00

Hillman Minx, 1958 .... 15.00

Horse van, #40, MOC 15.00

International Ltd., trailer, 1979 .... 2.00

Jaguar.. 50.00

M

Jennings cattle truck, 4-1/2" l 36.00

Knightrider car.................... 12.00

Korean Airlines Airbus, Sky Busters, 1988, MOC, 4-1/4" l
.... 35.00

Land Rover fire truck, 1966.. 10.00

Maserati, 1958......................... 10.00

Mercedes, container truck, #42 18.00

Nightmare on Elm Street, 1999
.... 5.00

Nissan, 300 ZX Turbo, 1986....... 1.00

Peterbuilt, cement mixer........... 8.00

Plymouth, Grand Fury police car, white body, black detailing, 1979
.... 5.00

Rallye Royale, #14, 1980, MOC
.... 12.00

Rig, 1993, NRFP......................... 6.00

Setra Coach, #12, 1970............. 5.00

Stake truck, #4......................... 5.00

Train car, green, 1978............. 28.00

Untouchables car.................... 15.00

Wells Fargo truck, #69, 1978
.... 24.00

Matchbox Toys, top to bottom: ambulance; red Chevy truck; blue Firebird with flame striping; racing car, N.A.R.T. Delainey Sampson, NRFP, **$20** to **$45.**

Matchcovers

Matchcovers have been on the scene since the early 1900s, but any examples from before the 1930s are considered scarce.

Match covers, Hunt's Tomato Sauce, 1963, **$3.**

Air Force, Officers' Club, Victorville, CA, Lion Match 6.00

Benetz Inn, gold and maroon ... 1.25

Bob's Home of the Big Boy, lists 10 CA locations, 1950s............... 12.00

Bond Bread, Wildcat fighter, Navy plane set, Lion Match, 1942
.... 10.00

Brass Rail Bar & Cocktail Lounge, Central Great Falls, Mont., Diamond Match 8.00

Broadway Limited, Pennsylvania Railroad, Safety-Speed-Comfort, Diamond Match 8.00

Bucks County Bank & Trust Co
. ... 2.50

Buy More War Bonds, We Must Win, Our First Duty 4.50

Champion Spark Plugs, 1930s 2.00

Dr. Pepper, 1930s 25.00

Dutch Boy Paint, Ulrich Paint & Glass 3.00

Elect Willkie, Preserve Your Freedom Be Thankful You Can Still Do It, Win with Willkie, Lion Match Co., unused.......................... 50.00

Enron 1.00

Howard Johnson....................... 7.00

Military design, shows barracks and flagpole, World War II vintage, Universal Match Corp., San Francisco 6.00

Nu-Grape 9.00

R & S Diner, 50th Anniv............. .50

RPM Motor Oil, Chevron Supreme Gasoline, unused 6.50

San Diego, souvenir type........... 4.00

Watch the Phillies, 1940, 1-1/2" x 2"
.... 15.00

Match covers, Dakota Motor Hotel, Winnipeg, Canada, Indian maiden, unused, **$3.**

Match Holders and Match Safes

Matches were precious commodities many years ago. Care had to be taken to keep matches dry, but still handy. Match holders can be found in almost every medium, ranging from table or mantle top containers to wall containers. Match safes, on the other hand, are small containers used to safely carry matches in a pocket. Many are figural and can be found in many metals. Some match safes will also have a striking surface.

For additional listings, see *Warman's Antiques & Collectibles.*

Match holders, figural, chick, painted pot metal, hinged head, sticker on base, repainted, 3" h, **$50.**

Advertising

Advance Traction Engine, celluloid wrapped, multicolored graphics, 2-3/4" x 1-1/2" 300.00

Anheuser Busch, engine and coal tender, falling lid type, by C. J. Hauck, nickel plated brass, patent Aug. 14, 1883, 3" x 1-5/8" 250.00

Biscuit, figural, Huntley & Palmer, orig paint on brass, 2-1/8" d 125.00

Cameron Pumps, adv, by Whitehead & Hoag Co., celluloid wrapped, black and white graphics, 2-3/4" x 1-1/2" 110.00

Ceresota Prize Bread Flour, 5-3/8" x 2-1/2", figural, diecut, tin litho, boy slicing bread 300.00

Diamond Match, bee and flower dec, by Ginna & Co., multicolored litho tin, 1-1/2" x 2-1/2" 55.00

Hunter Baltimore Rye, multicolored graphics, celluloid wrapped, by Whitehead & Hoag, 2-3/4" x 1-1/2" 135.00

Red Top Rye, orig white and red highlights, thermoplastic, 2-7/8" x 1-1/8" 115.00

Agate, black, brown, white banded agate, brass trim, engine turned design, push button lid release, abrasive striker inside lid, 2-3/4" x 1" 75.00

Book shaped, double ender, ivory, sterling initials, 1-3/4" x 1".... 35.00

BPOE, fob type, red, white, and blue enameled clock, by Simons Bros. & Co., sterling, 2-5/8" x 1-1/2" 275.00

Brass, open design over glass, rect, 2" x 1-3/8" 155.00

Candle matches, image of young lady, Roche & Cie, Grand Prix Paris 1900, complete with matches, 3-1/8" x 1-5/8" 30.00

Channel Fleet at Blackpool, nickel plated, enameled lettering, 1-7/8" x 1-1/2" 75.00

Cherub and wishbone motif, by Wm. Kerr Co., cat. #6, sterling silver, 2-5/8 x 1-1/2" 135.00

Cherry tree motif, by Wallace, silver plate, 2-1/2" x 1-1/2" 150.00

Clover motif, by Whiting Mfg., cat. #419, sterling silver, 2-5/8" x 1-3/8" 95.00

Compass, pocket watch shape, swivel ring at top, brass, 2" d 195.00

Match safes, pocket, four cigars, band across center reads "Havana," brass with nickel plating, 1-3/8" x 1-5/8", **$295.**

Match holders, hanging type, cream painted metal, black silhouette of girl with parasol in garden, **$35.**

Dangerfield's self-igniting, nickel silver, by Harvey Blakeslee, patent June 22, 1880, 1-3/4" x 3-1/4" 95.00

Door, hinge design, by Webster Co., sterling silver, gold wash inside, 2-3/4" x 1-5/8" 195.00

Dragon on rampage, nickel plated brass, 2-5/8" x 1-3/8" 95.00

Flask, figural, top nickel plated brass, bottom glass, 2-3/4" x 1-3/8" 150.00

Goldstone, rect, rounded end, brass trim, 3" x 1-1/8" 135.00

Horseshoe, mkd "Good Luck," enamel applied to nickel plated brass safe, 1-7/8" x 1-3/8" 45.00

Knight, in armor, holding lance, castle background, sterling silver, 2-3/4" x 1-3/8" 185.00

Overalls, figural, pewter, 2-7/8" x 1-1/4" 125.00

Pig running, figural, hinged at hind quarter, plated brass, ¾" x 2-1/4" 175.00

Scottish thistle, figural, brass, 2" x 1-1/2" 115.00

Seahorse, figural, brass, glass eyes, 2" x 1-1/8" 195.00

Stoneware, Whites Utica, salt-glazed American Brew Co., Rochester, N.Y., eagle inside badge, small impact fracture on rim, 2-3/4" h 220.00

Plain, tooled pattern, minor surface roughness, mold mark #1, 3" h 45.00

Westcott & Parker, Dealers in Coal & Wood, Utica, N.Y., 3" h 275.00

Tartan Ware, McBeth design, cylindrical, vesta socket on top, 2-3/4" x 7/8" 115.00

Wooden, barrel-form, brown and tan sponge-painted, 2-1/8" h 115.00

World's Fair, 1904 Exposition, Palace of Manufacturing & Palace of Mines & Metallurgy, metal.............. 65.00

McCoy

The J.W. McCoy Pottery was established in Roseville, Ohio, in 1899. Initially, the company produced stoneware and some art pottery. In 1911, three area potteries (Brush Pottery Company, J.W. McCoy Pottery Company, and Nelson McCoy Sanitary Stoneware Company) merged to create the Brush-McCoy Pottery Co. The new company produced all kinds of utilitarian ware, including cookie jars, garden items, and kitchenware.

For additional listings see, *Warman's Antique & Collectibles*, *Warman's Americana & Collectibles*, and *Warman's American Pottery & Porcelain*.

Reproduction alert.

McCoy Pottery, console bowl, green and white pebbly lobed exterior, creamy yellow interior, scroll handles, marked, **$35.**

Brush-McCoy

Bird bath 48.00

Center bowl, 5-1/2" h, Classic Line, pedestal, turquoise, brushed gold 35.00

Jardiniere, swallows, brown and green matte glaze, 7" d 85.00

Jug, Onyx, brown, with stopper, 10" h 120.00

Lantern, cat, patio type, 12-1/2" h 95.00

Mug, Davy Crockett, cream and brown glaze 45.00

Pitcher
Keg shape, brown glaze........ 70.00
Kolor Kraft, #331, dark-green glaze, 6-1/2" h.............................. 85.00

Planter
Duck, yellow, 3" h 15.00
Frog, green, 5-1/2" l.............. 40.00

House and Garden, green glaze, 5" h, 11" l 50.00
Peanut, matte glaze 40.00

Vase
Art Vellum Fawn, red glaze, 5" h, 6" d 100.00
Gladiola, pink, 12" h............. 70.00
Onyx, green 70.00
Ringed, #508, white, 8" h 40.00

McCoy

Ashtray, Seagram's VO, Imported Canadian Whiskey, black, gold letters 15.00

McCoy Pottery, planter, zebra, 1950s, McCoy USA Mark, 8-1/2" l, **$800+.**

Baker, oval, Brown Drip, 9-1/4" l 12.00

McCoy Pottery, two vases, pink flower, green foliage, ivory ground, **$50.**

McCoy Pottery, jardinière, arches with block motif, mottled brown glaze, marked, **$95.**

Bank, Centennial Bear, sgd, numbered 110.00

Basket, black and white, emb weave ext., double handle 25.00

Bean pot, brown, #2 .... 35.00

Console bowl, Garden Club, peach 45.00

Cookie jar
Colonial Fireplace 150.00

Kookie Kettle, black 55.00
Log Cabin 175.00
Potbelly stove, black 50.00
Puppy, with sign 135.00

Cornucopia, yellow 20.00

Creamer, Brown Drip, 3-1/2" h 6.00

Decanter, Apollo Mission 45.00

Hanging basket, stoneware, marked "Nelson McCoy," 1926 .... 20.00

Jardiniere, green and pink, small 85.00

Mixing bowl, medium and large, tan, blue and pink stripes 40.00

Planter
Bird, double cache pot 45.00
Duck, 1940s 35.00
Gondola, black, 11-1/2" l 40.00

Salt and pepper shakers, pr, figural, cucumber and mango, 1954 .... 20.00

Spoon rest, butterfly, dark green, 1953 .... 15.00

Tankard, Buccaneer, green, 8-1/2" h 80.00

McCoy Pottery, pitcher, ice lip, embossed floral on sides, deep pink glaze, marked "McCoy, Made in USA," **$75.**

Teapot, Grecian, 1958 .... 30.00
Vase
Bird of Paradise, green, 8" h. 45.00
Lily, single flower, three leaves, 7-1/2" h 48.00
Sailboat, pedestal, blue 50.00

Wall pocket, trivet 50.00

Wash bowl and pitcher, blue, medium size 95.00

McDonald's

It might be the sight of those golden arches, or it might be the growling of your tummy that convinces you to head to McDonald's. In any event, if you've got children with you when you go, you'll most certainly go home with a fast-food collectible.

For additional listings, see *Warman's Americana & Collectibles.*

Action figure, Big Mac, Remco Toys, MOC 20.00

McDonald's, plastic tumbler, Ronald McDonald, **$3.**

Activity booklet
Ronald McDonald Goes to the Zoo, Number Two, 9-1/4" x 12-1/4", ©1968 .... 18.00
Ronald McDonald's Travel Fun, 8-1/4" x 10-3/4", 12 pgs, c1970 .... 15.00

Ashtray, 3-1/2" x 6", metal, green, 1970 logo in yellow, street address in silver 18.00

Bank, 1953 Ford delivery van, Ertl, 1/25 diecast, ©1996, orig box and key 25.00

Coloring book, 17" x 22", *Ronald McDonald Giant Story Coloring Book,* ©1978, unuscd 25.00

Doll, Hamburglar, played-with condition 15.00

Employee cap, garrison style, 1963, unused 20.00

Hand puppet, 9-1/2" w, 13-1/4" h, Ronald McDonald, vinyl, c1970 .... 12.00

Happy Meal Prize, Genie and Building 5, from Aladdin and the King of Thieves, MIB 4.00

McDonald's, Happy Meal Dalmatian premiums, **$1** each.

McDonald's, mug, smoked glass, Ronald McDonald tossing football, **$3.**

Lunch box, Sheriff of Cactus Canyon, Aladdin, 1982, orig thermos, orig hang tag 175.00

Map, Ronald McDonald Map of the Moon, 1969 .... 7.50

Mask, prototype, 15" w, 9" h, Hamburglar, white vacu-form plastic, Collegeville Costumes, unmarked 35.00

Patch, cloth, Ronald McDonald, red, white, blue and yellow stitching 2.00

Photo, 5" x 6-1/2", glossy full color, facsimile signature "To all my friends, Ronald McDonald," c1970 .... 18.00

Premium ring set, six 1" x 1-1/4" yellow relief plastic rings, each with smiling Ronald faces, diecut eye holes, sic different colored soft vinyl ring base, Specialty Premiums, 1971 .... 60.00

Punch out sheet, Ronald McDonald's Bank for Little Savers, 11-3/4" x 13-3/4" still paper, full color, late 1960s 24.00

Record, 7" d, 45 rpm, maroon and silver label with logo and "Compliments of McDonald's Drive-in Restaurants," The Night Before Christmas, late 1950s-early 1960s 18.00

Salt and pepper shakers, pr
Original building shape 16.00
Speedy Fries and Shake, 4-1/2" h 18.00

Snow globe, 101 Dalmatians, MIB 25.00

McDonald's, Happy Meals display, Marvel Super Heroes, eight toys, **$35.**

Teeny Beanie Babies, 1998 series, Pinchers, Happy, Bongo, Mel, Inch and Twigs, set of six 50.00

Toy, parachute, 1/2" d x 7-1/2" l cardboard blow tube with full color paper wrapper, plastic parachute, late 1960s 8.00

Tray, 4-1/2" x 6-1/2" x 1/2" h, pale yellow plastic, center full color image of Big Mac, lightly incised inscriptions of copyright arch and Arabic, Japanese, and Chinese characters, 1970s 15.00

Medals

One way to honor a hero was to present him with a medal. Many of these awards were passed down through families as treasured mementos. Other medals include those that are commemorative in nature.

Medals, Liberty, 1776-1996, Bicentennial, pewter, original box and brochure, **$8.50.**

Commemorative
Dwight D. Eisenhower Inauguration, 1953, bronze, Medallic Art Co., 2-3/4" d 80.00
Mercedes Benz, South American dealerships, shows airplane, auto and boat, mkd 1885-1913 .... 17.50
Pan American Games, Sao Paulo, Brazil, 1963, bronze, in Portuguese, 2" d 14.50

Military
American Legion, 1-1/4" d ... 12.00
Bronze Star, engraved name, with ribbon bar and lapel pin, 1960s, in presentation case 50.00
Connecticut Foot Guard, 1st Company of Foot Guards, five years of service 35.00
USS Puget Sound, orig box .. 40.00

Religious
St. Dominic Pray for Us, Virgin Mary with infant Jesus, mkd Italy, 1" x 5/8" 2.00
St. Jude Thaddeus Intercede for Us, Infant of Prague Shrine New Haven, Conn., brass-colored, 5/8" d 2.00

Sports, 1-1/8" d
Basketball 12.00

Medals, George Washington, bronze, rim embossed "Washington, Soldier, Statesman, Freemason, The Supreme Council, **$5.**

Rowing 10.00
Swimming 10.00
Tennis 12.00

Medical Items

Ouch! Collectors of medical items certainly aren't squeamish as they search flea markets for new items to add to their collections. Some folks concentrate on medical apparatus and instruments, while others focus on other aspects of the profession.

Medical items: Need your eyes checked? This optometrist's case is filled with glass optics to correctly measure what strength eyeglasses you may need, **$150.**

Advertising trade card, 13" x 7-1/2", Kidd's Cough Syrup, diecut cardboard, Victorian woman and product advertising **110.00**

Bleeder, three folding blades, copper and brass, 18th C, 3-3/4" l ... **225.00**

Blood pressure kit, orig manual, 1917 .... **55.00**

Book
 Allergy in Adults, Med Clinics of N. America, 1974 .... **7.50**
 Anatomy & Physiology, C. Gray, and D. Dimber, 1931, 8th ed., 629 pgs **25.00**
 Diseases of the Blood, Roy R. Kracke, 1941, 2nd ed., 54 color plates, 46 illus, 692 pgs **25.00**
 The People's Common Sense Medical Adviser in Plain English, or Medicine Simplified, Pierce, 1889, illus, 100 pgs **19.95**

Box, Red Cross Sterilized Gauze, Johnson & Johnson **8.00**

Dental sterilizer, 11-3/4" x 7" x 8", paneled mahogany case, nickeled brass fittings, compartment with alcohol burner, steam boiler fitted in large zinc copper cavity, three removable wood slat racks, 19th C **230.00**

Doctor's bag, leather 40.00

Mortar and pestle, brass 70.00

Order form, Crawford's Drug Store, Atlantic City, N.J. 8-1/2" x 10-1/2" 20.00

Paperweight, oversized aspirin, orig box 10.00

Photograph
 Medical training type, students with skeletons 80.00
 Unidentified doctor's office interior 30.00

Medical items: Tired from walking all day at the flea market, perhaps you feel like you need one of these: an antique wheel chair, oak, caned back and seat, refinished, quilts laying on seat, **$50.**

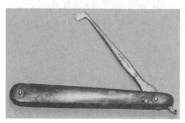

Medical items, folding scalpel, A.L. Hernstein, plastic tortoiseshell case, 5-7/8" l (open), **$60.**

Pinback button
 Dental Manufacturers Club, red on white celluloid, oval, early 1900s 12.00
 Luden Cough Drops, black and white celluloid, center package of Luden's Menthol Cough Drops, two gold fabric 1-1/2" unmarked ribbons on back 10.00

Medical items, cabinet, center compartment marked "Sterlizer," mirrored back, small fitted drawers with brass knobs, **$195.**

Meissen

Meissen is a fine porcelain with a long and interesting history. Briefly, the original factory dates to 1710 in Saxony, Germany. Over the years, decorating techniques were developed that led to the creation of beautiful pieces that are eagerly sought by collectors today. Each period of the Meissen story features different styles, colors, and influences. The factory is still in business today.

Many marks have been used by Meissen over the years. Learning to read those marks and ascertain the time period they represent will enhance a collector's knowledge of this lovely porcelain.

For additional listings and background information, *see Warman's English & Continental Pottery & Porcelain* and *Warman's Antiques & Collectibles.*

Reproduction alert.

Meissen, Onion Meissen pattern, soup plate, scalloped edge, cobalt blue decoration on white, marked "Meissen" with star, 9-3/4" d, **$45.**

Ashtray, Onion pattern, blue crossed swords mark, 5" d 80.00

Bread and butter plate, Onion pattern, 6-1/2" d 75.00

Cup and saucer, painted and encrusted forget-me-nots, blue mark, late 19th C 125.00

Dessert dish, painted red rose and foliage center, bouquets at corners, c1770 .... 225.00

Figure, young man and woman gathering eggs from under tree, white glaze, blue crossed swords mark, late 19th C 275.00

Hot plate, Onion pattern, handles 125.00

Platter, rect, blue painted flower bouquet, scattered small sprays and insects, 20" l 350.00

Soup plate, multicolored enameled scattered German flower bunches, ozier-molded border, gilt lined rim, blue mark, c1755 .... 250.00

Toothpick holder, Red Dragon, 2-1/2" h 250.00

Tray, 17-3/8" l, oval, enameled floral sprays, gilt trim, 20th C 400.00

Vase, floral dec, 20th C, 3" h 80.00

Meissen, figurine, woman holding caged dove and love letter, sheep at her feet, multicolored, 6-7/8" h, **$450.**

Vegetable dish, cov, Onion pattern, 10" sq 150.00

Metlox Pottery

After its formation in 1927, Metlox manufactured outdoor ceramic signs. During the Depression, the company reorganized and began producing dinnerware. During World War II, the factory was again retooled so that workers could make machine parts and parts for B-25 bombers. After the war, dinnerware production resumed along with the creation of some art ware. The factory finally closed in 1989.

For additional listings and history, see *Warman's Americana & Collectibles* and *Warman's American Pottery & Porcelain.*

Appetizer serving dish, Poppytrail, divided, basketweave pattern bowls, rooster with holes for toothpicks, 11" l 90.00

Bean pot, Homestead Poppy Trail, 9-1/2" h 150.00

Metlox Pottery, dinner set, service for six, California Ivy, green ivy on white ground, green Metlox stamped marks, **$90.**

Bowl
Ivy, 5-1/2" d 20.00
Sculptured Grape, 8-1/2" d... 16.00

Bread tray
Poppytrail 35.00
Red Rooster, 9" l 100.00

Canisters, cov, set of four, Red Rooster 250.00

Carafe, warmer, Red Rooster, six-cup 140.00

Casserole, cov, Sculptured Grape, one-qt 50.00

Cereal bowl, Sculptured Daisy 12.00

Chop plate
Palm..................................... 10.00
Rose-A-Day 8.00

Cookie jar, Clown................. 200.00

Creamer, Poppytrail................. 40.00

Cup and saucer
California Provincial 17.50
Sculptured Grape................. 10.00

Dinner plate, Della Robbia 8.00

Gravy boat, Peach Blossom..... 80.00

Hen on nest, Poppytrail......... 120.00

Milk pitcher, Poppytrail, shaped green handle.......................... 50.00

Mustard jar, Red Rooster........ 48.00

Platter, Provincial Rose............ 70.00

Salad bowl
California Strawberry........... 55.00
Red Rooster, 11-1/8" d 95.00

Salad plate, Sculptured Grape, 7-1/2" d 8.00

Metlox Pottery, Camellia plate, 9" d, **$5.**

Salad set, Sculptured Daisy, Metlox, 12" d bowl, matching fork and spoon 165.00

Soup bowl, Camellia California 17.50

Sugar, cov, Sculptured Grape ... 22.00

Teapot, Navajo, metal handle. 130.00

Vase, Poppytrail, chartreuse, 12" h 125.00

Vegetable bowl, divided, Poppytrail 40.00

Mettlach

Most collectors think of steins when they hear the name "Mettlach," but this German company also produced very fine pottery, including plates, plaques, bowls, and teapots. One of its hallmarks is underglaze printing on earthenware, achieved by using transfers from copper plates. Relief decorations, etched decorations, and cameos were also used. Individual pieces of Mettlach are well marked.

For additional listings, see *Warman's Antiques & Collectibles.*

Coaster, drinking scene, print under glaze, mkd "Mettlach, Villeroy & Boch," 4-7/8" d..................... 150.00

Loving cup, 7-3/8" w, 6-3/4" h, three handles, musicians dec 185.00

Plaque
#1044-542, portrait of man, blue delft dec, 12" d 125.00
#1108, incised castle, gilt rim, c1902, 17" d.................... 230.00

Stein
#171, cameo relief with musicians, 1/4 liter........................... 110.00

Mettlach, fruit bowl with matching underplate, open lattice work edges, early creamware, 7-1/2" d bowl, 10" d bowl, impressed mark, **$100.**

#1027, relief, face and floral dec, beige, rust and green, inlaid lid, 1/2-liter 215.00
#2057, etched, festive dancing scene, inlaid lid, 1/2-liter 325.00
#2833B, 1/2-liter................. 350.00

Teapot, 3-1/2" h, #3051, etched, Art Deco repeating design, lid missing 95.00

Vase, #1808, stoneware, incised foliage dec, 10" h, pr............ 230.00

Microscopes

Microscopes are included in the field of scientific instrument collecting, a category that has really taken off recently. If considering a purchase of a microscope, check to see that all the necessary parts are included. And remember, value is enhanced by original documentation, boxes, slides, etc.

Microscopes, three lenses, 8" h, Sears, **$15.**

Booklet, Gilbert microscope, 1960, 75 pgs.. 5.00

Catalog, *Biological and Chemical Supplies and Apparatus*, 1930s, microscope cover, 24 pgs 24.00

Microscope
Gilbert, toy, 1956, orig box... 50.00
New Gem Microscope, Bausch & Lomb Optical Co, Rochester, 75-300x. 7-1/4" h.................. 80.00
Regency, 100-400x, dovetailed wooden box, 7-7/8" h....... 75.00
Spencer, mkd "CENCO/Spencer/USA," double optical turret, orig case, 11"......................... 175.00

Unknown maker, compound monocular, 3-1/2" d stage with condenser and diaphragm, double mirror on calibrated rotating arm,

Microscopes, E. Leitz-Wetzler, No. 34459, 6 objective, wood case, **$200.**

japanned and lacquered brass, case, mkd "3373," c1885, 12" h 575.00

Militaria

Throughout history, men have marched off to war. Those who return often bring mementos of their travels. Years later these treasures end up at flea markets where eager collectors find them.

For additional listings, see *Warman's Antiques & Collectibles* and specific topics in this edition.

Reproduction alert.

Autograph album, GAR, 4-1/2" x 7", most pages signed at Milwaukee Reunion, Aug. 29, 1889, maroon velvet cover.......................... 110.00

Book
A Soldiers Recollections, Leaves from the Diary of a Young

Militaria, U.S. War Department identification, issued 1945, 2-3/4" x 4", **$10.**

Confederate, McKimm, 1910, black leather, 362 pgs....... 45.00

Militaria, uniform jacket, green wool, original insignias, **$65.**

Regimental History of the 316 Infantry............................. 25.00

Calendar plate, 1920, The Great World War, 1914-1919, flags and

Militaria, manual, Recognition Pictorial Manual, Bureau of Aeronautics, Navy Department, Washington, DC, June 1943, silhouettes, technical information on allied and axis aircraft, black and white, 80 pages, 6" x 10", **$40.**

globe in center, coats of arms of countries and calendar pages around border, gold lettering "Compliments of Luther Schoch, Ackermanville, PA" 35.00

Cartridge box, leather, white cloth strap, very worn, missing plate 70.00

Fife, 15-1/2" l, sgd "Firth, Pond & Co., Broadway, NY," large "C" below signature, brass ends, nickel silver and pewter mouth piece...... 175.00

Handkerchief, machine-stitched emblem of Strategic Air Command 22.00

Hat badge, infantry, brass, crossed krag rifles, 2" l 55.00

Map, Pacific Theater, Esso premium 18.00

Menu, US Forces in Thailand, Thanksgiving, 1963, 4 pgs..... 12.00

Newspaper, *The Wardial*, April 14, 1945, military base newspaper for Ward Island, Corpus Christie, Texas, 16 pgs........................ 15.00

Paperweight, West Point, sulphide, marching cadets holding two flags, 3" d....................................... 35.00

Pennant, felt
Camp Pickett, Va., red background with eagle, 25" l............... 25.00
West Point, logo of eagle on shield, 26" l 25.00

Pin, Naval officer insignia, eagle over shield and pair of anchors, sterling silver with gold wash, 1" d 32.00

Poster, World War I, "Join the Red Cross," Howard Chandler Christy, creases, edge wear 25-1/2" x 19-1/2" 250.00

Shoes, leather, pegged sole, brass buckle, stitching reads "H. S. Shawner, CT"...................... 150.00

Tie tack, R.C.A.F. Reserves, 3/4" sq 25.00

Token, U.S. Marine Corp, Third Battalion, brass...................... 10.00

Wings, Army Air Force, AWS, 1-1/8" l 28.00

Miniature Bottles

Flea markets are great places to find these clever bottles. Often they are samples, or they were designed to provide single servings for restaurant or commercial use.

Miniature bottles, Pabst, 4-1/4" h, **$17.50**.

Acme Beer, decal 6.50
Budweiser, paper label 17.50
Carstairs, lipstick shaped, 1950s 8.00
Fort Pitt Beer 3.00
Gold Bond Beer..................... 20.00
Hamms Preferred.................... 5.00
J & B Scotch........................... 10.00
Maple Farms, Vt., maple syrup. 1.00
Old Dutch.............................. 24.00
RC Cola 3.50
Tavern Pale 12.00

Miniature bottles, Pepsi, Nationally Famous Beverages, six bottles in original cardboard carrier, **$25**.

Miniatures

The world of tiny objects is truly a fascinating one. Some collectors are attracted to the craftsmanship shown by these tiny treasures, while others are more interested in finding examples to display. Keep scale in mind when purchasing miniatures for use in a doll house.

Armoire, tin litho, purple and black 35.00

Bed, four-poster, mahogany stain, hand-made 40.00

Bench, wood, rush seat 25.00

Bird cage, brass, bird, stand, 7" h 65.00

Chair, golden oak, center splat, upholstered seat, German, c1875, pr 75.00

Clock, metal.............................. 40.00

Decanter, two matching tumblers, Venetian, c1920 .... 35.00

Desk, Chippendale style, slant front, working drawers................... 65.00

Fireplace, Britannia metal fretwork, draped mantel, carved grate 65.00

Miniatures, tea set, Occupied Japan, six pieces plus lids, some damage, tray 3-1/2" d, **$30.**

Living room set, Empire style, sofa, fainting couch, two chairs, four pcs 350.00

Piano, grand, wood, eight keys, 5" h 35.00

Quilt, Whig Rose pattern, hand-made 125.00

Sewing table, golden oak, drawer, c1880 .... 100.00

Sofa, porcelain and metal 35.00

Stove, Royal, complete 120.00

Table, tin, painted brown, white top, floral design 35.00

Umbrella stand, brass, ormolu, emb palm fronds, sq 65.00

Urn, silver, handled, ornate 100.00

Vanity, Biedermeier 90.00

Wash bowl and pitcher, cobalt glass, minor chips 275.00

Miniatures, mantel clock, china, white, purple numerals, gold highlights, probably European, 2-3/4" h, **$35.**

Mirrors

Mirror, mirror on the wall… Mirrors are something we all depend on, and many of us use them as decorative accents in our homes and offices. Flea markets are great sources for interesting examples in almost every decorating style.

Hand mirror
Bakelite with rhinestones, butterfly design 40.00
Celluloid, Art Deco design ... 35.00
Celluloid, plain, beveled glass 25.00

Hanging
Chippendale style, mahogany, molded frame, gilt phoenix, loss to crest 300.00
Curly maple, frame and liner, 20th C, 17-1/2" h, 27-1/2" w ... 220.00
Gold leaf, carved florals and scrolls, beveled mirror 300.00
Mahogany veneer frame, rect, some loss to silvering 200.00
Reverse painted scene over beveled mirror, architectural pediment frame 250.00

Mirrors, pocket, Ludlow Ambulance Service, **$45.**

Tramp art frame, dark finish over varnish, stepped sawtooth border, stacked geometric designs, 15" h, 17-1/2" w 275.00

Pocket mirror, advertising
Bee Hive Overalls Best Maid, 1-3/4" w, 2-3/4" h, made by Whitehead & Hoag, Newark, NJ, c1910, bright image of girl modeling blue overalls 280.00
Berry Bros. Varnishes, 2-3/4" l, 1-3/4" h, little boy in overalls, straw hat, pulling dog in wagon 140.00
Lava Soap, celluloid centered by image of gray soap bar, opened container box, yellow ground, early 1900s 35.00
Mascot Tobacco, multicolored portrait of dog, red rim, white lettering 85.00
National Life Insurance, pink and white celluloid centered by replica of policy certificate, inscriptions for representatives located in Kansas City 25.00
Tydol Veedol Petroleum Products, celluloid, birthstones, 2" d 80.00

Shaving mirror, mahogany veneer on pine, line inlay, bowfront case, turned feet, two drawers, adjustable

mirror with turned posts, repairs, 23-1/2" h, 18-1/2" w, 7-1/2" d 145.00

Vanity mirror, three sections, folding, delicate engraving at top 150.00

Mirrors, Art Nouveau, quadruple plate, Christmas Angel, holly, and star, 6" w, 10-1/4" l, **$90.**

Model Kits

Plastic scale models were introduced in England in the mid-1930s. The popularity of these kits reached a high in the 1960s, but the oil crisis of the 1970s caused a setback in the industry. Understand that the character the model is based on has more to do with determining value than does the kit itself.

Apollo spacecraft, Revell, unbuilt 50.00

Catwoman Returns, Horizon, 1990s 10.00

Corvette, 1989, AMT Ertl, MIB 10.00

Cutty Sark, Scientific Model Airplane Co., carved wood hull, cast metal fittings.................................... 65.00

Flipper, Revell, 1965 .... 18.00

KLM 747, Matchbox, 1988, diecast, orig bubble pack, 3-3/4" wingspan, 4-3/8" l 35.00

Lufthansa 747, Matchbox, 1988, diecast, orig bubble pack, 3-3/4" wingspan, 4-3/8" l.................. 35.00

Mercedes-Benz 500K roadster, 1935, paperboard, Wrebbit, MIB 30.00

Model T, 1909, Gabriel, unbuilt 45.00

Pan Am 747, Matchbox, 1988, diecast, orig bubble pack, 3-3/4" wingspan, 4-3/8" l.................. 35.00

Penguin Returns, Horizon, 1990s 10.00

Robin, The Boy Wonder, Revell, 1999 rerelease, MIB........................ 15.00

Sense of Taste, Lindbergh Line, 1973, instructions, unbuilt.... 35.00

Star Trek Vulcan Shuttle, AMT/ Ertl, 1984, sealed 55.00

TWA 767-300, Herpa, German, scale 1:500, MIP 35.00

USS Constitution, Revell, 1966, unbuilt 80.00

Visible Man, Revell, dated 1977, unbuilt 15.00

Vostol, first Russian spacecraft, Revell, unbuilt 70.00

Model kits, Chopped Mini model kit, Model Products Corp., each **$15**.

Morton Potteries

Morton Pottery Works was established in Morton, Illinois, in 1922. Production of dinnerware, earthenware, and table accessories continued until 1976. The company also specialized in kitchenware and novelties for chain stores and gift shops.

Morton Potteries, miniatures, left to right: coffeepot, covered, brown Rockingham glaze, 3-1/2" h, **$75;** milk pitcher, cobalt blue glaze, 3-3/4" h, **$60;** brown glazed creamer, **$35;** green glazed creamer, **$40.**

Bank, acorn, green, Acorn Stove Co. adv, 3-1/2" h............................ 60.00

Cookie jar
Basket of fruit....................... 40.00
Panda.................................... 75.00

Drip-o-lator, brown Rockingham glaze, three pcs....................... 60.00

Dutch jug, three-pint, brown Rockingham glaze................. 60.00

Flowerpot soaker, calla lily, yellow and green............................... 18.00

Jardiniere, green, leaf dec, 4" h 45.00

Mug, pint, brown Rockingham glaze
.... 60.00

Pie baker, yellow ware, 10" d
.... 125.00

Planter
Covered wagon...................... 55.00
Young Davy Crockett, bear beside stump................................ 50.00

Toothpick holder, chick, white, black wash............................. 75.00

Morton Potteries, vase, white parrot with red, yellow, and green feathers, perched on purple grapes, green leaves, 8-1/2" h, **$45.**

Motorcycle Collectibles

Most people who are interested in motorcycle collectibles either ride this unique form of transportation or did so in the past. Whatever their motivation, it's a field that is growing, and these collectibles are sure to increase in value.

Motorcycles, toy, cast iron, Harley Davidson, painted blue, silvered wheels, 7" l, 4-1/2" h, **$120.**

Catalog, Harley-Davidson Motorcycles, accessories catalog, blue and yellow accents, 1954, 36 pgs, 8-1/2" h, 11" w................ 25.00

Department 56, Harley-Davidson showroom.............................. 65.00

Flyer, Harley-Davidson Motorcycles, Christmas, accessories, Baltimore, Md. dealer imprint, some inked notations, 6" x 9".................. 10.00

Key chain, Tour Award, 1960 .. 25.00

Magazine tear sheet
Harley-Davidson, *Farm Life*, 1919
.... 2.00
Honda Mini Trail, 1969, large sheet
.... 2.50

Patch, Harley-Davidson Motorcycles, embroidered, gold trademark in center, flanked by silver wings on black felt ground, early 1950s, 7-1/2".. 75.00

Stationery, white sheet, 2" red, pink and gray logo, Indian Motorcycles Dealer, profile of Indian head at left, text "Motorcycles for Sport, Business, and Police," wheel and wing design across top, Alabama dealer imprint, 3-digit phone number, c1920, 8-1/2" x 11"
.... 20.00

Toy
Corgi, stunt motorcycle, Corgi Rockets race track, gold cycle, blue rider, c1971.............. 70.00
Dinky, AA Motorcycle Patrol, motorcycle and side car... 30.00
Hubley, cast iron, replaced handle bars, 60% orig paint....... 200.00

Movie Memorabilia

Going to the movies has always been a fun event. Today's collectors actively seek memorabilia from their favorite flicks or items that are related to a particular star or studio.

Arcade card, Jackie Coogan, black and white portrait, tan ground 2.00

Autograph
Photo, Linda Blair, Exorcist, 8" x 10"..................................... 40.00
The Spirit of Notre Dame Movie Herald, sgd by Lew Ayres, Bucky

O'Connor, Sally Blane, Wm Bakewell, 5-3/4" x 8-1/2", black and white, 4 pgs, 1930s.... 45.00

Big little book, *Eddie Cantor in An Hour With You,* Whitman, #773, ©1934..................................... 40.00

Book
Crime Movies: An Illustrated History, 1980, softcover 9.00
Encyclopedia of Western Movies, 1984................................. 25.00
Ginger Rogers and the Riddle of the Scarlet Cloak, Lela E.

Rogers, Whitman 2378, 1942 .... 15.00
James Bond Show Book, Purnell & Sons, Ltd., London, c1960 20.00

Chair, War of the Worlds, director's chair, Gene Barry 150.00

Christmas stocking, *ET*, cotton 15.00

Cookbook, Gone With The Wind, Pebeco Toothpaste premium, c1939 .... 45.00

Game, Jaws Action Game, Just Toys, 1989 .... 15.00

Handbill
Men Are Not Gods, Miriam Hopkins, 6 x 9", 1930s 20.00
Spellbound, Gregory Peck and I Bergmann, 8 x 11", 4 pgs . 25.00

Movie memorabilia, car, Spy Kids, Spy Mobile, radio controlled, Radio Shack, MIB, **$30.**

Handkerchief, Gone With The Wind, Scarlet O'Hara, floral design, yellow, rose, green, black, white, and gold, black diecut foil sticker, early 1940s, 13" sq 60.00

Lobby card
Chick Carter, Detective, 11" x 14", bluetone photo, Chapter 1, Chick Carter Takes Over, 1948 Columbia Pictures serial.. 25.00
Gone with the Wind, set of six, first Italian release, 1948 .... 130.00
Lost Horizon, Mexican release, 12-1/2" x 16-1/2" 35.00
Miss Tatlock's Millions, Robert Stack, Dorothy Wood, 1948, framed 45.00
Rawhide Rangers, Johnny Mack Brown, Universal 20.00

Movie memorabilia, tin, Gloria Swanson, **$20.**

Magazine
Life, Woody Allen, March 21, 1969 .... 9.00
Look, Bing Crosby and family, June 7, 1960 .... 13.00
Teen Screen, Annette Funicello 22.00

Pinback button, Beau James, Bob Hope, 1957, 2-1/2" d.............. 38.00

Press book, *Mary Poppins,* Julie Andrews................................. 15.00

Program, Cleopatra, 1963........ 10.00

Sheet music, *As Time Goes By*, Casablanca, 1942, cover shows Humphrey Bogart, Ingrid Bergman and Paul Henreid................... 65.00

Mugs

While no one is sure when the first mug was produced, many early pottery manufacturers did include mugs in their patterns. Collectors tend to focus on advertising mugs or those related to a particular character.

Mugs, British Royalty commemorative, Queen Elizabeth II coronation, Issfield Pottery, England, multicolored image, gold banding, 3-7/8" h, **$20.**

Mugs, fraternal, souvenir of Atlantic City, July 13, 1904, Syria, Pittsburgh, glass, figural fish shaped handle, 3-1/2" h, **$65.**

Advertising
Hires, plastic.......................... 2.50
Mr. Peanut, plastic, yellow, 1970s 12.00
Nestle's Quik Rabbit, three-dimensional hard plastic, c1970 .... 12.00
Nipper, RCA Victor, plastic 8.00
Yum-Yum Donuts, white opaque glass.................................... 6.00

Beer mug, Barber Shop Whistle Stop, "For Good Cheer, Whistle for Your Beer," applied googly eyes, barber pole handle with whistle, mkd "G. C....Japan," 5-1/4" h 50.00

Boy scout, Coffee mug, "Blackhawk Area Council" and "Appreciation 72"... 12.00

British commemorative, Royal

Mugs, A&W Root Beer, 4-1/2" h, **$7.**

Silver Jubilee, 1952-1977, mkd
Royal Grafton 28.00

Glass, root beer type.................. 5.00

Lusterware, emb "Present," violets
deco, base mkd "J.C.S. Co.,
Germany" 55.00

Pottery
Bennington, brown Rockingham
glaze, double ring handle. 25.00
Unmarked, cobalt blue mirror
glaze, loop handle, set of four
.... 40.00

World's Fair
A Fair Size Mug, white glass, red
art and inscriptions, New York

World's Fair, 1964, 3-1/4" d,
3-1/4" h.............................. 10.00
Coffee Break, brown on white
china, coffee-related art and
slogans on reverse, New York
World's Fair, 1964-65, 4" h
.... 12.00
Coffee Hound, ceramic, colorful
art of cartoon dog, brown
inscriptions, inner wall with
pictorial gauge, New York
World's Fair, 1964-65, Japan foil
sticker, 4-1/2" d, 3-3/4" h
.... 15.00

Mulberry China

Mulberry china is similar to flow blue, but the design is a dark purple that appears almost black in some cases. The name derives from the resemblance of the color to crushed mulberries. Many of the same factories that produced flow blue also manufactured mulberry items.

Creamer
Corean 120.00
Marble, Wedgwood 90.00
Nankin, Davenport.............. 75.00

Cup plate, Ning Po, Hall 75.00

Dessert dish, Bryonia 30.00

Gravy boat, Calcutta.............. 110.00

Honey dish, Nankin, Davenport
.... 60.00

Milk pitcher, Ning Po, Hall, restored
spout 175.00

Plate
Avon, 9-3/4" d...................... 40.00
Berry, Ridgways, 10" d 145.00

Blackberry Lustre, Mellor Venables,
9" d 95.00
Calcutta, Edward Challinor,
8-1/2" d................................ 95.00
Corean, Podmore Walker & Co,
7-3/4" d................................ 50.00
Ning Po, Hall, 7-1/2" d 40.00
Pelew, E. Challinor, 8-1/2" d
.... 115.00
Strawberry, Walker, 9" d..... 110.00
Washington Vase, Podmore Walker
& Co., 8-3/4" d................ 100.00

Platter
Foliage, A. Walley, 15-1/4" l
.... 275.00
Washington Vase, Podmore Walker
& Co., 17-3/4" l............... 300.00

Teacup and saucer, handleless
Cyprus.................................. 100.00
Floral.................................... 80.00

Mulberry china, Cypress pattern,
Davenport, platter, c1850, 13-1/2" x
14-1/4", **$120.**

Music Boxes, Novelty Types

Music boxes were invented by the Swiss around 1825. They can now be found in many shapes, sizes, and materials. When buying a music box at a flea market, ask the dealer if it works properly and perhaps you'll hear the pretty tune.

Alice in Wonderland, Alice
and White Rabbit, "I'm Late,"
Disneyland, wood, 1980s 25.00

Ballerina, pink, metal base, some
wear 50.00

Birdcage, singing bird, German
.... 250.00

Children on merry-go-round,
wood, figures move, plays "Around
the World in 80 Days," 7-3/4" h
.... 30.00

Christmas tree, revolving, German
.... 65.00

Cuff links, pr, gold plated, one plays
Brahms Lullaby 125.00

Evening in Paris, illus of different
cosmetics, velvet and silver box
.... 125.00

Hummel
Joyful, #IV/53, trademark 6 150.00
Playmates, #IV/58, trademark 6
.... 150.00

Jewelry box, celluloid, French music box, red velvet lining, 3-1/2" w, 6-1/2" h **180.00**

Lucy, Anri, "Love Story," 1971, 5" **80.00**

Nancy, United Feature, ceramic, 1968 .... **80.00**

Nativity, bisque, O Holy Night, Lefton **65.00**

Piano, silver-plated, red velvet lining **45.00**

Pink Panther, Royal Orleans, 1983 .... **30.00**

Schroeder, Anri, "Beethoven's Emperor's Waltz," 1971, 5" **90.00**

Snowball, glass, Frosty the Snowman,

Music boxes, gilded cage with two wind-up birds, one red, one green, 8-1/4" square base, 15-1/4" h, **$495.**

red wooden base, 5" h **12.00**

Snoopy, Quantasia, "Blue Hawaii," 1985 .... **20.00**

Teacup, ceramic, TDL, 1980s ... **45.00**

Wizard of Oz, Dorothy, Schmid, plays Over the Rainbow, 1983 .... **25.00**

Music Related

Perhaps you're the type who likes to whistle while browsing at a flea market. Bet you'll find some music-related collectibles while you regale your fellow shoppers with a happy tune.

Also see Sheet Music and related categories in this edition.

Music related, figurine, Beethoven at piano, black wooden base, marked "Kauba," Geschutzt #4156, Austria, 9-1/4" h, **$850.**

Book
   History of English Music, London, 1895 .... **20.00**
   Songs for the Family, yellow hardcover, c1960 .... **10.00**

Bookends, pr, brass, musical notes **35.00**

Bookmark, figural grand piano, celluloid, printed adv **25.00**

Calendar print, dogs playing piano **5.00**

Catalog
   Hamilton Piano Co., Chicago Heights, IL, c1910, 8" x 10-1/2" **45.00**
   Kohler & Campbell, New York, NY, 1920, 5-1/2" x 8", pianos **32.00**

Guitar case, canvas, brown, leather bound edges, strap, buckle, and handle, 1890 .... **20.00**

Guitar pick, used **1.00**

Hat, marching band, blue and white, white plume, worn **10.00**

Music stand, chrome, folding type **2.00**

Music related, pin, costume jewelry, 2-1/2" h, **$5.**

Piano instruction book, beginner, green cover **2.00**

Pitch pipe, walnut, book form, paper label on int, "WN," crack, 6" l **200.00**

Player piano roll, orig box **5.00**

Sign, emb tin, Mason & Hamlin Grands & Upright Pianos, Boston, New York, Chicago, shows grand piano, framed, 19-1/2" x 27" **300.00**

Musical Instruments

The musical instruments generally found at flea markets have been used as practice instruments, or have been under the ownership of children. Expect to find wear, and understand that your purchase will probably need some repairs before it can make music again.

Musical instruments, hand-painted "Mexico" maraca, wooden handle, **$12.**

The Rudolph Wurlitzer Co. USA, stamped "P21766," fitted case, two period mouthpieces, turning crook and mute............................ 150.00

Cymbals, leather handles, American, c1900, 10" d 90.00

Drum, worn orig varnish and transfer dec of eagle and shield, labeled "Carl Fischer, New York," 16-1/2" d, replaced ropes and leather, old heads, two drum sticks . 330.00

Flute, Firth Hall and Pond, eight keys, crocus wood and nickel silver mounts, inlaid lip plate, nickel-silver keys with salt spoon cup cover, adjustable stopper c1855, stamped "Firth, Hall & Pond, Franklin Sq, New York, 1242," fitted mahogany case, 26-1/4" l 230.00

Melodeon, rosewood veneer, lyre shaped ends, ivory and ebony

Musical instruments, roller organ, Victorian Era, walnut, gold painted trim, **$250.**

Musical instruments, accordion, pearlized case, "E" in center, case, working condition, **$185.**

keyboard, 4-1/2 octaves, mkd "Carhart & Needham, New York," wear and veneer damage, lyre and bench mismatched, one bellows rod is missing, 28" h, 32-1/2" w, 16-1/4" d 175.00

Pianola, Aeolian, quartersawn oak, foot pedals, repairs required to bellows, 60 orig rolls, 36" h, 45" w 400.00

Recorder, tenor, Moeck, maple body, brass key 175.00

Saxophone, baritone, Buescher, Elkhart, IN, case and music stand 500.00

Trombone, Concertone, SP, gold plated bell, satin finish 300.00

Ukulele, The Serenader, B.&G., N.Y., double binding, celluloid fingerboard and head 250.00

Zither, Columbia, 47 strings, c1900 .... 275.00

Accordion, black lacquer, brass, silver and abalone inlay, keys and decorative valve covers with carved mother-of-pearl, needs repair 95.00

Banjo, Bacon Banjo Co., Style C, 17 fret neck, hard-shell case 185.00

Bassoon, 15-keyed, maple, brass mounts and keys, c1900, 50-1/4" l 460.00

Bugle, nickel-plated, minor dents, wooden case with black paint 100.00

Clarinet, 10-keyed boxwood, key of C, brass mountings, brass keys with round covers, c1860, orig mouthpiece, 21-1/2" l.......... 400.00

Cornet, silver-plated brass tubing, engraved at the bell, three piston valves with pearl buttons, Lyric,

Napkin Rings

Figural napkin rings are useful collectibles. Victorian silver and silver plate napkin rings, including examples having a whimsical nature, often are available at flea markets.

Napkin rings, International Silver, rings with repoussé design, set of four, MIB, **$45.**

Aluminum, souv of Washington DC, three scenes 10.00

Bakelite
Angelfish, marbled blue, c1940 .... 70.00
Bird, butterscotch 40.00
Elephant, navy blue, c1940 .... 95.00

Ceramic
Bird perched on ring, Japan 10.00

Fitz & Floyd, White Classic pattern 15.00
Franciscan, Fresh Fruit pattern 28.00
Pfaltzgraff, Yorktown pattern, set of four 10.00

Chrome plated, 1-1/2" d, 1" w, Art Deco, unengraved presentation panel, engine turned herringbone and squares engraving 25.00

Pewter, kewpie, 2-1/2" h 115.00

Plastic
Chili pepper, red 2.00
Oval, clear, carved floral dec.. 5.00

Porcelain
Chintz, Thistle pattern, Wade 18.00
Sunbonnet girl, mkd "Erphila Czechoslovakian," 2" x 4" 72.00

Silver
Beaded edge, plain center 95.00
Eagle, Meriden, 2" h 125.00
Leaf and barrel, tarnished.... 45.00

Silver plated
Billy Goat, nursery rhyme motif 85.00
Flowers on lily pad, top emb with fan and flowers, sgd "Middletown Quad Plate #97" 100.00

Napkin ring, silver plated, cupid in center, pepper shaker, open salt, round napkin ring, all mounted on footed shaped base, Victorian, **$200.**

Ring, engraved ferns 10.00
Swans, pair with ring on backs 175.00

NASCAR

It's a pretty cool sport when you think about guys racing cars that, except for the abundance of colorful advertisements, look like they could have come out of your driveway. When it comes to racing collectibles, nothing's hotter. Are you racing off to a flea market? You should find plenty of good NASCAR collectibles to choose from.

Ashtray, Penske Racing, 1984 Indy 500 Winner, helmet shape..... 15.00

Autograph, promotional card with photo of car and drivers in front, bios and stats on back, sgd in black sharpie, 8-1/2" x 11"
Force, John........................... 10.00
Skuza, Dean, Matco Tools 10.00

Bank
1991, Jeff Gordon, Carolina Ford Dealers, NASCAR Club Bank 65.00
1998, Terry Labonte, Monte Carlo, Kellogg's Corny Bank, 1:24, MIB 60.00

Barbie, 50th Anniversary Nascar Barbie, MIB 30.00

Book, *NASCAR: The Thunder of America!* NASCAR 50th anniversary, hardcover, orig dj, illus 30.00

Calendar, 1995, Winston Cup Series, different driver and car for each month 8.00

Cap, *Indianapolis Motor Speedway Inaugural Race,* limited edition, Aug. 6, 1994, blue, gold lettering, orig hang tag, never worn 15.00

Diecast car
CAT, #96, David Green, 1997 Chevrolet Monte Carlo, black and yellow, Revell Club, 1:24 scale, NRFB 48.00

NASCAR, die-cast car, Richard Petty, Team Transport, 1/87 scale, Road Champs, NRFC, **$15.**

Citgo, #21, Michael Waltrip, 1997 Ford Thunderbird, white and red, Revell Club, 1:24 scale, NRFB............................... 48.00

Dallenbach, Wally, #75, Power Puff Girls, 2000, Action Racing, 1:24 scale, MIB......................... 15.00

Nadeau, Jerry, #9, Cartoon Network, Power Puff Girls, 1998, Action Racing, 1:24 scale, MIB 18.00

Winn Dixie, #60, Mark Martin driver, Revell Club, 1:18 scale 90.00

Zerex, numbered edition, certificate of authenticity, Racing Champions, 1:24 scale, NRFB 45.00

Display card, 10-3/4" x 13-3/4", full color, cardboard easel counter type, May 16, 1976, Mason-Dixon 500 at Dover Downs International Speedway, DE, bicentennial theme art 20.00

Drinking glass, 2-1/4" d, 4-1/2" h, clear, Indy 500 Mayor's Breakfast, black and gold art for 500 Festival, slogan "Indy-Where It's At" 15.00

Helmet, miniature, facsimile signature, Simpson, made in China, 2-1/2" x 3"
Earnhardt, Dale 18.00
Gordan, Jeff, #24 .... 12.00

Key chain, Kelloggs, plastic, car-shape.. 8.00

License plate, plastic, Bill Elliott, Ford Taurus, #94, sponsored by McDonald's, 1998, 19" l, 8" h .. 8.00

Mug, *Slim Jim Racing Team*, glass, Busch Series Champions 1991 & 1994, c1996, 6-1/2" h............. 10.00

Pinback button, *Indianapolis Speedway*, 1-1/4" d, shaded blue and white ground, judges stand with two bright yellow racing cars, overprinted with large black and white checkered flag, c1950 .. 12.00

Program, 1927 Official Indy 500 .... 300.00

Seat cushion, Indy 700, orange and black, officially licensed product of Indianapolis Motor Speedway. 8.00

Stein, Winston Cup 25th Anniversary, 1995, limited edition, pictures of Kulwicki, Wallace, Earnhardt, Elliott, Allison, Petty, Yarborough, Parson, Waltrip, LaBonte, 5-1/2" h 10.00

Watch, men's, Jeff Gordon, #24 .... 125.00

Nautical

Anchors away! Nautical items can encompass things with a nautical theme or items that were actually used on a ship.

For additional listings, see *Warman's Antiques and Collectibles Price Guide.*

Book, George Goldsmith-Carter, *Sailors, Sailors,* 1966.............. 5.00

Nautical, naval compass, c1900, **$350.**

Bookends, pr
Anchors, brass, mounted on faux stone base, 8" h 47.50
Whale's Heads, bronze verdigris finish, 5-1/2" h 50.00

Charm bracelet, silver tone, fish, sailfish, shell, and seahorse charms 24.00

Chart, Boston Harbor, George W. Eldridge, 1876, 17" x 24" 195.00

Clock, wall, anchor, brass, bronze finish, battery operated......... 25.00

Coasters, set of four, each with different lighthouse.............. 20.00

Key chain, ship's wheel, leather attached to medallion, "VN Balboa," 1" d... 25.00

Lifeboat compass, 8" sq, 7-1/4" h, boxed, 20th C...................... 175.00

Plaque, White Star Line, thick brass plate, engraved words, mounted on varnished mahogany board, 18" x 7".. 375.00

Porthole, green, rubber seal 50.00

Print
Clippers *Ariel & Taiping*, M. Dawson, 26" x 31"............ 65.00
Cutty Sark, Racing Home, M. Dawson, 20" x 28" 65.00

Nautical, clipper ship card, Derby, Sutton & Co., Dispatch Line for San Francisco, blue lettering, white ground, printed by Nesbit & Co., Printers, NY, 6-3/8" x 3-9/16", **$315.**

Ship *Triumphant,* Frank Vining Smith, 22" x 32"................ **38.50**

Ship compass, 10" d magnetic compass, teakwood box, polished brass gimball ring, US Navy, World

War II era, made by John E. Hand & Co.. **750.00**

Ship's bell, 8" d, *Alister Hardy,* brass, dated 1953 .... **145.00**

Tablecloth, cotton, printed red tall ships and lighthouses, 1940s **30.00**

Table lamp, brass boat cleat-ships wheel, sea navigation chart lamp shade, 15" h **235.00**

New Martinsville Glass

Founded in 1901, the New Martinsville Glass Manufacturing Company was located in West Virginia. Its glassware products ranged from pressed utilitarian wares to some innovative designs and colors.

New Martinsville Glass, cake plate, Prelude etch, pedestal base, **$50.**

Animal
Baby bear, head straight....... **60.00**
Seal, holding ball, light lavender, candle holder **75.00**

Ashtray, Moondrops, red......... **35.00**

Basket, Janice, black, 12" l, 7" w, 9-1/2" h **190.00**

Bitters bottle, Hostmaster, cobalt blue **75.00**

Bookends, pr, clipper chips **95.00**

Bowl, Teardrop, crystal, three ftd, 11" d, 4" h **45.00**

Cake plate
Janice, 40th Anniversary silver overlay............................. **45.00**
Prelude, pedestal foot........... **10.00**

Candlesticks, pr
Janice, red........................... **200.00**
Radiance, 2-lite................... **230.00**

Candy box, Radiance, three-part, amber, etch #26 .... **160.00**

Champagne, Moondrops, red . **40.00**

Celery dish, swan, 8" l neck, 6" h **25.00**

Cigarette holder, cart shaped **20.00**

Console bowl, Janice, ftd, crystal **38.00**

Console set, Radiance, crystal, 12" bowl pr 2-lite candlesticks .. **125.00**

Cordial, Janice, red, silver trim **40.00**

Creamer and sugar, Addie, red **65.00**

Cup and saucer
Hostmaster, red **15.00**
Janice, red............................. **30.00**
Radiance, amber.................. **30.00**

Decanter, Moondrops, amber . **80.00**

Figure, crystal
Baby Bear, 3-1/2" h.............. **65.00**
Polar Bear, 4" h.................... **95.00**
Squirrel, 5" h........................ **55.00**

Goblet, Diamond Thumbprint. **12.00**

Iced tea tumbler, Prelude etching **17.50**

Lamp, 10" h, Art Deco style, pink satin, black enamel accents... **45.00**

Mug, Georgian, red.................. **18.00**

Nappy, Prelude, 5" d, heart shaped, handle **20.00**

Pitcher, Oscar, red................. **100.00**

Punch cup, Radiance.............. **15.00**

Relish, Radiance, amber, three-part **15.00**

Swan, Janice, crystal **80.00**

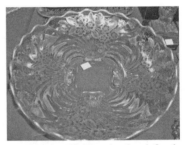

New Martinsville Glass, low bowl, floral silver overlay, **$35.**

Tumbler
Amy, #34, ftd **22.50**
Janice, red, 10 oz, ftd............ **35.00**
Moondrops, cobalt blue, 5 oz **24.00**
Oscar, red.............................. **20.00**

Vanity set, three-pc, Judy, green and crystal or pink and crystal **100.00**

Vase
Art deco style, black, 8-1/2" h **90.00**
Shell, leaded crystal, 5" h **70.00**

New Martinsville Glass, candlesticks, 2 lite, #18, amber, **$40.**

Newspapers

Saving a newspaper about a historic event or memorable occasion seems like such an easy thing to do. Happily for newspaper collectors, folks have been doing that for centuries. Flea markets are a great place to find these interesting publications.

American Journal, April 12, 1945, Roosevelt dies 45.00

Cincinnati Weekly Herald and Philanthropist, Nov. 22, 1843, feature on "Mr. Adams and the Colored People" 45.00

City Journal, Scopes Trial, July 10, 1925 .... 48.00

Dallas Morning News, Nov. 22, 1963, Kennedy slain 35.00

Hagerstown Daily Mail, Hagerstown, Md., April 6, 1964, Hero's Homage Paid MacArthur..................... 25.00

Havanna Post, Cuba, Oct. 7, 1926, National Foreign Trade Committee 25.00

Metropolis Planet, Metropolis, Ill., June 28, 1973, Superman souvenir edition..................................... 35.00

New York Times May 22, 1927, Lindbergh Does It 375.00

July 21, 1969, Man Walks on the Moon 30.00

The Fiery Cross, Indianapolis, IN, Feb. 14, 1924.......................... 20.00

The Post Standard, Dec. 8, 1941, Japan Declares War After Attacking US 65.00

The Washington Daily News, July 12, 1972, FAREWELL headline, final edition of publication............ 30.00

The Youths Medallion, Boston April 17, 1841 .... 40.00

Wilmington Home Weekly, May 2, 1886 .... 10.00

Newspapers, headline editions, Roosevelt Dies, Times-Herald, Newport News, VA, April 12, 1945, Vol. 46, No. 81, **$40.**

Niloak Pottery

Niloak Pottery was located near Benton, Ark. The founder of the company, Charles Dean Hyten, experimented with native clays and tried to preserve their natural colors. By 1911, he had perfected a method that gave this effect, a product he named Mission Ware. The pottery burned but was rebuilt. It reopened under the name Eagle Pottery and by 1929 was producing novelties. Several different marks were used, helping to determine the dates of pieces. By 1946, the company went out of business.

For additional listings, see *Warman's Antiques and Collectibles Price Guide, Warman's Americana & Collectibles,* and *Warman's American Pottery and Porcelain.*

Ashtray, blue glaze, hat shape.. 12.00

Bud vase, Ozark Dawn glaze, 7-1/4" h 65.00

Candlestick, Mission Ware, 10" h 245.00

Creamer, Ozark Dawn 35.00

Ewer, Ozark Dawn, 16-1/2" h . 150.00

Figure
Frog, matte green 30.00
Polar Bear, matte white 45.00

Planter
Deer, blue.............................. 35.00

Elephant, pink 30.00
Fox, red................................. 27.50
Swan, blue............................. 45.00

Strawberry vase, pink, gray-green glaze, opening with turkey, tail feathers spread out, orig paper label, sgd................................. 65.00

Vase, Mission Ware
Flared lip, 4" h 90.00
Hourglass form, 5-1/2" h.... 165.00

Vase, Ozark Dawn
Cylindrical, 8-3/4" h 200.00
Twisted handle, 6" h 155.00

Niloak Pottery, vase, tulips and leaves, purple glaze, white clay body, center opening surrounded by four additional openings, 6-1/4" h, **$30.**

Nippon China

From 1891 until 1921, *Nippon* was the mark Japan used on hand-painted porcelain made for export. However, in 1921, the United States required all imported Japanese wares to be marked *Japan*.

There are more than 200 documented marks or backstamps for Nippon. For some makers, the color of the mark helps determine the quality of the piece. Green was used for first-grade porcelain, blue for second-grade, and magenta for third-grade. Other types of marks were also used.

Sadly, today there are marked reproductions that can be very deceiving. Carefully examine any piece, study the workmanship, and thoroughly investigate any marks.

For additional listings, see *Warman's Antiques and Collectibles Price Guide*.

Reproduction alert.

Buyer beware!

Don't believe everything you see.

That's good advice when it comes to buying antiques and collectibles. It's not that a person should be cynical. However, the existence of reproductions, fakes, forgeries and fantasy items have led collectors to approach the marketplace knowledgeably and with caution.

The phrase "caveat emptor"—let the buyer beware—is especially true for anyone interested in Nippon porcelain. Fewer areas of the antiques market have been plagued by more reproductions bearing more fake marks than Nippon.

One of the best resources providing information about such bogus items is *Antique & Collectors Reproduction News*, a monthly newsletter. For information, write to ACRN, P.O. Box 12130, Des Moines, IA 50312-9403, or check the on-line database at www.repronews.com.

Nippon China, condensed milk server and underplate, cobalt blue, turquoise, green, pink, and gold decoration on white ground, **$85.**

What is a condensed milk server anyway? It was used to hold a whole can of condensed milk, when it was stylish to serve that type of milk, especially in regions where the fresh milk supply wasn't as plentiful as it is today. To remove the can, there is a hole in the bottom of the server.

green M in wreath mark, 18" l, minor gold wear 50.00

Hatpin holder, shaped, raised beading 65.00

Ashtray, black cat on roof 125.00

Basket, handle, hp roses, stippled gilt ground, 7-1/2" h 90.00

Nippon China, celery set, 12-1/2" master dish, six 4" l matching salt dips, pink and blue flowers with green leaves on tan band, gold scroll decoration, purple stamp M in wreath mark, **$65.**

Bowl, scalloped edge, floral and gold border, green "M" in wreath mark, 7-1/2" d 20.00

Box, cov, 4-1/2" d, floral dec, green maple leaf mark 115.00

Cake plate, floral design, gold trim, green "M" in wreath mark, 11" d 40.00

Candlestick, hand painted gold highlights, light green ground pedestal base, green maple leaf mark, 11" h 115.00

Candy dish, divided, scenic design, blue rising sun mark 50.00

Celery tray, pink flowers 60.00

Cup and saucer, Orange Blossom pattern, gold trim, blue mark 30.00

Dresser tray, delicate hp pink floral design, gold trim, closed handles,

Nippon China, cider set, four mugs, matching pitcher, Art Deco type multicolored decoration, **$130.**

Mayonnaise set, underplate, spoon, floral border, magenta "M" in wreath mark 50.00

Mustard pot, scenic design, green "M" in wreath mark, 3-1/2" h 40.00

Nut bowl, raised nut design, ftd, green "M" in wreath mark, 7" d 85.00

Plaque, Waiting by Shore, Dutch mother and two children looking over bay, dec rim, blue M in wreath mark, 10" d 100.00

Plate, two handles, floral and gold border, red and green mark, 10-1/2" d 35.00

Relish, cov, scenic design, gold trim, matching spoon, green "M" in wreath mark, 4" h 50.00

Serving tray, center handle, floral dec, magenta "M" in wreath mark 20.00

Sugar shaker, ecru and white ground, blue and yellow butterfly 80.00

Tea set, 6" h cov teapot, creamer, sugar, six cups and saucers, hp

swans in pond, mill in background, gold trim and beading, green M in wreath mark 150.00

Toothpick holder, 2" h, Woodland, white, green "M" in wreath mark 115.00

Vase
Double handles, Lilac pattern, gold trim, blue maple leaf mark, 8-1/2" h............................ 150.00
House and trees scene, ivory ground, gold painted grape leaves, green Morimura mark, 8" h 375.00

Nodders and Bobbin' Heads

Here's a collecting category that folks never seem to tire of. Perhaps it's the whimsical nature of these pieces or the idea that there is constant motion. Whatever it is, there are plenty of examples to be found at flea markets.

Nodder
Alligator, mkd "Made in Japan," c1940, 4-1/2" h 95.00
American League umpire, 8-1/2" h 45.00
Cowboy, Japan, 5" h 65.00
Chinaman, Japan, 6-1/2" h... 65.00
Elephant, green overalls, Hong Kong, 4" h.......................... 35.00
Fighting Irish, football player, made in Hong Kong, 1970s, 5-1/4" h 30.00
Goose, S.A. Reider & Co., U.S. Zone, Germany, 1-1/2" h, 3-1/2" l 65.00
Hawaiian boy or girl, Let's Kiss, Japan, each 85.00
Lion, fleece, plastic teeth...... 22.00
Oakland Athletics, 1988, 8-1/2" h 45.00
Orchestra conductor, hp, large mustache, top hat, tuxedo coat

with tails, late 1930s, 3-1/4" h 95.00
Peter Pan, 1950s, 6" h........... 75.00
Raggedy Ann, 5-1/2" h 175.00
Robin Hood, Japan, 6" h....... 85.00
Seattle Supersonics, composition, sticker "American Sports Sales Ltd, Made in Korea," late 1970s, 7" h 25.00
Woody Woodpecker, 1950s 50.00

Nodder/bank
Black policeman, Nassau, black pants, white hat and jacket, doubles as bank.............. 145.00
Colonel Sanders, plaster, 7-1/2" h 165.00
Nodder/clock, flamingo, pink and green, quartz clock, mkd "Japan," 1985, 10" w, 6-1/2" h 195.00

Nodder, Oriental woman, seated, holding fan, bisque, pale blue, gold trim, 3-3/4" h, **$120.**

Noritake China

Noritake China was founded by the Morimura Brothers in Nagoya, Japan, about 1904. The company produced high-quality dinnerware for export and also some blanks for hand painting. Although the factory was heavily damaged during World War II, production resumed and continues today. There are more than 100 different marks to help determine the pattern and date of production.

Ashtray, Tree in the Meadow, green backstamp, 5-1/4" d.............. 35.00

Bowl, autumn leaves, molded filbert nuts, ftd, turned-in sides, 7" sq 80.00

Bread plate, ear of corn dec, 12" l 50.00

Noritake China, dinner set, Allston pattern, gray leaves, blue and pink flowers, gold rim, **$45.**

Butter dish, cov, Tree in the Meadow, orig insert 65.00

Candlesticks, pr, gold flowers and bird, blue luster ground, wreath with "M" mark, 8-1/4" h 95.00

Celery set, celery holder, six matching salts, gold trim, green wreath marks......................... 85.00

Creamer, Chandon, #7306....... 42.00

Cup and saucer
Chelsea pattern..................... 30.00

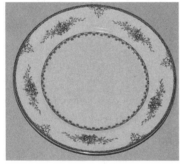

Noritake China, Castella plate, 9-7/8" d, **$10.**

Margarita pattern 12.00
Roanne, #6794..................... 18.00

Demitasse cup and saucer, Tree in the Meadow 48.00

Dinner plate, Margarita pattern, 9-7/8" d 18.00

Dish, handle, red and gold flower border, gold trim, red wreath mark, 5-1/2" w 28.00

Easter egg, yellow hat with blue trim, blue and pink flowers, dated 1976, satin lined box, 3" h............... 26.00

Hair receiver, Art Deco geometric designs, gold luster, wreath with "M" mark, 3-1/4" h................ 50.00

Jam jar, cov, basket style, figural applied cherries on notched lid 55.00

Lemon dish, Tree in the Meadow, 5-1/2" d................................. 35.00

Platter
Asian Song, medium 85.00
Carolyn, small 80.00
Tree in the Meadow, two handles 45.00

Potpourri jar, blue and white, pierced cov with red and yellow rosebud finial, 6" h 85.00

Salt, swan, white, orange luster 12.00

Soup bowl, Margarita pattern 18.00

Sugar bowl, cov, Margarita pattern 18.00

Vase, medallion with landscape scene on one side, florals on reverse, gold moriage, black background covered with tiny gold roses, gold edge at

Noritake China, nut dishes, pink and white apple blossoms, green foliage, gold trim, three small legs, green mark, set of four, **$38.**

bottom, some wear to gold, green "M" in wreath mark, c1920, 6" h 90.00

Vegetable bowl, cov, Bamboo 115.00

Wall pocket, orange luster, figural bird 180.00

Noritake China, server, center handle, cobalt blue, yellow, and green, brown wreath Japan mark, **$45.**

Noritake China, Azalea Pattern

In the 1920s, the Larkin Company of Buffalo, N.Y., became a prime distributor of Noritake China. Two of the most popular patterns it promoted were Azalea and Tree in the Meadow, causing them to be the most popular with collectors today. The design of Azalea pattern includes delicate pink flowers, green leaves on a white background. Many pieces have gold trim, especially on handles and finials.

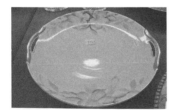

Noritake China, Azalea pattern, platter, two self handles, gold trim, **$20.**

Bon bon.................................... 48.00
Cake plate 40.00
Casserole, cov 75.00
Creamer 25.00
Dinner plate 24.00
Egg cup.................................... 55.00

Noritake China, Azalea pattern, condiment set, salt and pepper shakers, mustard in center, shaped tray, **$40.**

Lemon tray 30.00
Luncheon plate 15.00
Platter, oval............................. 20.00
Salad bowl, 10" d 37.50
Teapot..................................... 100.00
Vase, fan................................. 150.00
Vegetable dish, cov 75.00

Noritake China, Azalea pattern, lemon plate, ring handle, wear to gold trim, **$30.**

Nutcrackers

Clever devises to release the tasty part of a nut were invented as far back as the 19th century. Collectors today seek out interesting examples in various metals and wood.

Nutcracker, toy soldier, wooden, blue uniform, red hat, Steinbach, Präfent, Volkskunst, original tag, **$35.**

Bear, wooden, Black Forest, glass eyes, curved tail with lever that operates the mouth, 4-1/2" h, 8" l 165.00

Boy Scout............................... 210.00

Dentist.................................... 210.00
Dog, graniteware over cast iron, white on black base, black tail and lower jar, 5-3/4" h, 10-1/2" l 115.00
Eagle's head, wooden, Swiss, glass eyes, levered beak, 6-1/2" l 310.00
Fireman, wooden 25.00
Irishman, wooden.................... 25.00
Man's head, A. B. Hagen, patent Oct 17, 1950, aluminum 50.00
Marionette maker, wooden ... 25.00
Pliers type, cast iron, c1930..... 20.00
Rabbit, cast iron 20.00
Sailing ship, brass, English, 1939 .... 75.00
Santa, Bavarian, orig wooden gift box 60.00

Nutcracker, dog, cast iron, **$40.**

Squirrel, cast iron, 4-1/2" h, 5-1/2" l 100.00
St. Bernard, metal, advertises L.A. Althoff Makers of Headlight Stoves and Ranges Chicago, Ill., 5-3/4" h, 11" l..................................... 275.00
Sugar Plum Chef................... 20.00

Nutting, Wallace

The story of Wallace Nutting is a fascinating tale of an enterprising American. Born in 1861, he attended Harvard University and several theological seminaries. In 1904 he opened a photography studio in New York, later other branch studios. By the time he moved to Framingham, Mass., in 1913, he was employing more than 200 colorists, framers, and support staff. Nutting photographed the images that were to be hand colored under his specific directions. Nutting died in 1941, but his wife continued the business. After her death, the business continued until 1971, when the last owner ordered the glass negatives destroyed.

Although the listings here are devoted to his pictures, remember that he also published several books and sold silhouettes and furniture.

Wallace Nutting, picture, A Pilgrim Daughter, hand colored, original mat, pen signature and title, 26" x 33" original frame, c1915-25, dark mat, considerable frame damage, **$100.**

A Birch Grove, c1915-25, orig mat, pen signature and title, 15" x 13" period frame........................... 35.00

A Delicate Stitch, c1915-25, orig mat, pen signature and title, 14" x 11" new frame 80.00

A Garden of Larkspur, c1915-25, orig mat, pen signature and title, 10" x 12" orig frame, orig back paper..................................... 100.00

A Pilgrim Daughter, c1915-25, orig mat, pen signature and title, 15" x 12" orig frame...................... 100.00

At Paul Revere's Tavern, c1915-25, orig mat, pen signature and title, 15" x 13" period frame 160.00

A Virginia Reel, c1915-25, orig mat, pen signature and title, 16" x 14" orig frame.............................. 90.00

A Woodland Cathedral, c1915-25, orig mat, pen signature and title, 8" x 16" orig frame..................... 45.00

Billows of Blossom, c1915-25, orig mat, pen signature and title, 20" x 16" orig frame, orig backing paper 90.00

Coming Out of Rosa, c1915-25, orig mat, pen signature and title, 17" x 14" orig frame........................ 65.00

Dell Dare Road, c1915-25, orig mat, pen signature and title, 14" x 12" orig frame............................... 70.00

Height of Spring, c1915-25, orig mat, pen signature and title, 11" x 14" orig frame, new backing paper 55.00

In Tenderleaf, c1915-25, orig mat, pen signature and title, 12" x 16" orig frame, no backing paper 25.00

In Upland New England, c1905-10, orig mat, pencil signature and title, 15" x 10" orig frame, new backing paper..................................... 80.00

Old Wentworth Days, c1915-25, orig mat, pen signature and title, 14" x 17" orig frame, new backing paper..................................... 100.00

On the Slope, c1915-25, orig mat, pen signature and title, 16" x 10" orig frame, no backing paper 80.00

Patti's Favorite Walk, c1915-25, orig mat, pen signature and title, 12" x

Wallace Nutting, picture, By the Stone Fence, titled on original matting, original frame, 8" x 10", some water staining, **$75.**

Wallace Nutting, picture, Lichfield Minster, England, hand colored, original mat, pen signature and title, 18" x 22" original frame, c1915-25, **$125.**

10" orig frame, no backing paper 80.00

Tea at Yorktown Parlor, c1915-25, orig mat, pen signature and title, 16" x 10" orig frame, orig backing paper..................................... 100.00

The Hurrying Saranac, c1915-25, orig mat, pen signature and title, 10" x 12" orig frame, no backing paper..................................... 50.00

The Mills at the Turn, Holland, c1915-25, orig mat, pen signature and title, 12" x 10" orig frame, no backing paper 80.00

Untitled exterior, Connecticut, c1915-25, orig mat, pen signature and title, 9" x 7" orig frame, orig backing paper 35.00

Untitled exterior, Heart of Maine, c1915-25, orig mat and pen signature, 7" x 9" orig frame, orig backing paper 35.00

Waters meet, c1915-25, orig mat, pen signature and title, 20" x 16" orig frame............................... 70.00

Nutting-Like Pictures

Because Wallace Nutting's pictures were so successful, copycats soon appeared on the scene. Some artists had worked for Nutting and learned the techniques. These pictures are starting to catch the eye of collectors.

Davidson, David
  A Puritan Lady 70.00
  A Real D.A.R...................... 150.00
  Berkshire Sunset.................. 80.00
  Heart's Desire 30.00

  Her House In Order.............. 75.00
Haynes, F. Jay
  Old Faithful, 8" x 10" 95.00
  Great Falls, Yellowstone Park, 13" x 18" 150.00

Sawyer
  At the Bend of the Road....... 35.00
  Crystal Lake.......................... 65.00
  Echo Lake, Franconia Notch
  .... 50.00

Indian Summer 35.00
Lake Morey........................... 30.00
Lake Willoughby 50.00

Thompson, Fred
Calm of Fall 50.00
Fernbank 35.00
Fireside Fancy Work........... 140.00
Golden Trail.......................... 40.00
High and Dry........................ 45.00
Knitting for the Boys.......... 160.00
Lombardy Poplar................ 100.00
Miniature exterior, c1910-20, 2" x 3"
    orig frame, grade 3.5, mat stain
    .... 30.00
Miniature interior, c1915-25, 4"
    x 3" orig thin metal frame,
    close framed, orig Thompson
    backstamp, hanging calendar
    missing, grade 3.75 .... 45.00
Mother's Reveries, c1910-20, 17" x
    14", orig frame, grade 3.5, mat
    stains 50.00
Nature's Carpet 50.00
Neath the Blossoms, c1910-15, orig
    mat, pencil signature and title,
    11" x 7" orig frame, grade 4.0
    .... 200.00
Peace River 30.00
Portland Head 440.00
Roadside Brook, c1910-15, 20" x
    16" orig frame, orig Thompson
    stamp on back, grade 3.75
    .... 100.00

Wallace Nutting-like pictures, Fred Thompson, Olde Tyme Way, pencil signature and title, 7" x 5", c1910-15, **$25.**

Wallace Nutting-like pictures, Rabel, hand colored photo, exterior New England scene, 9" x 7" original frame, original backing, c1910-15, **$35.**

Wallace Nutting-like pictures, Standley, "Ute Pass, Manitou, Colorado," hand-tinted photograph, image size 7-3/4" x 3-1/4", **$70.**

Occupied Japan

To help repair its devastated economy after World War II, the Japanese made items to export, including porcelain, toys, and all kinds of knickknacks. Today savvy collectors know that items made during the occupation time period might be marked "Japan," "Made in Japan," or "Occupied Japan," as well as "Made in Occupied Japan."

Occupied Japan, opera glasses, 3-3/8" h, 4-1/8" l, **$45.**

Ashtray, souvenir from Florida, shaped like state, black letters, gold trim 15.00

Basket, figural roses and leaves . 7.50

Bell, chef holding wine bottle and glass 27.50

Demitasse cup and saucers, Dragonware, yellow and white, brown, green, and white enameled dragons, stamp mark, 2" d cup, 4" d saucers, price for set of four 175.00

Doll, bisque, black, painted eyes and mouth, fabric hair, arms and legs slightly loose, imp "Made in Occupied Japan," 4" h 75.00

Egg timer, maid, mkd 45.00

Figure
Colonial gentleman playing violin, 9-1/2" h 120.00

Colonial lady playing accordion, 9-1/2" h 120.00
Colonial lady, sitting on bench, holding fan, 9" h 125.00
Santa, 7-1/2" h 60.00

Flower frog, bisque, girl with bird on shoulder, pastel highlights, gold trim 48.00

Mug, boy-shaped handle 15.00

Parasol, paper, multicolored, large 150.00

Planter
Black cat, red ribbon 15.00
Cherub riding dragon's back, peach, lime green, and white, bisque 95.00

Plate, Gold Castle, set of six ... 165.00

Reamer, strawberry shape, red, green leaves and handle, mkd, 3-3/4" h 90.00

Rice bowl, hand painted, bright orange and yellow flowers, budding orange flower on back, mkd "Made in Occupied Japan," and ISCO in red triangle, 4-1/2" d 30.00

Salt and pepper shakers, pr, Hummel type boy and girl 95.00

Tape measure, pig, stamped "Occupied Japan" 45.00

Teapot, figural, squirrel on corn, yellow kernels, green foliage, brown squirrel handle and finial, mkd, 7" w, 5-1/4" h 120.00

Tea set
Aichi China, pink florals, cov teapot, creamer, cov sugar, six

Occupied Japan, porcelain figurine with vase, 3-1/8" h, **$8.50.**

7-7/8" d plates, six cups and saucers 165.00
Cottage, cov teapot, creamer, cov sugar 125.00

Toy, celluloid wind-up
Dancing couple, 4-1/2" h.... 125.00
Kitten with green ball.......... 35.00
Parrot, white wire bird cage 100.00

Vase, ballerina, white vase, burgundy trim, figural 7" h ballerina in white and burgundy tutu, 8" h 125.00

Vegetable, cov, Royal Embassy, Rutland pattern, 10" l 95.00

Wall pocket, lady with hat, 5" h 45.00

Ocean Liner Memorabilia

The thought of a leisurely ocean cruise has enticed many to try this mode of travel, and of course they brought back souvenirs. Today collectors are glad they did as they discover these mementoes at flea markets.

Ashtray, *Normandie*, Opalex Glass, France, 1945, 3-3/8" x 2-3/4". 55.00

Baggage tag, French Line, first class, unused 7.50

Book, *USS Triton SSRN 586 First Submerged Circumnavigation*, Government Printing Office,

Washington, DC, 1960, 1st printing 50.00

Ocean Liner collectibles, souvenir spoon, R. M. S. Adriatic, enamel and sterling silver, hallmarked, **$20.**

Brochure, Cunard Line, Getting There is Half the Fun, 16 pgs, 1952 .... 7.50

Deck plan, *RMS Queen Elizabeth,* Cunard, plan of first class accommodation, cream-colored folder, gold and brown lettering, 1952 .... 50.00

Dish, Cunard *RMS Queen Mary,* ceramic, oval, color portrait, gold edge, Staffordshire, 5" l 37.50

Fan, Cie Galen Transatlantique French Line, chromolithograph of Spanish style lady overlooking Mediterranean, watching ocean liner sail past, paper on wood, orig tassel, artist sgd, 1919 .... 85.00

Itinerary card, 3-1/4" x 6" State Line for Europe, full color, Castle

Gardens port, New York, text on reverse 20.00

Map, Norwegian Cruise Lines, *M/S Southward,* map of West Indies and Caribbean Sea, routes, antiquities images, 1970s, framed, 18" x 24"................................. 40.00

Menu
   Norddeutscher Lloyd, Bremen, tall sailing ship with smaller sailboat nearby on cov, four pgs, April, 1903 .... 35.00
   SS Leonardo Da Vinci, January, 1973 .... 6.00
   SS Lurline, Matson Lines, Commodore's Dinner, March 3, 1959, 12" x 9" 22.00

Newspaper Supplement, *Queen Mary, the World's Wonder Ship,* 20" x 24", acid free mat 125.00

Passport cover, Red Star Line, fabric, ship illus 27.50

Pencil, *S/S Oceanic,* Caran D'ache lead pencil, plastic case 25.00

Pennant, *R.M.S. Queen Elizabeth,* gray felt, blue, red, white, and black, some fading, 26-1/2" l. 25.00

Pinback button, 5/8" d, litho, Alpha Rally Day, steamship in bright red, blue and white sky and water, 1920s 2.50

Playing cards, Eastern Steamship Corp., full color deck, showing ship at sea, revenue stamp attached to edge flap of orig box, c1950 .. 15.00

Poster, *Nord-Lloyd Bremen* and *Europa,* marketed for American

Ocean Liner collectibles, cup and saucer, Porsgrund, Norway, white, multicolored flag, dark green and gold rim borders, **$10.**

transatlantic travel, conservation framed, 6-1/2" x 9-1/2"........ 150.00

Program, Charity Fete, *De La Salle,* French Lines, benefiting Central Lifeboat Society, Marine Welfare Society, Society Aid to Families of French Shipwrecked Mariners, and Transatlantique Maternity Fund, five color images by Jean Droit, Dec. 24, 1927 .... 50.00

Souvenir spoon, Cunard *White Star,* demitasse, silver plated 20.00

Tie clasp, Cunard Line *RMS Queen Mary,* gold tone, red, white, and blue enameled ship................ 18.00

Tobacco bag, 4-1/2" x 6-1/4", Oceanic Cut Plug Chewing Tobacco, white cloth, color image of steamship on green ocean, early 1900s 25.00

Track chart, Anchor Line, *SS Anchoria,* voyage from New York to Glasgow, 10-1/2" x 6" 75.00

Opalescent Glass

Opalescent glass is a type of clear or colored glass that has milky white decorations, and usually looks fiery or opalescent when held to light. This effect was achieved by applying bone ash chemicals to designated areas while a piece was still hot and then refiring it at extremely high temperatures. Opalescent glass was produced in England in the 1870s. Northwood began American production in 1897 at its Indiana, Pennsylvania, plant. Jefferson, National Glass, Hobbs, and Fenton soon followed with opalescent glass formulas of their own.

Banana boat, Jewel and Fan, green 115.00

Berry bowl, master
   Alaska, blue 195.00
   Tokyo, green 75.00

Bowl
   Argonaut Shell, vaseline, shell ftd 100.00

Beaded Stars, low base, green 45.00
Beatty Rib, blue, rect 65.00
Diamond Spearhead, 9" d, blue 45.00

Butter dish, cov
   Beatty Rib, white 95.00
   Drapery, blue, gold trim..... 215.00
   Fluted Scrolls, blue............. 200.00
   Jackson, blue...................... 155.00

Celery vase
   Alaska, blue, dec................ 150.00
   Diamond Spearhead, green 275.00
   Wreath and Shell, vaseline, dec 140.00

Compote
   Diamond Spearhead, vaseline 150.00
   Intaglio, vaseline.................. 70.00

Opalescent glass, jar, covered, blue, white swirling stripes, matching cover with blue ball finial, **$75.**

Tokyo, blue 60.00

Creamer
Alaska, blue, 3-1/2" h 75.00
Fluted Scrolls, blue 70.00
Hobnail, rose 110.00
Inverted Fan and Feather, blue
.... 125.00
Intaglio, white...................... 85.00
Paneled Holly, white............. 70.00
Scroll with Acanthus, green
.... 65.00

Goblet, Diamond Spearhead,
cranberry 85.00

Jelly compote
Diamond Spearhead, vaseline
.... 85.00
Everglades, blue, gold trim .. 85.00
Intaglio, blue........................ 55.00
Iris with Meander, vaseline.. 95.00

Match holder, Beatty Rib, white
.... 35.00

Mug, Diamond Spearhead, cobalt
blue 85.00

Pitcher
Beatty Swirl, canary yellow 195.00
Fern, white, sq top.............. 190.00
Fluted Scrolls, vaseline....... 300.00
Intaglio, blue....................... 215.00

Rose bowl
Beaded Drape, blue 60.00
Fluted Scrolls, vaseline....... 115.00

Salt, open, individual
Beatty Rib, white 42.00
Wreath and Shell, blue 65.00

Sauce
Alaska, white 20.00
Argonaut Shell, blue............. 40.00
Circled Scrolls, blue.............. 50.00
Drapery, Northwood, dec, blue
.... 35.00
Iris with Meander, yellow..... 25.00
Jewel and Flower, white........ 25.00
Regal, green 65.00

Spooner
Beatty Rib, white 45.00
Flora, blue........................... 110.00
Fluted Scrolls, blue, dec 70.00
Intaglio, white....................... 45.00

Sugar bowl, cov
Alaska, vaseline 155.00
Circled Scroll, green 85.00

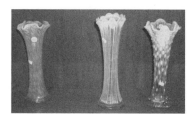

Opalescent glass, three vases, all green, white opalescent decoration, each **$35.**

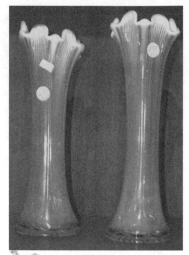

Opalescent glass, two blue vases, pulled ribbed type, white opalescent at tips, each **$45.**

Intaglio, blue.......................... 75.00

Toothpick holder
Beatty Rib, white 30.00
Diamond Spearhead, green.. 75.00
Iris with Meander, blue 115.00
Ribbed Spiral, blue............... 90.00

Tumbler
Alaska, vaseline 85.00
Beatty Rib, white 35.00
Beatty Swirl, white 45.00
Everglades, vaseline.............. 50.00
Fluted Scrolls, vaseline......... 75.00
Intaglio, white...................... 45.00
Jackson, green 50.00
Jeweled Heart, blue 85.00
S-Repeat, blue....................... 45.00

Opera Glasses

Ever get the feeling someone is watching you? Opera glasses were designed to do just that, allowing opera goers a better view of what was going on the stage and also who was wearing what and seated with whom in the other opera boxes. Today these discreet opticals are showing up at flea markets.

Opera glasses, brass frame, abalone shell decoration, **$65.**

Aluminum, burnished, tortoise
shell eye pcs, mkd "Kornblum,
Pittsburgh".............................. 85.00

Brass frame, abalone shell dec 65.00

Metal, center focus dial, settings for
theater, field, and marine, orig case,
c1920, 4-1/2" w..................... 85.00

Metal, mkd "3X, Made in Occupied
Japan," slight wear, 4" l.......... 90.00

Opera glasses, aluminum, burnished, tortoise shell eye pieces, marked "Kornblum, Pittsburgh," **$85.**

Owl Collectibles

Whoo, whoo, who collects owl items? Lots of folks! Some are enchanted with the wisdom of this regal bird, while others find owls fun and whimsical. Lucky for them, artists and designers have been incorporating the owl's image into items for years.

Owl collectibles, plate, Bavarian Forest, limited edition by Goebel, original box, 1980, **$20.**

Owl collectibles, match holder, porcelain, **$20.**

1970, 7" sq 25.00

Pin, Avon, solid perfume sachet, goldtone, 2" h......................... 10.00

Print, Mottled Owl, hand-colored, Beverly Robinson Morris, from *Birds of Great Britain*, 1895, slight stain, foxing, 10" x 6-3/4" 20.00

Spoon rest, ceramic, souvenir of San Francisco, shows cable car, has kitchen prayer, 7" x 4-1/2"..... 20.00

Tape measure, brass, glass eyes, mkd "Germany"............................. 40.00

Tin, Red Owl allspice, Red Owl Stores 18.00

Ashtray, ceramic, three cut owls, figural 30.00

Badge, 4-3/4" brass bar, 3" x 6" dark blue on cream ribbon, gold cord with bow above, large brass tassels on each side of bar, third at bottom, owl design, "National Editorial Association, Fifth Annual Convention, Aug. 27, 28, 29, 30 at Detroit 1889"......................... 60.00

Blotter, "Whoo? Oswald, I told you we couldn't get away with that bone!," two puppies under a tree, owl sitting on branch, Harry N. Johnson, Real Estate & Insurance, Highlands, NJ 10.00

Book rack, expandable, owl on each end 55.00

Brooch, Mandle, japanned mounting, clear rhinestones for the body and head, dark greet eyes and ears, 2-1/4" h, 1" w 50.00

Candy container, owl on branch 50.00

Figure, glass, alpine blue, Boyd, 3-1/2" h 12.00

Letter opener, brass 25.00

Napkin ring, standing owl, silver plated 150.00

Notepad holder, chalkware, figural,

Owl collectibles, message pad holder, wooden, Mother and baby owl with stained highlights, green stained ivy leaf decoration, worn merchant's advertisement with name and address at top, **$21.**

Paden City Glass

Founded in Paden City, W.Va., in 1916, this company made glassware until 1951. Paden City's wares were all hand made until 1948. The glass was not marked, nor was it heavily advertised. Much of its success laid with blanks supplied to others to decorate. Many of the company's wares were sold to institutional facilities, restaurants, etc. Paden City is known for rich colors in many shades.

For additional listings see *Warman's Antiques & Collectibles*.

Animal
Bunny, ears down, cotton dispenser 95.00
Goose 60.00
Pheasant, light blue 170.00
Pony, tall 100.00

Bowl, two-handled serving type
#215 Glades, Trumpet Flower etch, crystal 115.00
#220 Largo, ruby 65.00
#411 Mrs. B., Gothic Garden etch, crystal 45.00
#412 Crow's Foot Square, green 35.00
#412 Crow's Foot Square, Ardith etch, yellow 50.00
#881 Gadroon, Rose & Jasmine etch, crystal 50.00

Cake salver, footed
#191 Party Line, high footed, cheriglo 65.00
#191 Party Line, low, etched & gold encrusted border, crystal 30.00
#210 Regina, Black Forest etch, ebony or green 75.00
#215 Glades, ruby 45.00
#215 Glades, Spring Orchard etch, crystal 65.00
#220 Largo, high footed, crystal 50.00
#300 Archaic, Cupid etch, cheriglo 125.00
#330 Cavendish, gold encrusted border etch with roses, crystal 50.00
#411 Mrs. B, Ardith etch, green 85.00
#412 Crow's Foot Square, 8-1/4" w, 5-1/2" h, ebony 40.00
#411 Mrs. B, Gothic Garden etch, cheriglo 50.00

Candleholders, pr
#210 Regina, Black Forest etch, ebony 95.00
#220 Largo, Garden Magic etch, light blue 90.00
#411 Mrs. B, keyhole style, Ardith etch, ebony 50.00
#412 Crow's Foot Square, mushroom style, no etching, yellow 30.00

Candy box, cov, #191 Party Line, pink 50.00

Cologne bottle
#191 Party Line, dauber stopper, green 40.00
#215 Glades, amber stopper. 20.00

Comport, footed, open
#211 Spire, Trumpet Flower etch, crystal 50.00
#215 Glades, 6-1/2" wide, Forest Green 40.00
#300 Archaic, turquoise blue 45.00
#411 Mrs. B, 7" h x 7" w, Gothic Garden etch, yellow 35.00
#412 Crow's Foot Square, 7" w, low footed, mulberry 45.00

Console bowl, #881 Gadroon, Frost etch 65.00

Creamer and sugar
#411 Mrs B, Gothic Garden etch, crystal 45.00
#412 Crow's Foot Square, mulberry 42.00
#701 Triumph, Nora Bird etch, crystal 80.00

Cup and saucer, Largo, red 32.50

Goblet
#991 Penny Line, mulberry, low foot 18.50
#994 Popeye & Olive, 6-1/8" h, cobalt blue 35.00

Ice bucket, #191 Party Line, Peacock & Rose etch, amber, metal bail handle 120.00

Iced tea tumbler, #991 Penny Line, 12 oz, amethyst 22.50

Marmalade, cov, Emerald Glo, coppertone lid 40.00

Napkin rings, Party Line, set of six 60.00

Parfait, #191 Party Line, ftd, green 20.00

Plate
#210 Regina, 8", Black Forest etch, cheriglo 40.00
#220 Largo, 9", amber 10.00
#300 Archaic, 8-1/4", Nora Bird etch, green 35.00
#881 Gadroon, 8" plate, ruby 15.00

Relish, #890 Crow's Foot Round, three-part, 11" l oblong, crystal, star cut 35.00

Sherbet
#69 Line, Georgian, ruby 12.50
#191 Party Line, pink 8.50

Syrup pitcher, #185, gold encrusted band etch, amber 40.00

Tray, center handle
#221 Maya, light blue 30.00
#411 Mrs. B, Gothic Garden etch, yellow 30.00
#412 Crow's Foot Square, Orchid etch, crystal 50.00
#881 Gadroon, Irwin etch, ruby 50.00

Tumbler
#191 Party Line, 5-3/4" h, cone shape, pink 10.00
#210 Regina, 5-1/2" h, Black Forest etch, pink 80.00
#890 Crow's Foot Round, amber 35.00
#991 Penny Line, 3-1/4" h, ruby 10.00

Vase
#182, 8" h, elliptical, crystal, Trumpet Flower etch 115.00
#184, 10" h, bulbous, Peacock and Rose etch, Cheriglo . 165.00
#210 Regina, 6-1/2" h, Harvesters etch, ebony 145.00
#503 dome footed fan vase, ruby 95.00
#513 Black Forest etch, 10" h, crystal 195.00
#994 Popeye & Olive, 7", ruby 50.00

Paden City Glass, Orchid pattern, center handled sandwich server, red, **$125.**

Paint-by-Number Sets

For those of us who aren't artistically inclined, paint-by-number sets open a world that turns anyone into a first-class artist. Popular-culture figures are favorite subjects. Collectors look for sets that are mint in box. However, buyers are also snapping up many finished products, especially those with unusual subjects.

Paint by number set, mill scene, 9" x 12", **$2.**

Autumn mill, 19-1/4" x 15-1/2" 22.50

Barbie and Rockers, unused, MIP 15.00

Blond boy kneeling in prayer, beagle puppy, Simpson 10.00

Blue jays, framed, 13" x 10-1/2" 20.00

Deer scene, 24" x 18" 24.50

Desert scene, cactus, prospector, 15-1/2" x 11-1/2" 28.00

Hunting dogs, 16-1/2" x 20-1/2" 17.50

Impalas, drinking at African water hole, framed, 12" x 16" 32.00

Jesus and children, framed, 21-1/2" x 27-1/2" 7.50

Little boy praying, beagle by his side, Simpson's order label on back, 12-1/2" x 6-1/2" 10.00

Lighthouse, framed, 10" x 14". 16.50

Nude, woman sitting on rocks on beach, 12" x 16" 55.00

Paint by number set, Goldie Locks and the Three Bears, 11-1/2" x 5 1/2" each, pair, **$5.**

Paint by number set, covered bridge scene, 12" x 16", **$4.**

Popeye, Hasbro, set of five pictures, 12 paints, MIB 75.00

Roses, still life, 1958, PP Corp, two paintings, MIB......................... 7.50

Ship, 15-1/2" x 19-1/2".............. 15.00

Super heroes, Transogram, 16 watercolors of super heroes, 44 action scenes, unused kit, MIB 75.00

Winter landscape, 13" x 17" 15.00

Paintings

Need something to hang over the sofa, or perhaps brighten a wall in your dining room? Flea markets offer all kinds of paintings. Some famous artists' works have been found for real bargain prices at flea markets; it just takes some searching. Plus it's possible to find great works by unknown local artists at many flea markets. They might not have the "big name" appeal of a Renoir, but if you like the painting, why not buy it? Look for something that appeals to you and fits the size you need. Be sure to ask the dealer if he knows anything about the artist or where the painting came from. Knowing that kind of information can add to the value if you decide to sell it later. If the painting is unframed or framed in something you don't care for, consider how much you'll need to spend to reframe it before you make a purchase. The listings here are a very small sampling of what's available at flea markets.

Doskow, Israel, Surf, oil on board, sgd lower left 300.00

Greenleaf, Jacob, Surf at Andrews Point, oil on board, sgd lower left 350.00

Helverson, Dorothy, primitive farm scene, sgd, barn board frame, small 150.00

Painting, oil on canvas, still life of purple, yellow, and white pansies with green leaves spread on white cloth, gold frame partially obscures artist's signature, **$45.**

Kilbert, Robert, autumn landscape, oil on canvas, sgd lower right 460.00

Lamb, Adrian, landscape with scattered clouds, oil on board, sgd lower right 375.00

Ruth, Calvin, Geryville Store, watercolor, framed 350.00

Schlichter, Dick, winter scene, oil on board, framed, 6" sq 15.00

Thurston, John K., harbor scene, watercolor on paper, sgd lower right 435.00

Ripp, W. C., Rotterdam seaport, sgd, dated, lower right, watercolor and gouache on board, framed .. 500.00

Unsigned
Antiques shop, fall scene, watercolor, 24" x 36" 125.00
General store, primitive, oil on canvas, framed 20.00

Yerger, winter scene with house and barn, oil on canvas, ornate gold frame 250.00

Pairpoint

Here's a name that can confuse flea market dealers. Some associate Pairpoint with the Pairpoint Manufacturing Company or Pairpoint Corporation, a leader in silver-plated wares. Others associate it with National Pairpoint Company, a company that made glassware and aluminum products such as windows, and other commercial glassware. Today lead crystal glassware is still made by Pairpoint.

Basket, silver plated, 12-5/8" l, 9-1/4" w, 9-1/4" h, mkd "Pat applied for 12/1904," some wear to plating 295.00

Bowl, amethyst glass, silver label, unused 75.00

Compote, peachblow, hp florals, paper label, 6-3/4" d 160.00

Ferner, elongated mold blown oval body, purple and crimson pansies dec, emb metal lid with two ring handles, numbered "5126-211" 400.00

Fruit tray, silver plated, birds, cherries, and leaves, 11" x 14" 195.00

Mustache cup, silver plated, elaborate floral design, mkd "Pairpoint Mfg Co., New Bedford, Mass, Quadruple Plate, 2060," 3-1/4" h 45.00

Perfume bottle, amethyst, painted butterfly, teardrop stopper, "P" in diamond mark, 6-3/4" h...... 375.00

Tea set, silver plated 300.00

Tray, silver plated, designer Albert Steffin, 14" l, patented June 28, 1904 .... 195.00

Pairpoint, calling card receiver, swan on square top, 5-3/4" w, 6" h, **$175.**

Paper Dolls

Paper dolls date to the 1880s. Several early magazines, including *McCall's,* used to include paper dolls in every issue. The book form of paper dolls came into favor in the 1950s. Look for interesting characters and vintage clothing styles.

Paper dolls, Barbie & Ken, Whitman, original box, **$20.**

Advertising, McLaughlin's Coffee, five paper dolls, two dresses, die-cut horse, ©1894 .... 35.00

Alice Paper Dolls, Whitman #4712, 1972 .... 15.00

Amy Carter, Toy Factory, 1970s 15.00

Annie Oakley, 1956, uncut..... 65.00

Archies, Whitman, 1969 .... 25.00

Baby Sparkle Plenty, Saalfield, #1510 .... 22.00

Ballet Cut-Out, Whitman #1962, uncut...................................... 65.00

Paper dolls, Lennon Sisters, Whitman, **$24.**

Barbie, Peck Aubrey, 1994, MIP **15.00**

Betsy McCall Cut-Out/Punch-Out Paper Dolls, Saalfield #1370, ©1965 .... **24.00**

Blondie, Whitman, 1944 .... **80.00**

Bonnie Braids, Saalfield, #1559, 1951 .... **25.00**

Cinderella, Saalfield, uncut **20.00**

Heart Family, Golden Book, 1985, uncut...................................... **15.00**

Madeline, Viking, 1994, uncut .. **5.00**

Miss America Magic Doll, Parker Bros, 1953, uncut **24.00**

Nanny and the Professor, Artcraft, 1971 .... **24.00**

Peter Pan, Whitman, 1952....... **50.00**

Pony Tail, Samuel Gabriel & Sons, uncut...................................... **24.00**

Sandra Dee, Saalfield, 1959..... **30.00**

Shirley Temple, Whitman, #1986, 1976 .... **8.00**

Stand-Up, National Syndicate Display, 1942, uncut **45.00**

The Wedding Party, Samuel Gabriel & Sons, uncut **35.00**

Tuesday Weld, Saalfield, 1960 **30.00**

Paperback Books

Mass-marketed paperback books date to the late 1930s. Collectors tend to focus on one type of book or a favorite author.

Paperback book, *The True Mother Goose: Replica of the Original Antique Published 1833*, **$8.**

A Little Princess, Frances Hodgson Burnett, Apple, 1987 .... **4.00**

Favorite Christmas Carols, Firestone Tire and Rubber Co., 1955 ...... **5.00**

First Lady, Charlotte Curtis, Pyramid Book, 1962, 1st printing........ **12.00**

Flying Saucers in Fact and Fiction, Hans Stefan Santesson, 1968 .... **6.00**

Folk Medicine, D. C. Jarvis, MD, Crest Book, 4th printing.................. **3.00**

For Your Eyes Only, James Bond, 1st ed., 1981 .... **5.00**

Growing Up, Karl de Schweinitz, Collier Books, 1965 .... **5.00**

John F. Kennedy: War Hero, Richard Tregaskis **15.00**

Little Women, Louisa May Alcott, Apple, 248 pgs, book club edition **1.00**

Number 1, Billy Martin (autographed) and Peter Goldenbock, Dell, 1st printing, 1981 .... **20.00**

Saddle Man, Matt Stuart, Bantam, Sept. 1951, 1st printing **8.00**

Super Eye Adventure Treasure Hunt, Jay Leibold, Ray zone and Chuck Roblin illus, Bantam Skylar Books, 1995 .... **5.00**

U-Boats In Action, Robert C. Stern, 1977 .... **10.00**

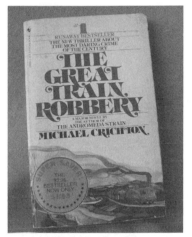

Paperback book, *The Great Train Robbery*, Michael Crichton, Bantam Books, 7th printing, 1979, **$1.**

They Were Expendable, W.L. White, 1941 .... **15.00**

Wings of Joy, Joan Winmill Brown, World Wide Publications, 1977 .... **5.00**

Paper Money

Here's another one of those topics where thousands of examples exist, and collectors should be critical of condition. There are many good reference books to help with both issues.

Bank of State of Georgia, 1857 .... **20.00**

Bank of Tennessee, 1861, 5 cents **10.00**

Consecutive Numbers, set of five, $1, CU FRNS, 1995 Star, District B **20.00**

It's a record

As noted in the *Bank Note Reporter,* an auction record was set when an 1890 $1,000 Treasury note sold for $792,000. The note is commonly known as the Levitan Grand Watermelon. Only three Grand Watermelons are known to be in private hands.

Continental Note, Philadelphia, Feb. 17, 1776, $2, decorative border,

woodcuts 85.00

Egypt, 10 pounds, 1958 .... 48.00

Lesbian and Gay, $3, 3-3/4" x 8-1/2", sponsored by Greater Gotham Business Market, Nov. 21-22, 1987, yellow 5.00

State of Florida, $1 .... 26.00

State of North Carolina, $2 note, 1861 .... 24.00

Tecumseh, Michigan, $1 .... 30.00

Paper money, Broken bank note, James River Kanawha Company, Five Dollars, Danforth, Underwood & Co., NY, engravers, 1861, 7-1/45" x 3-1/4", **$60.**

Paperweights

About the same time folks invented paper, they needed something to hold it down, so along came the paperweight. They can be highly decorative or purely practical. Look for ones of interesting advertising, perhaps a unique shape, or showing an interesting location.

For additional listings of traditional glass paperweights, see *Warman's Antiques and Collectibles Price Guide* and *Warman's Glass.*

Paperweights, Masonic, Syria Temple, Pittsburgh, Atlantic City Pilgrimage, 1924, George E. Meyer, Illustrious Potentate, 2-1/2" x 4", **$45.**

Cast iron
    Puppy, painted red collar, white stripe around head, late 1940s, 1-1/2" h 15.00
    Skeleton hand, 7-1/2" l 125.00
    Squirrel, painted soft brown to orange, off-white accents, 1930s, 2" h 25.00

Glass, rect, advertising
    Burlington Venetian Blind Co., Burlington, VT 70.00
    Coutes Clipper Mfg., Worcester, MA, illus of pair of clippers, 2-1/2" w, 4" l 75.00
    Dayton Ball & Co., Albany, NY, Manufacturers of Lasts 60.00
    Donnelly Machine Co., Brockton, MA, scalloped edge, illus of vintage factory, 3" w, 4-1/2" l 50.00
    Heywood Shoes, shoe illus, titled "Heywood is in it," 2-1/2" w, 4" l 40.00
    J. R. Leeson & Co., Boston, Linen Thread importers, spinning wheel image 80.00

Paperweights, Jim Davis, 1995, 3-1/2" h, **$7.**

Paperweights, spider, real hairy brown spider captured in round domed paperweight, **$25.**

    PP Van Vleet, President, Van Vleet Mansfield Drug Co., Memphis, TN 30.00
    Waite, Thresher Co., Providence, RI 70.00

Glass, antique
    Clichy, millefiori, complex millefiori canes set in colorless crystal, 1-3/4" d, 1-3/8" h 375.00
    Sandwich Glass, dahlia, c1870, red petaled flower, millefiori cane center, bright green leafy stem, highlighted by trapped bubble dec, white latticino ground, 2-1/2" d, 1-3/4" h 650.00

Glass, modern

Ayotte, Rick, yellow finch, perched on branch, faceted, sgd, and dated, 1979 .... 750.00

Baccarat, Peace on Earth, sgd 130.00

Banford, Bob, Iris and rose, purple, blue, and pink irises, center pink roe, recessed diamond-cut base, "B" cane at stem, 3" d..... 250.00

Caithness, Chai, gold symbol, translucent blue background, faceted front window, 3-1/4" d 210.00

Kaziun, Charles, millefiori spider lily, green ground, pedestal 365.00

Lundberg Studios, Art Nouveau design, irid orange, gray, and black flower, central millefiori star canes, irid dark green ground, sgd "Lundburg 73," 2-3/4" d........................... 225.00

Murano, cluster of green and white daisies, pink and white cushion, signature cane "Fili Tosi," 2-3/4" d 300.00

Perthshire, miniature bouquet, yellow flowers, pink buds, basket of deep blue canes, green and pink millefiori canes cut to form base, orig box and certificate, 2-1/2" d 160.00

St. Clair, pink flowers, green and white ground 60.00

Whittemore, Francis, two green and brown acorns on branch with three brown and yellow oak leaves, translucent cobalt blue ground, circular top facet five oval punties on sides, 2-3/8" d 300.00

Souvenir

Acrylic, torch inside made from materials from Statue of Liberty, 1886-1996, round, 4-1/2" d 20.00

Globe, Chicago World's Fair 1893-1933, 1-1/2" d colorful tin litho spinning globe, 4-3/4" h chrome accent white metal base, eagle medallion in low relief on front 28.00

Trylon and Perisphere, New York World's Fair, 2" x 4" x 1-1/8" h, dark brown Syroco Wood foil sticker on reverse 25.00

Parrish, Maxfield

Like many illustrators, Maxfield Parrish did commercial work. Today, some of those commercial illustrations are highly sought by collectors.

Bookplate print, 8" x 10"

The City of Brass 65.00

The Fisherman and the Genie 65.00

Wynken, Blyken & Nod 65.00

Calendar top, Edison Mazda Reveries, 1927, framed, 6-3/4" x 10-1/4" 175.00

Magazine cover

American Heritage, December 1970 .... 25.00

Scribner Magazine, 1902...... 55.00

Matchbook, Old King Cole, St. Regis Hotel, Newy Ork, wooden matches 25.00

Playing cards, The Waterfall, advertise Edison Mazda Lamps, boxed single deck 120.00

Print

Chancellor and the King, c1925, orig 9" x 12" frame 65.00

Dinky Bird, c1915, 5" x 7" frame 55.00

Hilltop, c1927, 6-1/4" x 10", framed in period 9" x 12" blue and gold frame, sgd lower left, titled lower center, "House of Art" lower right................................ 195.00

Lady Violetta in the Royal Kitchen, c1925, 9" x 12" orig frame 65.00

Prince Codadad, c1906, 9" x 11" print, orig 11" x 14" mat, orig blue and gold frame, "Copr P. F. Collier & Son" lower left 70.00

Rose Bower, c1920-25, unsigned, 10" x 15" period blue and gold frame, orig paper label preserved on back.............................. 65.00

Rubaiyat, c1917, 28-1/2" x 7" print in 33" x 11" orig brown and gold frame, "copyright 1917 C. A. Crane Cleveland" lower right, "Reinthal & Newman, New York" imp lower left 250.00

Maxfield Parrish, print, three maidens in garden setting, original frame, **$65.**

Patriotic Collectibles

Three cheers for the red, white, and blue! And three cheers for the collectors who thrive on this type of material. There are lots of great examples just waiting to be found at America's flea markets.

Patriotic collectibles, cup plate, deep amber glass, eagle in center with stars, **$15.**

Bank, Uncle Sam, Puriton 32.00

Bottle, Statue of Liberty, Avon, 7-1/2" h 10.00

Button, Liberty Bell, plastic shelf shank, 3/4" d 2.50

Candy container, drum, litho tin, red, white, and blue 65.00

Change tray, 4" d, Hebbrun House Coal, eagle in center, holding banner, wood grain ground 50.00

Costume jewelry
Flag pin, Coro, sterling silver, enamel and rhinestones, 1-1/2" h 75.00
"USA" pin, red, clear and blue rhinestones, 1-3/8" h 15.00

Dresser scarf, embroidered, Uncle Sam's top hat, c1940 .... 18.00

Eagle, pot metal, gold paint, 6" h 35.00

Envelope, Civil War, 2-3/4" x 5-1/8" 22.00

Fan, America First, diecut shield, red, white and blue cardboard, sailor raising deck flag, warships in background, biplanes overhead, 7" x 9" 45.00

Liberty Bell, Spirit of America, Pennsbury Pottery, 3-1/2" h .. 35.00

Magic lantern slide, American flag, 3-1/4" x 4" 48.00

Magazine tear sheet, Greyhound Presents A Grand New Super-Coach, Uncle Sam waving at bus, 1939 .... 15.00

Medal, Victory Liberty Loan, U.S. Treasury Dept. 15.00

Patriotic collectibles, Revolution Calendar, 1776-1896, eagle in center, New York City Chapter DAR, Louis Prang, red, white, and blue ribbon, **$90.**

Patriotic collectibles, flag plate, "Compliments of Holstein Mercantile Co., Holstein, Nebr.," 9-1/2" d, **$35.**

Needle book, World's Best, Statue of Liberty, airplane, ship, world, 6 needle packets 20.00

Paperweight, pair of US flags over upright red and green lily, four speckled lilies, 4-1/2" d 325.00

Pencil clip, Reddy Kilowatt Power, V, 1942 .... 10.00

Postcard
Betsy Ross sewing flag 5.00
Santa Claus toasting the holidays with Uncle Sam, Christmas Greetings, early 1900s 40.00

Sheet music, Liberty Bell Time To Ring Again, 1918 .... 10.00

Statue, Statue of Liberty, goldtone metal, 4-1/2" h 10.00

Tumbler, red, white and blue bands, gold eagle, 1970s, 4" h 2.00

Peanuts

The comic strip Peanuts has been bringing smiles to faces since 1950. Snoopy, Charlie Brown, Lucy and the rest of the gang are all creations of Charles M. Schulz. Peanuts collectibles are licensed by Charles M. Schulz Creative Associates and United Features Syndicate.

Activity book, *Peanuts Projects*, Determined, 1963 .... 30.00

Address book, United Feature Syndicate, Inc., 3-3/4" x 2-1/2" 6.00

Bank, Snoopy and Woodstock, lying on jack-o-lantern, Whitman Candies, 4-1/2" h 10.00

Book, *Speak Up, Charlie Brown Talking Storybook*, Mattel, 1971 .... 60.00

Peanuts, Snoopy, bowl, **$2.**

Bubble pipe, Snoopy's Fantastic Automatic Bubble Pipe, Chemtoy, Model #126, 1970s 5.00

Coloring book, *Peanuts: A Book to Color*, Saalfield, #4629 .... 25.00

Costume, Snoopy, flying ace, Collegeville 15.00

Doll
Charlie Brown, Determined, 1970s
.... 45.00
Linus, Hungerford Plastics, 1958, 8-1/2" h 50.00
Lucy, Ideal, 1976 .... 25.00
Peppermint Patty, Ideal, 1976
.... 30.00
Pigpen, Hungerford Plastics, 1958, 8-1/2" h 65.00
Schroeder and piano, Hungerford Plastics, 1958, 7" h 125.00

Snoopy, Determined, 1970s
.... 25.00
Game, Lucy Tea Party Game, Milton Bradley, #4129, 1972 .... 25.00
Music box
Lucy and Charlie Brown, Anri, plays Rose Garden, 4" h ... 75.00
Peanuts, Schmid, ceramic characters revolve around Christmas tree, plays Joy to the World, 1984, 8" h 85.00
Snoopy, Schmid, ceramic, lion tamer, plays Pussycat Pussycat, 1986, 6" 45.00

Nodder, Charlie Brown, Japanese, 5-1/2" h 75.00

Play set, Determined, Model #575, 1975 .... 90.00

Push puppet
Charlie Brown, Ideal, 1977 ... 20.00
Joe Cool, Ideal, 1977 .... 20.00

Peanuts, book, It's the Great Pumpkin Charlie Brown, Charles M. Schultz, **$10.**

Peanuts, thermos, Snoopy and Charlie Brown playing ball, original white cap, **$10.**

Puzzle, Schroeder, Charlie Brown, Snoopy and Lucy on baseball mound, Milton Bradley, 1973
.... 10.00

Radio, Snoopy Hi-Fi, Determined, Model #405, 1977 .... 35.00

Top, Snoopy and gang, Ohio Art, 5"
.... 10.00

Viewmaster gift set, Charlie Brown, GAF, 1970s, cylindrical container, viewer and seven reels 20.00

Wristwatch, Charlie Brown, Determined, 1970s 65.00

Pedal Cars

Pedal cars date to about 1915, when they were made to closely resemble automobiles of the day. War-time material supplies curbed growth for a few years, but these popular toys gained popularity again, just in time for special cars issued to tie into television programs of the 1950s and 1960s.

Pedal car, fire truck, red metal body, white lettering "Hook and Ladder, No. 1," original wood ladder, as found condition, **$195.**

Airplane, gray body, blue and white decals, red seat, restored 195.00

Blue Streak, blue and white, BMC
.... 450.00

Champion Straight Side, Murray, professionally restored 1,325.00

Coca-Cola truck, red and white, AMF 500.00

Comet, Murray 775.00

Earthmover, Murray 1,100.00

Fire truck, orig ladders 325.00

Junior Trac, AMF 250.00

Lincoln Zephyr, Garton, 1937, restored 4,500.00

Locomotive, Fast Mail, Toledo Wheel Goods, orig paint, 1920s . 3,500.00

Mustang, AMF 800.00

Pontiac sedan, Skippy Line, Gendron, 1935, orig paint 4,000.00

Safari wagon, AMF 50.00

Studebaker, Midwest Industries, restored 950.00

Tin Lizzy, green, Garton 500.00

Pennants

Rah Rah! Pennants used to be the flag of choice for sporting events and parades. Today they have become colorful collectibles.

Atlantic City, scenes Steel Pier, Convention Hall and bathing, 27" l 45.00

Atlanta Falcons, dark red and black on white 4.00

Captain Marvel, felt, yellow, Fawcett, 1940s 80.00

Cincinnati Redlegs, 1 tassel missing, 29" l 55.00

Cleveland Indians American League Champions 140.00

Democratic National Convention, Atlantic City, 1964, black and white picture of Linden Johnson in shield, 29" l 30.00

Empire State Building, "The tallest man-made structure in the world, 102 floors, 1,472 ft. high, Souvenir of Empire State Building, New York City," 26-1/4" l 15.00

Hemisfair, 3-1/2" x 7", day-glo blue, pink, orange, and yellow, San Antonio fair logo, 1968 .... 5.00

Howe Caverns, dated 1958, shows pagoda, 17-1/4" l 18.00

Lumbermen's Memorial, image of lumberjacks, 1940s, 26" l 25.00

Mt. Washington, White Mountains, N.H., World's First Cog Railway, 1957, 17-1/4" l 18.00

National Baseball Hall of Fame and Museum, Cooperstown, N.Y., 12" l 18.00

Navy, yellow and blue, 5-1/2" l. 15.00

New Jersey Turnpike, 25" l 22.00

New York Mets, 1969, team-signed 60.00

New York World's Fair, 9" x 25-1/2", white felt, blue and orange lettering,

multicolored exhibit buildings, 1964-65 .... 12.00

Philadelphia Eagles, 1940/50, 28" l 35.00

Pittsburgh Pirates, schedule of games, 1936 .... 50.00

South Carolina, black boy sitting on bales of cotton, 27" l 45.00

Souvenir of Gettysburg Battlefield, panorama of the Gettysburg Battlefield and monuments, 1930s/40s, 28" l 26.00

Univ of Wisconsin 20.00

Pennants, felt, French Lick, Ind., red and white, **$12.50.**

Pennsbury Pottery

Taking its name from the close proximity of William Penn's estate, Pennsbury, in Bucks County, Pa., this small pottery lasted from 1950 until 1970. Several of the owners had formerly worked for Stangl, which helps explain some of the similarities of design and forms between Pennsbury and Stangl.

Pennsbury Pottery, casserole, covered, Delft pattern, blue and white, **$35.**

Ashtray, Doylestown Trust 30.00

Bird
Audubon Warbler, #122, JR 150.00
Blue Ray, #108 .... 375.00
Gnat Catchers, #107, IM, 6-1/2" h 175.00
Hummingbird, #125 JR 325.00

Bowl
9" d, Hex, small heart dec on inside rim 45.00
11" d, Dutch Talk 70.00

Pennsbury Pottery, relish tray, Holly, five sections, Christmas tree shape, 14-1/2" l, **$35.**

Pennsbury Pottery, plate, Lower Bucks County Band, tulips and birds decoration, 11" d, **$24.**

Candlesticks, pr, 5" h, Hummingbird, white 65.00

Candy dish, 6" x 6", Hex, heart shape 10.00

Pennsbury Pottery, dealer's sign, nuthatch, 5" x 4-1/2", **$175.**

Cider set, 12" h decanter with six individual mugs..................... 75.00

Cigarette lighter, Black Rooster 5.00

Cigarette tray, 7-1/2" x 5", eagle sculpted in bas relief 12.50

Coffee mug, Falls Township, Bucks Co, 275th Anniversary 7.50

Creamer, Rooster, 4-1/2" h 45.00

Cup and saucer, Black Rooster 20.00

Desk basket, 5" h
Bird over Heart, 2013-68...... 15.00
Eagle, 2013-286 .... 25.00

Dinner plate, Hex.................. 17.50

Eggcup, Red Rooster 25.00

Figure
Slick Bunny, 5-1/2" h 85.00

Slick Chick on colored gourd, brown bird, 5-1/2" h 95.00

Milk pitcher
Amish Family, 6-1/2" h 175.00
Yellow Rooster, 7-1/2" h 150.00

Mug, Schiaraflia Filadelfia, owl and seal... 30.00

Pen holder, eagle, 5 stars......... 35.00

Pie pan, 9" d, mother serving pie 40.00

Plaque, railroad
Baltimore & Ohio RR Lafayette, 2103-10............................. 17.50
Camden & Amboy RR, 2103-8 9.50
Camelback & NYC & HRRR 999, 7-1/2".................................. 35.00
Central Pacific 2103-9 .... 9.50
Central RR of NJ..................... 9.50
Iron Horse, 7-1/4" x 5-1/2", 1960 .... 15.00
NYC & HRRR 999, 2103-7 ... 25.00

Plaque, ship
Baltimore Schooner, 2113-277 .... 20.00

Pennsbury Pottery, Baltimore & Ohio RR, Lafayette, 2103-10, **$15.**

Pennsbury Pottery, pair of wall pockets, square, green borders, left with bleeding heart type decoration, **$18;** right with PA Dutch tulips, **$24.**

Flying cloud, 1851, 2115-281 40.00
Sailing, black border 25.00
The Bark Charles W. Morgan 35.00
The Packet Dreadnought...... 10.00

Pretzel bowl, 12" x 8"
Amish, 1077-33 .... 25.00
Eagle, 1077-296 .... 30.00
Red Barn, 1077-75................ 35.00

Relish tray
14-1/2", Holly, five sections 30.00
14-1/2", Red Barn 55.00

Tea tile, 6" d, skunk "Why Be Disagreeable"......................... 60.00

Tray, Yellow Rooster, 8" l 50.00

Wall pocket
Antique Auto, 6-1/2" h 20.00
Bellows, eagle dec, high relief, 10" l 25.00
Clown, 6-1/2"........................ 30.00
Eagle, 21-1/2" wingspan....... 50.00
Floral, blue, light green border, 6-1/2".............................. 25.00

Pens and Pencils

Before computers, folks actually wrote letters with pens and pencils! Today some collectors find interesting examples at flea markets.

Pen
Cartier, 14k, large, two dents 260.00

Pens and pencils, ink blotter with advertisement for Van Dyke No. 600 drawing pencil, Griesemer Stationery Co., Allentown, PA, unused, 5-3/4" x 3-1/4", **$3.**

Conklin, Endura Model, desk set, two pens, side-lever fill, black marble base 135.00
Dunn, black, red barrel, gold filled trim, c1920...................... 45.00
Fisher Space Pen, 5" l, chrome finish metal pen, Fisher Co., Forest Park, IL, orig paper and box................................... 25.00
Moore, lady's, black, three narrow gold bands on cap, lever fill 75.00
Sheaffer Lifetime Stylist, gold filled metal, professionally engraved clip, 1960s........................ 35.00

Wahl, lady's, ribbon pen, double narrow band on cap, 14k #2 nib, lever fill, 1928.................. 80.00
Waterman's, black, gold trim, clip, unused............................. 50.00

Pencil
Brown-McLaren MFG. Co., Hamburg, Mich., Detroit

Pens and pencils, advertising pencil, "Colonial is good Bread," unused, 7-1/2" l, **$1.**

Office-7340 Puritan Ave., Phone
UNiversity 3-3520, Redipoint,
USA, celluloid 10.00
Conklin, rolled gold, initials
engraved on clip.............. 85.00

Mr. Peanut, engraved on both sides
of clip, some paint missing from
top hat 12.00
New York Rangers, 6" l mechanical
pencil, transparent upper barrel
over brown/tan scene of hockey

game, hockey player advances
puck, 1970 .... 10.00
Set, Cross, Ertl emblem, service
premium for 10 years of service,
MIB 75.00

Pepsi-Cola

"Pepsi Cola Hits The Spot!" That was part of a popular jingle the 1950s. Pepsi collectibles today are hot, just as the beverage itself has remained popular since first it was introduced in the late 1890s.

Pepsi
collectibles,
limited-edition
reproduction
bottle, 12-
ounce, **$4.**

Clock
Bottle cap shape, plastic, "Drink
Pepsi-Cola, Ice Cold," white
ground, 11" d.................. 165.00
Light-up, glass face, metal case, "say
Pepsi please" 16" sq........ 200.00

Cooler, metal, "Drink Pepsi-Cola" in
white, blue ground, 18-1/2" h,
18" w, 13" d 80.00

Door handle, "Drink Pepsi-Cola,
Bigger-Better," red, white, and blue
backplate, Bakelite handle... 145.00

Glass, clear with syrup line, 1930/40,
two-color decor, 10 oz 10.00

Menu sign, "Have a Pepsi" beside
bottlecap, "Pepsi-Cola, the Light
Refreshment" at bottom, black
chalkboard area, yellow/white
striped ground, 1950s, 30" h, 20" w
.... 75.00

Pinback button, Diet Pepsi For Girls
Girl Watchers Watch, 3" d cello,
flasher google eyes, 1960s 35.00

Salt and pepper shaker, plastic,
one-pc, "The Light refreshment"
under bottlecap logo, 1950s, orig
box 60.00

Serving tray, bottle cap, red, white,
and blue, 1940s.................... 230.00

Sign
Celluloid, button-type, "Ice Cold
Pepsi-Cola Sold Here," red name,
white text, blue/white/blue
ground, 1940s, 9" d 330.00
Tin, die-cut, bottlecap shape,
"Pepsi-Cola," crazing, 14" d
.... 140.00

Advertisement, Pepsi, 1956, woman
and man carving turkey in very
1950s setting, 11" x 14" 10.00

Bottle opener, metal, bottle shape,
"America's Biggest Nickel's Worth,"
rust, 2 3/4" l 45.00

Carrier, six-pack, wooden, "Buy
Pepsi-Cola," red and blue, 1930/40
.... 95.00

Pepsi collectibles, receipt, Durham
Pepsi-Cola Bottling Co., printed, black,
white, and red, double dot logo, 1950s,
3-3/8" x 5-5/8", **$5.**

Thermometer, tin
"Have a Pepsi" at top, bottle cap
"The Light refreshment" at
bottom, yellow with V-shaped
white area, 1950s, 27" h . 235.00
"Pepsi-Cola" bottlecap logo at top,
"More Bounce To The Ounce" at
bottle with red, white, and blue
ribbon, white ground, rounded
top and bottom, 27" h, 8" w
.... 275.00

Perfume Bottles

Decorative and figural perfume bottles have remained a popular area of collecting for generations. Perfume bottles can be found in a variety of sizes, shapes, and colors, as well as price ranges. Look for examples with matching stoppers and original labels.

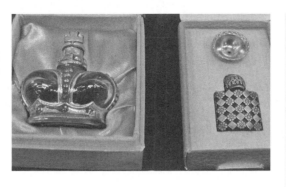

Perfume bottles, left: Prince Machibelli, cobalt blue and gold crown bottle, original fitted box, **$45;** right: unidentified maker, silver checkerboard pattern with flowers, small sterling funnel, original fitted box, **$65.**

Perfume bottles, white opalescent swirl glass, plastic lid, 3-3/4" h, **$8.**

Atomizer

Baccarat, amethyst panels, clear cut daisies, acid etched mark, 5-7/8" h............................ 125.00

Cambridge, stippled gold, opaque jade, orig silk lined box, 6-1/4" h 150.00

Czechoslovakian, cobalt blue, large enameled and faceted crystal stopper, c1930, 8" h 80.00

Devilbiss, clear, threaded dec, 4" h, #127 .... 45.00

Boxed set

Evening In Paris 135.00

Hudnut, Sweet Orchid, 3" h, 1920s 45.00

L'Heure Bleue, fluted and scrolled design, Guerlain fitted box 90.00

Cut glass

Cut glass, Button and Star pattern, rayed base, faceted stopper, 6-1/2" h 125.00

Figural

Decanter shape, glass, opaque blue ground, enameled white leaves and grape garlands, dragonfly in center, three gold applied ball feet, clear ground stopper 125.00

Genie slippers, glass, cork stoppers, paper labels, "Rose Oil and Cologne by H. P. & C. R. Taylor, Phila," some damage to orig labels, pr........................ 125.00

Glass

Cobalt blue, sheared top, c1890, 3" h 65.00

Mary Gregory, cranberry ground, white enameled girl dec, colorless ball stopper 175.00

Melon ribbed body, emb, lacy gold enameled fern leaves, colorless cut faceted stopper, 4-1/2" h 165.00

Quintessence Glass Studios, violet blue shading to clear, 1996, 4-1/2" h............................. 80.00

Satin, lay-down type, Diamond Quilted pattern, shading yellow to white, 6" l 400.00

Pet Equipment

One new area that was very apparent during this past summer's flea market season was the increasing number of pet related items. Most are slightly used, but might be good enough for a new pet owner to start with. Why not surprise Fido or Fluffy with a new bed to snuggle down on, they are always glad to see what you've bought at the flea market too!

Aquarium, 10 gallon, complete with heater, air filtration system ... 15.00

Bed, cat, removable fleece covering 5.00

Bed, dog, plaid waterproof covering, down filled............................ 15.00

Bird cage, white metal, white glass watering and feeding dishes, removable bottom tray.......... 20.00

Brush, dog grooming, wood handle, sturdy bristles.......................... 5.00

Car seat for small dog 5.00

Cat carrier

Cardboard, folding................. 1.00

Plastic, metal door, carrying handle on top 5.00

Cat lounger, to fit at windowsill, sheepskin-type fabric, plastic supports................................... 2.00

Clothing

Dog boots, set of four 6.00

Dog coat, felt, small dog......... 8.00

Dog coat, polar fleece, greyhound size.................................... 12.00

Halloween costume, small dog, coat, hat, bowtie with elastic 15.00

Collar

Choke-chain type 2.00

Leather, large dog................. 12.00

Leather, small dog, rhinestone trim 15.00

Pet equipment, watering dish, clear plastic dish with two swimming goldfish, multicolored chips on bottom, white plastic base with black paw prints, battery operated, **$5.**

Crate
Folding, metal, medium dog size
.... 20.00
Stationary, wood and metal, large
dog size.............................. 45.00

Dog house, wood, home made, for
medium sized dog................ 45.00

Dog igloo, plastic, for medium sized
dog.. 35.00

Feeding station, plastic platform
on legs, chrome or plastic feeding
bowls...................................... 20.00

Grooming items
Grooming platform, collapsible
.... 40.00
Nail clippers......................... 15.00

Hamster cage, metal 5.00

Hamster habitat, plastic, action and
exercise elements..................... 5.00

Leash
Cat type, braided harness....... 3.00
Leather, hand tooled, for small dog
.... 12.00
Woven nylon......................... 10.00

Training video 2.00

Vehicle harness 4.00

Water dish, continuous feed, plastic
.... 2.00

PEZ

PEZ was invented in Austria as a cigarette substitute. Eduard Haas hoped his mints would catch on when he named it PEZ, an abbreviation for *Pfefferminz*. By 1952, a tabletop model arrived in America, but it was not until the container was redesigned for children that the candy caught on. Many popular characters get periodic design updates, giving collectors variations to search for.

Aardvark, orange stem 10.00

Ant, green stem........................... 8.00

Aral, Gas, blue hat and shoes 6.00

Baloo, blue-gray head 20.00

Barney Bear, 1970s 12.00

Boy with hat, Pez Pal, 1960..... 12.00

Bugs Bunny, black stem, late 1970s
.... 15.00

Clown, Merry Melody Maker, MOC
.... 5.00

Cow B, mid-1970s 85.00

Donald Duck, MIP.................. 27.50

Donatello, feet 3.00

Dumbo, blue trunk, yellow base and
hat.. 60.00

Foghorn Leghorn, feet, early 1980s
.... 60.00

Fozzie Bear, 1991 .... 3.00

Goofy, green hat, feet, late 1980s
.... 3.00

Icee Bear................................... 5.50

Inspector Clouseu, yellow stem
.... 6.00

Kermit, mkd "Made in Hungry"
.... 7.50

Lamb, mkd "Made in Yuglosavia"
.... 6.00

Mariner, blue hat, black shoes... 7.50

Miss Piggy, early 1990s 10.00

Muselix, orange stem 12.00

Parrot, Merry Melody Maker, MOC
.... 8.50

Pebbles Flintstone, mid-1990s
.... 2.00

Penguin, Melody Maker, MOC
.... 12.00

Peter Pez, red stem, 1990s 3.00

Pilot, white hat, black shoes....... 6.00

Pink Panther, pink stem 12.00

Rabbit 7.50

RD-D2 .... 5.00

Santa, mkd "Made in Yuglosavia"
.... 8.00

Shell Gas, yellow hat, red shoes
.... 7.00

Smurf, Papa, red stem 3.00

Tom 6.00

Tuffy.. 7.50

Whistle, 1960s........................... 2.50

Woodstock, 1990s...................... 4.00

PEZ, whistle-shaped dispenser, with feet, red, white and blue, **$3.**

Pfaltzgraff

Here's a name most flea marketers associate with dinnerware. Do you know that Pfaltzgraff originally started as a stoneware company? By the early 1950s, company officials realized their future was in dinnerware production, and production successfully shifted toward that goal.

New Series

Pfaltzgraff has announced a new series of miniature replicas. The series will continue through 2011 as a celebration of the founding of the first Pfaltzgraff pottery in 1811 in York, PA. The first replica will be a stoneware jug with a simulated Bristol glaze. The miniatures will be issued in a gift box, which contains a certificate of authenticity.

Pfaltzgraff, pitcher, white shading to green, angular handle, **$10.**

Bean pot, cov, Gourmet 100.00
Butter dish, Village 10.00
Candlesticks, pr, Wyndham 25.00
Canister, coffee, Yorktowne 12.00

Casserole, cov
   Aura, 12" x 8" 14.00
   Meadow lane 48.00
   Oatmeal, three qt 40.00

Child's mug, bear faces 10.00

Coffeepot, Gourmet, metal and wood
   stand 125.00

Creamer, Wyndham 30.00

Cup and saucer
   Christmas Heirloom 7.50
   Yorktowne 5.00

Custard, Village, set of four 12.00

Dinner plate
   Gazebo 10.00
   Gourmet 12.00
   Windsong 12.00
   Yorktowne 10.00

Goblet, Village, set of four 14.00

Gravy boat with underplate,
   Wyndham 35.00

Honey pot, cov, Village, 5-1/4" h
   .... 20.00

Platter, Folk Art, oval, 14" l 10.00

Pfaltzgraff, dinnerware set, service for 10, accessory pieces, Village pattern, brown decoration on tan ground, **$75.**

Pfaltzgraff, dinnerware set, service for six, accessory pieces, Arbor Vine pattern, blue, green, and red decoration on white ground, **$45.**

Salad bowl, Village, set of 8 ..... 10.00
Salt and pepper shakers, pr
   Gourmet 30.00
   Wyndham 24.00
Sugar bowl, cov, Secret Rose 35.00
Teapot
   Gourmet 40.00
   Heritage 38.00
   Yorktowne 15.00
Vegetable dish, cov, Blue Tulip
   .... 35.00
Vegetable dish, divided, Yorktowne
   .... 12.00

Phoenix Bird China

Phoenix Bird China a blue-and-white dinnerware made from the late 19th century through the 1940s. The china was imported to America, where it was retailed by several firms, including Woolworth's, and wholesalers such as Butler Brothers.

For additional listings and a detailed history, see *Warman's Americana & Collectibles.*

Bread and butter plate, 6" d 8.00
Butter pat 10.00
Cereal bowl, 6" d 9.00
Coffeepot 55.00
Creamer 18.00
Cup and saucer 10.00
Dessert plate, 7-1/4" d 8.00
Dinner plate, 9-3/4" d 25.00

Eggcup, double cup 15.00
Luncheon plate, 8-1/2" d 12.00
Platter, oval, 14" l 45.00
Rice tureen, cov 55.00
Salt dip, scalloped 16.00
Sauce bowl, 5-1/2" d 6.00
Soup bowl, 7-1/4" d 10.00
Sugar bowl, cov 22.00

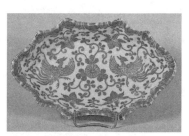

Phoenix Bird China, ice cream dish, 6-3/4" x 4" x 1-1/2" h, **$35.**

Teapot, cov.................................. 35.00   **Tea tile**, 6" d............................. 25.00   **Vegetable bowl**, oval 45.00

Photographs

Photograph collecting certainly is one way to add "instant ancestors" to those picture frames you'd like to hang. Many photographs are found at flea markets. Look for photographs that have interesting composition or those that give some perspective to the way an area once looked.

Photographs, postcard, real photograph of school children posed in front of Quakertown, PA, elementary school, names of each child neatly written on back, dated 1910, **$45.**

Albumen print
Baseball game, mounted, 5-1/4" sq **125.00**
Buffalo Bill, cabinet card.... **360.00**
Cowboy on horse with dog doing a trick on back of the horse, 1920-1930s, mounted, 5" x 7" ... **48.00**
Man with horse-drawn moving van in front of building with sign for "Pacific Transfer Company," dated 1913, identified in pencil as Portland, Ore., mounted, 5" x 7" **60.00**
New Jersey shorebird, Arthur Dill, 1983, framed, presentation documentation attached **15.00**

Cabinet card
Admiral Dot, dwarf, sepia, E & H. T. Anthony & Co., New York City, late 19th C, 2-1/2" x 4-1/4" **28.00**

Circus, fat lady in frilly dress straddling chair, black and white, Obermuller & Son, NY, 1880s, 4-1/4" x 6-1/2", ... **28.00**
Annie Russell As Elaine, sepia, New York photographer, late 1800s, 7-1/2" x 13" **12.00**
Mrs G. H. Gilbert, died 1904, sepia, New York photographer, 7-1/2" x 13" **10.00**

Carte de viste (CDV)
Boy on toy rocking horse, Louisana, Mo., imprint **45.00**
Girl with bisque doll............. **14.00**
Postmortem, baby **40.00**

Glossy, black and white, 29 photos of "The Delaware and Hudson 1930 Student Engineering Corps Railroad Field Trip".............. **25.00**

Sepia tone
Wagons, 4-1/2" x 6-1/2" photo mounted to 7" x 9" cardboard with charcoal gray tin paper, office and buildings, J. A. Creighton & Co., four loaded Creighton Lime wagons drawn by early steam tractor in foreground, reverse inked "Thomaston, Maine," early 1900s **25.00**
Moving truck, 6" x 8" photo of three men posed at primitive truck, inscribed on side "Long Distance Moving, Phil. Hertel, Public Truckman, 142 Washington Ave, R.B., Auto Vans," c1910 auto in background, mounted on 10" x 12" gray mat board............. **5.00**

Photographs, eagle cabinet card, Jones Studio, Madison, Wis., 6-1/2" x 4-1/4", **$90.**

Tintype
Civil war era soldier, unidentified **45.00**
George Washington, 2-1/2" x 4" card, centered 1-1/4" x 1-3/4" oval opening over 1-3/4" x 2" tintype with octagonal edges, attributed to 1876 Centennial **125.00**
Young woman, swatch of twill from jacket, 1-5/8" gold filled engraved locket case **85.00**

Pickard China

Wilder Pickard founded this company in 1897 in Chicago. China blanks imported from Europe were hand-painted by company artists. Signed pieces are especially sought.

For additional listings, see *Warman's Antiques and Collectibles Price Guide* and *Warman's American Pottery & Porcelain.*

Pickard China, pitcher, hand painted cherries on cream ground, gold rim, base, and handles, marked "Pickard China," 7-1/4" h, **$250.**

Bon bon, basket style, four sided, gold 45.00

Bowl, red and white tulips, gold dec, Limoges blank, 10" d 230.00

Cabinet plate
Heavy gold enameled border, Limoges blank, 8-1/2" d. 175.00

Lilies, gold background, artist sgd "Yeschek," 9" d 100.00

Cake plate, open gold handles, Desert Garden pattern 185.00

Celery set, two handled oval dish, five matching salts, allover gold dec, 1925-30 mark 125.00

Creamer, red and yellow currants, green leaves, unsigned, 1905-10 mark 165.00

Demitasse cup and saucer, Gold Tracery Rose & Daisy pattern, green band, 1925-30 mark 40.00

Hatpin holder, allover gold design of etched flowers, c1925 .... 50.00

Perfume bottle, yellow primroses, shaded ground, artist sgd and dated 1905, gold stopper 200.00

Plate
Blackberries and leaves, sgd "Beitler" (Joseph Beitler), 1903-15, 8-1/2" d 90.00
Currants, 7-1/2" d 75.00
Gooseberries dec, sgd "P. G." (Paul Gasper), 1912-18 mark, 8-1/4" d 45.00

Pickard China, celery dish, gold floral design, marked "Pickard, Deco, Made in USA, #418" 11-3/4" l, 5-1/2" w, **$80.**

Grapes and leaves, etched gilded border, sgd "Coufall," 1903-05 mark, 8-1/2" d 195.00
Peaches, gilded and molded border, sgd "S. Heap," 9-1/8" d ... 110.00

Platter, roses, gilded border, sgd "Seidel," 12" d 275.00

Vase
Scenic, sgd "E. Challinor" (Edward Challinor), 1912-18, 8-1/4" h 425.00
Three large dark poppies, gold, rust, and brown dec, sgd "Gasper," 9-1/4" h 365.00

Picture Frames

Here's a topic few people admit to collecting, but most of us have many of these in our homes. Flea markets are a good place to find interesting frames. Make sure you take measurements if you're looking for a certain size frame.

Celluloid, 8" x 6-1/4" 70.00

Curly maple, good curl, 16-1/4" x 16" 385.00

Grain-decor, pine, 17" x 14" 385.00

Horseshoe-form, white paint, gilt liner, 17-1/4" x 13-1/2" 95.00

Mahogany, gilt and black liner, 12" x 16" 75.00

Oak
Cross-corner, leaves in corners, 17" x 15" 45.00
Gesso border in gold, 30" x 25-1/2" 90.00

Primitive, painted black frame, red corner blocks, 18" x 24" 150.00

Shells, 8-1/2" x 6-1/2" 65.00

Silver, sterling, easel back, holds 6" x 8" 45.00

Tramp art
Cross-corner, 7" x 6" 115.00
Divided for two photos, gold paint, 13-1/2" h, 26-1/2" w 250.00

Walnut
Cross-corner, gilt liner, 8" x 7" 125.00
Oval, deep, 13-1/2" x 11-1/2" 40.00

Shadowbox type, gilt liner, 14-1/2" h, 12" w 75.00

Picture frames, celluloid, pair, one with original photo of woman, grained, easel back, **$60.**

Pig Collectibles

This little piggie went to market... Actually lots of piggies are heading to flea markets so that collectors can give them a new home. Some collectors specialize in famous characters, like Babe or Porky Pig, while others prefer figurines.

Pig collectibles, planter, A Present from Southend on Sea, 5-1/2" l, **$165.**

Advertising, cutting board, Arnold Kent Feeds, wood, pig shape . 22.00

Ashtray, green ceramic base, figural pink pig.................................. 5.00

Bank
Heart, green, two pigs on each side of sheet music, mkd "Germany" 85.00
Pig shape, ceramic, pink and white, multicolored flowers, curly tail, 1950s 30.00

Crock, orange pig along side, 3" h 85.00

Cutting board, pig shape, home made, well used 5.00

Figure
Black bisque pig jumping over fence, 4-1/2" l, 3-1/2" h 80.00
Lobster pulling leg of red pig 115.00
Pig riding in canoe, c1930.... 65.00
Purse, black bisque pig sitting on top of green purse, 2-1/4" h 80.00

Shoe, two pigs inside............ 85.00
Water trough, surrounded by four pigs, 4" l........................ 110.00
Wishing well, baby pig inside, large pig at side, 3-1/2" h 120.00

Inkwell, pink pig sitting on top of green inkwell, 3" h............... 100.00

Match holder, pair of pink bisque pigs, "Scratch My Back" and "Me Too"...................................... 120.00

Pinback button, Swift's, multicolored carton of smiling pig wearing rope noose while seated in frying pan, c1901..................................... 45.00

Pin dish, horseshoe, yellow and green, pink pig, stamped "Made in Germany," 5" w 85.00

Pocket mirror, Newtown Collins Short Order Restaurant, St. Joe, MO, yellow and orange, 2-1/8" d 55.00

Toaster cover, padded fabric, white background, pink pigs, Ulster

Pig collectibles, "My System" bisque figurine, Germany, 2-3/4" h, 3-3/4" w, **$40.**

Weavers, Ireland, 12" w, 9" h 15.00

Toothpick holder
Egg, two little pigs, 2-3/4" h 75.00
Lawn Tennis, pig with racquet, 3-3/4" h.......................... 85.00

Pig collectibles, bank, cast iron, seated pig holding sign with verse, "The Wise Pig," ©J. M.R., 6-3/4" h, **$80.**

Pinback Buttons

Here's a form of advertising that was an instant hit and is still popular. Look for interesting pinback buttons with advertising and political slogans of all types. Many early manufacturers included a paper insert that further exclaimed the virtues of the product. An insert adds value to a pin. Bright colors and good condition are also important.

Amoco, Join The American Party, American Gas, litho tin 18.00

Annual Summer Suit Sale, black and orange sweating man next to thermometer, c1930 .... 15.00

Big Chef White Bread, black, white, and red, white lettering, 1930s 12.00

Buster Brown Bread, multicolored, red rim lettering, Buster as sign painter, "Resolved that the Best

Bre(a)d People eat Buster Brown Bread" 24.00

Calif Dairy Industries Assn, white on red, 1935, St. Louis back paper 10.00

Cameo Gum, five angels among clouds, c1898 .... 20.00

Ceresota, trademark young boy seated on stool slicing giant bread loaf, c1900-12 .... 20.00

Chocolate Mason Mints, blue on silver, slogan "Soothing Cooling Flavor," 1940s.......................... 8.00

Cinderella Stoves and Ranges, multicolored, red, white, blue, and gold accents 15.00

Dakota Gold Turkey, blue and yellow design, red lettering, 1940s 12.00

Diamond C Hams, celluloid, 1-1/2" d 95.00

Pinback buttons, Lockport, NY, flight on Erie Canal, Whitehead & Hoag Co., 7/8" d, **$35.**

Falcon Flour Grocers Picnic, flour sack with company logo, 1899 .... 15.00

I'm a Chicken Dinner Candy Kid, blue text, red center chicken, yellow ground, c1930 .... 12.00

Lucky Strikes Again, 2-1/2" d 25.00

Meet Me At The Bon-Ton, Santa Claus, 1-1/4" d 28.00

Minnesota House Paints, red, white, black, yellow, and green, Whitehead & Hoag back paper, 1900-12 .... 35.00

Official Mickey Mouse Store, 1-1/4" d 18.00

Pfeiffer's Beer, red, white, and blue, yellow ground, 1930s 20.00

Ritz Crackers 14.00

Royal Typewriter Entrant, blue and white typewriter, blue text on dark red rim, white ground, Dawson Co. Photo Contest 25.00

The Freshest Thing in Town, Johnny Lawrence wearing derby, red text, bright yellow ground, 1930s 12.00

Vote for Betty Crocker, red, white, and blue, 1970s........................ 8.00

Pinback buttons, Ella Cinders, New York Evening Journal, red letters, black numbers, white ground, Offset Granure Corp, NY, 1-1/2" d, **$15.**

White Rose Bread 10.00

Yale Bread Wins, blue and white image of pennant, yellow ground, blue lettering, solid tin reverse 18.00

Planters

Flea markets are great places to find planters of every type. Unfortunately, many of us have brown thumbs and are soon left with a pretty container and little foliage. However, with careful inspection, you just might find out that your favorite planter is a piece of Westmoreland glass or McCoy pottery. Start to think about finding other uses for neat planters. They can be used in a powder room to hold guest towels, in a kitchen to hold utensils, etc.

Additional listings for planters can be found throughout this book; look under specific companies and also Lady's Head Vases.

ABC block, pastels..................... 8.00
Angel on gift 10.00

Baby, sitting on large shoe planter, pink and white, Relpo Ceramics, Japan, 1950s.......................... 25.00

Bambi, mkd "Walt Disney Productions".......................... 65.00

Bootie, blue, unmarked.............. 4.00

Butterfly on log, brown and white, glossy glaze, mkd "Shawnee USA 524"....................................... 12.00

Caboose, Mrs. Claus, Orion..... 12.00

Cactus and cowboy, natural colors, Morton................................. 17.50

Cat, coral glaze, green box, McCoy, 1950 .... 12.00

Christmas girl, Relco.............. 25.00

Elf on shoe, 8" l....................... 25.00

Fawns, standing pair, McCoy, 1957 .... 35.00

Flamingos, facing pair, 10" l.. 150.00
Frog, Norcrest 35.00

Girl in sleigh, red outfit, white sleigh, Napco 35.00

Planters, figural, chicken, Shawnee, 6-1/2" h, **$30.**

Planters, jardinière, maroon, self handles, honeycomb embossed border, vertical stripes, marked "USA," **$20.**

Planters, jardinière, blue and white floral design, smaller detailed blue and white dec on rim, remnants of gold trim, unmarked, some int. crazing from use, **$125.**

Gondola, yellow, McCoy 20.00

Mallard, head down, Royal Copley 22.00

Noel, children each holding letter, candy cane as base, Napco 35.00

Oriental style, green floral design, gold fish, white ground, large 25.00

Parrot, white, orange accents... 15.00

Pink, rect, unmarked.................. 5.00

Pipe, brown, black stem 9.00

Puppy, polka dot bowtie and beanie, 7" l... 30.00

Rooster, 6-1/2" h 20.00

Santa, face, Inarco, 6" h 20.00

Santa, figural, fur trim, Napco, 5-1/2" h 20.00

Santa on skis, Ucago Co., 4-1/2" h 15.00

Snow lady, red jacket, black hat with red rose, yellow umbrella...... 18.00

Snowman in car, Shafford, 4-1/2" h 20.00

Planters, jardinière, green, brown florals with mauve colored butterflies, unmarked, **$150.**

Planters, donkey, dark brown glaze, unmarked, **$5.**

Springer spaniel, black and white, unmarked 10.00

Straw hat, yellow, blue ribbon . 17.50

Swan, ceramic, white glaze......... 5.00

Teddy bear, sitting, pastels, mkd "7970 Japan" 6.00

Telephone................................... 8.00

Turkey, brown, Morton............ 15.00

Whale, glossy brown, gold trim 15.00

Wishing Well, McCoy, orig chain 30.00

Planters Peanuts

The Planters Nut and Chocolate Co. was founded in Wilkes-Barre, Pa., in 1906. In 1916, the company held a contest to find a mascot, and Mr. Peanut came to life. He has remained a popular advertising icon.

For additional listings, see *Warman's Americana & Collectibles.*

Reproduction alert.

Bank, plastic, set of four, solid colors, red, cobalt, green, tan 175.00

Belt buckle, peanut shape 15.00

Bobbing head, Mr. Peanut, composition, smiling, waving, plastic cane, 5-1/4" h 150.00

Bookmark, diecut cardboard, 1939 NY World's Fair, yellow, black, and white, 6-1/2" h 25.00

Box, cardboard
Planters Roasted Peanuts, oval red medallion shows peanut lettered "The Peanut Store," 10" h, 6-1/4" sq 55.00

Planters Salted Nuts, Fresh, Roaster To You, shows bowl of peanuts, 1940s-1950s...................... 15.00

Can, litho tin, Planters Pennant Brand Salted Peanuts, red pennant with Mr. Peanut, 5 lb, 8" h, 6-1/4" d 55.00

Coaster, tin, Mr Peanut in center, 3-1/2" d 10.00

Coloring book
50 States, 1970s 12.00
American Ecology, 1970s 12.00
Presidents of the United States, unused............................. 15.00

Coin, Mr. Peanut, Olympics, 1980 .... 10.00

Jar, glass, countertop
Four Corners Peanut jar, bottom mkd "Made in U.S.A." 215.00
Six-sided jar, yellow printing on all sides, bottom mkd "Made in U.S.A.".......................... 265.00
Eight-sided jar, embossed on all sides.............................. 125.00
Fired-on enamel label, "Planters Peanuts 5¢," and Mr. Peanut, red and blue, embossed back, orig red tin lid, c1940, 7-5/8" d, 9" h 200.00

Planters Peanuts, Mr. Peanut, figural red plastic salt and pepper shakers, pr, **$15,** and bank, silver trim, **$40.**

Lighter, Bic, 1970s................... 15.00

Mechanical pencil, 1970s....... 15.00

Postcard, Planters Peanuts at Times Square, 1940s scene, unused 20.00

Radio, transistor, plastic, yellow Mr. Peanut design, unused, orig box/ mailing carton, mint, 10" h, 5" w 110.00

Toy, plastic, windup, Mr. Peanut figure walker, tan body, black arms, legs, and hat, 1950s, 8-1/2" h 400.00

Whistle, figural, 1970s 15.00

Planters Peanuts, tin, Planter's Cocktail Peanuts, 1938 copyright, 3" h, 3-1/4" d, **$10.**

Plastic

It's hard to imagine life without plastics. Today collectors actively search for early plastics, including acrylics, Bakelite, and celluloid.

For a more detailed history and additional listings of plastics, see *Warman's Americana & Collectibles* and Bakelite and Celluloid in this edition.

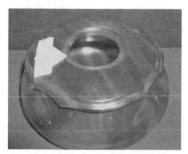

Plastics, hair receiver, imitation tortoise shell coloring, two pieces, **$20.**

Alarm clock, key wind, Black Forest works, octagonal translucent green case 30.00

Bag handle, Blue Cross, white, blue lettering .... .50

Barette, child's, pink chick with blue bow 2.00

Business card holder, seashells suspended in rect acrylic base 6.50

Dress clip, green opaque Lucite, triangular, chevron design, rhinestone trim 20.00

Mirror, hand, beveled acrylic handle and frame, U-shaped mirror, sterling silver floral ornament, c1946...................................... 55.00

Mug
Green, Del Val University....... 8.00
Purple, Nexium advertising ... 4.00

Napkin ring, translucent Lucite, sq shape, rounded edges, circular center, c1960, four-pc set 12.00

Paperweight, translucent Lucite cube, suspended JFK half dollar, c1965...................................... 10.00

Picture frame
Lucite, faux tortoise shell, lime green and brown, rect, wavy sides, linen backing, holds 3" x 5" picture 25.00
Plastic, molded, simulated wood grain, Nu-Dell Plastics, Chicago, 10-1/2" x 13".................... 15.00

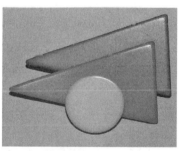

Plastics, pin, costume jewelry, 2-5/8" l, **$5.**

Pin, figural Santa face, American Greeting Cards........................ 1.00

Push puppet, Santa, holding bell, mkd "Made in Hong Kong for Kohner" 60.00

Salt and pepper shakers, pr, Mr. Peanut, red, 3" h 15.00

Wall shelf, translucent neon pink, 30" l, 6" d, 1970s 25.00

Playboy

Everyone smiles when someone tries to convince them that they really only read *Playboy* for the articles, since we all know this enterprise has grown into a mega business. Dedicated Playboy collectors know there is more to this interesting collectible as they scour the flea market landscape for that distinctive bunny logo.

The first *Playboy* magazine was released in December of 1953. Owner and publisher Hugh M. (Marston) Hefner did not put a date on the cover because he was not sure if there would be another copy. The popular Femlin was introduced into Party Jokes section of the August 1955 magazine.

The first Playboy club opened in 1960. In just over a year it had become the most visited nightclub in the world. After yielding a seemingly endless supply of ashtrays, mugs, swizzle sticks and other collectibles, the last stateside club closed in 1988.

Playboy, magazine, **$65.**

Ashtray, smoked black glass, Femlin logo in center, 3-3/4" x 3-3/4" 12.00

Bar set, sterling silver, four pcs 65.00

Book, *Playboy's Host & Bar Book*, Thomas Mario, Playboy, 1971, hard cover, 339 pages..................... 25.00

Calendar, Miss March, Stella Stevens, 1961 .... 65.00

Cocktail shaker, plastic, 9" h.. 40.00

Crock, stoneware, beige, red logo, 3" d... 32.00

Earrings, pr, clip, goldtone, 1" d 65.00

Eggcup, Jackson China, tan ext., white int., logo on front, Playboy Club around rim in black lettering, mkd "Jackson China, HMH Publishing Co., Inc.," 1960s... 22.00

Key charm, goldtone, black logo, 3-3/4" l 45.00

Magazine, *Playboy*, with centerfold intact
1955, September................. 180.00
1955, November 130.00
1957, March....................... 175.00
1985, September, Madonna on cover, last stapled issue.... 15.00
1994, November, Pamela Anderson on cover, autographed, mint 50.00

Money clip, Playboy Casino, 1-1/2" d 75.00

Mug, clear, black rabbit head logo, 9-3/4" h 12.00

Pin, gold plated, rhinestone eyes, 1-1/4" h 85.00

Playboy, magazine, February 1954, **$45.**

Puzzle, 1968, centerfold, Playmate Jean Bell, canister, opened 15.00

Ring, 14kg yg, logo in center.... 85.00

Shot glass, Femlin dec 18.00

Swizzle stick, black or white, Playboy on side, each 1.00

Telephone calling card, prepaid, limited edition...................... 50.00

Wall calendar, 1963, Playmate, orig envelope, mint...................... 55.00

Playing Cards

What we know today as playing cards were developed in 1885 by the U.S. Playing Card Company of Cincinnati. However, Americans had been using cards for games and entertainment since they first arrived in the 1700s. Look for interesting designs, complete sets, and orig boxes.

American Airlines, US mail plane, c1960-80, 2-1/4" x 3-1/2" box 10.00

Apollo 11, Kennedy Space Center, Florida, 1969, MIB 18.00

Boys Town, double deck, shows the famous "He ain't heavy, Father, he's my brother" scene, Brown & Bigelow, mint......................... 60.00

Chessie System, double deck, sealed 40.00

Delta Airlines, white pyramid, c1960-80, 2-1/4" x 3-1/2" box.. 8.00

Playing cards, birds, original box with foil label, **$10.**

Eastern/Ryder, text, logo, c1960-80, 2-1/4" x 3-1/2" box 8.00

Frisco Railroad, sealed 22.00

Jeff Gordon, double deck, collector's tin, 1999, NRFB 12.00

Our Airliner Miss Budweiser, DC 3, Anheuser-Busch logo, 1953, sealed 18.00

Ozark, snow-covered Rockies, c1960-80, 2-1/4" x 3-1/2" box........... 10.00

Quilt design, Patchwork, double deck, Hallmark, one joker missing, plastic box............................... 8.00

Raggedy Ann, Hallmark, orig box 25.00

Texas souvenir deck, Historical facts about Texas, Home of the President of the United States, mid-1960s, sealed 24.00

TWA collectors series, Douglas DC-9, 1966, c1960-80, 2-1/4" x 3-1/2" box 12.00

Playing cards, Autumn Leaf, made to match Hall's famous china pattern, some wear to cards and original box, **$20.**

U.S. Military, vertical vehicles, double deck, Vertol Aircraft Corp., Morton, Pa., plastic holder.... 40.00

Woman with dogs, double set, Congress 28.00

Playskool

Remember Mr. Potato Head? How about wooden Lincoln Logs and Tinkertoys? Does anyone recall Weebles, which wobble but don't fall down? Those are some of the most popular toys made by Playskool, which was founded in 1928. Playskool products are still largely designed for children 6 years old and under. Flea markets are a prime hunting ground for all manner of Playskool toys, both vintage and contemporary.

Colored blocks, cardboard canister, 1972 .... 22.00

Doll
Dressy Bessy, 1970, stuffed cloth, 18" h 40.00
Raggedy Ann, Christmas dress 65.00

Magazine tear sheet, black and white, 1952, shows round block stack, Peggy ball pull, Nok-out bench, etc., 11" x 14" 6.00

Play set, Gilligans Island, 12" w x 8" h island, raft, row boat, orig figures, mkd "Filmation," 1977 .... 60.00

Pounding bench, wooden, solid colored pegs, some play wear 10.00

Puzzle
Airplane, #330-16, 15 pcs 12.00
Bird, wood, 9-1/2" x 11-1/2" 18.00

Cookie's Sesame Street Number, Sesame Street, train motif, #105, five pcs 15.00
Dipsy and La La, Teletubbies, wooden............................... 3.00
Mary had a little lamp, wood 6.00
Po and Winky, Teletubbies, wooden 3.00
Snoopy leaning on bat, Model #230-27, 1979 .... 5.00
Steam Shovel, #360-29, 18 pcs 12.00

Skaneateles train, track and blocks set, 1960s, orig box, #S950, 55 pcs 90.00

Snoopy Slugger, ball, bat, and cap, Model #411, 1979 .... 15.00

Zoo, late 1960s/early 1970s, complete with animals.......................... 95.00

Playskool, Lincoln Logs, No. 892, 165 pieces, original container and contents, **$15.**

Pocketknives

Pocketknives have been made in various forms and with different types of handles and blade materials. Some collectors search out pocketknives from specific makers, while others specialize in certain handles or advertising knives.

Pocket knives, Coca-Cola, red with white lettering, **$45.**

Advertising, Canadian Club, Best in the House, mkd "Stainless Steel, Japan," normal wear **20.00**

Barlow, blade mkd "Colonial Prov. USA," two-blade, 3-1/2" l folded **95.00**

Camillus
Babe Ruth, facsimile signature on side, 2-1/2" **125.00**
#702, stainless **17.50**
Four-line stamp, black composition handle, mkd "Camillus Cutlery,

Camillus, NY, USA," three-blade, pre 1942............................. **18.00**

Case
XX 1 Dot, #A62351/2, two-blade, bone handle...................... **25.00**
XX 2 Dot, #6347HP, three-blade, bone stag handle **35.00**
XX 6 Dot, #640045R, four-blade, bone stag handle **30.00**

Cattaraugus Cutlery Co., three-blade, stag handle.................. **75.00**

Forestmaster, blade mkd "Colonial," four blades, used, some rust, 3-3/4" l folded **25.00**

Gerber, two-blade, wood and sterling silver handle **35.00**

Hammer Brand, loop missing, 2-1/4" l **10.00**

Hoffritz, Switzerland, stainless, two blades and scissors, adv "American Greetings," 2-1/4" d **25.00**

Parker Edwards, two-blade, wood handle, etched "Eagle Brand Knives," stamped "Parker Edwards Alabama, USA," orig box....... **30.00**

Remington, UMC, three-blade, smooth black handle **35.00**

Schrade Cutlery, Captain DL-2, Dura Lens diamond nail file, precision scissors, pen blade, mkd "Snap On" **12.00**

Thornton, red handle, two blades, well used, 3-1/2" l.................. **55.00**

Ulster, Ulster Mark 40 engraved on blade, stamped "Ulster Knife USA," bone stag handle **15.00**

Winchester, cattle, three-blade, celluloid handle, worn inscription on handle, sharpened.......... **265.00**

Zippo, two-blade, adv "Trio Mfg Co., Inc.," 2" l................................. **18.00**

Pocket Watches

Pocket watches never go out of style and currently are quite fashionable. When shopping for a pocket watch at a flea market, ask a lot of questions as you carefully examine the watch: who made it, when, where, has it been repaired or cleaned recently, does it keep the proper time, etc.

American Waltham Watch Co.
Gold filled case, size 16, Roman numeral dial, elk on back, c1891, open face **250.00**
Silver, Deuber coin silver, model 1883 movement, size 18, open

Pocket watch, hunter, size 6, Illinois, 14k solid gold case, 15 jewels, **$300.**

face, c1891, small chip and ding to case............................. **295.00**

Aurora, Size 18, Roman numeral dial, lever set 15 jewel gilt movement #38691, Grade 3 1/2 Guild, second model, yellow goldfilled hunting case #5161726..................... **200.00**

Burlington, Size 16, open face Arabic numeral dial, lever set 17 jewel nickel movement #3447536, Illinois, yellow goldfilled case #5001237 .... **100.00**

Champney, S. P., Worcester, MA, 18k yg, openface, gilt movement, #8063, key wind, white dial, Roman numerals, subsidiary seconds dial, hallmarks, orig key, c1850, dial cracked, nicks to crystal...... **250.00**

Elgin National Watch Co.
Size 6, Roman numeral dial, pendant set 7 jewel nickel movement #10652232, first model, yellow goldfilled Wadsworth hunting case #316391 .... **120.00**
Size 16, open face Arabic numeral dial, lever set 19 jewel nickel movement #21235315, B.W. Raymond, yellow goldfilled case #8048 .... **215.00**

Size 16, Roman numeral dial, pendant set 17 jewel nickel movement #10374226, model 6, 3 Finger Bridge, silverode hunting case **85.00**
Size 18, Arabic numeral dial, lever set 17 jewel nickel movement #6146026, B.W. Raymond Ad, FP, yellow goldfilled Keystone hunting case #2403421 .. **150.00**

Eterna, pendant, 18k yg, rect form, black line indicators, hallmark **230.00**

Hamilton
Size 16, open face Arabic numeral dial, lever set 21 jewel nickel movement #427186, Grade 992B, 10 karat yellow rolled gold plate case #561340 .... **300.00**
Size 18, Arabic numeral dial, lever set 16 jewel nickel movement #35152, Grade 931, for R.G. Allison, St. Johns, Michigan, coin silver hunting case #606853 .... **300.00**

Hampden
Size 16, Arabic numeral dial, lever set 17 jewel nickel movement #1890116, William McKinley,

BRDG, in a yellow goldfilled hunting case #6028660 .. **165.00**
Size 18, Roman numeral dial, lever set 17 jewel nickel movement #1332191, Adjusted, silverine Dueber hunting case #2942431 .... **90.00**

Howard, 14k white gold, 17 jewels, matching chain, open face **450.00**

Illinois
Size 16, open face Arabic numeral dial, pendant set 17 jewel nickel movement #3136048, Texas Special, yellow goldfilled case #6287230 .... **120.00**
Size 18, Roman numeral dial, lever set 11 jewel nickel movement #231676, yellow goldfilled hunting case #143231 .... **150.00**

Montgomery Ward
Size 18, open face Roman numeral dial, lever set 21 jewel nickel movement #1448074, Grade 61, sixth model, 10 karat yellow rolled gold plate Illinois case #7769495 .... **175.00**

Size 18, open face Roman numeral dial, pendant set 11 jewel nickel movement #757650, 20th C, silverine Dueber case #4280 .... **75.00**

New York Standard, Size 16, open face Dan Patch stop watch Arabic numeral dial, pendant set 7 jewel nickel movement #0, 10 karat yellow goldfilled horse engraved Keystone case #9687884...... **225.00**

Rockford, Size 18, open face Roman numeral dial, lever set 17 jewel nickel movement #624324, Belmont, coin silver Fahys case **120.00**

Thomas, Seth, Size 18, Roman numeral dial, lever set 7 jewel gilt movement #44595, second model, gold plate Keystone hunting case #1220445 .... **60.00**

Vacheron & Constantin, 18k gold, hunting case, white enamel dial, Roman numerals, gilt bar movement, cylinder escapement, sgd on cuvette, engraved case, 10 size **350.00**

U.S. Watch Co., 14k yg, hunter, size 6, white dial, black Roman numerals, subsidiary seconds dial, engraved floral and scroll motifs on case **250.00**

Waltham
Lady's, 14k yg, hunting case, white enamel dial, Arabic numeral indicators, subsidiary seconds dial, Lady Waltham jeweled nickel movement by A.W.W. Co., floral engraved case no. 224709, 0 size, gold ropetwist chain **300.00**
Size 14, Roman numeral dial, pendant set 13 jewel nickel movement #3127180, Chronograph, first model, coin silver American hunting case #21280 .... **150.00**
Size 18, open face Arabic numeral dial with 24-hour time, lever set 21 jewel nickel movement #10559638, Crescent St., first model, yellow gold-filled American case #405850 .... **215.00**

Political and Campaign Items

As the cost of getting elected to political office continues to spiral upward, we can thank our forefathers for establishing the practice of creating items with their image or slogan. Intended to passively generate votes, these political items are now eagerly sought by collectors.

For additional listings, see *Warman's Antiques and Collectibles Price Guide* and *Warman's Americana & Collectibles,* as well as specific topics in this edition, including John F. Kennedy, Abraham Lincoln, and Presidential.

Reproduction alert.

Badge, 4", Wendell Wilkie, black and white portrait **25.00**

Bank, 11" h, figural hollow plaster peanut shell, Carter facial features **35.00**

Bumper sticker, 3" x 5", Nixon-Agnew '68, red, blue, and silver flag, yellow lettering, unused **3.50**

Campaign tie, 1960s, orig cardboard store hanger
Let's Back Jack, slogan in white on dark blue **48.00**
USA Likes L.B.J., slogan in white down center, medium gray ground.................................. **8.00**
Vote Republican, slogan in white, medium purple ground **5.00**

Cocktail napkins, 4-3/4" x 4-3" x 1-1/4" deep red, white, and blue box with elephant on lid, The Peoples Choice Of Course, 36 4-1/2" sq folded white napkins, each with black and white art by cartoonist Richard Taylor, elephant cartoon in center, political quotes in each quadrant, copyright 1952 Richard Taylor, Errett Smith Inc., NY, unused **5.00**

Cuff links, pr, McKinley, real photo, brass frame, clear celluloid over sepia portrait, c1896............. **18.00**

Dart board, 14" d, large 7" x 10" black and white paper photo of Agnew mounted in center..... **15.00**

Desk calendar holder, 3-1/2" x 6" two-sided cardboard, full-color illus on back, diecut holder for small desk calendar, blue front, gold lettering, Eisenhower, c1956 . **14.00**

Election day hand-out
3" x 8" blue cardboard, black type, Eisenhower-Nixon, hand-out from "First Teen-Age Republican Club in Pennsylvania," 1952 .... **5.00**
4" x 8-1/4", Democratic Republican Ticket, New Hampshire Governor Daniel Marcy of Portsmouth, other candidates, c1890 .... **5.00**

Golf tee, Eisenhower, 1-1/2" x 2" red, white, and blue pack of three Ike golf tees................................. **18.00**

Political and campaign items, pinback buttons, Nixon for President, red, white, and blue; Don't Settle for Peanuts, Ford, gray elephant, red, white, and blue; Get America Moving Again, Carter in '76, photo center, green and white; The Grin Will Win, Jimmy Carter for President, '76, peanut center, green and white, prices range from **$3** to **$5.**

Hot pad, 6" sq, Vote for Congressman Jerry Ford Who Works For You in Congress, white, red and white checkered border, 1960s........ **25.00**

Inauguration ticket, Nixon, black and white photos of Nixon and Agnew, seating info, $20, 1973, unused **7.00**

Jugate
Ford-Reagan, black and white photos, white background, red top lettering, blue bottom lettering, red stars, pre-convention, 1976.............. **35.00**
Goldwater/Miller, black and white photos in center, white background, red, white, and blue lettering.............................. **5.00**
Johnson-Humphrey, bluetone photos, red, white, and blue background, blue stars....... **8.00**

Lapel stud
Harrison, 1/18", white and blue enamel flag, white enamel background, blue enamel ribbon design with brass letters "R.L.U.S.," c1888 .... **12.00**
McKinley, diecut, white metal, black finish, cut-out circle surrounding portrait, c1896 .... **10.00**

License plate, 6" x 12" shape of PA, yellow and blue plastic, Humphrey/Muskie **15.00**

Memo pad holder, 4" sq, polished silver finish, Bill Clinton, facsimile signature, presidential seal, MIB **65.00**

Money
Bush Campaign, "Bill is Good For One New President," copyright 1999 Slick Times **8.00**

Clinton impeachment, satirical, $3, black, white, and red front, green and white reverse, front inscription "This Bill Is Tender For All Gals Public and Private," reverse with image of White House with red and white U-Haul truck parked in front, 2-1/2" x 6"......................... **15.00**

Newspaper article, "Nixon Admits He Hid Facts," Aug. 6, 1974 issue of *New York Daily News*, illus, bold front page headlines, 11" x 15" **3.00**

Paperweight, 3-1/2" x 4-1/2", Bush Quayle Reunion, pewter colored metal, raised horseshoe design, facsimile signatures in center, Jan. 18, 1990 .... **20.00**

Pennant, 12" x 29", brown felt, white letters, fleshtone portrait of Eisenhower in pale turquoise suit, gray necktie, yellow-gold trim band and streamers, 1953 .... **24.00**

Penny, 2" d white cardboard disk, black lettering "New Nixon Penny-Getting Smaller-Smaller," cellophane window at center with tiny brass facsimile of 1¢ piece with Nixon caricature on one side, c1972 .... **3.00**

Pinback button
Au H20 – Goldwater for President, 3-1/2" d, black and white photo, blue and red lettering, 4-1/2" bright gold on purple fabric ribbon.............................. **25.00**
I'm for Nixon, 3-1/2" d, 1960 .... **25.00**
It's LBJ All The Way, 4" d, red, white, and blue celluloid, portrait **12.00**

Political and campaign items, jugate postcard, Taft and Sherman, "Our Choice," **$14.**

Political and campaign items, plate, Governor Rendell, back marked "For the Advancement Of Community Leadership, The WHYY President's Dinner Honoring Edward G. Rendell, Governor, Commonwealth of Pennsylvania, June 4, 2004, Education and Opportunity, Lenox," **$45.**

Poster
11" x 17", Bush for President, red, white, and blue paper, red stripe at top, blue stripe at bottom, 1980................................... **12.00**
16" x 20", Carter in wheat field, brown and white, inspirational quote, facsimile signature, 1976 .... **12.00**
16" x 22", Keep Him On the Job, black and white portrait of Hoover............................. **50.00**
35" x 45", I Ask Your Help, Nixon-Agnew, blue tone photo and inscription in blue and red at top, lower half with enlarged image of Nixon letter "To My Fellow Americans," 1968 .... **25.00**

Program
9-1/2" x 12", Nixon Night in Philadelphia, Oct. 5, 1960, four pgs, black and white photo of Nixon family and Republican luminaries, text and program schedule **8.00**
11" diecut football, eight diecut pgs, Republican Victory Kick-Off Dinner, Convention Hall, Philadelphia, PA, Oct. 4, 1955 .... **14.00**

Sample ballot
4" x 11", black and white, "McGovern for President/Manhattan/Tues Nov. 7th, 6 A.M.-9 P.M.," Democratic slate from President to district assembly person................. **5.00**
4-1/4" x 12-1/2", black on pale green, 6th Congressional District of PA, April 26, 1960 primary, front shows Nixon along with

Republican Congressional candidate, horizontal crease lines 9.00

Shopping bag, 13" x 16", "Humphrey's My Bag," paper, handles imprinted on both sides in red, white, and blue, 1968 ..... 10.00

Sign, 12" x 18", "No Parking" during Reagan inauguration, white cardboard, blue and red printing, blue shield, 1981 .... 35.00

Sticker
5-3/4" x 6", red, white, and blue shield shape, "LBJ USA," day-glo, blue tone photo in center, white

silhouette of country, copyright D.N.C. 1964 .... 4.00

8" x 11", 30 1-3/4" circular peel-off stickers used in 1968 because of delay in delivery of Humphrey buttons, read "If I Had A Button It Would Say Humphrey/Muskie," unused 3.00

Poodles

In the 1950s, poodles were supreme! From poodle skirts to television lamps, they were the favorites of many kids. Collectors enjoy reliving some of that nostalgia at flea markets by finding those friendly pink, white, or black poodles they loved as a kid.

Poodles, pair of lamps, each with white ceramic poodle, applied "coleslaw"-type fur, wooden base, original wiring and lamp shade, **$45.**

Ashtray, black, some wear to ear and face, 4-1/2" 5.00

Autograph dog, white vinyl, signatures, 1950s, 4-1/2" x 7" 18.00

Beanie Baby, Gigi, MWBT and protector 18.00

Cookie jar, American Bisque .. 65.00

Figure, white, pink tongue, gold accents, Norcrest, 7-3/4" h 30.00

Jewelry box, wood, white, poodle dec, sgd "Kellerman Jewel Case, Japan," 1960s, 10" x 6" 25.00

Lamp, television type, poodle and puppy, mkd "Kron," 1950s, 13" h 160.00

Pin
Beau, sterling, 1-1/2" x 1-3/4" 35.00
Stein, Parisian Poodle, orange body, ivory pom poms, purple hair bow, mkd "Lea Stein, Paris" on clasp, 1-1/2" x 1-1/2" 95.00
Tortolani, gold-tone, faux pearls and red rhinestone eye, 1-1/2" x 2-1/4" 85.00

Pillow, poodle design, tiny rhinestone accents, tassels on each corner, 16" sq 165.00

Pincushion, metal and fabric, nodding head and tail 35.00

Planter, ceramic, pink, c1940, 6-1/2" h, 8-1/2" w, 3-1/2" d.... 45.00

Playing cards, yellow and blue backgrounds, Congress Playing Cards, Cell-U-Tone Finish, used 35.00

Purse, wool, gold embellishment, large 50.00

Salt and pepper shakers, pr, egg shape, one with yellow poodle,

Poodles, figure, one poodle pulling cart with female passenger holding matching umbrella, white, applied "coleslaw" type fur, 4-1/2" l, 5-1/4" h, **$130.**

other with blue poodle, flowers, butterfly, raised relief, orig plastic stoppers and Enesco stickers 25.00

Toy, pink poodle talking on phone, wind-up 50.00

Wall plaque, chalk, white head, illegible imp mark, 4-1/2", 4-1/4" w 30.00

Popeye

Popeye! Popeye the Sailor Man, started as a supporting character in the comic strip *The Thimble Theatre* on January 17, 1929. This comic strip was drawn by Elzie Seager and revolved around the life of Olive Oyl who most of us identify as Popeye's main squeeze. By 1933, he was seen with another woman on the silver screen when Fleischer Studios paired him up with Betty Boop. After nearly 600 cartoons, our hero Popeye is still faithful to his gal Olive Oyl and his pal Wimpy. Today the Fleischer cartoons are available on video and often seen on Superstation TBS and the Cartoon Network, as well as striding into collectors open arms at our favorite flea markets.

Bank, Popeye sitting, silver, Leonard, 1980 .... **15.00**

Belt buckle, Popeye with spinach, Lee, 1980.................................. **8.00**

Big little book, Whitman
Ghost Ship to Treasure Island, 1967 .... **8.00**
Popeye and the Jeep Book, 1937 .... **25.00**
Wimpy the Hamburger Eater Book, 1938.................................. **25.00**

Book
Adventures of Popeye, Saalfield, 1934................................ **35.00**
Little Pops the Spinach Burgers Book, Random House, 1981 .... **5.00**
Olive Oyl and Swee' Pea Wash Up Book, Tuffy Books, 1980.... **4.00**

Bookends, pr, Popeye and Brutus, ceramic, Vandor, 1980........... **20.00**

Bowl, National Home Products, plastic, 1979............................ **6.00**

Card game, House of Games, 1978 .... **8.00**

Charm, celluloid, 1930s **15.00**

Chocolate mold, metal, 1940s **35.00**

Christmas ornament, Season's Greetings, Presents, 1989........ **8.00**

Colorforms, Popeye the Weatherman, 1959 .... **20.00**

Coloring book, *Popeye and Swee' Pea Coloring Book*, Whitman, #1056-31, 1970 .... **7.00**

Doll
Brutus, Presents, 1985.......... **12.00**
Olive Oyl, Dakin, 1960s, 8" h **25.00**
Popeye, Chicago Herald American, 1950s **30.00**

Egg cup and mug, Magna, Great Britain, 1989 .... **15.00**

Game, Popeye's Sliding Boards and Ladders, Warren Built-Rite, 1958 .... **12.00**

Give-A-Show Projector, Kenner **35.00**

Gumball machine, Hasbro, 1968 .... **10.00**

Jack in the box, Mattel, 1961 .. **60.00**

Mechanical pencil, Eagle, 1929, 10-1/2" l **30.00**

Mirror, Popeye lifting weights, Freelance, 1979........................ **7.00**

Paint book, *Giant Paint Book*, Whitman, 1937...................... **75.00**

Paperweight, Popeye Eats Del Monte Spinach, 1937 .... **50.00**

Pencil case, Hassenfield Bros, red, 1950s...................................... **25.00**

Snow globe, Olive Oyl and Swee' Pea, Presents, 1989......................... **7.00**

Squeeze toy, Wimpy, Cribmates, 1979 .... **12.00**

Suspenders, Popeye and Olive Oyl, KFS, 1979, blue........................ **6.00**

Toss game, Rosebud Art, 1935 **50.00**

TV tray, KFS, 1979..................... **8.00**

Umbrella, KFS, 1979, blue and white **12.00**

Porcelier

Porcelain light fixtures, small appliances and a variety of tableware were some of the items produced by Porcelier Manufacturing Company, which was in business between 1926 and 1954. Collectors look for flawless items, wanting any gold trim to be unworn and items such as light fixtures to have their original pulls.

Coffeepot
Basketweave pattern, wildflower decal **75.00**
Dutch couple, 12-3/4" h **85.00**

Coffee set, percolator, sugar and creamer, lavender-blue bell platinum design................... **130.00**

Creamer, Hostess Field Flowers, platinum trim........................ **17.50**

Light fixture
Ceiling-mount, two sockets, white

Porcelier, teapot, nautical motif, 7-1/2" h, **$20.**

with pink lilacs, needs rewired, no mounting hardware, 11" x 6-1/4"................................. **30.00**
Wall-mount, circular back, socket arm, white with red roses, gold accents, rewired, replaced socket **100.00**

Salt and pepper shakers, pr, floral design, 3-1/2" h **12.00**

Teapot
    Chevron, orange, three cup.. **60.00**
    Nautical, shows sailboats, 8" h
        .... **48.00**

Hearthside, rim chip, 6-3/4" h
    .... **25.00**

Waffle iron, Barock-Colonia, gold
    dots variation...................... **160.00**

Postcards

Ever wonder what happened to all those postcards tourists have sent over the decades? Postcard collectors are searching flea markets for them. Some buyers specialize in local history cards, while others seek a specific maker or artist. Most are reasonably priced, but recently some rare postcards have sold for record prices.

Postcard, real photo, swimmers, unused, **$5.**

Advertising
    Case Stem Tractor, salesroom,
      Columbus, OH **60.00**
    Ford, 3-1/2" x 5-3/4", black, white,
      gray, and orange, cartoon with
      couple speeding down road in
      Ford convertible, "If you own a
      Ford the world laughs at you or
      with you," man at lower right
      without shoes says "Where did
      you get that roller skate," artist
      sgd "Cobb X. Hinn," Wellsboro,
      PA, Aug 1915 postmark ... **20.00**
    Kellogg's, Tony the Tiger, Tony with
      camper's gear, pointing to sign
      post, mid-1960s, 3-5/8" x 5-5/8"
      .... **15.00**

Airline, issued by airline, unused
    Pluna, Uruguay, Boeing 737... **6.00**
    Trans-Canada Airlines, Viscount
      at Windsor Airport, Windsor,
      Ontario, Canada................. **8.00**

Bank, Buffalo, NY, Buffalo Savings
    Bank, Buffalo Square, 1900s ... **6.50**

Baseball, Palace of Fans Ballpark,
    Cincinatti, stamped "Sept 18 1908"
    .... **125.00**

Cats, four kittens, "Greetings from the
    Kills," early 1900s **6.00**

Christmas, little girl and doll, silk
    insert, Wolf and Co., NY, writing on
    back **10.00**

Dogs
    Happy Birthday, "We're sending
      these puppies to say, Have

a Happy Birthday," photo of
    beagles by Roberts **6.00**
    Pekingese, "Just a Few Lines," B B
      London, Series No. G 53, printed
      in Germany **9.00**
    Scottish Terriers, sgd "M. Gear,"
      published by Valentine & Sons,
      Ltd., Dundee and London,
      unused.............................. **30.00**

Easter, Easter angel, early 1900, never
    used **12.00**

Happy Birthday, 3-1/2" x 5-1/2",
    embossed, colorful flowers, early
    1900s...................................... **4.50**

Hold to light, used
    Art Nouveau couple dancing
      .... **35.00**
    Cat and Mouse, kissing couple
      .... **15.00**
    Cinderella, 1900, Belgium.... **85.00**
    Girl with Umbrella **30.00**
    US Treasury Building, Washington,
      DC **25.00**

National Air Races, 3-1/4" x
    5-1/2", glossy black and white,
    1935, unused **20.00**

NY Yankees, 3-1/2" x 5-1/2", glossy
    color, player, facsimile signature,
    Dexter Press Inc., 1971.......... **12.00**

Pretty lady
    Cowgirl on horseback, The Belle of
      the Plain, traces of glue...... **8.00**
    Dear Heart, pretty lady wearing
      large hat, copyright 1908,
      previously glued into album
      .... **10.00**

Postcard, New National Museum,
Washington, D.C., 1913 postmark, **$3.**

Postcard, Christmas, Merry Christmas, striped kitten in heart, holly and gold trim, German, **$9.**

Railroad, chrome
    Erie Railroad **3.50**
    Milwaukee Railroad **3.00**
    Southern Pacific Limited **3.00**
    Southern Pacific Railroad **3.00**
    Steam Town USA.................... **2.00**
    Vista-Dome Zephyr................ **3.50**

Restaurant, Hollywood Cabaret
    Restaurant, Broadway, 48th, NYC
    .... **10.00**

School scene, children posed in front
    of brick building, names identified
    on back, 1910, real photo...... **20.00**

Socialist Labor Party, 3-1/2" x
    5-1/2", black and white, scene
    "Solidarity of Labor," c1920, unused
    .... **25.00**

Street scene
    Red Lion Inn, Quakertown, PA,
      trolley, passengers............ **30.00**
    Santa Fe, chrome................... **3.00**

Valentine
    Cupid with arrows, "You stole a
      heart! Love's law is plain, that
      bids you part, with one again"
      .... **6.00**
    Two cupids tending love fire, 1900
      .... **8.75**

Posters

Posters have long been an effective communication tool. Their size, bright colors, and great illustrations caught the attention of many passersby. Today they are treasured and becoming more available at flea markets.

For additional listings, see *Warman's Antiques and Collectibles Price Guide* and *Warman's Americana & Collectibles,* as well as Movie Posters in this edition.

Poster, Grateful Dead, April 1988, Centrum, Worcester, Massachusetts, hot pink and blue, **$50.**

Abbie Hoffman, Steal This Poster, May 13, 1982 lecture at New York Univ, 11" x 17" 75.00

Air France - North Africa, Villemot, stylized imagery of mosques and minarets, lavenders, yellow, and blues against sky blue background, plane and Pegasus logo, c1950, 24" x 39" 225.00

Bridge of Peace, Venette Willard Shearer, anti-war poster from American Friends Service Committee, National Council to Prevent War, children of all nations play beneath text of song of peace, c1936, 16" x 22" 125.00

Buddha and Heartstone, Polish magician performing tricks, English and Polish text, c1914, 14" x26" 100.00

Carry On With Franklin D. Roosevelt, portrait in gravure,

black letters against white ground, framed, 1936, 9" x 11" 15.00

Clyde, Beatty-Cole Bros Combined Circus, the World's Largest Circus, Clyde Beatty in Person, Roland Butler, Lion tamer, 19" x 26" 90.00

Democratic, national and PA state candidates, 1984, glossy paper, 17" x 22" 20.00

Ediswan Electric Home Iron, full color, showing 1930s electric iron, c1935, 11" x 18" 60.00

Family Fun Night, Disneyland, May 16, 1971, 12" x 9" 45.00

Fight For Women's Liberation, Vote Socialist Workers 1970 NY State Campaign, red, black, and white, 11" x 17"...................... 45.00

Give It Your Best, 48-star U.S. flag, World War II, 28-1/2" x 20"... 60.00

I Want You, Uncle Sam Army recruiting poster, 1975, 14" x 11" 80.00

Poster, Golden Gate International Exposition, 1940, 18" x 13-1/2", **$575.**

Poster, orange and blue, psychedelic, **$35.**

Launch of USS Ronald Reagan CVN 76 aircraft carrier, July 12, 2003, full color, 27" x 40" 25.00

Patty Hearst, Wanted by the FBI, black and white photos, 1974, 10-1/2" x 16", ... 45.00

The World of Pogo, Walt Kelly's menagerie of characters from Okefenokee Swamp, made for exhibit held at the Museum of Fine Arts, Springfield, MA, 1971, 17" x 11"... 55.00

This Home is For Hoover, black and white, 8-1/2" x 11-1/2" ... 30.00

Welcome President Nixon to Pekin, dark blue on bright orange on white, 1973, 14" x 20"....... 25.00

Women's Action Pentagon, Washington, DC, Sunday, Nov. 16, 1975, black, white, and brown, 9-1/2" x 16-3/8" 45.00

Powder Jars

Containers to hold powder were a staple of a lady's dressing table. The boxes were often decorative or whimsical. Today collectors are charmed by them.

Celluloid lid, frosted green glass jar base, wear to emb black design on top, 3-1/2" h, 4-1/4" w 28.00

Glass

Clear, elephant on top, raised trunk 28.00

Clear, lady sitting in front of beveled mirror 55.00

Clear, lady's portrait under lid, reverse painted highlights, box shape, wear to paint, 3" x 4" 85.00

Clear, My Pet 40.00

Frosted, green, Art Deco lady 250.00

Frosted, green, Cameo lady 225.00

Frosted, green, Crinoline Girl 145.00

Frosted, green, hand painted flowers 30.00

Frosted, pink, elephant, trunk down 65.00

Frosted, pink, lovebirds........ 60.00

Hobnail, clear, opalescent white hobnails, 4-3/8" d............. 25.00

Iridescent, marigold, figural poodle on top 32.00

Pink, Annette 75.00

Musical, silvertone metal, 8-1/2" h 60.00

Powder jar, colonial lady, blue opaque glass, **$65.**

Precious Moments Figurines

Created by Samuel J. Butcher in 1978 and produced by Enesco, Precious Moments is now in its third decade of production. This popular line of collectibles features cute kids with inspiring messages. The collectibles include figurines, mugs, ornaments, and plates. Collectors should enjoy their Precious Moments, but not hope to reap great rewards on the re-sale of these objects.

Bell, 1994, Christmas................ 10.00

Bookmark, brass, Your Love is So Uplifting, 2-1/2" h, MOC......... 6.00

Cake top, Lord Bless You and Keep You, bride and groom, 6" h ... 65.00

Christmas ornament

God bless you this Christmas, seal 15.00

Holiday expressions, 1995.... 12.00

May your Christmas be gigantic, elephant........................... 15.00

Doll

Boy, 8" h................................ 10.00

Graduate 15.00

Figure

Angel, blowing trumpet 30.00

Birthday Club, Clown Drummer, Charter Member, 3-3/4" h 80.00

Blessing of Showers, elephant and mouse 25.00

Boy in overalls, candy canes in flowerpot.......................... 35.00

Bride 20.00

God Understands, triangle mark, string tag 125.00

Healing Begins with Forgiveness 40.00

Jonathan and David, it's what inside that counts 90.00

Love Lifted Me, older boy helping younger friend tumbling from wagon, 5-1/2" h 80.00

Peacemaker, 1979, 5" h......... 55.00

This is Your Day to Shine, little girl being helped by kitten and puppy, 6" h 80.00

Thou Art Mine, little boy and girl with turtle, writing in sand, 5-1/4" h............................. 70.00

We All Have Bad Hair Days 30.00

You Can't Take It with You 20.00

Mug, 1992 .... 5.00

Stationery, note cards and envelopes, assorted designs, orig box....... 5.00

Precious Moments, children reading, **$60.**

Precious Moments, doll, clutching baby in blanket, **$35.**

Precious Moments, clown with balloons, **$50.**

Presley, Elvis

"You ain't nothin' but a hound dog…" Elvis was quite a hit in his day. Even after his death in 1977, memorabilia sales remain strong. Fans still flock to his home and swoon when they hear his songs.

Album, LP
Elvis, RCA Victor, 1964 .... **30.00**
Elvis Fun in Acapulco, RCA Victor, 1963 .... **40.00**
Elvis Presley, calendar insert for Girls! Girls! Girls, RCA Victor, 1963 .... **70.00**
Personally Elvis, blue label, double pocket, silhouette **50.00**
Spinout, black label, DOT, RCA, white top **35.00**

Barbie, Barbie Loves Elvis, 1996, MIB **130.00**

Book, *Operation Elvis,* Alan Levy, Henry Holt & Co., 1960, hardcover, dj **35.00**

Calendar, 1977, Tribute to Elvis, Boxcar Enterprises, 12" x 13" **50.00**

Cookie jar, riding in car **90.00**

Decanter, McCormick Distillery, porcelain

Music box base plays "Blue Hawaii," Aloha Elvis, shows Arizona Memorial, 16" h **295.00**
Music box base plays "Loving You," mkd "Young Elvis '55," 16" h, MIB **275.00**
Portrait bust, orig booklet titled "1935-1977, The End of an Era," 15" h, MIB **275.00**
Singing pose, 14" h, MIB.... **275.00**

Flicker button, black and white photos of Elvis playing guitar, titled "Love Me Tender," ©1958 Elvis Presley Enterprises, 2-1/4" d. **25.00**

Magazine, *Saturday Evening Post*, July/August, 1985, "Legends that Won't Die" **10.00**

Menu, Sahara Tahoe, 1972 .... **72.00**

Necklace, Love Me Tender, heart shaped pendant, ©Elvis Presley Enteprises 1956, 13-1/2" l, MOC **215.00**

Paperback book, *Elvis Presley: The King is Dead*, Martin A. Grove, 1977 .... **6.00**

Pinback button, Baltimore Loves Elvis Presley, Charm City USA, 1977, 3-1/2" d **40.00**

Portrait, sgd by artist Ivan Jesse Curtin, mounted on wooden frame, c1960.................................... **125.00**

Puzzle, The King, Springbok, 1992, 1000 pieces **50.00**

Sheet music, *Love Me*, 1954 ... **35.00**

Tab, litho tin, blue, gold lettering, "I Love Elvis," metallic gold background, 1970s, 2" d........ **15.00**

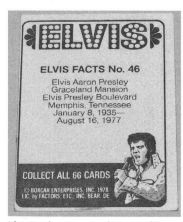

Elvis Presley, Facts Card No. 46 of 66, Boxcar Enterprises, 1978, **$10.**

Elvis Presley, clock, figural, legs swing, **$40.**

Elvis Presley, poster, autographed, **$750.**

Princess Diana

Her tragic death in 1997 stopped the world for a brief time. Collectibles ranging from things made during her lifetime, such as wedding commemoratives, and later memorial pieces, are readily available at flea markets.

Ale glass, Royal Wedding......... **32.00**
Beanie baby, purple bear **32.00**

Beer can, Felinfoel Brewery, Wales, 1981, official Royal Wedding

commemorative, bottom opened **15.00**

Brooch, memorial heart pin, orig card 50.00

Calendar, 1998, still sealed...... 10.00

Coach replica, Matchbox, replica of coach used in wedding, made for Her Majesty's 40th Anniversary, limited edition, MIB.............. 65.00

Doll, porcelain, flower girl, pastel yellow dress, white roses, Danbury Mint, 11" h........................... 175.00

First-day cover, Marshall Islands 3.00

Princess Diana, card game, British Monarchs, made to commemorate royal wedding July 29, 1981, Grimaud Playing Cards, ©J. M. Simons, June 1981, **$10.**

Postcard, birthday card type, photo of Diana and Charles, unused 10.00

Slippers, figural head of sleeping Diana and Charles, c1980, unused, orig tags 48.00

Tea towel, Irish linen, portraits of Diana and Charles, Prince of Wales plumes, 28-1/2" x 18-1/2"...... 20.00

Tin, engagement photo, banner on top "Royal Wedding, July 1981," mkd "Regent Ware, Made in England".............................. 20.00

Trading card set, full unopened package, Press Pass................ 95.00

Prints

Prints are a great way for the common folk to have copies of fine artwork for their homes or offices. Currier & Ives was one of numerous publishers that reproduced a variety of artwork. Today's limited-edition prints compete for the same collector dollars.

For additional listings, see *Warman's Antiques and Collectibles Price Guide.*

Reproduction alert.

Prints, "The Christmas Martyrs," photogravure, Gebbie & Husson Co., 10-3/4" x 16-1/4", **$25.**

Baille, James, publisher, colored lithograph, period frame
The Marriage, 1849, 12" x 8-1/2" 115.00
The Young Bride, 1848, 17" x 13" 75.00

Boileu, Philip, child, c1914, "The Associated Sunday Magazines" cover, Feb. 1, 1914, sgd lower right, 16" x 20 frame 45.00

Currier & Ives
A Scene on the Susquehanna, C#5415, farm on one side of river, flock of sheep, damage to modern gilt frame, repaired tears, 21-1/4" w, 18-1/4" h 175.00

Jay Eye See, Record 2:10, cherry frame, stains, minor damage, edge repair, 13-3/8" x 17-5/8" 165.00
Lady Washington, period veneer frame with chips, slight stains, 1 small pc missing from margin 275.00
Meeting of the Waters, 14" x 10" orig frame, orig wooden backing 75.00

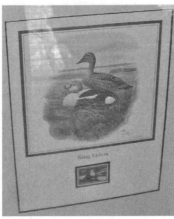

Print, framed and matted 1992 Federal King Eiders duck, **$15** stamp, print, numbered #452/1000, pencil signed "Balke," **$125.**

Print, Cherokee Chief Sequoyah, hand colored engraving, framed, **$45.**

Fox, R. Atkinson
A Perfect Melody, c1920-25, pseudonym sgd "DeForest" lower right, title lower center, 7" x 9" orig frame......................... 50.00
Clipper Ship, c1920-25, unsigned, 20" x 12" period frame..... 40.00
The Old Mill, c1920-25, unsigned, 9" x 12" frame.................. 60.00

Kellogg & Comstock
The Angler, girl reading letter to man fishing, grain-decor frame, margin tear, stains, fold line, 9-3/4" x 14"..................... **120.00**
The Fruit, walnut cross-corner frame, short margin tear, 10" x 14"............................... **60.00**
Napoleon, hand-colored, 1870, 17" x 13"................................ **225.00**

Pressler, Gene, *Cinderella*, c1920-25, sgd lower right, titled, 8" x 11" orig metal frame **45.00**

Remington, Frederick, *Indians in Canoe*, c1900, sgd lower left, 16" x 12" period frame, damaged mat **35.00**

Soyer, Raphael, *Bust of a Girl*, lithograph in black, red and blue on paper, edition of 300, sgd "Raphael Soyer" in pencil lower right,

numbered "86/300" in pencil lower left, image size 18-3/8" x 13-5/8", framed, over 1" margins...... **210.00**

Unsigned, New Castle church, 1939, matted, framed..................... **15.00**

Walker, George H. and Co., publisher, Joe L. Jones, lithographer, *Deacon Jones' One Hoss Shay, No. 2*, lithograph in blue and black, hand coloring, on paper, identified in

Punch Boards

Feel like taking a chance? For those lucky collectors who enjoy finding punch boards, flea markets often offer several choices.

Ace High, 13" x 17", deck of cards jackpot **90.00**

Barrel of Cigarettes, 10" x 10", Lucky Strike Green **44.00**

Basketball Push Card, 6" x 9", 1¢, candy prize **10.00**

Big Game, 8" x 10-1/2" **30.00**

Candy Special, 4-1/2" x 7-1/2", penny candy board................ **24.00**

Extra Bonus, 13" x 12" **40.00**

Five on One, 11" x 11"............. **18.00**

Good Punching, 9-1/2" x 10", cowboy motif......................... **36.00**

Home Run Derby, 10" x 12", green baseball park **75.00**

Jackpot Bingo, 10" x 8", thick card jackpot **10.00**

Lu Lu Board, 10" x 11", colored tickets **28.00**

More Smokes, 10-1/2" x 10-1/2" **24.00**

Nestle's Chocolate, 9" x 8-1/2", 2¢ board............................... **45.00**

Odd Pennies, 6-3/4" x 11", 2¢ and 3¢ board................................... **45.00**

Palm Chart, 20" x 11-1/2", 1936, orig envelope................................... **8.00**

Pocket Board, 2" x 2-3/4"......... **8.00**

Professor Charley, 1946, Superior Mfg. Typical 25¢ cash board **18.00**

Speedy Tens, 10" x 13"............. **18.00**

Tavern Maid, 9-1/2" x 13-1/2", cans of beer prize........................... **55.00**

Win A Buck, 4-1/2" x 7-1/2" ... **12.00**

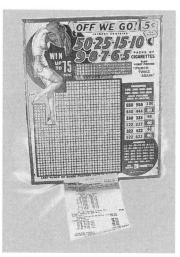

Punchboards, Off We Go!, 5¢ punch, unused, 10" x 12-1/2", **$35.**

Puppets

Puppets come in all shapes and sizes, from hand operated to elaborate marionettes to ventriloquist dummies and little push puppets, giving collectors a real variety. The fun part about collecting puppets is that all probably have made people laugh and smile, and probably still have lots of smiles left to share with their new owners.

Hand, all used condition
Babes in Toyland, Gund **35.00**
Boxers, 8-1/2" h, fabric, soft vinyl or rubber painted head, one with ivory fleshtone color, molded crew cut hair, second with charcoal fleshtone, molded black hair, 1960s, price for pr.... **20.00**

Bugs Bunny, rubber head, Zany, 1940s **35.00**
Casper, Commonwealth Toys, 1960s **15.00**
Droop-A-Long, vinyl head, Ideal **25.00**
Elmer Fudd, rubber head, Zany, 1940s **30.00**

Flora, Fairy Godmother, 1958 .... **60.00**
Foghorn Leghorn, rubber head, Zane, 1940s **30.00**
Gumby, Lakeside, fabric and soft vinyl, 1965, 9" h **15.00**
Magilla Gorilla, Ideal **40.00**
Prince Charming, Gund, 1959, 10" h **20.00**

String puppet, Pinocchio toymaker, celluloid head, wood body, **$35.**

Red Rose Chimp, 8" h, fabric and soft vinyl, yellow cap inscribed "Red Rose," 1960s **20.00**
Sylvester, rubber head, Zany, 1940s **32.00**
Tweety, rubber head, Zany, 1940s **30.00**
Woody Woodpecker, Mattel, pull string voice box, 1963 ...... **35.00**

Marionette, all used condition
Batman, 15" h, painted plaster head and hands, wood body and legs, fabric costume, 1960s 40.00
Clown.................................... 42.00
Howdy Doody, cloth body, vinyl head and hands, body mkd "Goldberger Doll Co., Made in Hong Kong," head mkd "Eegee," 12" h 500.00
McCarthy, Charlie, composition, 12" h 125.00
Pinocchio, Walt Disney Enterprises, composition, 12" h 125.00
Princess Winter, Spring, Summer, Fall, 14" l 500.00
Siamese Temple Dancer 130.00

Hand puppet, plush, wolf, felt tong and fangs, glass eyes, **$5.**

String puppet, Wonder Woman, Madison Ltd., Hackensack, NJ, MIB, **$20.**

Push puppet, used condition
Atom Ant.............................. 25.00
Cowboy on white horse, by Kohner, Socko label 45.00
Donald Duck 30.00
Mickey Mouse 30.00
Olive Oyl............................. 35.00
Pluto 25.00
Popeye 35.00
Santa Mouse 35.00
Terry the Tiger 30.00

Ventriloquist dummy, all used condition
Bozo.................................... 42.00
Jerry Mahoney...................... 60.00
Three Stooges 100.00
Willie Talk, Horsman 42.00

Purinton Pottery

Purinton Pottery is another Ohio pottery company that made dinnerware and some table wares. Founded in Wellsville, the company was in business from 1936 to 1959.

For additional listings see *Warman's Americana & Collectibles.*

Bank, Raggedy Andy, 6-1/2" h . 80.00

Casserole, cov, Apple, oval....... 25.00

Cereal bowl
Intaglio 12.00
Pennsylvania Dutch.............. 15.00

Chop plate, Apple.................... 20.00

Coffee mug, Plaid...................... 3.00

Coffeepot, cov, Apple.............. 60.00

Creamer
Apple.................................... 12.00
Normandy Plaid 40.00

Cruet set, Intaglio.................... 36.00

Cup and saucer
Estate 12.00
Normandy Plaid 17.50

Dinner plate
Fruits 15.00
Intaglio 16.00
Normandy Plaid 20.00
Plaid.................................... 15.00

Dutch jug, Apple, 6" h, 8" w 35.00

Grill plate, Apple, 12" d 25.00

Honey jug, Red Ivy 35.00

Marmalade, cov, Maywood 32.00

Purinton Pottery, canister set, revolving, each section labeled and decorated with different fruit motif, **$65.**

Purinton Pottery, flour canister, 9-1/2" h, **$50.**

Pitcher
Apple.................................. 45.00
Fruits 32.00

Platter, Intaglio, 12-1/2".......... 22.00

Relish dish, Fruits, divided, three parts, handle........................ 18.50

Roll tray, Intaglio.................... 35.00

Salt and pepper shakers, pr
Apple.................................. 18.00
Plaid................................... 15.00

Serving dish, Intaglio, 11-1/4" 22.00

Snack set, Apple 32.50

Sugar, cov, Apple, 5" h.............. 38.50
Teapot
Maywood............................. 35.00
Red Ivy.............................. 35.00
Tumbler, Apple 20.00
Vegetable
Intaglio 25.00
Normandy Plaid, divided..... 50.00
Wall pocket, Apple, 4" h........ 130.00

Purses

Here's an item most ladies wouldn't be without. Collectors are intrigued with the styles, colors, and different textures of purses from bygone eras.

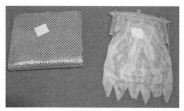

Purses, evening bags, both Whiting & Davis, left: silvered fabric, clutch type, **$45;** right: enameled pastel Art Deco type design, gold-toned frame, original fringe, **$65.**

Alligator, brown, designer type 50.00

Bamboo, boxy style, 13" x 14" . 65.00

Beaded
Enameled pink, blue, and yellow, frame stamped "Whiting and Davis" 200.00
White with pastel colored beaded flowers, mkd "Made in Hong Kong," 9" x 5"................... 40.00

Evening
Brocade, Art Deco, engraved gold filled frame...................... 75.00
Faille, black, marcasite set mounting, gold onyx monogram, c1930 .... 70.00
Satin, pink, silver bugle beads, ivory colored seed pearls, silver frame and clasp, trimmed in white rhinestones, silver chain handle, Jolle Original, 9" x 7-1/2" x 1"................................. 110.00

Leather, tooled
Mexican, brown, white inserts 45.00
Saddle shape........................ 60.00

Lucite, trapezoid, cream colored, gold-tone frame, rigid handle, snap clasp, navy lining and side gussets, c1950, 8" w........................... 185.00

Macramé, yellow twine, olive colored wooden beads, shoulder type, hand made 5.00

Mesh, silver and enamel, R. Blackington & Co., mesh link bag, frame enameled with white

Purses, coin, imitation alligator skin, **$5.**

geometric pattern, green squares, lavender border, interior engraved with name, silk cord strap, early 20th C, 6" w 250.00

Plastic, white opaque, applied pink rose, green leaves, goldtone fittings 25.00

Straw, two handles, gold-tone ball type clasp, c1950................... 20.00

Puzzles

What's got lots of pieces and hours of fun? Puzzles. Puzzles have been around about as long as the America, starting as ways to keep children occupied. By the 1890s, adults wanted to have some fun too, leading the creation of more intricate examples. Ask the dealer if the puzzle is complete and if any pieces are damaged. Missing pieces can drastically reduce the price.

For additional listings, see *Warman's Antiques and Collectibles Price Guide.*

Jigsaw puzzle, A Constructional Victory Jigsaw Puzzle, Union Castle Liner, lithograph of ocean liner on box, red plaid sides, **$295.**

Aquaman and Merz, Whitman, 100 pcs, 1968 .... 20.00

Babes in Toyland, Jaymar, 1961 .... 20.00

Blondie & Dagwood, Featured Funnies, 1930s 50.00

Captain Marvel, Reed & Associates, 1940s, orig envelope 50.00

Cunard Line, Queen Mary in Trafalgar Square, Chad Valley, W. McDowell artist, 1936, 300 pcs, replaced box, 11-1/2" x 16" ... 65.00

Dudley Do-Right, Whitman, 1975 .... 15.00

Dumbo, Jaymar Specialty 11" x 14" 15.00

Evening on Grand Canal, Venice, #2, Pastime Puzzles, Parker Brothers, plywood, c1930, 150 pcs, 20 figural pcs, orig box, 9-3/4" x 10" 60.00

First In The Heart Of His Countrymen, Corker Picture Puzzle, Whitman Publishing Co. 15.00

Game of Chess, Pickwick, Hoadley House, 1930s, 365 pcs, four replaced, replaced box, 17-3/4" x 13-3/4" 75.00

Journey to the moon, Life series, ©1969 by Time Inc., 500 pcs, orig box 15.00

Land of the Midnight Sun, W. E. Bryant, 160 pcs, one figural pcs, "B" signature pc, orig box, mail lending library, 12" x 10" 50.00

Lending Library, Painting the Vase, Goddard artist, Eugene Sexton, orig box, 16" x 21-3/4" 150.00

Mother Goose, 1954, Sifco Co., 10" x 8" 16.00

Premier, Kidnapped (bear), Milton Bradley, 200 pcs, eight figural pcs, orig box, 12" x 9" 50.00

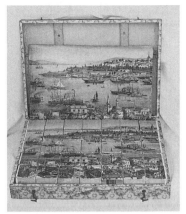

Block puzzle, German, five original lithographed scenes included in original box, 18" x 13-1/8", **$295.**

Sunset, #7, Pastime Puzzles, Parker Brothers, plywood, c1928, 126 pcs, 12 figural pcs, orig box, 7" x 9" 55.00

Vatican Pavilion, New York World's Fair, 1964-65, 10" x 14-1/4" frame tray 12.00

Pyrex

Pyrex was developed by the researchers at Corning Glass in the early 1910s. By 1915, Corning launched its Pyrex line with a 12-piece set. Fry Glass Company was granted permission to produce Pyrex under its Fry Oven Glass label in 1920. Cooks today still use many Pyrex products. This kitchenware collectible is just starting to become popular with many people. Don't overlook advertising and paper ephemera dealing with Pyrex.

Baker, cov, delphite blue, 6-3/4" x 4-1/4" 22.00

Bowl, tab handles, bright red ext., gold pinecone dec 45.00

Bean pot, cov, clear, two-qt 12.00

Casserole set, set of three graduating from 1 to 2-1/2 quarts, pink and white, clear glass lids, 1950s 90.00

Coffeemaker, Flameware, #7826B, octagonal stick handle, closed loop lid, aluminum basket and pump 75.00

Dinner plate, white, lime green borders, 12-1/2" d, set of six . 90.00

Double boiler, mkd "Flameware" 17.50

Freezer server, Butterprint 12.00

Mixing bowl set
   Primary colors, set of four nested bowls, solid colored exterior, white int., slight wear 90.00
   Shenandoah, set of three, NRFB 85.00

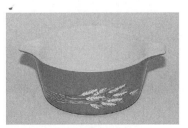

Pyrex, serving dish, wheat pattern, 7-1/2" d, **$8.**

Pie plate, clear, 10" 10.00

Refrigerator set, eight pcs
   Butterprint 45.00
   Early American pattern, 1961 .... 60.00
   Primary colors, two small, one medium, one large, clear glass lids 75.00

Saucepan, two qt, straight glass handle, pouring lip 65.00

Serving dish, Bluebelle 20.00

Vegetable dish, divided, red ext. 20.00

Pyrography

It's an interesting concept: give someone a hot tool and tell him to go burn a design on a piece of wood. That is essentially what pyrography was all about. Skilled artisans introduced the form to America in the mid-1800s, but it became a hobby for the masses around the turn of the century, when several companies began offering items with designs stamped on them for burning. The Flemish Art Company of New York was the largest producer of pyrography products, and the term Flemish Art has become synonymous with burnt wood pieces of that era. The hobby was most popular from 1890 to 1915.

Bench, small child holding ball, another child in high chair, red poinsettia flowers, lift seat **75.00**

Book rack, folding, 18" l **80.00**

Box
Book-shaped, woman wearing crown, two pcs, 1905, 4" x 3-1/2" x 1-1/2" **45.00**
Hand-painted, cherries design **42.00**

Game board, triangle-design surface, owl on reverse, 11" x 14" **110.00**

Glove box, cov, poinsettias, leaves, and "Gloves" on top and inside hinged lid, red painted poinsettias, 10-1/8" w, 3-1/2" d, 2" h **38.00**

Handkerchief box, cov, poinsettias, leaves, and "Handkerchiefs" on top and inside hinged lid, red painted poinsettias, 6-3/4" l, 6-3/4" w, 1" h **32.00**

Plaque
Dutch girl with cookie jar, painted floral border, 12" x 9" **65.00**

Pyrography, box, hand-painted cherries and leaves, broken clasp, 2-1/2" h, 6" square, **$10.**

Gibson Girl, 10" d **165.00**
Indian maiden in headdress, oval **85.00**
Young lady, oval, mkd "Flemish Art Co., New York, No. 859," 1910, 12-1/2" x 8" **95.00**

Plate, ornate design, sgd on back in French **12.00**

Plate rack, fruit motif, 12" h, 42" l **220.00**

Spoon holder, three dancing Dutch girls, slots for eight spoons ... **55.00**

Tray, Dutch couple walking along canal, semi-opaque painted primary colors, 15-1/2" x 9" .. **40.00**

Utensil box, 3" h, 12" w, 9" d . **135.00**

Wastebasket, woman's bust and grapes decor, square, scalloped top, 14" h **70.00**

Quilts

Colorful bits and pieces of material sewn together make up quilts. Wonderful examples can be found at flea markets, from vintage, handmade, one-of-a-kind quilts to newer designer quilts. Carefully examine any quilt before purchasing, look at the design for its aesthetic quality as well as colors. Make sure the fabrics are stable. Check the binding and the back. Feel how heavy the inner layer is to help determine warmth. And don't be afraid to give it a sniff test, too. Depending on the age, design, and fabrics, you probably can't toss an antique quilt into the washer and dryer, so make sure your potential purchase is appealing to all your senses. Remember fabrics may age differently, making some more fragile than others, sometimes in the same quilt. Do consider using quilts for more than bed coverings, they make great wall hangings, informal slipcovers and table coverings, as well as cuddly throws to snuggle under.

There are many excellent quilt identification books available to collectors. Many collectors are also quilt makers and may find the quilt books by KP Books of interest, including Patricia J. Morris and Jeannette T. Muir's *Worth Doing Twice, New Quilts from Old Tops.*

For additional listings, see *Warman's Antiques & Collectibles.*

Quilt, appliqued red and green strawberries, yellow embroidered blossoms, white ground, **$100.**

Broken Star, orange, yellow, green, red, brown, blue, and white painted calico patches, red and white calico Flying Geese border, PA, 19th C 475.00

Crazy, pieced velvet and cotton, multicolored, some embroidery, 1920s, wear and loss to fabrics 75.00

Cross and Crown, yellow, red, and olive patches, yellow borders, red backing, 84" x 83" 450.00

Diamonds, polychrome calico bars forming concentric diamonds, white backing, white edge binding, quilting follows bars, 74" sq 300.00

Eight patch star, red and black bandanna prints, yellow ground 130.00

Floral medallions, pastel pink, green and yellow appliqués, swag border, minor stains, 82" x 90" 420.00

Flying Geese, variant 190.00

Four Patch, green, brown, red, and blue printed calico horizontal panels, diamond and zigzag quilting, Mennonite, PA, 9th C 230.00

Grandmother's Fan, pinks and greens, some fading, staining 45.00

Irish Chain, pink, green, and peach calico, straight green and pink borders, brown calico backing, embroidered with red "B" in lower left hand corner, 6'10" x 6'11" 225.00

Log Cabin, yellow, brown, red, green, brown, pink, and white bars, broad red and black borders, rope quilting, red, yellow, and green calico backing, 81" x 81" 250.00

Martha Washington's Flower Garden, calicos and printed fabrics, predominately yellows, red and tan borders, hand stitched, minor wear, 66" x 86" 300.00

Nine Patch, variation, blue, gray, and tan, white background and backing, 73" x 72" 365.00

Oak Leaf, red and green printed fabric vine border, white ground, late 19th C, 72" x 88", minor stains, marker lines 300.00

Pineapple Medallion, pink calico and white, 76-1/2" x 94 .... 395.00

Pinwheel, red and white 115.00

Serrated Square, pink and green calico, shell and diamond quilted, 82" x 84" 325.00

Shoofly, variant, pink calico, green zigzag 125.00

Star, large eight pointed star in pastels, white ground, white backing, repair at corner, 69" sq 200.00

Starbursts with blocks and bars, multicolored starbursts, pink blocks and bars, complex quilting, reverse stamped "M. A. Darby," paper tag states c1865, PA, scattered staining front and back, one star worn through, 82" x 90" 350.00

Quilt, log cabin, made from reds, black, and purple cotton, scalloped border, **$325.**

Sunbonnet Sue, some wear, 1930s
.... 125.00

Tulips, right pink and green tulips, white ground, figure eight quilting in border, white back, 80-1/2" x 92"
.... 300.00

Quimper

Known for its colorful peasant design, Quimper is a French faience that dates to the 17th century. As times and styles changed, patterns were also influenced but still continued to have a certain charm that is special to Quimper.

For additional listings, see *Warman's Antiques and Collectibles Price Guide* and *Warman's English & Continental Pottery & Porcelain*.

Ashtray, 4-1/2" l, 2-1/2" w, octagonal, male peasant in center, scattered four dot designs, typical florals, blue sponged border, indented rests, yellow striped base, "HB Quimper France C.D. 1154" mark
.... 45.00

Bell, 3-1/4" h, bagpipe-shape, frontal view of female peasant, yellow centered blue dot florals, red and green foliage, molded brown pipe, blue ribbon, bluets on reverse, Porquier Beau Normandy, hairline
.... 85.00

Bowl, cov, band of single stroke red and green florals on bowl, female peasant vertical florals and border band of single stroke florals, yellow and blue lined rim, blue knob, blue dash and yellow outlined scroll handles, mkd "HenRiot Quimper, France," 9" w 195.00

Cake plate, pedestal base, black haired male peasant playing bagpipes, surrounded by floral sprays and floral garland border, pattern repeated on underside and base, mkd "HR Quimper" on front
.... 385.00

Chamberstick, 5" sq, male peasant with staff on one side, single branch of red tipped single stroke flowers on opposite, scattered blue dot designs, rolled blue streaked and orange borders, blue streaked ring handle 170.00

Charger, 15-3/4" w, octagonal, seated male peasant playing bagpipe, standing peasant blowing horn, blue acanthus on yellow border, "HB Quimper" mark 225.00

Cider jug, cov, 7" h, male peasant on front under spout, blue sponged trees and vertical rushes, scattered four blue dot designs, single stroke florals, blue sponged overhead

handle, spout, and knob, mkd "HB Quimper" under spout 210.00

Cup and saucer, male peasant on cup, green and red horizontal single stroke foliage, yellow-centered blue dot flowers, scattered four blue dot designs, blue banded rim, green sponged handle, mkd "HR Quimper" 85.00

Egg cup, 2-3/4" h, attached underplate, female peasant on cup, band of red, blue, and green foliage on base, blue lined wavy rim on cup, "HenRiot Quimper France" mark 175.00

Inkpot, 3" h, 4" w, three lobes, seated female peasant on front, scattered red and green foliage, blue and orange lined rims, blue button know, "Quimper Made in France" mark 295.00

Knife rest, 3-1/2" l, triangle shape, male or female peasant and foliage, blue dash edges, blue sponged ends, mkd "HenRiot Quimper France" on front, price for pr 90.00

Mustard pot, cov, 3-1/2" h, 4" d, band of single stroke orange, red, blue, and green, foliage and flowers on cover and body, blue lined rims, blue dash applied arched handles, "HenRiot Quimper France" mark
.... 145.00

Plate

Center crowing rooster, red and green single stroke floral and yellow-centered blue dot florals in center, border band of single stroke red, green, and blue florals and foliate, mkd "HB Quimper," 9-3/8" d 195.00

Male peasant, green, yellow, blue and rust florals, green and rust border with blue dots, yellow, green, and blue lined rim, "HB" mark, 9" d 300.00

Porringer, 7-1/2" w handle to handle, male peasant in center, vertical foliage, yellow and blue striped border, blue sponged handles, "HB Quimper" mark 165.00

Teapot, 8" h, Breton Broderie pattern, bands of cobalt blue and raised orange chevrons, green enamel dots, white body, "HB Quimper" mark, c1930 .... 295.00

Tray, Breton Broderie pattern, male and female portraits facing each other in center, wide cobalt blue border with raised orange dashes and dots, scalloped rim, "HB Quimper" mark 325.00

Wall pocket, figural bagpipe-shape, typical male peasant, molded blue ribbon at top, brown pipe at side, yellow glaze, "HB Quimper" mark
.... 110.00

Quimper, cereal bowl and underplate, pink and green bands, pink and yellow flowers, tab handles, **$30.**

Radio Characters and Personalities

The golden age of radio created a whole cadre of heroes and characters for the listeners. Like the stars of today, these folks had fan clubs and created premiums and memorabilia to meet the demands of the earliest collectors.

Autograph
Fibber McGee and Molly, Brown Derby menu 120.00
Jones, Spike, radio photo...... 75.00
Lyman, Abe, 8" x 10" glossy black and white fan photo, 1934 .... 10.00

Award certificate, H.C.B. (Hot Cereal Breakfast) Club Grand Award, orig manila mailing envelope, Cream of Wheat text, typed recipient's name, May 4, 1931 .... 15.00

Bank, Uncle Don's Earnest Saver Club, oval, paper label, photo and cartoon illus, Greenwich Savings Bank, New York City, 1930s, 2-1/4" h...... 40.00

Blotter, The Shadow, orange, blue, and white, red silhouette, 1940s 28.00

Book
All About Amos 'n' Andy and Their Creators Correl & Gosden, 1929, 128 pgs, illus 55.00
'R' You Listening? Tony Wons, radio scrapbook, CBS, Reilly & Lee, 1931, 1st ed., dj 9.00

Booklet, Zenith Radios, Burns & Allen, Boswells, 1930s 45.00

Figure, Free Speech Mike, KMPC, Los Angeles, painted plaster figure, top half radio microphone, patriotic hat, call letters 710 KC on base, late 1960s, 5-3/4" h...................... 60.00

Flashlight, Jack Armstrong, cardboard, red metal ends, c1939 .... 25.00

Game, Charlie McCarthy Radio Party Game, orig envelope............. 65.00

Greeting card, get well card, black and white photo of Amos n' Andy, Hall Brothers, 1931, 4-1/2" x 5-1/2" 32.00

Magazine, *Post*
Arthur Godfrey, 1955 .... 10.00
Jack Benny article, 1963 .... 15.00

Map, Jimmy Allen, full color, printed letter on back, 1934 .... 125.00

Membership badge, Pilot Patrol, Phantom 32.00

Newsletter, Jimmy Allen, red, white, and green holiday design and signatures on front cover, black and white photos on back, four pgs 65.00

Patch
Captain Midnight 30.00
Jack Armstrong, Future Champions of America, 1943 .... 20.00

Pencil sharpener, figural, Charlie McCarthy, diecut plastic, color decal, 1930s 70.00

Photo, Fiber McGee and Molly, black and white glossy, cast members, late 1930s, 8-1/4" x 12" 40.00

Pinback button
Adventurers Club, Frank Buck, 1936................................... 20.00
Magic Club, Mandrake the Magician.......................... 60.00
Uncle Don, Taystee Bread 55.00

Puzzle, Amos n' Andy, Pepsodent premium, 1931 .... 40.00

Ring, Jack Armstrong, Dragon's Eye, crocodile design, green stone, 1940 .... 150.00

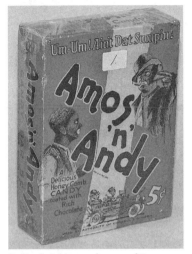

Radio characters and personalities, Amos 'n' Andy, candy box, cardboard, Williamson Candy Co., 12" h, 8-1/2" w, **$280.**

Sheet music, *Lonely Heart*, Today's Children cast, Eilene's wedding party, ©1936 Pillsbury 8.00

Stamp album, Jimmie Allen Flying Club Stamp Album, stamps mounted inside, 1936............ 85.00

Valentine, Joe Penner, mechanical diecut, Joe holding duck on shoulder, inscribed "I'll Gladly Buy A Duck," c1935 .... 30.00

Whistle, Jimmie Allen, brass, c1936 .... 30.00

Radios

Today a radio brings us news, weather, and some tunes. But to generations past, it brought all those things plus laughter, companionship, and entertainment. The mechanical device that allowed connection to this new exciting world was developed and refined at the beginning of the 20th century. New technology caused changes in the shapes and materials of early radio receivers.

Also see: Transistor Radios.

Radio, Philco, floor model, **$95.**

Admiral, #18, leatherette 40.00

Arvin, #522A, ivory metal case, 1941
.... 65.00

Atwater Kent, table, 55 Keil .. 200.00

Bulova, clock radio
#100 .... 25.00
110 .... 25.00

Crosley
Bandbox, #600, 1927 .... 80.00
Liftella, 1-N, cathedral 185.00
Super Buddy Boy 115.00

Dumont, RA346, table, scroll work,
1938 .... 110.00

Emerson
274, brown Bakelite 165.00
#570 Memento 100.00
#888 Vanguard 80.00

General Electric
#410 .... 30.00
#515, clock radio 25.00

Motorola
Jet Plane 55.00
Jewel Box 70.00
Pixie 45.00
Ranger, portable 30.00

Novelty
Green Giant 30.00
Pet evaporated milk can 48.00
Radio Shack D-cell battery ... 38.00
Twix candy bar, orig box 60.00

Philco
T1000, clock radio 80.00
#20, cathedral 200.00

Radio, GE table model 409, bakelite
case, **$65.**

RCA Victor
#17, Radiola 75.00
#33 .... 60.00

Silvertone - Sears
#1, table 75.00
#1582, cathedral - wood 200.00
#1955, tombstone 115.00

Zenith
Table, #6D2615, boomerang dial
.... 95.00
Trans-Oceanic 100.00
Zephyr, multiband 95.00

Raggedy Ann

Who's always got a smile? Of course, it's Raggedy Ann. This happy creation of Johnny Gruelle has lived on for decades. You can find Raggedy Ann, Andy, their dog and friends in children's literature and all kinds of decorative accessories.

Raggedy Ann, dolls, left: Raggedy Andy, two Raggedy Anns, played-with condition, each **$20.**

Children's book
Raggedy Ann & Hoppy Toad,
McLoughlin, 1940 .... 95.00
Raggedy Ann & Marcella's First Day
At School, Wonder Book, #588
.... 22.00
Raggedy Ann Stories, Volland,
1918, 1st ed., Johnny Gruelle,
color pictures 65.00

Raggedy Ann and Andy, pair, 15" h, **$25.**

Sweet and Dandy Sugar Candy
Scratch and Sniff Book, Golden
Press, 1976, well read 15.00

Cookie jar
California Originals, incised mark
on lid and "859 USA," 13-3/4" h
.... 125.00
Certified International, 11" h 95.00

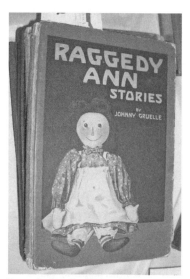

Raggedy Ann, book, *Raggedy Ann Stories*, by Johnny Gruelle, **$75.**

Creamer, figural, foil label, Royal Sealy, 4-1/2" h 35.00

Cup, Johnny Gruelle, 1941, Crooksville China 65.00

Doll
Georgene Novelties, 1947, 19" h 265.00
Hasbro Commemorative Edition, 1996, 12" h 40.00

Knickerbocker, Raggedy Ann and Andy, 1960s, 30" h 250.00

Game, Raggedy Ann's Magic Pebble Game, Milton Bradley, copyright 1941 Johnny Gruelle Co., orig box 95.00

Hand puppet, Dakin, 1975 ..... 15.00

Lunch box, plastic, Raggedy Ann and Andy on front, orig thermos 75.00

Music box, ceramic, Raggedy Andy, plays Do-Re-Me, Schmid 75.00

Nodder, 5" d head, 5-1/2" h ... 175.00

Paint by number canvas, 1988, unused 18.00

Print, copy of orig Johnny Gruelle drawing, 6" x 9" 35.00

Pop-up book, *Raggedy Ann & the Daffy Taffy Pull*, 1972.......... 15.00

Railroad Collectibles

All Aboard! Transportation of goods and passengers across this great country was a dream of the early railroad men. Today, we take it for granted that these giants will keep moving along tracks laid so many years ago. Collectors can tell you about their favorite rail lines or types of collectibles.

Railroad collectibles, steam whistle, brass and copper, mounted on keystone shaped wooden plaque along with cast iron railroad spike, **$95.**

Baggage check, Texas Central RR, 1-5/8 x 2", brass, Poole Bros, Chicago 38.50

Railroad collectibles, button, Brotherhood Railroad Trainmen, **$5.**

Bank, 1-1/2" w, 2-1/2" h, hard plastic replica of streamliner engine "6304," stylized lettering, Canadian-Global Marketing, Exclusive Supplier of Via Souvenirs, 1960s 25.00

Blanket, Canadian Pacific 85.00

Booklet
By The Way Of The Canyons, Soo Line, 1907 .... 20.00
Union Pacific RR, 1926 .... 15.00

Box, tin, black, paper attached to handle reads "Pittsburgh, Cincinnati, Chicago, St. Louis Railway Co., June 15, 1901" .. 40.00

Brochure, 8-1/2" x 11", Union Switch & Signal Co., ©1944, 32 pgs.... 5.00

Button, 2-1/4" d, black on cream, Brotherhood of Locomotive Engineers meeting, "Visitor B. of L. E. Union Meeting Lincoln Neb June 29 & 30, 1909" 15.00

Calendar, Burlington Zephyr, 1943 .... 90.00

Railroad collectibles, valentine, I'm 'Train'ing to be your Valentine," fold-down with red tissue paper, printed in US, **$35.**

Railroad collectibles, print, PRR locomotive, #9604, framed, **$125.**

Calendar card, 2-1/4" x 3-3/4", Union Pacific System, "Most Popular Route to Yellowstone National Park," back with red, white, and blue shield log for Overland Route and 1922 calendar 15.00

Car inspector's record, D & RGW, Ridway, filled in, 1928........... 10.00

Catalog, Erie Railroad, Co., New York, NY, 32 pgs, 1918 .... 42.00

China
Creamer, B & O, Centenary pattern, Scammell's Lamberton China, 3-1/2" d, 3-3/4" h............ 210.00
Cup and Saucer, B & O, Capital 60.00
Demitasse Cup and Saucer, CMSTP & P, Traveler, Syracuse, backstamped 85.00
Dinner Plate, B & O, Shenango, 10-1/2" d........................ 120.00

Christmas card, Santa Fe RR, 1944, unsigned 7.50

Railroad collectibles, two PRR cast iron plaques, each **$45;** employee's pinback button, white ground, red logo, black lettering and employee number, **$35.**

Coaster, Central RR, New Jersey, Statue of Liberty logo, set of six 15.00

Drinking glass, 2-1/2" d, 4-3/8" h, clear glass, maroon inscription "Milwaukee Road Host No. 18/ American Legion," 1930s 15.00

Folder
100 Years of Progress in Modern Railroading, Pennsylvania RR, 1934 .... 15.00
The Royal Scot, Century of Progress Expo, Chicago, 1933, sponsored by London Midland and Scottish Railway 6.00

Hat, 8-1/2" x 10-1/2", Amtrak, paper diecut, red, white, and blue, 1980s 15.00

Head rest cover, PRR, tan ground, brown logo, 15" x 18" 15.00

Lantern
Dietz, Nightwatch, deep red globe, some wear 60.00
Penn Central RR, red globe with logo, Adlake, 10" h 95.00

Magazine
Baltimore & Ohio, 1929 .... 20.00
Railroad Magazine, 6-1/2" x 9-1/2", 1951 .... 6.50

Membership card, American Association Railroad Ticket Agents, 1931 .... 10.00

Menu, Amtrak, Good Morning, single card, 7" x 11" 3.50

Napkin, linen
Burlington Route, 20" sq, white, woven logo 10.00
C & O, blue monogram 8.50

Padlock, Rock Island, orig key 35.00

Pass
Ft Wayne, Cincinnati & Louisville and White Water, 2-1/2" x 3-3/4" white card, green accents, purple ink stamp facsimile signature of president, 1889 .... 12.00
Ohio, Indiana, and Western, 2-1/4" x 3-3/4", black and white, ornately printed, signed in ink by general manager, 1889 ..... 12.00

Patch, South Shore Line, embroidered, 3-3/8" x 1-1/2" .. 9.00

Playing cards
Chessie 20.00
Denver & Rio Grande Railways 35.00
EJ & ERR 20.00

Postcard
Fresh Air Pullman, giant grasshopper in open cargo car, Multrakrom Postcard Co., Dodge City, Kansas, c1950 .... 10.00
White River at Sharon, VT, New England States Limited, scenic, 5-3/4" x 3-3/4" 22.00

Ribbon, Brotherhood of Railroad Men, Grand Union Picnic, Harrisburg, PA, June 27, 1901, 1-7/8" x 3-3/4", beige, gold accent lettering 10.00

Sign, Seaboard RR, "Explosives," 1948 .... 20.00

Spike, chromed, Chesapeake & Ohio RR, engrave 1944-1970, retirement presentation, 6" l 25.00

Step, Pullman RR Station, wood, hand cut out on top, 21" w, 10" h 25.00

Sugar tongs, Canadian Pacific, SP, mkd "England" 20.00

Timetable
Atchison, Topeka & Santa Fe, 1954 .... 12.50
Erie Railroad, 1907 .... 32.00
L&N Kansas City Southern, 1955 .... 8.50
Southern Pacific RR, 1915 ... 22.00

Tour souvenir, Flying Scotsman, 1969 USA tour, flannel print, 17" x 20", image of engine 4.00

Ramp Walkers

Here's a collectible where the prices might be a surprise to you. Remember those little plastic toys we all played with as a kid, no batteries required, just a sturdy surface that we could tilt so the little critter could walk away? Well, today collectors are walking all over flea markets to find them.

Cow, plastic, 2-1/4" h 45.00
Cowgirl, plastic, c1945, 6-1/2" h 95.00
Donald Duck, pushing wheelbarrow, Marx, plastic, 1950s 120.00
Elephant, plastic, Hong Kong, 2-1/4" h 65.00
Farmer, plastic, 2-5/8" h 60.00
Fireman, with hose, Marx...... 110.00

Ramp walker, rriceratops, blue plastic, white horns and eyes, black wind-up knob, marked "Made in Hong Kong, No. 7820," **$4.50.**

Hop and Hop, marching soldiers, Marx, 2-3/4" h 20.00

Little girl, plastic, orig weight ball, 6-1/2" h 115.00

Nanny, pushing carriage 22.00

Penguin, plastic, Hong Kong, 2-5/8" h 60.00

Popeye and Wimpy, plastic, Marx, ©1964, MIB 80.00

Soldier, wood and cloth, c1920, 4-3/4" h 65.00

Reamers

Feel like putting the squeeze on something? How about an orange, lemon, or grapefruit? Reamer collectors know just how to make their favorite juice and end up sweetly smiling when making a new purchase to add to their collection. They will tell you that reamers can be found in all types of materials, shapes, and sizes.

China
Austria, white, pink flowers, green trim, 3-3/4" h 95.00
Bavaria, white, red, yellow, and green flowers dec, gold trim, two-pc type 60.00
Czechoslovakia, orange shape, white, green leaves, mkd "Erphila," two-pc, 6" h 65.00
England, white, orange, and yellow flowers, 3-1/2" h 90.00
Germany, Goebel, yellow, 5" d 95.00

Japan, lemon, yellow, white flowers, green leaves, 4-3/4" h 60.00
United States, Ade-O-Matic Genuine, 8" h, green 145.00

Glass
Crystal, Criss-Cross, Hazel Atlas, tab handle, small.............. 25.00
Lime green, Anchor Hocking, 6-1/4" d.......................... 35.00
Pink, Jennyware, Jeanette... 145.00
Transparent green, pointed cone, tab handle, Federal 30.00

Reamer, Criss Cross, green, 6" d, **$15.**

White, embossed "Sunkist," McKee 15.00

Metal
Aluminum, Pat, 8" l, 161609, Minneapolis, MN 5.00
Dunlap's Improved, iron hinge, 9-1/2" l............................. 45.00
Gem Squeezer, aluminum crank handle, table model two-pc 12.00
Kwicky Juicer, aluminum, pan style, Quam Nicholas Co. 10.00
Nasco-Royal, scissors type, 6" l 8.00
Wagner Ware, cast aluminum, skillet shape, long red seed dams beneath cone, two spouts 45.00

Reamer, swan, yellow body, red roses, green leaves, illegible mark, **$45.**

Records

Spin me a tune! Records have evolved from early cylinders for Thomas Edison's first phonographs to the vinyl disks of today. This music can cross into other collecting areas devoted to specific artists such as Elvis or because of the subject matter on the record's album sleeve or protective box. Quickly gaining in popularity are children's records that have an image imprinted on the vinyl.

Aaron, Hank, The Life Of A Legend, 33-1/3 rpm, single record on Fleetwood label, interviews and

career highlights, mid-1970s, unopened.............................. 10.00

ABC Wide World of Sports, 33 rpm, 1970, narrated by Jim McKay 25.00

Records, Bing Crosby, Favorite Hawaiian Songs, Vol. 2, Decca, A-461, 1946, **$20.**

Ballad of the Green Berets, The, Staff Sgt Barry Sadler of US Army Special Forces, RCA, 7" sq jacket, 45 rpm, unused 20.00

Belafonte, Harry, LP, Streets I Have Walked, 1963 .... 35.00

Berry, Chuck, Johnny Bgoode, 78 RPM, Chess 10.00

Blue Ridge Mountain Girls, She Came Rolling Down The Mountain, Champion 12.00

Brooklyn Tabernacle Choir, Rejoice 15.00

Bye Bye Birdy, Columbia, orig cast, 1980 .... 17.50

Campbell, Glen, Christmas with Glen Campbell, Capitol, SL 6699, black label with pink colorband 8.00

Checker, Chubby, Limbo Party, Parkway, LP, 1962 .... 20.00

Cline, Patsy, Crazy, Who Can I Count On, Decca 31317, 1961, 45 ...... 3.00

Crosby, Bing, The Songs I Love, six long play records, mint in orig case 75.00

Day, Doris, Wonderful Day, Columbia Records XTV 82022, 1960s 8.00

Disneyland Davy Crockett, record storybook, copyright 1971, 24 pgs 35.00

Doody, Howdy, Christmas 24.00

Dragnet, 78 rpm, Jack Webb cover 30.00

Ellington, Duke, Jubilee Stomp, Okeh, 41013, 1938 .... 15.00

Empire State Observatory Voiceogram, 6" record, 6-1/8" sq envelope, 1930s 20.00

Griffith, Andy, Goober Sings 35.00

Higitus Figitus, Walt Disney Productions, Little Golden Record, 1938 .... 8.00

Hot Rod Granny, Hanna-Barbera 50.00

Johnny Quest, Hanna-Barbera, 45 rpm 28.00

Little Nipper Giant Storybook, RCA Victor, 1951 .... 50.00

Liverpool Five, Out of Sight, RCA LSP-33682, German imp, LP... 8.00

Lulu, To Sir with Love, Epic LN 24339, LP, mono, 1967 .... 6.25

Miller, Glenn, Glenn Miller Story, Unbreakable, LP, Decca, 1954 .... 22.00

Oklahoma, Decca, orig cast, 1953 .... 42.00

Presidential Profiles, The Presidents Speak, John F. Kennedy, narrated by Art Baker, 7" sq jacket, 33-1/3" rpm, unused 15.00

Presley, E., Touch of Gold, Volume 2, EPA-5101, maroon label........ 85.00

Return of the Pink Panther, United Artists, 1970s, 45 rpm 30.00

Rogers, Roy, Dale Evans, Jesus Loves Me, Camden, 1960, LP 30.00

Secret Squirrel, Hanna-Barbera, 45 rpm 30.00

Squiddly Diddly, Hanna-Barbera, 45 rpm 35.00

Teardrops, The Stars Are Out Tonight, Josie.......................... 30.00

Welling & McGhee, Ring the Bells of Heaven, Champion, 16660 .... 17.50

Wells, Kitty, Country Music Time, Decca DL 74554, black label with rainbow band through center 8.00

Williams, Hank, Reflections of Those Who Loved Him, MGM-Pro-912, three LPs, promotional box set, 1975 .... 60.00

Wynette, Tammy, Your Good Girl's Gonna Go Bad, Epic LN 26305, LP, stereo, 1967.............................. 5.00

Red Wing Pottery

Red Wing is a generic term that covers several manufacturers that produced utilitarian stoneware and ceramic dinnerware in Red Wing, Minn. The trademark red wing is the most recognizable symbol used in Red Wing, but other marks also identify the pottery.

For additional listings, see *Warman's Americana & Collectibles* and *Warman's American Pottery & Porcelain.*

Red Wing Pottery, wing ashtray, **$45.**

Ashtray, horse head, ochre 75.00

Bean pot, cov, stoneware, adv 85.00

Bread and butter plate
Bob White.............................. 12.50
Random Harvest 7.50

Candy dish, three-parts, hexagon, semi-gloss gray...................... 18.00

Red Wing Pottery, handled gravy, Bob White, 9-1/2" l, **$25.**

Red Wing Pottery, vase, two handles, gray matte ground, four relief panels of brown semi-glazed trees, marked "Red Wing Union Stoneware Co., Red Wing, Minn.," 9-3/4" h, **$50.**

Celery dish, Lotus pattern, Concord shape, 11-1/4" l 35.00

Chop plate, Capistrano, 12" d 26.00

Crock, two-gallon, large wing 100.00

Custard cup, Fondos, green and pink 18.00

Dinner plate
  Bob White 15.00
  Lotus 12.50

Figure
  Cowboy, rust 175.00
  Cowgirl, #B1414, white 175.00

Nappy, Lotus 9.50

Pitcher

Blue Deco, orig label, 5-1/8" h 325.00
Bob White, 12" h 65.00

Planter
  Cart, butterscotch 75.00
  Lamb, white 30.00

Platter, Random Harvest, 13" l 30.00

Salt and pepper shakers, pr, Town and Country, dark green 65.00

Soup bowl, Lotus pattern, Concord shape, 6-3/8" d, set of six 70.00

Vase
  Art Deco lady and deer, #1151, turquoise semi-gloss glaze, white crackle glaze int., asymmetric handles 65.00
  Ribbon, #1169, soft green 85.00

Redware

American colonists began making redware in the late 17th century, using the same clay as for bricks and roof tiles. Ready availability of the clay meant that items could be produced in large quantities. The lead-glazed items retained their reddish color, hence the name redware, although various colors could be obtained by adding different metals to the glaze; 2004 saw some record prices set at auction for vintage redware. Often when this type of news hits the flea market circuit, dealers will include some in their inventory, especially if they tend to specialize in country or primitive wares. Modern craftsmen, like Lester Breininger, have kept the redware tradition alive and can be found working in several parts of the country today.

For additional listings, see *Warman's Antiques & Collectibles.*

Bank, apple shape, red and yellow paint, 3-1/4" h 160.00

Bowl, Foltz Pottery, bowl, tulip sgraffito decor in cobalt, 1980, 14-1/2" d 145.00

Canning jar, John Bell, orange glaze, cylindrical shape, impressed "J.

Redware, cat figure, molded by R. R. Stahl, blue glaze, oval base, dated 1/6/1950, 3-3/4" h, **$185.**

Bell" on bottom, side repairs, chips, 5-5/8" h, 4-5/8" d 425.00

Charger, large, sgraffitto, eagle dec, Lester Breininger 300.00

Compote, int. with black glaze, bird dec, Lester Breininger, 1986 .... 100.00

Crock
  3-1/2" d, 2-1/2" h, molded rim, manganese brown int. glaze 250.00
  6" d, 4" h, molded rim, red-orange and green glaze 360.00

Dog figure, basket by paw, Lester Breininger, 1988 .... 275.00

Fish mold
  Stahl Pottery, mottled brown glaze, dated 1939, glaze imperfections, 3" h, 11" l 165.00
  Unmarked, vintage, spiraled flutes, scalloped rim, brown sponging on pinkish-amber ground, wear, slight hairline, 8" d 145.00

Flower pot, 5-5/8" h, mottled green and brown glaze, rust ground,

crimped rim, attached saucer, attributed to John Bell 275.00

Jar
  New England, flared rim on sloped shoulder, brownish-green glaze with lighter spots and dark brown streaks, attributed to New England, late 18th/early 19th C, 7" h, minor wear to glaze on rim 360.00
  Stahl Pottery, dark reddish-brown glaze, ovoid, shoulder handles, mkd "Made in Stahl Pottery by Thomas Stahl, April 16, 1936," 3-3/4" h 90.00

Jug, applied handle
  Bulbous, applied handle, molded spout, brown manganese glaze, 7-1/8" h 250.00
  Incised banding at center, brown manganese glaze, 6-1/4" h 200.00

Pie plate
  Two-line swag decor, yellow slip, imperfections, 11-1/2" d 220.00

Three-line, yellow slip, wavy decor,
wear, hairlines, 8-1/2" d
.... 440.00

Turk's head mold, mottled red and
dark brown glaze, c1830, 10" d
.... 150.00

Regal China Corporation

Here's a chinaware maker that was owned by Jim Beam Distilleries. Its wares include those wonderful
decanters you think of as Beam bottles, plus several types of advertising wares and items made for clients
including Quaker Oats and Kraft Foods.

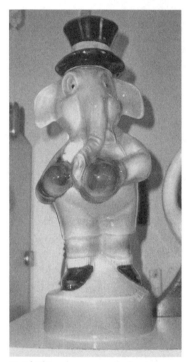

Regal China, lamp, gray elephant
dressed as boxer, wearing black top hat,
brown boxing gloves, turquoise shorts,
$30.

Canister, Old McDonald's Farm, gold
trim
Coffee, horse lid 235.00
Flour, Grandpa lid 225.00
Pretzels, Grandma lid......... 300.00
Sugar, Grandma lid 225.00

Cookie jar, cov
Baby pig, wearing diaper, holding
rattle, #404 .... 275.00
International Assoc Jim Beam
Bottle & Specialties Club 125.00
Quaker Oats........................ 125.00

Creamer, Old McDonald's Farm,
rooster, #383, 6" h................ 135.00

Decanter, Jim Beam, empty
Antique Trader, 1968............ 10.00
Cat, 1967.............................. 10.00
Cherubs, 1974....................... 10.00
Ford, 1978............................. 25.00
Hawaii, 50th State................. 15.00
Ohio 10.00
Sailfish, 1957, 14" h 10.00
Telephone, 1979.................... 10.00

Lamp base, 12-3/4" h, Davy Crockett
.... 125.00

Salt and pepper shakers, pr, Old
McDonald's Farm
Barrels, red, gold trim, #385, 4" h
.... 125.00
Boy and girl, #392 .... 120.00

Regal China, whiskey decanter, The
Appaloosa, issued by Jim Beam, **$25.**

Shot glass, blue, raised molded
lettering "Jim Beam 1980," 2-3/4" h
.... 14.00

Teapot, Old McDonald's Farm, duck,
7-1/2" h 300.00

Tobacco jar, Fox, Jim Beam..... 60.00

Religious Collectibles

Hunting for religious collectibles at flea markets is a great idea, but not in lieu of going to church services.
(Well, perhaps before or after Sunday services.) However, no matter when you shop, you're likely to find
something of interest.

Bible, Bohemian, decorative celluloid
cover, latch closure, 1884, 3-1/4" x
4-1/2" 195.00

Book
Gospel Hymns, Biglow & Main Co.,
The John Church Co., 1894
.... 50.00

Hark the Harold Angel Sings, Rev
Charles Wesley, M.A., E. P.
Dutton, 1886, gilt edges
.... 100.00
*History of the First Presbyterian
Church of Bellefontaine*, Ohio,
1900, hardcover.............. 120.00

*International Sunday School
Lessons*, 1918.................... 15.00
*Mother Lee's Experience in Fifteen
Years' Rescue Work*, Richard
Artmus Lee, 1906, black and
white photos.................... 50.00
Sunday School is Fun, 1948, with
dustjacket 7.50

The Earth Gods, Kahlil Gibran, 1931, hardcover, 12 illus 35.00

Candleholders, angels, brass, graduating in size from 12" h to 18" h, set of three................ 300.00

Charm, Chai, 14kt yg, 1-1/4" 165.00

Children's book
A Child's Life of Christ, 1920s, 167 pgs, illus 7.00
Children's Missionary Story Sermons, Hugh T. Kerr, DD, Pastor of Shadyside Presbyterian Church, Pittsburgh, 1915, Fleming H. Revell Co., 54 sermons, beige hard cover 7.00

Doorstop, church door, painted cast iron, 6" h 165.00

Figure
Plastic, Madonna, blue rhinestone halo, 3-3/4" h...................... 5.00
Precious Moments, Jesus Loves Me, 1976.................................. 55.00

Religious collectibles, wall hanging, Christ praying, night scene of village below, original frame, **$45.**

Flagon, stoneware, with incised and blue glazed "Star of David," pewter lid, German, late 19th C, 8" h 150.00

Folk art, Wedding Feast, carved and painted wood and plaster, sgd J.J. Stark, 11-1/2" x 17-1/4" 275.00

Magazine, *Sunday School Magazine*, November 1881, Southern Methodist Publishing House.. 3.50

Marriage box, pewter, circular, scene of couple, inscribed "Mazel Tov," 19th C 250.00

Matzoh bag, embroidered silk, cream ground, colorful lion, crown, and foliage, Europe, early 20th C, 15" d 200.00

Matzoh plate, Tepper blue transfer dec, vignettes of the Seder, identified in Hebrew and English, Ridgways, early 20th C, 10" d 180.00

Menorah, porcelain, Lenox, 6" h, 12" l 100.00

Paperweight, Star of David design, white stardust canes, millefiori

garland, cobalt blue ground, Perthshire, 2-1/2" d 110.00

Picture, Sacred Heart, litho tin, framed, 23-1/4" w, 29-1/4" h 200.00

Pinback button, Vacation Bible School, 3/4" d.......................... 3.00

Postcard, Rally Day, 1924 .... 3.50

Santos, carved wood, polychrome and gesso, Spanish
Crucified Christ, 14" h 200.00
Infantata, 7-3/4" h 375.00
St. Mary in Glory, standing on cloudwork with seraphim, 10" h 115.00

Songbook
Bradbury's Golden Shower of Sunday School Melodies, 1862 .... 18.00
Sunday School Songbook, 1870 .... 15.00

Religious collectibles, planter, three singing nuns, black habits, gold cross and details, **$28.**

Religious collectibles, plaque, "My Kitchen Prayer," **$15.**

Road Maps

Today's road maps are a far cry from the early guide books that provided written descriptions of how to get from Point A to Point B. While most maps are readily affordable, earlier examples, especially those with colorful covers, have taken the hobby to a new price level. Using old road maps as decorative elements has taken off recently. Look for inexpensively priced ones to use as a colorful addition to a plain desk—spread the maps out, then top with a piece of glass the size of the desk top. Other ideas to decorate with maps would include making lampshades, boxes, etc. out of them.

California, Chevron, 1973......... 3.00

Central & Western United States, Deep Rock Gasoline, 1960s... 10.00

Georgia, Texaco, 1965................ 5.00

Hawaii, Shell Oil Co., 1961....... 10.00

Illinois, Conoco, 1970 .... 3.00

Indiana Official Highway Map, 1970-71 .... 3.00

Kentucky and Tennessee, Ashland Flying Octanes, 1950s 15.00

Mid-Atlantic Region, Delaware, Maryland, Virginia and West Virginia Road Map with Pictorial Guide, Esso, 1952 .... 7.50

New Jersey, shore points on reverse 2.50

Road map, Texaco, 1928, **$350.**

New York World's Fair, 1963-64, Esso 12.00

Ohio, AAA triptik 4.00

Pennsylvania Official Highway Map, 1972-73 .... 3.00

South Dakota Official Highway Map 4.00

Trails through New Hampshire and Vermont, Tydol, 1930s 12.00

USGS Quadrangle, Norristown, PA, framed 20.00

Wyoming, Mobil Oil Co. 5.00

Road map, Maryland, official highway map, photo and message from Governor William Donald Schaeffer on other side, published by Maryland Department of Transportation, **$.50.**

Robots

These mechanical marvels have delighted moviegoers and science fiction buffs for years. The first documented robot is Atomic Robot Man, created in 1948. The Japanese dominated the robot market. By the 1970s, production had moved to Hong Kong and other foreign countries.

For additional listings, see *Warman's Americana & Collectibles.*

Action figure, Robot Zone, five 2-1/2" h figures, 1985, mkd "Made in British Colony of Hong Kong," MOC 25.00

Bank, wind-up, plastic, dumps coin in slots when revolving, mkd "Made in Hong Kong," orig box 25.00

Figure
Lost in Space, chrome version, Trendmasters Classic 60.00
Rosie, Jetson's, plastic, Applause, orig sticker, 1990 .... 25.00

Top, Shogun Rocket, plastic, Mattel, 1978, MIP 15.00

Toy
Biliken Ultra 7, tin litho wind-up, Japan, MIB 300.00
Cosmos Robot, battery-op, plastic, Kamco, China, 1980s, MIB, 12-1/2" h 40.00
Fighting Robot, tin litho, battery operated, Japan, 1960s ... 200.00
Flying Man Robot, litho tin wind-up, SY, orig box, 6" x 3" base, 11" h 350.00
Lost in Space, battery operated, Remco 685.00

Magic Mike II, tin litho, battery operated 100.00
Moon Stroller, wind-up, arms swing, moving radar, mkd "Made in Hong Kong," MIB 35.00
Rascal, wind-up, mkd "1978, Tomy Corp., Made in Taiwan," MIP, 2" h 20.00
Robot Sentinel, battery operated, walks, arms move, lights, four shooting missiles, plastic, mkd "Made in China by Kamco," 1980s, 13" h, MIB 55.00
Saturn, battery operated, walks, lights up eyes, mkd "Made in Hong Kong by Kamco" 40.00
Sentinel Robot, plastic, Kamco, China, 1980s, MIB 35.00
Silver colored, wind-up, mkd "Made in Hong Kong," MIB 35.00
SP-1, friction, blue and red space ship, Japan, 1950s, 6-1/2" l 300.00
Sparky Robot, wind-up, silver and red, flashes, 1950s, Japan, 8" h 375.00
Star Strider, litho tin 175.00
Tang, General Foods, 7-1/4" h 30.00

TR2 Talking, mkd "Made in Hong Kong," orig box 65.00

Robots, Mr. Machine, working condition, some play wear, **$125.**

Rock 'n' Roll

"Rock, Rock, Rock Around the Clock!" Remember the good ol' days with American Bandstand and the great singers Dick Clark introduced us to? No matter what kind of music you associate with rock 'n' roll, chances are good that some neat collectibles will be rocking at your favorite flea market.

Rock 'n' roll, Bruce Springsteen, poster, early, **$750.**

Action figure, Paul Stanley, The Jester, Psycho Circus.............. 12.00

Book
Mike Jagger: Primitive Cool, Christopher Sanford, St. Martin's, 1994................................. 12.00
Rock Elvis, 1994, 240 pgs 24.00
Picture Life of Stevie Wonder, A. Edwards and G. Wohl, 1977 .... 7.00

Book cover, orange and red title paper, three black and white book covers, one with Pat Boone, one with Sal Mineo, third generic signer, 1958 Cooga Mooga Products, Inc., NY, unused in clear plastic bag............................. 18.00

Bracelet, gold chain link, burnished gold disc with raised Monkees

guitar symbol, orig retail card, ©1967 .... 27.50

Colorforms, KISS, MIB 27.50

Comic book
AC/CD, early 1990s.............. 15.00
Frank Zappa, #32, 1991........ 20.00
Jane's Addiction, early 1990s 15.00
Janis Joplin, #63 .... 15.00
Queensryche, early 1990s 20.00

Cuff links, pr, Dick Clark, MIB 35.00

Figure, Dave Clark Five, Remco, Rick, Mike, Dennis 95.00

Game, Duran Duran into the Arena, Milton Bradley, 1985 .... 18.00

Lunch box, The Osmonds, metal, orig thermos, unused, 1973 .... 95.00

Magazine, Hit Parader, February 1960, Paul Anka cover............ 5.00

Nodder, twisting man, gold base, "Let's Twist" decal, Japan sticker, c1960..................................... 75.00

Pinback button, black and white photo
Bob-a-Loo, WABC, disc jockey 70.00
Dick Clark, dark green ground 15.00
Frankie Avalon-Venus, bright pink ground............................. 25.00

Photo, promotional, Brothers Four, 8-1/2" x 11" black and white 6.00

Poster
Grateful Dead, skeleton and roses theme, 1983, 45" x 54"... 250.00
Hot Tuna, Orange County Jam, June 13, 1975, 15" x 23"......... 150.00

Rock 'n' roll, comic book, The Monkees, Dell, 12-533-809, September, **$15.**

Puzzle, frame tray
Bee Gees 20.00
KISS, 1964 .... 25.00

Record case, cardboard, full color photo and signature of Dick Clark, blue, white plastic handle, brass closure, holds 45 RPM records 45.00

Salt and pepper shakers, pr, ceramic feet, mkd "Rock-N-Roll Indiana," mkd "Japan," 2-3/4" l 6.00

Scarf, AC/DC, EuroTour, 1980-81 .... 60.00

Tie clip, Dick Clark American Bandstand, gold-tone metal 15.00

Window card, 22" x 14", Rolling Stones, Gimme Shelter, blue, yellow, and white 165.00

Wrapper, Freddie & the Dreamers, Donruss, c1965, 5-1/4" x 6-1/4" 8.00

Rockwell, Norman

One of America's most beloved artists, Norman Rockwell was born 1894. By the time he died in 1978, he had created more than 2,000 paintings. Many of these paintings were reproduced as magazine covers, illustrations, calendars, etc. Rockwell's ability to capture the essence of everyday life has attracted people to his work for generations. Besides the artwork, many of Rockwell's illustrations have been used in designs of limited-edition collectibles.

Norman Rockwell, limited edition collector plate, Triple Self Portrait, Gorham, **$20.**

Bell, Love's Harmony, 1976, wooden handle, 9" h............................. 45.00

Dealer sign, porcelain figure standing next to plaque, c1980, 5-1/4" h................................. 125.00

Figure
Dave Grossman Designs, Inc., The Graduate, 1983................. 35.00
Gorham, Jolly Coachman, 1982 .... 40.00

Lynell Studios, Cradle of Love, 1980 **45.00**
Rockwell Museum, Bride and Groom, 1979 .... 75.00

Ignot, Franklin Mint, Spirit of Scouting, 1972, 12-pc set **275.00**

Magazine cover
Boys' Life, June, 1947............ 45.00
Family Circle, Dec. 1967....... 15.00
Red Cross, April 1918 .... 25.00
Saturday Evening Post, April 19, 1950................................. 85.00
Saturday Evening Post, Sept. 7, 1957 .... 35.00
Saturday Evening Post, Jan. 13, 1962 .... 20.00
Scouting, Dec. 1944 .... 15.00

Plate
Dave Grossman Designs, Huckleberry Finn, 1980 .... 35.00
Franklin Mint, The Carolers, 1972 .... 75.00
Gorham, Boy Scout, 1975 .... 45.00
Knowles, Grandma's Courting Dress, 1984, MIB.............. 15.00
Lynell studios, Mother's Day, 1980 .... 15.00
River Shore, Jennie & Tina, 1982 .... 15.00

Norman Rockwell, magazine cover, *Saturday Evening Post*, June 7, 1958, **$30.**

Rockwell Museum, First Prom, 1979................................. 15.00
Rockwell Society, A Mother's Love, first edition, 1976.............. 18.00
Royal Devon, One Present Too Many, 1979 .... 10.00
Royal Manor Porcelain, Scotty's Stowaway, 10" d................ 10.00

Rogers, Roy

This popular cowboy hero made a positive impression on many young minds. Today collectors are drawn to Roy Rogers' memorabilia to remember and commemorate the morals and honesty he stressed.

Roy Rogers, plastic figural cup, Quaker Oats, **$20.**

Autographed photo, Roy Rogers and Dale Evans, 8" x 10"........ 65.00

Box, Yankiboy, Dale Evans Queen of the West Official Cowgirl Outfit, 11" x 14", c1948 .... 75.00

Calendar, 1960, Roy Rogers Ranch, Nestle Quik premium, 10" x 14" 95.00

Cap pistol, Kilgore, white metal, Roy's name in s ript on one side of frame, white plastic grips, late 1950s.................................... 100.00

Cereal kit, Roy Rogers Riders Club, Post Cereals, orig mailing envelope, 1951-52, orig unused contents 195.00

Child's book
Roy Rogers and the Desert Treasure, Alice Sankey, color ills by Paul Souza, Whitman Cozy Corner Book, 1954 .... 20.00
Roy Rogers Trigger to the Rescue, Whitman Cozy Corner Book, #2038, 1950 .... 35.00

Figure, Marx playset, vinyl Dale Evans, holding hat, cream, 2-1/4" h............................. 18.00

Roy Rogers, pocket knife, Roy Rogers and Trigger, **$45.**

Roy Rogers, gun drawn, red, 2" h
.... 40.00

Gloves, pr................................ 150.00

Guitar, orig box, 1950s........... 140.00

Horseshoe game, hard rubber
horseshoes 190.00

Lantern, tin litho, 7-1/2" h....... 65.00

Pop gun, Roy Rogers Cookies, diecut
paper, c1951........................... 45.00

Raincoat, cap, child's oilcloth over
canvas fabric, mid 1950s..... 150.00

Ring, branding iron, brass, 1948,
Quaker 195.00

School bag, Roy Rogers King of the
Cowboys, vinyl, 10-3/4" x 13-3/4"
.... 125.00

Sweater vest, image on front and
back of Roy on Trigger, name at
lower right, label "Official Roy
Rogers 100% Virgin Wool By

Pauker Brothers Wear," 1950s
.... 95.00

Tie slide, metal, 2" l, 1950s 30.00

Wristwatch, Roy Rogers and Trigger,
Ingraham, flicker image dial, back
of case inscribed "Many Happy
Trails, Roy Rogers and Trigger,"
chrome accent metal expansion
band, 1960 .... 150.00

Rookwood

Founded in 1880, Rookwood Pottery underwent a metamorphosis as produced a varying line of wares that ranged from highly detailed artist-decorated vases to production-line figural paperweights. The distinctive mark used indicates the clay or body mark, the size, the decorator mark, a date mark, and the factory mark. Learning to accurately read these marks will enhance your understanding and appreciation for Rookwood Pottery.

Rookwood, ashtray, center baseball design with "Jim Reninger" and "MacGregor Gold Smith," medium blue, 1949, 5-3/4" d, **$90.**

Ashtray, owl, green high glaze, 1950, 4-1/4" h 125.00

Bowl, standard glaze, almond husk shape, by Grace Young, 1899, incised golden flowers, brown ground, flame mark/279A-Y/ G.M.Y., 6" d, crack and several nicks..................................... 100.00

Chamberstick, standard glaze, painted by Jeannette Swing, yellow violets, flame mark, artist's cipher, 1894, 3" h 350.00

Cornucopia vase, satin blue, #27645 .... 300.00

Ewer, standard glaze, oak leaves on shaded brown and umber ground, by Sadie Toohey, flame mark, 1899, 11" x 8"................................. 415.00

Lamp base, celadon green, #6775, 1945, 9-1/2" h 225.00

Paperweight
Canary, white, 1946, 3-5/8" h
.... 145.00
Gazelle, white, 1934, 4-1/2" h
.... 250.00
Rooster, 1946, 5" h.............. 350.00

Pitcher, light standard glaze, squatty, leaf handle, painted by Constance Baker, daisies dec, flame mark and "CAB," c1890, 3-3/4" h 265.00

Vase
Lily, turquoise, #6314, sgd "65," 1945, 7-1/4" h................. 200.00

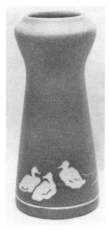

Rookwood, vase, wax resist duck motif, blue tones, artist signed "Kath-Van Horne," 1910, #1659E, 7-3/8" h, **$900.**

Standard glaze, red poppies, green leaves, dec by Mary Luella Perkins, c1896, 5" h........ 350.00
Vellum glaze, grape decor, Margaret McDonald, 1912, 6-7/8" h
.... 660.00

Rose Bowls

A rose bowl is defined as a round or ovoid bowl with a small opening. Crimped, pinched, scalloped, petaled, and pleated designs are common. They held potpourri or rose petals.

Rose bowl, satin glass, white body, yellow scissors-cut top, hand painted violets, Mount Washington, 3-3/4" d, 2-3/4" h, **$195.**

Amethyst, squatty, enameled dec, fluted top 115.00

Blenko, transparent amethyst, free blown, 30 tight rolled crimps, rough pontil, 3-5/8" h............ 30.00

Bohemian, amber stained cut to clear, grape and vine dec, 3-1/2" h 25.00

Fenton
Beaded Melon, white with yellow interior, eight crimps, collar base, 3-1/2" d.................... 45.00
Fenton Flowers, ftd, green carnival glass................................ 125.00

Imperial, Imperial Star and File, dark marigold carnival glass 45.00

Northwood, Leaf and Beads, ftd, purple carnival glass 85.00

Pattern glass, Puritan pattern, 2-1/4" h 50.00

Porcelain, blue glaze over white base, white int., oval scene captioned "Water St., Shullsburg, Vt," gold outline.................................... 40.00

Satin glass
Light green, embossed apple blossoms in glass, eight crimps, ground pontil, 3-3/4" d
.... 150.00
Shaded pink to white, soft white interior, undecorated, eight crimps, ground pontil, 3-1/2" d
.... 45.00

Westmoreland, Concave Flute, green carnival glass 135.00

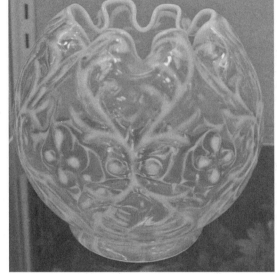

Rose bowl, opalescent, Seaweed pattern, **$85.**

Roseville Pottery

In 1892, the J.B. Owens Pottery was renamed Roseville Pottery Co., taking its name from the Ohio town where the manufacturer was based. From the late 19th century until the business was sold to Mosiac Tile Co. in 1854, Roseville produced a vast quantity of art pottery and dinnerware.

In the 1930s and 1940s, the company hit full stride with numerous lines of mass-produced pottery that remain highly popular with collectors today. Unfortunately, reproductions of many of those designs were reproduced in the 1990s. Although those imported reproductions can be easily detected by knowledgeable collectors, the fakes continue to fool many people who see the name Roseville and think they're buying a vintage piece of pottery.

For additional listings, see *Warman's Antiques and Collectibles Price Guide*, *Warman's Americana & Collectibles*, and *Warman's American Pottery & Porcelain*.

Reproduction alert.

Basket
Bushberry, blue 400.00
Mock Orange, # 911-10, 10" h
.... 180.00

Bookends, pr
Burmese, green, raised marks, 4-3/4" w, 6-3/4" h 255.00

Iris, book shape, blue, raised mark, No. 5, 5-1/4" w, 5-1/4" h
.... 290.00

Roseville pottery, vase, #446-4, white magnolia flowers, apricot ground, two handles, 4-1/4" h, **$65.**

Bowl
Blueberry, #412-6 .... 130.00
Peony, #428-6 .... 95.00
Rosecraft Panel, rolled rim, c1920,
  8" d, 2-3/8" h 140.00
Water Lily, #663, blue 100.00

Bud vase, Dahlia Rose, double
.... 175.00

Candlesticks, pr
Carnelian I, blue-green, c1910
.... 150.00
Freesia, #1160-2, green 100.00
White Rose, #114-1, pink... 100.00

Console bowl, Bushberry, #414-40
.... 350.00

Cornucopia
Snowberry, #100-8 .... 125.00
Tourmaline, white 90.00

Flower frog, Carnelian II, 1921
.... 50.00

Flowerpot and saucer, Zephyr Lily,
  green, #672, 5" h.................. 255.00

Jardiniere
Bushberry, #657-3, brown.. 110.00
Florentine, cream and green, 8" h,
  12" d 325.00
Fuchsia, bulbous, blue, imp mark,
  No. 645-8"....................... 350.00

Mug, Dutch 110.00

Pitcher
Blended Landscape, 7-1/2" h
.... 140.00
Pinecone, ball jug shape..... 495.00

Planter, Florentine, brown, rect,
  11-1/4" l, 5-1/4" h 290.00

Roseville pottery, iris basket, pink to green glaze, 10" h, **$180.**

Roseville pottery, tea set, Magnolia, blue glaze, **$325.**

Plate, Raymor, #154, autumn brown
.... 20.00

Urn, Carnelian II, mauve and purple
.... 230.00

Vase
Bittersweet, #881-1, gray.... 100.00
Bleeding Heart, #951-4 ...... 125.00
Dahlrose, bulbous, black paper
  label, 5" d, 8-1/4" h......... 290.00
Freesia, #119-7, green 115.00
Iris, #917-6, pink................ 115.00
Magnolia, #89-7, brown 115.00
Ming Tree, green, #581, 6" h
.... 175.00
Peony, #6308, yellow 150.00
Pine Cone, gold and brown, #838,
  6" h 265.00
Rosecraft Vintage, RV ink mark,
  small tip chip, 8-1/2" l.... 265.00

Wall pocket
Gardenia, brown, 8" h 150.00
Maple Leaf, 8-1/2" h 75.00
Snowberry, blue, 8" h 180.00

Royal Bayreuth

Another Bavarian firm, Royal Bayreuth traces its history to the late 1790s. The company is still in business, producing dinnerware. Royal Bayreuth is well known to collectors for its figural lines that were popular in the late 1880s. One interesting type of porcelain Royal Bayreuth introduced is Tapestry Ware. Placing a piece in fabric, then decorating and glazing and firing the item caused the texture of this ware.

For additional listings, see *Warman's Antiques and Collectibles Price Guide* and *Warman's English & Continental Pottery and Porcelain.*

Ashtray, elk 225.00

Bell, peacock dec, 3" h 275.00

Bud vase, two necks joined by small
  handle, Dutch children scene
.... 125.00

Candy dish, Lobster 140.00

Celery tray, Tomato pattern.... 95.00

Chamberstick, Corinthian, 4-1/2" h
.... 60.00

Creamer, figural
Bird of Paradise 225.00

Clown, red 275.00
Devil & Cards, 4" h, blue back
  stamp............................... 115.00
Eagle 200.00
Frog, green.......................... 250.00
Lamplighter, green 250.00

Creamer, tapestry
Brittany women, double handle,
  4" h 125.00
Mountain sheep, hunt scene, 4" h
.... 110.00

Cup and saucer
Boy with turkey.................. 125.00

Royal Bayreuth, creamer, figural lobster, blue mark, **$85.**

Royal Bayreuth, vase, 5-1/4" h, **$285.**

Man in boat fishing............ 125.00

Hair receiver, boy with donkey
.... 125.00

Match holder, tapestry, Arab scene
.... 100.00

Milk pitcher
Little Boy Blue.................... 200.00
Mountain sheep, pinched spout
.... 125.00

Mustard, cov, tomato, figural leaf
underplate 125.00

Pin dish, Arab scene 75.00

Plate
Boy and donkeys.................. 95.00
Hunter walking in brook with five
dogs 75.00
Little Bo Peep 125.00
Man in boat fishing.............. 95.00
Soccer scene 85.00

Portrait plate, 9" d, Arab and camel,
green back stamp 125.00

Powder box, cov, Cavalier Musicians
.... 175.00

Ring box, cov, pheasant scene, glossy
finish...................................... 85.00

Salt and pepper shakers, pr
Grape clusters, figural, purple
.... 150.00
Rose Tapestry, pink roses... 375.00

Sugar bowl, cov, Brittany Girl dec
.... 100.00

Vase, tear drop shape, floral dec,
5-1/2" h 125.00

Wall pocket, Strawberry........ 265.00

Royal Bayreuth, vase, white roses, ivory ground, blue mark, 8-1/2" h, **$210.**

Water pitcher, figural
Conch shell 500.00
Lobster................................. 395.00

Royal China

Manufactured in Sebring, Ohio, from 1924 to 1986, Royal China made a large variety of dinnerware patterns. Collectors today are particular fond of several patterns, including Currier & Ives, Bucks County, Colonial Homestead, Fair Oaks, Memory Lane, Old Curiosity Shop, and Willow Ware.

For additional listings and more detailed history, see *Warman's Americana & Collectibles.*

Ashtray, Colonial Homestead
.... 10.00

Beverage tumbler, Currier and Ives
.... 10.00

Bread and butter plate
Bucks County 3.00
Colonial Homestead............... 2.50
Old Curiosity Shop 3.00
Willow Ware 4.00

Breakfast plate
Colonial Homestead............. 12.00
Currier and Ives.................... 15.00

Butter dish, cov
Bucks County 40.00
Colonial Homestead............. 25.00
Willow Ware 25.00

Calendar plate, 1974, Currier and
Ives... 12.00

Casserole, cov, Bucks County
.... 75.00

Cereal bowl
Currier and Ives.................... 12.00
Memory Lane 8.00

Coaster, Willow Ware 30.00

Coffee mug
Colonial Homestead............. 15.00
Old Curiosity Shop 30.00
Willow Ware 15.00

Creamer
Currier and Ives..................... 7.50
Willow Ware 5.00

Cup and saucer
Bucks County 4.00
Colonial Homestead............... 4.00
Currier and Ives..................... 6.00
Memory Lane 4.00
Willow Ware 5.00

Dinner plate
Bucks County 4.00
Colonial Homestead.............. 4.00
Old Curiosity Shop 4.50
Willow Ware 4.00

Royal China Co., plate, Old Curiosity Shop, 10-1/8" d, **$4.50.**

Fruit bowl
Bucks County 3.00
Old Curiosity Shop 3.00

Grill plate, Bucks County 15.00

Gravy boat, underplate, Memory
Lane 15.00

Juice tumbler, Bucks County
.... 15.00

Old fashioned tumbler, Memory
Lane 10.00

Pie plate, 10" d
Currier and Ives, Grist Mill .. 30.00
Memory Lane, Old Swiss Mill
.... 30.00
Willow Ware 25.00

Platter
Colonial Homestead, 11-1/2" l
.... 20.00
Willow Ware, 11" d 30.00

Salad plate
Bucks County 8.00
Willow Ware 10.00

Salt and pepper shakers, pr
Bucks County 20.00
Old Curiosity Shop 25.00

Soup bowl
Colonial Homestead 8.00
Willow Ware 10.00

Sugar bowl, cov
Bucks County, tab handles
.... 20.00

Currier and Ives, angled handles
.... 15.00
Memory Lane, angled handles
.... 15.00

Teapot, cov
Colonial Homestead 90.00
Old Curiosity Shop 100.00

Tidbit, three tiers, Willow Ware
.... 50.00

Vegetable bowl, 9" d
Old Curiosity Shop 15.00
Willow Ware 20.00

Water tumbler, Old Curiosity Shop
.... 15.00

Royal Copenhagen

Many collectors think of Royal Copenhagen as making blue-and-white Christmas plates. However, this Danish firm has also made dinnerware, figurines, and other tablewares.

Royal Copenhagen, Christmas plate, 1975, original box, **$35.**

Bowl, reticulated blue and white,
round 125.00

Butter pat, Symphony pattern, six-pc
set... 35.00

Candlesticks, pr, blue floral design,
white ground, bisque lion heads,
floral garlands, 9" h 160.00

Christmas plate, 1976............. 40.00

Cream soup, #1812 .... 75.00

Cup and saucer, #1870 .... 75.00

Figure
Girl knitting, No. 1314, 6-3/4" h
.... 350.00
Lady with deer, 9-3/4" h..... 350.00

Inkwell, Blue Fluted pattern,
matching tray 150.00

Royal Copenhagen, dish, Langeline, green trademark, three wavy blue lines, green "4228," impressed mark, **$24.**

Royal Copenhagen, Anniversary plate, 1775-1995, original box, **$50.**

Pickle tray, Half Lace pattern, blue
triple wave mark................... 70.00

Plate, #1624, 8" d 50.00

Platter, 14-1/2" l, #1556.......... 140.00

Vase, sage green and gray crackled
glaze, 7" h 150.00

Royal Copley

Royal Copley was a trade name used by the Spaulding China Company of Sebring, Ohio. Concentrating on the table ware and novelty market, Royal Copley was sold through retail stores to consumers who wanted a knick-knack or perhaps something pretty to use on their table.

Royal Copley China, planter, teddy bear by tree, **$20.**

Ashtray, black and pink, 5-1/4" l
.... 10.00

Bank, piggy 25.00

Candleholder, angel with star
.... 40.00

Figure
   Cocker Spaniel..................... 24.00
   Mallard ducks, pr 60.00
   Parrot, 8" h 55.00
   Wren 30.00

Lamp, Flower Tree.................. 70.00

Pin dish, flower, leaf................ 12.00

Pitcher, pink, blue flowers, partial
   paper label, 7-1/4" h 45.00

Planter
   Boy and girl leaning on barrels,
     deep blue and yellow, 6" h
     .... 55.00
   Cow...................................... 20.00
   Deer and fawn head, 9" h..... 40.00
   Elephant and ball 25.00
   Kitten with yarn, c1942-57 .. 42.00
   Mallard Duck....................... 30.00
   Peter Rabbit........................ 25.00
   Puppy and mailbox 15.00

String holder, bird on branch
   .... 75.00

Vase
   Fish, green and brown, gold
     highlights, 8" h................ 35.00
   Floral dec, 4-1/4" h 20.00

Royal Copley China, planter, red bird perched on red and yellow apple, green leaves, **$25.**

Wall pocket
   Angels, blond, blue gown, 6-1/4" h
     .... 25.00
   Apple, red 85.00
   Hat 48.00
   Rooster 35.00

Royal Doulton

This English firm has had a long and interesting history. The company produced a variety of figurines, character jugs, toby jugs, dinnerware, Beswick, Bunnykins, and stoneware. One popular dinnerware line is known as Dicken Ware, named for the Dickens characters included in the design. The listings here are a sampling of Royal Doulton found at flea markets.

Animal
   Brown Bear, HN2659 .... 175.00
   Bunnykins, Aerobic............ 150.00
   Cat with Bandaged Paw, 3-1/4" h
     .... 45.00
   Dalmatian, HN1113 .... 250.00
   Elephant, Flambe, HN489A
     .... 200.00
   Pine Martin, HN2656......... 275.00

Character jug
   Cardinal, large 150.00
   Pickwick, miniature 85.00

Christmas Carol plate
   #1, 1982 .... 35.00
   #2, 1983 .... 35.00

Figure
   Affection, HN 2236 .... 70.00
   Balloon Seller, HN 1743 ..... 135.00
   Beachcomber, HN 2487...... 100.00
   Buttercup, HN 2399.............. 80.00
   Cavalier, HN 2716................ 145.00
   Christmas Morn, HN 1992
     .... 165.00
   Coralie, HN 2307.................. 85.00
   Darling, HN 1985 .... 30.00

   Daisy, HN 3802..................... 90.00
   Gentleman from Williamsburg, HN
     2227 .... 120.00
   Grace, HN2318 .... 100.00
   Janet, NH 1537 .... 80.00
   June, HN 2790 .... 60.00
   Lady Pamela, HN 2718....... 140.00
   Laurianne, HN 2719........... 125.00
   Master, HN 2325.................. 195.00
   Peggy, HN 2038 .... 50.00
   Sara, HN 3219 .... 70.00
   Sir Henry Doulton, HN 3891
     .... 75.00
   Summertime, NH 3137 ...... 100.00

   Valerie, HN 2107 .... 65.00

Mug, mermaid handle 65.00

Plate
   Alfred Jingle 145.00
   Bottom from Mid Summer's Night
     Dream............................. 185.00
   General store 30.00
   Gullivers 95.00
   Henry VIII.......................... 135.00
   Orchids 85.00
   Skater................................... 90.00

Toby jug, small, Farmer John
   .... 50.00

Royal Doulton, figures, left: Old Balloon Seller, HN1315, **$250;** right: The Balloon Man, HN1954, **$330.**

Roycroft

Roycroft is a familiar name to Arts and Crafts collectors. The Roycrofters were founded by Elbert Hubbard in East Aurora, New York. He was a talented author, lecturer, and manufacturer. Perhaps his greatest contribution was the campus he created with shops to teach and create furniture, metals, leather working, and printing.

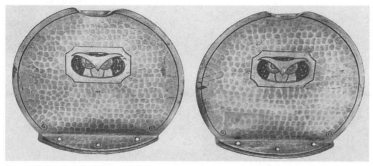

Roycroft, bookends, hammered copper, brass finish, owl motif, impressed and stamped "Roycroft," 5-1/2" w, 4-1/2" h, **$90.**

Roycroft, chair, straight, oak, green leather seat, wear to original finish, **$250.**

Billfold, matching change purse, lady's, 3-1/2" x 6-3/4", tooled leather, emb foliate motif, mononngrammed "RK," orig mirror, pencil, and notepad, orb and cross mark 425.00

Bookends, pr, model #309, hammered copper, rect, riveted center band suspending ring, dark brown patina, imp Roycroft orb, minor wear 225.00

Book, *Elbert Hubbard's Scrapbook,* emb leather cov, orig glassine dust jacket, fitted box, c1923, 228 pgs 90.00

Box, cov, tooled leather and suede lined, lid emb with poppy medallion, orb and cross mark, 1-1/2" x 4" x 4", some scuffs and wear to corners.................... 475.00

Bracelet, hammered sterling silver 225.00

Bud vase, 10-1/2" l, wall hanging, hammered copper, cut-out frame 200.00

Candle lamp, blue art glass, baluster form, flaring foot, stamped "Roycroft," electrified 175.00

Humidor, brass, acid-etched finish, 5" h, discoloration 200.00

Letter holder, perpetual calendar, copper, acid-etched border, orb and cross mark, 3-1/2" x 4-3/4" x 2-1/4", normal wear to patina......... 150.00

Motto, orig Roycroft frame, matted "Do Not Keep Your Kindness...," 17-1/4" x 12-1/2" .... 350.00 "Happiness is a Habit, Cultivate It," 23" x 19" 350.00

Sugar bowl, cov, china, hp by Bertha Hubbard, sgd "B. C. Hubbard" 200.00

Tray, 17" d, octagonal, hammered copper, two handles, orb and cross mark, cleaned patina, slight bend to one edge............................... 290.00

Vase, model #212, copper, tall cylindrical form, rim border of stylized dogwood flowers within diamonds, brass wash with green accents around rim, orb on base, all over wear to brass wash, 10-1/4" h 460.00

R.S. Germany

R. S. Germany wares are also known as Schlegelmilch porcelain, in reference to the brothers whose potteries in the Thuringia and Upper Silesia region of Poland/Germany produced wares from the 1860s until the 1950s. Generally R. S. Germany porcelain is decorated with florals and detailed backgrounds. Handles and finials tend to be fancy.

Biscuit jar, cov, roses dec, satin finish, loop handles, gold knob, 6" h 95.00

Bowl
5-3/4" d, scenic, bird dec, Prov Saxe ES mark 35.00
10" d, shaped petal border, red roses and buds, gold edge, light green mark 100.00

Bread plate, Iris variant edge mold, blue and white, gold outlines, steeple mark 115.00

Calling card receiver, lily mold, blue RSG mark, 5-1/2" l 35.00

Celery vase, handles, multicolored florals, gold trim, RSG steeple mark, 12-1/4" l 80.00

Chocolate pot, white rose florals, blue mark 95.00

Demitasse cup and saucer, pink roses, gold stenciled dec, satin finish, blue mark 95.00

Lemon plate, cutout handle shaped as colorful parrot, white ground, gold trim, artist sgd "B. Hunter" 60.00

Nappy, stage coach scene, Prov Saxe ES mark 70.00

Nut bowl, cream and yellow roses, green scalloped edge, 5-1/4" d 65.00

Plate, white flowers, gold leaves, green ground, gilded edge, dark green mark, gold script signature, 9-3/4" d 45.00

Sugar shaker, floral dec, gold trim, RSG steeple mark 70.00

Tea tile, peach and tan, green-white snowballs, RM over faint blue mark 165.00

R. S. Germany, grapefruit bowl, hand painted rim with grapefruits, foliage, and blossoms, signed "E. B. Jahn," blue R. S. Germany mark, **$40.**

R.S. Prussia

Like R. S. Germany, R. S. Prussia was porcelain made by Reinhold Schlegelmilch in the same region. Designed to be used for export, the wares are mostly table accessories or dinnerware. Pieces of R. S. Prussia tend to be more expensive than R.S. Germany, primarily because of better molds and decoration.

Reproduction alert.

Bowl
10" d, Mold #128, red roses, satin finish, red RSP mark...... 250.00
10-3/4" d, red and pink roses, gold trim, red RSP mark........ 150.00

Celery dish, green florals 175.00

Chocolate pot, cov, green and yellow luster, pink flowers.............. 325.00

Creamer and sugar, florals, blue arched panels........................ 100.00

Ferner, mold #876, florals on purple and green ground, unsigned 175.00

Hair receiver, green lilies of the valley flowers, white ground, red mark 95.00

Plate, poppies dec, raised molded edge and gilt trim, 8-3/4" d 75.00

Shaving mug, mold #609, floral dec, fleur-de-lis, floral dec, red RSP mark 115.00

Spoon holder, pink and white roses, 14" l...................................... 200.00

Syrup, cov, underplate, green and yellow luster, pink flowers 125.00

Toothpick holder, pink and white roses, green shadows, jeweled, six small feet, red mark 250.00

Vase, poppies and snowballs dec, red RSP mark, 6" h 250.00

R. S. Prussia, cake plate, pink, white, yellow, and purple flowers, shaded ground, gold highlights, green wreath mark, 10-7/8" d, **$165.**

Russian Items

Flea markets are great places to find Russian collectibles. From beautiful amber from the Baltic region to pieces commemorating events, there is a lot of variety. Russian craftsmen were known for their exquisite work in silver, enamels, and lacquer.

Beads, amber, graduated, screw closure, 28" l 350.00

Belt, turquoise cloisonné links spaced with silver gilt links, large turquoise clasp, hallmarks.................. 185.00

Blood cup, 4" h, enameled, gilt and transfer dec, Imperial double headed eagle, cipher of Czar Nicholas II above date 1896 .... 260.00

Box, lacquer, Fedoskino, Tzar surveying wonders of Dvidon's Country................................ 575.00

Commemorative coin, Russian scientist A.C. Popov, 1984, 1 Rubl 25.00

Compact, sterling, Catherine the Great on front...................... 175.00

Match safe, patinated, applied plaque with Russian characters, 3" l 125.00

Plate, double-headed eagle crest, hand-painted, 12" d.............. 95.00

Purse, 14k yg, curved frame gypsy-set with eleven old mine-cut and old European-cut diamonds,

Russian items, samovar, brass, several Russian hallmarks stamped on front, scrolled handles with wood hand grips, **$50.**

approx. total wt. 3.00 cts, further set with gypsy-set oval sapphires and circular-cut rubies, mesh body, trace link chain, 95.2 dwt, Russian hallmarks............................. 200.00

Stool, painted, top with geometric strapwork dec, turned tapered legs, early 20th C, 13-1/2" w, 9-1/4" d, 8-7/8" h 125.00

Sugar scoop, 4-1/2" l, silver, cloisonné enamel dec, hallmarked Moscow, dated 1891, maker's mark "G.K." for Gustav Klingert ... 300.00

Wine cup, silver, Slavic flowers decor, 19th C, 2-1/2" h 125.00

Russian items, papier-mâché boxes, left: cigar case, St. Petersburg type scene, **$45;** right: calling card case, royal palace scene, titled and signed in Russian on front, black border and background, **$65.**

Salt and Pepper Shakers

What table would be complete without a pair of salt and pepper shakers? Flea markets are great places to spot novelty and decorative sets. Most can add a smile to even a sleepy head! Generally the salt shaker has larger holes or more holes than the pepper.

For additional listings, see *Warman's Antiques and Collectibles Price Guide* and *Warman's Antiques & Collectibles.*

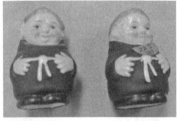

Salt and pepper shakers, pair, monks, Goebel, **$20.**

Apples	10.00
Barn and silo	10.00
Baseball and glove	12.00
Birds on nest	10.00
Bride and groom, Goebel	55.00
Chicks, emerging from egg-shaped cups, script mark "Japan," 4-1/2" h	60.00
Cowboys, Vandor	10.00
Dachshund and tire	18.00
Dobbin horses, Japan	18.00
Duck and egg, 3-1/4" h	27.50
Exxon Tiger, plastic	15.00

Feet	5.00
Frogs	7.00
Granny, in rocking chair, Norcrest	22.00
Indian chief and squaw, 3-1/4" h, both mkd "1947 copyright, Multi Products"	18.00
Lawn mower, moving wheels and pistons, 1950s	30.00
Lemons	5.00
Lennie Lennox, 4-1/2" h, painted ceramic, Lennox Furnace Co., ©1950	95.00
Martians, green, Japan	35.00
Milk cans, copper	20.00
Minnie Mouse and vanity	15.00
New York World's Fair, 1939, 3-1/4" h Trylon shaker, 1-3/4" d Perisphere shaker, 3" x 4-1/2" oval silvered base	18.00
Parrots, Fitz & Floyd	35.00
Penguins, black and white body, orange bill and webbed feet, mkd "Japan," c1930s, 3" h	10.00
Pluto and doghouse	15.00

Salt and pepper shakers, pair, covered wagons, pottery, original label reads "Arrow, Jersey City, NJ, Made in Japan," **$18.**

Poodles	40.00
Rabbits, yellow, snuggle type, Van Telligen	42.00
Refrigerators, GE, 1930-style refrigerator, milk glass	30.00
Sammy Seal, Metlox	75.00
Skunks, Enesco	12.00
Teapot and coffeepot, brown, Japan	12.00
Thermos and lunch pail	35.00

Salts, Open

Before the advent of salt shakers, open salt containers were used on tables. Frequently there was a master salt to hold this precious condiment. Another way of dispensing salt was individual salts, often called salt cellars, with one per place setting, along with a tiny spoon. The individual salts were originally sold as sets and can be found in silver, silver plate, and various types of glassware. Open salt collectors can be found searching flea markets for individual examples to add to their growing collections.

Amethyst-tinted glass, sun-colored	5.00
Bavaria, lavender ext., gold int., mkd "Bavaria," 1-1/2" d	18.00
Cut glass, master, green cut to clear, silver plated holder, 2" h	120.00

Intaglio, individual, bronze basket frame with "jewels," burnished gold scene on body, eight-sided	80.00
Limoges, peach flowers, white ground, gold trim, three small feet	30.00
Lusterware, swan, mkd "Made in Japan by Noritake," 2" h	24.50

Milk glass, top hat, Daisy and Button pattern	20.00
Pattern glass, individual	
Fine Rib, flint	35.00
Hawaiian Lei	35.00
Three Face	40.00
Pattern glass, master	
Barberry, pedestal	45.00

Salts, open, group of 24 matching salts, pressed glass, clear, octagonal, paneled sides, price for set, **$65.**

Salts, open, individual, Nippon China, light blue exterior, white interior with purple flowers, gold trim, three legs, 1-1/2" w, 1" h, **$10.**

Jacob's Ladder, pedestal base 40.00
Snail, ruby stained............... 75.00

Pewter, master, cobalt blue liner, pedestal.................................. 70.00

Porcelain, octagonal, master, blue and white paisley design 10.00

Royal Bayreuth, individual, lobster claw....................................... 85.00

Silver plated, cobalt blue glass liner, 2-1/2" d 22.00

Slag glass, Chick, Spring Surprise, red and gold slag, Boyd, 2".... 10.00

Sterling silver, whale, crystal salt, mkd "Sterling, Germany," 3-1/2" h 60.00

Sand Pails

Bright lithographed metal sand pails have gained in popularity in recent years. Made by several of the major toy manufacturers, they were designed with all types of characters and childhood scenes. Look for ones with bright colors. Most collectors prefer very good examples, but will tolerate some dents and signs of use.

Beach scene, German, 1950s 115.00

Cowboy, chased by Indian, Ohio Art, with shovel........................... 100.00

Easter scene, bunnies and chicks, 6" h.. 85.00

Flower cart, 6" h 35.00

Flowers, metallic blue, Ohio Art, 1960s, 9-1/2" h....................... 40.00

Humpty Dumpty, Ohio Art ... 50.00

Mecki Hedgehog, German 40.00

Mickey Mouse, Donald dressed as commander on homemade warship, desert island setting, "Farm Crest" text around bottom, copyright Walt Disney Enterprises, Ohio Art Co., c1937..................................... 250.00

Red Riding Hood, Ohio Art, 7-7/8" h 75.00

Under the Sea design, Ohio Art, 9-1/2" h 42.00

Sand pail, Captain Hook, Ohio Art, **$65.**

Satin Glass

A type of art glass frequently found at flea markets is known as satin glass. It was first produced in the late 19th century, as an opaque art glass with a velvety matte (satin) finish achieved through treatment with hydrofluoric acid. Most pieces were cased or had a white lining, known as "mother-of-pearl." The most common colors are yellow, rose, or blue. Examples with blended rainbow-like colors are the most desirable. As the glass was made, the glass blowers would create patterns in the bodies that resemble diamond quilting or herringbone patterns, giving the glassware a further descriptive name.

Today, Fenton Art Glass makes interesting examples of satin glass and compliments it even further with hand decorating, reminiscent of the type of decorating the original Victorian consumers favored.

For additional listings, see *Warman's Antiques & Collectibles* and *Warman's Glass*.

Reproduction alert.

Basket
   Blue, herringbone patterned body, mother-of-pearl, applied frosted camphor feet, 5-1/2" h, 4" w 95.00
   Pink shading to white, applied twisted and frosted rope handle, 4-3/4" h, 4" w 95.00

Bowl, raindrop, crimped ruffled rim, white ext., robin's egg blue int., 7" d 60.00

Bud vase, bulbous, small tapered neck, opaque white, price for pr, 7-1/2" h 90.00

Cologne bottle, long dauber, green, oval foot, green, Lancaster Glass 95.00

Cream pitcher, blue, raindrop patterned body, mother-of-pearl,

frosted blue reeded handle, white lining, bulbous, round mouth 195.00

Dish, 5-1/4" d, raspberry ground, ivory ruffled rim 65.00

Ewer
   Blue shading to white, herringbone patterned body applied clear crimped handle, 8-3/8" h 150.00
   Red shading to pink, multicolored enamel floral dec, applied clear crimped handle, 10" h.... 150.00

Paperweight, diamond quilted, turquoise blue, attributed to Fenton 60.00

Perfume bottle, pink, swirl patterned body, mother-of-pearl, white and orange flowers dec,

4-1/2" h, atomizer missing 150.00

Pitcher, bulbous
   Light blue, multicolored enamel floral dec, applied frosted handle, polished pontil, 7" h 140.00
   Pink, yellow plated interior, applied frosted handle, polished pontil, 7-1/2" h.......................... 160.00
   Yellow shading to white, herringbone patterned square body, applied clear handle, polished pontil, 6" h....... 170.00

Rose bowl
   Bright yellow to white, enameled berries, leaves, and stems, Victorian, 4-1/2" h 145.00
   Mottled pink, polished pontil, 2-1/2" h............................ 50.00
   Shaded blue, herringbone patterned body, mother-of-pearl int., 6 crimp top, 4" h 195.00

Toothpick holder, yellow, diamond quilted patterned body, 2-1/2" h 160.00

Tumbler, diamond quilted patterned body, 3-3/4" h
   Blue.. 70.00
   Pink.. 60.00
   Yellow 60.00

Vase
   Blue, raindrop patterned body, frosted amber edge ruffled fan top, 5-1/2" h 145.00
   Rose pink fading to pale pink at base, diamond quilted patterned body, hp spray of carnations, long green stems, 10-3/4" h 175.00
   Shaded pink, diamond quilted patterned body, blue flowers and morning glory dec, bee in flight, 7" h 125.00

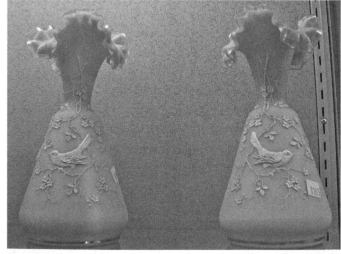

Satin glass, ewers, yellow shading to white base, crimped rims, white birds perched on flowering branches, price for pair, **$165.**

Scales

Whether it's the scales of justice or a candy scale, collectors like to find interesting examples to add to weight their collections.

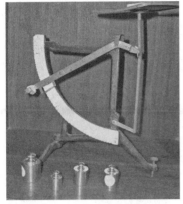

Scale, balance, enameled dial, four brass weights, European, **$25.**

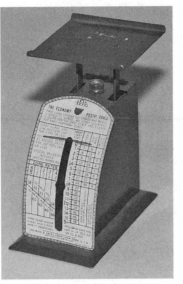

Scale, Economy Postal Scale, No. 500, 1st-class postage was three cents per ounce, original box in rough condition, **$12.**

Scale, hanging type, marked "L F & Co., New York" with three in diamond, suspended hook, **$45.**

Baby, white metal base, white wicker basket, 1950s 65.00

Balance, V.W. Brinckerhoff, New York, cast iron, scroll designs, brass pans, 7-1/4" h, 14-3/4" w....... 85.00

Candy scale, white enamel, 2-lb capacity, Eureka Automatic Scales, No. 35864, with pan, 20" h, 13" w 195.00

Kitchen scale
Montgomery Wards Family Scale, 25-lb capacity 35.00
Universal Family Scale, 24-lb. capacity, 1865 patent date 40.00

Platform, Peerless Junior, Peerless Weighing Machine Co., porcelainized steel, tiled platform, gold lettering, 63" h 350.00

Postal, Nolan Scale Co., Boston, nickel plated, sq pan, dial graduated 0-7, 1889 patent date, desk clamp, 4-1/2" h 175.00

Spring
Fray's Improved Spring Balance, brass and iron, 48 lb, 14-3/8" l 30.00
Penn Scale Mfg. Co., brass and iron, 100 lb., 17-1/2" l, wear 35.00
Morton & Bremner, iron, brass face, 24 lb., 9-1/4" d round tin pan, 11" l 35.00

Store, Hanson Weightmaster, cast iron, gold case with ground, black lettering and indicator, 6" x 14" x 10"... 60.00

Scotties

Scotties are one of the most recognizable dog breeds. Some attribute this to President Franklin Roosevelt and his dog, Fala. Others identify Scotties with Jock from Lady and the Tramp. Many Scottie collectibles are found with black dogs and red and white accents. Scottie images can be found on every type of item, and they bring a smile with their always-happy-wagging tails.

Ashtray, combination ashtray and cigarette holder, mkd "Made in Japan," 4" x 4" x 3" 80.00

Bank, cast iron, Hubley 115.00

Calendar, 1959, Texaco, Scottie and girl on telephone 20.00

Christmas card, two black Scotties on front, single-sided, 1930s... 6.00

Cocktail glasses, set of six 55.00

Dog food dish, emb, McCoy ... 15.00

Doorstop, cast iron, two Scotties, orig paint, 6" h, 8-3/4" l....... 225.00

Ice tub, glass, eight black Scotties around outside, red checker border, 1940s, 4-1/4" h...................... 55.00

Ink blotter, milk glass, chips to ear 65.00

Nodder, celluloid, windup, Occupied Japan 125.00

Pin, gold filled, rhinestone eye and collar 25.00

Powder jar, frosted green glass 85.00

Salt and pepper shakers, pr, figural
Black and white 32.00
Orange Scotties playing
instruments 75.00

String holder, figural 125.00

Toothbrush holder, porcelain, three
Scotties, Japan, 4" h 125.00

Toy, tin wind-up, Marx, orig box
.... 215.00

Scotties, ashtray, chrome Scottie, black enamel base, marked 'Frank Art Inc., Pat Appld For," **$85.**

Sebastian Miniatures

Marblehead, Mass., was the home for Prescott Baston's Sebastian figurines. He started production in 1938 and created detailed historical figurines or characters from literature. Finding a figure with the original label adds to the value of these little charmers.

Sebastian Miniatures, The Skipper, ©1966, P. W. Baston, 3-3/4" h, **$45.**

Abraham Lincoln 18.00

**America Remembers Family
Reads Aloud** 32.00

Aunt Betsy Trotwood 24.00

Building Days Boy, blue label
.... 35.00

Colonial Carriage 80.00

Confederate soldier 22.00

Cow hand, ©1950, MIB 25.00

Dealer plaque, Colonial man,
©1951, MIB 48.00

Ezra, yellow label 30.00

Gibson Girl 90.00

House of Seven Gables 100.00

In the Candy Store, green and silver
Marblehead label 135.00

Mrs. Cratchit, light blue label,
2-1/2" h 30.00

New England Town Crier, figure
standing next to dealer's plaque
.... 25.00

Pecksniff, red label 20.00

Peggoty, blue label 20.00

Sailing Days Girl, red label 35.00

School Days, boy or girl, sitting by
open desk, 3" h 30.00

Sea Captain, #132 .... 30.00

Snow Days Girl, #6253, orig box
.... 35.00

Mark Twain 120.00

Sebastian Miniatures, John Alden, **$30.**

William and Hannah Penn
.... 200.00

Sesame Street

"Sunny day...Everything's A-OK!" That's the song Sesame Street collectors sing as they gleefully search through flea markets for the growing number of items related to Big Bird, Elmo, and the rest of the Sesame Street gang. Wise collectors know to watch for knockoffs: cheap, unlicensed imitations of Sesame Street products. Most of the copycats aren't worth adding to a collection.

Sesame Street, banjo, child's, white plastic body, green, character, played with condition, **$1.**

Sesame Street, Big Bird figurine, Gorham, with original box, 7-1/2" h, **$22.50.**

Bank, Cookie Monster, sgd Jim Henson, orig Sesame Street box 24.00

Book, *Sesame Street L & M Book,* Funk & Wagnalls, copyright 1978, hardcover 4.00

Candy box, tin, Sesame Street Friends for Life, 7" d 4.00

Cookie jar, Big Bird, pale yellow, 11-1/2" h 55.00

Cup, plastic, Cookie Monster 5.00

Fast food premium, McDonald's, Kermit the Frog, NHL, 1995 . 10.00

Figure, Grover, ceramic, Gorham, 1976, 5-1/2" h 22.00

Game, Walk Along Sesame Street, Milton Bradley, orig box, c1975 .... 20.00

Halloween costume, child's, Big Bird, orig costume, mask, box 10.00

Lamp, child's, Big Bird 15.00

Little Golden Book, *Sesame Street The Together Book,* #1978 ..... 5.00

Sesame Street, Tickle Me Ernie, Tyco, original tags, some play wear, **$5.**

Lunch box, metal, Aladdin, plastic, orig thermos, 1985 .... 15.00

Patch, sew-on, Big Bird, 4-1/2" h 9.00

Plush toy
Baby Piggy, 1987 .... 8.00
Christmas Elmo, Tyco, 1997 .... 18.00
Cookie Monster, laughs, says "Oh Boy Oh Boy," 1996 .... 18.00
Grover, Tyco 5.00
Kermit the Frog, Fisher-Price, 1976 .... 15.00
The Count, Tyco, 1997 .... 6.00

Pop-up book, *Grover's Superprise,* 1978 .... 12.00

Puzzle, wooden tray, Hen Pen Men, Playskool, 1973 .... 8.00

Record, Hits from Sesame Street, Vol. III, Peter Pan Records, 45 rpm 4.00

TV Guide, Cookie Monster on cover, July, 1971 .... 15.00

Toy, car, Big Bird driving, ©Mattel Inc., Sesame Street Muppets, ©Henson, Made in China 1.00

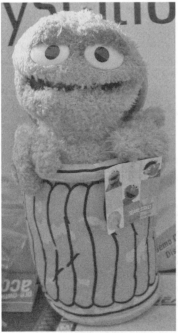

Sesame Street, Oscar the Grouch in his trash can, plush, original tags, **$8.**

Sesame Street, child's feeding dishes, mug, bowl, and plate, all with Cookie Monster, letters, numbers, and shapes as borders, **$15.**

Sevres and Sevres-Type China

Sevres porcelain at a flea market—sure, not every dealer carries it, but some pieces of this fine French porcelain show up at flea markets. Just like today, when Sevres porcelain became so popular, imitations were made. Those are often considered "Sevres type" and are also found at flea markets. Carefully check the mark and decoration of an item before buying it. Many reproduction Sevres pieces exist, including some older fakes.

For additional listings, see *Warman's Antiques and Collectibles Price Guide* and *Warman's English & Continental Pottery & Porcelain*.

Reproduction alert.

Bowl, genre dec top panel, landscape face panel, turquoise blue ground, gilt floral ornamentation, bun feet, entwined "L" mark, date mark "L," 3-1/2" l, 2" w, wear to gilt **180.00**

Clock, 17" h, emb metal case, five inset painted porcelain panels, three are scenic, frontal pc with young lovers, c1900 .... **815.00**

Compote, polychrome transfer printed figural landscapes, bronze mounts, 20th C, 5-1/4" h, price for matched pr **175.00**

Ewer, urn body with courting scene, pastel French colonial dress, sgd "Le Duc," ormolu handles and base, dome lid, mkd, 16" h **375.00**

Luncheon plate, central gilt six-pointed star, border with hunt scenes, 9-3/4" d, price for six-pc set **325.00**

Patch box, cov, 3-1/4" l, shaped ovoid, green ground, hinged lid with hand painted scene of Napoleon on horseback, sgd lower right "Morin" **250.00**

Pin box, cov, cartouche of romantic couple on cover, blue ground, oval, 6-1/2" l **275.00**

Portrait plate, Mme Duchatelet, sgd "G. Perlex," cobalt blue border

with floral panels and gilt accents, scalloped rim, entwined "L" mark, dated "BB" **125.00**

Salt, hp roses, paneled blue and white ground **35.00**

Vase, gilt ground, enamel Art Nouveau stylized leaf and flower design, printed mark, 6" h .. **445.00**

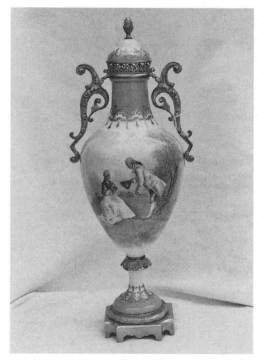

Sevres China, ewer, urn body with courting scene, pastel French colonial dress, signed "Le Duc," ormolu handles and base, dome lid, marked, 16" h, **$375.**

Sewer Tile

Also called sewer pipe, sewer tile was produced from about 1880 through the early 20th century. Draining tiles and sewer tiles were produced at the factories, but the workers often spent their spare time creating other items of utilitarian or whimsical nature. Although some molded pieces were made, much of the production was one-of-a-kind items. Pieces that are signed and/or dated are especially prized.

Ohio is recognized as the leading producer of sewer tile, but other states, including New York, Pennsylvania, and Indiana, all had a strong presence in the sewer tile market.

Sewer tile, spaniel, 10" h, **$250.**

Alligator, Ohio, 15" l 440.00

Bank, dog, seated Spaniel, probably Tuscarawas County, Ohio, 10-1/2" h, minor glaze flakes
.... 220.00

Cat, seated, glaze with copper speckles, small chips, one front foot missing, 7" h 330.00

Dog, seated, spaniel
5-1/2" h, minor edge chips
.... 195.00
8-1/4" h, incised detail up the back, over the head and down the front leg, incised collar and chain, deep-brownish red glaze, oval base, minor base chips
.... 275.00
10-1/2" h, light-brown glaze
.... 330.00

Owl, perched on log, 20th C., 8-1/2" h
.... 165.00

Planter, stump, three branches, hand tooled bark, 9" d, 26" h 225.00

Sewer tile, rabbit, olive green glaze, impressed mark "AR," 5" square, **$40.**

Umbrella stand, tree trunk design, applied roses, chips on flowers, 25-1/2" h 330.00

Sewing Collectibles

"A stitch in time saves nine," or so thought Ben Franklin. Today collectors find lots of sewing memorabilia at flea markets. From tiny needle holders to interesting sewing machines, it just takes a little hunting, like finding a needle in a haystack.

For additional listings, see *Warman's Antiques and Collectibles Price Guide* and *Warman's Americana and Collectibles.*

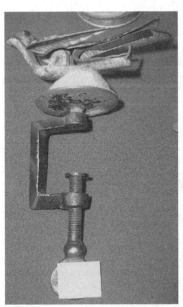

Sewing items, sewing bird, tin litho bird, cast iron base, wear, **$65.**

Bag, printed cotton, mauve, green, lilac, and beige floral design, late 1920s 25.00

Basket, wicker, round, beaded lid
.... 27.50

Book, *American Needlework, 1776-1976*, Leslie Tillett, NY Graphic Society, 1975 .... 15.00

Catalog
New Home Sewing machine, New York, NY, c1900, 12 pgs ... 12.00
United Thread Mills, New York, NY, c1930, 7 pgs 18.00

Crochet hook, metal, capped
.... 15.00

Darning egg
Ebony, sterling handle 100.00
Porcelain, marbleized finish, one piece, 5-1/2" l 12.50
Wood, 5-1/2" l, age crack 10.00

Dress form, wire and cloth 50.00

Embroidery scissors, stork shape, steel, Germany, c1900 .... 25.00

Instruction manual
Domestic Sewing Machine, model 725 .... 10.00
Singer Sewing Machine 400w, 106, 107, 108, 109 and 110, dated 1948 .... 10.00

Machine
Chasige, blue body, child's ... 35.00
Davis, electric 25.00
Greyhound Electric 45.00
Howe, AB, treadle, cast iron base, c1880 .... 100.00
Rowley Electric Automatic, c1935
.... 200.00

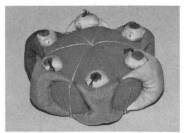

Sewing items, pincushion, Chinamen, 3-1/2" d, **$35.**

Sewing items, Singer sewing machine, small size, original case and accessories, **$480.**

Singer Featherweight, Model 221, black case, attachments, c1941 .... 400.00
Singer, New Family, treadle, cast iron base, c1872 .... 100.00
Weed, Family Favorite, treadle, cast iron base, 1873 .... 175.00
White, #2, electric 10.00

Wilcox & Gibbs, electric, c1930 .... 150.00

Needle book
Hartford Federal Savings & Loan, Pocket-Rocket, litho paper 12.00
Sears Roebuck and Co, A Gift to you from Kenmore - Fine Needlework, Japan 10.00
Sewing Circle, four ladies sewing, six needle packets and threader 10.00

Needle case, egg shape, wood, mkd "The Columbian Egg," Germany, orig needles 155.00

Pincushion
Apple, satin, red and yellow, green leaves and stem, 2-1/2" h, 3" d 65.00
Calico dog, holding flower pin cushion, mkd "Made in Japan," 3" l, 2-1/4" h 30.00
Chinese figures surrounding cushion............................. 35.00

Quilt frame, large, fancy scroll work ends 150.00

Scissors, emb florals on handle, German................................. 30.00

Sewing bird, gilt finish, pin cushion 180.00

Sewing items, Singer sewing machine, child size, **$125.**

Sewing card, child's, Alice in Wonderland, Whitman, 1951 .... 30.00

Spool, woolen, mill type, 8-1/2" h, old blue paint............................... 10.00

Tape measure, figural
Apple, hard plastic, red, leaf pull 24.00
Dress form 50.00
Pig, pink, mkd "Japan" 65.00

Tracing paper, Singer, unopened back, c1960.............................. 4.00

Shaving Mugs

"Shave and a hair cut, two bits!" Oh how we'd love to pay those prices again. And probably finding a barber who still uses old-fashioned shaving mugs might just be harder than finding vintage shaving mugs at a flea market. There are several different types of shaving mugs: fraternal, generic, scuttles. By far the most popular are the occupational-style mugs, made exclusively for use in barbershops in the United States. Introduced shortly after the Civil War, they were still being made into the 1930s. Unlike shaving mugs used at home, these mugs typically had the owner's name in gilt. The mug was kept in a rack at the barbershop, and it was used only when the owner came in for a shave. Occupational shaving mugs, which have a hand-painted scene depicting the owner's line of work, are especially prized.

For additional listings, see *Warman's Antiques and Collectibles Price Guide* and *Warman's English & Continental Pottery & Porcelain.*

Reproduction alert.

Floral and scrolls, transfer design, late 19th C., 3-3/4" h.............. 45.00
Fraternal
Loyal Order of the Moose, gold circle with gray moose head, purple and green floral dec, gilt rim and base, mkd "Germany" 220.00

United Mine Workers, clasped hands emblem flanked by crossed picks and shovels, floral dec, rose garland around top, mkd "Germany" 125.00
Hunting
Duck hunting, 3-1/2" x 3-1/2", hp, duck hunter and dog in boat 275.00

Ducks, 3-5/8" x 3-5/8", hp, two colorful ducks at water's edge, mkd "J. & C Bavaria"...... 100.00
Hunting dogs, 4-1/8" x 3-3/4", hp, two hunting dogs, brown background, mkd "St Louis Electronic Grinding Co., Barber Supplies," some wear to gold trim, crack in ring handle 120.00

Rabbit hunting, 3-1/2" x 3-01/2", hp, large rabbits in foreground, hunter walking through snow, factory in background ... **120.00**

Sportsman, 3-5/8" x 3-5/8", hp, caught fish, fishing rod, shot gun, leafy sprigs, scene of men fishing in background, name in scroll, V D Austria **130.00**

Occupational, hand-painted
Express wagon, 4" x 3-3/4", hp, man driving horse drawn wagon, word "Express" on side, floral springs, gold rim and name **400.00**

Finish carpenter, man planing a board, name above, floral sprigs on sides **250.00**

Hotel clerk, clerk at desk, guest signing register **325.00**

Three shaving mugs, all unmarked, left: burgundy surround, floral trim, name in gold **$35;** center: blue ground, dated 1913, **$50;** right: pink ground, dated 1902, **$45.**

Oil driller, 3-5/8" x 3-5/8", hp, detailed oil well scene, T & V France............................ **220.00**

Shoemaker, hp, scene of shoemaker in shop, gilt foot and swags around name **195.00**

Writer, black desk inkwell with sander, pen, and brass handle **350.00**

Patriotic, flying bald eagle with U.S. flag and leaves/berries in claws, gilt ribbon across flag with name, wear, 3-1/2" h **220.00**

Scuttle
Coronation of H M King Edward VII, 18th May 1937, British seal with monarch, flags on reverse **40.00**

Fish shape, green and brown **75.00**

Shawnee Pottery

From 1937 until 1961, Shawnee Pottery operated in Zanesville, Ohio. The company made kitchenwares, dinnerware, and some art pottery. Two of its most recognized patterns are Corn Queen and Corn King.

For additional listings, see *Warman's Antiques and Collectibles Price Guide.*

Shawnee Pottery, ice-lip pitcher, Sunflower, 7-1/4" h, **$55.**

Bookends, pr, cattails and ducks **75.00**

Bowl, 8-3/4" l, oval, Corn King, #95 .... **45.00**

Butter dish, cov, 7" l, Corn King, mkd "#72, Oven Proof" **165.00**

Coasters, pastels, set of four **50.00**

Cookie jar
Happy, Dutch boy **385.00**
Mugsey, blue scarf **500.00**
Smiley Pig, red flowers **200.00**

Cornucopia, blue **30.00**

Creamer
Cat, yellow and green **55.00**
Corn King, #70 .... **25.00**
Puss-n-Boots **85.00**

Figure
Goldfish, 3-1/4" h **16.00**
Elephant, yellow, 3-1/4" h **18.00**
Raccoon, 3-1/2" h **60.00**

Fruit dish, Corn King, #92 ...... **40.00**

Incense burner, Chinaman, blue base, mkd "USA" **30.00**

Pie bird, Pillsbury, 5-1/2" h...... **85.00**

Shawnee Pottery, planter, Old Mill, olive green glaze, marked, **$40.**

Shawnee Pottery, cookie jar, Smiley Pig, holding purse, rosebuds on hat, green ruffle at neck, **$95.**

Pitcher
Bo Peep, 1940s, mkd "Patented Bo Peep USA" **195.00**
Chanticleer **250.00**

Fern............................. 65.00
Smiley Pig, clover dec, red
   bandanna 165.00

Planter
Deer and fawn 27.50
Fish 70.00
Flying goose......................... 35.00
Old Mill 40.00

Pixie boot, green, gold trim . 15.00

Salt and pepper shakers, pr
Chanticleer 50.00
Corn King, tall..................... 35.00
Dutch Couple....................... 70.00
Milk Cans 24.00
Smiley Pig............................ 75.00
Swiss kids 40.00

Spoon holder, flower pot, mkd
   "patent pending" 15.00

Teapot, Granny Ann.............. 175.00

Vase, white, 10" h..................... 35.00

Wall pocket, birdhouse 35.00

Sheet Music

Here's a topic that might get you humming along. Sheet music is especially popular today, perhaps because the nostalgic appeal of the old tunes or the interesting cover art. You might want to check that old piano bench to see what titles are stored there.

A Woman In Love, Guys & Dolls, photo of Brandy & Sinatra 25.00

Blue Christmas, 1964 .... 2.50

Coast Guard Forever.............. 15.00

Couldn't Sleep A Wink Last Night 12.50

Down Yonder, Spade Copley.... 10.00

Father of the Land We Love, 1931 .... 8.00

Five Minutes More 12.50

G.O.P. March, red, white, and blue cover, elephant beating bass drum, blue and white images of Landon and Knox, "For President/For Vice President," text at bottom "Sold to Help Finance The 1936 Campaign" 80.00

Heart of My Heart, 1926............ 3.75

I Don't See Why I Cannot Stay At Home, front cover with oval sepia photo of waif-like newsboy in winter clothing, ©1915 .... 10.00

Keep 'Em Flying 15.00

Lady Madonna, Beatles 18.00

Love & Marriage..................... 12.50

Sheet music, *The Midnight Fire Alarm*, written by Harry J. Lincoln, arranged and published by E. T. Paull, ©1907, **$25.**

McKinley and Hobart Grand March, Boston Weekly Journal of Sheet Music, July 8, 1896 .... 20.00

Milkman Keep Those Bottles Quiet, Broadway Rhythm, Tommy Dorsey, 1944 .... 5.00

No Orchids For My Lady......... 15.00

Now Is The Hour, Bing Crosby 12.00

One Zy, Two-Zy, 1964 .... 12.00

Paper Doll, Sinatra.................... 15.00

Sidewalks of New York, "Complete with Campaign Choruses," tan, brown, and white, Al Smith and facsimile signature 40.00

Soconyland Is Everywhere You Go, color cover with map of New York and New England states, eight pgs, ©1928 Standard Oil Co. of NY 20.00

The Marines' Hymn, 1942 .... 15.00

Thicker than Water, Andy Gibbs 4.00

Welcome Back, John Sebastian 4.00

When My Prince Charming Comes Along, Ellis, 1935 .... 10.00

White Christmas, 1942............... 4.50

Shenango China

New Castle, Pennsylvania, was the site of the Shenango China Company from 1902 until 1961. It was bought out by Anchor Hocking in 1979, after having merged with Castleton China between 1940 and 1968. By 1991, the factory closed, causing a hole in the heart of the whole town. Shenango China is typically a full-bodied china, often found as restaurant ware. Look for a bold mark, often including an Indian brave, as well as the company name and pattern name.

Shenango Pottery, butter pat, Blue Willow pattern, colored Indian mark, 3-1/2" d, **$12.**

Ashtray, Golden Door, International Arrivals Building, Idlewild Airport, black logo, white ground, 4" d 15.00

Bicentennial plate, Washington crossing Delaware, multicolored underglaze print, harvest gold filigree border 20.00

Bowl, black spatter border, center black silhouette of horses and a carriage with driver 6.50

Butter pat, Blue Willow, multicolored Indian mark, 3-1/2" d 12.00

Coffee mug, Steak n Shake, mkd "Shenango China USA ©Interpace T-34," 3-1/2" h 28.00

Cookies for Santa plate, center image of jolly Santa 24.00

Cup and saucer
Navy, blue and gold trim, gold Dept of Navy insignia, mkd "Shenango China USA" 16.00
Nestle's, Inca Ware, Indian mark 18.00
Restaurant style, turquoise ext., white int. 15.00
Western Round Up 85.00

Cup, Summer Daze, black backstamp with Indian, RimRol, Welroc N-22, c1960 .... 10.00

Dinner plate
Christmas, dark blue, white etched winter scene 20.00
Waldorf-Astoria, green and purple oak leaf wreaths, hotel logo 24.00
Western Round Up 90.00

Gravy boat, Quartermaster, 10" l., 4-1/2" h 22.50

Grill plate, red and white coach scene, cabbage rose rim, sitting Indian stamp mark, 10-1/4" d 28.00

Salad plate, Waldorf-Astoria, green and purple oak leaf wreaths, hotel logo 18.00

Sauceboat, Parliament Gold, Staffordshire shape, ivory, mustard band, gold trim 15.00

Service plate, Sheraton Hotel, floral center, wide green border, gold logo and trim 22.00

Serving bowl, restaurant ware, white, dark green lines, 9-5/8" l, 7" d 15.00

Soup bowl, Turf Catering, 9" d 8.50

Sugar bowl, cov
Restaurant ware, white body, dark green lines, mkd "Rim Rol, Wel-Roc," orig box 16.00
Western Round Up, tan Inca Ware body, western motif, green back stamp "Shenango China, New Castle, PA, U.S.A. Rimrol Welroc U15" 125.00

Signs

Advertising signs have been a staple of flea markets for many years. With the many signs available, great examples can be found in all price ranges and made from different types of materials. Bright colors and appealing graphics are important, but condition is always critical.

Reproduction alert.

Sign, Coca-Cola, metal, round, red, white lettering, **$175.**

American Field Hunting Garments, diecut cardboard counter type, mallard, 1940-50 .... 140.00

Bell System, Public Telephone, bell logo in center, porcelain flange, 18" sq 275.00

Butternut Bread, Gee! But It's Dandy Bread, 7" x 10", cardboard diecut, repairs.................................... 20.00

Columbia Records, cardboard, Columbia Phonograph cylinder packages on either side of highly emb American eagle standing stop stars and stripes shield, 11" x 14-1/2"..................................... 200.00

Creamsicle, Enjoy This Delicious Treat, boy holding Popsicle, tin 15.00

Edgemont Tobacco, linen, shows two colorful packages, framed, 36" x 12" 70.00

Entrance, reverse-painted glass, 3-3/4" x 18" 22.00

Goody Root Beer, tin, c1940 .... 95.00

Hawaiian Pineapple Juice, Surf Rider, tin.................................. 15.00

Helmar Turkish Cigarettes, porcelain, 24" x 12"................. 80.00

Independence Indemnity Insurance, tin litho, 15" x 18" 55.00

Kellogg's Corn Flakes with Bananas, cardboard stand-up, easel back, 30" x 20" 275.00

Kramer's Full Flavored Beverages, 9" x 20", tin, red, black, and green on white, c1960 .... 40.00

Signs, Kurfees Paints, flange porcelain sign, 14" x 20-1/4", **$30.**

Merkle's Blu-J Brooms, emb tin, shows Blu-J sitting atop broom, framed, some damage, 13" h, 9-1/2" w 175.00

Nu-Wood Insulating Wall Board and Lath, porcelain, house among trees, mfg. by Veribrite Signs, 22-1/2" x 35" 100.00

Park Lane Frocks, 7-1/2" x 15", reverse glass, gold, brown, green, white, light green, Price Brothers, Inc., Chicago-NY 20.00

Purity Butter Pretzels, diecut cardboard, easel back, smiling blond boy carrying giant pretzel against black background, white lettering, early 1930s, 22" h, 12-1/4" w 70.00

Rainbow Is Good Bread, 2-1/2" x 18", emb tin 15.00

Red Coon, Sun Cured Chewing Tobacco, heavy paper, red and black raccoon, yellow ground, black lettering, 18" x 22" 60.00

Segal Key, double sided, diecut tin litho, key shape, 31" l 170.00

Vienna Pudding, paper, comical dinner guests looking as family dog runs between butler's legs, spilling the Vienna Pudding, border trimmed, 12-1/4" x 9" 80.00

Wells Fargo Lamont Gloves, 9-1/2" x 23-1/2", 1950s 25.00

Silhouette Pictures

Silhouette pictures are decorative plaques with rounded or convex frames over a black image. Having foil or colored backgrounds, they were a later generation's answer to the old hand-cut silhouettes, thus the name.

Dresser box, wood, red metal trim, large heart shaped cut-out on top with dancing silhouettes, lined int. with mirror, 8-1/2" x 6-1/2", wear 50.00

Picture, convex glass type
Equestrian jumping fence 40.00
Fairies, painted background, 1929 .... 35.00
Girl with doll 30.00
Hearts, shows suitor, mkd "Deltex" 24.00

Lady, seated at vanity, hairbrush in hand 40.00
Lady with bird in cage, pale pink background, silver stars, 8-3/4" x 10-1/2" 60.00
Lovebirds, boy courting girl, two lovebirds watching, foil accents on dress and boy's suit 30.00

Southern belles, one holding parasol and sniffing flower, other bending to pick flower, pr 35.00

Silhouette pictures, black reverse painted silhouettes on white glass, Martha and George Washington, names in script, wooden frame, **$60.**

Silhouette pictures, black and white silhouette, gent on bended knee, holding hand of lady with fan in other raised hand, framed, **$20.**

Silhouette pictures, top: pair of round miniature silhouettes, both with fashionable ladies walking dogs, **$40;** lower: man in tree picking apples for lady with checkered apron, titled "Ripe Apples" on sign, **$35.**

Thermometer and scene
Dick's Café Manchester, Maryland, ducks taking flight from autumn setting pond, gold metal frame, 5" w, 4" h........................... 15.00
Two women sitting by fireplace, one in rocking chair knitting, other at spinning wheel, 1941 calendar 40.00

Silver, Plated and Sterling

Every flea market has great examples of silver in sterling and also silver plate. Look for hallmarks and a maker's mark to determine the age of a piece, its silver content, and perhaps the country of origin. Also check for signs of silver polish hidden in crevices, often an indication that a piece has been polished for years. When examining plated silver, some wear is acceptable if it doesn't detract from the overall appearance.

For additional listings, see *Warman's Antiques and Collectibles Price Guide.*

Silver plated, water pitcher with ice lip, **$50**; silver plated tray with raised scalloped border, **$95**.

Silver plate

Baby rattle, bells, rocking horse on one side, blocks on other, 4-1/2" l 25.00

Bank, clown with umbrella 35.00

Butter dish, cov, glass insert, mkd "Sheridan, Silver Plated," 3-1/2" h 45.00

Candelabra, pr, three-light, tapering stem issuing central urn-form candle-cup and two scrolling branches supporting wax pan and conforming candle-cup, oval foot with reeded border, vertical flutes, Continental, 12" h 150.00

Champagne bucket, cylindrical, bracket handles, applied scroll border band, monogram, Simpson, Hall, Miller & Co., 9" h 275.00

Child's mug, two handles, engraved 30.00

Comb case, emb floral design, faux tortoiseshell comb, 5" l 30.00

Crumb set, brush and tray, mkd "Quadruple Plate, Crescent Silver Co. 94" 25.00

Entree dish, oval, gadrooned rim, detachable foliage handles, monogrammed, American, 11-1/2" l 80.00

Salt and pepper shakers, pr, Oneida, weighted bases, 4-3/4" h 20.00

Teapot, Derby Silver Co., emb floral motifs and arabesques, 8" h .. 60.00

Toast rack................................ 45.00

Tray, rectangular, center chased with scrolls, trellis, and foliage, gadrooned and foliate handles, English, 27" l........................ 150.00

Wine cooler stand, Art Deco, Reed & Barton 200.00

Silver, sterling

Baby spoon, ornate curled handle
Cupid 65.00
Mother Goose....................... 60.00

Basket, reticulated, sides with scrolls and diapering, scroll rim, three scroll feet, fluted base, monogrammed, Whiting Mfg Co., 9" d....................................... 460.00

Child's mug, single handle, engraved bands, monogram 45.00

Cigarette/compact case, chain, allover scrolling.................. 110.00

Creamer, tapered cylindrical, short spout, scroll handle with shell terminal, applied stepped base, monogrammed, Paul Storr, London, 1831, side mkd "Storr & Mortimer," 2-7/8" h 200.00

Glove hook, ornate handle...... 30.00

Silver, sterling, Christmas ornament, Dove of Peace, Heritage House Christmas Heirloom Collection, original box and certificate of authenticity, original red hanging ribbon, tarnished, **$25**.

Grape shears, grape motif dec 90.00

Ladle, 11" l, oval bowl, curved tapered handle with floral and beaded trim, mkd "Made by - Ramirez," Mexican government eagle mark, "Sterling," "Hecho en Mexico".............. 415.00

Meat skewer, George III, Thomas Whipham & Charles Wright, London, 1761-62, tapering, plain loop terminal, engraved "V," mkd, 3.90 oz, 12-3/4" l................. 210.00

Nail file, head of woman as handle, 6-1/2" l 30.00

Order, Austrian, 1929-30, traces of gilt, inscribed "HM 1929/30," marked, 6" l, 1.30 oz............ 120.00

Punch ladle, scrolling foliage, monogrammed, 9-1/2" l...... 100.00

Salad serving fork and spoon, Chambord pattern, Reed & Barton, monogrammed, 9" l 200.00

Salt and pepper shakers, pr, 3-1/2" h, Spratling, domed forms on angular wooden bases, maker's marks 500.00

Salt, open, 4" l, Walker & Hall, Sheffield, 1902-03, Edward VII, cobalt blue glass liner, mkd. 180.00

Teapot, Kingston pattern, Wallace 250.00

Tea service, marker's mark "H.F.," London, 1914, George V, reeded borders, 9-1/4" h teapot with wood handle and finial, creamer and open sugar, 19.45 ozs 300.00

Travel clock, plain rect case with rounded corners, eight-day movement, oct goldtone engine-turned face, black Roman numerals, silver surround with engine turning, engraved scrolls and floral sprays, monogrammed cover, Wm Kerr & Co., 3-5/8" l 200.00

Whistle, chain, Reed and Barton, sterling, MIB.......................... 45.00

Sleds

You won't find the infamous "Rose Bud" sled at a flea market, but you might be able to find some other interesting examples. There are many variations of sleds, some made for boys, girls, singles, doubles, and even some with wheels for those who lived in "snowless" climates. Don't overlook sled-related collectibles.

Inkstand, brass, sled figural, glass well....................................... 195.00

Pencil box, sled shape, wooden, 8-1/2" l 200.00

Postcard, Christmas Greetings, two children on sled, 1915 postmark 15.00

Sled, wooden
Dog, oval decal and "Wagner Make," 30-1/2" l.............. 300.00

Dutch, oak, woven fabric seat, 1960s 160.00
Flexible Flyer, No. 60J, 1960s, 60" l 40.00
Hustler, painted on red ground 360.00
Rocket Plane, Flexible Flyer type, 51" l 55.00
Running horse design, 19th C., 26" l 150.00
Yankee Clipper #10, Flexible Flyer 75.00

Sled, L L Bean, wood, for small child, **$45.**

Smurfs

Smurfs made their debut in 1958, as secondary characters for a story illustrated by Pierre Culliford, better known as Peyo. It wasn't long before these little blue guys and gals were taking center stage. Collectors know to watch for figurines, toys, records and other Smurf memorabilia at flea markets.

Animation cel, matted, mkd "#240 21 65," 11" x 14".................... 95.00

Bicycle license plate, Smurfs Ride Free, 1983 .... 3.50

Book, *Smurfing in the Air*........ 3.50

Card game, 1982, MIB 12.00

Dexterity puzzle, Smurf girl shooting PEZ into Papa Smurf's mouth, green case, European, 1980s 10.00

Figure
Drummer, plastic, 1966.......... 6.00
Olympic Smurf 40.00
Smurf with Go-Cart, MIB 15.00
Super Smurf, with hobby horse, MIB 15.00
Tennis player, plastic, 1981 .... 4.00

Key chain, figural, 2-1/4" h........ 5.00

Lunch box, plastic, Thermos Co.,1987.................. 32.00

Mushroom cottage, Peyo Schleich, orig box, description in English, French and German, 1970s, MIB 55.00

Ornament, wearing red hat, 1978 .... 1.25

Smurfs, book, *The Hundredth Smurf*, Random House, 1982, **$2.50.**

PEZ
Boy, blue stem 3.00
Papa, red stem 3.00
Smurfette, yellow stem 14.00

Playset, Smurf Village 8.00

Stuffed toy
Amour Smurf 12.00
Baby Smurf, pink, 16" l 20.00
Baseball Smurf, baseball shirt, baseball in hand, orig side tag, 1982................................... 12.00
Blue, 1979, 16" h................... 20.00
Papa, sitting, 10" h................. 12.00
Smurfette 12.00
St. Patrick's Day 14.00
Sweetheart Valentine............ 12.00

Telephone, mkd "H. G. Toys," 1982 .... 20.00

Wind-up toy, blue and white, mkd "Wallace Berry Co., Hong Kong," 1980 .... 12.00

Snack Sets

A snack set is the combination of a plate or tray with an indent to hold a cup. Perfect for a snack in front of that new invention, television, or perhaps just the item to serve refreshments on the patio. Many glass and dinnerware services included these items in the 1950s. Whole sets can be found in original boxes, perhaps attesting to the fact that although they were a great wedding present, the idea never really caught on.

Snack set, milk glass, 10-1/4" x 7-1/4" tray, set of six, **$27.50.**

Anchor Hocking
Classic 10.00
Grape, clear, grape and leaf design,
  orig box 26.50
Primrose, Anchorglass, milk glass,
  11" l plate, eight-pc set..... 25.00
Wheat, eight-pc set 65.00

Bavaria, bone china, purple roses
dec, 7-1/2" d plate.................. 15.00

California Pottery, bright orange,
1960s, four pcs, orig sticker "Cal-Style Ceramics Torrance Calif
#2433".................................... 40.00

Federal
Red rose dec 5.00
Yorktown, orig boxed set 24.00

Fire-King
Fleurette................................ 24.00
Soreno, green, 9-3/4" d plate,
  2-1/2" h cup....................... 5.00

Hand painted, pink flowers with
yellow centers, green leaves, gold edge, artist sgd "G. H. T. 1940,"
8-1/2" x 7-1/4" plate, 3-1/2" d x
1-7/8" h cup 24.00

Hazel Atlas
Apple Waffle Block 10.00
Capri Sea Shell pattern, light blue
  .... 18.00
Sea Shell, crystal, 10" x 6-1/2" tray,
  3-1/2" d x 2-1/2" h cup..... 20.00

Indiana
Harvest Grape, milk glass 9.00
Kings Crown, amber 12.00

Lancaster, Daisy and Button, olive
  .... 18.00

Lefton China
Poinsettia.............................. 20.00
Summertime......................... 24.00

Noritake, red rose, gold trim ... 15.00

Shelley, Flowers of Gold, pattern
#141287, Dainty shape........ 130.00

Steubenville, Woodfield pattern, two
Tropic Green, two Salmon Pink,
four Dove Gray, 9" plate, 4-1/4" w x
2-1/2" h cup, 16-pc set, one chipped
plate 60.00

Soda

Getting thirsty? Collectors from around the country tend to call carbonated beverages by different names: it's "soda" to some, "soda pop" to others, and "pop" in other regions. Whatever your passion, flea markets are a great place to find collectibles that will "wet your whistle."

Advertising trade card, 5" x 6-1/2",
Hires Root Beer, full color portrait
of young lady holding package of
powdered "Hires Improved Root
Beer," brown and white text on
reverse, late 1800s 15.00

Blackboard, Frostie Root Beer, tin,
1950s..................................... 75.00

Carton ad, 6-3/4" x 7-1/2", Squirt,
diecut thin cardboard, © 1961
Pilgrim and turkey, smiling Squirt
Boy, Turkey Day Treat with
Squirt................................. 10.00

Smiling Santa carrying sack
  with Squirt Boy inside, Merry
  Christmas from Squirt..... 10.00

Construction sheet, Tiny Nehi
Animal Show, 9" x 12-1/2" stiff
paper, full color circus performer,
animals, clowns, ringmaster, and
bareback rider, Nehi Bottling Co.,
1930s-40s, unused................ 30.00

Cooler, Drink Dr. Pepper, airline
style, 16" h, 18" w, 9" d 190.00

Counter bin, 9" x 13-3/4" x 4-1/4",
Quaker Brand Salted Peanuts
  .... 42.00

Coupon, Hires Root Beer, druggist
stamp on front, 1-3/4" x 3".... 95.00

Door pull, Enjoy Kist Beverages,
Here's Refreshment, litho tin 60.00

Fan, 75 Years Good, Dr. Pepper, Good
For Life, cardboard.............. 100.00

Mug, 4" d, 6-1/2" h, Richardson Root
Beer Rich, clear glass, frosted white
letters, 1940s.......................... 20.00

Soda collectibles, Richardson Root Beer, Rochester, NY, cone shaped wax coated container, 9-3/4" h, **$15.**

Poster, 13" x 19", 7Up Fresh Up Family, full color of father reading bedtime story to sons, all enjoying bottle of 7Up, ©1948 .... 20.00

Sidewalk marker, Enjoy Grapette, Walk Safely, brass, round, 1940s-50s.. 50.00

Sign
Ask For Orange-Crush Carbonated Beverage, embossed tin, 1940s, 12" x 20" 165.00
Drink Barq's, It's Good, embossed tin, 12" x 30".................. 100.00

Drink Canada Dry, metal flange, white shield with crown, 14-1/2" x 17-1/2"........................ 100.00
Drink Sun Spot, tin, 9-3/4" x 12" 185.00
Enjoy Orange Crush, celluloid, 9" d 75.00

Thermometer, Drink NuGrape Soda, A Flavor You Can't Forget, tin, rounded top and bottom, shows six bottles, 16" x 6-3/4" 100.00

Soda Fountains

Soda fountains are another icon of a bygone era. However, a variety of soda fountain collectibles draw keen interest on today's collectibles market.

Ashtray, Breyers, 90th Anniversary, 1866-1956 .... 22.00

Barbie, Soda Fountain Sweetheart Barbie, Coca-Cola, 1st in series, MIB...................................... 250.00

Can, Abbott's Ice Cream, half gallon, Amish girl, c1940 .... 15.00

Dispenser, Buckeye Root Beer, tree trunk shape.......................... 375.00

Display card, 5" x 8-1/2", 7-Up, diecut cardboard, full color image of infant in red playsuit, copyright 1950 .... 15.00

Glass, Hershey's, clear, 5-3/4" h, pr 22.00

Ice cream scoop, Indestructo No. 4 .... 50.00

Jar, Borden's Malted Milk, glass 175.00

Magazine cover, *Saturday Evening Post,* young soda jerk talking to girls at counter, Norman Rockwell, Aug. 22, 1953........................ 15.00

Menu, Rush's Luncheonette, 1955 .... 5.00

Milk shake glass, hard plastic, soda fountain style, premium, Quik rabbit and blue "Nestles Quik," 16-oz, 6-3/4" h, pr 12.00

Milkshake machine, Hamilton Beach, triple head, green....... 75.00

Paper cone dispenser, glass tube, metal holder, "Soda Fountain

Drinks & Ice Cream Served in Vortex," gold label, wall mount, 11" l.. 40.00

Pinback button, Sanderson's Drug Store, blue and white, soda fountain glass illus, "Ice Cream, Soda/Choice Cigars/Fine Candies," 1901-12, 1" d 28.00

Seltzer bottle, cobalt, Babad's Miami Seltzer Co............................. 100.00

Soda fountain collectibles, fan, heart shaped cardboard diecut, pretty girls on front, back with advertising, **$45.**

Sign, Orange County Fountain, porcelain on steel, yellow oval center, blue and white lettering, dark blue ground................ 110.00

Back of fan with advertising, "Mission Shop, Compliments of Thos. H. Hollingshead, Wholesale and Retail Dealer in Ice Cream and Confectionary, Sole Agent in Moorestown for Breyer's Ice Cream, printer: Harvey M. Bates, Calenders, etc. Phila, Pa," thin wood stick..

Spoon, Wm A Rogers, 1900s, 5" l 15.00

Straw holder, pressed glass, clear
Cradle shape, 1910s............ 250.00
Cylindrical, red metal lid, 1950s
.... 175.00

Sundae glass, tulip shape, clear,
5-3/4" h 15.00

Syrup jar, white porcelain, metal lid/
pump, set of four 125.00

Tray, 13" x 11", Schuller's Ice Cream,
ice cream sodas and cones .. 200.00

Whipped cream dispenser, mkd
"Kidde Mfg Co.," 10" h 35.00

Souvenir China

These porcelain souvenirs have images of places or events. Early examples were hand-painted in England and Germany, and specially made for merchants in the United States. Souvenir china can be found in a variety of forms, from ashtrays and pitchers to plates and vases.

For additional listings, see *Warman's Americana & Collectibles* and *Warman's Antiques and Collectibles Price Guide*.

Bank, Marion, VA, Smith County
Courthouse, barrel shape, 3" h
.... 80.00

Box, cov, Rushville, IL, Wester School,
black transfer, made by Wheelock
.... 70.00

Chamberstick, Brant Rock, MA,
National Electric Signalling Co.,
From Bluefish Rock, Aladdin style,
2-1/4" h, 6-3/4" l 160.00

Condiment set, Gettysburg, 1863,
hp, salt and pepper shakers,
condiment jar with lid and spoon,
5-1/4" x 5-1/2" base, orange, yellow
flowers, green leaves, gold, irid
slate blue, and white accents, mkd
"Nippon," 1930s 25.00

Cup and saucer
Niagara Falls, marked "Carlsbad,
Austria" 18.00
Wildwood by the Sea, NJ,
multicolored scenes, mkd "Hand
Painted Japan" 30.00

Demitasse cup and saucer, Hotel
Roosevelt, New Orleans 35.00

Souvenir china, plate, View of Million Dollar Pier, Atlantic City, NJ, multicolored, gold reticulated border, **$45.**

Souvenir china, plate, Ocean Yacht Race, Newport 1964 Bermuda, map of Bermuda in center, **$25.**

Plate
Along 101 The Redwood Highway,
maroon, Vernon Kilns 25.00
America's Playground, Florida
Sunshine Flowers, The Singing
Tower, brown and white, Jonroth
.... 25.00
Birmingham, AL, The Industrial
City, maroon, Vernon Kilns
.... 20.00
Boston, MA, Filene's, brown,
Vernon Kilns 20.00
Carlsbad Caverns, White's City, New
Mexico............................. 25.00
Delaware Tercentenary Celebration,
1938, black and white, Spode
.... 35.00
Denver, CO, state capital in center,
blue, Vernon Kilns 20.00
Franconia Notch, NH, Cannon
Mountain, aerial passenger
tramway, Jonroth 20.00
Greenville, SC, blue, Vernon Kilns
.... 20.00
Luray Caverns, colorful center, gold
rim.................................... 25.00

Nevada, The Silver State, Hoover
Dam in center, brown, Vernon
Kilns 20.00
New Mexico, picture map 20.00
Plymouth Rock, Plymouth, MA,
brown and white, Jonroth
.... 25.00
San Diego County Fair, Delmar, CA,
Don Diego Welcomes You, blue
.... 35.00
West Virginia, state capital in
center, brown 20.00
World's Fair, Century 21-Seattle
World's Fair-1962, black
lettering, center with yellow and
green grounds illus, sponsor
inscription "Made Expressly For
Frederick & Nelson-Seattle"
.... 12.00

Match holder, Grand Falls, NE,
cobalt, Germany 50.00

Teapot, Little Falls, NY, High School,
5-1/2" h 100.00

Toothpick holder, Alexandria, VA,
Christ Church, 2-1/2" h 50.00

Souvenir china, plate, "Regent Spring, Excelsior Springs, Mo.," Wheelock China, 3-7/8" d, **$45.**

Vase, Cripple Creek District, CO, The Independence Mine, cobalt, two handles, Germany, 3" h 130.00

Souvenir Spoons

Collecting souvenir spoons has become more popular in the past few years. Collectors are starting to admire the tiny treasures often for their colorful decoration as well as the place they honor. The following is a sampling of sterling silver souvenir spoons.

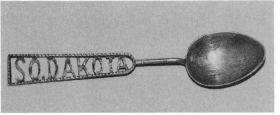

Souvenir spoon, "So. Dakota," **$30.**

Souvenir spoons, assorted, each **$15** to **$45.**

Souvenir spoon, Queen Victoria Diamond Jubilee, sterling silver, gold wash, coronation scene in bowl, elaborate decoration on both sides of handle, 6-1/4" l, **$170.**

Alaska Yukon Pacific Expo, emb "Alaska" on front, dog tem, huskies, and skagway on back, emb "A.Y.P. Expo, 1907," 5-1/2" l 115.00

Atlantic City, oar shape, shows sailing ship and lighthouse, Codding Bros. & Heilborn, 4" l 18.00

Colorado Springs, script name in bowl, handle of columbine flowers, prospector, Balance Rock, state capitol crest, Federal post office and Mining Exchange on back..... 55.00

Houston, engraved in bowl, mkd "Wallace Silversmiths, Watson Co., Texas".................................... 45.00

Kennedy, bust of JFK, "35th President 1961-1963," bowl emb "Friendship 7," Wm. Rogers Mfg. Co., silver plated.................... 25.00

Mormon Temple, Salt Lake City, engraved in bowl, block letters handle, 5-1/8" l 45.00

New York City, Statue of Liberty, city seal in bowl, Shiebler, 4-1/4" l 75.00

New York World's Fair, 1939, lettered inscription on handle, detailed image of Trylon, Perisphere, and Theme Building, Exposition Silver Plate, 6" l... 12.00

San Diego Skyline, mission, fruit, Paye & Baker, Old Palms, 5-5/8" 50.00

St. Louis, Missouri, corn stalks, hay, "United We Stand, Divided We Fall," St. Louis engraved in bowl, American eagle and Justice on back, 5-1/2" l 85.00

Summerville, SC, double-sided full-figured black man holding melon, engraved bowl 110.00

Tacoma, WA, Old Church, gold-washed bowl, state handle, Mayer Bros., 5-3/8" l........................ 30.00

Vermillion, SD, gold-washed bowl, view of the university building, Whiting, 5" l 24.00

Space Adventurers, Fictional

Space adventurers have always fascinated folks, from Buck Rogers in 1929 to the early awaited sequels to Star Trek. We're spellbound by their adventures—taken to new places and returned safely at the journey's end.

For additional listings, see *Warman's Americana & Collectibles*.

Action figure, Cylon Centurian, Battlestar Galactica 50.00

Activity book, *Planet of the Apes*, Saalfield, © 1974, unused 12.00

Big Little Book, Whitman
Buck Rogers in the City of Floating Globes, 1933 .... 70.00
Buck Rogers, 25th Century A. D., 1938, Cocomalt premium 48.00

Book, *Tom Corbett's Wonder Book of Space*, Marcia Martin, Wonder Books, 1953 .... 12.00

Booklet, *Meet Major Matt Mason-Mattel's Man in Space Mattel's Man In Space*, 1965 .... 18.00

Card game, E. T., Parker Bros, ©1982 Universal City Studios 8.00

Code wheel, Captain Midnight 20.00

Coloring book
Planet of the Apes 10.00
Rocky Jones, Space Ranger, Whitman, cockpit cov, 1951 .... 40.00

Comic book
Battlestar Galactica, Marvel, Vol. #1, #1, March, 1979 .... 5.00
Micornauts, Marvel, Vol. 1, #1, 1978 .... 5.00
Space Ghost, 1987, Hanna-Barbera 7.00

Cookie jar, space capsule, decal "A Lasting Reminder of the Space Age," and "Gateway to the Stars, Cape Kennedy," Capitol Pottery, 1965, 8-1/2" h 225.00

Crayon box, Buck Rogers Crayon Ship, cardboard, six colored pencils, c1930.................................... 175.00

Die-cast, Lost in Space Jupiter 2, with bonus film clip, MOC 5.00

Direction finder, Battlestar Galactica, 2" d plastic compass with paper insert, Larami Corp, ©1978 Universal City Studios, MOC .. 8.00

Figure, Buck Rogers, Buck, Dr. Huer, Dale, Friend, Monster, painted lead, each....................................... 40.00

Flashlight, Captain Astro, wrist type, Bantamalite, c1967, MOC 45.00

Game, battery operated, space ship saves the world, plastic and cardboard, 1970s 115.00

Gun, Captain Video Secret Ray Gun, red plastic flashlight, secret message instructions, Power House Candy premium 90.00

Lid, Rocky Jones Space Ranger, painted red, white, and blue, center rocketship, planet, and stars, text "On TV every Sunday at 5:30 on WTTG/Channel 5" (Washington DC), threaded, c1954, 2-3/4" d 40.00

Light, E. T., finger, battery operated, Knickerbocker, ©1982 Universal City Studios, MOC................. 20.00

Lunch box
Buck Rogers in the 25th Century, metal, with plastic thermos, 1979, Aladdin.................. 55.00
Space 1999, metal, with thermos 45.00

Mask, Wicket W. Warrick, latex rubber, brown and black, 1983 Lucasfilm Ltd. ©, Don Post Studios Inc.. 12.00

Space adventurer, fictional, Tom Corbett, bed spread, chenille, twin size, **$150**.

Movie poster, 2001: A Space Odyssey, 1968 .... 175.00

Pinback button, Rocky Jones, Space Ranger, membership type 45.00

Pop gun, Buck Rogers, XZ-31 Rocket Pistol, cardboard, full color, Cocomalt premium, 1934, repairs to paper insert, some discoloration and damage to one side......... 35.00

Punching bag, Buck Rogers Official Punch-O-Bag, unopened tan envelope with rubber balloon, Morton's Salt premium, Lou Fox, Chicago, 1935 .... 40.00

Salt and pepper shakers, pr, boys in space suits, 1950s 40.00

Viewmaster gift set, E. T., red hard plastic viewer, ©1982 Universal City Studios, unopened................. 15.00

Wallet, Battlestar Galactica, vinyl, 1971, Larami, MOC............... 18.00

Space Exploration

In a day when space shuttle flights are commonplace, we've lost the excitement associated with early space flights. Nonetheless, space-related memorabilia, from the days of Sputnik to today's missions to Mars, is available to collectors. Flea markets are a great place to find such items.

For additional listings, see *Warman's Americana & Collectibles.*

Badge, 6" d celluloid, full color portrait of Apollo XI astronauts rimmed in upper red and lower blue, white lettering, cardboard insert with unused diecut easel, bar pin fastener........................... 20.00

Card, 10-1/2" x 13-1/2", cardboard, multicolored, 3-D image of astronaut and landing module floating above moon crater, printed in Japan for W. C. Jones Publishing Co., Los Angeles, ©1966 .... 28.00

Calendar plate, 1984, Columbia space shuttle, "Hail Columbia," Spencer Gifts, 9" d 9.00

Charm bracelet, 7-1/2" l brass, 11 colorful enamel charms, Apollo missions 7-16, generic NASA Apollo charm, Rocket Jewelry Box, Inc., MIB.............................. 15.00

Commemorative cover, 3-3/4" x 6" envelope from stamp club, Apollo 11 images, not stamped or canceled 4.00

Drinking glass, 4" h, Apollo 13, continuous red, white, and blue scene, 1970 .... **5.00**

Flight commemorative, 3-1/2" celluloid pinback, black and white photo, red, white and blue border, gold lettering on 2" x 4" purple ribbon "Astronaut Gordon Cooper, Welcome Back to Earth in Faith 7/22 Orbits Around the World May 15, 1963" **20.00**

Greeting card, happy birthday, Space Patrol Man, diecut, full-color, transparent green helmet, orig envelope.................................. **25.00**

Hanger, 11" d thin plastic replica of lunar surface, craters, elevation ridges, valleys, glows in dark, 1969 .... **12.00**

Key holder, 1-3/8" d bright gold luster metal key ring and clip, Apollo II, orig box, 1969 .... **14.00**

Map
  Hammond's Guide to the Exploration of Space Map, 7-1/4"

Space explorers, *Apollo, Man on the Moon Coloring Book*, Artcraft, 1969, 11" x 8-1/2", unused, **$20.**

x 10-1/2" folded, opens to 29" x 45", 1958.......................... **25.00**
  Lunar space map, 20" x 24", full color, Lipton premium, 1969 .... **15.00**

Medallion, First Man on Moon, brass **8.00**

Mug, 6" h, glossy white hard plastic, western boot shape, red, white, and blue flag above red and blue inscription "NASA/Houston, Texas," c1970..................................... **10.00**

Pass, 2-1/2" x 4", Distinguished Guest, NSA space shuttle flight 51-1, laminated plastic, spring clip fastener, 1985......................... **24.00**

Pennant
  5" x 10-1/2", First Men on Moon, thin vinyl, blue, white, gray, and black, red, white, and blue flag, top margin with Armstrong's "One Small Step" statement **14.00**
  29" l, red, white, and blue felt, illus of Apollo 11 moon landing **5.00**

Pinback button, 3-1/2" d, Astronaut John Glenn, New Frontier, 1962 .... **20.00**

Placemat, 10" x 14", textured paper, bright red, white, and blue design, used by TWA at Kennedy Space Center, 1976............................. **5.00**

Playing cards, 2" x 3", Space Shuttle, Kennedy Space Center, FL, c1980, sealed in orig cellophane....... **10.00**

Postcard, 5" x 7-1/8", full color NASA photo of earth, Apollo 8, unused **5.00**

Print, 10-3/4" x 15-1/4", Challenger Tragedy, black and white illus on parchment-like paper, dated Tues Jan 28, 1986, New York Daily News

Readers Care, titled "Per Ardua Ad Astra"...................................... **10.00**

Record, 33-1/3 rpm, NASA Radio Presentation, scheduled for weekly broadcast week of Oct. 18, 1976 .... **5.00**

Sticker, 3-3/4" d
  Apollo 11, peel-off paper, winged eagle landing on moon, 1969, unused................................ **3.00**
  Apollo 15, red, white, blue, gray, and black, cardboard, logo for July 1971 mission............... **4.00**

Token, 1" d, aluminum, bright gold finish, Apollo 11, lunar landing on one side, Armstrong's quote on other, July 20, 1969................. **3.00**

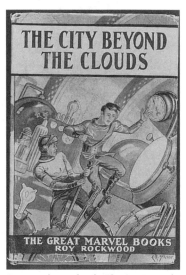

Space explorers, book, *The City Beyond The Clouds*, Roy Rockwood, Cupples & Leon Co., New York, 1925, **$15.**

Space Toys

Now that we've done some imagining about space adventurers and real space heroes, how about some toys to round out our experience? Flea markets are sure to yield some out-of-this-world treasures.

Also see Robots.

Action figure, Commander Sisko, Deep Space Nine, 1994, MIB, 5" h **8.00**

Astronaut, Mark Apollo Astronaut, Marx, jointed plastic, orange space suit, white helmet, plastic

accessories, orig instructions and box, 7-1/2" h **175.00**

Bagatelle game, space theme, rockets and moon graphics, 14" x 8" **25.00**

Bendee, Close Encounter of the Third Kind, Alien, MOC.................. **45.00**

Colorforms, Battlestar Galactica **35.00**

Flying saucer, litho tin, space pilot, revolving antenna, swivel lighted engine **325.00**

Space toy, space tank, marked "Made in China, MIB," **$45.**

Game

Moon Blastoff, Schaper, unused,
sealed, MIB 48.00
Planet Patrol, 1950s 75.00

Gun

Jet Space Gun, KO, Japan, tin litho,
1960s, 10" l 55.00
Junior Jet Play Gun, open faced box
with Space Girl graphics
.... 45.00
Rocket Jet Space Gun, silver plastic,
7" l 45.00
Space Fazer, Kusan, 12" l 65.00
Space Flash, battery operated,
plastic, 6" l, MIB 65.00

Helmet, Space Patrol, cardboard,
1950s 215.00

Kite, Gayla Space Craft, unused, MIP
.... 35.00

Model, AMT, Apollo Spacecraft,
c1969, 5" x 7" x 1", unused 12.00

Moon lander, 10" x 17" header card,
cellophane bag holding 10" x 10-
1/2" rigid cardboard lunar surface
target, plastic "LEM" thrower, eight
extended sprockets, each tipped
with rubber suction cup, made in
Hong Kong, 1970s 18.00

Play set, Space Shuttle Space Set,
plastic, 11 pcs, 1984, Hong Kong,
unsealed 25.00

Puzzle, 500 pcs, Journey to the Moon,
Life series ©1969 Time Inc., 8" x
11" x 2" box, orig poster missing
.... 10.00

Space ships

Apollo, battery-op, Japan, MIB
.... 275.00
Gemini, litho tin, plastic windshield
broken, 6" h 100.00

Space toy, torpedo boat, friction, marked
"Made in China, MIB," **$40.**

Space toy, radar rocket, black, red, and
yellow plastic console, silver paper
accents, Remco, original box, **$40.**

Space capsule, inflatable,
Friendship 7, Puralator
premium, 1962, 22" x 22" x 20"
.... 30.00

Top, Space Top, litho tin, 1950s
.... 45.00

Yo-Yo, Orbit, small white plastic
satellite, green plastic ball used to
represent Earth, string, copyright
1969 Tom Boy Inc., blue, white, and
orange blister card 10.00

Whistling moon whistle, 3" h
rocket replica, yellow plastic nose
cone, red plastic base, center blue
paper wrapper, Japanese maker,
instructions for use, 1950s 12.00

Spongeware

Ever see pottery that looked like someone had taken paint and just sponged all over the piece? Well, that's spongeware. Extensively produced in England and America, spongeware items were most commonly blue and white, but yellowware with mottled tans, browns, and greens was also popular. The design was achieved by sponging, spattering, or daubing on the color, and it was generally applied in an overall pattern. Care should be taken when examining a piece of spongeware, as modern craftsmen are making some examples that rival their antique ancestors.

For additional listings, see *Warman's Antiques and Collectibles Price Guide* and *Warman's Country Price Guide.*

Reproduction alert:

Reproductions and contemporary examples are quite common.

Bank, pig, brown and green sponging,
pierced eyes and coin slot, 6" l
.... 220.00

Bowl
11-1/2" d, green and brown
sponging, glaze flakes 300.00
12" d, blue sponging above and
below blue stripe 275.00
12" d, blue sponging overall
.... 415.00

Butter crock, Good Luck pattern,
blue dec, 5" h, 7-1/2" d 225.00

Carpet ball, 3-1/4" d
Brown 85.00
Green 75.00
Red and white plaid 90.00

Chamber pot, handle, overall blue
sponging, 10" d 125.00

Cup and saucer, blue flower dec on
cup 60.00

Dish, blue and white, serpentine rim,
6-1/2" x 8-1/2" 200.00

Milk pitcher, black sponging, white
ground, 7-1/2" h 185.00

Mixing bowl, blue and white, 8" d
.... 175.00

Pitcher

Barrel shape, green, gold, and brown sponge, 10" h **110.00**

Chicken wire design, blue sponging, 9" h, T-shaped tight through line **165.00**

Lattice design, brown and green sponging, yellow body, rim chips, 9-1/4" h **85.00**

Spongeband, large, Red Wing **195.00**

Rolling pin, Wildflower, cobalt blue dec **290.00**

Salt shaker, Spongeband, blue dec, white glaze, Red Wing **120.00**

Spittoon, blue bands, imperfections, 5" h, 7-1/2" d **100.00**

Sugar bowl, cov, floral reserve, brown sponge, English, 19th C, 4" h **95.00**

Whimsy, figural cowboy hat, dark blue sponging, c1900, some glaze crazing, 5-1/2" l **45.00**

Spongeware, bowl, tortoise shell pattern, amber ground, brown and black striations, **$85.**

Sporting Collectibles

Whatever sport is your passion, you're bound to find some interesting examples of ephemera and other collectibles while browsing a flea market.

For additional listings, see *Warman's Antiques and Collectibles Price Guide, Warman's Americana & Collectibles,* and specific categories in this edition.

Sporting collectibles, cigarette case, contoured, black gun metal, sterling silver relief of soccer player, gemstone catch, 3-7/8" x 3-1/4", **$185.**

Autograph

Gallo, Bill, 6-1/4" x 9", Boxing Writers Assoc Dinner program, Waldorf-Astoria, NY, 1968 .... **18.00**

Hagler, Marvin, 8-1/2" x 11" black and white photo, mkd "Courtesy of KO Magazine," captioned with name and "World Middleweight Champion," autographed "To Chuck, Best Wishes World Champion, Marvelous Marvin Hagler #84" **20.00**

Patterson, Floyd, 3-1/4" x 5-1/4" greentone photo arcade card, black ink "All the best, Floyd Patterson," c1960.............. **25.00**

Pep, Willie, 8" x 10" glossy black and white Wide World photo, 1940s **35.00**

Specht, Bobby, 8" x 10" glossy black and white photo, Ice Capades, 1957 .... **8.00**

Belt, glossy plastic, clear plastic buckle, black images of golfer, tennis player, boxer, and baseball player, 1950s, 34" l, 1" w, slight darkening **10.00**

Bumper sticker, Kentucky Colonels, ABA ball, team logo, name in blue and white, unused, 1974-75, 15" l **20.00**

Cabinet photo, 4-1/4" x 6-1/2" card, sepia tone photo of young male skater in competition uniform, 1890s..................................... **15.00**

Lamp, 14-3/4" h bowling pin, 9" h metal figure of bowler, white shirt, dark blue pants, brown belt and shows, "Sensenich Golden Eagle Nylonized" decal, bowling ball with red "ABC," 1950 .... **60.00**

Sporting collectibles, pocket scorer, The Chicago Tribune, celluloid, American Art Works, Conshocton, Ohio, **$40.**

Sporting collectibles, postcard, Soldier Field and Field Museum, Grant Park, Chicago, 1937 postmark, **$5.**

Magazine article, *Sports Illustrated*, Muhammad Ali **9.00**

Matchbook, Bowl for Your Health, 1930, 1-1/2" x 2", unused **2.00**

Original art

11" x 11" white sheet, crisp black ink of Cuban bantamweight champion Lorenzo Safora, by "Lewis," early 1940s **24.00**

12" x 16-1/2", Swedish heavyweight Ingemar Johansson on the night of June 20, At New York's Polo Grounds, by Gene Basset for Sporting News, artist sgd lower right corner **40.00**

Patch, fabric

3" x 3-1/2", Bowling League Champion, c1966 .... **1.50**

3-1/2" d, white, red and blue stitching, "W. R. Hearst Citizen Rifle Teams-Junior" **8.00**

Pinback

2-1/4" d, Madison Regatta, 1980 admission badge, full color, Budweiser sponsored speed boat race 2.50

3" d, Unlimited Hydroplane racing boat, Atlas Van Lines 8.00

Pin set, Smokin Joe's, Winston Cup Competition, Camel Cigarettes,

4" x 7" colorful high gloss enamel cardboard folder holding set of six driver portrait pins 15.00

Photo, 8-1/4" x 10" glossy black and white of Jack Demsey, US Army Signal Corps, dress uniform, 1944 .... 12.00

Print, 11" x 14", portrait of Tex Rickard by Charles M. Quinlan, c1930 .... 15.00

Weight lifting award, 1-1/2" d dark bronze-like medal, inscribed "Weight Lifting," engraved "Awarded to Bob Hoffman-Cyr Bell-Bent Press-1936" 20.00

Sporting Goods

So, you'd rather participate in sports than watch? Need some kitschy decor items for your family room? Well, head for the flea market and look for some of these neat collectibles.

Baseball cap, autographed, game used

Jackson, Bo, 1994 CA Angels 85.00

Walker, Larry, 1995 Colorado Rockies 165.00

Baseball glove, professional model

Del Ennis, Wilson 60.00

Joe Dimaggio, Spalding 50.00

Pee Wee Reese, pre-World War II 75.00

Basketball, autographed

Archibald, Nate 100.00

Bird, Larry 200.00

Bradley, Bill 150.00

Catalog

Melrose Boat Works, Melrose Park, IL, c1930, 19 pgs, You Won't Go Wrong With the Melrose Boat Way! Build Your Own Boat with Our Blue Prints, cuts of cabin cruisers, sail boat, etc....... 40.00

National Target & Supply, Washington, DC, 1930s, 131

Sporting collectibles, Keds basketball shoes, **$35.**

pgs, 8-1/2" x 11", Handbook & Catalog, cuts of targets..... 40.00

Old Town Canoe Co., Old Town, ME, 1973, 28 pgs, Old Town Discovery, The Finest in Canoes, Kayaks & Power Boats 35.00

Shakespeare Co., Kalamazoo, MI, 1959, 32 pgs, 7" x 10", Angler's Catalog 24.00

Spaulding, A. G., & Bros., Chicopee, MA, 1911, 52 pgs, Catalog X, steel playground apparatus 55.00

Football, autographed

Bergey, Bill 70.00

Ditka, Mike 125.00

Flaherty, Ray...................... 150.00

Hockey stick, game used, autographed

Cashman, Wayne, Sher-wood, uncracked....................... 175.00

LeBlanc, J. B., Koho, cracked 50.00

Minnow bucket, green canvas, collapsible, No. 08, Mfd. by the Planet Co., West Field, Mass., 7-1/2" h 155.00

Roller skates, Glove Roller Skates No. 197, Marvel Beginners Ages 2-5, orig box, one leather strap missing 35.00

Shot holder, James Dixon & Son 35.00

Skis, pr, wood, early, hand made, leather straps 150.00

Staffordshire Items

The Staffordshire district of England is well known for the quality porcelain produced there through the centuries. This region was home to many potteries that supplied dinnerware, table items, and novelties such as mantel figures and toby jugs.

For additional listings, see *Warman's Antiques and Collectibles Price Guide* and *Warman's English & Continental Pottery & Porcelain.*

Bank, cottage shape, 5-1/4" h, repairs 195.00

Chamber pot, cov, 9" h, Columbia, mkd "W. Adams," short hairline in bottom 80.00

Creamer, cow, blue and dark red splotch polychrome dec, pearlware, early 19th C, 7" l 235.00

Cup and saucer, handleless, dark blue transfer of vase with flowers,

imp "Clews," small chips, wear 95.00

Cup plate

Polychrome floral wreath border, spring center, imp "TT" 145.00

Staffordshire items, figure, milkmaid and cow, oval base, polychrome enamel decoration, **$125.**

Sheltered Peasants, dark blue, flower and fruit border, mkd with title 110.00

Two hunters, one seated, hunting dog, light blue, border with gun and bag, imp "D" 100.00

Figure

Scottish couple, matching green feathered caps, man wearing green and orange tartan, holding horn, woman holding basket 115.00

St. Patrick, standing, hand to heart, base titled, enamel and gilt dec, Victorian, c1860 .... 215.00

Templars, modeled as three officials, two women flanking bearded man, raised initials I.O.G.T. (International Order of Good Templars), Victorian, c1870 .... 200.00

Victoria and Victor Emmanuel II, modeled standing figures, man

in military attire with hound by his feet, woman in formal dress, base titled "Queen & King of Sardinia," gilt trim, Victorian, c1855, crazing 200.00

Whippet holding rabbit in its mouth, Victorian, second half 19th C, price for pr, one with leg damage 425.00

Mantel ornament, cottage, Potash Farm, hairlines, 9" h 175.00

Mug, pearlware, black transfer print of Hope in landscape scene, silver luster highlights, minor imperfections, 3-3/4" h 60.00

Plate

Dr. Syntax Disputing his Bill with the Landlady, blue and white transfer, James and Ralph Clews, Cobridge, 1819-36, 10-1/2" d 125.00

Staffordshire items, plate, Harper's Ferry from the Potomac Side, from American Scenery series, light blue decoration on white, marked "John & Wm Ridgeway," 9-1/4" d, **$85.**

Staffordshire items, plate, red transfer, **$15.**

New York, US, medium red, eagle and cornucopia mark, 5-7/8" d 95.00

Shannondale Springs, Virginia, US, medium red, eagle and cornucopia mark, 7-7/8" d 70.00

Toddy plate, 4-13/16" d, multicolored view of thatched cottage at foot of hill, surmounted by castle ruins, sepia butterfly border, imp "P" 90.00

Undertray, Death of Punch, Dr. Syntax literary series, blue and white transfer, James and Ralph Clews, Cobridge, 1819-36, 10" x 5-3/4", crazing on reverse 85.00

Vase, cow and calf with tree trunk vase, facing pair, Victorian, c1870, 10-3/4" h 470.00

Waste bowl, Forget-Me-Not, red transfer, edge roughness, 5-5/8" d 60.00

Stangl

Stangl Pottery was an active pottery in the Flemington, N.J., area. It produced colorful dinnerware and tablewares and is well known for its interesting bird figurines.

For additional listings, see *Warman's Antiques and Collectibles Price Guide* (Stangl Birds) and *Warman's Americana & Collectibles* (dinnerware).

Basket, #3414 .... 20.00

Butter dish, cov, Garland 45.00

Cake stand, Fruit and Flowers 60.00

Candy jar, Terra Rose 60.00

Carafe, Colonial, wooden handle 65.00

Casserole, Fruit, 8" d 85.00

Chop plate, Magnolia, coupe shape 40.00

Cigarette box, cov, Daisy 50.00

Coffeepot, Blueberry 100.00

Creamer
Blueberry 15.00

Blue Rooster 27.50
Fruit 25.00

Cup and saucer
Colonial 12.00
Country Garden 20.00
Fruit 18.00
Harvest 22.00
Terra Rose 24.00
Town and Country, brown ... 20.00

Stangl Pottery, server, center metal handle, original foil label, **$35.**

Dinner plate
Arbor 22.50
Country Garden 45.00
Fruit...................................... 25.00
Terra Rose............................ 15.00
Water Lily 15.00

Eggcup, Country Garden 15.00

Gravy boat
Golden Harvest.................... 15.00

Stangl Pottery, sugar and creamer, Town and Country, brown and white, pair, **$30.**

Thistle.................................... 24.00

Mug, Town and Country, blue
.... 22.00

Pitcher, Amber Glo, pint.......... 40.00

Platter
Blueberry, 14" d.................... 75.00
Fruit, 12-1/2" d..................... 35.00

Punch cup, Jeweled Christmas Tree
.... 25.00

Salad bowl, Orchard Song....... 50.00

Salt and pepper shakers, pr,
Blueberry.............................. 24.00

Teapot
Bachelor Button................... 40.00

Stangl Pottery, dinnerware set, White Dogwood, 51 pieces, **$250.**

Stangl Pottery, dish, flower, detailed center, turquoise glaze, **$28.**

Harvest 80.00
Terra Rose............................. 60.00

Tidbit tray
Bittersweet, 10" d................. 45.00
Morning Blue........................ 45.00

Vase, Antique Gold, orig sticker, 5-1/2" h 45.00

Vegetable bowl
Blueberry.............................. 50.00
Orchard Song, divided 25.00

Stangl Pottery, Kiddieware, divided feeding dish, chicks and bunny, **$85.**

Stanley Tools

Some of the finest tools were created by the Stanley Tool Co. Today they are increasingly collectible. Look for examples free of rust and damage, but expect to find some wear from usage.

Adjustable scraper, wooden handle 65.00

Stanley tools, miter box, #150, cast iron, some wear, **$65.**

Brace, No. 923, 8" l 45.00

Chisel, No. 750, 5/8" bevel edge, mkd "Stanley, D, Made in USA," 9-1/4" l 35.00

Clapboard marker, No. 88, 80% nickel remains 25.00

Doweling jig, No. 59, nickel-plated, orig box................................. 30.00

Folding measure
No. 27, 24" 10.00
No. 38, 24" 20.00

Hammer
Claw, 7 oz, bell face 25.00

Magnetic tack, No. 601, orig decal 40.00

Jointer, No. 7, 22" l 85.00

Level
No. 27, 9" l 10.00
No. 104.................................. 40.00

Pick, No. 7 .... 45.00

Plane
No. 3, c1950, made in USA logo, rosewood handle............ 100.00
No. 4, type 11, three patent dates cast in bed, dark rosewood handle............................ 115.00
No. 25, block, 9-1/2" l......... 250.00
No. 45.................................. 150.00

No. 48, tongue and grove ... **120.00**

No. 62........................... **400.00**

No. 90, rabbet plane, orig box

.... **165.00**

Pocket level, patent date June 23 '96, 3" l.. **75.00**

Putty knives, Handyman, cocobolo handles, six-pc set, orig box

.... **95.00**

Ratchet brace, No. 2101, Yankee, 14" l....................................... **75.00**

Router, No. 71-1/2..................... **60.00**

Saw set, No. 43, pistol-grip, orig box

.... **60.00**

Vise, No. 700 .... **45.00**

Yard rule, No. 41, maple, 36" l

.... **45.00**

Star Wars

"May The Force Be With You" as you search for collectibles from this series of science-fiction movies. George Lucas brought such special effects to the screen that fans of all ages were mesmerized. Twentieth Century Fox was clever enough to give Kenner a broad license to produce movie-related toys and items, creating a wealth of Star Wars materials for collectors.

Action figure

Chewbacco, weapon, pouch and ammunition belt, 1978, mint, 12"

.... **70.00**

Chief Chirpa, Return of the Jedi, MOC................................. **35.00**

Darth Vader, 12" h, Kaybees Exclusive, MISB **60.00**

Hoth Snowtropper, Empire Strikes Back, MOC **150.00**

Imperial Commander, loose .. **8.00**

Luke Skywalker, 1st issue, 12" h, MISB.............................. **38.00**

Bank, Darth Vader, black vinyl, Adam Joseph Industries, ©1983 Lucasfilms Ltd., orig box....... **20.00**

Cereal box, Kellogg's, Star War C-3PO, 1984 .... **35.00**

Clock, Bradley, 1980-84 .... **45.00**

Earrings, pr, figural, metal, C-3PO, Weingeroff, ©1977 20th Century Fox **5.00**

Figure, Darth Vader, hp bisque, Sigma, © 1983 Lucasfilm Ltd., orig string tag and box.................. **20.00**

Game

Escape from Death Star Game, 1977

.... **35.00**

Ewoks Save the Trees, 1984, sealed

.... **25.00**

Model, Klingon Battle Cruiser, Star Trek: The Next Generation, AMT Ertl, MIB................................. **35.00**

Pencil tray, C-3PO, Sigma **50.00**

Play set

Hoth Generator Attack, white hard plastic ice base, generators,

Scout Walker vehicle, six diecast metal figures, Kenner, ©1982 Lucasfilms Ltd., MIB........ **30.00**

Imperial Attack Base, snow base, action levers, Kenner, ©1980 Lucasfilms Ltd., MIB........ **75.00**

Poster art set, Star Wars 3-D Darth Vader, Craftmaster, ©1978 20th Century Fox, 17-1/2" x 22" sealed box **15.00**

Record, Star Wars, 24-page read-along book, 33-1/3 rpm record, Buena Vista.............................. **5.00**

Shampoo, Yoda, 6-1/2" h **35.00**

Star Wars, action figure, Ewok, Urgah Lady Gorneesh, Kenner, **$22.50.**

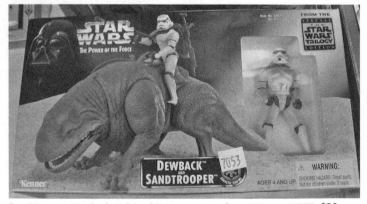

Star Wars, toy, Dewback and Sand Trooper, action figure, Kenner, NRFB, **$20.**

Steiff

Steiff bears and toys are recognized by their button ear tag. Steiff's first teddy bear appeared in 1903 and was an instant hit. The company remains in business, and collectors know the name means quality and a well-made toy.

Steiff, bear, modern, beige fur, red ribbon, round metal tag, **$40.**

Arco German Shepherd, mohair, 1950-60 .... 70.00

Beaver, Nagy, mohair, chest tag, post WWII, 6" l............................. 95.00

Bunny, Manni, button.............. 85.00

Circus seal, with ball, on stand 85.00

Cocker Spaniel, Cockie, black and white mohair, 1950-60 .... 90.00

Donkey, Grissy, gray Dralon, black plastic eyes............................. 30.00

English Sheep Dog, long white pile mohair, 1950s 40.00

Fawn, straw stuffed, glass eyes, ribbon collar 30.00

Frog, 3-3/4" l, velveteen, glass eyes, green, sitting, button and chest tag 125.00

Goat, 6-1/2" h, ear button....... 150.00

Hen, gold and black spotted feathers, yellow plush head, felt tail, black button eyes, c1949 .... 85.00

Kangaroo, plush, glass eyes, two plastic Joeys in pouch........... 70.00

Koala, glass eyes, ear button, chest tag, post WWII 135.00

Leopard 90.00

Llama, white, brown spots 110.00

Owl.. 75.00

Parakeet, Hansi, bright lime green and yellow, airbrushed black details, plastic eyes, button tag, chest tag, plastic beak and feet 115.00

Penguin, Peggy, glass eyes, ear button, chest tag, post WWII 95.00

Pony, brown and white mohair, glass eyes, 1960s............................. 60.00

Rabbit, jointed, mohair, 6-1/2" h 110.00

Steiff, cocker spaniel, tan and white, original ribbon tag, **$35.**

Seal, tan mohair, gray spots, black eyes, 1950-60 .... 30.00

Squirrel, Perri........................... 45.00

Teddy bear

Blond mohair, glass eyes, ear button, brown embroidered nose, mouth and claws, excelsior stuffed, felt pads, c1930, 13" h 150.00

Light brown plush, glass eyes, jointed, c1950................. 350.00

One Hundredth Anniversary Bear, ear button, gold mohair, fully jointed, plastic eyes, orig box, 17" h 200.00

Tan mohair, ear button, chest tag, jointed, c1980.................. 75.00

Stein, Lea

A French lady by the name of Lea Stein is taking over the jewelry market! Her creations use a secret method of layering colored sheets of plastic, then cutting fanciful shapes. She started her jewelry business in Paris in 1969 and continues today, releasing a new design every year. Look for her signature on the closure to make sure it's a genuine piece of Lea Stein jewelry.

Bracelet, bangle, dark green and red swirled peppermint stick swirls 75.00

Earrings, pr, clip, bright green swirls on pearly white, stamped on back, 1-3/8" d 75.00

Pin, signature Lea Stein-Paris V-shaped pin back
Bacchus, cat, pearly silver and black, 2-3/8" w, 1-1/8" h... 65.00
Bee, transparent wings with gold edge, faux ivory body and head, topaz colored glass edge eye, 2-3/8" wingspan 70.00
Blueberries, peach lace, 2-7/8" l 65.00

Cicada, irid red wings, striped body and head, 3-3/8" l, 1-1/4" w 75.00
Flamingo, pink, 1-7/8" w, 2-3/8" h 55.00
Flower pot, two flowers, one aqua lacy turquoise, other purple lacy, dark blue leaves, turquoise lacy pot, 1-1/2" w, 2-1/2" h 65.00
Mistigri Kitty, caramel, 4" 2, 3-7/8" h............................. 70.00
Panther, pearly ivory harlequin, medium faux tortoiseshell, 4-1/4" l, 1-3/4" h............... 65.00
Swallow, pink and white lace wings, 2-3/4" w, 1-3/8" h 60.00
Swan, silvery glitter neck, black

Lea Stein, brooch, cat, Atilla, blue, **$75.**

beak and a faux-coral seashell body, 1-7/8" w, 2-7/8" h ... **85.00**

Three ducks, orange lace bodies, dark royal blue heads, dark blue wings, 1" w, 2-1/4" h **85.00**

Steins

Finding steins at flea markets is great fun. Look for advertising or novelty steins, and don't overlook the limited ones made to commemorate a special event, such as a fire truck housing.

For additional listings, see *Warman's Antiques and Collectibles Price Guide.*

Stein, Budweiser, 1988 Collectors Series, **$22.**

Anheuser-Busch
Berlin, Great Cities of Germany, MIB **30.00**
Candy Cane, Coca-Cola, MIB **30.00**
Christmas, MIB **70.00**
Civil War, Abraham Lincoln, MIB **95.00**
Saddle Bronc, Winchester Rodeo, MIB **30.00**
Wild Mustang, Animals of the Prairie, MIB **35.00**

Avon, vintage automobiles, 1979 .... **14.50**

Budweiser
Bald eagle, Endangered Species series, MIB **240.00**
50th Anniversary, 1933-1983, 3rd in Holiday series, Clydesdales on snow scene with cabin **90.00**
Basketball, 1991, orig box **15.00**
Frog, Albert Stahl and Co., 9-1/2" h **190.00**
NASCAR, Bill Elliot, MIB..... **55.00**
Peregrine Falcon, Birds of Prey, MIB **65.00**

Figural
Ape, dressed in hobo tuxedo jacket, top hat, drinking from stein, smoking pipe, pewter thumb rest, 9-1/2" h................... **100.00**
Jolly Man, sitting on stump, playing accordion, pewter thumb rest and lid rim, 9-1/2" h **150.00**
Monk, #3, fat monk with book, pewter handle, by Gertiz, West Germany, 7" h **125.00**

McCoy, Spirit of '76, 8" h **35.00**

Mettlach
#171, half liter, figures representing monthly activities, blue background, inlaid top, pewter rim and thumb rest, 9-1/2" h, minor rubbing.................. **90.00**
#1032/2333, gnomes drinking from horn, pewter lid **185.00**

Oakland Raiders, National Football League Collector's Stein 7-1/2" h **15.00**

Stein, cobalt, silver-plated lid, 4-1/4" h, **$35.**

Oktoberfest, German beer garden scene, Ceramarte, 1996, 5-3/4" h **20.00**

Olympics, deep relief, full color, official logo, Atlanta, 1996, mkd "Made in Brazil, Ceramarte," 5-3/4" h **25.00**

Regimental, 1/2 liter, porcelain
11 Armee Corps, Mainz 1899, names to Res. Doring, two side scenes, plain thumblift, strap tear repaired, lines in lithophane, 10" h **485.00**
30 Field Artillery, Rastatt 1897-99, named to Freund Hilfstromp, two side scenes, roster, thumblift missing............................ **375.00**

Stocks and Bonds

Just as today's Wall Street stocks and bonds fluctuate, so do the prices of vintage stocks and bonds, just not as quickly. Many collectors enjoy researching the companies that issued stock; some enjoy the intricate vignettes.

American Locomotive Co., 50 shares, canceled, 1947 .... **20.00**

Atlas Powder Co., 8" x 12", Security Banknote Co., 100 shares

of preferred stock, stamped "Specimen" twice in red **20.00**

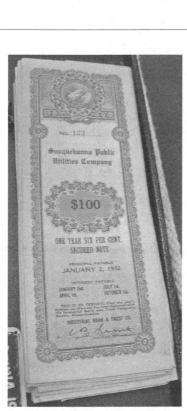

Stocks and bonds, Susquehanna Public Utilities, $100 One Year Six Per Cent Secured Note, Industrial Bank & Trust Co., 1932, **$5.**

Baldwin Co., Ohio, 1919, orange, common, odd shares, no vignette, fancy border, punch cancel 8.00

Buffalo Niagara & Eastern Power Co., NY, 1926, common, less than 100 shares, blue and black, vignette at top of Niagara Falls, 2nd vignette of workman with oil can standing beside giant turbine, issued, punch,

cancelled, American Bank Note Co. 18.00

California Street Cable RR Co., San Francisco, CA, 1884, unissued, cable car vignette 35.00

City of Los Angeles, 1911, Street Improvement Bond Series 1, Blake Ave, California state seal on title panel in blue and gray, black printing, orange border, punch canceled, no coupons 12.00

Deer Lodge Investment Company, Deer Lodge, MT, common, unissued, black, violet border, violet seal, low issue number, vignette of elk, shares $10 each, GOES ... 12.00

Engineers Petroleum Co., DE, 1921, 100 shares, eagle on rock vignette, orange green border design, Security Bank Note Co., Phila 18.00

Great Divide Oil Co., Colorado, 1930s, oil field, gushers, train, and buildings, common, odd shares, green, unissued 8.50

Hornell Airways Inc., issued and canceled, NY, two women and sun rising over mountains vignette, 1920s 65.00

International Business Machines Corp, issued, brown 5.00

Milwaukee Street Railway, incorporated under the laws of New Jersey, c1880 .... 50.00

Packard Motor Car Co., August 7, 1951, one share 30.00

Pennsylvania New York Central Transportation Co., 100 shares, blue on white, black vignette, Sept. 11, 1968 .... 50.00

Pennsylvania Salt Manufacturing, c1880, eagle, shield, arrows, olive branch, orange gray border, hand stamped cancel, Wm M Christy's Sons, Philadelphia 15.00

Pepsi-Cola United Bottlers, vignette of goddess holding world globe and Pepsi bottle, issued 15.00

Rochelle & Southern, Illinois, 1900, unissued, black and white 12.00

Sentinel Radio Corp, issued and canceled, green, goddess and two radio towers vignette 5.00

Susa Corp, Co, 1972, corporate logo at top center, green border, corporate seal, Rocky Mt Bank Note Co 7.50

Universal Motors Co., DE, 1916, orange "Temporary Stock Certificate," issued, Common, ornate border, no vignette, uncancelled, emb company seal lower left corner, sgd by officers 10.00

Vose Mining Co, Townsend, MT, c1890, common, odd shares, unissued, arched title, black, fancy gold border, green diamond shaped vignette of mining scene, very thin paper, 11-1/4" x 7-1/8" 20.00

Washington Gas Light Co., Washington, DC, 1987, 19th C style vignette, company works at top center, men on horses, man with wheelbarrow, bystanders, and blacksmith, Washington Monument at right, American Bank Note Co. 15.00

Western Union Telegraph Co., 100 shares, 1969 .... 15.00

Stoneware

Crocks and jugs are forms of stoneware. Early potters boasted of its durability and added cobalt blue lettering to advertise their location, or perhaps a flower or bird as decoration. Pieces which exhibit slightly pitted surfaces are referred to as having an "orange peel" glaze. Stoneware items are impervious to liquid and extremely durable, making them ideal for food preparation and storage. The most desirable pieces are those with unusual cobalt blue decorations.

For additional listings, see *Warman's Antiques & Collectibles.*

Batter pail, unsigned, attributed to White's, Utica, c1865, six quarts, imp "6," oak leaf design under spout, orig bale handle, short tight hairline 330.00

Bottle, imp and blue accented "B. F. Haley California Pop Beer 1889," 10" h, glaze drip at shoulder to right of imp name 135.00

Canning jar, unsigned, c1850, 1 gal, four wide accent stripes across front, 9-1/2" h, stack mark, glaze burns on left side 110.00

Stoneware, jug, New York, S & Co., Fort Edwards, NY, cobalt blue flourish and dot trim, strap handle, **$115.**

Chicken waterer, unsigned, probably PA origin, c1840, 1 gal, imp "I" at shoulder, brushed blue accents at button top and inner and out rim of watering hole, 11" h............. 415.00

Cream pot
Brady & Ryan, Ellenville, NY, c1885, six quarts, singing bird on dotted branch, imp "6" below maker's name, 8-1/2" h, extensive glaze flaking at rim and spots on back 180.00
Roberts, Binghamton, NY, c1860, one gal, bird on branch, ext., 7-1/2" h, rim chip on back 770.00

Stoneware, crock, "Home Made Preserves," **$50.**

Stoneware, mixing bowl, blue bands, decorative edge, 14" d, **$95.**

Crock
Brady & Ryan, Ellenville, NY, c1885, two-gal, singing bird on plume, 9" h, professional restoration 550.00
Lyons, c1860, two-gal, double tulip dec, blue accents at name and ears, 9" h, stained from use 165.00
D. Mooney, Ithaca, NY, c1862, pail shape, brushed blue dec, 8" h, somewhat overglazed in the firing............................... 330.00

Jug
America, early 19th C, imp "2" below top, cobalt blue bird with high comb and long bill perched on large leaf, 13" h, light staining 420.00
J Fisher & Co, Lyons, NY, c1880, two-gal, bee stinger dec, 13-1/2" h, minor glaze burning, large glaze drips at shoulder and back 180.00
S Hart Fulton, c1875, three-gal, signature double love birds, 13-1/2" h, staining from use, long J-shaped glued crack on back 500.00
Lyons, c1865, two-gal, large brushed leaf design, 13-1/2" h, some over glazing at shoulder 165.00
J & E Norton, Bennington, VT, c1855, three-gal, compote of flowers, thick glassy cobalt, 16" h, professional restoration, some staining from use 550.00
Whites, Binghamton, c1860, two-gal, dotted double poppy dec, 12-1/2" h, professional restoration to tight line 275.00

Stoneware, water cooler, covered, original spigot, cobalt blue stripes, crown mark with "4," **$75.**

Pitcher
Unknown American maker, ovoid, applied handle, brushed cobalt blue flower with long leaves, three flourishes around rim at handle, interior with brown glaze, 7" h, hairline at base 675.00
Whites Binghamton, incised line around middle, raised rim, cobalt blue polka dot floral dec, 10" h 615.00

Whistle, figural, Rockingham glaze, c1870
1-1/2" h, bird, chips in glaze 90.00
3-1/2" h, owl on stump....... 220.00

Stoneware, jug, brown top, blue name "John G. Best, Bath, Pa," **$90.**

Strawberry Shortcake

Who's that freckle-faced kind in the puffy bonnet? It's Strawberry Shortcake, of course. Strawberry Shortcake memorabilia is both available and affordable, meaning it's perfect flea market material as well as a great collectible for children and adults.

Strawberry Shortcake, metal lunch box with plastic thermos, **$20.**

Carrying case, strawberry shape 15.00

Jewelry
  Charm set, Apricot, Lemon, Custard, some wear........ 100.00
  Necklace, Strawberry Shortcake, hand over mouth.............. 25.00
  Ring, Strawberry Shortcake 20.00

Comforter, Strawberry Shortcake, some wear.............................. 15.00

Doll
  Angel Cake with Souffle, MIB 45.00
  Apricot with Hopsalot, MIB 65.00

  Lem & Ada with Sugar Woofer, MIB 90.00
  Mint Tulip with Marsh Mallard, MIB 80.00
  Strawberry Shortcake, 1st ed., MIB 75.00

Game, board, slight play wear
  Berries to Market Game, American Greetings Corporation, copyright 1979.................................. 35.00
  Strawberry Shortcake Berry-Go-Round, Parker Brothers, copyright 1981 .... 25.00

Lunch box, Aladdin 25.00

Pillow panel, Strawberry Shortcake train, uncut............................ 15.00

Play set
  Lime Chiffon, Dance n' Berry-cise, 1991, MIP........................ 35.00
  Strawberry Shortcake, Berry Beach Park, 1991, MIP 45.00

Record, 1980, LP 20.00

Sleeping bag, Strawberry Shortcake 15.00

String Holders

The string holder developed as a useful tool to assist the merchant or manufacturer who needed tangle-free string or twine to tie packages. The early holders were made of cast-iron, with some patents dating to the 1860s. Among the variations to evolve were the hanging lithographed tin examples with advertising and decorative chalkware examples. In the home, string holders remained a useful kitchen element until the early 1950s.

Look for examples that are bright and colorful, free of chips or damage, and include the original hanger.

Apple, chalkware, 7-3/4" h 95.00

Balloon bunch, ceramic, Fitz & Floyd 50.00

Bird, pottery............................. 85.00

Black man and woman, chalkware, matched pair 275.00

String holder, cat, chalkware, 6-3/4" h, **$75.**

Boy, top hat and pipe, chalkware, 9" h 125.00

Bride, ceramic, mkd "Made in Japan" 140.00

Cast iron, ball shape, designed to be hung from ceiling................. 75.00

Cat, ball of twine, white cat, red/orange ball, chalkware, 7" h 75.00

Chef
  Black, chalkware, 8" h 165.00
  White, chalkware, 7-1/4" h 145.00

Dove, white, ceramic 50.00

Dutch girl, chalkware, 7" h.... 100.00

Elephant, ceramic, yellow, Hoffritz Co... 35.00

Hippo, ceramic 75.00

Mammy, holding flowers, chalkware, 6-1/2" h 185.00

Monkey, sitting on ball of string, chalkware............................ 225.00

Mouse, ceramic, Josef Originals 55.00

Pear, chalkware, 7-3/4" h.......... 85.00

Pineapple, face, chalkware, 7" h 165.00

Strawberry, chalkware, 6-1/2" h 115.00

Teapot, ceramic, parakeet dec, Japan 85.00

Witch, sitting on pumpkin, broom and book in hand, pottery 60.00

String holder, ceramic, cat face, white, pink and black trim, Holt Howard, **$95.**

Stuffed Toys

Steiff was the originator of stuffed toys. By the middle of the 20th century, stuffed toys of every type, color, and animal were made. Some were sold in stores, others used for carnival prizes. Today many of these animals find their way to flea markets, hoping someone will give them a new home.

Stuffed toys, Lamb Chop, white, green and white Macy's cap, **$15.**

Stuffed toys, rhino, plush, darker markings, **$10.**

Alf, talking, 18" h 75.00

Bear, blue, red, white, and blue Union Pacific shield logo on chest ... **20.00**

Bucky Badger, University of Wisconsin mascot, Animal Fair, 1960s, 23" h 36.00

Cat, tiger-striped, Purrfection, Gund, 1985 Collectors Classic Limited Edition #1174, 15" h 16.00

Dinosaur, Animal Fair, late 1970s, 26" l 15.00

Dumbo, Character Novelty Co., 14" h 85.00

Elephant, mohair, wooden tusks 45.00

Fozzie Bear, tan hat with felt holly trim, Tyco 15.00

Goosey Gander, velveteen and

Stuffed toys, squirrel, 7-1/2" h, **$15.**

brocade vest, top hat, 24" h ... **30.00**

Lion, standing, Animal Fair, 1979, 15" h 24.00

Michigan J Frog, Warner Bros 24.00

Paddington Bear, 16" h 16.00

Penguin, black and white, orange beak, button eyes................... 35.00

Phillies Phanatic, 19" h 35.00

Polar bear, Always Coca-Cola emblem, 7" h 10.00

Sock Monkey, home made...... 20.00

Tickle Me Ernie 20.00

Velveteen Rabbit, Toys R Us... 25.00

Super Heroes

Shazam! Super heroes have been influencing the minds and checkbooks of collectors for decades. Batman, Green Hornet, Captain Midnight, Superman, etc., and all kinds of villains have come to life from comic books, radio, television and movie tales.

For additional listings, see *Warman's Americana & Collectibles* and related topics in this edition.

Super heroes, comic book, *Captain America*, Marvel, #343, July, **$2.**

Super heroes Left: Wonder Woman mirror, Avon, ©1987, DC Comics, original box, **$15;** Doll, Wonder Woman, no box, **$12.**

Action figure, Aquaman, MOC 35.00

Bank, Batman, plastic, full color, arms crossed 75.00

Big little book, *Aquaman Scourge of the Sea*, Whitman, 1968 ... 15.00

Book, *Adventures of Superman*, Random House, Armed Services edition, 1942 .... 100.00

Button
Batman and Robin Fan Club, 1960s 10.00
Hawkman Superhero Club, 3" d 20.00
Superman Muscle Building Club, 1954 .... 50.00

Card game, Marvel Superheros, Milton Bradley, 1978 .... 20.00

Clock, wall, Superman, New Haven, 1978, battery operated 30.00

Colorforms, Marvel Superheroes, 1983 .... 10.00

Coloring book
Spider-Man, The Arms of Doctor Octopus, Marvel, 1983...... 10.00
Superman to the Rescue, Whitman, 1964 .... 25.00

Drinking glass, Wonder Woman, Pepsi, 1978, 6" h 10.00

Easy Show Projector, Marvel Superheroes, Kenner, 1967 ... 75.00

Figure, Superman, Presents, 15" h 25.00

Hair brush, Superman, Avon, 1976, MIB 25.00

Paint set, Superman, American Toy Works, 1940, unused 250.00

Pin, Superman Junior Defense League, diecut, 1940s 75.00

Pop-up book, *Superman,* Random House, 1979, hardcover 15.00

Puppet, Spider-Man, Imperial, vinyl head, 1976 .... 15.00

Record
Superman, the Movie, 1978, two-record set, LP 24.00
Wonder Woman, Peter Pan Records, 33-1/3 rpm 10.00

Tattoo, Aquaman, Topps, 1967 .... 20.00

Telephone, Superman, ATE, plastic 150.00

Water gun, Superman, 1967 .... 30.00

Wrapper, Super Heroes Stickers, Philadelphia Chewing Gum Corp., ©1967 Marvel Comics Group, 5" x 6" 5.00

Wristwatch, Superman, 1977 .... 35.00

Super heroes, comic book, *Fantastic Four*, Marvel, #31, June, **$90.**

Swankyswigs

Collectors never seem to tire of finding these little glasses. Kraft Cheese Spreads were originally packed in these colorful juice glasses as early as the 1930s. Over the years many variations and new patterns have been introduced.

Antique, brown coal bucket and clock, 3-3/4" h........................... 5.00

Bands, red and black.................. 3.00

Bustlin' Betsy 5.00

Deer and squirrels, brown, 3-3/4" h
.... 8.00

Dots and circles, black, blue, green, or red 4.50

Elephants and birds, red, 3-3/4" h
.... 8.00

Kiddie Cup, pig and bear, blue . 2.00

Modern flowers, dark and light blue, red or yellow
Cornflower............................... 3.25
Forget-me-not 3.25

Jonquil 3.00

Roosters, red, 3-1/4" h 6.00

Swankyswigs, left: Antiques series, brown decoration, 3-3/4" h, **$5;** right: Kiddie Cups series, black and white decoration, **$5.**

Swarovski Crystal

The Swarovski family traces its glassmaking tradition to Austria in 1895. Today the company is still identified with high-quality crystal. Look for a swan logo on most pieces. The original box and packaging add to an items value.

Charm, musical clef note, enamel and crystal, 1-3/4" h 15.00

Christmas ornament, snowflake, MIB
1992 .... 250.00
1996 .... 195.00
1997 .... 160.00

Cigarette holder, #7463NR062, sculpted crystal, SC or swan logo
.... 175.00

Clock, table, Helios, # 0168003, artist Borek Sipek, 3-3/8" h........... 355.00

Swarovski crystal, Pegasus, **$85.**

Crystal City, retired Dec. 1994
Cathedral, City Gates, or Town Hall, each 215.00
Poplar trees........................ 175.00

Figure
Baby beaver, sitting, retired Dec. 1999................................. 215.00
Baby lovebirds 115.00
Cat, flexible metal tail, SC or swan logo.................................... 75.00
Dachshund, large, 3" l 125.00
Dragon, Society member, "Fabulous Creatures," 1997 .... 595.00
Elephant, large, frosted tail 115.00
Harp, MIB.......................... 295.00
Kiwi, 1956, 1-3/4" h............ 200.00
Mouse, spring tail, 2-1/2" h 195.00
Rabbit, large 250.00
Squirrel, 10th anniversary . 275.00

Paperweight, pyramid, helio, small, 1990, orig box and certificate
.... 595.00

Pendant, red and black enameled child's sled, crystal on top, 2" h
.... 35.00

Pineapple, rhodium metal foliage, 2-1/2" h 200.00

Schnapps glass, 2" h, SC or swan logo, Europe, set of three 200.00

Star
1994, MIB 225.00
1995, MIB 275.00
1999, MIB 235.00

Treasure box, removable lid, round Butterfly on lid, SC logo..... 300.00
Flowers on lid, SC or swan logo
.... 300.00

Vase, sculpted crystal, three frosted crystal flowers, SC or swan logo, 2-7/8" h 220.00

Swarovski crystal, grape cluster, **$45.**

Swizzle Sticks

Here's another example of something people tend to save as a souvenir. Who hasn't tucked one into their pocket? After awhile you've got a collection started, so why not search for some more examples during your next trip to a flea market.

Aluminum, golf club shape, "O'Donnell's Sea Grill" on shaft, "Stolen in Washington, D.C." on other side, pr 15.00

Commemorative, plastic
Alaska Airlines, white, gold lettering "Gold Coast Alaska Airlines," 5-1/2" l 3.00
American Airlines, blue, 6" l.. 5.00
Continental Airlines, Continental to Hawaii, yellow 4.50
Hard Rock Café, guitar at top, 9" l 2.00
Hotel Statler, champagne glass, white lettering on red 10.00
Howard Johnson's, 5-1/2" l..... 1.00
Lawrence Welk Welkome Inn, 6" l 1.00
Mirage, Las Vegas, 6" l 1.00
Playboy, 8" l...................... 5.00
SAS, light blue, 6" l............ 4.50
San Francisco, white, cable car on one side, "San Francisco, the

Swizzle stick, Indianapolis Motor Speedway Motel, 6-1/4" l, **$2.**

Friendly Skies" on other, 5" l 3.50
SS Independence, 5-1/2" l...... 1.00
The Sands, Las Vegas 1.00
TWA, airplane on top........... 10.00

Glass
Advertising, colored 3.50
Amber...................................... 1.50
Black 2.00
Christmas, set of six 25.00
Man, top hat 3.50
Seagull 12.00

Souvenir, Hotel Lexington, amethyst, 1939 World's Fair 20.00
Spatter knob, clear stirrer 1.00

Plastic
Ballerina, yellow 65.00
Hawaiian girl 2.50
Leprechaun, green, shamrock on hat.................................... 3.00
Mr. Peanut, Everybody Loves A Nut 5.00
Santa 5.00
Sword .... .25

Syracuse China

Founded in Syracuse, N.Y., in the mid-1800s, this china company is still in operation. Along with the many dinnerware patterns produced over the years are pieces for commercial accounts, such as the C&O Railroad. The company's restaurant wares are especially popular with collectors.

Ashtray, Irish setter in center, front mkd "Stuart Bruce," some hairline cracks from use, 4-1/2" d 10.00

Bread and butter plate
Army Medical Dept, tan, Econo-Rim, c1940 .... 10.00

Syracuse China, creamer, white, turquoise blue decoration, marked "Syralite, by Syracuse, 96-D, U.S.A.," **$5.**

Norfolk & Western Railroad, dogwood pattern.............. 12.00

Coffee cup
American Airlines 20.00
BPOE Elks, restaurant gauge, Nov. 1936 backstamp 7.00

Creamer, Chessie, C & O Railroad 40.00

Cup and saucer
Adobe Ware, Rodeo Cowboy, stenciled "Adobe Ware, Syracuse China, 5-EE USA," c1950 . 40.00
Biltmore Hotel, gold trim....... 7.00

Demitasse cup and saucer, mauve airbrush dec, scallop rim, Nov. 1955 backstamp.............................. 12.00

Dinner plate
Airbrush, stenciled chrysanthemum, mauve, 11" d, 1943.................................. 35.00
Biltmore Hotel, gold trim..... 10.00
George Washington Hotel, Jacksonville, FL, 1959, 10" d 20.00

Roosevelt Hotel, gold trim ... 10.00

Platter, Sabella, fish chef logo, green mark, 12" x 9-1/2" 35.00

Salad plate, Castaways Restaurant, maroon fan dec, 7-1/4" d 30.00

Side dish, restaurant style
American Airlines, 3-3/4" d 18.00
Floral dec 8.00

Soup bowl, Anderdsen Restaurant, Pea Soup Characters, Hap-Pea and Pea-Wee, 9" d........................ 45.00

Sugar bowl, cov, Coralbel, Winchester shape 190.00

Teapot, cov
Coralbel, Virginia shape...... 275.00
Sante Fe RR, California Poppy, 4" d 200.00

Vegetable, cov, Bracelet, gold rim 200.00

Taylor, Smith & Taylor

Taylor, Smith & Taylor was started by W. L. Smith, John N. Taylor, W. L. Taylor, Homer J. Taylor, and Joseph G. Lee in Chester, W.Va., in 1899. By 1903 the firm reorganized and the Taylors bought out Lee. By 1906, Smith bought out the Taylors. The company continued making dinnerware and table wares until 1981, when the plant closed. The Smith family sold its interest to Anchor Hocking in 1973.

For additional listings, see *Warman's Americana & Collectibles* and LuRay pattern in this edition.

Bowl
Autumn Harvest.................. 40.00
Vistosa, cobalt blue, 8" d 65.00

Breakfast set, Cape Cod, toast plate, creamer, sugar, salt and pepper shakers................................... 35.00

Butter dish, cov, Empire.......... 20.00

Cake plate, Laurel, 10-1/4" d ... 12.00

Calendar plate, 1911, horseshoe with horse head center, adv for PA tinsmith, stove, roofing company, 7" d.. 45.00

Casserole, cov
Autumn Harvest.................. 38.00
Sea Shell, 8" d 50.00

Chop plate
Plymouth 20.00
Stagecoach 35.00
Vistosa, light green, 11" d 85.00

Coffeepot, cov
Autumn Leaves, stain on handle
.... 65.00
Boutonniere, 10" h 70.00

Creamer and sugar
Break O'Day.......................... 55.00
Vistosa, light green.............. 45.00

Taylor, Smith, Taylor, plate, small yellow roses, black trellis design, **$5**.

Cup and saucer
Marvel................................... 6.00
Vogue 6.50

Dinner plate
Empire, 10" d........................ 12.00
Fairway, 9-1/2" d 8.50
Pebbleford, 10" d 10.00

Dish, Autumn Harvest, 12-1/2" l, 9-7/8" w 60.00

Egg cup, Vistosa, cobalt blue ... 25.00

Gravy boat
English Abbey 60.00
Paramount............................ 12.50

Luncheon plate, Vistosa, light green
.... 17.50

Platter
Autumn Harvest, 13-1/2" l... 45.00
Golden Jubilee 42.00

Salad bowl, Marvel................. 17.50

Salt and pepper shakers, pr, Versatile 6.00

Sauce boat, underplate, Pattern #1377 .... 45.00

Soup bowl, Vistosa, deep yellow
.... 24.00

Sugar bowl, cov
Dwarf Pine, yellow 125.00
Golden Jubilee 40.00

Teapot
Laural.................................... 32.00
Vistosa, deep yellow 85.00

Vegetable dish, cov
Autumn Harvest.................. 40.00
Silhouette.............................. 95.00

Teapots

To devoted tea drinkers, the only way to properly brew a cup of tea is in a teapot. Thankfully there are many wonderful examples of teapots available to collectors. From decorative porcelain teapots to whimsical figural teapots, the array is endless.

For additional listings, see specific companies, such as Hall China, in this edition.

Figural
Betty Boop........................... 35.00
British Bobby, English.......... 35.00
Dickens character, Beswick, English
.... 85.00
Doc....................................... 35.00
Elephant, plastic, Hong Kong, 1960s
.... 12.00
Gone shopping, chair, Gucci shoes, handbag, hat, English 110.00
Lucy 50.00

McCormick, black 35.00
Minnie Mouse 35.00
Popeye, Cardew 100.00

Porcelain or pottery
American Bisque, Red Rose, gold trim 55.00
Blue Ridge, Appleyard, teapot, cov
.... 95.00
Dragonware, mkd "H. Katu, Pearl China, Nagoya, Japan"...... 75.00

English, Countess, Grindley, flow blue............................... 350.00
English, Wade, paisley chintz pattern, c1925 .... 650.00
Frankoma, Wagon Whccls, Prairie Green glaze, six-cup size.. 80.00
German, Royal Hanover, hand painted 75.00
Homer Laughlin, Rhythm, 5" h
.... 45.00
Japan, hand painted scene ... 40.00

Teapot, silver luster, white floral and foliage decoration, **$65.**

Occupied Japan, turquoise ground, white flowers 30.00
Royal Albert, Old English Rose, 5-3/4" h 350.00
Shawnee, Granny Ann........ 250.00

Teapot, brown over white, "Jas. Van Dyk, Tea Importer," 3-1/2" h, **$40.**

Taylor, Smith and Taylor, Vistosa, light green 95.00

Teapot, aluminum, chased floral and scroll decoration, black wooden handle and knob, two-cup size, **$12.**

Teleflora, white ground, raised pink rose, brown handle 40.00

Teddy Bears

Everybody has loved one of these at some time in their lives, and many collectors start by buying one or two that reminds them of a childhood companion. Whatever the motivation, teddy bears are still one of the hottest collectibles. Look for teddy bears that are in good condition, perhaps showing a sign or two of a little loving. Some collectors are more discriminating about condition and know they may pay a premium.

For additional listings, see *Warman's Antiques and Collectibles Price Guide,* as well as Steiff and other categories in this edition.

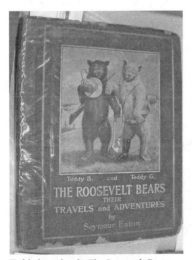

Teddy bear, book, *The Roosevelt Bears, Their Travels and Adventures*, Seymour Eaton, **$65.**

Boyds, panda, black and white, jointed.................................... 15.00
Brooklyn Doll and Toy Co., brown plush, plastic eyes and nose, 1982 .... 25.00

Teddy bear, Raikes Originals, Buttercup, NRFB, **$25.**

Campbell's Super Chief bear 25.00

Teddy bear, Gund, black plush, original box, **$25.**

Dakin, sailor, plush, plastic eyes 35.00
Dean, Ernest, black mohair, glass eyes, orange ribbon, jointed 60.00
Fisher-Price, light brown, gingham dress, plastic eyes, suede nose 25.00
Gund, Theo, light brown 20.00
Hermann, 1995 Munich Oktoberfest, jointed, growler 150.00

Hershey's Cocoa 85.00

Jeane Steele Original, 11-1/2" h, straw hat, felt collar, big fabric bow, jointed, tag "Kent Collectibles/Jeane Steele Originals/©1985" 48.00

Koala Me, store display, 10" h 75.00

Laveen bear, Shug, long gray fur, blue corduroy vest, large blue

marble eyes, leather snot and paw pads, orig hang tag, 18" h.... 165.00

Musical, Swiss, 16" h, mohair 350.00

Petsey, Steiff, blond, button 95.00

Raikes, Robert, Winter Fairy, wooden face, gossamer wings............. 60.00

Tara Toys, Ireland, light gold mohair, fully jointed, plastic eyes, Rexine

pads, mouth opens and closes by squeezing knobs on back of head, early 1950s, cloth label sewn in foot seam, pads worn, fur loss around mechanism, replaced nose, 16" h 175.00

Teddy Ruxpin, orig box, two tapes, orig books............................ 100.00

This Bear, Possum Trot, brown plush, orig tags 75.00

Telephones and Related

Talk, talk, talk, that's what we've been doing since this wonderful invention caught on with our ancestors. As technology changes, some folks are starting to notice that perhaps telephones are something to collect. Add to that some interesting ephemera, and you've got a great collecting area.

Telephone, Mickey Mouse, rotary dial, black, red, yellow, and white, **$95.**

Calendar, 1947, Illinois Bell Telephone, wallet size, adv on front, calendar on back 10.00

Candy container, Miniature Dial Telephone, glass candlestick telephone, 4-1/4" h 55.00

Charm, figural telephone, enamel dial, gold.............................. 150.00

Cufflinks, pr, goldtone............. 15.00

Lighter, desk phone motif, Occupied Japan 220.00

Paperweight, Bell Telephone logo, 3-1/4" h 55.00

Planter, figural white porcelain telephone, roses, leaves, gold trim, Lefton 10.00

Postcard
Bell Telephone Co. Building, Kansas City, MO, 1924.................... 5.00
Christmas, girl using candlestick telephone, 1913 postmark 7.50

Salt and pepper shakers, pr, pink wall telephone, orig box mkd "Party Line," c1950 .... 25.00

Sheet music, *Hello Central Give Me Heaven*, cover shows girl with phone.................................... 15.00

Sign
Bell Telephone, blue enamel, flange 90.00
New York Telephone Co., porcelain, trademark bell, 8" d 150.00
United Utilities System, Public Telephone, porcelain, two-sided, L-shape, flange.............. 200.00

Stock certificate, Associated Telephone Co, 1945 .... 10.00

Telephone
Candlestick, Kellogg........... 300.00
Co-pay, gray, box with key ... 95.00
Desk, rotary, blue plastic, Bell System 30.00
Figural, Bozo, no lights when rings, Telemania, 12-1/2" h........ 60.00

Figural, '57 Chevy, red, push-button, modular plugs, unused 35.00
Figural, Mickey Mouse, 1978, Western Electric............. 150.00
Figural, Pizza Inn, cartoon figure of mustache-wearing pizza maker, touch-tone, Taiwan, late 1970s, 10" h 25.00
Figural, Snoopy, push button dial 75.00
Wall, Chicago Telephone Supply Company, 26" h 220.00
Wall, single box, Kellogg, refinished 200.00
Wall single box, Kellogg, oak case, 25-1/2" h........................ 200.00
Wall, single box, Western Electric 190.00

Telephone almanac
1940, Bell System Telephone Subscribers, American Telephone & Telegraph 5.00
1959, Michigan Bell Telephone Co., slight discoloration 2.50

Telephone book
Beloit, WI, 1954..................... 5.00
Villisca, Iowa, 1962 .... 17.50

Toy
Fisher-Price telephone pull toy, #2251, 1993 .... 7.50
Junior Phone, battery operated, Modern Toys, Japan, 1950s, two large hard plastic phones, orig wiring, instructions, and fold-out display box 60.00

Yellow Pages, Washington, D.C., March 1948............................. 55.00

Television Characters and Personalities

"Now on with the show" was Ed Sullivan's promise to the audience that waited to be entertained. Today's flea markets are a great place to find vintage items relating to early television and the many characters who became stars.

For additional listings, see *Warman's Americana & Collectibles*, plus other categories in this edition.

Television characters and personalities, book, *I Spy, Message from Moscow,* **$24.**

Activity pad, Popeye, Merrigold Press, 1982 .... 3.50

Bank, Romper Room, Do-Bee, Hasbro 55.00

Big Little Book, *Lassie Adventure in Alaska*, Whitman, 1967 ... 15.00

Card game
Beverly Hillbillies, Milton Bradley 24.00
Howdy Doody, orig slide-out box 45.00
Mork & Mindy 18.00

Cigar band, Hawaii Five-O, full color 2.50

Colorforms, Family Affair, #515 .... 20.00

Coloring book, unused
Beverly Hillbillies, Whitman, 1963 .... 24.00
Dennis the Menace, 1973 ...... 15.00
Family Affair, Whitman 40.00

Comic book, *I Love Lucy*, Dell, #3, 1954 .... 135.00

Cookbook, *Buffy's Cookbook,* Jody Cameron, Family Affair 15.00

Diecast car, Starsky & Hutch, 3" l, metal and plastic, 1970s 35.00

Doll
Cher, Mego, 12" h 50.00
Six Million Dollar Man, 1973, MIB 35.00

Flip book, Television Motion Pictures, Universal Toy & Novelty, 1930s, 1-1/2" x 2-1/4" 35.00

Game
A-Team, 1984 .... 25.00
Down You Go, Selchow & Righter Co., ©1954........................ 18.00
Family Ties 25.00
Lost in Space...................... 180.00
Mister Ed, Parker Brothers, ©1962, missing dice and markers 45.00
Road Runner, Milton Bradley, Warner Bros, 1968 .... 65.00

Guitar, Moniees, Mattel, 1966 . 40.00

Gum card wrapper, 5" x 6" waxed paper wrapper
Dark Shadows, Philadelphia Chewing Gum, ©1968 Dan Curtis Productions, black, white, dark pink.......................... 40.00
Mash, Donruss, ©1982 20th Century Fox...................... 8.00

Halloween costume, child's, orig costume, mask, box, Mr. Ed 115.00

Hat box, Buffy, Family Affair, pink plastic, 1969, 10-1/2" d 45.00

Inflatable canoe, Daniel Boone, Fess Parker, Multiple Toy Makers, 1965, MIP 50.00

Lunch box
Andy Griffith, labeled "Barney Fife Security," 8" x 6" 18.00
Bewitched 18.00
I Dream of Jeannie 18.00

Magazine, *TV Junior,* March 1959 .... 20.00

Medic set, M*A*S*H, Ja-Ru, ©1981, 20th Century Fox Film Corp, MOC 18.00

Mirror, Miss Piggy, Sigma, glazed ceramic, easel back and hook for hanging, early 1980s 80.00

Television characters and personalities, comic book, *Beverly Hillbillies*, Dell, **$100.**

Night light, Flintstones, Fred and Barney..................................... 25.00

Nodder, Dr. Kildare, Lego...... 125.00

Paint set, Rocky and Bullwinkle Presto Sparkle, Kenner, 1962 .... 30.00

Photograph, Robert Redford in "Jeremiah Johnson," ABC Sunday Night Movie, Dec. 19, 1976... 10.00

Pinback button
Ben Casey, white, blue letters 15.00
Bullwinkle for President, red, white, and blue flag, ©1972, 2-1/4" d 40.00

Playing cards, Man from U.N.C.L.E., Ed-U-Cards, 1965.................. 20.00

Play set
Baywatch, Lifeguard Training Set, Toy Island, 1997 .... 25.00
Ben Casey, play hospital, Transogram, 1960s........... 50.00

Television characters and personalities, dolls, Donnie and Marie Osmond, Mattel, NRFB, **$20.**

Pull toy, Leakin' Lena, pound and pull, Pressman, 1960s............ 60.00

Push puppet
Huckleberry Hound 45.00
Pebbles................................. 50.00

Puzzle, frame tray, Mighty Mouse and TV Pals 10.00

Record
Knight Rider, record storybook 15.00
Lewis, Shari, Party Record, Allied Creative Services, Inc., c1950 .... 25.00

Ring, Sky King, adjustable, sq red plastic television box............. 90.00

Television characters and personalities, doll, Vanna White, MIB, **$15.**

Sneakers, Mighty Mouse, children's, orig box................................. 25.00

Sticker book, *Mrs Beasley,* Whitman, ©1972 Family Affair 20.00

Toy
Bonzo scooter, wind-up 130.00
Mighty Mouse Dynamite Dasher, Takara, 1981 .... 50.00
Pink Panther, plastic, walking wind-up, trench coat, glasses 10.00

Television characters and personalities, Golden All-Star book, *Welcome Back Kotter*, 1977, **$5.**

Wilma Flintstone friction car, Marx, 1962.................................... 90.00

TV Guide cover, framed, 16" x 20" tan wood frame, white cardboard mat, Alistair Cooke, Nov. 11-17, 1972 cover............................. 15.00

Wallet, CHIPS, orig display card, MGM, MOC........................... 20.00

Wall plaque, Wally Walrus, ©Walter Lantz, Napco, 1958 .... 75.00

Waste can, Batman, tin litho, 1966, 10" h....................................... 30.00

Whistle, Dragnet...................... 15.00

Tennis Collectibles

Tennis anyone? Here's another sport where the collectibles are starting to command increased attention. Look for ephemera and equipment with endorsements by famous players.

Autograph, Billie Jean King, 8" x 10" photo...................................... 25.00

Book, *How to Improve Your Tennis*, Harry "Cap" Leighton.............. 7.50

Cigarette card, 1931 Lawn Tennis series
Lakeman, Jan Fry 10.00
Wilmer Allison..................... 10.00
Jacques Brugnon 7.00

Cuff links, pr, sterling, mkd "Fenwick & Sailor" 135.00

Decanter, Erza Brooks, tennis player, 1973, 14" h 20.00

Doll, Annalee Mobilitee, tennis player mouse holding tennis racket, ball hanging form racket, orig green tag, 1965 .... 15.00

Figure
Goebel, rabbit with tennis rackets 95.00
Precious Moments, boy tennis player, olive branch mark, 1985, 5-1/2" h............................. 35.00

Pin, tennis racket, green enamel, mkd Gerry's, 2-1/2" l........................ 4.00

Photo, 4" x 6", glossy black and white, Ichiya Kumajaya and Hachishiro Mikami, added inscription "Our

Japanese Tennis Champions, Who After A Long And Friendly Match with American Team in United States Returned today To Japan And Had Tremendous Welcome By Their Brethren," 1920s 3.00

Tennis balls
Dunlop, can of three, Planter's Peanuts adv 25.00
Dunlop, Vinnie Richards...... 25.00
MacGregor, red and white plaid can 25.00
Spaulding, Pancho Gonzales, blue label.................................... 20.00
Wilson, Jack Kramer illus, red and white................................. 55.00

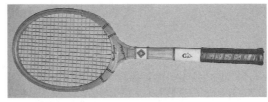

Tennis, racket, Frank Parker autograph model, MacGregor, **$25.**

Tennis, trophy, Doubles Consolation, Muskogee, 1921, silver-plated, 4-7/8" h, **$37.50.**

Tennis racket

Dayton, 1923 patent 70.00
Knickerbocker, wood 45.00
Spaulding, needs restringing 10.00
Wilson Sporting Goods, Maureen
    Connolly, full color portrait on
    handle, 1950s 25.00
Wright & Ditson Championship,
    26" l 50.00

Thimbles

Thimble, thimble, who's got the thimble? Collectors do! And, they enjoy their tiny treasures. Finding thimbles at flea markets is probably easier than it sounds since there are so many different kinds of thimbles — advertising, commemorative, political, porcelain, and metal.

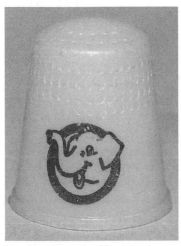

Thimble, plastic, Republican, local candidate's name on back, **$.25.**

Thimbles, sterling silver, left: embossed leaf design, **$45;** center: center band with swirl design, lilypad design around base, **$65;** monogrammed, **$50.**

Aluminum, plain 4.00

Commemorative
California, gold-tone, white
    background with bear, 3/4" l
    .... 10.00
HRH Prince William of Wales, to
    commemorate his 1st birthday,
    portrait of Prince and Mother,
    June, 1983 .... 27.00

Mackinac Bridge, copper-tone,
    showing bridge................. 10.00
World's Greatest Porcelain Houses,
    Royal Doulton, tea roses and
    blue bonnets, Franklin Mint
    .... 12.00

Figural, ceramic, 2-1/4" h
Donald Duck 15.00
Goofy 15.00
Minnie Mouse 17.50

Pewter
Always Coca-Cola................. 12.00
Hummingbird on top, raised
    flowers with crystal centers,
    Comstock Creations......... 10.00

Porcelain
Anniversary, violet flower, gold
    band, mkd "Fine Bone China,
    Ashleydale, England"......... 8.00
Blossom by Blossom the Spring
    Begins, Royal Grafton, England,
    1970s 10.00
Blue and red flowers, mkd "Avon"
    .... 6.00
Bird 5.50
Franciscan, Desert Rose, Franklin
    Mint, 1982........................ 15.00
Pink and blue flowers............. 6.00

Silver
Gold band, Simons Bros....... 20.00
Greek Key band 25.00
Plain, 5/8" l 5.00

Tiffany Studios

Louis Comfort Tiffany was an interesting man. While he was a patron of arts and crafts, he was also a skilled craftsman. Although he worked in many mediums, he is most acclaimed for his glass creations and designs. Flea market shoppers should be aware that most "signed" Tiffany glass pieces were not signed by Louis Tiffany. Never buy a piece of Tiffany glass based solely on the signature. Make sure things sold with "genuine Tiffany" boxes originally came in that box as many things originating at the famous New York City store find their way back to the secondary market via flea markets.

For additional listings, see *Warman's Antiques and Collectibles Price Guide* and *Warman's Glass.*

Reproduction alert.

Box, bronze, etched metal grape vine pattern, imp "Tiffany Studios New York 816," c1900, 6-1/2" l, three Favrile panels damaged, hinge detached 550.00

Bowl, Favrile, irid gold, sgd "L.C.T.," 6" d...................................... 100.00

Calling card receiver, bronze, mkd "Tiffany Studios" 75.00

Candlestick, heavy walled amber glass stick, 10 prominent swirled ribs, fine gold luster, inscribed "L. C. T.," labeled, 6-3/4" h 400.00

Champagne flute, Favrile, pale yellow with deep green yellow opalescent finish, highly irid, sgd "L. C. T. Favrile #1806," 5" h 350.00

Desk accessories, Zodiac pattern, bronze, wear to patina
Calendar holder.................... 95.00
Rocker blotter..................... 120.00

Letter opener, Grapevine pattern, bronze and green slag glass. 450.00

Nut dish, 2-3/4" d, ruffled rim, irid gold, sgd "L.C.T. Favrile"..... 175.00

Paper rack, bronze, Chinese pattern, dark patina, some green wash in pattern recesses, three-tier, imp "Tiffany Studios New York 1756," some metal corrosion.......... 260.00

Salt, open, ruffled rim, shallow bowl, amber glass, irid gold, polished pontil, initialed "L.C.T." on base, 2-1/2" d 250.00

Serving fork, sterling silver, Wave Edge pattern 150.00

Tile, pressed molded irid blue glass, stylized blossom motif, imp "Patent Applied For," 4" sq 375.00

Vase
Elongated bulbous body, 10 prominent ribs below flattened rim, gold irid, inscribed "L. C. Tiffany Favrile," and number, 7-1/4" h........................... 525.00
Oval body, teal blue, lined in opal white glass, smooth matte lustrous surface, inscribed "L. C.

Tiffany Studios, crystal award vase, engraved "Pennsylvania Horse Breeders Association 1993 Iroquois Award, Pennfield Farms, Inc., breeder of Fleeced," **$125**.

Tiffany Favrile 1753E," 5-3/4" h 750.00

Tiles

Tiles have been used as a functional design element for decades. Collectors have also recognized the beauty of tiles and search them out. Examples range from inexpensive souvenirs to more pricey art pottery examples.

American Encaustic Tiling Co., white, black design of horseman riding through brush, 4-1/4" sq 48.00

Art pottery, 6" h, 12" w, landscape with birds and moose in foreground, dark green high gloss glaze..................................... 175.00

Batchelder, imp bird design, blue ground, imp mark, 6" sq, price for pair...................................... 175.00

California Art, landscape, tan and green, 5-3/4" sq 65.00

J. & J. G. Low, Chelsea, MA 4-1/4" sq, putti carrying grapes, blue, pr 75.00

6" d, circular, yellow, minor edge nicks and glaze wear........ 35.00

Marblehead, blue and white ships, 4-5/8" sq, price for pair 125.00

Minton Hollins & Co., urn and floral relief, green ground, 6" sq 45.00

Tile, Mercer Pottery, Bucks County, PA, red clay, green glazed Pennsylvania German tulip design, **$20.**

Mosaic Tile Co., Delft windmill, blue and white, framed, 8" sq 55.00

Pardee, C., portrait of Grover Cleveland, gray-lavender, 6" sq 125.00

Souvenir
    Mount Vernon, multicolored 6.00
    Myrtle Beach, S.C., boating and beach scene, blue on white 6.00
    Old Deerfield, Massachusetts, black on white............................. 5.00
    Washington, D.C., Bicentennial, 1776-1976, 200 Years of Progress 6.00
    West Dennis, Mass., The Lighthouse Inn.................. 6.00

Tile, Rebekah, National Tile Company, 4-3/8" square, **$20.**

Tile, Grueby, turtle with brown shell, green leaves, yellow ground, 6" square, **$495.**

Tile Art Originals, Jane Tallman, Miami, FL, colorful hand-painted parrot, 7" sq 5.00

U. S. Encaustic Tile Works, flowered wreath, light green, 6" sq 20.00

Wedgwood, Tally Ho, man riding horse, blue and white, 8" sq 85.00

Tins

One of the most decorative aspects of collecting vintage advertising is to collect tins. They were designed to catch the consumer's eye with interesting graphics and/or colors. Today collectors seek them out for many of the same reasons.

For addition listings, see *Warman's Advertising*.

Angelus Shoe Polish Company Los Angeles, Cal., 3-1/2" d, black on cream, man and woman bowing their heads in front of bell, c1920-40, full...................................... 7.50

Babbitt's At Your Service, Trademark Cleanser, 4-3/4" h, orange, blue, white, and black, center graphic with uniformed saluting character in white suit, hat and gloves, unused.................. 8.00

Bower's Old Fashioned Peanut Crunch, brown and tan....... 30.00

Buster Popcorn, 10 lb, 9-1/2" h 75.00

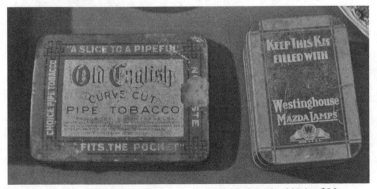

Tins, left: Old English Curve Cut Pipe Tobacco, red, black, and gold litho, **$20;** Westinghouse Mazda Lamps, orange and black litho, **$15.**

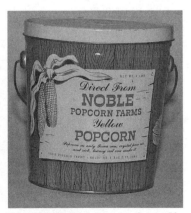

Tin, Noble Popcorn Farms pail, 6-1/2" h, 5-7/8" d, **$20.**

Calcox Tooth Powder, 2-1/2" d 85.00

Campfire Marshmallows, Campfire Kitchens, 7-1/4" d, 2" h 70.00

Capitol Mills, Lincoln, Seyms & Co., 5-1/2" h 60.00

Charlie Chips, tan and brown 20.00

Colgate Talc for Men, Invisible, Soothing, Refreshing, blue on white, 3-1/4" h 27.50

Crouthamel Potato Chips, red, white, and blue 25.00

Crisp-N-Good Potato Chips, 20 oz 35.00

Elite Powder, A Perfect Foot Powder, 4-1/8" h 30.00

Evening In Paris, round, 5" h . 10.00

Italina Antacid, 1930s 30.00

Johnson & Johnson Baby Talc 60.00

Kodak Developer, 3-1/2" h 40.00

Lucky Strike, flat fifty 35.00

Monarch Cocoa, 3" h 50.00

Mount Cross Coffee, J. S. Brown Mercantile Co., 3 lb, 7-1/2" h 70.00

National Biscuit 15.00

Old Berma Coffee, Grand Union Co., 1 lb, 6-1/4" h 50.00

Omar Cigarettes 15.00

O-So-Easy Mop, 1920s 50.00

Plee-zing 7.00

Rawleigh's Cocoa, sample, 2-1/4" h 60.00

Red Pepper Silver Buckle Spices, cayenne, 2-1/2" h 25.00

Red Rooster Coffee, keywind, 1 lb 72.00

Rose Kist Popcorn 48.00

Runkel's Cocoa, sample, 1-1/4" h 65.00

Shur-Fine 7.00

Sovereign Toffees, hinged, full color American Indian scene, c1950, 3" x 3-1/2" x 5-3/4" 38.00

State of Vermont Maple Syrup, one gal 24.00

Sudan Spice 9.00

Tom Thumb Crescent Crackers, blue and silver litho, red ground, two pound size, 7" h 60.00

Uncle Sam Shoe Polish, 3-1/2" d 75.00

Whitman's Salmagundi, hinged, Art Nouveau design of young lady, ©S. F. W. & S. Inc., 1920s, 4-1/4" x 7-1/2" x 2" 20.00

Tinware

Edward and William Pattison settled in Berlin, Conn., in 1738, becoming America's first tinsmiths. Before that time, the pieces of tinware used in the Colonies were expensive imports. It wasn't until the discovery of tin near Goshen, Conn., in 1829 that tinplate was produced in America. The industrial revolution ushered in machine-made, mass-produced tinware, and, by the late 19th century, the handmade era had ended. Tinware with painted decorations is known as toleware. Look for signs of age when buying vintage tinware as today's craftsmen make many fine examples following the old styles.

Toleware brings high prices

Some new high prices for toleware were set at auction in 2004 when the collection of Eugene and Dorothy Elgin was sold to Conestoga Auction Company, Inc., in April. A 6-1/4" d, 2" h chamberstick with an applied handle, japanned ground, polychromed floral decoration, yellow, red, green, and white, yellow banding, sold for $22,000. A 10-1/2" h, 6-3/8" d, 9-1/2" w coffeepot with a gooseneck spout, red ground, central medallion with floral motifs, yellow, black, blue, green, and tan, brought a stunning $55,000. A covered sugar bowl, 4" d, 3-3/4" h, with a scrolled finial, japanned base, floral polychrome, yellow, green, red, and white band decoration, brought $11,550. Many pieces the Elgins sold of their long time collection had been acquired at local flea markets and estate auctions.

Book box, remnants of painted design, 9-1/4" l 125.00

Bread tray, toleware, black ground, red flowers, green leaves, gold trim 45.00

Candle mold, 10" h, 6-1/4" l, twelve-tube, applied handle, hanger ring, two wick holders 250.00

Candlestick, 6" h, 4-1/4" d, adjustable push-up, scallop grip ring handle, round base 330.00

Candle sconces, pr, semicircular, candle socket and tall back with crimped crest, later white and green flowers, yellowed varnish, 12-7/8" h 250.00

Coffeepot
Gooseneck, flared gallery foot, inverted conical top, stamped banding, arched tapered ribbon handle with handle brace, rounded hinged lid, wooden turned finial, 10" h 250.00
Punched heart and floral motif, V-shaped spout, 10" h 550.00

Comb holder, hanging, mirrored 95.00

Cream pail, stamped banding around sides, arched bail handle,

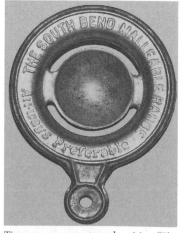

Tinware, egg separator, advertising, "The South Bend Malleable Range, All-ways Preferable," **$20.**

Tinware, comb holder, hanging type, mirror, two containers, embossed floral design, plating almost completely worn off, **$35.**

early solder repair, 8-3/4" h, 5-3/8" d 60.00

Dust pan, 13-1/2" w, 16-1/2" l, bell shaped, crimped molding,

compass wheel and various stamps, anniversary type, wooden handle 440.00

Flour bin, from Hoosier cabinet, 31" h...................................... 125.00

Lunch kettle, hinged lid, 2 hinged brass handles, mkd "Champion," 1917 patent date, interior with removable tray and insulated container, minor rust, 5-7/8" h, 9-3/4" w, 6-1/4" d................... 75.00

Quilt template
4-5/8" d, star 30.00
7" d, flower 35.00

Skater's lantern, light teal-green globe, 6-3/8" h 225.00

Tray, painted village scene, "Concord 1839," copper-painted rim with flowers, 15" x 18-1/2" 195.00

Wall pocket, large arched top with crimped rim, flanked by two small

Tinware, silent butler, painted red strawberries, gold leaves, **$35.**

circular elements, full-width rect pocket, some rust, 5-1/8" w, 7-5/8" h 200.00

Tip Trays

Tip trays are small colorful trays left on a table so that a patron could leave a tip for the wait staff. Their colorful lithographed decoration makes them an interesting collectible to many collectors. Because many of these little beauties saw a lot of use, carried coins, etc., expect to find signs of wear, perhaps some denting.

Reproduction alert.

Tip tray, Jack Daniels Old No. 7 Old Time Tennessee Whiskey, square, multicolored tin lithograph, **$65.**

Bull Brand Feeds, Maritime Milling Co., Buffalo, NY, rect 185.00

C.D. Kenny, Baltimore, boy with turkey, round 90.00

Clysmic, King of the Table Waters, woman with bottle, oval........ 80.00

El Verso Cigar, man smoking in den 60.00

Fraternal Life & Accident Insurance, rect, 4-7/8" x 4-1/4" 135.00

Globe-Wernicke Sectional Bookcases And Household Goods, Horace Prentice & Son, Kalamazoo, Mich, Chas W Shonk, Chicago, c1910...................... 45.00

National Cigar Stands Co., beautiful lady in center, 6" d 195.00

Prudential Insurance, 2-1/2" x 3-1/2" 20.00

Quick Meal Ranges, oval, 4-1/2" x 3-3/8" 250.00

R. D. Hubbard Flour, gold and black on simulated wood grain, text, detailed center graphic of flour sack, 4-1/8" 45.00

Success Manure Spreader, Kemp & Burpee Mfg. Co., Syracuse, early 1900s, 3-1/4" x 4-3/4" 140.00

World's Best Table Water, White Rock, scantly clad female kneeling,

Tip tray, tin, "New Store, New Goods, Anthony & Cowell Co., At the Old Stand," **$15.**

looking into water, rect, 6-1/8" x 4-1/8" 100.00

Titanic Collectibles

There are two types of Titanic collectibles. The older are those that were generated when the great ship was built and first launched. The public then was eager for news about this disaster just as we would be today. There were newspaper reports, books written, and other memorabilia. The second classification of Titanic memorabilia relates to the recent movie and its popularity.

Book, *Wreck & Sinking of the Titanic*, Marshall Everett, 1912, worn condition 150.00

Key chain, Titanic, White Star Line, MOC 3.95

Magazine, *National Geographic*, December, 1985 .... 2.25

Model kit, Minicraft 350 scale, Japan, 30" l, MIB.............................. 55.00

Movie prop, certificate of authenticity
Oar Lock, brass.................. 450.00
Passageway Lamp, brass..... 250.00

Newspaper, Daily Mirror 35.00

Photograph, movie set, set of 27 4" x 6" photos, showing film crews, actors, 1977 .... 35.00

Print, 6" d round sealed bubble frame, shells and seaweed dec on frame 250.00

Reverse painting on glass, minor paint flaking 145.00

Ticket stub, Titanic Artifact Exhibit, Franklin Institute, Phila 2.00

Video, 1977 movie..................... 3.00

Titanic collectibles, reverse painting on glass, Titanic about to collide with iceberg, original frame, some flaking to paint, **$75.**

Tobaccoania

Tobaccoania is a term coined to reflect the joys of smoking, and includes cigar, cigarette, and pipe smoking. As a collectible, tobaccoania seems to be as strong today as it was several years ago.

Crate label, multicolored graphics, 6-3/4" x 13-1/2"
Sailor's Hope, Maclin-Zimmer-McGill Tobacco, Petersburg, VA, lady holding binoculars and parasol, early 1900s.......... 24.00
Welcome Nugget, T. C. Williams Co., VA, prospector holding gold nugget, early 1900s 24.00

Folder, Mail Pouch Chewing Tobacco, black and white, diecut of baby laying on blanket next to Mail Pouch tobacco package, ©1938 .... 15.00

Humidor, cov, figural, Devil head, majolica, 6" h......................... 85.00

Lunch box, Central Union Cut Plug, The United States Tobacco Co., Richmond, VA, 4-1/4" x 7" x 4-5/8" 210.00

Pipe
Meerschaum, dog and puppy 75.00
Meerschaum, fairy, wings wrap around bowl.................. 225.00
Meerschaum, lion's head, orig case 115.00
Unknown maker, dark brown bowl with New York World's Fair in low relief, top of bowl smooth while bottom textured, black stem, "Wally Frank Ltd" name on side, red and white paper sticker, 5-1/2" l.............................. 60.00

Plate, tin, Havana Post, Morning English, La Tarde-Castello, woman holding jug 150.00

Pouch, orig contents
Arrow.................................. 15.00

Bigger Hair, 5" h 30.00
Buckeye, Mellow Chewing Tobacco, 5" h 5.00
Harp................................... 15.00
Sure Shot, 5" h 20.00

Tobaccoania, tobacco jar, terrier head, porcelain, matte finish, marked "N588," blue stamped "R" in diamond, 5-5/8" h, **$195.**

Tobaccoania, smoking stand, Depression-era, walnut, carved door, copper lined interior, refinished, **$75.**

Uncle Daniel, 3-1/2" h 15.00

Sign
Red Coon Tobacco, cardboard
.... 250.00
Edgeworth Tobacco, metal over
cardboard, 9-1/4" x 13-1/4"
.... 475.00

Tobacco cutter
Enterprise Mfg. Co., Philadelphia,
April 13,1875 patent 195.00
Drummond's Good Luck Tobacco
Cutter, American Machine Co.,
16" l 185.00
Griswold, Erie, PA 70.00

Tobacco jar
Crystal, hammered copper top,
Roman coin dec, sgd "Benedict
Studios" 250.00
Fisherman........................... 275.00
Mandarin, papier-mâché...... 95.00
Scotsman 295.00

Tobacco silk, zebra, 2" x 3"...... 10.00

Tobacco Tins

Everybody remembers the old joke about letting Prince Albert out of the can. Today's collectors of tobacco tins search for Prince Albert and many other colorful characters who grace the front of tobacco tins.

Tobacco tin, Sweet Mist Chewing Tobacco, Scottish Dillion Co., gold ground, red and black decoration, **$195.**

C.H.Y.P. Inter-Collegiate Mixture,
2-1/4" x 4-1/2" x 3-3/8"........ 160.00

Dill's Best, vertical pocket tin,
4-1/2" h 44.00

Edgeworth Junior, Extra High
Grade Tobacco, vertical pocket tin
.... 70.00

Fashion Cut Plug Tobacco, lunch
box, 4-1/2" h, 7-1/2" w 385.00

Golden Rod Plug Cut, 1-3/8" h,
4-3/8" w, 3-3/8" d.................. 40.00

Golden Sceptre, vertical pocket tin,
rounded corners 250.00

Guide Pipe & Cigarette Tobacco,
Larus & Bros., vertical pocket,
4-1/4" x 3" x 7/8".................. 230.00

Hi-Plane Smooth Cut Tobacco,
round, 6-1/4" h 220.00

Long Distance, Scotten Dillon Co.,
pail, multicolored graphics with
battleship, 6-1/2" x 5-1/2" ... 170.00

Lucky Strike Roll Cut, vertical
pocket tin, 4-1/4" h................ 90.00

North Pole Tobacco, United States
Tobacco Co., hinged box, 3-1/8" x
6-1/8" x 3-7/8" 220.00

Pat Hand, Globe Tobacco Co.,
vertical pocket, full, 2-3/4" x 2-1/2"
x 1-3/8" 130.00

Picoback, The Pick of Tobacco, screw
lid, 1/2-lb, round, 4-1/2" h 35.00

Qboid Cube Cut, vertical, plantation
illus, 4" x 3-1/2" 190.00

Century, horizontal, 1-1/4" x 2-1/8" x
3/8".. 170.00

Tobacco tin, pocket size, vertical, Qboid, both sides concaved, 4" h, **$190.**

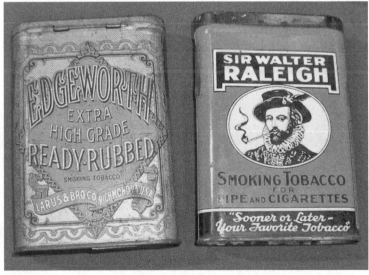

Tobacco tins, pocket size, left: Edgeworth High Grade, Ready Rubbed, blue and white, **$70**; right: Sir Walter Raleigh, orange and black, **$15.**

Tokens

Tokens are small medallion or coin-like objects. Some tokens were used in lieu of currency for transportation, such as a railroad token. Other tokens were forms of advertising or perhaps were used for admission to an event. Look for tokens where you tend to find coins and medals.

Token, "The Cathedral Church of St. John the Devine, Souvenir of Pilgrimage, New York," gold, 1-1/2" d, **$35.**

Boy Scout, good turn token..... 30.00

Chief Of The Sixes, Product Of General Motors...................... 25.00

Chuck E. Cheese Pizza Time Theatre, Ogden, Utah / In Pizza We Trust, 1980, 1" d 1.00

Cracker Jack, Woodrow Wilson 8.00

General Motors Motorama, 1956 .... 20.00

Houston Transit Authority, Houston skyline, 7/8" d 2.00

Ford, 30th Anniversary, 1933, copper 30.00

Fountain of Youth, St. Augustine, FL... 10.00

Green River Whiskey, goldtone 1-1/4" d 45.00

Metropolitan Transit Authority 4.00

North Shore Animal League, 1945-1975, gilded bronze.............. 20.00

Old Golden Nugget Gaming, Laughlin, NV 15.00

Pierce-Arrow, brass, 1-3/4" d . 60.00

Token, "Good Luck Souvenir, Pan-American Exposition, Buffalo, N.Y.," encased 1901 Indian-head penny, 1-1/2" d, **$10.**

Token, Pittsburgh Bicentennial, 1758-1958, bronze, original plastic box, **$25.**

Rockford, Illinois Transit Co., good for one city fare 5.00

Spokane United Railways, school fare... 8.00

Union Pacific, "A sample of the aluminum in the new Union Pacific Train built by Pullman Car & Mfg. Corp., ALCOA Aluminum Co. of America," 1-1/4" d 10.00

Washington, Member Friendship Fire Co., bronze 25.00

World's Fair and Expositions
1939 New York World's Fair, brass, Communications Building 15.00
Expo '74, Spokane, Wash., U.S. Pavilion, silver, 1-1/2" d 8.00

Tonka

Tonka Toys were built to last, and many a male flea market shopper has been known to get weak in the knees over seeing vintage Tonka Toys. Remembering all those hours of happily building roads and playing with cars and trucks can make a fella real nostalgic, especially when you realize Tonka first introduced it's full line of trucks in 1949 and is still in business today—that's a lot of trucks—all built for hours of play.

Army Jeep 45.00

Backhoe, 21" l........................... 50.00

Baggage tractor, trailer 50.00

Bulldozer, #3906, lever to adjust blade, sun umbrella.............. 24.00

Camper, #1070, purple metal, white plastic camper top, mini, 1970s, MIB... 90.00

Cement mixer, 1970s............ 150.00

Crane, #2940, yellow, black boom 15.00

Crawler, 1970s 150.00

Dump truck, red and green, Tonka, 1955 .... 100.00

Dune buggy, #2445, bumper chain, 1970s, MIB 90.00

Loader, #2920, lever operated bucket 24.00

Motor home, #3885, Winneabago 25.00

Pickup, red body, white roof.. 225.00

Ruff rider, #1045, green, mini 5.00

Snowmobile, 7" l 7.50

Tonka, truck, green and white, Star Kist Foods Inc., original decals, played-with condition, **$24.**

Sportsman pick-up 75.00

Trencher, #1089, mini, yellow . 10.00

Universal Jeep, MIB 125.00

Wrecker, #3915, dual hoists, white 60.00

Tools

Considering this great country was built from the ground up, tools have been with us for a long time. Treated properly, good tools last for years, many eventually making their way to flea markets. Tool collectors tend to find flea markets to be like gold mines when they are searching for something new to add to their collections.

Adjustable wrench, Crescent, 4" l 65.00

Anvil, Compliments of John Fink Metal Works, San Francisco and Seattle Wash, 4" l 30.00

Archimedian drill, bit, c1915 50.00

Axe head, single bit, Black Raven 20.00

Blow torch, Montgomery Ward 85.00

Book
Delta Power Tools 1940 Catalog, Delta Mfg. Co., Milwaukee, 48 pgs 25.00
Working Wood, A Guide for the Country Carpenter, Mike & Nancy Rubel, Rodale Press, 1977 .... 24.00

Brace
P. S. & W., No. 1202, 12" sweep, Samson patent ball bearing chuck, 1895 patent date, rosewood handle.............. 40.00
Yankee, No. 2101-10, 10" sweep 65.00

Broad ax, W. Hunt, 6" h, orig handle 50.00

Buck saw, wood, worn varnish finish, mkd "W. T. Banres," 30" 45.00

Draw knife, D. R. Barton 1882, 22" l, orig finish 85.00

File, half round, 20" l 15.00

Foot measure, Korrecto 30.00

Hammer, claw type, Winchester 55.00

Hand drill, Yankee.................. 40.00

Ice saw, 78" l 85.00

Jointer and raker gauge, Simonds, No. 342, adjustable 30.00

Measuring tape, Lufkin, 100'.. 65.00

Monkey wrench, Coes Wrench Co, Worcester, MA 95.00

Nut wrench, Boos Tool Corp, Kansas City, MO, screw adjust, orig box, 6" l.. 85.00

Pipe wrench, Erie Tool Works #8, angled 60.00

Tools, Craftsman tool chest, multi-levels, on wheels, red, locking, **$150.**

Tools, levels, wood, brass plates, price for pair, **$80.**

Plane
Doscher Plane & Tool Co., Saugatuck, Conn., 9-1/2" l 55.00
Record, No. 050, "Improved Combo," metallic, Sheffield, England, orig cutters, orig wood box, 9" l 185.00
Stanley, No. 3, c1950, made in USA logo, rosewood handle ... 100.00

Pliers, W. Schollhorn, Bernard's patent, parallel jaws, top nippers, blued, 6-1/2" l 25.00

Saddle maker's knife, H. G. Comph & Co., Albany, NY, crescent shape, rosewood handle, orig tooled leather scabbard 45.00

Saw vise, Sears, Roebuck & Co., No. 4920, Dunlap, orig box, 11" l. 55.00

Screwdriver, flat wood handle, round sides, 9" blade 35.00

Socket chisel, 9/16" gouge, mkd "Lakeside" 15.00

Square, double, Starrett #13, 4" 35.00

Tap and die set, Greenfield No. AA-4, two pc adjustable die screw plate 45.00

Upholstery tack hammer, Fairmount #22 .... 50.00

Wire gauge, Starrett Co., No. 283, US standard, 3-1/2" l 15.00

Toothpick Holders

Here's another accessory that has been present on the table or sideboard since Victorian times. Typically they are high enough for a toothpick to stand on end and large enough to hold many toothpicks. Over the years, toothpick holders have been made in all different types of materials.

Toothpick holder, reproduction, swan motif, carmel slag glass, 2-1/2" h, **$5.**

Bisque, skull, blue anchor shape mark 65.00

China
Japan, Figaro and Pinocchio standing next to basket.... 10.00

Japan, pig, basket along side, wearing top hat 65.00
Occupied Japan, cornucopia .. 5.00
Royal Bayreuth, elk 120.00
R. S. Germany, white mother-of-pearl luster 40.00
R. S. Prussia, pink and green luster ground, floral trim 45.00

Glass
Carnival, Flute pattern, purple 70.00
Carnival, Kittens pattern, marigold 95.00
Cut Glass, pedestal, chain of hobstars dec 150.00
Milk Glass, parrot and top hat, c1895 .... 45.00
Pressed, top hat 12.00

Pattern glass
Daisy and Button, blue 75.00
Jewel with Dewdrop 50.00
Texas, gold trim.................... 50.00

Silver plate, chick standing next to egg, engraved "Just Picked Out," Victorian, plate very worn 25.00

Toothpick holder, Pomona Glass, Flower & Pleat pattern, yellow stain decoration, 2-1/4" h, **$60.**

Torquay Pottery

This English pottery is often called Motto Ware because it usually contains a motto written into the clay. Some of the sayings are quite humorous. The pieces were hand decorated and usually well marked.

Bowl, Allervale, "Du'ee mak yerzel at 'ome," 3-3/4" d........................ 18.00

Butter tub, tab handles, cottage dec 85.00

Candlestick, "Many are called but few get up," 3-1/2" h 100.00

Cheese dish, "Cheese" on one side, "Comfort is better than pride" on other, 6-1/2" x 5-1/4" x 3-1/2" h 175.00

Creamer and sugar
"Du'ee Be Aisy" on creamer, "Du'ee Ave Zum Sugar" on sugar, red clay body, blue geometric slip dec 75.00
"Go Aisy Wi' It" on creamer, "Elp Yersel' Tu More" on sugar, 1930s 115.00

Dish, "Waste Not Want Not," cottage dec, 3-3/4" d 48.00

Egg cup, "Fresh Today," cottage dec 30.00

Finger bowl, "Time Ripens All Things," 4-1/4" d.................... 28.00

Jug, cov, "Kind words are the music of the world," 5-3/4" h 180.00

Jug, open, cottage dec, 4" h "Better to sit still than rise to fall" 85.00
"Time ripens all things" 85.00

Nappy, "When friends meet, hearts warm," cottage, 4-3/4" d 70.00

Planter, mottled black and brown

Torquay Pottery, pot with lid, 4-1/2" h, **$40.**

ext., blue flowers, green leaves, 6-1/2" d 80.00

Plate, cottage, "To thine own self be true" 75.00

Salt and pepper shakers, pr, egg shape, painted shamrocks, "The Shamrock of Ireland" on one, other with "The Land Where the Shamrock Grows" 50.00

Shaving mug, scuttle, "The nearer the razor, the closer the shave," Dad on back, 6-1/2" l 215.00

Tea cup and saucer, "Early Sow Early Mow," c1916 .... 70.00

Teapot, small, house dec, 4" h 120.00

Tulip vase, hand painted, cobalt blue ground, hummingbird and floral design, black mark and #32, 7-1/2" h 95.00

Vase, peacock, raised details, three handles, 9-1/2" h 125.00

Tortoiseshell Items

The mottled brown design known as tortoiseshell was so popular with Victorians that many items were made of actual tortoise shells as well as being imitated in glassware and pottery. With the invention of celluloid and plastics, imitations saw a revival. Today, real tortoiseshell falls under the protection of the Endangered Species Act. But, remember when many vintage tortoiseshell items were made, the entire tortoise was being used for food and other purposes, so the shell was also used.

Tortoise shell items, cigarette case, brass clasp and hinges, 3-1/2" x 2-7/8", **$40.**

Box, cov, circular, painted figure by riverscape, French, late 19th C, minor losses, 3" d 495.00

Calling card case, mother-of-pearl and ivory inlaid dec, c1825, 4" x 3" 225.00

Cigarette case, domed oval, applied central carved monogram, Continental, late 19th/early 20th C, 4-1/4" l 325.00

Coin case, matching calling card case with ivory writing pad, lined with blue silk, monogrammed, in 7-3/4" fitted case............................. 425.00

Dresser box, cov, rect, 4-3/8" l 250.00

Glove box, domed lid, ornate ivory strapping, sandalwood int., 3-1/2" h 375.00

Snuff box, oval, silver dec, 1-1/2" x 3" 325.00

Tea caddy, rect, hinged lid, small brass plate and escutcheon, int. fitted with tortoise shell veneered cover, English, late 18th/early 19th C, some small losses, 4-3/4" w, 3-3/8" d, 4-3/8" h 885.00

Travel set, case, comb, nail file, hand mirror, shoe horn, hair brush, soap box, toothpaste box, toothbrush box, powder box, nail buff, monogrammed "B.M.A," case worn 40.00

Toys

Every toy at a flea market is collectible, although some are worth more than others. Factors that influence price include age, condition, the original box, desirability, and maker. Probably the most deciding factor in the purchase of an antique toy is the one that makes the heart of the collector skip a beat, something that says that toy is important. The sampling below is just a mere peak into the giant toy box that many flea markets represent to collectors.

For additional listings, see *Warman's Antiques and Collectibles Price Guide, Warman's Americana & Collectibles,* and *Toys & Prices,* 12th edition, as well as specific company listings in this edition.

Toys, Drumming Animal Clockwork, black and white panda in red shirt playing chimes, green ground, marked "Made in China," MIB, **$20.**

Airplane, Buddy L, orange wings, aluminum propeller, c1930 ... 95.00

Airport fire tender, Dinky, #276, MIB 90.00

Airport tractor, Doepke 125.00

Austin delivery truck, Arcade #173, 1932 .... 100.00

Bristol helicopter, Dinky, #715, MIB 65.00

Bunny, three-wheeler bike, litho tin wind-up, mkd "MTU, China" 65.00

Burlington bus, Way of the Zepher, Corgi, MIB 45.00

Butterfly, litho tin friction, Alps 100.00

Camper truck, tin, litho, friction, 8" l, MIB 175.00

Carousel, Disney, Linemar, litho tin wind-up 150.00

Toys, Suzy Homemaker plastic oven, electric, 1968, Deluxe Topper Corp., 14" h, 9-1/2" w, **$25.**

Cessna airplane, plastic and tin, battery operated, Bandai, MIB 125.00

Child in stroller, litho tin, converts from stroller to high chair, 2-1/4" h 150.00

Chimpee the One Man Drummer, Alps, MIB.............................. 75.00

Coupe, rumble seat, A. C. Williams, 4-3/4" l, c1930, small chip on bottom of seat 195.00

Dipper bug, pull toy, 1950s, MIB 85.00

Dairy transport truck, Duo-Tone slant design paint, red and white, opens in back, orig decal, Buddy L, 26" l 75.00

Delivery truck, Betty Boop, tin litho 15.00

Drive-in theater, Snoopy, Kenner, 1971 .... 95.00

Dump truck, Smith Miller, #109, metal, red............................ 415.00

Easy Bake Oven, Kenner's, 1960, orig mixes and box.............. 140.00

Erase-O-Board and Magic Screen set, Popeye, Hassenfield Bros, 1957 .... 30.00

Express parcels delivery, litho tin wind-up, separate tin driver figure, built-in key, 1-3/4" h 195.00

Evel Knievel Skycycle, Ideal Toys, diecast, MIB........................ 125.00

Farm produce wagon, Dinky, #343, MIB... 75.00

Ferris wheel, colorful seats and graphics, Ohio Art.............. 295.00

Fire chief car, Acme Toy 45.00

Fire ladder wagon, Doepke.. 100.00

Fire truck, red, rubber, Auburn 25.00

Flat tire wrecker, yellow, Buddy L 125.00

Flying patrol set, Tootsietoy, MIB 175.00

Ford Cortina police car, Corgi, #402, MIB 15.00

Give A Show Projector, Kenner, boxed 35.00

Go-Go Turtle, plastic wind-up, Daito, 1960s, MIB................. 35.00

Grain elevator scoop, Model Toys 160.00

Grand Prix Special, racer and trailer, Nylint 50.00

Toys, Autobus A Imperialale, double-decker bus, friction, marked "Made in China," MIB, **$20.**

Greyhound Scenicruiser bus, tin, friction, Japan, 1960s 70.00

Horse van, yellow, red, Sun Rubber, 1935 .... 40.00

Jack in the box
Popeye, Nasta 12.00
Sleeping Beauty, Enesco....... 40.00

Jet roller coaster, Wolverine, orig box 145.00

Jumpy Rudolph, Asahi Toys, 6" 155.00

Knockout Electronic Boxing Game, Northwestern Products, #777 .... 95.00

Lincoln Van Lines Trans Canada Service Truck, 18 wheeler, 23" l 150.00

Merry Grinder, litho tin wind-up, 1920s, 4" h 175.00

Musical clown, Mattel, MIB 210.00

Outdraw the Outlaw, Mattel 165.00

Police car, Acme Toys............. 45.00

Policeman on motorcycle, tin, friction, MIB......................... 75.00

Punching clown, Romper Room Happy Jack, Hasbro, MIP 17.50

Race car
Auburn Rubber 65.00
Remco, Shark, 19" l 70.00
Schuco, green, key wind, MIB 190.00

Racing motorcycle, litho tin, friction, Japan, 1960s, 3-3/4" l 18.00

Toys, two tops, both brightly colored lithograph on tin, left: **$8,** but has some play damage; right: Ohio Art, **$12.**

Toys, taxi, Yellow Taxi, No. 361, yellow, black, and white litho tin, marked "Made in USA," play wear, **$85.**

Toys, guns, assorted, play wear, ranging from **$5** to **$25.**

Rhythm set, Romper Room, Hasbro, MIB 20.00

Road grader, Kenton, worn orig paint and tires 90.00

Roadster, red and black, Wyandotte, 7" l 175.00

Rolykin, Mickey Mouse, Marx 12.00

School bus, Cragston, litho tin, battery operated, orig box ... 100.00

Squeak, Scooby Doo, Sanitoy, 1970s 20.00

Star of the Circus Clown, litho tin friction, Cragston 190.00

Texaco tanker, Buddy L, red, white letters 75.00

Top
Mickey Mouse and Three Pigs, Lackawanna, 9" d 35.00
Snoopy and Peanuts Gang, Ohio Art 10.00

Truck, plastic, Hershey's Milk Chocolate, two removable Hershey kisses, Buddy L, 1982, mkd "Made in Japan" 15.00

UPS truck, hard plastic, clicker on front tiers, ©UPS, Made in China, 1977, 5-1/2" l 45.00

Vegas T-Bird, Corgi, #348, MIB 85.00

VW Beetle, Dinky, #181, MIB . 95.00

Whirlybird, 25 men attack team, Remco, 1960s, orig box 275.00

Toys, Gilbert, Erector set, no. 8-1/2, all electric set, metal box, C.8, **$175.**

Toys, locomotive, International Express, friction, marked "Made in China," MIB, **$25.**

Toy Dimestore Soldiers

Children have been fascinated with three-dimensional lead, iron, rubber, and plastic toy soldiers for many years. About the time of World War II, dimestores started to carry soldiers, which immediately became popular with youngsters. The toys could be purchased one at a time, making each set unique, unlike the English lead soldiers, which were sold in sets.

Toy dime store figures, Indian, kneeling, bow and arrow, Barkley, **$6.**

Aircraft spotter, Manoil 27.50

Army motorcycle, with sidecar, Barclay 50.00

Bandit, hands up, Grey Iron 40.00

Baseball player, Auburn Rubber 35.00

Bicycle dispatch rider, soldier, Manoil 25.00

Bomb thrower, two grenades in pouch, Manoil 20.00

Boy, traveling suit, Grey Iron ... 10.00

Bugler, pre-war, tin helmet, Barclay 20.00

Cadet officer, Grey Iron.......... 20.00

Charging soldier, tommy gun, Auburn Rubber 12.00

Toy dime store figures, box of assorted soldiers, green uniforms, three black horses, **$45.**

Colonial soldier, Grey Iron 17.50

Cowboy, mounted, firing pistol, Barclay 24.00

Crawling soldier, Barclay 15.00

Deep sea diver, 65 on chest, Manoil 18.00

Farmer, sowing grain, Manoil . 20.00

Flag bearer, post-war, Manoil . 24.00

Football player, Auburn Rubber 35.00

Indian chief, Barclay 12.00

Knight with pennant, Barclay 15.00

Lineman, football player, Auburn Rubber 25.00

Machine gunner, kneeling, Auburn Rubber 15.00

Marine officer, pre-war, marching, sword, blue uniform, tin hat . 27.50

Navy doctor, white uniform, Barclay, flat underbase 15.00

Nurse, white uniform, Barclay 24.00

Officer, post war, pot helmet, Barclay, orig sword............................ 175.00

Pirate, Barclay........................... 15.00

Policeman, raised arm, Barclay 15.00

Sailor, blue uniform, Barclay 15.00

Soldier, gas mask and with flare gun, Manoil 20.00

Wounded soldier, Manoil 17.50

Toy Train Accessories

Toy train accessories, like Plasticville houses, tunnels, miniature figures and fences, are often found at flea markets. Look for these tiny treasures to add to your train set-up.

Trains, accessories, sign, Athearn, Trains in Miniature, HO scale, lithograph on cardboard, oak frame, **$35.**

Airport hanger, Lionel 36.00

Bachman Hotel, Plasticville, HO 6.00

Barnyard animals set, Plasticville, 1940s, MIB 26.00

Billboard, American Flyer, #566, whistling, 1951-55 .... 20.00

Bridge, plastic, brown 7.00

Catalog, Lionel, accessories
1953, 9" x 6", 15 pgs 35.00
1959, 34 pgs......................... 15.00

Eureka Diner, American Flyer, #275, 1952-53................................. 45.00

Fence and gate, Plasticville....... 3.25

Foot bridge, Plasticville, #1051 .... 7.00

Gas station, Esso/Shell, Plasticville 18.00

Greenhouse, Plasticville, MIB 65.00

House, Plasticville
Brick-look............................... 8.00
Cape Cod 10.00
Ranch...................................... 5.00

Manual, How to Operate Lionel Trains and Accessories, 1957, 64 pgs, 8-1/2" x 5-1/2" 15.00

Milk car platform, Lionel....... 75.00

Moving and storage van, Plasticville, NRFB................. 35.00

Outhouse, Plasticville, O or S gauge 10.00

People kit, #2809-149 Citizens, Plasticville 15.00

Spruce trees, pr, Plasticville 8.00

Trainmaster remote command controller, Lionel, O gauge 40.00

Trains, accessories, gas station, Plasticville, #1800/149, **$18.**

Train signal, cast metal, 10-1/2" h 20.00

Trestle set
American Flyer, #780 .... 40.00
Lionel, #111 .... 24.00

Union Station, Plasticville 18.00

Waiting room, American Flyer, metal...................................... 30.00

Water tower
American Flyer, red and white checkerboard sides, bubbling type................................. 100.00
Lionel..................................... 80.00

Toy Trains

Toy trains are one of the most popular types of toys that collectors invest in today. Early toy trains were cast iron and quickly progressed to well-crafted examples using different types of metals and materials. American Flyer, Ives, and Lionel are among the most recognized makers. The prices listed are for sets of trains.

Trains, Lionel, locomotive, #1655, original box, **$60.**

American Flyer

American Legion Ltd, S gauge, #4019 locomotive, #4040 box car, American pullman, Pleasant View observation car, maroon litho and roofs............... 660.00

Freight, O gauge, 2-6-4 locomotive, eight-wheel tender, flat bed car, box car, derrick car, tank car, gondola, caboose, 1930s 450.00

Freight, O gauge, black steeple cab electric locomotive, orig paint and lettering, four litho cars, green gondola marked "Pennsylvania System" and "PRR 1116," automobile box car mkd

Trains, John Deere HO Scale Train Set, **$400.**

Trains, Lionel, hopper car, #2601, Detroit & Toledo Shore Line, Expressway for Industry, MIB, **$35.**

"American Flyer Fast Freight 1115," caboose mkd "American Flyer #1114" 175.00

Freight, O gauge, #476 gondola, #478 boxcar, #480 tank car, #484 caboose.......................... 130.00

Freight, S gauge, Northwestern, #4677 diecast locomotive and tender, #3207 sand car gondola, #3025 wrecker car, #3211 caboose, 10 pcs curved track, 1938, some wear from use 400.00

Passenger, O gauge, #253 locomotive, two #610 cars, #612, dark green, maroon inserts, 1924 .... 295.00

Passenger, S gauge, #4331, #4331, #4332.............................. 300.00

Bachmann, N gauge, Spirit of 1776 commemorative set, diesel locomotive, caboose, and three box cards, MIB 135.00

Ives, passenger set, locomotive, tender, three cars, S gauge 150.00

Trains, Lionel, locomotive, #682, Pennsylvania tender, original box, **$110.**

Lionel

Flying Yankee, #616 locomotive, three #617 coaches, #618 observation car, gunmetal and chrome, 1935.................. 275.00

L.A.S.E.R., #1150, chromed DC switcher locomotive, Ram-Jet A.C.L.M. car, glow-in-the-dark radar tracking car, survelliance helicopter car, glow-in-the-dark "Laser Gun Security Car," DC power pack, orig tract, play mat, 36" x 54 set up, orig box 250.00

Passenger, #252 electric locomotive, #529 coach, #530 observation, olive green, c1926 .... 175.00

Marx, black locomotive, #551 Union Pacific tender, #91257 Seaboard gondola, #3724 Union Pacific caboose, track, battery operated, orig box, c1955 .... 125.00

Trains, Lionel, freight car, BN 637500, Norfolk and Western Railway, MIB, **$40.**

Tramp Art

Here's a hot part of the flea market scene! Now considered to be folk art by some, these pieces were crafted by someone with limited materials, tools, and sometimes skill. By adding bits and pieces together, layers became objects such as picture frames, boxes of all kinds, etc.

Box, hinged cover, dove, heart, and anchor dec, 4-1/4" w, 1-3/4" h 200.00

Cabinet, hanging, shaped crest, two pierced doors....................... 175.00

Comb box, hanging, arched scalloped back with layered notch-carved rosette in center accented with small round white porcelain knobs, front of open box slopes forward and has scalloped top edge, double dart-shaped ornament on front, dark-red paint, 10-1/8" h, 8-3/4" w 110.00

Crucifix, wooden pedestal base, wooden carved figure, 16" h

Tramp art, cross, carved multi-layers, 15-1/2" h, 8-1/4" square base, **$65.**

.... 185.00

Frame
12-1/2" h, 10-1/8" w, applied notch-carved molding with hearts and Xs around sides, stained finish 110.00
14" x 12", hearts and diamonds, painted gold 255.00

Jewelry box, hinged lid, 4 square layered notch-carved feet, one back foot missing, 6" h, 14" w, 8-1/4" d 140.00

Match safe, strike surface, open holder for matches 75.00

Mirror
Crown of Thorns pattern, diamond shaped frame with outset corners, 19" w, 19" h 175.00
Frame with dark finish over varnish, stepped sawtooth border, stacked geometric designs, 15" h, 17-1/2" w 275.00

Vase, Crown of Thorns, rect, 13" h 175.00

Wall pocket, open work and porcelain buttons, 9" w, 7" h . 95.00

Trays

Trays are another type of advertising collectible. Like tip trays, expect to find interesting lithographed scenes and advertising for all types of products. Also expect to find some signs of usage.

Reproduction alert.

Tray, Hornung Beer, Jacob Hornung Brewing Co., Philadelphia, gold French horn in center, 12" d, **$50.**

Bartlett Spring Mineral Water, 13" d...................................... 150.00

Beamer Shoes, Victorian woman, c1900...................................... 75.00

Beam, Jim, plastic, 17" x 11"....... 9.00

Bozo, TV tray, some rust.......... 30.00

Buffalo Brewing Co., scratches and soiling, 13" d........................ 100.00

C.D. Kenny Co., Christmas motif of girl with doll, holly border, 10" d 230.00

Coors Beer, yellow, white, and black, 13" d....................................... 15.00

Donaldson's Dept. Store, tin litho 48.00

Eiffel Tower Brand Camembert, pressed aluminum, black printing, image of waiter serving wine, cheese, and bread, text "The Best Cheese That Experience, Care And Money Can Produce," Mercury, Nov. Co., 318 Bway, NY, c1900 .... 24.00

Falstaff Brewing, merry group of cavaliers, c1920, 24" d 95.00

Tray, tin, Shurtleff's Ice Cream, red and white, 12" x 17", **$65.**

Tray, papier-mâché, Samurai warriors in battle, pagodas in background, rectangular form with rounded corners, Japanese, 24-3/4" x 19", minor wear, **$165.**

Greyhounds, running.............. 15.00

Happy Birthday Mickey Mouse, Cheinco, 1978, 14" d.............. 45.00

Hires Root Beer, orange and yellow parrot, green ground............ 30.00

Knickerbocker beer, metal, 13" d 15.00

Maier Brewing, woman in orange outfit, Maier trademark on side, ©1909, Kaufmann & Strauss Co. litho, some overall scratching 100.00

Moerlein Beer, trademark "Crowned Wherever Exhibited" in fancy filigree, rim shows different expositions, Chas. W. Shonk Co., minor inpainting 50.00

National Brewery Co. White Seal Beer, factory scene, horse drawn wagon, early blob top bottle, Griesedieck Bros, proprietors, chipping and scratching 185.00

Pacific Brewing & Malting Co., Mt. Tacoma illus, orig 1912 work order from Chas. W. Shonk Co. on back 50.00

Park Brewing Co., factory scene, early railroad, horse drawn carts, and automobiles, Chas. W. Shonk

Co. litho, some inpainting, 12" d 60.00

Scottish and Newcastle Breweries, Ltd. blue, tan, and red, 12-1/2" d 25.00

Stahley's Flour, horse and girl, 1905 .... 50.00

Stegmaier Brewing Co., factory scene, early railroad and automobiles, minor scratching and rubbing 70.00

Terre Haute Brewing Co., room full of colonials raise their empty glasses to flying cherubs 125.00

Valley Forge Beer, Washington and men raising flag at headquarters, 12" d 40.00

Wolverine Toy Co., c1920, 4" x 6" 95.00

Woodward's The Candy Man, litho, black and white center image of midget couple holding box of chocolates, red and white peppermint sticks on sides, text with name, statistics, selling slogans, bottom rim printed "Made by John G. Woodward & Co., Council Bluffs, Iowa," 1920s, 5" x 7" 45.00

Trivets

Trivets are handy for holding hot irons and pots. Over the years, some have become quite decorative.

Note: All trivets listed are cast iron, unless otherwise noted.

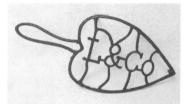

Trivet, cast iron, heart, loop handle, "L & Co." in center, three feet, 8-1/8" l, **$40.**

Iron rest
Double Point, IWANTU, Comfort Iron, Strause Gas Iron Co., Phila. Pa., embossed image of gas iron 40.00

Humphrey Gas Iron & General Specialty Co. 40.00

Kitchen
Cupids, two cupids in center, 4-3/4" w, 8-1/2" l 12.00
God Bless Our Home, gold, green, red and black paint, 4-1/4" d 10.00
Good Luck, horseshoe with star in center, mkd 9-35 and VCM, 7" x 4-1/4" 50.00
Griswold, #7, 7-1/4" 45.00
Peacock, brass 15.00
Souvenir of San Francisco, hand painted tile in cast iron frame 10.00
Wilton #2, love birds, hearts, brooms and star, painted gold 20.00

Trivet, cast iron, Gothic arch with filigree and trumpet flowers, scroll handle, 9 1/4" l, **$20**.

Trolls

These funny looking characters marched onto the scene in the 1960s. With their bright colors and busy hair, they have been bringing collectors good luck.

Caveman, Mop-Pets by Sarco, 1960s, 5" h 25.00

Cinderella, 12" h 15.00

Marx, talking troll, 18" h 45.00

Russ Berrie Troll, baby in pajamas, 7-1/2" h 6.00

Treasure Troll, Ace Novelty Co., baby, 11" h 15.00

Wooden, hand-carved, Henning, Norway, 5" h 32.00

Trolls, a young flea market vendor included a troll doll in their "This stuff for 50¢ each" box—a bargain for whomever found the troll first.

Trophies

How many of us have received a trophy for some event and it now resides in the back of a closet? Some trophies find their way to flea markets and then attract new buyers. Look for interesting names or dates on a trophy.

Bowling, Bakelite, 1960s........ **100.00**

Boy Scouts, figural metal boy on plastic base, 8-1/2" h **35.00**

Dog
Best Breed at Perth County Kennel Club, Canada, 1964, 5-1/2" h
.... **18.00**
Best Hound 1962, cup style, silver-plated............................... **220.00**

Garfield, on his knee, Arlens holding needle, "Get the point," Enesco Corp., 4-1/2" h **25.00**

Golf
Crystal Lake Country Club, 1931, silver-plated, runner-up, 5" h
.... **5.00**
Figural golfer on marble base, 1973
.... **60.00**

High school
Mercury figure on black base, District Champ, SDHS

Exclamatory League, 1933
.... **110.00**
Triumph figure on black base, District High School Exclamatory, 1930.......... **125.00**

Tennis, Smithville 1938-1939, name engraved on back **25.00**

Trap shooting, Pennsylvania Trap Shooting, 1930, 6-1/2" h...... **185.00**

Trophies, women's bowling, 9" h, **$9.**

Trophies, Cedarbrook Country Club, Senior Champion, 1990, Waterford covered jar, **$65.**

Trophies, First Prize, Special, Speed Boat Race, Hackensack River, Sept. 24-16, Won By Bubble, sterling silver, figural speed boat on top, tarnished, **$20.**

Tupperware

Tupperware was one of the first household products introduced to modern housewives at parties. By gathering with friends, housewives could see the latest in plastic wares and have a good time too. Today, Tupperware is especially sought in Japan and many European countries. Related booklets and other paper ephemera are destined to become collectibles of tomorrow, just as Tupperware is beginning to show up at flea markets; 2004 saw Tupperware opening retail stores, so more examples may be coming to a flea market near you.

Advertisement, full color, 1970s, 8" x 10"... **18.00**

Bar set, four tumblers, ice bucket, tray, black **25.00**

Bowl, cov, bright green, 8" d, 3-1/2" h
.... **6.00**

Cake carrier, cov, 9-1/2" x 13"
.... **20.00**

Coasters, pastel, set of six in orig holder, 2-7/8" d...................... **15.00**

Condiment caddy set, eight pcs
.... **20.00**

Child's cup, solid and sippy lid
.... **6.00**

Tupperware, child's play set, 26 pieces, orange, green, yellow and brown plastic, **$15.**

Child's playset
Mini-mix set, 1979, complete, MIB
.... **20.00**
Mini-party set, 1980, complete, MIB **20.00**

Collector plate, Chrissy's Favorite Toy, little girl with bowl on head, orig certificate, 1993, 7-1/4" d. **6.00**

Cookbook, *Stacked Cooked Meals*, Meredith, 1990, microwave system
.... **10.00**

Cup, Super Bowl XXIX, January 2, 1995, Joe Robbie Stadium, orig top, 7-1/4" h..................................... **7.50**

Deviled egg carrier **15.00**

Figure, Tupperware lady, 7-3/4" h 65.00

Iced tea spoon, pastels, 12" l, set 10.00

Jello mold, green, three pcs..... 12.00

Microwave set, three qt, unused 18.00

Mustard container, mkd, 7-1/2" h 5.00

Pastry sheet, 18" w, 21-1/2" l..... 5.00

Pepper shaker, light blue, 2-3/4" h 4.00

Salad tongs, blue-green hard plastic, mkd "Tupperware" on handle, 1958, orig box........................ 15.00

Sandwich set, carrier, four 6-1/4" sq containers, one each pink, blue, yellow, and green, 9" h carrier 25.00

Snack trays, set of six 12.00

Stacking set, 13 pcs 18.00

Turtle Collectibles

Turtle collectors will not find a flea market slow going. There will probably be several interesting examples to add to their growing collections.

Turtle, candle, 3" l, **$1.**

Unknown maker, green and clear rhinestones, 2" l 40.00
Unknown maker, gold and black enamel, 1-1/4" l................ 20.00

Pincushion, green and brown velvet, worn.......................... 5.00

Paperweight, cast iron 35.00

Pill box, sterling silver, 1-1/2" l, 1-1/8" w 35.00

Planter, McCoy........................ 40.00

Tape measure, brushed gold metal, red rhinestone eyes, 3" x 2-1/2" 130.00

Toy, Uncle Timmy Turtle, Fisher-Price #437, 1942 .... 100.00

Bolo tie, figural turtle, crushed turquoise inlay and sterling silver, marked ".925 Taxco," 3" d...... 65.00

Dish, cov, figural, green, 5" d 45.00

Earrings, pr, sterling silver, 1" l 8.50

Figure, Shawnee Pottery, 3-1/2" l 30.00

Hat, child's, green 5.00

Napkin ring, pewter, figural turtle with ring on back, 2-1/2" h ... 28.00

Nodder, 3-1/2" l........................ 25.00

Pin
Ciner, yellow enameled shell, green rhinestones, red rhinestone eye, 1-1/2" x 1-1/4"................. 50.00

Turtle, pull toy, litho tin shell, plastic body, metal walking strap, **$35.**

TV Guides

These little television-oriented magazines have been steadily growing in value. There is usually an article about the star featured on the cover, plus other interesting tidbits for television memorabilia collectors.

TV Guides, Feb. 14-20, 2004, collectible NASCAR racing cover, Dupont car, #24, **$3.**

1953, Queen Elizabeth.............. 12.00

1960, Washington County Schools, close circuit edition................ 4.00

1961, Lawrence Welk............... 15.00

1963, Jackie Gleason, Dec 15-21 .... 5.00

1964, America's Long Vigil, Kennedy assassination........................... 4.00

1964, Dick Van Dyke, Jan. 4 .... 8.00

1966, Adam West as Batman, March 26-April 1............................. 75.00

1966, Flipper, Vol. 14, #28 .... 5.00

1967, Ed Sullivan 7.50

1967, Huntley and Brinkley, Vol. 15, #26 .... 5.00

1967, Barbara Walters, Vol. 15, #31 .... 5.00

1973, Bill Cosby 10.00

1975, Tony Orlando and Dawn 6.00

1976, George Kennedy............... 5.00

1976, Sonny and Cher.............. 18.00

1977, Frank Sinatra................... 5.00

1981, Archie Bunker.................. 6.50

1982, Michael Landon 7.50

1983, M*A*S*H........................ 8.00

1984, Pierce Bronsan 12.50

1985, Cheryl Ladd..................... 4.00

1986, Farrah Fawcett 5.00

1986, Nicollette Sheridan 7.50

1986, Lucille Ball..................... 15.00

1997, Xena, May 4.00

1998, Winter Olympics, set of four 30.00

1999, Star Wars, set of four 30.00

Typewriters and Accessories

Tap, tap, ding. Remember the bell that used to ring as you pecked away on a typewriter? Some collectors still hearing that sound. You can find them searching flea markets for vintage typewriters, accessories and related ephemera. Vintage typewriters are another example of where you should thoroughly inspect the keys, motor, and wiring, before trying to use it.

Advertisement
IBM Electric Typewriters, 1952, 11" x 14"................................... 12.00
Royal, 1962 .... 15.00
Royal Portable, 1970s............. 5.00

Charm, 14k yg, moveable carriage 95.00

Lighter, adv, Typewriter Sales & Service, Inc., Bristol, TN, Orbit lighter 45.00

Oil can, Smith Premier Typewriter Oiler, 3-1/2" h 24.00

Postcard, Remington Plant...... 15.00

Ribbon tin
Allied Carbon & Ribbon Mfg Corp., NY 35.00
Carter's Midnight Typewriter Ribbon, Carter's Ink Co., Boston 16.00
Columbia Twins 15.00
Eberhard.............................. 10.00
Hallmark, Cameron Mfg Co., Dallas 20.00
KeLox, KeLox Manuf Co. 24.00

Typewriters, Underwood Standard, #5, **$45.**

Panama................................ 20.00
Remington............................. 7.50
Seagull 20.00
The Webster Star Brand, F. S. Webster Co. 20.00
Thorobred, Underwood Corp, Burlington, NJ.................. 25.00
Vogue Royale 5.00

Swarovski, figure, crystal, #208886 .... 40.00

Toy, Junior, Marx 30.00

Typewriter
Adler 7, oak case 335.00
Blickensderfer, #7, 1897 ..... 300.00
Bing #2, German, with case 150.00
Corona, folding, #3, 1912..... 95.00
Empire, 1892 .... 200.00
Harris Visible, #4, 1913...... 300.00
Imperial, Model B, 1908..... 250.00
International Electromatic, IBM, 1930............................... 120.00
L. C. Smith #8, 12" carriage.. 20.00
L.C. Smith & Corona, Comet 65.00
National, #5, 1920 .... 225.00
Remington, Noiseless, portable, orig case, 1950s................ 50.00
Royal, Model 1, 1906.......... 200.00
Simplex................................ 50.00
Tom Thumb, orig case.......... 15.00
Underwood #5.................... 155.00
Woodstock, 1914 .... 45.00

Uhl Pottery

This Evansville, Indiana, pottery was founded in 1854 by two German immigrants, August and Louis Uhl. Their production gradually shifted from utilitarian stoneware to pottery dinnerware and household goods. Their miniature novelty items were very successful. The company closed in 1944. Several family members brought the company back to life in the late 1980s and began to produce a limited number of miniatures and Acorn Ware crocks.

Bottle, water, hand-turned 60.00

Bowl, #119, tulip, yellow 80.00

Casserole, cov, 8" d, 3-1/2" h, brown, incised "529," stamped "Uhl Pottery Co., Huntingdon, Ind." 30.00

Christmas jug
1939, beehive jug, brown over white, "Merry Xmas 1939" 200.00
1942, squat jug, brown over white, "Merry Christmas 1942" 225.00

Churn, two-gal, Bristol glaze, Acorn Wares ink stamp, ... 150.00

Cookie jar, light blue, 9-1/4" h 120.00

Flower frog, #624 .... 45.00

Flowerpot, Egyptian, terra cotta 30.00

Mug
Barrel form, tan, mkd "16" .. 10.00
Grape leaves, dark brown stoneware, c1910, 5" h 26.00

Pitcher
#124, blue, 8-1/2" h 65.00
#181, grape design, blue....... 75.00
#197, blue 75.00

Planter
Cat, black 110.00
Rabbit, #167, blue.............. 127.50

Spittoon, blue 70.00

Teapot, #132, dark turquoise, 5" h, blue underglaze stamp 90.00

Vase
#113, blue 75.00
#123, mauve......................... 40.00

Union Collectibles

Remember the jingle "look for the union label?" Today collectors are still looking for that label, and also items relating to their favorite union. Many interesting examples of union-related collectibles can be found at flea markets, especially if you look in showcases that usually contain smalls.

Autograph, John L. Lewis, 5-1/2" x 7-1/2" glossy black and white reprint photo of United Mine Workers leader, miner's clothing and helmet, face covered by coal, 3-1/2" x 5-3/4" white card with large ornate signature in blue ink, tiny pencil date "2/58" on back 45.00

Book, *Henry Ford vs Labor, The Flivver King*, Upton Sinclair, 5-3/4" x 7-1/2", 120 pgs, 1937, softcover 35.00

Delegate badge, IAMAW, Seattle, bronze, emb space capsule 35.00

Notepad, 2-1/2" x 4-1/2", celluloid cov, 52 lined paper pages, pro-union and other inform, calendars for 1907, 1908, 1909, graphic of man in brown suit, showing clothing's union label 28.00

Pencil clip, Vote UAW, black lettering, white ground 5.00

Pinback button, Labor Day March for Human and Labor Rights, Sept. 6, 1976, Raleigh, North Carolina, black and white sketch of people with signs, 3" d 14.00

Pocket knife, Case, XX 8 Dot, #3318SH, SP, three-blade, yellow composition handle, red lettering, logo, United Steel Workers of America on handle 20.00

Print, 12-1/2" x 15-1/2", black and white, portraits of Teddy Roosevelt and John Mitchell as "The World's Leading Champions of Arbitration and Fair Play," 1902 coal strike settlement, United Mine Workers of America 190.00

Shaving mug, United Mine Workers, clasped hands emblem flanked by crossed picks and shovels, floral

Union collectibles, pinback button, International United Automobile Workers of America, center lavender gear, red border, 1" d, **$20.**

dec, rose garland around top, mkd "Germany".............................. 125.00

Universal Pottery

Organized in 1934 by the Oxford Pottery Company, in Cambridge, Ohio, the firm merged and bought several other small potteries over the years. Universal Pottery made dinnerware and kitchenware until 1960, when the company closed. Because of the mergers, several different brand names were used, including Oxford Ware and Harmony House.

For additional listings, see *Warman's Americana & Collectibles* and *Warman's American Pottery & Porcelain.*

Universal Pottery, Calico Fruits pattern, top row, covered casserole, **$30;** cup and saucer, **$20;** range shaker, **$20;** platter, **$45;** batter jug with lid, **$60.**

Batter jug, Cattails 45.00

Bowl
    Ballerina, dove gray, 7" d........ 7.00
    Moss Rose, 5-1/2" d 7.00

Bread and butter plate
    Ballerina, pink........................ 3.50
    Moss Rose.............................. 6.00

Bread box, Cattails................... 40.00

Butter dish, cov, Cattails.......... 40.00

Casserole, cov, Cattails............. 20.00

Cup and saucer
    Camwood.............................. 12.00
    Woodvine 12.00

Custard cup, Calico Fruit.......... 6.50

Dessert bowl, Iris 3.00

Dinner plate
    Ballerina, chartreuse 7.00
    Moss Rose.............................. 7.50
    Rambler Rose 10.00

Drip jar, Bittersweet 25.00

Egg cup, Ballerina, jade green . 12.00

Gravy boat
    Highland............................... 35.00
    Rambler Rose 12.00

Milk jug, Calico Fruit............... 30.00

Mixing bowl, Woodvine, one qt
    .... 22.50

Pie server, Cattails 24.00

Platter
    Bittersweet............................ 35.00
    Cattails.................................. 35.00

Valentines

Collecting Valentine's Day sentiments is a pleasure for many folks. The earliest cards were hand made. After the greeting card business became more fully developed, valentines were included. Many collectors prefer die-cut cards, which are sometimes found with layers or pull-down decorations. Others like mechanical or animated cards, which have a moving part.

For additional listings, see *Warman's Antiques and Collectibles Price Guide* and *Warman's Americana & Collectibles.*

Character, Batman and Robin, 1966
.... 10.00

Charm string, four hearts, ribbon
.... 45.00

Honeycomb tissue
  Children playing house, 1920s, 8" x
    5" 25.00
  Cupid and flower basket, 1926
    .... 32.00
  Girl with tennis racket and bag of
    balls, German, 1920s, 5" h
    .... 25.00

Mechanical
  Boxer, "You sure are a Knockout
    Valentine," 8-3/4" h, 8" w
    .... 24.00
  Baseball player swinging bat, "I'd
    sure go to bat for a Valentine
    Like You," 6-1/4" h 22.00
  Saxaphone player, "My dear
    Sweetheart I'm making a big
    noise about you," 5" h 10.00

Pop-up, 4" x 4-1/2" heart shaped stiff
  diecut paper, young girl holding
  ring of roses at waist, winged girl
  cherub on floral bicycle, bouquet
  of pansies and violets accented by
  red tissue accordion-cut paper, mkd
  "Printed in Germany," early 1900s
  .... 10.00

Valentines, Barbie Valentines, Cleo, MIB, **$15.**

Postcard, 3-1/2" x 5-1/2", full
  color, lightly embossed, German
  publisher, early 1900s
  Cherubs 3.50
  Children.................................. 2.50

Pull-down, German
  Car and kids, 1920s 35.00
  Dollhouse, large, 1935 .... 45.00

Valentines, assortment, each **$10-$20.**

Stand-up, easel-back
  Automobile, windows open . 12.00
  Cat with parachute, 4-1/2" x 3-1/2"
    .... 24.00
  Flower basket, pasteboard, 1918
    .... 10.00

World's Fair, Brussels, 1958, First
  World's Fair of the Atomic Age,
  #B7604, orig envelope 15.00

Van Telligen

Designer Ruth Van Telligen created some fun characters for the Royal China and Novelty Company of Chicago. Produced by Regal China, the items were limited to a few cookie jar designs and salt and pepper shakers. The cookie jars were made in limited numbers and tend to be hard to find.

Salt and pepper shakers, pr
  Bears, yellow, 3-1/2" h 45.00
  Black boy and dog 185.00
  Bunnies, hugging 25.00
  Ducks.................................... 75.00
  Dutch boy and girl, 3-3/4" h
    .... 80.00
  Mary and lamb 85.00
  Peek-A-Boos, red and white
    .... 170.00
  Snuggle Hug Love Bugs...... 125.00

Van Telligen, duck salt and pepper shakers, chips, **$75.**

Vending Machines

Got a penny for a gumball? Vending machines with gumballs, peanuts, and other goodies captured many pennies and loose change. These simple vending machines date to about 1910.

Vending machine, Ajax, hot nut vendor, with side cup holder, top lights up, 1940, **$800.**

Aspirin, Certified, c1950, 12 for 25¢ 50.00

Candy
Hershey, c1950, 1¢................ 75.00
Mills, automatic, c1936 ...... 100.00
Victor, Topper, c1950 .... 90.00

Cigar, Malkin Phillies, steel meal, 10¢, 1930s 95.00

Combs, Advance machine, Model #4, 10¢, 1950s 45.00

Confection, Master, c1923, 1 cent, 16" h 200.00

Gum
Adams, c1934, four column, tab gum vendor, chrome, decal, 22" h 100.00
Ford, round globe with Ford decal, chrome finish 150.00
Victor, 1940s, aluminum front, cylindrical glass, 17" h restored 245.00

Matches, Edwards Mfg Co, c1930, Diamond, one to four books, 13-1/2" h 225.00

Nut
Atlas Bantam tray vendor, 1940s, restored, 11" h 395.00
Eldridge, aluminum, 1936, 8-1/2" h, 4-1/2" w, 4" d 195.00

Pens, Servend, c1960 .... 75.00

Postcard, Exhibit Supply, 1¢, 1930s 125.00

Stamps, Shipman Stamp, c1960 .... 45.00

Vending machine, peanut, "Eat 'em Hot," **$350.**

Vernon Kilns

Founded in Vernon, Calif., the firm was formerly called Poxon China. After it sold to Faye Bennison in 1931, it was renamed Vernon Kilns. The company then flourished and made high-quality dinnerware and other items. Souvenir plates were among their more successful products. The company folded in 1958, when it sold its trade name, molds, and remaining stock.

Berry bowl, Calico 8.50

Vernon Kilns, sugar bowl, Chintz, **$12.50.**

Bread and butter plate
Hawaiian Flowers 20.00
Homespun 3.00

Cake plate, Organdie, 12" d 20.00

Chowder bowl, Moby Dick, dark blue 30.00

Coffeepot, Style 165.00

Creamer and sugar, Raffia..... 22.00

Cup and saucer
Chatelaine, topaz 40.00
Moby Dick, brown 22.00

Demitasse cup and saucer,
Organdie.............................. 20.00

Dinner plate
Chatelaine, jade 20.00
Chintz 48.00
Dolores, 10-1/2" d 18.00
Gingham 8.00
Hawaiian Flowers, blue, 9" d 32.00

Egg cup
Gingham 18.50
Organdie 27.50
Tam O'shanter...................... 30.00

Figure, Unicorn, Fantasia, gray glazed ceramic, mkd "Vernon Kilns," 1940 .... 350.00

Flower pot, matching saucer, Tam O'shanter 80.00

Vernon Kilns, dinnerware set, Plaid pattern, olive green and brown on white ground, **$90.**

Mug, Brown-Eyed Susan 25.00

Pitcher
Barkwood, two-qt................. 60.00
Bel Air, two-qt 70.00
California Heritage............... 70.00
Raffia, two-qt........................ 40.00
Tradewinds, qt...................... 60.00

Platter
Brown-Eyed Susan, 12" d 12.00
Modern California Orchid, 16" l
.... 75.00
Painted Rose, oval, 16" l 95.00

Salad bowl, Tam O'shanter 25.00

Salad plate
Chatelaine, topaz 25.00
Chintz 18.00

Salt and pepper shakers, pr,
Gingham 15.00

Souvenir plate
Georgia, 10" d 15.00
Lookout Mountain, made for
Livelys Lookout Museum, deep
red, 10-1/4" d 20.00
Nebraska University 30.00
Texas Southwest Methodist
University, Dallas, backstamp
"Made exclusively for Titche-
Goettinger Co." 35.00

Teapot, Linda......................... 125.00

Tid-bit tray, Organdie, two tiers
.... 25.00

Vegetable bowl, Tam O'shanter,
divided.................................. 20.00

Vietnam War

With the passing of time since the Vietnam War, there is growing interest in military and civilian items related to the conflict. Items from "The Nam" and those from back in "The World" are seen with increasing frequency at flea markets, where good pieces an still be found at reasonable prices.

Belt buckle, Vietnam in Honor of the men and women of the armed forces of the United States who served in the Vietnam War, image of man with hand on Vietnam Memorial Wall, couple hugging, rose, ©1992, 2-1/4" x 3-1/4"
.... 30.00

Book
William D. Blankenship, The Leavenworth Irregulars, Bobbs-Merrill, 1974, 1st ed., orig dj
.... 50.00
Josiah Bunting, Lionheads, 1972, orig dj 75.00
Edward Doyle and Samuel Lipsman, The Vietnam Experience, America Takes Over, 1965-1967, Boston Publishing, 1982................................. 15.00

Collector plate
Armor, Roger Redford, Nilsson, 1990, MIB........................ 30.00
Vietnam Veteran's Memorial, Islandia............................. 35.00

Comic book, issued by Army for operation and maintenance of M16A1 rifle, 1969.................. 20.00

Flag, POW, black and white, some use
.... 15.00

Gas mask, Wilson, canister, straps, coupling, metal case 50.00

Magazine
American Quarterly Review, Oct. 1967, Vol. 36, No. 1, Asia After Viet Nam, 14-pg article by Richard M. Nixon 50.00
Life, Oct. 20, 1967, "U.S. Prisoners in North Viet Nam"............ 5.00

MIA bracelet, red aluminum, "Maj Horace H. Fleming III, FL. USMC 10 May 68 SVN" 25.00

Lighter, Zippo, Vietnam 68-69 Qui Nhon, enamel decor............ 300.00

Pinback button, Out Now Nov. 6th, Demonstrate Against the War NPAC, 1-3/4" d 20.00

Poster, cardboard, Vietnam Moratorium Oct. 15 No Business As

Usual Until The Troops Are Home, 13" x 10".................................. 15.00

Shoulder tab, RV Ranger, white silk, light-red border, 23 Vietnamese Ranger Bn 75.00

Uniform
Flight jacket, G-1, US Navy, leather, size 40............................. 260.00
Flight suit, coveralls, US Army/Marines, summer, size 36 55.00
Overcoat, USAF, blue, #1549, double breasted, shield buttons, 1974................................. 40.00
Trousers, green BDU, field, cotton, adjustable waist................ 50.00
Trousers, green tropical, cotton, summer weight, Golden Mfg Co., Inc., Golden, MS, adjustable waist 45.00

Uniform patch 5.00

Welcome home packet, issued by Chapter 154 Vietnam Veterans of America, Mt. Clemens, MI.... 15.00

Viking Glass

Located in New Martinsville, W.Va., this glass company has recently ceased production under the last of the original family owners, Dalzell-Viking. Viking produced various brightly colored glassware items through the years and also made some crackle glass. Look for a silver and pink foil label on some items.

Viking Glass, candy dish, dome covered with pointed finial, deep orange-red, original label, **$25.**

Ashtray
Amber, crackle glass, 7" l 15.00
Teal blue, triangular, orig foil label, 3-3/4" w 17.50

Basket, blue, 5-1/2" x 7" 35.00

Bell, red, 3-1/2" h 15.00

Bookends, pr, owls, dark green, 7" h
.... 65.00

Bowl
Amethyst, 1950s 25.00
Tangerine 40.00

Bust, Madonna 30.00

Candy dish, olive green, Teardrop pattern, 8" h 15.00

Cigarette lighter, amber 35.00

Compote
Amber, part of orig sticker, 8-1/2" d, 7" h 35.00

Amberina, 4-3/4" h, 8-3/4" d
.... 35.00

Cruet, applied handle, orig stopper, 6-1/2" h, amber or green 30.00

Fairy lamp, red satin 55.00

Figure
Bird, red 50.00
Duck, dark blue 40.00
Elephant, frosted 20.00
Penguin, dark blue 65.00

Goblet, orange and gold, 4-5/8" h
.... 12.00

Juice set, cobalt blue, five pcs .. 30.00

Pitcher, orange, applied clear handle
.... 30.00

Vase, Epic Ruby, 16-1/2" h 35.00

Wagner Ware

Wagner Manufacturing made cast-iron hollow ware, brass castings, and aluminum cookware among other household items. The company prospered from 1891 to the late 1950s under the care of the Wagner family. The firm was bought in 1959 by Textron, which held it until 1969.

Ashtray, skillet shape, 3" d 40.00

Corn stick pan, 13" l 65.00

Dutch oven, Magnalite, six-qt . 45.00

Frying pan, #5 .... 15.00

Muffin pan, 11-hole, 7-1/4" x 10-1/2"
.... 55.00

Roaster, #4285, 15-3/4" l 75.00

Scoop, #912, 9-1/4" l 24.00

Skillet
No. 3, pie logo 24.00
No. 6 .... 35.00
No. 8 .... 30.00
No. 12 .... 60.00
No. 1101A, sq 45.00

Spoon, aluminum, long handle, #710
.... 35.00

Teakettle, wire handle, 6" h ... 150.00

Waffle iron, wooden handles
.... 30.00

Wagner ware, ashtray, cast iron, 6-1/4" x 4-3/4", **$20.**

Wall Pockets

Wall pockets are clever pottery holders designed to hang on walls. Potteries such as Roseville and Weller made wall pockets in the same lines as their vases, bowls, etc. Collectors search for these potteries plus interesting examples from lesser-known makers. Wall pockets were very collectibles a few years ago, driven by the decorator market. Today they are becoming easier to find at flea markets, but the prices haven't declined.

Wall pocket, Pennsbury Pottery, bellows shape, green eagle, blue stars, red trim, **$60.**

Frankoma
Acorn, light brown, mkd
"Frankoma 190" 25.00
Cowboy Boot, blue and white,
speckled, mkd "Frankoma 133"
.... 30.00

Gilner, fish, yellow stripes, mkd
"Gilner Calif C" 25.00

Holt-Howard
Santa King 35.00
Santa ornament 55.00
Sunflower 100.00

Japan, Harlequin heads, boy and girl
.... 65.00

McCoy
Apple on leaf 50.00
Fan, white, pink floral 60.00
Leaf, blue and pink 40.00
Morning Glory 50.00
Post Box, green 50.00
Sunflower, bird 45.00
Tulip, white 40.00
Yellow, pink floral dec 40.00

Morton Pottery, cockatiel, pastels
.... 35.00

Occupied Japan
Butterfly 35.00
House 15.00
Parrot 15.00

Pennsbury Pottery, bellows-shape,
eagle motif 60.00

Roseville
Foxglove, brown, #1296-8"
.... 190.00

Wall pocket, owl, made in Japan, 7-1/2" h, **$10.**

Gardenia, brown, #666-8"
.... 150.00

Green, matte, 8" l 120.00
Maple Leaf, 8-1/2" 75.00
Three sided, green, 11" l 110.00
Tulips, emb flowers, white ... 60.00

Royal Copley
Angel 25.00
Cocker spaniel 20.00

Shawnee, teapot, pink apple dec
.... 32.00

Thames, trio of Christmas carolers
.... 45.00

Unmarked
Acorn, majolica 95.00
Cornucopia shape, cattail and duck
dec, blue, 6" h 40.00

Plaster, yellow iris dec, homemade,
8" l 20.00

Weller
Blue, emb leaf, 7" l 60.00
Iris, blue, 8-1/2" l 50.00

West Coast Pottery, peacock, mkd
"USA-441" 45.00

Watch Fobs

A watch fob is a useful and/or decorative item that is attached to a man's pocket watch by a strap. Its main function is to assist the user in removing the watch from his pocket. The heyday of watch fobs was late in the 19th century, when many manufacturers created them to advertise products, commemorate special events, or serve as decorative and useful objects. Most watch fobs are made of metal and struck from a steel die. Some are trimmed with enamel or may have a celluloid plaque. When found with their original watch strap or original packaging, the value is enhanced.

For additional listings, see *Warman's Americana & Collectibles.*

Reproduction alert.

Watch fob, advertising, Indian Motorcycles, brass fob, black leather strap, **$90.**

symbol and name on back, c1950
.... 25.00
General Motors, diesel engine,
bronze luster, block logo on back,
engraved dealer name 15.00
Green River Whiskey 45.00
Joliet Corn Shellers 150.00
Kelly Springfield Tires, white metal,
raised illus of female motorist,
"Kelly Springfield Hand Made
Tires" on back, 2" d 80.00
Lima Construction Equipment,
copper luster, large excavation
tractor, world continents
background, inscribed "Lima/
Move The Earth With a Lima,"
back text for shovels, draglines,
clamshells, and cranes 25.00
Martin-Senour Paints, silvered
brass, 1" d multicolored celluloid
insert, text on back 65.00
Pontiac, with key chain, 3/4" d
.... 45.00
Red Goose Shoes, enameled red
goose 100.00
Studebaker, enameled tire design
.... 50.00
Ward's Fine Cakes, white porcelain,
bluebird, silvered beaded rim
.... 45.00

Commemorative
American Legion, Cleveland State
Convention, 1946, diecut brass
.... 35.00
Princeton University, brass, 1908
.... 48.00
Souvenir Chicago Camp, June
19-23, 1918, Municipal Pier,
Chicago 30.00

Watch fob, advertising, State Farm Mutual Auto Insurance Co., enameled metal, black leather strap, **$50.**

World Championship Rodeo
Contest, Chicago 45.00

Political
Bryan, Our Next President ... 40.00
Democratic National Convention,
Baltimore, 1912, silvered brass,
center shield with eagle ... 20.00
Republican National Convention,
brass, 1920, bust of Lincoln
.... 40.00
Taft and Sherman, 1-1/4" jugate
portraits, leather fob 45.00

Advertising
Anheuser-Busch, diecut silvered
brass, enameled red, white, and
blue trademark, 1-1/2" d .. 60.00
Caterpillar, MacAllister Machinery
Co., Ft Wayne-Indianapolis,
Plymouth, IN, 1-1/2" 45.00
Corby's Canadian Whiskey
.... 175.00
Foundry & Machine Exhibition Co.,
1-3/4" x 1-1/2" 48.00
Gardner-Denver Co, jackhammer,
silvered brass, tool replica,

Waterford Crystal

Waterford is easily identified with high-quality crystal. The firm was started in 1729 in Waterford, Ireland. Look for a finely etched mark or a foil type label. Waterford continues to make exquisite glassware today.

For additional listings, see *Warman's Antiques and Collectibles* and *Warman's Glass.*

Waterford Crystal, decanter set, decanter, four tumblers, fitted wooden tray with brass trim, **$195.**

Ashtray, 5" d............................ 95.00

Bowl, allover diamond cutting, 6" d
.... 70.00

Bud vase 60.00

Cake plate, 10" d, 5-1/4" h, sunburst center, geometric design 85.00

Candlesticks, pr, pear shape, hollow center, horizontal oval cuts on wafers, rayed base, looped cross cuttings, 7" h........................ 175.00

Christmas ornament, c1995.. 17.50

Clock, ABC block 60.00

Creamer and sugar, Tralee pattern
.... 85.00

Figure
Dolphin............................. 110.00
Eagle 140.00
Lion.................................... 150.00
Rocking horse..................... 80.00

Shark................................... 125.00

Frame, ABC block, 4" x 6"........ 55.00

Goblet, Colleen......................... 65.00

Honey jar, cov......................... 70.00

Letter opener........................... 45.00

Napkin rings, eight-pc set..... 165.00

Paperweight, Capital 90.00

Rose bowl, 5-1/2" d, laurel border, spike diamond band.............. 50.00

Vase, bulbous, top to bottom vertical cuts separated by horizontal slash cuts, sgd, 7" h...................... 140.00

Watering Cans

Here's a topic that was really hot at last summer's flea markets. It seemed like everywhere you looked there was a watering can. Again, it's the decorator influence encouraged those with a country-style interior to add a few watering cans. And, while all this flower watering has been going on, more children's vintage lithographed-tin watering cans also appeared on the scene. They, too, have become an eagerly sought item.

Brass, small dings, 4-3/8" h, 9-3/8" l
.... 8.00

Ceramic, Czechoslovakian, white ground, blue-green shading and trim, two swans swimming, 5-1/4" h 60.00

Child's, litho on tin
Ohio Art, turquoise and orange flowers, pink hearts, yellow ground, 8-1/4" h............... 35.00
Super Smurf in Shower 10.00
Victorian children in garden, handle loose, scratches, wear, 8" h 60.00

Copper, round, long narrow spout, round closed sprinkler head
.... 60.00

Miniature, doll house size, metal, painted red, flower dec, 1" h ... 5.00

Sterling silver, narrow spout, small size 45.00

Tin
Brass head............................. 35.00
Dover, orig label, no sprinkler
.... 25.00
Painted green, wear, orig round sprinkler, long loop handle
.... 40.00
Unmarked, some age darkening
.... 30.00

Watering cans, miniature, ceramic, maroon glaze, ring handle, incised decoration, **$5.**

Watt Pottery

Although the name Watt Pottery wasn't used until about 1920, founder W.J. Watt was involved in the pottery business as early as 1886. He worked at several pottery companies before purchasing the Crooksville, Ohio, Globe Stoneware Company. With the help of his sons Harry and Thomas, son-in-law C. L. Dawson, daughter Marion Watt, and numerous other relatives, he began production of this uniquely American pottery. Most Watt dinnerware features underglazed decorations on a sturdy off-white or tan body. Much of Watt dinnerware was sold by Safeway, Woolworth, and grocery chains. A fire destroyed the factory in October 1965, and it was never rebuilt.

For additional listings, see *Warman's Americana & Collectibles*.

Reproduction alert.

Watts Pottery, cookie Jar, Apple pattern, **$75.**

Baker
Autumn Foliage.................... 90.00
Starflower, #67.................... 165.00
Westwood, #96 .... 45.00

Bean pot, Autumn Foliage, #76
.... 50.00
Berry bowl, Cherry, #4 .... 25.00
Bowl
Apple, #04.............................. 95.00
Raised Pansy, #9 .... 135.00
Rooster, #6.......................... 100.00
Tulip, #64 .... 175.00
Casserole, individual, Raised Pansy
.... 145.00
Cereal bowl, Apple 24.00
Cookie jar, Autumn Foliage, #76
.... 95.00
Creamer
Apple, #62............................ 175.00
Bleeding Heart...................... 75.00
Tulip, #62 .... 225.00
Mixing bowl, Rooster, #5 .... 85.00

Mug, Starflower, #61.............. 285.00
Pepper shaker, Autumn Foliage,
hour-glass shape.................... 90.00
Pie plate, Pansy, #33, adv......... 60.00
Pitcher
Apple, #15............................ 165.00
Bleeding Heart, #15.............. 55.00
Cherries, #15, with advertising
.... 180.00
Rooster, #15........................ 145.00
Teardrop, #15....................... 65.00
Salad bowl
Double Apple, #73 .... 60.00
Teardrop 75.00
Two-Leaf Apple 85.00
Spaghetti bowl
Cherry, #39 .... 50.00
Teardrop 165.00

Weather Vanes

Weather vanes were originally designed to indicate the direction of the wind, showing farmers which way a potential weather system was coming. Look for large weather vanes made of copper, sheet metal, cast or wrought iron, wood, or zinc. Because so many reproductions exist, it's the type of collectible that it is important to ask the dealer about the provenance of the piece, and don't be too timid to examine it carefully. Expect to find some signs of weathered wear on vintage weather vanes.

For additional listings, see *Warman's Antiques and Collectibles Price Guide*.

Reproduction alert:

Reproductions of early weathervanes are being expertly aged and then sold as originals.

Arrow, copper, ball finial, dents, 13" h, 25" l 350.00

Banner, zinc and wrought iron, banner/arrow finial, 54-1/2" h 700.00

Eagle, copper, full bodied, cast zinc feet, wooden base, 21" wing span, 18-1/2" h, one foot loose, arrow bent 250.00

Fish, flat sheet metal, applied fins, green glass eyes cracked, gilt loss, 13-3/4" h, 16" l 995.00

Horse
Prancing, cast aluminum, over arrow, bullet holes, small size 50.00
Running, sheet metal, holes, wear, 16" h, 28" l 220.00

Running, tin, full-bodied, on arrow, 24" l 825.00
Standing, sheet metal, large tail to vane, 26" l 110.00

Rooster, sheet iron, reinforced with riveted iron straps, 36-1/2" h, 27-1/2" l 980.00

Schooner, 39" l, 23-3/8" h, wooden, hull painted red and black, cream-colored sail, wire rigging, America, 20th C, wooden stand, wear 275.00

Weather vane, rooster, copper, later wooden base, 22" l, 21-1/2" h, **$2,750.**

Wedgwood

Wedgwood is another name that usually denotes quality. Josiah Wedgwood built a factory at Etruria, England, between 1766 and 1769, after having been in the ceramics business for a few years. Wedgwood's early products included caneware, unglazed earthenware, black basalt, creamware, and jasperware. Bone china was introduced between 1812 and 1822. Over the years these and other wares have been made, marked, and well used. Today, Wedgwood still continues its tradition of fine quality.

For additional listings, see *Warman's Antiques and Collectibles Price Guide* and *Warman's English & Continental Pottery & Porcelain.*

Ashtray, jasper, white portrait in center, Wedgwood Society collector edition 20.00

Basket, Queen's Ware, oval, undertray, basketweave molded bodies, pierced galleries, green and black enamel oak leaves and trim, imp mark, early 19th C, 9" l 290.00

Wedgwood, Jasperware, left: black covered jar, white classical figures, **$75;** center: lilac dip vase, white classical figures, **$95;** right: light blue covered jar, white classical figures, **$65.**

Wedgwood, plate, modern dinnerware production, green transfer print with yellow accented roses, **$5,** representing a good buy to someone who uses this pattern and needs an extra plate.

Biscuit jar, cov
Basalt, black, engine-turned body below band of children playing in relief, silver plated rim, handle, and cov, imp mark, late 19th C 520.00
Jasper, three color dip, central dark blue band bordered in light blue, applied white classical figures, silver plated rims, cov, and handle, imp mark, handle damaged 250.00

Bowl
Luster Ware, fish dec, mottled blue ext., mother of pearl int., printed mark, c1920, 4" d 350.00
Unique Ware, Norman Wilson, moonstone ground exterior, interior with translucent green glaze shading to blue center, impressed mark, 1930-60, 8-1/8" d 400.00

Calendar plate, 1996, Peter Rabbit, 8" d............ 32.50

Celery dish, bone china, gilt diamond border, printed mark, foot rim, light gilt wear, c1820 .... 175.00

Cheese dish, cov, jasper, dark blue dip, applied white classical and foliate relief, imp mark, mid-19th C 350.00

Child's feeding dish, Peter Rabbit 20.00

Creamer, jasper, blue, relief of Classical figures making offerings to gods 60.00

Crocus pot, 6" h, hedgehog, oval shaped pierced body, green majolica glaze, impressed mark, c1865, missing undertray, slight footrim chips 400.00

Cup and saucer, dinerware
Cathay.................................. 20.00
Royal Blue........................... 10.00
Windbrush........................... 32.00

Dinner plate
Blue Willow 20.00
Devon Spray 18.00
Royal Blue........................... 12.00

Fruit plate, majolica, turquoise basketweave, 6-1/2" d.......... 250.00

Game pie, caneware, oval, molded, rabbit finial, imp mark, 1865, 7" l, orig liner cracked 445.00

Match box, jasper, dark blue ... 90.00

Wedgwood, plate, multicolored, characters standing in arches, back marked "Shakespeare Characters, All The World's A Stage, This plate shows the Globe Theatre Bankside and historic roles played by the actors listed below in the plays of William Shakespeare, Poet and Playwright, born 1564 Stratford –upon-Avon England, died 1616, Mr Shuter as Falstaff, Mr Garrick as MacBeth, Mr Smith as Richard III, Miss P Hopkins as Lavina, Mrs Lessingham as Ophella, Mr Garrick as King Lear, Mr Grist as Othello, Mr Kean as Hamlet, Mrs Hopkins as Volumina, Mrs Balkley as Mrs Ford, In Association with the Shakespeare Birthplace Trust, Wedgwood & Barlaston of Etruria, Made in England," original box, **$45.**

Medallion, jasper, light green dip, oval, portrait of Admiral Richard Howe, imp title and mark, 3-1/2" x 4-1/4" 260.00

Mustard pot, cov, jasper, yellow dip, attached underplate, applied black fruiting grapevine relief, pot with lion masks and rings, silver plated cover, impressed mark, c1930, rim chip, stained interior, dish rim restored................................ 325.00

Pitcher, black basalt, club, enameled floral dec, imp mark, c1860, 6-1/2" h 350.00

Plaque, jasper, solid black, applied white classical relief of muses, imp mark, 19th C, wood frame, rect 490.00

Tureen, cov, fig finial, white ironstone 115.00

Urn, jasper, blue, scene of Classical figures in relief, two handles, acanthus borders, 11" h....... 275.00

Vase
Creamware, molded grape vines and foliage, painted band of strawberries, mid 19th C, minor damage, 6" h...................... 90.00
Jasper, black jasper dip, applied white classical relief, Portland, imp "Marshall Field & Co. Wedgwood Exhibition 1918," price for pr, 4" h 690.00
Wine cooler, redware, fruiting vines on molded body, raised mask handles, imp mark, early 19th C, 10" h 550.00

Weller Pottery

Samuel Weller opened a small pottery factory near Zanesville, Ohio, in 1872, originally producing utilitarian stoneware. By 1882, he moved to larger quarters and expanded his lines. As the years continued, more designers arrived and the lines were expanded to include commercial wares. As art pottery became popular, Weller developed lines to answer that need. Today, some of the art pottery lines are highly sought. The company stayed in business during World War II, but by 1948 it had ceased operations.

For additional listings, see *Warman's Antiques and Collectibles Price Guide, Warman's Americana & Collectibles,* and *Warman's American Pottery & Porcelain.*

Ashtray, Roma.......................... 35.00

Basket
Melrose 155.00
Warwick............................... 125.00

Bowl
Cameo.................................... 95.00
Roma 95.00
Scandia 75.00

Bud vase, Woodland 195.00

Console bowl, Sydonia, 17" x 6" 90.00

Cornucopia, Softone, light blue 45.00

Ewer
Cameo, white rose 65.00
Panella 55.00

Flower frog
Marvo, blue............................ 55.00

Silvertone............................. 100.00

Mug, Claywood......................... 75.00

Pitcher
Bouquet 60.00
Pansy.................................... 110.00

Planter
Forest Tub, 4"....................... 135.00
Woodrose.............................. 60.00

Vase

Art Nouveau, 5" h 160.00
Atlas, 6-1/2" h 165.00
Dogwood, 9-1/2" h 125.00
Forest, fan-shape, blue, tan, and
  green matte glaze, imp mark,
  c1920 .... 200.00
Louwelsa, 6-5/8" h 180.00

Scenic 65.00
Souevo, 7" h 115.00
Viola, fan shape 65.00

Wall pocket

Blue, emb leaf 60.00
Pearl, 8-1/2" l 160.00
Sydonia, blue 225.00
Woodrose 110.00

Weller Pottery, vase, Hudson line, decorated by S. Timberlake, 9-1/2" h, **$450.**

Weller Pottery, wall pocket, owl, greens and browns, 11" h, **$170.**

Vase with flowers, 7-1/2" h, **$775.**

Weller Pottery, Cameo vase, tan glaze, 13" h, **$75.**

Western Collectibles

The American West has always held a fascination. Whether you're a collector interested in history or a decorator striving to achieve a western motif using authentic items, flea markets yield many items rustling up.

For additional listings, see *Warman's Americana & Collectibles.*

Belt buckle, bucking bronc, MIB 40.00

Book
  Cowboys North and South, Will James, 1924 .... 45.00
  Famous Sheriffs and Western Outlaws, William MacLeod Raine, Doubleday, 1929, 1st ed., 294 pgs 12.00

The Keeper of Red Horse Pass, W. C. Tuttle 7.50

Bolo, figural 3" d turtle, crushed turquoise inlay, mkd ".925 Taxo" 65.00

Bookends, pr, End of the Trail, tired Indian on pony, cast metal 75.00

Coasters, cowboy, set of four in holder 15.00

Cowboy hat, Stetson, orig box 150.00

Figure, cowboy, Stetson 35.00

Glass, frosted, painted cowboy on bucking bronco, 1950s 25.00

Holster, leather, double, studs, jewels, 1950s 65.00

Western Americana, wagon set, wood bench, cast iron, upholstered back support and seat, **$115.**

Western Americana, assorted western-themed magazines, prices range from **$2** to **$5.**

Western Americana, badge, US Marshall Deputy, Arizona Territory, **$25.**

Pennant, Grand National Livestock Show and Rodeo, San Francisco, 1960s...................................... 35.00

Pillow cover, Souvenir of Cheyenne, cowboy motif......................... 20.00

Plate, steer head, Western Enamel, 10" d....................................... 20.00

Saddle, western style, tooled decor, 1970s.................................... 225.00

Saddle blanket, Pendleton, Indian style print, 1970s 125.00

Saddle stand, wood 100.00

Salt and pepper shakers, pr, figural covered wagons 10.00

Scarf, horses motif, rayon, 28" sq 24.00

Spurs, pr, Mexican style, silver inlay, large rowels.......................... 450.00

Vase, wagon wheel shape, stamped "Frankoma" 35.00

Wall lamp, cast iron silhouette of bronco buster 30.00

Wrapper, Wild West Picture Puzzle, 5" x 7" waxed paper wrapper, Gum Inc., 1930s.............................. 48.00

Western Stoneware

Western Stoneware, Monmouth Pottery, was founded in Monmouth, IL in 1906. The well-known dinnerware designer, Eva Zeisel, developed a stoneware dinnerware line in 1954 for this company. One of the most popular patterns of this company is known as Marcrest Ware, each stoneware piece is covered in a rich chocolate brown glaze.

Western Stoneware, bean pot, brown glaze, raised diamond motif, lid missing, **$10.**

Bowl, 8" d, Marcrest 12.00

Casserole, Marcrest.................. 12.00

Cup and saucer
  Blue dec on white ground 12.00
  Marcrest................................. 7.50

Dinner plate
  Blue dec on white ground 15.00
  Marcrest................................. 6.50

Mug, Marcrest............................ 5.00

Platter, blue repeating dec of roosters, birds, and fish, white ground, 16" l 24.00

Teapot, blue dec on white ground 28.00

Western Stoneware, milk pitcher, Marcrest, brown glaze, 6" h, **$25.**

Westmoreland Glass

Founded in 1899 in Grapeville, Pa., the Westmoreland Company originally made handcrafted high-quality glassware. During the 1920s, the company started to make reproductions and decorated wares. Production continued until 1982. Pieces were made in crystal, black, and colored milk glass, among other colors. Milk glass pieces bring the most interest from collectors today.

For additional listings, see *Warman's Americana & Collectibles.*

Westmoreland Glass Co., Della Robbia pattern, tumblers, each **$30;** sherbets, each **$22;** stemware, each **$28.**

Animal dish, cov
Eagle on nest, aqua carnival glass
.... 35.00
Hen on nest, milk glass 60.00
Swan on nest, milk glass 185.00

Appetizer canapé set, Paneled
Grape, milk glass 80.00

Basket
Princess Feather, 7-1/4" d... 125.00
Thousand Eye, clear, 8-3/4" h
.... 300.00

Bowl
Dolphin, milk glass, 12" d
.... 145.00
Hobnail, blue, ftd, two handles,
8" d 160.00
Paneled Grape, milk glass, 10" d
.... 50.00

Bud vase, Roses & Bows, milk glass,
10" h, paneled grape dec 45.00

Butter dish, cov, Old Quilt, milk glass
.... 28.00

Cake stand, Paneled Grape, milk
glass 95.00

Candlesticks, pr
English Hobnail, pink 60.00
Old Quilt, milk glass, 3" h 20.00

Candy dish, cov
Della Robbia, 7" h 100.00
Old Quilt, milk glass, sq, high foot
.... 30.00

Cheese dish, cov, Old Quilt, milk
glass 45.00

Cologne bottle, Paneled Grape, milk
glass 45.00

Compote, vaseline, 7" h 145.00

Console set, Crystal Wedding, milk
glass, cov compot, pr 4-1/2" h
candlesticks, orig label 150.00

Creamer, Paneled Grape, milk glass
.... 16.00

Cruet, Old Quilt, milk glass 25.00

Cup and saucer
Paneled Grape, milk glass 22.50
Plain, beaded edge, milk glass
.... 12.00

Dresser tray
Daisy, milk glass 20.00
Sunflower, milk glass 30.00

Goblet
Della Robia, milk glass 18.00
English Hobnail, crystal 10.00
Paneled Grape, milk glass 18.00
Thousand Eye, crystal 12.00

Honey dish, cov, Beaded Grape, milk
glass, sq 20.00

Iced tea tumbler
Old Quilt, milk glass, 5-1/4" h, ftd
.... 18.00
Paneled Grape, milk glass, 12 oz
.... 22.00

Pin dish, square, milk glass 7.00

Pitcher, Paneled Grape, milk glass
.... 45.00

Plate
English Hobnail, amber 10.00
Old Quilt, milk glass, 8" d 32.00
Rabbit, horseshoe and shamrock
border, blue carnival 15.00

Punch set, Della Robia, crystal bell
shaped punch bowl, six cups
.... 45.00

Salad plate
Della Robia, crystal, dark stained
fruit 24.00
English Hobnail, crystal 6.00

Relish, three-part, Paneled Grape,
milk glass 40.00

Sugar, cov, English Hobnail, ice blue
.... 55.00

Tidbit, Beaded Grape, milk glass, 2
tiers 45.00

Tray
Heavy Scroll, allover gold dec
.... 25.00
Maple Leaf, 9" d 12.00

Tumbler, milk glass, ftd
Apple 20.00
Old Quilt, 4-1/4" h 10.00
Peach 20.00

Vase, Grape and Lattice, milk glass,
10" h 115.00

Westmoreland Glass Co., Blackberry pattern, candy dish, covered, milk glass, signed on lid, 1955, 5-3/4" h, **$20.**

Whirligigs

A variation of the weathervane, whirligigs indicate wind direction and velocity. Often constructed by the unskilled, they were generally made of wood and metal and exhibited a rather primitive appearance. Flat, paddle-like arms are characteristic of single-figure whirligigs, but multi-figure examples are usually driven by a propeller that moves a series of gears or rods. Three-dimensional figures are commonly found on 19th-century whirligigs, but silhouette figures are generally indicative of 20th-century construction. The prices listed below are for vintage whirligigs, expect to pay much less for modern 20th century examples.

Indian in canoe, carved and painted wood, paddle arms, 14" h, 18" l **440.00**

Man sawing logs, cut tin, wooden base, old worn gold, red, green and black paint, directional in green and black, propeller in green and orange, 32-3/4" l **145.00**

Patriotic motif, black man with hat pumping water for woman in polka-dot bandana and with washboard, wooden, propellers in red, white and blue with stars on the ends, white stars along the base, compass stars on the directional, repairs, weathering, 26-1/2" l **1,000.00**

Roosters, two facing each other, on tower made resembling an oil derrick, wooden, painted wood, 62" h.................................... **110.00**

Soldier, painted wood, black, gray, and white, wooden stand, wear, 9-5/8" w, 13" h **355.00**

Woman washing clothes, painted wood, 1930s, 12" h, 15" l **185.00**

Whirlgigs, primitive, pine, directional arrow, 15-1/4" l, 10-1/2" h, **$45.**

Whiskey Bottles, Collectors Edition

The Jim Beam Distillery started a craze in 1953 when it issued its first Christmas special edition bottle. During the 1960s, the craze had caught fire with collectors and the whiskey manufacturers were only too happy to create more and more bottles. Many folks bought each new bottle as it was issued, enjoying the bottle and often the contents too. By the 1980s, the fire was out as speculators were beginning to try to cash in and the market became flooded. Today there are a few collectors looking to complete a series, but on the whole, the bottles are worth much less now than in the late 1960s.

Before putting out figural collector bottles on your flea market table, check the local liquor laws, some states may require you to have a special license to sell a bottle with its original contents.

For additional listings, see *Warman's Americana & Collectibles*.

Cyrus Noble
Sea turtle, 1979..................... 50.00
Whitetail deer, 1979 .... 35.00

Double Springs
Bentley, 1927 model............. 40.00
Cadillac, 1913 model............ 35.00
Ford, 1940 model 30.00

Ezra Brooks
Casey at Bat, 1973 .... 15.00
Clown with balloons, 1973... 20.00
Club Bottle #1, Distillery, 1970
.... 12.50
Clydesdale, 1974................... 10.00
Lion on Rock, 1971 .... 10.00
Masonic, fez, 1976................ 10.00

Motorcycle, 1971 .... 17.50
Quail 12.00
Reno Heritage, 1968.............. 18.00
Spirit of St. Louis, 1977 .... 12.00
Train, Iron Horse, 1969 .... 12.00
Vermont Skier, 1973.............. 12.00

Jim Beam
Akron, Rubber Capital, 1973
.... 24.00
Barney's Slot Machine, 1978
.... 20.00
Bass fish................................. 18.00
Buffalo Bill, 1970s 10.00
Cat... 20.00
Cowboy, 1981 .... 12.00
Elks Centennial 8.00

Irish Setter 18.00
Key West, FL........................... 6.00
Order of the Blue Goose....... 18.00
Remington 20.00
Republican Elephant, 1972 .. 30.00
San Francisco Trolley 8.00
Saturday Evening Post, 1970s
.... 15.00
Springer Spaniel 18.00

Lionstone
Barber, 1976 .... 40.00
Bartender, 1969 .... 30.00
Baseball Player, 1974............ 24.50
Cherry Valley 20.00
Dove of Peace, 1977.............. 40.00
Eastern Bluebird, 1972......... 20.00

Hockey Player, 1974 .... **20.00**
Indian, squaw, 1973.............. **25.00**
Riverboat Captain, 1969....... **12.00**
Stutz Bearcat, miniature, 1978
.... **15.00**

Ski Country
Ebenezer Scrooge, 1979, miniature
.... **24.00**
Jaguar, miniature.................. **30.00**
Koala, 1973 .... **40.00**
Mountain Goat **25.00**
Submarine, 1976, miniature
.... **20.00**

Tom Thumb.......................... **30.00**

Wild Turkey
Series #1, No. 5, with flags, 1975
.... **40.00**
Series #2, No. 2, lore, 1980 ... **30.00**
Series #3, No. 5, with raccoon, 1984
.... **40.00**

Whiskey bottle, collector edition, Cyrus Noble, assayer, miniature, ©1974 Haas Brothers, **$20.**

Whiskey bottle, collector edition, Double Springs, owl, brown, **$10.**

Whiskey bottle, collector edition, Wild Turkey, No. 1, miniature, **$22.**

Wicker

Wicker furniture evokes a summertime feeling, even in the cold of winter. Wicker can be found in natural rattan or painted. The Victorians loved it. Today the look is still popular. Look for pieces with original upholstery in good condition and without too many layers of paint. Many pieces of wicker cannot be stripped without damaging the materials.

Baby basket, painted white, wooden stand with wheels................ **150.00**

Chair
Arm, wide flat arm rests continue to back, broad seat, repainted
.... **200.00**

Wicker, doll carriage, with original white cotton parasol, **$225.**

Boudoir chair, lady's, wicker, ornate curliques, bead garlands
.... **335.00**
Photographer's, elaborate scrolled back and arms, painted white
.... **450.00**

Chest of drawers, dark finish, six drawers, wooden pulls **300.00**

Ferner, white, metal liner, rectangular, repainted several times
.... **185.00**

Footstool, upholstered seat, painted
.... **195.00**

Lamp, hanging, shaped shade over ball type white plastic shade, dec gold hanging chain............... **25.00**

Music stand, Wakefield Rattan Co., three shelves, orig paper label, c1883.................................... **285.00**

Picnic basket, suitcase shape, plastic

Wicker, rocker, ornate high back, ornate patterned back and seat, scrolling arms, balloon-type ornaments on front stretcher, as found condition, **$190.**

tableware held in place with leather straps 25.00

Rocking chair, Wakefield Rattan Co., serpentine edges, braided trim, wooden rockers, painted white 265.00

Stool, Heywood-Wakefield, orig label 150.00

Suite, sofa, two matching arm chairs, ottoman, some damage to wicker, worn old upholstery, as found condition 300.00

Table, round wooden top, re-painted 120.00

Wine rack, natural, 26" h......... 60.00

Winnie the Pooh

A. A. Milne's "tubby little cubby all stuffed with fluff" has become a best friend to countless children. It's no wonder Pooh, Piglet, Eeyore, and the rest of the gang are eagerly sought by collectors. Mass marketing of Pooh in recent years has brought a flood of newer collectibles into the market. However, buyers can still find a fair share of vintage Pooh items at flea markets.

Big Golden Book, *Winnie-The-Pooh and Eeyore's Birthday,* E. Dutton, copyright 1964, 1965 by Walt Disney Productions....... 35.00

Book
Winnie The Pooh, Fat Bee, puppet included, produced for Buena Vista home video, 1994, mint 12.00
Winnie the Pooh and Tigger Too, Disney's Wonderful World of Reading, Grolier, hardcover, 1975, orig cardboard mailer 20.00

Figure, Eeyore, stamped "Walt Disney Productions Japan," 4" l......... 45.00

Lamp, Dolly Toy, 1964.............. 35.00

Magic slate, Western Publishing, 1965 .... 22.00

Little Golden Book, Walt Disney Presents Winne-The-Pooh, The Honey Tree, 1977, 19th printing 2.00

Pinback button, Winnie, Disneyland, c1960 .... 12.00

Plush toy, Winnie, tags removed, 12" h...................................... 15.00

Puzzle, frame tray, Whitman, 1964 .... 10.00

Record, Winnie the Pooh and Christopher Robin Songs, Disney, 78 rpm, Decca Records 40.00

Sand pail, tin litho 7.50

Snow globe, musical................ 15.00

Teapot, Cardew...................... 100.00

Toy, white knob wind-up, Winnie the Pooh in safari clothing, exclusive to Disney Animal Kingdom 6.50

Wall decoration
Train, Disney, particleboard, 35" l 12.00
Winnie, Tiger, Eeyore, heavy cardboard, c1960.............. 40.00

Winnie the Pooh, book, *Winnie The Pooh's Bedtime Stories*, by Bruce Talkington, illustrations by John Kurtz, Walt Disney, **$5.**

Wizard of Oz

MGM gave birth to an institution when it released "The Wizard of Oz" in 1939, although L. Frank Baum's stories of Oz date to the early part of the 20th century. While vintage Oz items are competitively sought and can be pricey, a variety of contemporary collectibles fit into any person's budget. Among the newer items are numerous pieces commemorating the film's 50th anniversary in 1989.

Book
The Road to Oz, Junior Edition, Rand/McNally & Co., 1939 copyright, 5-1/2" x 6-3/4" 24.00
The Road to Oz, L. Frank Baum, Reilly & Lee, 1909 .... 90.00

Christmas ornament, Bradford Novelty, 1977, 4-1/2" h
Cowardly Lion 5.00

Dorothy.................................... 7.50
Scarecrow 5.00
Tin Man 5.00

Collector's plate, If I Only Had a Brain, Scarecrow, 1977, orig box, 8-1/2" d 18.00

Comic book, *Tales of the Wizard of Oz*, Dell, 1962........................ 10.00

Cookbook, *The Wonderful Wizard of Oz Cookbook*, Monica Bayley, hardcover, 1st ed, 1981.......... 48.00

Costume, Cowardly Lion, Collegeville, 1989 .... 10.00

Doll
Cowardly Lion, Ideal, 1984 .... 20.00

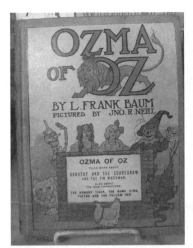

Wizard of Oz collectibles, book, *Ozma of Oz*, by Frank L. Baum, illustrations by Jno. R. Neill, **$95.**

Wizard of Oz collectibles, book, *The Lost Princess of Oz*, by Frank L. Baum, illustrations by Jno. R. Neill, **$185.**

Wizard of Oz collectibles, doll, Tin Man, Effanbee, original box, **$25.**

Dorothy, Madame Alexander, 1991 .... 24.00
Mayor of Munchkinland, Presents, 1989 .... 18.00

Scarecrow, Mattel, talking 40.00
Tin Man, Largo, 1989 .... 10.00

Drinking glass, Scarecrow, Coca-Cola, 50th anniversary commemorative, 1989, 6" h .. 10.00

Game, Return to Oz, Golden Press, 1985 .... 8.00

Lunch box and thermos, Aladdin, 50th anniversary 65.00

Paint by number set, Craft Master, 1968 .... 20.00

Play set, Wizard of Oz, Mego, complete 250.00

Photograph, Judy Garland, black and white, checkered Wizard of Oz dress, 1940s, 8" x 10" 8.00

Puppet theater, Proctor and Gamble, 1965 .... 40.00

Sheet music, *Over the Rainbow*, 1939 .... 40.00

Toy
Squeak, Wizard, Burnstein, 1939 .... 125.00
Wind-up, Cowardly Lion, Durham Industries, MOC 15.00

Wristwatch, Eko, quartz, Emerald City on face 15.00

Wizard of Oz collectibles, book, *The Purple Prince of Oz*, by Ruth Plumly Thompson, Founded on and Continuing The Famous Oz Stories by Frank L. Baum, illustrations by Jno. R. Neill, **$300.**

Wizard of Oz, *The Emerald City of Oz*, Reilley & Lee Co., 1910, **$125.**

World War I

Fueled by the assassination of Austrian Archduke Franz Ferdinand by a Serbian national in June of 1914, World War I was set off with Germany invading Belgium and France. Shortly after that, Russia, England, and Turkey joined the war. By 1917, the United States and Italy had become involved. When peace was reached in 1919, millions had died and damage was wide spread. Memorabilia relating to World War I was carefully laid aside, hoping it would be the last war. Alas, it was not.

Badge, American Red Cross-Military Welfare, cap, enamel **24.00**

Banner, Welcome Veterans, white fabric, red edging, center red and blue image for sponsor Disabled American Veterans, c1918, 11" x 17-1/2" **25.00**

Bayonet, orig case **24.00**

Belt, some emblems.................. **35.00**

Gas mask, carrying can, shoulder strap, canister attached to bottom, German................................. **50.00**

Grave marker, unused, bronze, Hampden Bros Aluminum Co. **45.00**

Handkerchief, Remember Me, soldier and girl in center, red, white, and blue edge.............. **24.00**

Helmet, US, 3rd Army insignia **72.00**

Leather flight cap **60.00**

Magazine, *Red Cross Magazine*, October 1918, battle-scene cover **15.00**

Medal, British, King George V **65.00**

Photograph, Officer Training Camp, Chickamuga Park, GA, 1917, 7" x 31".. **85.00**

Piano manual, *Manual of Arms and Fingers for Boys At the Piano*, John Thompson, Willis Music Co., ©1929, 38 pgs, music, black and white illus, 24 military theme piano exercises, each with place for stamp, unused **15.00**

Postcard, real-photo, soldier in uniform.................................... **5.00**

Poster, *Liberty Loan Honor Button*, blue and white image of pinback button, cardboard, 10-1/2" x 14" **25.00**

Ribbon, Ladies G.A.R., 1912, black lettering on 8" l silk ribbon ... **20.00**

Scarf, silk, sweetheart, white, eagle, flag, sweethearts, etc. **40.00**

Sheet music
American Patrol March, 1914 .... **15.00**
If We Had A Million Like Him Over There, tribute to George Cohan **15.00**
What Kind of an American Are You?, Uncle Sam design ... **20.00**

Trench art, pencil holder, shell affixed to base of three crossed bullets, 4-3/8" h **95.00**

Watch fob, flag on pole, USA, beaded, blue **48.00**

World War I collectibles, real-photo postcard, soldiers on parade, unused, **$10.**

World War II

Several world events came together in 1939, leading to World War II. The German Third Reich was engaged in an arms race; the Depression compounded the situation. After Germany invaded Poland, Allied and Axis alliances were formed. From 1942 to 1945, the whole world was involved; almost all industry was war-related. Peace was not achieved until August 1945. Today collectors are discovering artifacts, equipment, and remembrances of this war. The recent unveiling of the World War II memorial has caused many collectors to think about why they are so passionate about collecting this type of memorabilia.

Ashtray, Mussolini as vulture in tree limb, two circling vultures **50.00**

Belt buckle, Navy, Okinawa, 1945, mkd "Solid Brass, Made in USA" **24.00**

Book
Army Songs, 1941, 64 pgs..... **35.00**

World War II collectibles, arm band, Nazi, red, black, and white, **$195.**

Pilot Rating Book, CAA, US Dept of Commerce **20.00**

Candy container, tank, Victory Glass, no closure.................... **30.00**

Card, diecut, Happy Birthday Soldier, image of soldier wearing baggy uniform.................................. **12.00**

Container, Stand Firm, red, white, and blue thin waxed surface cardboard, Winston Churchill quote and bulldog, lists people and companies from Montreal and Toronto involved in manufacturing **25.00**

Dexterity puzzle, Atom Bomb, silhouette of Japan, A. C. Gilbert Co., 1946............................. **150.00**

Dogtag, scarce early version with next of kin name/address...... **20.00**

Drinking glass, Remember Pearl Harbor, artwork of Pearl Harbor and Hawaiian Islands, warships, and aircraft, 4-3/4" h **65.00**

Envelope, shows pilot delivering letter to solider parachuting to ground, caption reads "High-Ho, A Letter for…," unused, 8-7/8" x 3-7/8" **8.00**

World War II collectibles, booklet, *Hello Buddy, Comics of War, Faces of Service, Remember the Unemployed War Veterans*, red and blue print on pulp type paper, **$15.**

Medal, campaign and service medal, orig box.................................. 25.00

Pencil sharpener, BASDD, plastic airplane.................................. 35.00

Photo brochure, At Work to Win, Buick Motor Division, General Motors Corp, ©1943.............. 25.00

Picture frame, gold accent tin litho frame, black scroll line work, red, white, and blue etched glass, image of American flag in center, shield with space for photo, 5-1/2" x 7-1/2" 20.00

World War II collectibles, knapsack, other side, **$90.**

Pillow cover, Armored Force Keep 'em Rolling, Fort Knox, KY, red, white, and blue, red fringe, 20" sq 20.00

Poster, *For Freedom's Sake Buy War Bonds,* Liberty Minuteman statue, US Government Printing Office, 1943 .... 60.00

Punch-out kit, Model Battleship, 7" x 10", full color envelope with scene of battleship on open sea, colorful thin cardboard sheet, Reed & Associates, early 1940s, unused 45.00

Salt and pepper shakers, pr, figural, Gen MacArthur, glazed ceramic, 2" x 2-1/2", tan hat, long yellow pipe 85.00

Sheet Music, *What Do You Do In The Infrantry*...................... 15.00

World War II collectibles, knapsack, green canvas body, pony fur covered flap and back, brown leather, aluminum fittings, stamped "Maury & Co., 1936," also signed on back by German soldier, "Uffz Hamen," **$90.**

Songbook, *Army Song Book,* 1941, 64 pgs....................................... 30.00

Toy, Eagle Bomb Sight, Toy Creations, 1940s, red, white, and blue orig box 50.00

View-Master reel, Naval Aviation Military Training Division, hand-lettered, #51, Fiat G-50 Italian fighter 30.00

Window ad card, Flying Civilian Pilots Fight the Submarine, ad for July issue of *Flying Magazine* 30.00

Wyandotte

Playthings a kid could be rough with, Wyandotte's heavy-gauge steel toys were a favorite with children. The company began in 1921, taking its name from the town of Wyandotte, Mich., where it was located. At first the firm just made toy pistols and rifles, but soon moved to a line of cars and trucks with wooden wheels. Wyandotte went out of business in 1956.

Wyandotte, steam shovel, blue cap, red and yellow claw and base, remnants of original decal, played-with condition, **$65.**

Airplane, blue and red, white wooden wheels, metal propeller, wings fold at hinges, 1940s, 9" wingspan 145.00

Army truck, 22" l................... 115.00

Coupe, 1930s, 7-1/2" l............ 160.00

Ice truck, #348 .... 375.00

Rocket racer, #319................. 100.00

Ship, *USS Enterprise* 120.00

Shooting gallery, litho tin wind-up, tin target, orig darts 290.00

Station wagon, Cadillac, #1007, 21" l 275.00

Submarine 165.00

Wrecker, 10" l.......................... 110.00

Yo-Yos

Q: What keeps coming back when you toss it away? A: A yo-yo. Few people can truly throw away a yo-yo, which means there are many examples available on today's market. In addition to vintage items, look for contemporary yo-yos featuring popular cultural figures, advertising yo-yos and commemorative examples. Fantastic yo-yo collections can be seen at The Yozeum in Tucson, Arizona, and the National Yo-Yo Museum in Chico, California.

Baseball, white, red stitching dec 4.00

Big Con, plastic 4.00

Buzz Lightyear, 2" d 32.00

Coca-Cola, 1992 Summer Olympics 25.00

Duncan
Bowling ball, Duncan Sports Line Model, #1070, MOC 55.00
Butterfly, green, MOC 15.00
Campbell's Kids, Duncan 25.00
Glow in the dark 6.00
Wooden, black and red, 1930s 25.00

Eleyo, red, MIB 5.00

Grand Prix, wheel 5.00

Hot Wheels, Mattel, tire motif, red chrome hubcaps, 1990, MOC 12.00

The Iron Giant, Warner Bros., 1990 .... 12.00

Jurassic Park, 1992, MIP 20.00

Moon astronauts, 2-1/2" x 1-1/4" thick litho tin panels, H. F. Hong Kong, c1969 .... 15.00

NASCAR, Mark Martin 5.00

Nightmare Before Christmas, Spectra Star 10.00

Oreo Cookie 10.00

Planter's Mr. Peanut 20.00

Poll Parrot Shoes 10.00

Pro Flash Boy, pink plastic 8.00

Sea Rider 6.00

Steam Genie, metal 10.00

Yo-yos, Duncan Imperial, red plastic, 2-1/4" d, **$5.**

Zeppelins

Oh, those fanciful flying machines. Some folks call them dirigibles, while others refer to them as blimps. To collectors they are something to gloat about, especially when finding that rare piece to add to their coveted possessions.

Book
Mit Graf Zeppelin Um Die Welt, 1929, black and white photos, German text **65.00**
The Story of the Airship, 6" x 9" hardcover, 6th edition, ©1931, Goodyear Tire & Rubber Co., Akron **20.00**

Booklet, 4-1/2" x 5-7/8", *USS Los Angeles,* by Rell S. Clements, ©1926 .... **35.00**

Candy mold, Anton Reiche, Dresden, tin, two-pc clamp style **145.00**

Christmas light bulb, milk glass, painted green, red, white, blue, and gold, 1950s, 2-1/2" l, non-working **20.00**

First-day cover, San Francisco Greets *U.S.A.S. Macon* Upon Arrival at Home Base, 8 cent airmail stamp, postmarked "Moffett Field, Oct. 15, 1933" **30.00**

Flight schedule, from Germany to America, c1936 .... **60.00**

Magazine print, German *Graf Zeppelin* flying over NY skyscrapers, *New Yorker Magazine,* Haupt, 1930, 8" x 11" image, acid-free mat **125.00**

Pinback button, Lakehurst Naval Air Station, red, white, and blue, attached ribbon and aluminum airship, 1930s **95.00**

Postcard, 3-1/2" x 5-1/2", black and white, unused
Motorized cigar-shaped airship with propeller, tail rudder, single passenger, black text "Compliments of Helfrich Bohner & Co., Furnishers of High Grade Furniture, Allentown, Pa," c1910 ...... **25.00**

Zeppelin flying over Montevideo, Uruguay **20.00**

Stereoview, Zeppelin flying over German town during World War I, description on back **60.00**

Toy, plastic, hanging gondola, orig box with narrative printed in

German, English, and French, 13" l **125.00**

Whistle, tin litho, dark red, blue, yellow, and green airship with gondola below, mkd "Japan," 1930 .... **30.00**

Zeppelins, pamphlet, "Facts About the World's Largest Airships," **$15.**

Index

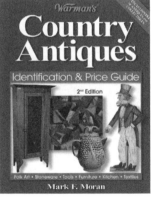